IP Address Management

IP Address Management

Second Edition

Michael Dooley & Timothy Rooney

IEEE Press
Series on
Networks and
Services Management

Dr. Veli Sahin and
Dr. Mehmet Ulema, *Series Editors*

IEEE PRESS

WILEY

Published by John Wiley & Sons, Inc., Hoboken, New Jersey.
Published simultaneously in Canada.

For general information on our other products and services or for technical support, please contact our Customer Care Department within the United States at (800) 762-2974, outside the United States at (317) 572-3993 or fax (317) 572-4002.

Wiley also publishes its books in a variety of electronic formats. Some content that appears in print may not be available in electronic formats. For more information about Wiley products, visit our web site at www.wiley.com.

Library of Congress Cataloging-in-Publication Data

Names: Rooney, Tim, author. | Dooley, Michael Earl, 1962- author.
Title: IP address management / Michael Dooley & Timothy Rooney.
Description: Second edition. | Hoboken, New Jersey : Wiley, 2021. | Series:
    IEEE press series on networks and service management | Timothy Rooney
    appears as the first named author in the first edition. | Includes
    bibliographical references and index.
Identifiers: LCCN 2020030601 (print) | LCCN 2020030602 (ebook) | ISBN
    9781119692270 (cloth) | ISBN 9781119692287 (adobe pdf) | ISBN
    9781119692300 (epub)
Subjects: LCSH: Internet addresses. | Internet domain names.
Classification: LCC TK5105.8835 .R66 2021 (print) | LCC TK5105.8835
    (ebook) | DDC 004.67/8–dc23
LC record available at https://lccn.loc.gov/2020030601
LC ebook record available at https://lccn.loc.gov/2020030602

Cover design by Wiley
Cover image: © Bill Donnelley/WT Design

Set in 9.5/12.5pt STIXTwoText by SPi Global, Chennai, India

10 9 8 7 6 5 4 3 2 1

Contents

Preface

The Covid-19 pandemic has abruptly reset many of our perceptions about what's really necessary and important in today's world. While we hope that it is but a distant albeit seminal memory by the time you read this, it is nevertheless an event of sea change proportions. Many of us have come to realize how we've taken for granted the people serving the critical essentials underpinning our daily lives. First and foremost, the doctors, nurses, hospital workers, and first responders willingly risk their own safety to rescue us should we need their help. Many others risk exposure to the virus by serving the broader community, such as those working at grocery stores, critical retail stores, delivery companies, food banks, and other core establishments. We are grateful for their courage and dedication in supporting our fundamental means of existence.

We also commend the other heroes, who lie further behind the front lines as auxiliaries, and while less susceptible to direct broad-based virus exposure, nonetheless serve an indispensable role in meeting basic needs of modern life that lie just above health, food, and shelter. This includes (but is certainly not limited to) those who work in financial institutions who are helping those sorely short of cash due to economic conditions, those in government supporting administration of key services, and those who, near and dear to our hearts, help keep the Internet and our Internet Protocol (IP) networks up and running.

In today's world, the Internet is indispensable for communication and interaction especially in times of quarantine (at least for those who have Internet access, though that's a subject for another book). We rely on the Internet for the web, email, video conferencing, streaming, mobile communications, managing our homes and personal lives, and much more. And the tireless efforts of network engineers, administrators, and operations personnel, collectively "IP managers," help assure all of our Internet devices work reliably wherever we are, whenever we need them. These IP managers have prepared in advance and keep close watch so your devices can connect to the Internet by obtaining IP addresses, and you can navigate your browser, email, and apps in human-readable language, not the numerical language of Internet devices.

These activities, comprising the practice of Internet Protocol address management (IPAM), encompass the application of network management disciplines to IP address space and associated network services, namely DHCP (dynamic host configuration protocol) and DNS (Domain Name System). The consequence of inadequately configuring DHCP is that end users may not be able to obtain IP addresses to access the network. Without proper DNS configuration, usability of the network will greatly suffer because the name-to-address lookup process may fail. Imagine having to navigate to a website or send an email or an instant message by IP address instead of by name!

It's equally important that these DHCP and DNS configurations be based on a common IP address plan, which maps out the IP address hierarchy, subnets, DHCP address pools, and DNS domains. The linkages among the IP address plan, DHCP server configuration and DNS server configuration are inseparable; a change of an IP address will affect DNS information and perhaps DHCP as well. These critical network functions provide the foundation for today's converged services IP networks, which comprise most enterprise and service provider networks, so they must be managed using a rigorous approach.

Like other heroes we've observed during this pandemic, IP managers' efforts go largely unnoticed and are taken for granted as users happily utilize these IPAM technologies unawares. Keeping these core Internet services provisioned properly, performing adequately, secured appropriately, and functioning accurately necessitates extraordinary effort. And demands on their efforts are not diminishing in the least. Today's IP networks are growing increasingly complex as new IP services and technologies are deployed.

Since the first editions of our IPAM books nearly a decade ago, we've observed both an underlying consistency in IP networks and IPAM technologies and techniques as well as a transformative evolution of certain aspects of IP networks and in the ways in which they are managed. Stalwart Internet technologies such as IPv6 and Domain Name System security extension (DNSSEC) have seen an increase in production deployments. Security focus, ever a network hallmark, has expanded with the use of IPAM technologies to enhance overall network security. Use of private and public cloud services and corresponding virtualization and "software-defined" automation technologies have exploded. And deployment of Internet-accessible devices within our workplaces, our homes, and even in rugged unstaffed environments has expanded the Internet to encompass this Internet of Things (IoT).

We have incorporated each of these topics into this edition to bring it up to date. We've also reorganized this book to improve the flow, transferring the nitty gritty protocol and related details to Part V, to keep the discussion at a consistent level throughout. We begin the book with an introduction to core IPAM technologies in Part I, then move on to IPAM mechanics in Part II. We cover IPAM and network security in Part III, then seek to provide practical information in Part IV, including an example use case, business case and current evolving trends from here.

This book is for those unheralded heroes who selflessly maintain the availability, reliability, and effortless use of the Internet and IP networks at large. We hope you find the material useful. And we thank you.

East Norriton, PA

Acknowledgments

We would both like to thank Thomas Plevyak, Veli Sahin, and Mary Hatcher, our editors at IEEE Press, as well as Paul Vixie, Greg Rabil, Andreas Taudte, and Paul Mockapetris for their time spent reviewing proposals and drafts of this book and for providing extremely valuable feedback.

Michael: I would like to thank my family, my wife Suzanne, my son Michael, and my daughter Kelly, for all their love and support while working on this book. I would also like to thank the following individuals who are my friends and co-workers. I have had the pleasure to work with some of the best and brightest people in the world, and I am truly blessed. In no particular order: Karen Pell, Steve Thompson, Greg Rabil, John Ramkawsky, Alex Drescher, David Cross, Marco Mecarelli, Brian Hart, Bob Lieber, and all my co-workers at Diamond IP, Lucent, and Quadritek. I would also like to acknowledge the original Quadritek leadership team that I had the privilege to work with as we helped to define and create the IP Address Management market back in the early years, specifically including Joe D'Andrea, Arun Kapur, and Keith Larson.

Timothy: I would first like to thank my family especially my wife LeeAnn and my daughters Maeve and Tess for their love and support during the development of this second edition. I would also like to thank the following individuals with whom I have had the pleasure to work and from whom I have learned tremendously about networking technologies among other things: Greg Rabil, John Ramkawsky, Andy D'Ambrosio, Alex Drescher, Steve Thompson, David Cross, Marco Mecarelli, Brian Hart, Frank Jennings, and those I have worked with at BT Diamond IP, INS, and Lucent. From my formative time in the field of networking at Bell Laboratories, I thank John Marciszewski, Anthony Longhitano, Sampath Ramaswami, Maryclaire Brescia, Krishna Murti, Gaston Arredondo, Robert Schoenweisner, Tom Walker, Charlene Paull, Frank DeAngelis, Ray Pennotti, and particularly my mentor, Thomas Chu. I also wish to acknowledge others who have otherwise inspired me to press on to complete this and prior books, including Peter Tsai, Howard Falick, Holly Weller, Steve Wheeler, Craig Hamilton, Scott Medrano, Bob Lieber, Chris Williams, Ken Schumaker and my esteemed co-author, Michael Dooley.

About the Authors

Michael Dooley – Michael is responsible for overall operations of the Diamond IP division of BT. Prior to joining the team, he was President and CEO of Diamond IP Technologies, a company that was acquired by INS, and in turn by BT. Before Diamond IP Technologies was formed, Michael was Vice President of Operations for the VitalSoft line of software products at Lucent Technologies, and Vice President of Engineering at Quadritek Systems. Michael has co-authored Wiley's IPv6 Deployment and Management and DNS Security Management books, and possesses more than 25 years of experience managing and developing large-scale software products. He is a graduate of Temple University in Philadelphia.

Timothy Rooney – Tim has worked with IP technologies in various capacities over the last 25 years, including systems engineering and development. He has an extensive background in IP, telecommunications, wireless services, and software. Prior to joining Diamond IP, Tim worked at AT&T Bell Laboratories, Triton PCS and Lucent. While at Diamond IP, Tim has managed the engineering development and market introduction of several IP address management systems and managed services. Tim has authored two IPAM books, co-authored two others with Michael Dooley, and holds a Bachelor of Science in Commerce and Engineering Sciences from Drexel and a Master of Science in Electrical Engineering from Rutgers University.

Part I

IPAM Introduction

This opening Part I of this book introduces IP and IPAM basics, providing an overview of IP networking, IP address structures and formats, IP addressing techniques, name-to-IP address resolution, and various uses or applications of IPAM technologies.

1

Introduction

There is no Internet without the Internet Protocol (IP). IP sets the rules for communicating among Internet connected devices and serves as the foundation for every Internet app. IP is not only the protocol for the Internet but is the de facto enterprise network protocol as well. This chapter introduces the basics of IP networking and motivations for managing IP addresses within your own network.

IP Networking Overview

Each party engaged in a communication, whether two people speaking or two computers exchanging information, must comply with a set of conventions that govern the rules of such communication. Language and culture generally guide such conventions for human conversation. A protocol defines these conventions for computers. And it's usually easier to get computers to comply with these conventions than people! A protocol dictates the sequence and syntax of communications as well as recovery mechanisms required in response to error conditions. There are actually several protocols or protocol layers that facilitate computer communications, each providing a specific set of functions to support a level of commonality for communicating over a variety of media. We'll delve more into this later in this chapter, but let's start out with a simple analogy to human communications to introduce the key aspects of IP addressing and why address management is important for those who manage IP networks.

When two people converse, one person may initiate the discussion in one of many ways: by physically approaching the other and speaking, calling him or her on their mobile, sending him or her an instant message, and so on. In each of these scenarios, the initiator of the conversation identifies and locates the intended

IP Address Management, Second Edition. Michael Dooley and Timothy Rooney.
© 2021 The Institute of Electrical and Electronics Engineers, Inc.
Published 2021 by John Wiley & Sons, Inc.

recipient, then attempts to begin a conversation using the chosen medium. When I want to talk to my friend Steve for example, I can look up his number on-line or in a phone book, dial his number, and when he answers the phone, I can identify myself and begin the conversation. At a basic level, IP communications follows a similar process. When an IP device seeks to communicate with another, it must identify and locate the intended recipient, then initiate communications over a link, while also identifying itself to the recipient in the process.

Perhaps the best, though admittedly trite, analogy for IP communications is that of postal letter delivery. Nevertheless, let's consider this process of "sneaker mail," then relate it to IP communications. The basic postal delivery process is depicted in Figure 1.1, beginning with me writing a letter to Steve and communicating it via postal mail.

After writing my letter, I enclose it in an envelope. This is step 1. Next, I write my return (From) address and Steve's (To) address on the envelope, and stamp it to pay my postal service provider. At this point, I'm ready to mail it, so step 3 consists of depositing my letter in my outgoing mailbox. After my mailperson picks up my letter, the fourth step entails forwarding of the letter within the postal system to the local post office serving Steve's address. After the letter has been delivered to the post office or distribution center serving Steve's address, a local delivery mailperson drops the letter in Steve's mailbox. When Steve walks out to the mailbox, he can open the letter and read my letter. Message delivered!

Let's map this postal message flow to sending a message over an IP network, referring to Figure 1.2. In this case, we're communicating electronically over the Internet, though this analogy holds whether communication ensues over a

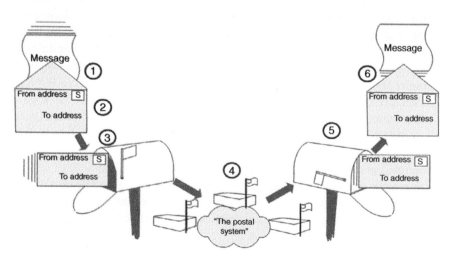

Figure 1.1 The postal delivery analogy.

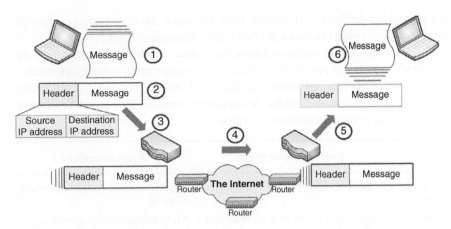

Figure 1.2 Internet protocol communications.

private enterprise, broadband, wireless, or home IP network or a combination thereof. Just as Steve and I have postal mail addresses, we both need IP addresses to communicate with each other over the Internet. No one else in the world has the same mailing address as Steve; likewise, no one else in the world has the same IP address as Steve (technically this isn't necessarily true when IP addresses are translated between me and Steve, but let's go with it for now). Let's assume that each of our computers is configured with its respective IP address and that I know Steve's IP address.

Step 1 entails the creation or typing of my message to Steve. In step 2, my computer, knowing my IP address and Steve's, places my message within a data packet, or specifically an IP packet. An IP packet is simply the message to be communicated (including upper layer headers), prefixed with an IP header. The IP header, like our letter envelope, contains my (From) source IP address as well as Steve's (To) destination IP address, among other fields. Having formulated my IP packet, I'm now ready to send it. From my home network, I have a broadband router, to which my computer transmits my IP packet as step 3. This transmission may occur over a cable or a wireless connection between my computer and the router.

In step 4, my router forwards my IP packet to the Internet via my broadband service provider (no stamp required, they'll bill me later). Devices in the Internet called routers forward my IP packet ultimately to Steve's broadband service provider and the broadband router in his house. Routers examine each IP packet's header information to determine where to forward the packet to reach its destination IP address efficiently. Having been delivered to Steve's broadband router, step 5 consists of forwarding the packet to Steve's computer, whose IP address matches the IP packet's destination IP address field. In step 6, Steve's computer strips off the IP header to yield the message I had typed. Message delivered!

In both postal and IP communications, the source and destination addresses are specified and are unique, an infrastructure of people and/or machines successively forward the message toward its addressed destination, and it is ultimately delivered to the recipient. The table below summarizes the key similarities among the postal and IP communications examples.

	Postal communications	**IP communications**
Message contents	Letter, package, or parcel	Application data such as an instant message
Message container	An envelope or box with To and From street addresses	An IP packet including an IP header with source and destination IP addresses
Sending of the message	Performed by depositing the letter in an outgoing mailbox	Performed by transmitting the IP packet from the device to the local router
Message routing	The letter is physically transported by air, sea and/or ground via one or more postal offices or distribution centers ultimately reaching the postal delivery center serving the To address specified	Routers forward the IP packet over a variety of media (e.g. fiber, copper, wireless) to other routers ultimately reaching the router serving the destination IP address
Message delivery	Postal personnel deliver the letter to the street address specified on the envelope	The local router delivers the IP packet to the computer configured with the destination IP address
Message receipt	The envelope is opened and discarded, and the letter is read	The IP header is stripped from the IP packet and the message or packet payload is delivered to the application (instant message window in this case)

The two core concepts common to these communications analogies are routing and addressing. As we've implied so far, routing is dependent on proper addressing! Let's examine this relationship in more detail.

IP Routing

The postal system operates by "routing" letters and packages as efficiently as possible to regional distribution centers, local centers, and finally to the curb. Scanning and tracking systems along the way direct parcels closer to their ultimate destination via various means of transportation through one or more distribution centers along the way. Typically, this routing is performed by first examining the "To" (destination) addressed country, postal code, city and state or province, and finally the street address. The encoding of the general (country, postal code) and the specific (street address) in the "To" address enables different entities in the postal system to use different portions of the address to route efficiently. Distribution centers can forward packages based only on country and postal code information; once the parcel arrives at a local center serving the destination postal code, the local center then needs to examine the street address for final delivery.

If Steve lives down the street, my letter will simply traverse my local post office, perhaps a distribution center and back to Steve's local post office for delivery. If Steve lives across the country, my letter will likely route from my local post office through one or more regional centers, then to Steve's local distribution center for delivery. If Steve lives in a different country, my letter will likely be required to enter the country through a customs agent. The customs agent may analyze the letter and either allow its further delivery within the country or deny it by returning it to the sender or confiscating or disposing it.

Routers perform analogous functions in routing IP packets. Routers mimic the scanning systems of the postal system by examining the network portion of the destination IP address within each IP packet and forwarding it on, getting closer to the destination with each hop. Upon reaching the local serving router, this router examines the full IP address in order to deliver it to the intended recipient. Hence, IP addresses are comprised of a network portion and a host portion, concatenated together as we'll discuss in the next chapter.

If the packet is destined for a network operated privately, e.g. by a corporation or enterprise, the packet will likely meet with examination analogous to the customs agent. And like the customs agent, this enterprise gateway or firewall can allow or deny further transmission of the packet to its destination. By the way, just as storms or other events can cause flight delays or mail reroutes in the postal system, routers can detect analogous outage or congestion events to reroute IP packets as needed. Yes neither rain, nor snow, nor dark of night will stop postal mail or IP packet delivery!

IP Addresses

As we've seen, each device on an IP network must be uniquely identifiable, by means of an IP address. Hence, each device desiring to communicate on an IP network requires an IP address. Your computer at home, your voice-over-IP phone at work, and your mobile all have IP addresses, at least at the time they're powered up and ready to communicate. In our example above, we assumed that the IP address of each computer was already programmed in, but how does this IP address get in there? The IP address for each device can be assigned and configured in each device either manually or automatically.

The manual address assignment approach using a fixed IP address works well for fixed infrastructure IP devices like routers and servers. But for the vast majority of IP addressable devices such as laptops and mobile phones, which are highly mobile, the fixed address assignment approach does not work well. This is because the assigned IP address must be relevant to the current network or subnet to which the IP device is connected. If these IP devices move about, they need to be IP-addressable within the context of their current location on the IP network, rendering the manual method very cumbersome. Even the postal service doesn't offer a "find me" service to deliver my mail to me wherever I happen to be!

To illustrate this location-sensitivity requirement, consider a small organization with three offices as illustrated in the left of Figure 1.3. To enable network communications among these sites, we interconnect them over a wide area network (WAN), which may be the Internet or in this case, a private network from a service provider. To enable communications and routing, we've installed at least one router in each location as illustrated in the right of Figure 1.3. This figure shows an overlay of a simple IP network among these locations.

To enable routing among these locations, we need to assign each location a unique set of IP addresses. In this way, the Branch Office will be home for one set of IP addresses (or one IP network), the Retail Store a different set, and Headquarters, yet another unique set of IP addresses. Let's use the set of IP addresses shown for each router as in Figure 1.4. Each router will support a set of IP addresses, from which individual IP addresses would be assigned to printers, laptops, voice over IP phones, and other IP devices in that location.

We'll describe the structure and format of both versions (IPv4 and internet protocol version 6 [IPv6]) of IP addresses in more detail in Chapter 2, but an IPv4 address is composed of four numbers, separated by decimal points or dots. Each of the four numbers can range in value from 0 to 255. In our example, IP address set 10.1.1.0–255 has been allocated to headquarters, 10.2.1.0–255 to the branch office, and 10.3.1.0–255 to the retail store. IPv6 addresses, also assigned to each location to support a dual-stack structure, are comprised of up to thirty-two hex

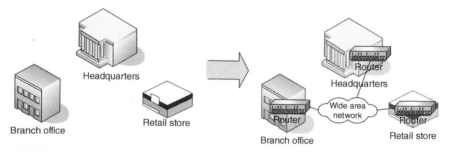

Figure 1.3 Organization's locations with IP network foundation.

digits, grouped into sets of four, and separated by colons, with strings of zeroes indicated by double colons. Each of these IP address sets is called a subnetwork or subnet, as each represents a portion or subset of the overall enterprise's set of IP addresses.

Note that each set of IP addresses falls within a contiguous IP address range which corresponds to the network portion of the IP addresses within each set. Recall from our postal analogy that the network portion of the address is analogous to the postal distribution center which is used for efficient routing until the post or IP packet in this case is delivered to the local serving router.

The interconnecting WAN also has a network address to enable inter-site communications. The routers in each location must be configured with this network information in order to properly route IP communications traffic. In this way, our Branch Office router is responsible for IP addresses 10.2.1.0–10.2.1.255 and 2001:db8:0:2::-2001:db8:0:2:ffff:ffff:ffff:ffff, so all IP packets with a destination IP address falling in these ranges will be forwarded to the Branch Office router. This partitioning of IP addresses to particular sites or routers is analogous to the splitting of geographic locations by zip code and corresponding postal distribution centers.

Now that we've partitioned our IP addresses and configured our routers in accordance with our addressing plan, let's look at address assignment for a given device, say my laptop. Let's say I'm in the branch office on Monday as signified by laptop-abc in Figure 1.4, I'll need an IP address from the branch office subnet, let's say 10.2.1.52 and 2001:db8:0:2::80e1:4d. This is because the Branch router "owns" the 10.2.1.0–255 and 2001:db8:0:2:: subnets and serves as my "local post office" for delivery of IP packets to devices in the branch office. When I send an instant message to a colleague at Headquarters, my messages are routed to a Headquarters router and responses are routed to me via the Branch Router.

Now let's assume I'm called to a meeting at the retail store on Tuesday. When I arrive at the retail store and connect to the store's network with my manually configured 10.2.1.52 and 2001:db8:0:2::80e1:4d IP addresses, I will quickly realize

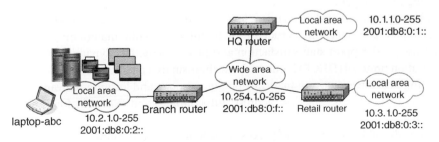

Figure 1.4 A more detailed IP network breakdown.

that I cannot communicate on the network. This is because my configured IP addresses are part of the branch office network, not the retail store networks or 10.3.1.0 and 2001:db8:0:3::. Thus, when I begin sending an IP communication, say by opening a web page, entering a www address, my web browser sends an IP packet to the destination website IP address, using my laptop's IP address, 10.2.1.52, as the source IP address. The web server acknowledges the communication and responds with the requested web page, addressing it back to IP address 10.2.1.52. The routers all "know" that the Branch Router serves IP addresses on the 10.2.1.0-255 subnet, so they route the response IP packet intended for my web browser back to the branch office!

From my perspective, I'm not getting a response from the web server. Is the network down or is the web server down? As I call the help desk complaining about the network outage, the network team quickly discovers that my IP address is not appropriate for the subnet to which I am connected. They walk me through the cumbersome process of manually changing my laptop's IP address to 10.3.1.187 or would you believe 2001:db8:0:3:7fe:d912:af99:3476, only to walk me back through the reverse process when I return to the branch office on Wednesday. Once my address is relevant to my location, I'm able to communicate bidirectionally with the web server and other IP application servers such as email servers because my address falls within the set assigned to the local serving router.

This simple example illustrates the importance of not only having an IP address for IP communications but one that's appropriate to the subnet to which you're connected. Thus, with even minimal mobility of associates going to meetings, visiting customers, or generally traveling about, the clumsy manual help desk process outlined above is impractical. To require people to call the help desk when they need a new IP address (not only when the network really is down) reduces end user productivity (and patience!), as well as increases the costs of help desk operations and network and server technical support. Plus, it's extremely difficult to walk a "technically challenged" person through the process of manually entering an IP address on a device! And as the variety of devices that people use to connect increases, the variety of IP address entry methods likely increases as well, adding to the support team burden.

Clearly, an automated mechanism for assigning a unique IP address relevant to the subnet of connection is crucial to reducing costs while maintaining overall end user and support staff satisfaction and productivity. The dynamic host configuration protocol (DHCP) is one such mechanism that enables an IP device connecting to a network to automatically obtain a unique and location-relevant IPv4 and/or IPv6 address. Stateless address autoconfiguration (SLAAC) for IPv6 is another.

Once the address assignment process is automated, we've eliminated the error-prone human entry of device IP addresses. But what about the destination IP address? Earlier, we glossed over the fact that I already knew Steve's IP address or that the www address I typed was magically translated into an IP address to enable creation of an IP packet. So, if communications on an IP network requires IP addresses, how do we get away with entering text names to send emails or connect to websites? The solution is the domain name system (DNS), which enables users to enter names for services, websites, or email boxes, obviating the need to enter IP addresses.

We generally take this for granted, which is a good thing! Imagine carting around the equivalent to an Internet phone book with websites and associated IP addresses. DNS works "behind the scenes" to provide a name-to-address lookup mechanism to bridge this gap between human consumable names to network consumable IP addresses. Unless you're a numbers wizard, entering http://www.ipamworldwide.com in your web browser is vastly simpler than entering (and remembering) https://192.0.2.201, let alone https://2001:db8:7e9:31a:ce00::90aa. Fortunately, this usability problem was recognized early in the development of the Internet and DNS was devised to automate this directory lookup function.

Once you type in a www address, your computer looks up the www address in DNS and obtains the corresponding IP address, which it then uses as the destination IP address in the IP header. Other forms of name-to-address translation have been developed over the years, including hosts files, Yellow Pages (YP), and Windows Internet Naming Service (WINS), but DNS has sustained its dominant status as the de facto, production network-proven name-to-address translation service for IP communications today. Before further exploring the core elements of IP address management (IPAM), namely IP address allocation, DHCP and DNS, let's take a more detailed look at the basics of IP networking by exploring the inner workings of how routers deliver IP packets to their respective destinations.

At this point, you may be wondering, why don't we just eliminate the routers and use one massive network that everyone can share instead of employing this subnetting process that leads to readdressing of my laptop when I move from location to location? After all, I could just use one IP address anywhere in the network. While this approach is theoretically possible utilizing a bridged network across all of these sites, this does not scale well because performance of communications will suffer with growing inter-site distance and number of devices on the network. This is due to that fact that in a shared or bridged network, every device's messages are sent to every other device on the network. And because the network is a shared medium, collisions may result when two or more devices attempt to send messages at the same time.

Collisions in the networking world have the same effect as those in interpersonal communications. As more members join the "conversation," collisions arise more frequently. As collisions occur, parties to the conversation (at least the polite ones) back-off momentarily before reattempting to initiate communications. The more parties involved in the conversation, the more frequently collisions occur, and the larger the backlog of messages awaiting communications. This attempt/back-off/reattempt process escalates quickly until ultimately no party attempting to communicate gets a message to a recipient. As the backlog of reattempts to communicate builds, frustration escalates and gridlock results. The same effect occurs when too many devices attempt to communicate on a large monolithic shared medium. And the same general solution, which for human conversation consists of groups naturally branching off from the main conversation into subgroups of smaller sets of people, can be applied to IP networks.

By reducing and limiting the number of parties communicating on the same medium, we can localize the collision domain and reduce the number of collisions and backlog on the network as a whole. The deployment of switches and routers supports this partitioning of the network into separate collision domains. Switches enable partitioning of the collision domain itself by virtue of interconnecting pair-wise switch ports, each of which is physically connected to a host. Routers provide collision domain boundary points by terminating yet interconnecting collision domains. Routers in particular leverage the concept of protocol layering to separate collision domains. Let's review the concept of protocol layering which will lead us back to a more detailed discussion of the roles of switches and routers.

Protocol Layering

The International Standards Organization (ISO) has defined a layered protocol model, separating responsibilities for different aspects of controlling communications [1]. The layered model consists of seven layers and is denoted the open systems interconnect (OSI) model. The term protocol stack refers to the fact that several protocol layers are "stacked" one upon another to usher data and commands from my web browser onto the wire or over the air and through the network to the destination. In fact, the Internet Protocol's ability to run over various media such as these and others is a powerful consequence of the use of a layered protocol stack. The OSI model enables a common implementation of the Internet Protocol across a variety of lower layer data link and physical layers, including cable, digital subscriber line (DSL), fiber, Ethernet, Wi-Fi, 5G, and so on. Figure 1.5 illustrates the OSI model with a brief summary of key functions of each layer.

Application layer (layer 7)   The application layer provides the primary end user exposure and functionality. For example, a web browser, file transfer program, or email client are examples of applications.

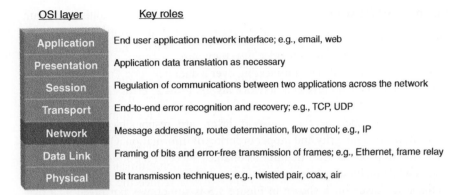

Figure 1.5 OSI protocol stack summary. Source: ISO/IEC [1].

Presentation layer (layer 6)   The presentation layer is responsible for defining the data format and syntax between application endpoints in the communication. For example, this layer specifies standard graphics formatting and translation for communications across the network.

Session layer (layer 5)   The session layer is responsible for regulating the end-to-end communications of applications across the network, providing such services as security and authentication. NetBIOS is an example of a session layer protocol.

Transport layer (layer 4)   The transport layer is responsible for end-to-end communications integrity, assuring flow control between the two endpoints, as well as data checking, requesting retransmissions, and proper ordering of information. Transmission control protocol (TCP) and user datagram protocol (UDP) are transport layer protocols within the TCP/IP stack.

Network layer (layer 3)   The network layer is responsible for the formatting of information into packets and/or packet fragments for communications and for routing over one or more networks. IP is a network layer protocol.

Data link layer (layer 2)   The data link layer is responsible for formatting of information into frames for communications over the physical network, including error checking for data integrity. Ethernet, Token Ring, and Wi-Fi are examples of data link layer protocols. The data link layer is commonly split into logical link control (LLC) and media access control (MAC) sublayers. The familiar term "MAC address" refers to a device's layer 2 or media access control address.

Physical layer (layer 1)   The physical layer defines the electronic interfaces and characteristics including voltage and current specifications for transmission of data and control (e.g. preamble) bits. EIA-232 (RS-232) provides an example of a physical layer specification.

OSI and TCP/IP Layers

These protocol layers not only permit interoperability for multiple applications and underlying physical networks but they also segment the responsibility required for successfully communicating over a data network. For example, some layers such as the data link and network layers, provide error checking and correction to facilitate accurate communications and reduce retransmission requirements. Others, such as the transport layer, are responsible for end-to-end communications integrity and proper ordering of information. Overall, the standardization of protocol layer definitions enables successful end-to-end communications while facilitating interoperability.

This seven-layer stack shown in Figure 1.5 is sometimes portrayed as a five-layer stack in the Internet context with the Application layer sitting above TCP, IP, data link, and physical layers, respectively, as shown in Figure 1.6. Protocol layering enables not only the transmission of IP packets over a variety of media but it also permits a variety of end user applications to communicate over IP, which in turn run over various lower layer protocols. For example, an email client application can communicate to an email server using a post office protocol version 3 (POP3) application, which is layered on TCP, and in turn IP, which can then be layered on an Ethernet, Token Ring, Wi-Fi, or other layer 2 protocol, and ultimately a particular physical layer. Another example illustrated in Figure 1.6 features hypertext transfer protocol (HTTP) (web browsing), TFTP (trivial file transfer protocol), and POP3 running over respective transport protocols and IP, Ethernet and 100BaseT. This provides a seamless end user experience in using

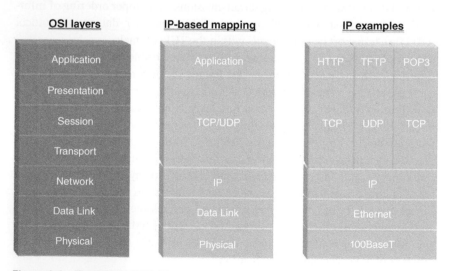

Figure 1.6 The OSI and TCP/IP protocol stacks.

common applications whether communicating over an Ethernet 1000BaseT network, an 802.11 wireless network, or an asynchronous transfer mode (ATM)-based network.

Layering also enables components of the stack to be developed and offered by different organizations. In practice, protocol layering works effectively at the application to TCP/IP boundary and the TCP/IP to data link boundary, though TCP and UDP generally operate exclusively with IP at the transport-network layer boundary. An application programming interface (API) enables a variety of applications from different vendors to utilize common function calls into the TCP/IP stack, which is commonly included with the operating system. The de facto API for TCP/IP applications is the *sockets* interface originally implemented on BSD UNIX (on which DNS BIND was also originally implemented). The sockets interface defines program calls to enable applications to interface with TCP/IP layers to communicate over IP networks. Microsoft's Winsock API is also based on the sockets interface.

TCP/UDP Ports

The "IP Examples" stack on the right of Figure 1.6 illustrates that a device may be running multiple applications, all reachable by its IP address. Once an IP packet has been successfully routed to the destination denoted by its IP address, the stack must deliver the packet to the correct application. Port or socket numbers for the source and destination are specified in the transport layer (TCP or UDP) header, which enable specification of a desired application. A given TCP/IP connection between two endpoints is defined by this four-tuple: {Source IP address, Source port, Destination IP address, and Destination port}. Sometimes the protocol, TCP or UDP is considered a fifth member of a five-tuple.

The source port is typically selected randomly by the sending device, while the destination port is defined by the corresponding application to which a connection is desired. Example "well-known" TCP/UDP ports include 53 for DNS, 67 for DHCP, 547 for DHCPv6, 80 for HTTP, and 443 for HTTPS. A device desiring to issue a DNS query would populate its source IP address, a random source UDP port, the DNS server's IP address within the Destination IP address field and port 53 as the destination port.

Intra-Link Communications

To get our arms around how data flows through these layers within protocol stacks, consider Figure 1.7. Beginning with the application data in the upper left of the figure, notice the addition of headers as the application data payload traverses down the stack. The data link frame that is transmitted on the local network

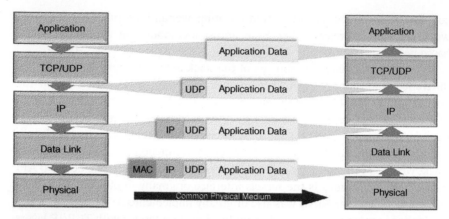

Figure 1.7 Protocol layering.

encloses the application data and upper layer headers. The frame recipient on the right side of the figure then processes and strips off each header at corresponding layers as the data is passed up the stack to the destination application. The headers and payload shown at each layer boundary are exactly the same on both ends of this intra-link communication.

As application data is prepared for transmission on an IP network using a TCP/IP stack, the application calls the sockets API to communicate the data down the stack. A TCP or UDP header is added based on application selection, and then an IP header is appended. Recalling our earlier postal analogy, we can now see that the IP header was just one such header added to a network message. The "message" to which the IP header was appended included the application data (e.g. the instant message text) plus the transport layer (TCP or UDP) header. In this multi-layered stack model, each layer adds a header to enable it to perform its respective function.

The application generally specifies the UDP or TCP header parameters, which consist of the application-specific port number as well as checksum, flow control, and other data. The IP header contains the sender's and the receiver's IP addresses. The sender's IP address is assigned manually or automatically (e.g. via DHCP or SLAAC), and the recipient's IP address is entered either via the application user interface or is fetched from a DNS server.

Below the IP layer, the IP packet, which itself comprises an IP header, a TCP or UDP header, and application data, is enclosed within a data link layer frame for transmission over the physical network. Communication on a given data link requires encapsulation of the IP packet within a data link frame, which itself requires source and destination data link (MAC) addresses. To transmit the IP packet within a data link frame, the transmitting host must determine the recipient's data link (MAC) address. So the device must map the destination IP address to a destination MAC address for transmission within a layer 2 frame on the physical network. But another wrinkle arises depending on whether the destination IP address is on the same data link as the sender.

Are We on the Same Link?

Generally, each device can determine if the intended recipient resides on the same link by virtue of its configured IP address and subnet address range. If the destination IP address falls within the same subnet range as the sender's IP address, the device is considered on the same link. Otherwise, if the intended recipient does not reside on the same subnet, the source device must identify a router on the link which can forward or route the data to the intended destination. Using either a routing table, or for most non-router devices, a configured *default route*, the device can determine the next hop to which to send the data. A default route is the next hop destination to which all packets are sent in the absence of a known next hop toward the intended destination address. This is kind of like my outgoing mailbox in the postal analogy, which is where I place all of my outgoing communiqués. This default route is typically the IP address of a router serving the subnet to which all outbound packets destined beyond the subnet are to be sent. This router is also referred to as the *default gateway*.

For example, as per Figure 1.4, if I use my laptop to transmit data to another device within the branch office, i.e. with destination IP address in the range of 10.1.1.0–10.1.1.255 or 2001:db8:0:2::, it can be sent directly (intra-link); if I transmit data to a device in HQ or the retail store, my laptop must send it to the branch router for routing to the destination via the WAN. Whether sending the data to an intra-link destination or a router, the sending device must determine the recipient's or router's data link (MAC) address in order to formulate and transmit the IP packet within a data link layer frame. This MAC address is generally the data link layer address for the intended device. But we determined the destination IP address from DNS, not the MAC address; so how is this MAC address determined?

The *address resolution protocol (ARP)* enables a device to determine the MAC address of a device on the same link corresponding to its IP address. The device transmitting the message knowing the intended next hop IP address (recipient on-link or router) formulates an ARP data link broadcast frame requesting MAC resolution of the IP address. A broadcast frame is a data link frame addressed to all devices on the link. For Ethernet data links for example, a broadcast frame uses the destination Ethernet address of all 1's, meaning the broadcast address for all devices connected to this Ethernet link. The device that is configured with the sought IP address responds with an ARP response frame indicating its corresponding layer 2 address. This enables the source device to formulate the Ethernet frame for transmission of the IP packet. Most devices cache this information in an ARP cache, providing a temporary storage of this IP-to-MAC address correlation to reduce the need for repeated ARP queries, e.g. for multi-frame or frequent communications.

Limiting Broadcast Domains

Data links like Ethernet comprise the collision domains (also referred to as broadcast domains) we referred to earlier. The data link layer is chiefly concerned with accessing the network for transmission, detecting collisions, and performing error checking on frames. All devices connected to a common data link receive frames sent from every other connected device. As the number of devices within the collision domain increases, and/or the number of communications attempts per device increases and/or the volume of communications per device increases, the more likely data collisions will occur, degrading network performance. If we can confine the number of participants in each collision domain, we can improve overall performance and end user productivity and satisfaction.

This brings us back to how switches and routers constrain broadcast domains. Historically, Ethernet local area networks (LANs) were deployed with wiring to each office, cubicle, or end station funneled back to one or more Ethernet hubs. Hubs literally broadcast frames received on any given port to every other port, thus comprising an indivisible collision domain. Switches were developed to directly interconnect (or switch) traffic between source and destination ports without blindly broadcasting all data to all ports. Switch ports effectively provide a direct point-to-point connection between the end device and its switch port. The switch detects the MAC address of each connected device then leverages this information to directly interconnect the port on which the frame is incoming to the appropriate destination port. This minimizes superfluous broadcast traffic to devices on all other ports. Of course, layer 2 broadcast traffic is broadcast to all switch ports, but this certainly offers an improvement!

Modern layer 2 switches have further evolved to enable definition of a subset of physical ports to a given broadcast domain. Thus, instead of hardwiring hub ports within a broadcast domain or LAN, one could partition which switch ports belong to independent broadcast domains. These independent broadcast domains are referred to as virtual LANs (VLANs), as the switch supports multiple logical LANs on one physical switch device. Broadcast traffic on ports within VLAN 1 will not be broadcast to switch ports associated with VLAN 2 for example. Consider Figure 1.8 for an example of VLAN segmentation. The figure shows the common implementation of associating different VLANs with different subnet addresses. This is contrasted against the single broadcast domain per hub shown on the left of the figure.

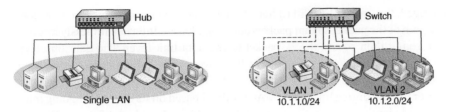

Figure 1.8   Hub vs. switch/VLAN architecture.

Interlink Communications

Switches certainly help reduce the scope of collision domains but there are only so many switch ports! The second method used to limit broadcast domains leverages protocol layering concepts and employs routers to separate layer 2 networks. Consider Figure 1.9, which is a recasting of Figure 1.7 with an intervening router. The left side of the figure is identical to that in Figure 1.7. Each protocol layer adds its respective header as the application data moves down the stack. Finally, the Ethernet frame is sent over the physical [layer] network to a router. The router also has a protocol stack, but it consists only of layers 1–3 (routers generally do provide a configuration "application" layer but the purposes of this discussion, we'll consider their routing functions only). As the router's data link layer checks the frame integrity, it strips off the layer 2 frame header (and footer if used) then passes the IP packet to the IP layer, the router analyzes the source and destination IP addresses (and potentially other IP header fields) to determine where next to route the packet. That is, the router is only an intermediate point on the way toward the ultimate destination, hence its protocol stack limitation to layers 1–3.

After the router determines where next to route the IP packet, it appends a modified IP header (note the differently shaded IP header in the figure – the source and destination IP addresses remain the same but at least one other field is

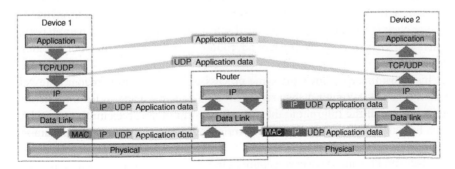

Figure 1.9   Protocol stacks with an intervening router.

changed, the time to live (TTL) field, which is decremented by each router along the path of the packet so that packets don't wander the Internet aimlessly forever). The router then passes the IP packet to the data link layer. The data link layer encapsulates the IP packet within a link layer frame appropriate to the corresponding link and physical layers over which the message will be transmitted. The router uses its source link layer (MAC) address based on its chosen outgoing interface and identifies the destination link layer address based on ARP or ARP cache mapping of the next hop IP address to its corresponding MAC address. Thus, the router may receive the incoming packet on the left over a wireless link, then transmit it as modified appropriately over an Ethernet link.

Upon receiving the link layer frame, Device 2's protocol stack processes each successive layer, passing it up its stack to the intended application. Note that the data link and IP layer frames and packets respectively vary link-by-link. However, the transport layer message and application data itself are identical at both the sending and receiving ends of the connection. Of course, the goal is to transmit the application data intact, and the identical TCP/UDP layer message enables the intended end-to-end processing required of the transport layer.

We can now conclude that the router serves to terminate the data link layer or collision domain on the left side of the figure, only to modify the IP and MAC headers then forward the message to a second collision domain on the right side of the figure. For this reason, routers are also known as *gateways*, serving as gateways between layer 2 collision domains and IP networks. While switches utilize port VLAN configurations to separate collision domains at layer 2, routers use IP subnets to differentiate collision domains at layer 3.

Worldwide IP Communications

Let's extrapolate our view from Figure 1.9 from two devices interconnected via a single gateway to a scenario where I'm using my computer at home over my broadband connection to access a web server halfway around the world, as shown in Figure 1.10. When I browse the website hosted on the server, the site address I type or click is captured and formulated into IP packets (thanks in part to DNS) that are then sent via my broadband router to my service provider's router, Router A.

This transmission follows the same process we reviewed as shown on the left half of Figure 1.9. Router A then routes my data packet via additional intervening routers through the Internet to the ultimate destination, served by Router G. On each link along the way, each router terminates the layer 2 frame and IP packet, determines where next to route it (next hop IP address from a particular outgoing interface) and formulates a corresponding frame for transmission to the next hop. Notice that there are multiple paths from my PC to the web server in Figure 1.10.

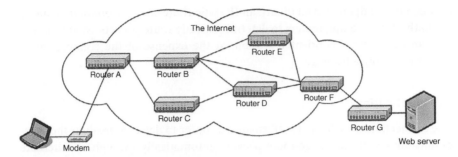

Figure 1.10   Simple view of an IP network such as the Internet.

One of my packets may travel from end to end over path A–B–E–F–G, while the next packet may take a different path, say A–C–D–F–G, and so on. Each IP packet is routed independently through the network.

Contrast this with an old-fashioned circuit-switched telephone call that temporarily "nails up" a dedicated connection through the traditional telephone network from my phone to the phone of the person I'm calling. Since our voice conversation requires setup of a connection which comprises a physical path through the telephone network for the duration of our discussion, this type of connection is referred to as "connection-oriented." At the IP layer, IP does not establish a connection prior to communicating, and each IP packet is routed independently: all packets may happen to follow a common end-to-end path, they may all take different paths, or more likely, somewhere between these two extremes. IP is therefore considered "connectionless."

Connection-oriented communications generally provide a more reliable method of communications at the expense of tying up network resources and not dynamically rerouting around intermediate failure points during the connection session. The term *reliable* in this context means that there are means to detect and recover from dropped packets or packet fragments. "Pardon me?" usually works during a voice conversation and certain protocols such as TCP include an analogous construct with positive acknowledgement. While IP itself is considered an unreliable datagram service, the transport layer above IP, namely the TCP, can be used to overlay connection-oriented controls to provide reliable communications between two devices or hosts. Without nailing up a physical connection, TCP provides mechanisms to properly order incoming IP packets and to request retransmission of IP packets should one or more get lost along the way. UDP is an alternative connectionless transport layer protocol within the TCP/IP protocol suite which provides unreliable data delivery. Conversely, a pseudo-layer 2 technology such as multi-protocol label switching, MPLS, could be used to logically "nail up" a connection path over which IP packets can be transmitted between two endpoints. And finally, an IP static route could be configured along the path of intervening routers to deterministically route packets. Static routing emulates a connection-oriented session, at the expense of the connectionless dynamic routing advantage.

Dynamic Routing

The connectionless scheme for IP enables a router to detect a break in the communications path and to re-route packets automatically through an alternate route, keeping the lines of communication open. If you've ever been on a phone call and the call dropped, you've experienced this disadvantage of connection-oriented communications: if a link along the path fails, the entire session fails. Connectionless communications provide automated routing around outages, and this resilience was in fact one of the key design goals of the Internet Protocol.

Each router along the communications path of an IP packet examines the destination IP address in the IP header to identify whether it directly serves the network on which the destination IP address resides, or failing that, to which router to forward the packet that is "closer" to the ultimate destination. Each router consults an internal routing table, which stores information about where next to route packets destined for various IP networks. The routing table within each router governs routing decisions on each incoming IP packet and generally indicates one or more next hops in the path for a given destination network. A next hop is another router to which a given router can forward the packet directly. That is, the next hop is an adjacent or directly connected router, which itself may be directly connected or be multiple (hopefully fewer) hops away from the destination. In this way, each router need not be aware of every other router on the Internet; instead a given router must simply know where next among its directly connected peers to send a packet to get it closer to its ultimate destination.

A *routing protocol* is used by each router to periodically communicate with its neighboring routers to obtain their current routing and reachability information to keep routing tables up-to-date. Hence, dynamic routing makes use of recently updated routing information to make next-hop routing decisions. If a link or router fails, reachability changes will be detected and updated reachability metrics will ripple through the routing infrastructure via the chosen routing protocol. Routing protocols define the format and rules governing this "background" communication among routers which enable each to maintain its routing table with the latest reachability information.

For example, considering Figure 1.10, Router B will receive advertisements of reachability to the network on which the web server resides from Routers A, D, E, and F. None of these routers directly serves this network but they offer an intermediate path. Using a simple hop count distance metric, router F advertises a hop count of 2, while routers D and E advertise a hop count of 3 and Router A a hop count of 4. Presumably, the chosen next hop will be closer to the intended destination, i.e. Router F, though other factors such as packet traffic congestion may come into play. More sophisticated metrics beyond hop count are now taken into account with modern routing protocols. Upon receiving the packet from Router B, the chosen next hop router then performs the same basic algorithm to determine whether it directly serves the IP network or if the packet must be sent on to another router, e.g. Router G. Ultimately, the packet should reach a router serving the intended destination IP address for delivery.

Two types of routing protocols are generally used by an organization. Interior routing protocols enable routers within an organization to communicate subnet reachability. Interior routing protocols include routing information protocol (RIP/RIP-2), Enhanced Interior Gateway Routing Protocol (EIGRP from Cisco Systems Inc.), and open shortest path first (OSPF), which is far and away the most popular. Exterior routing protocols, such as intermediate system to intermediate system (IS-IS) protocol or border gateway protocol (BGP), enable updating of reachability and metric information across organizations or routing domains. Reachability to my network is communicated by my routers (or my Internet service provider [ISP]) using an exterior routing protocol. BGP is the de facto Internet standard exterior routing protocol.

Organizations typically run an interior routing protocol like OSPF on their internal routing network and BGP on their externally facing router interfaces, e.g. those connected to their *ISPs*. However, BGP is not necessary for organizations with a single ISP connection not providing downstream routing, e.g. to other organizations. For example, BGP would not be required for a small office with a single-ISP connection. Such an end user is considered single-homed in contrast to a multi-homed organization with multiple Internet connections to one or multiple ISPs. BGP summarizes reachability information for the organization, which is identified via an autonomous system (AS) number. AS numbers are simply organizational identifiers and are distributed and managed by *Regional Internet Registries (RIRs)* to uniquely identify an organization or more accurately, a routing domain. We'll delve into the role of RIRs in Chapter 3.

What is meant by the statement that "BGP summarizes reachability information"? When communicating subnet reachability (known as *advertising*) to the Internet using an exterior routing protocol, the routers do not list every subnet by hop number. This would create a massive amount of messaging overhead. A process called summarization or aggregation enables the communication of a single network address on the Internet for each such contiguous set of IP addresses. This is kind of like routing letters to a zip code distribution center. The center at the other end of the country needs only route to the destination postal code center then allow that center to perform local delivery. Likewise, summarization enables routers to identify a contiguous set of IP addresses as a single network address along with its relative proximity or distance instead of communicating such reachability for every single IP address or subnet. Typically, an organization obtains a set of Internet addresses from an RIR or ISP and simply advertises reachability to all such addresses by network address. It's then up to the organization to carve up this network allocation internally for Internet reachability as needed. This block allocation process is one of the key processes of IPAM as we'll discuss in detail in Chapter 6. A similar summarization process is utilized by interior routing protocols as well.

Routers and Subnets

As routers serve as inter-link gateways and forward or route packets based on layer 3 (IP) information, each link needs to be assigned a set of IP addresses, i.e., a subnet address. Each device on a given link will require an IP address from the corresponding subnet address associated with the link and will generally utilize ARP to identify a MAC address corresponding to the IP address to which to transmit IP packets over the link. The process of IP subnetting entails the partitioning of an IP network into contiguous sets or blocks of IP addresses, which are then associated with each link or subnet. Based on the subnet plan, a key element of IPAM, routers can be provisioned accordingly.

Provisioning a subnet on a router is akin to the addition of a new housing development for postal delivery. Just as the postal system must be updated to reflect the newly available addresses, Internet routers must likewise be updated. Fortunately, in both cases, this is usually a simple process. In the postal case, most new neighborhoods fall within an existing postal code and as long as the rest of the "postal system" can continue to deliver letters to the postal distribution center serving this zip code, updating is limited to systems and personnel within the local center or zip code.

In the Internet world, each organization desiring to communicate on the Internet needs a set of Internet-unique IP addresses. An organization's set or block of IP addresses can be likened to a zip code. Any IP communications destined for devices within an organization's set of addresses are routed to the organization's routers, akin to zip code distribution centers. The organization's routers then handle "local delivery" within the organization. Hence, the addition of a subnet to a router's configuration affects only intraorganization routers, which need to be updated via the interior routing protocol to identify which router serves the new subnet.

Referring back to our example network in Figure 1.4, the Branch office router advertises direct reachability to the 10.2.1.0 network, not a listing of 0–255 IP addresses; this reduces the size of routing tables and update messages from 256 to 1 for each such subnet, thereby reducing overhead and improving router performance. Likewise, the advertisement of the 2001:db8:0:2:: network affords one route instead of 1.8×10^{19} individual IP addresses. And this is why we don't allow the Retail Store router to contend with the Branch office router for serving the IP address 10.2.1.52 when I'm at the Retail store for a day: the overhead in routing protocol messages would create needless traffic at the expense of end user productivity traffic. Overhead is also minimized by virtue of the fact that the router only analyzes up to the IP layer in the protocol stack. Without having to fully digest each frame, it is able to quickly discern where next to route the message.

In the case of our HQ networks, if three networks were served by a single router, the router could communicate its proximity to these networks in one statement instead of $3 \times 256 = 768$ for each IP address, or at worst just three, one for each network. Organizing your address space to promote this router aggregation is important to keeping routing protocol communications small to speed up communications of updates and routing outages while enabling scalability.

Within an organization, address space planning must consider address capacity needs for the IP device population in the context of the organization's routing topology. And as we'll see in later chapters, alignment of address allocations with routing topology produces an efficient address plan that will minimize routing protocol update traffic and routing table sizes.

Assigning IP addresses

The subnet and network plan serves as the foundation on which individual devices can obtain IP addresses(es) relevant to their respective points of connection. Tracking of address assignments is critical given that a duplicate IP address assignment would render communications impossible for both claimants to the duplicate IP address. While some devices like routers, switches, and servers may be manually configured with IP addresses, these addresses must be tracked to eliminate IP address duplications. For other devices such as end user devices, DHCP serves as the Internet standard protocol for server-based automated IP address assignment. DHCP is a client/server protocol which "leases" IP addresses to clients for a duration configurable by an administrator from a few seconds to forever.

SLAAC is an IPv6 feature which enables a device to determine the relevant subnet address based on information from the serving router to derive a full IPv6 address. Duplicate address detection (DAD) is a process whereby each IPv6 address, whether derived via SLAAC or leased from DHCP, is verified as unique on the subnet.

The Human Element

All of this discussion of IP addresses, subnets, routers, etc. is exciting for us and hopefully for you, dear reader, but what of your network users? They likely have little desire to even know about networking details underpinning their access to email and websites. Fortunately, thanks to the wonder of IP routing we've discussed in this chapter, IP packets can usually get from point A to point B on the Internet. And fortunately for end users, the DNS makes identifying point B as simple as typing a www address in a browser.

Often termed "the directory of the Internet" or similarly banal labels, DNS is essentially a distributed Internet database of information, commonly consisting of IP addresses associated with domain names. When users enter a web address into a browser, the browser initiates a DNS lookup for the entered web address in text form to retrieve its corresponding IP address, which the browser populates as the destination IP address within its IP packet to connect to the webserver. DNS certainly makes the Internet usable for humans, at least mere mortals not well versed in IPAM technologies!

Why Manage IP Space?

Given the necessity of users automatically obtaining relevant IP address assignments for their devices and easily navigating the Internet thanks to the DNS, network managers clearly should be monitoring, tracking, and configuring their DHCP and DNS services in conjunction with their overall IP address plans. The practice of IPAM entails the application of network management disciplines to IP address space and associated network services, namely DHCP and DNS. The linkages among an IP address plan and configurations of DHCP and DNS servers are inseparable. A change of an IP address will affect DNS information and perhaps DHCP as well. These services provide the foundation for today's converged services IP networks, which offer ad hoc anytime, anyplace communications.

If end user devices such as laptops or voice over IP (VoIP) phones cannot obtain an IP address via DHCP, they will be rendered unproductive and users will contact the help desk. Likewise, if DNS is improperly configured, application navigation by name, phone number, or web address will likewise impair productivity and induce help desk calls.

Effective IPAM practice is a key ingredient in an enterprise or service provider IP network management strategy. As such, IPAM addresses configuration, change control, auditing, reporting, monitoring, security, trouble resolution, and related functions as applied to the three foundational IPAM technologies:

1) *IP address subnetting and tracking* – maintenance of a cohesive IP address plan that promotes route summarization, maintains accurate IP address inventory, and provides an automated individual IP address assignment and tracking mechanism. This tracking of individual IP address assignments on each subnet includes those assigned by hard-coding, e.g. routers or servers, and others assigned dynamically, e.g. via DHCP or SLAAC.

2) *DHCP* – automated IP address and parameter assignment relevant to location and device type. This requires tracking address assignments configured on devices and setting aside dynamically allocated address pools. These address pools can be configured on DHCP servers in order to enable devices to request an IP address, and receive a location-relevant address in reply.

3) *DNS* – lookup or resolution of host names, e.g. www entries to IP addresses. This third key aspect of IPAM deals with simplifying IP communications for humans through the use of names, and the mapped IP addresses must be consistent with the IP address plan.

Basic IPAM Approaches

Early History

With the growth in prominence of the use of TCP/IP within enterprise networks and for service provider Internet offerings starting in the mid-1990s, organizations initially managed the three cornerstones of IPAM independently. Smaller organizations maintained a paper log, spreadsheet, or in-house database for tracking IP address space and subnet assignments. DHCP and DNS configuration files for the few DHCP and DNS servers operating on the network were generally configured manually using text editors. Larger organizations built home-grown systems or procured commercial software solutions for all or portions of these three areas to provide some degree of automation and consistency among these key areas. The focus historically had been on simply providing a repository of information for IP address tracking and usually for some level of DHCP and DNS configuration and tracking.

Most currently available IPAM tools provide a repository and, in some cases, automated creation of DHCP and DNS configuration information. Indeed, there are many tools available in the market today, each providing varying levels of integration and functionality. Thus, some organizations continue to use spreadsheets or databases for IP inventory, while utilizing a software tool with a graphical user interface (GUI) for DHCP and/or DNS management. Even the use of spreadsheets or databases has historically proven adequate for "first generation" monolithic IP networks.

Today's IP Networks and IP Management Challenges

Today, many organizations have deployed wireless, VoIP, unified communications services, cloud-based infrastructure, Internet of Things (IoT) devices and more IP service offerings are continually emerging. These organizations commonly configure their routers to provide a differentiated "class of service" to certain devices like VoIP devices than to data devices such as laptops or PCs. This translates to IP packets for voice traffic garnering higher priority queuing than data traffic for example. The delay sensitivity requirements of voice communications often necessitate such a configuration. For example, if my email takes an additional 30 seconds to reach my email server, I would rarely even notice. But if portions of my voice conversation are delayed by even half a second, the communication will be rendered totally useless. But how can each router distinguish VoIP vs. data traffic? As we discussed earlier in this chapter, routers can use information in the IP header to differentiate these packets, including in some cases the source IP address field. Considering the use of the source IP address field, the routers must be configured with which source IP addresses represent VoIP phones and which represent data devices. Of course, this maps back directly to the IP address plan afforded by the IP inventory and assignment aspect of IPAM.

This address segmentation may require the organization to partition its address space essentially into parallel address spaces – parallel in that they each service the same physical networks, albeit for different applications. They could carve out a portion of the data network for allocation for VoIP devices. This slice of IP address space must then be reflected in the router configurations for packet processing and in each subnet providing VoIP and data services to end users. In addition, VoIP phones utilize DHCP to obtain an IP address and configuration, so configuration of the data and VoIP address pools within DHCP servers in accordance with the address segmentation plan is required.

Along with the pool configuration, the DHCP server must be configured to recognize a VoIP phone from a data device while deciding what address to assign. This is generally performed using a construct referred to as client classes. Finally, many organizations desire to have VoIP devices reside on a different DNS domain for administrative purposes. Whether on a separate domain or one common to other devices on the subnet, generally DNS requires updating the relevant name to address information and possibly even telephone numbers and other device or application specific information as well.

The upshot of this discussion is that the introduction of a new IP service, such as VoIP, introduces a substantial ripple effect on how IP address space is managed. It affects IP inventory, in tracking and allocating what amounts to a parallel address space across the organization's sites, as well as DHCP and DNS configurations. While the overall address space within the organization may not have changed, the complexity and granularity of configuration required has essentially doubled. The introduction of additional IP services requiring "special treatment" in address assignment and configuration, such as video conferencing, would stimulate the requirement for a third parallel address space and the further increasing of management complexity.

Beyond the management complexity around the three basic IPAM cornerstones, an additional set of requirements has arisen. As more IP services are deployed, it's easy to see that the reliance on the IP network grows linearly if not exponentially. With more intraorganizational and even interorganizational communications relying on the integrity, performance, and availability of the IP network, as it extends into the cloud and perhaps into the field with IoT devices, the exigency to effectively manage it grows. With increased reliance comes increased risk to your organization should portions of your IPAM foundation degrade or fail. Securing your IPAM helps secure the foundation of your network. And you can employ several IPAM techniques to enhance to overall security of your network.

IPAM is a fundamental component of your overall IP network management strategy. The increasing dependence of your business on your IP network increases the importance of your IPAM processes, which must be reliable, highly available, accurate, secure, and ideally integrated into the broader IP network management processes and systems.

2

IP Addressing

Internet Protocol History

The Internet Protocol (IP) is the most widely deployed network layer protocol worldwide. Emerging from a US government sponsored networking project for the U.S. Department of Defense begun in the 1960s, protocols that evolved as the TCP/IP suite were initially implemented in the early 1970s. The fact that the Internet has scaled rather seamlessly from a research project to a network of over 4.5 billion users [2] is a testament to the vision of its developers and robustness of their underlying technology design.

IP was "initially" defined in 1980 in request for comments (RFC) 760 [3] and 791 [4], edited by the venerable Jon Postel. I've quoted "initially" because as Mr. Postel pointed out in his preface, RFC 791 is based on six earlier editions of the ARPA (advanced research projects agency, a U.S. Department of Defense agency) Internet Protocol, though it is referred to in the RFC as version 4 (IPv4). RFC 791 states that IP performs two basic functions: addressing and fragmentation. While this may appear to trivialize the many additional functions and features of IP implemented then and since, it actually highlights the importance of these two major topics for any protocol designer. Fragmentation deals with splitting a message into a number of packets so they can be transmitted over networks that have limited packet size constraints, and reassembly of packets at the destination in the proper order. Addressing is of course one of the key topics of this book, so assuring unique addressability of hosts requiring reachability is critical to basic protocol operation.

The Internet has become an indispensable tool for daily personal and business productivity with such applications as email, instant messaging, web browsing, content streaming, and wireless, video, and voice communications. The Internet has indeed become a core element of modern society. The term "Internet," evolved

IP Address Management, Second Edition. Michael Dooley and Timothy Rooney.
© 2021 The Institute of Electrical and Electronics Engineers, Inc.
Published 2021 by John Wiley & Sons, Inc.

from the lower-case form of the term used by the early developers of Internet technology to refer to communications among interconnected networks or "internets."

Today, "the Internet" refers to the global Internet that we use on a daily basis, and it truly is a massive network of interconnected networks. Most enterprise networks also utilize the TCP/IP protocol stack, as do broadband, wireless, and landline service providers. Getting all of these networks and hosts on them to cooperate and exchange user communications efficiently requires a robust set of rules for such communications. IP has proven remarkably robust, as well as extremely versatile and scalable.

The Internet Protocol, Take 1

In Chapter 1, we introduced the concept of protocol layering. The network or IP layer in our case adds a header to the data it receives from the TCP or UDP transport layer as illustrated in Figure 2.1. This IP header is analyzed by routers along the path to the final destination to ultimately deliver the IP packet to its final destination, identified by the destination IP address in the header. The source IP address is also encompassed in the IP header and may also be used in routing decisions.

The format of the IP header is detailed in Chapter 17 if you're interested in the details, but for our present purposes suffice it to say that the IP header contains two IP addresses: the source (sender) IP address and the destination IP address.

The IP address field is comprised of 32 bits. The familiar dotted-decimal notation for an IP address reflects the splitting of the 32-bit address into four [8-bit] octets. We convert each of the four octets to decimal, then separate them with decimal points or "dots." This is certainly easier than calculating these 32 bits as one huge number! Consider the 32-bit IP address in Figure 2.2. We simply split this into four octets, convert each octet to decimal, then separate the decimal representation of each octet by "dots." Hence the term, "dotted decimal."

Class-Based Addressing

RFC 791 defines three classes of addresses: A, B, and C. These classes are identified by the initial bits of the 32-bit address as depicted in Figure 2.3.

IP Header	IP packet contents

Figure 2.1   Basic IP packet.

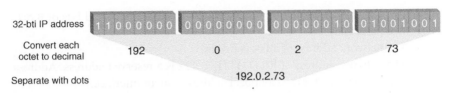

Figure 2.2 Binary to dotted decimal conversion.

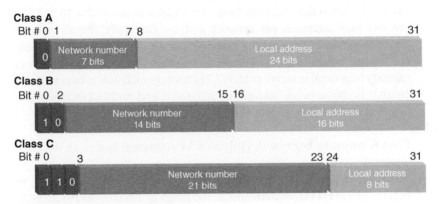

Figure 2.3 Class-based addressing.

Each class corresponds to a particular fixed size for the network number and local address fields. The local address field can be assigned to individual hosts or further broken down into subnet and host fields as we'll discuss later.

The division of address space into classes provided a means to easily define different sized networks for different users' needs. At the time, the Internet was comprised of certain U.S. government agencies, universities, and some research institutions. It had not yet blossomed into the de facto world-wide network it is today, so address capacity was seemingly limitless. The other reason for dividing address space into classes on these octet boundaries was for easier implementation of network routing. Routers could identify the length of the network number field simply by examining the first few bits of the destination address. They would then simply look up the network number portion of the entire IP address in their routing table and route each packet accordingly. Computational horsepower in those days was rather limited, so minimizing processing requirements was a key consideration. A side benefit of classful addressing was simple readability. Each dotted decimal number represents one octet in binary. As we'll see later with the case of classless addressing, this visual mapping is not as intuitive.

Examining this class-based addressing structure, we can observe a few key points:
  o Class A networks

- o Class A prefixes begin with binary 0 ($[0]_2$)[1] plus 7 additional bits or 8 network bits total.
- o The network address of all 0s is invalid[2]
- o The network address of $[01111111]_2 = 127$ is a reserved address. Address 127.0.0.1 is used for the "loopback address" on an interface.
- o This leaves us with a class A network prefix range of $[00000001]_2$ to $[01111110]_2 = 1 - 126$ as the first octet.
- o The local address field is 24 bits long. This equates to up to $2^{24} = 16,777,216$ possible local addresses per network address. Generally, the all 0s local address represents the "network" address and the all 1s is a network broadcast, so we typically subtract these 2 addresses from our local address capacity in general to arrive at 16,777,214 hosts per Class A network. Thus, 10.0.0.0 is the network address of 10.0.0.0/8 and 10.255.255.255 is the broadcast address to all hosts on the 10.0.0.0/8 network.
- Class B networks
  - o Class B networks begin with $[10]_2$ plus 14 additional bits or 16 network bits total.
  - o The range of class B network prefixes in binary is $[10000000\ 00000000]_2$ to $[10111111\ 11111111]_2$ or networks in the range of 128.0.0.0 to 191.255.0.0, yielding 16,384 network addresses.
  - o The local address field is 16 bits long for $65,536 - 2 = 65,534$ possible hosts per class B network.
- Class C networks
  - o Class C networks begin with $[110]_2$ plus 21 additional bits or 24 network bits total.
  - o The range of class C network prefixes is $[11000000\ 00000000\ 00000000]_2$ to $[11011111\ 11111111\ 11111111]_2$ or networks in the range 192.0.0.0 to 223.255.255.0, yielding 2,097,152 networks.
  - o The local address field is 8 bits long for $256 - 2 = 254$ possible hosts per Class C network.
- Class D networks (not illustrated in Figure 2.3)
  - o Class D networks were defined after RFC 791 and denote multicast addresses, which begin with $[1110]_2$. Multicast is used for streaming applications where multiple users or subscribers receive a set of IP packets from

---

[1] To differentiate a binary 0 (one bit) from a decimal 0 (7–8 bits) in cases where it may be ambiguous, we subscript the number with the appropriate base. Don't worry; we're not digressing into chemistry with discussion of oxygen molecules with the 0_2 notation, simply "zero base 2."

[2] Though some protocols like DHCP use the all 0s address as a placeholder for "this" address.

a common source. In other words, multiple hosts configured with a common multicast address would receive all IP traffic sent to the multicast group address. There is no network and host portion of the multicast network as members of a multicast group may reside on many different physical networks.

  o The range of class D networks is from [11100000 00000000 00000000 00000000]$_2$ to [11101111 11111111 11111111 11111111]$_2$ or the 224.0.0.0 to 239.255.255.255 range, yielding 268,435,456 multicast addresses.

• Class E networks (not illustrated in Figure 2.3)
  Networks beginning with [1111]$_2$ (Class E) are reserved.

Internet Growing Pains

With seemingly limitless IP address capacity, at least as it seemed through the 1980s, class A and B networks were generally allocated to whoever asked. Recipient organizations would then subdivide or subnet[3] their class A or B networks along octet boundaries within their organizations. Keep in mind that every "network," even within a corporation, needs to have a unique network number or prefix to maintain address uniqueness and maintain route integrity.

Subnetting provides routing boundaries for communications and routing protocol updates. Each network over which IP packets traverse requires its own IP network number (network address). As more and more companies sought to participate in the Internet by requesting IP address space, the Internet Network Information Center (InterNIC), the organization originally responsible for allocating IP address space prior to the formation of Regional Internet Registries (RIRs), was forced to throttle address allocations. Those requesting IP address space from RIRs soon faced increasingly stringent application requirements and were granted a fraction of the address space requested. In having to make do with smaller network block allocations, many organizations were forced to subnet on non-octet boundaries.

Whether on octet boundaries or not, subnetting is facilitated by specifying a *network mask* along with the network address. The network mask is an integer number representing the length in bits of the network prefix. This is sometimes also referred to as the mask length. For example, a class A network has a mask length of 8, a class B of 16, and C of 24. By essentially extending the length of the network number which routers need to examine in each packet, a larger number of networks can be supported, and address space can be allocated more flexibly. This is illustrated in Figure 2.4.

---

[3]The term *subnet* is frequently used as a verb as in this context, to mean the act of creating a subnet.

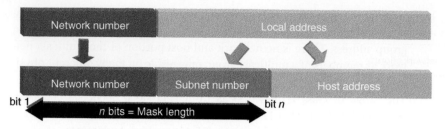

Figure 2.4 Subnetting provides more "networks" with fewer hosts per network.

Routers need to be configured with this mask length for each subnet that they serve. This allows them to "mask" the IP address, e.g. to expose only the indicated network + subnet bits within the 32-bit IP address to enable efficient routing without relying on address class. Based on this extended network number, the router can route the packet accordingly. Hosts on each subnet also require this mask configuration to discern which destination addresses fall within the same subnet for direct communications and which lie outside the subnet requiring transmission to the default gateway.

The network address and mask length were originally denoted by specifying the 32-bit mask in dotted decimal notation. This notation is derived by denoting the first n bits of a 32-bit number as 1s and the remaining 32-n bits as 0s, then converting this to dotted decimal.

For example, to denote a network mask length of 19 bits, you would

- create the 32-bit number with 19 1s and 13 0s: 11111111111111111110000000000000
- separate into octets: 11111111.11111111.11100000.00000000
- convert to dotted decimal: 255.255.224.0.

For example, the notation for network 172.16.168.0 with this 19-bit mask is 172.16.168.0/255.255.224.0.

Thankfully, this approach was superseded by a simpler notation: the mask is now denoted with the network address as: <network address>/<mask length>. While the notation is easier to read, it does not save us from the equivalent binary exercise! For example, the 172.16.0.0 class B network would be represented as 172.16.0.0/16. The "slash 16" indicates that the first 16 bits, the first two octets, represent the network prefix.

Here's the binary representation of this network:

Network address	Network prefix	Local address
172.16.0.0/16	*10101100 00010000*	00000000 00000000

Let's subnet this network using a 19-bit mask. Expanding this out into binary notation:

Network address	Network prefix	Subnet	Local address
172.16.0.0/19	*10101100 00010000*	*00*000000	00000000
172.16.32.0/19	*10101100 00010000*	*001*00000	00000000
172.16.64.0/19	*10101100 00010000*	*010*00000	00000000
172.16.96.0/19	*10101100 00010000*	*011*00000	00000000
172.16.128.0/19	*10101100 00010000*	*100*00000	00000000
172.16.160.0/19	*10101100 00010000*	*101*00000	00000000
172.16.192.0/19	*10101100 00010000*	*110*00000	00000000
172.16.224.0/19	*10101100 00010000*	*111*00000	00000000

Notice that the class B network bits are depicted under the Network Prefix column in italic font, and we highlighted the subnet bits in larger bold italic font in the Subnet column. Using this 3-bit extension, we effectively expanded the network number from 16 bits to 19. By incrementing the binary values of these 3 bits from $[000]_2$ to $[111]_2$ per the highlighted Subnet bits above, we can derive $2^3 = 8$ subnets with this three-bit subnet mask extension. Routers and hosts would then be configured to use the first 19 bits to identify the network portion of the address with the corresponding mask length, e.g. 172.16.128.0/19, then having the router communicate reachability to this network via routing protocols. This technique, called variable length subnet masking (VLSM) became increasingly more prevalent in helping to squeeze as much IP address capacity as possible out of the address space assigned within an organization.

The two-layer network/subnet model worked well during the first decades of IP's existence. However, in the early 1990s, demand for IP addresses continued to increase dramatically, with more and more companies desiring IP address space to publish websites. At the then current rate of usage, the address space was expected to exhaust before the turn of the century! The technical standards body of the Internet, the *Internet engineering task force* (IETF) cleverly implemented two key policies to extend the usable life of the IPv4 address space, namely, support of private address space (ultimately RFC 1918) and classless inter-domain routing (CIDR, RFCs 1517–1519 [5–7]). Of course, during this time, the IETF also began work on specifying IPv6 as the successor to IPv4, offering vastly larger address capacity.

Private Address Space

Recall our statement that every "network" within an organization needs to have a unique network number or prefix to maintain route integrity. As more and more organizations connected to the Internet, the Internet became a potential vehicle for hackers to infiltrate organizations' networks. Many organizations implemented firewalls to filter out IP packets based on specified criteria regarding IP header values, such as source or destination addresses, UDP vs. TCP, and others. This guarded partitioning of IP address space between "internal" and "external" address space dove-tailed nicely with address conservation efforts within the IETF.

The IETF issued a couple RFC revisions, resulting in RFC 1918 [8] becoming the standard document that defined the following sets of networks as "private:"

- 10.0.0.0 – 10.255.255.255 (10/8 network) – equivalent to 1 class A
- 172.16.0.0 – 172.31.255.255 (172.16/12 network) – equivalent to 16 class Bs
- 192.168.0.0 – 192.168.255.255 (192.168/16 network) – equivalent to 1 class B or 256 class Cs

The term *private* means that these addresses are not routable on the Internet. However, within an organization, they may be used to route IP traffic on internal networks. Thus, my laptop is assigned a private IP address and I can send emails to my fellow associates, who also have private addresses. My organization in essence has defined a private Internet, sometimes referred to as an intranet. Routers within my organization are configured to route among allocated private IP networks, and the IP traffic among these networks never traverses the Internet[4].

Since I'm using a private IP address, someone external to the organization, outside the firewall, cannot reach me directly. Anyone externally sending packets with my private address as the destination address in the IP header will not be able to reach me as these packets will not be routed by Internet and ISP routers. But what if I wanted to initiate a connection externally to check on how much money I'm losing in the stock market via the Internet? For employees requiring access to the Internet, firewalls employing *network address translation (NAT)* functionality are commonly employed to convert an enterprise user's private IP address into a public or routable IP address from the corporation's public address space.

---

[4]Technically, with the use of virtual private networks (VPNs) or tunnels over the Internet, privately addressed traffic may traverse the Internet, but the tunnel endpoints accessing the Internet on both ends must utilize public IP addresses.

Typical NAT devices provide address pooling features to pool a relatively small number of publicly routable IP addresses for use on a dynamic basis by a larger number of employees who sporadically access the Internet. The NAT device bridges two IP connections together: the internal-to-NAT device communications utilizes private address space, while the NAT device-to-the Internet communications uses public IP addresses. The NAT device is responsible for keeping track of mapping the internal private IP address to the public IP address used externally.

Many NAT devices also support use of single source IP addresses shared among multiple internal clients by varying the source UDP/TCP port number. This is referred to as address plus port (A+P) translation and is illustrated in Figure 2.5, with the internal network utilizing the 10/8 address space, and external or public addressing utilizing the 192.0.2.108 address. Per the figure, one device with IP address 10.1.0.1 source port 50555 has its source IP address and port mapped to 192.0.2.108, source port 60001; another connection from IP address 10.2.0.2 has its source IP and port mapped to 192.0.2.108, 60002. This A+P strategy effectively increases the size of the address field to encompass the IP address and at least a portion of the port field. The mapping state is maintained in the NAT device such that it can map packets received from the Internet (i.e. responses) to corresponding internal devices.

From a public IP addressing capacity requirements perspective, my organization only needs sufficient IP address space to support these ad hoc internal-to-Internet connections as well as Internet-reachable hosts such as web or email servers. This amount is generally much smaller than requiring IP address space for every internal and external router, server or host, to which I can assign private addresses. Implementation of private address space greatly reduced the pressure on IP address space capacity, as enterprises required far less public address space.

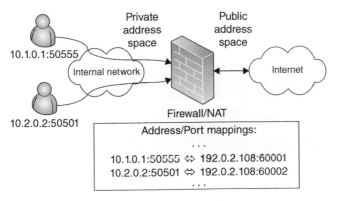

Figure 2.5 Example use of NAT to map private to public addresses and ports.

Classless Addressing

The second strategy enacted to prolong the lifespan of IPv4 featured the implementation of CIDR, which vastly improved network allocation efficiencies. Like VLSM, which allow subnetting of a classful network on non-octet boundaries, CIDR allows the network prefix for the base address block (allocated by an RIR or ISP) to be variable. Hence, a contiguous group of four class C's for example could be combined and allocated to a service provider as a single /22. This is illustrated in Figure 2.6. If the four contiguous blocks shown, 172.16.168.0/24 – 172.16.171.0/24 are available for allocation, they could be allocated as a single /22, that is, 172.16.168.0/22.

Notice that the darker shaded bits represent the network number, i.e. the first 22 bits, which is identical on all four constituent networks. The remaining ten bits represent the local address space for subnet and host assignment. Since the network address is indicated with all 0s in the local address field, the /22 network is identified as the bit string at the top, namely 172.16.168.0/22. As you can see, CIDR is very similar to VLSM in terms of the decimal to binary arithmetic required to calculate network addresses on non-octet boundaries. The extra step of filling in zeroes for local addresses outside non-octet boundary masks introduces an opportunity for error. In addition, VLSM can be applied to a CIDR allocation to further increase the chance of error. But as is usually the case, there's a price to pay for more flexibility. CIDR and VLSM broke down the class walls to provide truly flexible network allocations and subnetting.

Special Use IPv4 Addresses

In addition to private space, certain portions of the IPv4 address space have been set aside for special purposes or documentation. Such IPv4 address allocations include reservations for special use IP addresses, which are summarized below and defined in RFC 6890 [9].

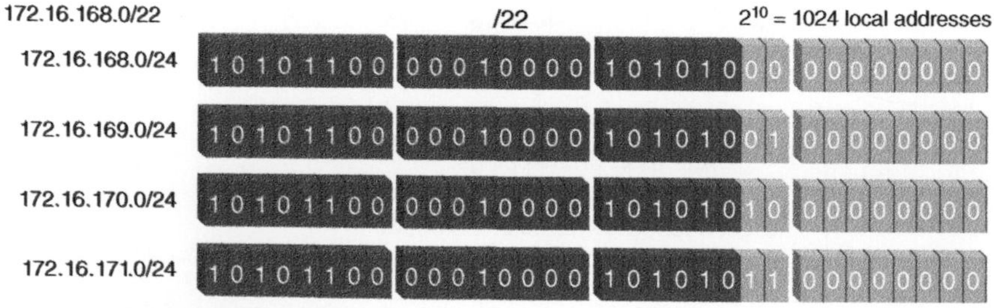

Figure 2.6 CIDR allocation example.

Address space	Special use
0.0.0.0/8	"This" network; 0.0.0.0/32 denotes this host on this network
10.0.0.0/8	Private IP address space, not routable on the public Internet per RFC 1918
100.64.0.0/10	Shared Address Space used by service providers to assign to customer edge routers for use with carrier grade network address translators (CGNs)
127.0.0.0/8	Assigned for use as the Internet host loopback address, i.e. 127.0.0.1/32
169.254.0.0/16	The "link local" block used for IPv4 auto-configuration for communications on a single link
172.16.0.0/12	Private IP address space, not routable on the public Internet per RFC 1918
192.0.0.0/24	Reserved for IETF protocol assignments
192.0.0.0/29	Dual-Stack Lite IPv4-IPv6 translation address space
192.0.2.0/24	Assigned as "Test-Net-1" for use in documentation and sample code
192.88.99.0/24	Allocated for 6to4 relay anycast addresses (see Chapter 17 for further discussion)
192.168.0.0/16	Private IP address space, not routable on the public Internet per RFC 1918
198.18.0.0/15	Allocated for use in benchmark tests of network interconnect devices
198.51.100.0/24	Assigned as "Test-Net-2" for use in documentation and sample code
203.0.113.0/24	Assigned as "Test-Net-3" for use in documentation and sample code
240.0.0.0/4	Reserved for future use (formerly Class E space)
255.255.255.255/32	Limited broadcast on a link.

Source: Based on RFC 6890 [9].

The Internet Protocol, Take 2

IP version 6[5] was originally specified in the mid-1990s to address a then-urgent need to supplement the rapidly diminishing IPv4 address space. At the time work was begun in earnest on defining IPv6 or IPng (IP next generation) as it was

---

[5]IP version 5 was never implemented as an official version of IP. The version number of "5" in the IP header was assigned to denote packets carrying an experimental real-time stream protocol called ST, the Internet Stream Protocol. If you'd like to learn more about ST, please refer to RFC 1819.

initially called, the Internet was just starting to catch on with the general public. More and more enterprises were expanding their internal networks to enable connection to the global Internet. Since every reachable host required a unique public IPv4 address, the demand for addresses skyrocketed.

Version 6 of the IP is an evolution from version 4 but is not inherently compatible with version 4. The primary objective for version 6 was to redesign version 4 based on the prior twenty years of experience at the time with IPv4. Real world application support added to the IPv4 protocol suite over the years was designed into IPv6 from the outset, though both protocols continue to evolve. This included support for security, multicast, mobility, and auto-configuration, among other features.

The most striking difference between IPv4 and IPv6 is the IP address field. Whereas IPv4 uses a 32-bit IP address field, IPv6 uses 128 bits. A 32-bit address field provides a theoretical maximum of 2^{32} addresses or 4.2 billion addresses. A 128-bit address field allows 2^{128} addresses (2^{96} IPv4 Internets!) or 340 trillion trillion trillion addresses or 340 undecillion (3.4×10^{38}, using the American definition of undecillion, 10^{36}, not the British definition which is 10^{66}). To put some context around this tremendously large number, consider that this quantity of IP addresses:

- averages to 4.5×10^{28} IP addresses per person on Earth based on a 7.5 billion population
- averages to 4.3×10^{20} IP addresses per square inch of the Earth's surface.
- amounts to about 14 million IP addresses per *nanometer* to the nearest galaxy, Andromeda, at 2.5 million light years

Like IPv4, not nearly every address will be usable due to subnetting inefficiencies, but a few undecillion of wasted addresses won't have much impact! Beyond this seemingly incomprehensible quantity of IP addresses, there are a number of similarities between IPv6 and IPv4. For example, at a basic level, the "IP packet," notion we discussed in Chapter 1 applies equally well for IPv6 as IPv4, as do the basic concepts of protocol layering, packet routing, and CIDR allocations.

IPv6 Address Types and Structure

Three basic types of IPv6 addresses have been defined. Like IPv4, these addresses apply to interfaces, not nodes. Thus, a printer with two interfaces would be addressed by either of its interfaces. The printer can be reached on either interface, but the printer node does not have an IP address per se. Many router and server products support the concept of a "box address" via a software loopback address. This loopback address, not to be confused with the 127.0.0.1 or ::1 loopback addresses, enables reachability to any one of the device's interfaces. Of course, for end users attempting to access a node, DNS can hide this subtlety by enabling a host name to map to one or more interface addresses.

- *Unicast* – the IP address of a single interface.
- *Anycast* – an IP address for a set of interfaces usually belonging to different nodes, any one of which is the intended recipient. An IP packet destined for an anycast address is routed to the nearest interface (according to routing table metrics) configured with the anycast address. The concept is that the sender doesn't necessarily care which particular host or interface receives the packet, but that one of those sharing the anycast address receives it. Anycast addresses are assigned from the same address space from which unicast addresses have been allocated. Thus, one cannot differentiate a unicast address from an anycast address by sight.

Anycast addressing of DNS servers has proven successful in providing *closest routing to the intended service*. This provides benefits in simplifying client configuration in always using the same [anycast] IP address to perform a DNS query, regardless of where on your network the client is connected. It has also proven effective in dispersing distributed denial of service (DDoS) attacks as we'll discuss in Part 3.

- *Multicast* – an IP address for a set of interfaces typically belonging to different nodes, all of which are intended recipients. Unlike IPv4, IPv6 does not support broadcasts. Instead, applications that utilized broadcasts in IPv4, such as DHCP, use multicast to a well-known (i.e. predefined) DHCP multicast address in IPv6.

A device interface may have multiple IP addresses of any or all address types. IPv6 also defines a link-local scope of IP addresses to uniquely identify interfaces attached to a particular link, such as a LAN. Additional scoping can be administratively defined per site or per organization for example.

IPv6 Address Notation

Recall that IPv4 addresses are represented in dotted decimal format where the 32 bit address is divided into four 8-bit segments, each of which are converted to decimal, then separated with "dots." If you thought remembering a string of four decimals was difficult, IPv6 may prove more challenging. IPv6 addresses are not expressed in dotted-decimal notation; they are represented using a colon-separated hexadecimal format. Jumping down to the bit level, the 128-bit IPv6 address is divided into eight 16-bit segments, each of which is converted to hexadecimal, then separated by colons. Each hexadecimal "digit" represents four bits per the mapping of each hex digit (0-f) to its four-bit binary mapping below. Each hex digit corresponds to four bits with possible values of:

0 = 0000	4 = 0100	8 = 1000	c = 1100
1 = 0001	5 = 0101	9 = 1001	d = 1101
2 = 0010	6 = 0110	a = 1010	e = 1110
3 = 0011	7 = 0111	b = 1011	f = 1111

Source: Based on RFC 6890 [9].

After converting a 128-bit IPv6 address from binary into hex, we group sets of four hex digits and separate them with colons. We'll use the terms *nibble* to represent a single hex digit and *hextet*[6] to refer to the grouping of four hex digits or 16 bits; thus, we have eight hextets separated by colons, rendering an IPv6 address appearing as:

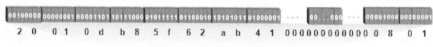

2001:0db8:5f62:ab41:0000:0000:0000:0801

Instead of dealing with four decimal values, each between 0 and 255, separated by dots in IPv4, IPv6 addresses consist of up to eight hextet values, each between 0 and ffff, separated by colons. There are two acceptable abbreviations when writing IPv6 addresses. First, leading zeroes within a hextet, i.e. between colons, may be dropped. Thus, the address above could be abbreviated:

2001:db8:5f62:ab41:0:0:0:801

The second form of abbreviation is the use of a double colon to represent one or more consecutive sets of zero hextets. Using this form of abbreviation, the address above can be further abbreviated as:

2001:db8:5f62:ab41::801

Isn't that much better?! Note that only one double colon may be used within an address representation. Since there are always eight hextet segments in the address, one can easily calculate how many of them are zero with one double-colon notation; however it would be ambiguous with more than one.

Consider the address: 2001:db8:0:56fa:0:0:0:b5. We can abbreviate this address as either:

2001:db8::56fa:0:0:0:b5 *or* 2001:db8:0:56fa::b5

---

[6]In our prior books, we've used the Latin version, *sedectet* but there is no "official" term for this 16-bit grouping so we'll go with hextet here.

We can easily calculate that the double colon denotes one hextet (8 total minus 7 hextets shown) in the first case and three (8 minus 5 shown) in the second notation. If we attempted to abbreviate this address as 2001:db8::56fa::b5, we could not unambiguously decode this, as it could represent any of the following possible addresses:

2001:db8:0:56fa:0:0:0:b5
2001:db8:0:0:56fa:0:0:b5
2001:db8:0:0:0:56fa:0:b5

Hence the requirement holds that only one double colon may appear in an IPv6 address.

Address Structure

As with IPv4, the IPv6 address is composed of a network and a host portion; however, experience with VLSM and subnetting in general has led to addition of a subnet field. The IPv6 address is divided into three fields:

The global routing prefix is akin to an IPv4 network number and is used by routers to forward packets to router(s) locally serving the network corresponding to the prefix. For example, a customer of an ISP may be assigned a /48-sized global routing prefix and all packets destined to this customer would contain the corresponding global routing prefix value. In this case, $n = 48$ per Figure 2.7. As with IPv4 CIDR notation, when denoting a network, the global routing prefix is written, followed by slash, then the network size, called the prefix length. Assuming our example IPv6 address, 2001:db8:5f62:ab41::801, resides within a /48 global routing prefix, this prefix address would be denoted as 2001:db8:5f62::/48. The network address is denoted with zero-valued bits beyond the prefix length (bits 49–128 in this case) as denoted by the terminating double colon.

The subnet ID provides a means to denote particular subnets within the network defined by the global routing prefix. Our ISP customer with a /48 may choose to use 16 bits for the subnet ID, providing 2^{16} or 65,534 subnets. In this case, $m = 16$ per Figure 2.7. This leaves $128 - 48 - 16 = 64$ bits for the interface ID (IID). The IID denotes the interface address of the source or intended recipient for the packet. As we'll discuss a bit later, the global unicast address space that has been allocated for use so far requires a 64-bit IID field.

Figure 2.7   IPv6 address structure. Source: Based on Internet Assigned Numbers Authority (IANA) 2019 [10].

One of the unique aspects of this IPv6 address structure in splitting a network ID consisting of the global routing prefix and subnet ID, from an IID, is that a device can retain the same IID independently of the network to which it is connected, effectively separating "who you are", your IID, from "where you are," your network prefix. As we'll see, this convention facilitates address autoconfiguration, though not without privacy concerns. But we're getting a little ahead of ourselves, so before we go there, let's jump back up to the macro level and consider the IPv6 address space allocated so far by the Internet addressing authority, the Internet Assigned Numbers Authority (IANA).

IPv6 Address Allocations

The address space that has been allocated so far by IANA represents less than 14% of the total available IPv6 address space (Table 2.1).

Table 2.1 IPv6 address allocations.

IPv6 prefix	Binary form	Relative size of IPv6 space	Allocation
0000::/3	000	1/8	Reserved by IETF – The "unspecified address" (::) and the loopback address (::1) are assigned from this block
2000::/3	001	1/8	Global unicast address space
4000::/3	010	1/8	Reserved by IETF
6000::/3	011	1/8	Reserved by IETF
8000::/3	100	1/8	Reserved by IETF
a000::/3	101	1/8	Reserved by IETF
c000::/3	110	1/8	Reserved by IETF
e000::/4	1110	1/16	Reserved by IETF
f000::/5	1111 0	1/32	Reserved by IETF
f800::/6	1111 10	1 / 64	Reserved by IETF
fc00::/7	1111 110	1/128	Unique local unicast
fe00::/9	1111 1110 0	1/512	Reserved by IETF
fe80::/10	1111 1110 01	1/1024	Link local unicast
fec0::/10	1111 1110 11	1/1024	Reserved by IETF
ff00::/8	1111 1111	1/256	Multicast

Source: Based on Internet Assigned Numbers Authority (IANA) 2019 [10].

2000::/3 – Global Unicast Address Space

The global unicast address space allocated so far, 2000::/3, represents 2^{125} or 4.25×10^{37} IP addresses. Given the 64-bit IID requirement defined in the IPv6 addressing architecture (RFC 4291 [11] as updated by RFC 7136 [12]), the global unicast address format defined in RFC 3587 [13] illustrated in Figure 2.7, with the "m" sized subnet id field becomes $(128-64-n) = 64-n$. An example of the segmentation for a /48, $n = 48$, is shown in Figure 2.8.

The first three bits are $[001]_2$ to indicate the global unicast address space allocated so far. These and the following 45 bits in this example comprise the global routing prefix, followed by the 16 bit subnet ID and 64 bit IID, respectively.

fc00::/7 – Unique Local Address Space

The unique local address (ULA) space, defined in RFC 4193 [14], is intended to provide locally assignable and routable IP addresses, usually within a site. RFC 4193 states that "these addresses are not expected to be routable on the global Internet." Thus, while not as stringent as RFC 1918 in defining private IPv4 address space, the ULA space is essentially private addressing, providing "local" addressing with a high probability of still being globally unique. The format of ULA space is as illustrated in Figure 2.9.

The first seven bits, bits 0–6, are $[1111\ 110]_2$ = fc00::/7, which identifies a ULA. The eighth bit, the "L" bit is set to "1" if the Global ID is locally assigned; setting the "L" bit to "0" is currently undefined. The 40-bit Global ID field is intended to represent a globally unique prefix and must be allocated using a pseudo-random algorithm, not sequentially. The subnet ID is a 16-bit field to identify each subnet, while the IID is a 64 bits.

fe80::/10 – Link Local Address Space

Link local addresses are used only on a particular link, such as an Ethernet link; packets with link local destination addresses are not routed. That is, packets

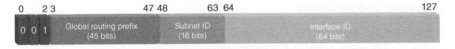

Figure 2.8 Currently allocated global unicast address format example with n = 48.

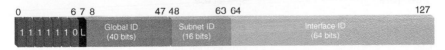

Figure 2.9 Unique local address format.

having link local addresses will not reach beyond the corresponding link. The format of link local addresses is:

The fe80::/10 link local prefix is followed by 54 zero bits and the 64-bit IID.

ff00::/8 – Multicast Address Space

Multicast addresses identify a group of interfaces typically on different nodes. All multicast group members share the same group ID and hence all members will accept packets destined for the multicast group. An interface may have multiple multicast addresses; i.e. it may belong to multiple multicast groups. The basic format of IPv6 multicast addresses is:

The prefix ff00::/8 identifies a multicast address. The next field is a 4-bit field denoted "Flags." The format of the multicast packet is dependent on the value of the flags. The Scope field indicates the breadth of the multicast scope, whether per node, link, global or other scope values. Some example multicast addresses follow.

- ff01::2 = node-local all routers address
- ff02::1 = link-local all nodes address
- ff05::1:3 = site-local all DHCP servers address
- ff08::101 = organization-local network time protocol (NTP) server address

Please refer to Chapter 17 for more details on IPv6 multicast addressing.

Special Use IPv6 Addresses

Specific IPv6 addresses or blocks set aside for particular special uses are summarized in the following table and defined in RFC 6890 [9].

Address space	Special use
::1/128	Loopback address
::/128	Unspecified address

Address space	Special use
64:ff9b::/96	IPv4-IPv6 translator well-known prefix
::ffff:0:0/96	IPv4-mapped address space
100::/64	Discard-only address block for remote triggered black holing (RTBH) for denial of service mitigation
2001::/23	Reserved for IETF protocol assignments including the following
2001::/32	Teredo, an IPv4–IPv6 translation mechanism
2001:2::/48	Allocated for use in benchmark tests of network interconnect devices
2001:db8::/32	Assigned for use in documentation and sample code
2001:10::/28	Assigned to the experimental ORCHID (overlay routable cryptographic hash identifiers) endpoint identifiers
2002::/16	6to4 IPv4–IPv6 tunneling mechanism

Source: Based on RFC 6890 [9].

IPv4–IPv6 Coexistence

With two versions of the Internet Protocol to choose from, which should you select? Despite the fact that IPv6 is now "the" Internet Protocol many networks support numerous IPv4-addressed devices. Implementing IPv6 is the right thing to do, but from a practical standpoint it may not make sense for your network right now. While every modern network device, operating system (OS) and application supports both IPv4 and IPv6, feathering IPv6 into an IPv4 network should technically be relatively straightforward.

Such a dual protocol network, or *dual stack* as its referred, enables support of both IPv4 and IPv6 packets and transactions. But operationally supporting two networking protocols is challenging. Validation of full device, OS and application support for both protocols is necessary, especially if you're running "legacy" applications. Training of network engineering, operations, and customer support staff is required to provide an adequate level of management competence. And speaking of management, network monitoring, security and troubleshooting tools, not the least of which includes your IPAM system, will need to support both protocols in a dual stack network. All of this may or may not represent significant issues for your environment.

On the positive side, supporting both protocols, at least within your Internet-reachable services, allows your Internet applications to serve the whole Internet. While the IP transactions of most IPv6-only devices such as modern mobile phones are translated from within a mobile provider's network from IPv6 to IPv4, there are many cases where pure IPv6 users are likely trying to reach your public Internet resources.

We'll explore this and discuss alternative approaches in more detail in Chapter 7.

3

IP Address Assignment

Recall our routing discussion from Chapter 1, particularly regarding route aggregation. Managing your address space in adherence to this principle is paramount to simplifying management tasks on an ongoing basis. As we'll also discuss in Chapter 6, proper IP address planning can facilitate not only management of route aggregation, but also the application of security policies, implementation of application-specific routing treatment, and governance of geographic-specific guidelines.

Address Planning

Regional Internet Registries

IP addresses must be unique on a given network for proper routing and communication. As with every seemingly authoritative statement, there are exceptions! Anycast addresses are typically assigned to multiple hosts, and multicast addresses likewise are shared. Private addresses are also commonly duplicated, even within an organization though packets using them are not routed on the Internet.

How is uniqueness of unicast addresses assured across the global Internet? The Internet Assigned Numbers Authority, IANA, is responsible for global allocation of IP address space for both IPv4 and IPv6, as well as other parameters used within the TCP/IP protocol, such as application port numbers. In fact, you can view these top-level allocations by browsing to www.iana.org/ipaddresses/ip-addresses.htm and selecting "Internet Protocol v4 Address Space" or "IPv6 Address Space."

IANA is, in essence, the top-level address registry, and it allocates address space to RIRs. The RIRs, listed below, are organizations responsible for allocation of address space within their respective global regions from their corresponding space allotments from IANA.

IP Address Management, Second Edition. Michael Dooley and Timothy Rooney.
© 2021 The Institute of Electrical and Electronics Engineers, Inc.
Published 2021 by John Wiley & Sons, Inc.

- AfriNIC (African Network Information Centre) – Africa Region
- APNIC (Asia Pacific Network Information Centre) – Asia/Pacific Region
- ARIN (American Registry for Internet Numbers) – North America Region
- LACNIC (Regional Latin-American and Caribbean IP Address Registry) – Latin America and some Caribbean Islands
- RIPE NCC (Réseaux IP Européens) – Europe, the Middle East, and Western Asia

The goals of the RIR system are as follows:

- *Uniqueness* – Each unicast IP address must be unique world-wide for global Internet routing.
- *Aggregation* – Hierarchical allocation of address space assures proper routing of IP traffic on the Internet. Without aggregation, routing tables become fragmented which could ultimately create debilitating bottlenecks within the Internet.
- *Conservation* – With IPv4 in particular but also for IPv6 space, address space needs to be distributed judiciously according to actual usage requirements.
- *Registration* – A publicly accessible registry of IP address assignments eliminates ambiguity and can help when troubleshooting. This registry used to be accessible using the *whois* protocol but now is reachable using the registration data access protocol (RDAP). Today, there are many address registration databases, operated not only by RIRs but by local internet registries (LIRs)/Internet service providers (ISPs) as well for their respective address spaces.
- *Fairness* – Unbiased address allocation based on true address needs and not long term "plans."

The general address allocation hierarchy is depicted in Figure 3.1. National Internet registries are akin to local Internet registries, but are organized at a national level.

Back in the 1980s and early 1990s many corporations (end users per Figure 3.1) obtained address space from a centralized Internet Network Information Center (InterNIC). With the explosive growth of the Internet and correspondingly, address requests, a regionalized approach creating the RIRs was adopted in the mid-1990s. The LIR/ISP layer was added during the transition to CIDR addressing to provide further delegation of address allocation responsibility. Today, most organizations obtain address space from LIRs or ISPs. The process for obtaining such address space is generally dictated by the LIR/ISP with whom you conduct business, though RIRs recommend use of consistent policies to maximize fairness and efficiency.

After an RIR allocates a given address space to an ISP, the ISP may advertise the address space on the Internet. The ISP may then assign portions of its given address space to its customers as they subscribe to the ISP's services. Customers in turn then allocate and assign their portion of the address space within their

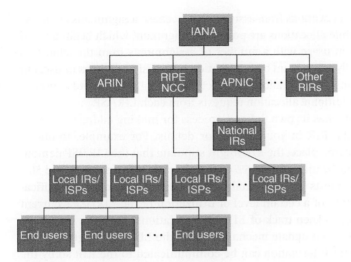

Figure 3.1 IP address allocation from the top down. Source: RFC 2050 [269].

respective organizations. The ISP need not modify its address space advertisement because customer-assigned IP address space "rolls up" within the bounds of this advertised space.

Going back to our postal analogy in Chapter 1, the allocation of space to an ISP is analogous to deployment of a new zip code to a postal region. Mail from outside this region destined to the new as well as former zip codes served by the region are forwarded to the corresponding distribution center. Likewise, as IP packets destined for an ISP's allocated space traverse the Internet, they are routed to the ISP for subsequent routing to the corresponding customer. Thus, the LIR/ISP layer helps aggregate route advertisements on the Internet. Multiple customers served by each ISP can be summarized in one route on the Internet. If business is good and the LIR/ISP requires more address space, the LIR/ISP can request additional space from their RIR.

RIR Address Allocation

From an RIR perspective, RIRs *allocate* space to LIR/ISPs, and LIR/ISPs *assign* address space to their customers. The term *allocate* technically refers to the provision of an IP address block to serve as a "pool" of address space that can be drawn upon for *assignment* to customers. Customers can then use the assigned address space by themselves allocating blocks and subnets from this space, then assigning IP addresses from allocated subnets to individual hosts. The mechanics of this allocation and assignment are based on procedures we'll discuss in Chapter 6.

RIRs differentiate allocations from assignments because assignments comprise addresses in use, while allocations are pools for assignment which begin unused but in theory grow in usage with a number of assignments from the allocation over time. Technically, RIRs count both allocations and assignments as in-use, but leave open the ability to audit allocated space for actual address utilization as needed to process additional allocation requests from each LIR/ISP.

Each RIR generally has its own defined process for making address requests, so please consult the RIR in your region for details. For example, to obtain address space in the first place, the RIR might stipulate that the LIR/ISP demonstrate the need for utilization of say 25% of the allocation immediately and 50% within one year. Requests for additional address space could require justification via demonstration of a certain level of utilization of the LIR/ISP's current allocations. In order to keep track of LIR/ISP allocations, the RIRs have each implemented REST-based update mechanisms. As the LIR/ISP assigns address space, the assignment information can be communicated to the RIR so by the time additional address space is requested, the RIR and LIR/ISP have common allocation information against which the RIR's threshold can be confirmed and approved.

Address Allocation Efficiency

During the development of IPv6, much thought went into deriving the 128-bit address size. While IPv4 provides a 32-bit address field which provides a theoretical maximum of 2^{32} addresses or over 4.2 billion addresses, in reality the theoretical maximum is much less than 4.2 billion. This is due to the hierarchical allocation of address space for multiple layers of networks, then subnets and finally hosts. RFC 1715 [15] provides an analysis of address assignment efficiency, in which a logarithmic scale was proposed as a measure of allocation efficiency, which was defined as the H ratio:

$$H = \frac{\log_{10}(\text{number of objects})}{\text{number of available bits}}$$

Assignment efficiency measurements for IPv6, with its massive address space, is not calculated based on the H ratio; a different ratio, the HD ratio [16], is used:

$$HD = \frac{\log_{10}(\text{number of allocated objects})}{\log_{10}(\text{maximum number of allocatable objects})}$$

The "objects" measured in the HD ratio for IPv6 are the IPv6 site addresses (/48s) assigned from an IPv6 prefix of a given size. The /48 address blocks are those commonly assigned to each end user by the LIR/ISP. So an LIR/ISP with a

/32 allocation which has allocated 100/48s would have an HD ratio of log(100)/log(65,536) = 0.415.

Multi-Homing and IP Address Space

The term *multi-homing* refers to the provisioning of multiple connections to the Internet via one or more ISPs. A multi-homing strategy seeks to improve the reliability and perhaps performance of an organization's Internet connectivity and provides several benefits:

- Business continuity providing sustained Internet connectivity in the event of a connection outage when connected over diverse links to one or more ISPs.
- Improved performance via load sharing of Internet traffic over multiple connections when connected over diverse links to one or more ISPs, e.g., in the form of "Internet breakout" in a software-defined wide area network (SD-WAN) deployment.
- Resiliency through ISP redundancy when multiple ISPs are subscribed to limit exposure in the event of an ISP outage
- Policy and performance benefits achieved through routing of traffic based on congestion or based on requirements to route traffic of differing applications to differing links or ISPs.

If you subscribe with a single ISP, you may want to consider deploying at least two connections into different ISP points of presence (POPs, i.e., locations) originating from different locations on your network as shown in the left half pane of Figure 3.2. In this scenario, your Internet connection can survive an outage of one interfacing router or switch on your network or one the ISP ingress or a link or connection outage between them. If the ISP itself suffers a broader outage which renders its service unavailable or performance-impaired, this would hamper your outbound and inbound connectivity to the Internet which could be devastating to your business.

A diverse connection to multiple ISPs adds ISP resiliency to the architecture as shown in the right pane of Figure 3.2. In both panes of the figure we illustrate the routing of Internet traffic in and out based on the IPv6 and IPv4 prefixes corresponding to your public address space. On the left half of the figure, ISP A has provisioned address space to you as illustrated by the routing of Prefix PA_a relevant packets. Since this space was carved out of the ISP's space that is was allocated from an RIR or another provider, it is referred to as provider aggregatable (PA) space. The PA_a notation indicates PA space from ISP A. Because this space is carved out of ISP A's address space, if you were to unsubscribe from ISP A, you would have to renumber your publicly addressable devices to use the new ISP's PA space and remove ISP A's PA addresses.

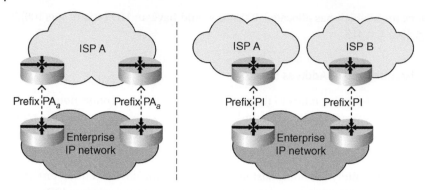

Figure 3.2   Multiple connections to one ISP (l); multi-homing with PI space (r).

In the general Internet model of end-to-end connections, i.e., without network address translation, the renumbering process would entail renumbering every device in your network within the new address plan based on space from the new ISP. Many IPv4 enterprise networks use NAT, enabling internal hosts to use private address space, and the resulting renumbering process entails updating NAT rules along with changing IP addresses for any hosts reachable from the Internet (e.g. web, email, and DNS servers). Network prefix translation for IPv6 is an experimental protocol which maps the internal address., e.g., ULA address, to a public global unicast address by mapping the first 64 bits of the address, retaining the original Interface ID for each device address.

On the right half of Figure 3.2, we illustrate the use of provider independent (PI) space which your enterprise may be able to obtain from an RIR or LIR. PI space enables you to advertise reachability to this address space via one, two, or any number of ISPs. You will need to obtain an autonomous system number (ASN) from your RIR as well and use the BGP to communicate routing reachability to your network from the Internet.

The use of PI space enables you to subscribe to any ISP and cancel ISP service without renumbering. While PI space offers numerous advantages to your IP planners, it does require that you advertise routes to your address space to routers within the global Internet as it is not assigned by your ISP. Thus, PA space maintains global Internet route aggregation while PI space does not.

If you are unable to obtain PI space due to your RIR policies, you can still connect to the Internet via two or more ISPs, leveraging their respective PA space allocations. As we show in Figure 3.3, the enterprise border routers interfacing directly to their respective ISP edge routers participate in an exterior routing protocol (e.g. BGP) to advertise reachability to the respective address blocks. Thus, the enterprise router connected to ISP A will advertise reachability to the address space provided to the enterprise by ISP A (PA_a), while the enterprise router

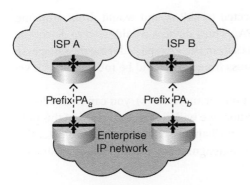

Figure 3.3 Multi-homing to two ISPs using PA space.

connected to ISP B will advertise reachability to the address space provided by ISP B (PA_b).

The two enterprise routers in Figure 3.3 also need to communicate with each other using an interior routing protocol via the enterprise IP network. In this manner, loss of connectivity to an ISP may be detected, though this is where things get interesting. One cannot simply route packets to/from ISP A through ISP B. Internet Best Current Practices [17, 18] call for denying incoming traffic from a source address not provisioned on a given router interface. For example, packets with a source address from PA_a incoming to ISP B from the enterprise network would be dropped (such traffic would only be accepted on links to ISP A). Such apparent spoofing of source IP addresses is a common vector for distributed denial of service attacks, ergo the best practice of ingress filtering. Therefore, when a link to the ISP or the ISP router fails, packets with corresponding addresses will be unrouteable.

If you are using NAT or NPT, though it defies the end-to-end principle, you would need to update translation rules to map only to available ISP address spaces. However, a recent RFC draft [19] specifies a solution to routing around the failure of an ISP link or router in a multi-homed deployment. This approach requires source address dependent routing (SADR) and hosts configured with addresses from both/all ISPs with the ability to select a source address within a prefix advertised by the next hop. SADR capability must be deployed at minimum on enterprise routers connecting to ISP(s) though extending this SADR domain to first hop routers (from end devices) can improve efficiencies despite the greater effort required to properly configure.

Referring to Figure 3.3, each enterprise network host would be assigned an IP address from both PA_a and PA_b address space. The enterprise routers connecting to respective ISPs would route only packets with a source address matching the connected ISP address space to the corresponding ISP. If the link to ISP A fails for example, the enterprise router connected to ISP A and would drop outbound packets with source addresses from PA_a. Thus, devices would need to detect the outage and use their source IP addresses from the PA_b space during the outage. In this manner, packets with source address from PA_b would be routed to ISP B via the corresponding enterprise router.

Once you've obtained IP space from one or more ISP(s), you can then allocate the address space within your organization. We will discuss the details of this public and private space allocation process in Chapter 6. But for now, we'll defer this and jump to the topic of endpoint address assignment within an allocated subnet.

Endpoint Address Allocation

In the early days of the Internet's existence, when hosts numbered in the hundreds, assigning an IP address to a device was fairly trivial. It was simply one of the configuration parameters entered manually on each host. This "once and done" or static address assignment process using a hard-coded IP address certainly was simple, but it inhibited the host's mobility among different networks or subnets. Enabling mobility required the cumbersome task of reconfiguring the host with a new IP address based on the present location or network to which connection was desired as we illustrated in Chapter 1.

Nonetheless, you will likely have a set of static addresses for devices on your network that do not require mobility, such as routers, servers, etc. It's imperative to keep track of which IP addresses on allocated subnets are statically assigned, which are assigned to address pools for dynamic assignment, and which are free or reserved for future use. Maintaining a subnet IP inventory will minimize duplicate or otherwise erroneous IP address assignments.

Server-based Address Allocation Using DHCP

The DHCP is a client-server protocol for devices connecting to an IP network to automatically obtain an IP address. DHCP has been a tremendous time saver for IP network administrators. It enables a device to multicast or broadcast its request for an IP address, and solicit one or more DHCP servers within the IP network to assign an IP address without user intervention. For most end user devices such as laptops, VoIP phones, mobiles, and others, the DHCP process transpires "behind the scenes" upon device boot-up or connection to a wireline or wireless network. DHCP also enables efficient use of IP addresses by allowing an IP address to be reused among devices within dynamically allocated address pools. A given IP address may be used by one device one day and a different device the next.

DHCP is supported for both IPv4 and IPv6. We'll discuss the IPv4 version first. DHCP is built on the foundation of an older protocol, the Bootstrap Protocol, referred to as BOOTP. BOOTP provides automation of address assignment but is restricted to pre-assigning a given IP address to a particular device, identified by its network interface (i.e. link layer MAC) address. Thus, a BOOTP server is configured with a list of MAC addresses and corresponding IP addresses. DHCP incorporates this functionality with the added capability of assigning IP addresses to clients without requiring *a priori* knowledge of each client's hardware address.

DHCP supports three types of IP address allocation:

1) *Automatic allocation* – the DHCP server assigns a permanent IP address to the client
2) *Manual allocation* – like BOOTP, the DHCP server assigns a "fixed" IP address based on the particular device's hardware address
3) *Dynamic allocation* – the DHCP server assigns an IP address for a limited time period, after which it can be reassigned, perhaps to a different device

Automatic allocation may be useful for a particular set of users or devices requiring a permanent IP address assignment via DHCP, where there's no requirement for a particular user or device to have a particular IP address. In other words, you may want to set aside a number of "permanent" addresses without directly associating each IP address with a particular hardware address. This is in contrast to Manual DHCP, which like BOOTP, associates a particular hardware address with a corresponding IP address.

Dynamic allocation enables the DHCP server to assign an IP address to a particular client for a given time period referred to as the *lease time*. When the IP address becomes available due to the expiration of the lease or the client relinquishing the address, the server can reassign the same address to a different client. Under dynamic allocation, the DHCP server leases its IP addresses to clients for a fixed period of time. As such, the lease time is one of many configurable parameters for your DHCP server.

Regardless of the DHCP address allocation type, the process by which a DHCP client obtains a lease is the same. The basic process begins with a DHCP client broadcasting a DHCPDISCOVER (Discover) packet. Since the client does not have an IP address, nor generally any information about the IP network, it inserts the all-zeroes address as the source address and the broadcast (all-ones) address as the destination address within the IP header. Let's assume that a DHCP server has been deployed on the same subnet to which the DHCP client is connected. Upon receiving the Discover packet, the DHCP server will determine if it has an address available on this subnet on which the Discover was received.

If an address is available in the pool, the DHCP server will send a DHCPOFFER (Offer) packet to the client, offering an IP address and associated configuration parameters, called *options*. Note that the client may request particular options in the initial Discover message. The DHCP client may receive more than one Offer if multiple DHCP servers are servicing this subnet. The client will select one configuration set and broadcast a DHCPREQUEST (Request) packet, specifying the selected DHCP server whose offer it has accepted. The selected DHCP server will acknowledge the Request with a DHCPACK (Ack) once it has recorded the lease information in non-volatile storage, thereby binding the IP address to the DHCP client. This basic message flow is sometimes referred to as the "DORA" process – Discover, Offer, Request, and Ack (Figure 3.4).

In this simple example, the DHCP server resides on the same subnet as the DHCP client. The client broadcasts the Discover packet on the network. Since the DHCP server resides on the same network, it receives the broadcast and processes the packet. Knowing the network from which the broadcast originated, the DHCP server can assign an available IP address on the network. But do you have to deploy a DHCP server on every subnet? Fortunately, no; the DHCP server simply must be reachable from the subnet via the IP routing infrastructure. The router(s) receiving the Discover broadcast packet will not propagate the broadcast as this would create excessive and needless IP packet traffic. Instead, the router will forward or *relay* the packet via unicast directly to the intended DHCP server. Each router configured to perform this relay function is referred to as a *relay agent*. Each relay agent must be configured with the IP addresses of each DHCP server serving the subnet. This configuration parameter, commonly referred to as the DHCP Relay address or helper address, enables the router to accept the Discover broadcast, look up the DHCP server(s) configured for DHCP Relay, and then route the Discover packet via unicast directly to each DHCP server as illustrated in Figure 3.5.

In the process, the router modifies the DHCP Discover packet to insert the IP address of the interface on which the Discover was received into the Relay Agent (Gateway) Interface Address field. This parameter enables the DHCP server to identify the subnet on which an address assignment has been requested. Note that when the gateway interface address (GIAddr) field is zero, the DHCP server assumes the subnet on which to assign the IP address is the same as that on which the Discover was received (via direct broadcast).

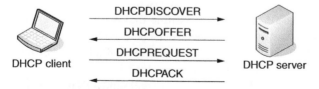

Figure 3.4 DHCP "DORA" process.

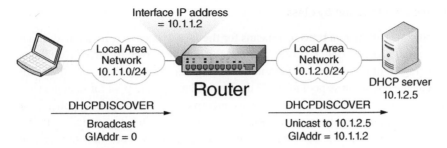

Figure 3.5 DHCP relay.

DHCP Servers and Address Assignment

Each DHCP server can be configured with multiple address pools serving several different subnets in various locations. In fact, for some DHCP server implementations, the same address pool can be configured on multiple DHCP servers for redundancy. The DHCP server keeps track of the state of all IP addresses across all of its configured address pools. When an address is leased to a client, the server generally tracks not only the lease time for the IP address, but an identifier for the client leasing the IP address. This identifier is typically the client hardware address (chaddr) field containing the layer 2 (MAC) address of the client, though the client-identifier field, option 60, may also be used.

The use of the client-identifier (client ID) option over the chaddr field was suggested to maintain an identifier for the device even if the link hardware is moved to another device. But in practice, most devices either do not provide a client ID or copy the value of the chaddr field into the client ID option.

The basic decision process used by DHCP servers in offering an address is based on the following.

- If the client has a leased address as recorded in the DHCP server, the server will assign this address.
- If the client previously had an address that is now expired or released but is still available, the server will assign this address.
- If the client includes an address in the Requested IP Address option, option 50, and the address is available, the server will assign this address.
- The server will assign an available address from a pool on the same subnet on which the Discover broadcast was received if the GIAddr field is zero, or on the subnet indicated by the GIAddr value if nonzero. Additional criteria based on parameters within the Discover packet may dictate from which pool the address gets assigned, if there are multiple pools serving the subnet in question. These parameters are generically referred to as client class parameters and are discussed next.

Device Identification by Class

Client class parameters provide a means for the DHCP client to provide additional information to the DHCP server, and for the DHCP server to recognize clients requiring unique IP address or parameter assignments. For example, you may want to dedicate one address pool for VoIP devices and a separate pool for data devices. This may be motivated by administrative concerns or by source routing policies for voice vs. data packets from the respective devices. Most DHCP servers, including those available from the Internet Systems Consortium (ISC) or Microsoft, enable specification of vendor class or user class values to enable such categorization as criteria in assigning an address from an address pool, along with associated options. This function is a key application for DHCP and we'll discuss it more in Chapter 5.

DHCP Options

As mentioned earlier, DHCP clients can request settings for particular options, and servers can assign these and other parameters based on the DHCP server configuration. DHCP administrators can define groupings of options to be assigned to all or certain DHCP clients based on the client's hardware address, client class value, or other DHCP packet parameter.

For example, we can set up two client classes corresponding to VoIP and data devices. Devices of these types will likely require different configuration parameters. For example, Cisco VoIP devices typically require option code 66 or 150, while Avaya VoIP devices require option 172, and data devices require neither of these. We can configure the DHCP server to distinguish different DHCP clients based on client class values provided by each client, and we can define DHCP options for each pool, which will be provided to clients receiving addresses in the corresponding pool associated with the respective client class. Alternatively, Manual DHCP address reservations enable mapping of a hardware address to a specific IP address, and associated DHCP options can also be defined for the device.

Please refer to Chapter 18 for a complete list of currently defined DHCP options.

DHCP for IPv6 (DHCPv6)

DHCP for IPv6 addresses is referred to as DHCPv6 and is defined in RFC 8415 [20]. Like DHCP for IPv4, DHCPv6 supports assignment of IPv6 addresses and configurations. In addition, the DHCPv6 protocol has been extended to support DHCPv4-over-DHCPv6 (DHCP 4o6) [21] to facilitate migration to IPv6 networks by enabling configuration of IPv4 devices via DHCPv6; for example when a residential IPv4 device requires DHCP configuration from a service provider running only IPv6. DHCP 4o6 provides for the encapsulation of DHCPv4 messages within

DHCPV4-QUERY and DHCPV4-RESPONSE message types. A current enumeration of DHCPv6 message types is provided in Chapter 18.

DHCP Comparison IPv4 vs. IPv6

DHCPv6 uses different message types and packet formatting than DHCP for IPv4 but is similar in many ways. The following table highlights these similarities and differences (Table 3.1).

Table 3.1 Comparison of DHCP for IPv4 and IPv6.

Feature	DHCPv4	DHCPv6
Destination IP address of initial message from the DHCP client	Broadcast (255.255.255.255)	Multicast to link-scoped address: All-DHCP-Agents address (ff02::1:2)
DHCP relay support	Yes using preconfigured relay agent addresses	Yes using All_DHCP_ Servers site-scoped multicast address (ff05::1:3)
Relay agent forwarding	Same message type code but inserts giaddr and unicasts to DHCP server(s)	Encapsulates client message in RELAY-FORW to DHCP server(s) and RELAY-REPL from server(s)
Message to locate server to obtain IP address and configuration	DHCPDISCOVER	SOLICIT
Server message to engage client	DHCPOFFER	ADVERTISE
Client message to accept parameters	DHCPREQUEST	REQUEST
Server acknowledgement of lease binding	DHCPACK	REPLY
Client message to leasing DHCP server to extend lease	DHCPREQUEST (unicast)	RENEW
Client message to any DHCP server to extend lease	DHCPREQUEST (broadcast)	REBIND
Client message to relinquish a lease	DHCPRELEASE	RELEASE
Client message to indicate that an offered IP address is already in use	DHCPDECLINE	DECLINE
Server message to instruct client to obtain a new configuration	DHCPFORCERENEW	RECONFIGURE
Request IP configuration only, not address	DHCPINFORM	INFORMATION-REQUEST

DHCPv6 Address Assignment

The DHCPv6 process begins with a client issuing a SOLICIT message, in essence requesting a "bid" from DHCP servers that can provide an IP address on the particular subnet to which the client is connected as shown in Figure 3.6. Instead of broadcasting this initial packet as in IPv4, the SOLICIT message is sent by the client to the All_Relay_Agents_and_Servers multicast address, ff02::1:2.

Any routers on the link configured as relay agents will receive the SOLICIT packet and will relay the packet to a DHCPv6 server(s). IPv6 relay agents do not require configuration of DHCP Relay addresses as in the IPv4 case, though they may enable such configuration. Instead, relay agents encapsulate the original Solicit packet within a Relay-Forw packet, which is then transmitted to the site-scoped All-DHCP-Servers multicast address (ff05::1:3). The Link Address field of the Relay-Forw packet indicates the link on which the client requesting an IP address currently resides. This information is used by the DHCP server in assigning an appropriate IP address for this link, in a manner similar to the DHCPv4 GIAddr field. This process is illustrated in Figure 3.7.

DHCPv6 servers on this subnet will receive the SOLICIT packet directly, and others responding to the site-scoped All_DHCP_Servers multicast address will receive the SOLICIT packet encapsulated within a RELAY-FORW packet. In either case, the DHCPv6 server may respond with an ADVERTISE packet, indicating a preference value. The preference value is intended to enable the client to

Figure 3.6 DHCPv6 address assignment.

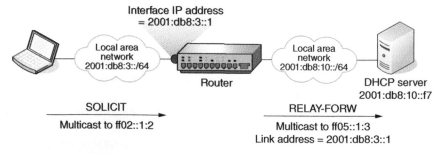

Figure 3.7 DHCPv6 relay.

select the server advertising the highest preference as configured by administrators. The server will alternatively indicate if it has no addresses available on the subnet. The ADVERTISE packet will be unicast to the client if the SOLICIT had been received directly using the client's source IP address from the SOLICIT packet (most likely the client's link local address). If the SOLICIT had been received by the server via a RELAY-FORW packet from a relay agent, the ADVERTISE message will be encapsulated in a RELAY-REPL packet and unicast to the corresponding relay agent.

The client analyzes the advertisements received, and selects a server from which to request an IP address, typically with the highest preference, and issues a REQUEST message to the server. The server will then record the address assignment and reply to the client with a REPLY message.

When the client receives a Reply packet to confirm the address assignment, the client must perform duplicate address detection (DAD) to assure no other device is already using the IP address due to autoconfiguration or manual configuration. If another device is using the assigned IP address, the client would send a Decline message to the DHCP server, indicating that the address is in use. The client can then reinitiate the DHCP process to obtain a different IP address.

In addition to the four-packet exchange outlined above, DHCPv6 features a rapid commit option. This halves the messaging requirements by enabling the server to simply REPLY to a SOLICIT packet. The client would include the rapid commit option in its SOLICIT message. Servers responding with an address assignment would issue a REPLY packet directly, also including the rapid commit option. Note that each server responding will assume the address it assigned is leased, so rapid commit should be used with either short lease times or for support by a limited number of servers.

DHCPv6 Prefix Delegation

DHCPv6 is used not only to assign individual IP addresses and/or associated IP configuration information to hosts, but can also be used to delegate entire networks to requesting router devices. This form of delegation via DHCPv6 is called *prefix delegation*. The original motivation for prefix delegation arose from broadband service providers seeking to automate the process of delegating IPv6 subnets (e.g. /48 to /64 networks) to broadband subscribers in a hierarchical manner. A requesting router device at the edge of the service provider network, facing subscribers, would issue a request for address space via the DHCPv6 protocol to a delegating router. Note the terminology: this is intended to be an inter-router protocol though a DHCPv6 server could perform the functions of the delegating router.

The prefix delegation process utilizes the same basic DHCPv6 message flow described above for address assignment per Figure 3.7: Solicit, Advertisement,

Request, and Reply. Additional information within the corresponding DHCPv6 messages can be used to determine an appropriate network for delegation. Like IP addresses, prefixes have preferred and valid lifetimes. The requesting router can request a lifetime extension via the DHCPv6 Renew and Rebind messages. We'll discuss address lifetimes at the end of this chapter.

Device Unique Identifiers (DUIDs)

Like DHCPv4, DHCPv6 servers must track the availability and assignment of IP addresses within their configured address pools, and identify requestors and holders of IP addresses. DHCPv6 utilizes the device unique identifier (DUID) to identify clients. DUIDs are used not only for servers to identify clients, but for clients to identify servers. The DUID is analogous to the client-identifier concept in that DUIDs are intended to be globally unique for a device, not an interface. DUIDs should not change over time, even if the device undergoes changes in network interface hardware. DUIDs are constructed in various manners automatically by IPv6 nodes. They consist of a two-octet type code followed by a variable number of octets based on the type. The following DUID type codes are currently defined:

- Type = 1 – Link layer address plus time (DUID-LLT)
- Type = 2 – Vendor-assigned unique ID based on enterprise number (DUID-EN)
- Type = 3 – Link-layer-based DUID (DUID-LL)
- Type = 4 – Universally unique identifier (DUID–UUID)

For those based on link layer address, they are to be used for *all* device interfaces, even if the hardware from which the link layer address was obtained is removed. The DUID is a device identifier, not an interface identifier.

Identity Associations (IAs)

While DUIDs are associated with all interfaces of a device and IP addresses are assigned to interfaces, you may be wondering how the device and server identify particular interfaces for a given DUID. The concept of the identity association (IA) provides this linkage between a DHCPv6 server and a client interface for individual address or prefix assignment. IAs are differentiated by type between those for temporary addresses (IA_TA), which are short-leased, nonrenewable addresses, those for non-temporary addresses (IA_NA), and those for prefix delegation (IA_PD).

Temporary address assignments assuage privacy concerns associated with autoconfigured addresses based on hardware addresses (i.e. modified EUI-64 interface IDs), which do not change over time. The concern is that a given Interface ID within an IPv6 address does not change unless the underlying hardware interface changes. Thus, even if the network upon which a device is connected changes from day-to-day, the interface ID does not. The ability to track the location of a device and thus its user, becomes relatively easy; hence the concern with privacy. The use of short-lived, non-renewable address assignments via DHCP can be one approach to address this concern, hence the concept of temporary addresses. We'll discuss this privacy issue in detail later in the chapter.

For individual address assignment, temporary or non-temporary, each client interface has an IA, identified by an IA Identifier, or IAID. The IAID is represented as four octets in client-server DHCPv6 communications and is chosen by the client. The IAID must be unique among all IAIDs associated with the client and must be stored persistently across client reboots or consistently derivable upon each reboot. The client specifies its DUID and IAID for which an address is being requested from the DHCPv6 server. The DHCPv6 server assigns an IPv6 address to the IAID, along with the corresponding T1 (renew) and T2 (reboot) timer values.

IA_PDs are not necessarily associated with a device interface. Recall that the requesting router is using DHCPv6 to obtain an IPv6 network delegation. The requesting router must derive one or more IA_PDs for use within DHCPv6, and it must be persistent across reboots or consistently derivable.

DHCPv6 Options

As with DHCP for IPv4, additional configuration parameters may be defined on a DHCPv6 server for assignment to corresponding DHCPv6 clients. Please refer to Chapter 18 for a complete listing of currently defined DHCPv6 options.

IPv6 Address Autoconfiguration

A key benefit of IPv6 features the ability for devices to automatically configure their own IPv6 address that is unique and relevant to the subnet to which they are presently connecting. Three basic forms of IPv6 address autoconfiguration are defined:

- *Stateless* – This process is "stateless" in that it is not dependent on the state or availability of external assignment mechanisms, e.g., DHCPv6. The device attempts to configure its own IPv6 address(es) without external or user intervention. This form is abbreviated as SLAAC (stateless address autoconfiguration).
- *Stateful* – The stateful process relies solely an external address assignment mechanism such as DHCPv6.

- *Combination stateless and stateful* – This process involves a form of stateless address autoconfiguration used in conjunction with stateful configuration of additional IP parameters. This commonly entails a device autoconfiguring an IPv6 address using the stateless method, then utilizing DHCPv6 to obtain additional parameters or options such as which NTP servers to query for time resolution on the given network.

At the most basic level, the autoconfiguration of an IPv6 unicast address was intent on concatenating the address of the network to which the device is connected (where you are) and the device's interface ID (who you are). But as we touched on earlier, the latter portion introduces glaring privacy concerns. Internet conglomerates such as content delivery networks (CDNs) and popular social media websites with access to large quantities of user IP traffic could easily track the source locations and destination endpoints for individuals' Internet sessions. Privacy extensions for the derivation of the Interface ID have been introduced to assuage such privacy concerns. We'll get to that in a moment but let's first consider how the device determines the address of the network to which it is connected.

Neighbor Discovery

The process of *neighbor discovery* in IPv6 enables a node to discover the IPv6 subnet address on which it is connected. Neighbor discovery in general also enables identification of other IPv6 nodes on the subnet, to identify their link layer addresses, to discover routers serving the subnet and to perform DAD. Discovery of routers enables IPv6 nodes to automatically identify routers on the subnet, negating the need to configure a default gateway manually within the device's IP configuration. This discovery process enables a device to identify the network prefix(es) and corresponding prefix length(s) assigned to the link.

Neighbor discovery entails each router periodically sending advertisements on each of its configured subnets indicating its IP address, its ability to provide default gateway functionality, its link layer address, the network prefix(es) served on the link including corresponding prefix length and valid address lifetime, as well as other configuration parameters.

The router advertisement also indicates whether a DHCPv6 server is available for address assignment or other configuration. The M bit (Managed address configuration flag) in the router advertisement indicates that DHCPv6 services are available for address and configuration settings. The O bit (other configuration flag) indicates that configuration parameters other than the IP address are available via DHCPv6; such information may include which DNS servers to query for devices on this link. Nodes can also solicit router advertisements using Router Solicitation messages, addressed to the link local routers multicast address (ff02::2). The following table summarizes the interpretation of these flags.

Flag	O = 0	O = 1
M = 0	No DHCPv6	DHCPv6 for configuration only
M = 1	DHCPv6 for address and configuration	DHCPv6 for address and configuration

Modified EUI-64 Interface Identifiers

Once a node identifies the subnet to which it is attached, it may complete the SLAAC process by formulating its Interface ID. The IPv6 addressing architecture stipulates that all unicast IPv6 addresses, other than those beginning with binary [000]$_2$ must use a 64-bit Interface ID. Interface IDs derived from the device's MAC address must be generated using the modified EUI-64 algorithm [12]. The "unmodified" extended unique identifier-64 algorithm entails concatenating the 24-bit company identifier issued by the IEEE to each network interface hardware manufacturer (e.g. the initial 24 bits of an Ethernet MAC address) with a 40-bit extension identifier. For 48-bit Ethernet addresses, the company identifier portion of the Ethernet address (first 24 bits) is followed by a 16-bit EUI label, defined as hexadecimal fffe, followed by the 24-bit extension identifier, i.e., the remaining 24 bits of the Ethernet address.

The modification required to convert an unmodified into a modified EUI-64 identifier calls for inverting the "u" bit (universal/local bit) of the company identifier field. The "u" bit is the seventh most significant bit in the company identifier field. Thus, the algorithm for a 48-bit MAC address is to invert the "u" bit and insert the hexadecimal value fffe between the company identifier and the interface identifier. This is illustrated in Figure 3.8 where a MAC address of AC-62-E8-49-5F-62 yields an interface ID of ae62:e8ff:fe49:5f62.

For non-Ethernet MAC addresses, the algorithm calls for use of the link layer address as the Interface ID, with zero padding (from the "left"). For cases where no link layer address is available, e.g., on a dial up link, a unique identifier utilizing another interface address, a serial number, or other device-specific identifier is recommended.

Opaque Interface IDs

Use of an Interface ID derived from a device's MAC address raises several privacy and security concerns:

- *Location tracking* – IPv6 addresses containing a deterministic (or static in general) interface ID could allow the tracking of the user's location based on the network prefixes to which the user's Interface ID is associated.
- *Activity tracking* – User activity may likewise be tracked by analyzing destinations accessed by the corresponding source IPv6 address containing the user's Interface ID.
- *Device targeting* – Decoding of the interface ID may allow an attacker to identify the manufacturer of the device's interface and thereby enable exploitation of known vendor vulnerabilities.
- *Address reconnaissance* – Determination of MAC vendors used within a network could aid attackers in reducing the search space from an entire /64 $(1.8 \times 10^{19}$ addresses) for a subnet to those containing portions of the Interface ID associated with known MAC vendors when identifying possible attack targets

Several alternative approaches to the modified EUI-64 algorithm have been devised to address these concerns, including the following.

- Cryptographically generated addresses (CGA) utilize an Interface ID which consists of a one-way hash of a public key and auxiliary parameters, cryptographically binding the public key to the corresponding IPv6 address [22].
- Temporary (privacy) addresses are supplemental addresses periodically generated using a random interface ID [23]. These are supplemental in the sense that these addresses are used only on outbound connections in order to reduce device identity exposure, so another stable form of interface ID derivation is also required. Temporary addresses have been found by some network managers as exacerbating the challenges of defining access control, auditing addresses, and troubleshooting network problems.

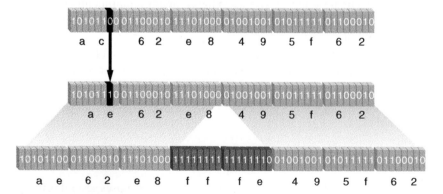

Figure 3.8 Modified EUI-64 interface ID example.

- Constant Interface IDs are not based on the modified EUI-64 algorithm but on some other form of pseudo random generation but is appended to its relevant prefix.
- Stable (non-temporary) semantically opaque addresses are based on a pseudo-random Interface ID that is the same every time the device connects to a given subnet, but is different for each subnet visited. In addition, they are not correlated with the device's MAC address [24]. This method is the IETF recommended approach to Interface ID generation for SLAAC instead of the modified EUI-64 method [25].

The following table offers a comparison of the resilience of each of these address assignment schemes against the major privacy and security concerns outlined at the beginning of this section [26].

| | **Vulnerability based on the IPv6 address[a]** | | | |
Mechanism	Location tracking	Activity tracking	Device targeting	Address reconnaissance
Modified EUI-64	During device lifetime	During device lifetime	Possible	Possible
Static (manual)	During address lifetime	During address lifetime	Depends on address derivation method	Depends on address derivation method
CGA	Not vulnerable	During address lifetime, e.g., until regenerated	Not vulnerable	Not vulnerable
Temporary	Not vulnerable	During temporary address lifetime	Not vulnerable	Not vulnerable
Constant	During address lifetime	During address lifetime	Not vulnerable	Not vulnerable
Stable	Not vulnerable	During use within a given subnet	Not vulnerable	Not vulnerable
DHCPv6	Not vulnerable	During address (lease) lifetime	Not vulnerable	Depends on address assignment method

[a] A device may be exposed to these vulnerabilities based on aspects other than its IPv6 address. Source: RFC 7721 [26].

Methods which utilize an unchanging Interface ID are more susceptible to location tracking given the deterministic association of the Interface ID with the user/device. Activity tracking of a session between two IP addresses is certainly possible while both addresses are in use, e.g., during the user/device address lifetime. And any method that is derived from a device's MAC address opens the door to device targeting as well as address reconnaissance. DHCPv6 assignment methods could also simplify address reconnaissance attempts if addresses are assigned monotonically if not otherwise deterministically.

Reserved Interface IDs

Upon derivation of an interface ID using any of the above algorithms, a node must confirm that it does not overlap with the set of Interface IDs reserved by IANA [27]:

Reserved interface identifier range	Reserved for
0000:0000:0000:0000	Subnet-Router anycast address
fdff:ffff:ffff:ff80 – fdff:ffff:ffff:ffff	Reserved subnet anycast addresses

The Interface ID may not be unique, especially if not derived from a unique 48-bit MAC address. Thus, the device must also perform DAD prior to committing the new address. Before completing the DAD process, the address is considered tentative.

Duplicate Address Detection (DAD)

DAD is performed using the neighbor discovery process, which entails the device sending an IPv6 neighbor solicitation packet to the IPv6 address it just derived (or obtained from DHCPv6) in order to identify a pre-existing occupant of the IP address. After a slight delay, the device also sends a neighbor solicitation packet to the solicited node multicast address associated with this address as well.

If another device is already using the IP address, it will respond with a neighbor advertisement packet, and the autoconfiguration process will stop; i.e., manual intervention or configuration of the device may be required to assign an alternate interface ID. If a neighbor advertisement packet is not received, the device can assume uniqueness of the address and assign it to the corresponding interface. Participation in this process of neighbor solicitation and advertisement is required not only for autoconfigured addresses but even for those statically defined or obtained through DHCPv6.

IPv6 addresses have a lifetime during which they are valid as illustrated in Figure 3.9. In some cases, the lifetime is infinite, but the concept of address

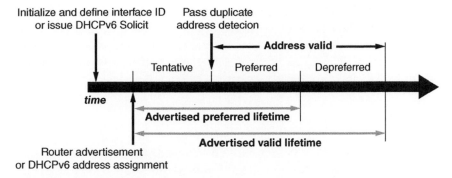

Figure 3.9 IPv6 address lifetimes. Source: Based on Microsoft 2009 [267].

lifetime applies to both DHCPv6 leased addresses as well as autoconfigured addresses. This is useful in easing the process of network renumbering. Routers are configured with and advertise a preferred lifetime and a valid lifetime value for each network prefix in their router advertisement messages. IP addresses that have successfully proven unique through the DAD process described above can be considered either preferred or deprecated. In either state, the address is valid, but this differentiation provides a means for upper layer protocols (e.g. TCP, UDP) to select an IP address that will likely not change during the ensuing session.

A device refreshes the preferred and valid lifetimes with each router advertisement message or lease renewal. When time expires on a preferred prefix, the associated address(es) will become deprecated, though still valid. Thus, the deprecated state provides a transition period during which the address is still functional but should not be used to initiate new communications. Once the valid lifetime of the address expires, the address is no longer valid for use. For example, to renumber a subnet, the router can be configured to advertise the new prefix, and devices on the network would undergo the autoconfiguration process using the new prefix as the lifetime of the old prefix expires.

Figure 5-9   IPv6 address lifetimes. Source: Based on Microsoft 2013[24].

4

Navigating the Internet with DNS

DNS represents the third cornerstone of IPAM and a foundational element of IP communications. DNS provides the means for improved usability of IP applications, insulating end users from communicating by entering IP addresses. Certainly, to communicate over an IP network, a device needs to send IP packets to the intended destination device; and as we have discussed, IP packets require source and destination IP addresses. DNS provides the translation from a user-entered named destination, e.g. web site address, to its IP address.

As a network service, DNS has evolved from simple host name-to-IP address lookup utility to enabling very sophisticated "look-up" applications supporting voice, data, multimedia, and security applications. DNS has proven extremely scalable and reliable for such lookup functions. We'll discuss how this lookup process works after first introducing how this information is organized.

Domain Hierarchy

The global domain name system is effectively a distributed hierarchical database. Each "dot" in a domain name indicates a boundary between tiers in the hierarchy, with each name in between dots denoted as a *label*. The top of the hierarchy, the "." or root domain provides references to top-level domains, such as .com, .net, .us, .ie, which in turn refer respective subdomains. Each of these top-level domains or TLDs is a child of the root domain. Each TLD has several children domains as well, such as ipamworldwide.com, with the ipamworldwide domain beneath the com domain, which in turn resides below the root domain. And these children may have children domains and so on.

IP Address Management, Second Edition. Michael Dooley and Timothy Rooney.
© 2021 The Institute of Electrical and Electronics Engineers, Inc.
Published 2021 by John Wiley & Sons, Inc.

As we read between the dots from right to left, we can identify a unique path to the host we are seeking. The text left of the leftmost dot is generally the host name (some environments allow dots within hostnames which is relatively uncommon though permissible), which is located within the domain indicated by the rest of the domain name. A *fully qualified domain name* (FQDN) refers to this unique full [absolute] path name to the node or host within the global DNS data hierarchy. Figure 4.1 illustrates a FQDN mapping to the tree-like structure of the DNS database. Note that the trailing dot after .com. explicitly denotes the root domain within the domain name, rendering it fully qualified. Keep in mind that without this explicit FQDN trailing dot notation, a given domain name may be ambiguously interpreted as either fully qualified or relative to the "current" domain. This is certainly legal and easier shorthand notation, but be aware of the potential ambiguity.

Name Resolution

To illustrate how domain information is organized and how a DNS server leverages this hierarchical data structure, let's take a look at an example name resolution. Let's assume I'd like to connect to a device named pc52 per the example in Figure 4.1. Thus, I enter the host domain name, `pc52.dev.ipamworldwide.com.` as my intended destination. The application into which I type this domain name (e.g. email client, web browser, etc.) utilizes the sockets[1] API to communicate with a portion of code within the TCP/IP stack called a *resolver*. The resolver's job in this instance is to translate the domain name I entered into an IP address that may be used to initiate IP communications.

The resolver issues a query for this host name to my local DNS server, requesting the server provide an answer. The IP address of this local DNS server is configured either manually, via DHCP using the domain servers option (option 6 in DHCP and option 23 in DHCPv6), or via a router advertisement recursive DNS server (RDNSS) option for SLAAC. This DNS server will then attempt to answer the query by looking in the following areas in the specified order and as illustrated in Figure 4.2.

We refer to this local DNS server to which the resolver issues its query as a *recursive server*. "Recursive" means that the resolver requests the DNS server locate the answer to its query if it does not know itself. From the resolver's viewpoint, it issues one query and expects an answer. From the recursive DNS server's

---

1 This API call is from the application to the TCP/IP layer of the protocol stack. The getaddrinfo() sockets/Winsock call initiates this particular process.

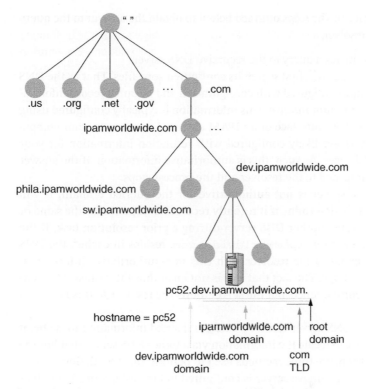

Figure 4.1 Domain tree mapping to a fully qualified domain name.

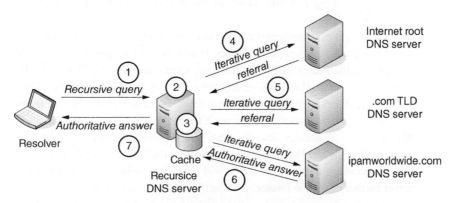

Figure 4.2 Recursive and iterative queries in name resolution.

perspective, it may need to issue several queries in an attempt to locate the answer for the resolver. The recursive server is the resolver's "portal" into the global domain name system. The recursive server accepts queries directly from client resolvers and performs the steps outlined below to obtain the answer to the query on behalf of the resolver.

1) The resolver initiates a query to the recursive DNS server.
2) The recursive server will first search its configured zone files. That is, the DNS server is typically configured with configuration and resource record information for which it is *authoritative*. This information is typically configured using text files, a Windows interface or an IPAM system. For example, your company's DNS servers are likely configured with resolution information for your company's IP devices. As such, this is authoritative information. If the answer is found, it is returned to the resolver and the process stops.
3) If the recursive server is not authoritative for the queried domain, it will access its cache to determine if it recently received a response for the same or similar query from another DNS server during a prior resolution task. If the answer for `pc52.dev.ipamworldwide.com.` resides in cache[2], the DNS server will respond to the resolver with this non-authoritative information and the process stops. The fact that this is not an authoritative answer is generally of little consequence, but the server alerts the resolver to this fact in its response.
4) If the recursive DNS server cannot locate the queried information in cache, it will then attempt to locate the information via another DNS server that has the information. There are three methods used to perform this "escalation."
   a) If the queried recursive server is configured to forward queries to another server, the server will forward the query as configured in its configuration or zone repository and will await an answer and return it to the querying client.
   b) If forwarding is not configured and the cached information referenced in step 3 yields a partial answer to the query, it will attempt to contact the source of that information to locate the ultimate source and answer. For example, a prior query to another DNS server, server X, may have indicated that DNS server X is authoritative for the `ipamworldwide.com` domain. The recursive DNS server may then query DNS server X for information leading to resolution of `pc52.dev.ipamworldwide.com`. Upon querying server X, the queried server will either resolve the query by providing the IP address(es) for `pc52.dev.ipamworldwide.com`. or will provide a referral to another DNS server further down the hierarchy "closer" to the sought FQDN.

---

2 Cache entries are temporary and are removed by DNS servers based on user configuration settings as well as the advertised lifetime (time-to-live, TTL) of a resource record.

c) If no information is found in cache, the server cannot identify a referral server, or forwarding did not provide a response[3] or is not configured, the DNS server will access its *hints* file. The hints file provides a list of *root name servers* to query in order to begin traversing down the domain hierarchy to a DNS server that can provide an answer to the query. The response from a root server is always a *referral* to a TLD DNS server which is authoritative for the TLD in the queried name. The root servers are "delegation-only" servers and do not directly resolve queries, only answering with delegated name server (NS) information for the queried TLD.

5) For cases 4b and 4c above, the recursive server *iterates*[4] additional queries based on responses down the domain tree until the query can be answered. Continuing with our example, upon querying a server which is authoritative for com., the answer received will be a referral to the name server that is authoritative for ipamworldwide.com., and so on down the tree until the DNS server(s) that are authoritative for the queried information are located.

Note that by issuing queries to other DNS servers to locate resolution information, the recursive server itself performs a resolver function to execute this lookup. The term *stub resolver* is commonly used to identify resolvers which do not iterate down the domain tree. Stub resolvers such as those within typical end user clients are configured only with which recursive DNS servers to query.

6) If the queried information exists within an authoritative server, the query response includes the answer to the query in the form of one or more *resource records* matching the queried name, class, and resource record type.

The recursive server generally updates its cache not only with the ultimate answer for the specific query, but with any additional information provided with the answer and referral messages received in the process. In this way, the recursive server caches the domain names and IP addresses for the .com and ipamworldwide.com domains. When the same or another stub resolver queries for another domain with the .com domain subtree, the recursive server can utilize its cache to query one of the .com name servers directly without needing to query the root server as mentioned in step 4c. If an answer cannot be found, the recursive server will also cache this "negative" information as well for use in responding to similar queries.

7) The recursive DNS server will provide the answer (or indication of no answer) to the stub resolver and the process ends.

We mentioned the use of DNS forwarders in step 4, where the server queried by stub resolvers forwards all or some queries to other DNS servers for recursion. You

---

3 If the forward only option is configured, the resolution attempt will cease if the forwarded query returns no results; if the forward first option is configured, the process outlined in this paragraph ensues, with escalation to a root server.

4 These individual "point-to-point" queries are also referred to as iterative queries.

might deploy this configuration if you have a consolidated set of internal caching servers through which you funnel external-bound DNS queries or if you're using a third-party DNS resolver service. In both cases, you can configure your forwarding DNS servers to resolve internal name space and forward other queries to your caching servers or to your service provider's DNS servers respectively. The forwarding DNS server generally caches resolution answers like recursive servers to minimize DNS message flow and improve resolution performance. We'll discuss this topology in Chapter 14.

In summary, the resolution process entails (a) locating a NS with authoritative information to resolve the query in question and (b) querying that server for the desired information. In our example, the desired information was the IP address corresponding to the domain name pc52.dev.ipamworldwide.com. This "translation" information mapping the queried domain name to an IP address is stored in the DNS server in the form of a resource record; if the name has multiple IP addresses, each is identified in respective resource records, collectively comprising a *resource record set*. The bottom line is that DNS servers are configured at all levels of the domain tree as authoritative for their respective domain information, including where to direct queriers further down the domain tree. In many cases, these servers at different levels are administered by different organizations. Not every level or node in the domain tree requires a different set of DNS servers as an organization may serve multiple domain levels within a common set of DNS servers.

Resource Records

Resource records provide the means to map the question to an answer. The type of resource record defines the desired result type; e.g. the A resource record type will provide an IPv4 address as an answer while the AAAA type will provide an IPv6 address. The answer may be "the final answer" or referral information that can be used to obtain the desired answer via additional queries or other means. When responding to a query for information, a DNS server will place the resource record information in the Answer section of a DNS message. The "on-the-wire format" dictated by the DNS protocol is illustrated in Figure 4.3.

When representing resource records in zone files, all of these fields may be entered except the RDLength field, which is inserted when the resource record information is placed in a DNS message by the DNS server. The textual representation of a resource record generally follows a common convention shown below. Most resource records are defined with the following general fields, though depending on the resource record type, the RData field may consist of multiple subfields.

Owner	Time to live	Class	Type	RData

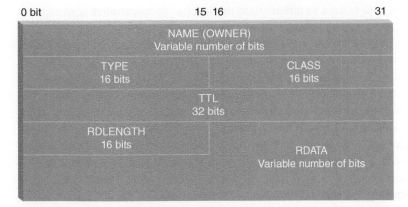

0 bit   15 16   31

NAME (OWNER)
Variable number of bits

TYPE
16 bits

CLASS
16 bits

TTL
32 bits

RDLENGTH
16 bits

RDATA
Variable number of bits

Figure 4.3   DNS resource record wire format. Source: Based on RFC 1035 [28].

- *Owner* (Name) – This field contains the information being queried.
- *Time to live* – The number of seconds for which the information contained in this resource record is valid for servers and resolvers caching this information. After the TTL expires, the resource record information must be removed from the name server and resolver cache. The TTL can be specified on a per resource record basis or if omitted, a zone level default TTL value is used.
- *Class* – The class of the resource record, usually IN for Internet.
- *Type* – The type of resource record corresponding to the type of information being sought
- *RData* – The "record data" or answer portion corresponding to the information being sought by matching the Owner (Name), class and type field contents.

Please consult Chapter 19 for a complete listing of currently defined resource record types and the applications they support.

Zones and Domains

While the top three layers of the domain tree typically utilize three sets of DNS servers under differing administrative authority, the support of multiple levels or domains on a single set of DNS servers is a deployment decision. This decision hinges primarily on whether administrative delegation is required or desired. For example, the DNS administrators for the `ipamworldwide.com` domain may desire to retain administrative control of the `eng.ipamworldwide.com.` domain, but to delegate `dev.ipamworldwide.com` to a different set of administrators and NSs.

The term *zone* is used to differentiate the level of administrative control with respect to the domain hierarchy. In our example, the ipamworldwide.com zone contains authority for the ipamworldwide.com, phila.ipamworldwide.com, and sw.ipamworldwide.com domains, while the dev.ipamworldwide.com zone retains authority for the dev.ipamworldwide.com domain as illustrated in Figure 4.4.

Thus, administrators for the ipamworldwide.com zone must configure all resource records and configuration attributes for the ipamworldwide.com zone, including subdomains within the ipamworldwide.com zone such as the sw.ipam-worldwide.com domain. At the same time, ipamworldwide.com administrators must provide a delegation linkage to any child zones, such as dev.ipamworld-wide.com.

By delegating responsibility for dev.ipamworldwide.com, the DNS administrators for ipamworldwide.com agree to pass all queries for dev.ipamworldwide.com (and below in the domain tree for any subdomains of dev.ipamworldwide.com) to DNS servers administered by personnel operating the dev.ipamworldwide.com zone. These dev.ipamworldwide.com administrators can manage their domain and resource records and any children autonomously; they just need to inform the parent domain administrators (for ipamworldwide.com) where to direct queries they receive as resolvers or other DNS servers attempt to traverse down the domain tree seeking resolutions.

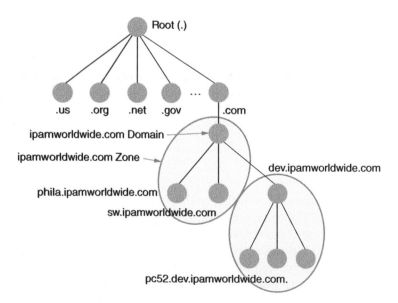

Figure 4.4 Zones as delegated domains.

When other recursive DNS servers around the world seek to resolve any domain names ending in ipamworldwide.com on behalf of their stub resolvers, their queries will require traversal of the ipamworldwide.com DNS servers then down to dev.ipamworldwide.com DNS servers thanks to this linkage. This linkage is realized with NS resource records within the ipamworldwide.com zone, which identifies the name servers authoritative for the dev.ipamworldwide.com delegated zone. These NS records provide the continuity to delegated child zones by referring resolvers or other name servers further down the domain tree. Corresponding address (A or AAAA) records called *glue records* are also usually defined to "glue" each resolved NS host domain name to an IP address for further queries since the NS record rdata field contains the domain name of the corresponding DNS server.

The process of delegation of the name space enables autonomy of DNS configuration while providing linkages via NS record referrals within the global DNS database. As you can imagine, if the name servers referenced by these NS records are unavailable, the domain tree will be broken at that point, inhibiting resolution of names at that point or below in the domain tree. If the ipamworldwide.com DNS servers are down, authoritative resolution for ipamworldwide.com and its children will fail. This illustrates the requirement that each zone must have at least two authoritative DNS servers for resiliency.

In summary, the administrators for the ipamworldwide.com zone need to configure their DNS servers with configuration and resource record information for the ipamworldwide.com, phila.ipamworldwide.com and sw.ipamworldwide.com domains. They also need to configure their servers with just the names and addresses of DNS servers serving delegated child zones, particularly dev.ipamworldwide.com in this case. They need know nothing further about these delegated domains; just where to refer the querying recursive DNS server during the resolution process.

Dissemination of Zone Information

Given the criticality of the DNS service, DNS server redundancy is a must. DNS server configuration information consists of server operational parameters and declarations of all zones for which the server is authoritative. This information can be defined on each server that is authoritative for a given set of zones. Additions, changes, and deletions of resource records, the discrete resolution information within each zone configuration file or repository, can be entered once on a master server, or more correctly, the server that is configured as master for the respective zone. The other servers that are likewise authoritative for this information can be configured as secondaries, and they obtain zone updates via the process of zone transfers. Zone transfers enable a secondary server to obtain the latest copy of its authoritative zone information from the master server.

Microsoft Active Directory-integrated DNS servers support zone transfers for compatibility with this standard process, but also enable DNS data replication using native Active Directory replication processes.

Zone versions are tracked by a serial number which must be incremented every time a resource record change is applied to the zone. Secondaries are configured to periodically check the zone serial number set on the master server by querying its start of authority (SOA) record; if the serial number is larger than its last known value for the zone, it will conclude that it has outdated information and will initiate a zone transfer. Additionally, the server that is master for the zone can be configured to proactively notify its secondaries that a change has been made, stimulating the secondaries to immediately check the serial number and perform a zone transfer to obtain the updates more quickly than awaiting the normal periodic update check.

Zone transfers may consist of the entire zone configuration file, called an absolute zone transfer (AXFR) or of the incremental updates only, called an incremental zone transfer (IXFR). In cases where zone information is relatively static and updated from a single source, e.g. an administrator, the serial number checking with AXFRs as needed works well. These so-called static zones are much simpler to administer than their counterpart: dynamic zones. Dynamic zones, as the name implies, accept dynamic updates, e.g. from DHCP servers updating DNS with newly assigned IP addresses and corresponding host domain names. Updates for dynamic zones can utilize IXFR mechanisms to maintain synchronization among the master and multiple secondary servers.

The popular ISC BIND DNS reference implementation utilizes journal files on each server to provide an efficient means to track dynamic updates to zone information. These journal files are temporary appendages to corresponding zone files and enable tracking of dynamic updates until the server writes these journal entries into the zone file and reloads the zone. Many server implementations load the zone file information into memory along with incremental zone updates, for fast resolution. Other approaches to storing zone information include use of a database such as is the case with the Microsoft, PowerDNS and Knot DNS implementations as well as ISC BIND.

Reverse Domains

We introduced the common domain name-to-IP address resolution process, comprised of locating a DNS server authoritative for the domain name, then seeking an authoritative response to the query. Another popular form of query is for IP address-to-name resolution. This "reverse" form of resolution is commonly used as a security check when establishing VPN connections or for general IP address-to-hostname lookups. Given an IP address, how does a DNS server traverse the domain tree to find a host domain name? Special top level domains are defined for IP address-based domain trees within the *address and routing parameter area* (arpa) domain: `in-addr.arpa.` is defined for IPv4 address-to-name resolution and `ip6.arpa.` is for IPv6 address-to-name resolution.

The only wrinkle in organizing IP addresses within a domain tree results from mapping an IP address, which reads left-to-right as less detailed (network) to more detailed (IP host), while reading a domain name left-to-right reads more specific (specific host, domain) to less specific (root). Therefore, the IP address is reversed to enable representation within the domain hierarchy, reading left-to-right as more specific to less specific. This is illustrated in Figure 4.5.

You may notice that the mapping of dotted decimal notation enables mapping of reverse domains to octet-boundary based network allocations. For example, if we've been allocated a "class C" network as our public space, 192.0.2.0/24, it is easy[5] to visualize the leaves of the `in-addr.arpa.` domain tree depicted above mapping to individual hosts. And like resolution of host names, traversal of the in-addr.arpa. domain tree follows a similar process to locate authoritative resolution of address-to-name queries. The Pointer or PTR resource record type provides a mapping from address to host, as we'll discuss in the next chapter.

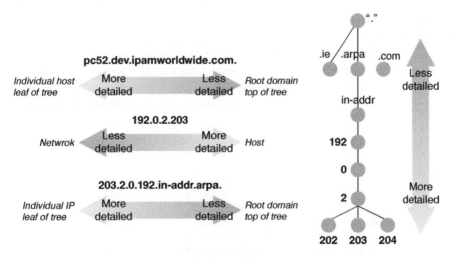

Figure 4.5 IP address (reverse) domain tree mapping.

---

5 Of course "easy" is a relative term, but once you get accustomed to reverse domains, at least such classful IPv4 networks are easily visualized as reverse domains.

But what if we had been allocated a subnet on non-octet boundaries? For example, if we had allocated a /25 instead of a /24. If the allocated subnet was smaller than a class C network, a more complex representation and zone configuration is required. Let's say for example that we allocate a subnet for a remote office as 192.0.2.0/25. If we try to represent the corresponding reverse domain as `2.0.192.in-addr.arpa`, this would encompass the desired half but also the "other half" of the 192.0.2.0/24 network, namely the 192.0.2.128/25 network. But this other half could be allocated to a different organization having its own DNS authority. In that case, who would administer the classful reverse zone since it's split across two authorities? The solution is to indicate that portion of the fourth octet to which the subnet applies in the reverse zone name.

RFC 2317 [29] specifies the use of the CIDR notation within the `in-addr.arpa` zone name. Thus, literally reversing the numbers between the dots of the allocated subnet, we arrive at the following: for network 192.0.2.0/25, the corresponding reverse domain is `0/25.2.0.192.in-addr.arpa`.[6] The "other half" of this class C would be `128/25.2.0.192.in-addr.arpa`. Subnets of smaller sizes would follow a similar notation, using the fourth octet of the network address, followed by /<cidr size>, followed by the remaining three octets from the IP address, reversed, then appended with `in-addr.arpa`.

When a resolver issues a PTR query, it will be in the form of `185.2.0.192.in-addr.arpa.`, so how do we map this query to the appropriate zone, `128/25.2.0.192.in-addr.arpa` in this case? The solution calls for the use of canonical name (CNAME) records in the parent (`2.0.192.in-addr.arpa.`) zone to selectively point to the proper delegated zone, each of which may be administered by separate DNS administrators. A CNAME record for each individual IP address needs to be created to map to a corresponding RFC 2317 style reverse domain.

Let's look at how this would work in our example case. Within the parent zone corresponding to this `2.0.192.in-addr.arpa.` zone, we would configure the following:

```
2.0.192.in-addr.arpa. IN SOA dns.ipamworldwide.com.
admin.ipamworldwide.com. ( 1 2h 30m 1w 1d )

0/25.2.0.192.in-addr.arpa.    IN NS dns.A1.ipamworldwide.com.
                              IN NS dns.A2.ipamworldwide.com.
-
1.2.0.192.in-addr.arpa.     IN  CNAME  1.0/25.2.0.192.in-addr.arpa.
2.2.0.192.in-addr.arpa.     IN  CNAME  2.0/25.2.0.192.in-addr.arpa.
3.2.0.192.in-addr.arpa.     IN  CNAME  3.0/25.2.0.192.in-addr.arpa.
```

---

6 While RFC 2317 specifies slashes within these domain names, many DNS administrators substitute dashes in order to associate zone names with zone file names, which cannot contain slashes. Hence, we could denote this zone as 0-25.2.0.192.in-addr.arpa defined in zone file db.0-25.2.0.192.in-addr.arpa. We'll stick to the RFC 2317 format here, but dashes work just as well.

```
. . .
127.2.0.192.in-addr.arpa.      IN   CNAME   127.0/25.2.0.192.in-addr.arpa.
128/25.2.0.192.in-addr.arpa.   IN NS dns.B1.ipamworldwide.com.
                               IN NS dns.B2.ipamworldwide.com.
129.2.0.192.in-addr.arpa.      IN   CNAME   129.128/25.2.0.192.in-addr.arpa.
130.2.0.192.in-addr.arpa.      IN   CNAME   130.128/25.2.0.192.in-addr.arpa.
131.2.0.192.in-addr.arpa.      IN   CNAME   131.128/25.2.0.192.in-addr.arpa.

. . .

254.2.0.192.in-addr.arpa.      IN   CNAME   254.128/25.2.0.192.in-addr.arpa.
```

The first line comprises the zone SOA record with zone parameters. See Chapter 19 for full details on this and all resource record types. The next entries declare the name servers authoritative for the 0/25.2.0.192.in-addr-apra zone. Next, individual resource records enumerating each IP address (in reverse domain format) within the first half of our /24 (0–127) refer to alias names by virtue of the CNAME type. Thus, a query for 3.2.0.192.in-addr.arpa resolves to a CNAME of 3.0/25.2.0.192.in-addr.arpa. The resolver would follow this CNAME by querying for this alias 3.0/25.2.0.192.in-addr.arpa., which resides in the 0/25.2.0.192.in-addr-apra zone. The resolver would then issue a third query to one of the name servers authoritative for this zone per the aforementioned NS records requesting resolution of 3.0/25.2.0.192.in-addr.arpa.

The corresponding `0/25.2.0.192.in-addr.arpa.` zone on these servers would contain the following:

```
0/25.2.0.192.in-addr.arpa. IN SOA dns.A1.ipamworldwide.com. admin.
ipamworldwide.com. ( 1 2h 30m 1w 1d )

0/25.2.0.192.in-addr.arpa.     IN NS dns.A1.ipamworldwide.com.
0/25.2.0.192.in-addr.arpa.     IN NS dns.A2.ipamworldwide.com.

1.0/25.2.0.192.in-addr.arpa.   IN   PTR   public1.ipamworldwide.com.
2.0/25.2.0.192.in-addr.arpa.   IN   PTR   public2.ipamworldwide.com.
3.0/25.2.0.192.in-addr.arpa.   IN   PTR   www.ipamworldwide.com.

. . .
```

Or in abbreviated format:

```
@ IN SOA dns.A1.ipamworldwide.com. admin.ipamworldwide.com. ( 1 2h 30m 1w 1d )
// Implicit domain origin 0/25.2.0.192.in-addr.arpa.
```

```
         IN NS dns.A1.ipamworldwide.com.
         IN NS dns.A2.ipamworldwide.com.

1    IN    PTR    public1.ipamworldwide.com.
2    IN    PTR    public2.ipamworldwide.com.
3    IN    PTR    www.ipamworldwide.com.
. . .
```

Querying this zone file for this referenced CNAME alias, to `3.128/25.2.0.192.in-addr.arpa.`, we find our PTR record pointing to the associated hostname wwwlo.ipamworldwide.com, completing the resolution.

For non-octet bounded networks larger than class C networks (i.e. /9–/15 and /17–/23), DNAME records can be used for mapping reverse domains. For example, the 172.16.0.0/14 network could be allocated and delegated to a customer administrator. Reverse queries on this network can be referred to the customer's DNS server, dns.customer.com per the following example, configured within the `172.in-addr.arpa.` zone file:

```
16/14.172.in-addr.arpa. IN   NS      dns1.ipamworldwide.com.
16/14.172.in-addr.arpa. IN   NS      dns2.ipamworldwide.com.
16.172.in-addr.arpa.        IN   DNAME  16.16/14.172.in-addr.arpa.
17.172.in-addr.arpa.        IN   DNAME  17.16/14.172.in-addr.arpa.
18.172.in-addr.arpa.        IN   DNAME  18.16/14.172.in-addr.arpa.
19.172.in-addr.arpa.        IN   DNAME  19.16/14.172.in-addr.arpa.
```

These entries delegate the reverse lookups for all four /16 networks comprising the customer's /14 to the customer's DNS servers as indicated by the first two records shown above. The next four records map these four /16 reverse domains to the `16/14.172.in-addr.arpa.` domain. Notice the RData field, which is the rightmost field of these four DNAME records are within the 16/14.172.in-addr.arpa. domain, served by dns1.ipamworldwide.com and dns2.ipamworldwide.com.

We've essentially inserted an artificial layer in the reverse tree to serve as a consolidation point. Thus, to resolve the PTR record for a host with IP address 172.18.45.94, the resolving name server would traverse down the `172.in-addr.arpa.` tree. The next node down, `18.172.in-addr.arpa.`, has a domain alias of `18.16/14.172.in-addr.arpa.` by virtue of the DNAME lookup. Next, by querying the dns1.ipamworldwide.com DNS server, which is authoritative for the `16/14.172.in-addr.arpa.` zone, we resolve the corresponding PTR entry within this zone: `94.45.18.172.in-addr.arpa. IN    PTR    host.ipamworldwide.com.`

IPv6 Reverse Domains

IPv6 reverse domain mapping follows a similar approach, albeit with much longer domain names. As with IPv4, the IPv6 address must be reversed, maintaining its hexadecimal format. But the IPv6 address must first be "padded" to the full 32 hex digit representation; that is, the two forms of abbreviation discussed in Chapter 2 must be removed by including leading zeroes between colons and filling in double colon-denoted implied zeroes. Figure 4.6 illustrates an example of the process for the IPv6 address 2001:db8:b7::a8e1. The address must be expanded or padded and the digits reversed. Then, this result must be "domain-ized" by removing the colons, inserting dots between each digit, and appending the ip6.arpa. upper level domains.

Figure 4.7 illustrates the logic in reversing the IPv6 address in order to be represented in a domain hierarchy as read left-to-right as more specific to less specific. This is directly analogous to Figure 4.5, which illustrates this concept for IPv4 addresses. The full 32-hex digit representation used in Figure 4.7 provides a unique, though lengthy, traversal down the ip6.arpa. domain tree (not shown).

Note that this example illustrates the reverse domain representation for a full 128-bit IPv6 address. Subnets can have corresponding reverse domain definitions as in IPv4. For a /64 allocation, only the first 64 bits (16 hex digits) would be included. Thus, for the host above, its /64 subnet reverse zone notation would be defined as:

`0.0.0.0.7.b.0.0.8.b.d.0.1.0.0.2.ip6.arpa.`

2001:db8:b7::a8e1

Expand

2001:0db8:00b7:0000:0000:0000:0000:a8e1

Reverse

1e8a:0000:0000:0000:0000:7b00:8bd0:1002

Domain-ize

1.e.8.a.0.0.0.0.0.0.0.0.0.0.0.0.0.0.0.0.0.0.0.7.b.0.0.8.b.d.0.1.0.0.2.ip6.arpa.

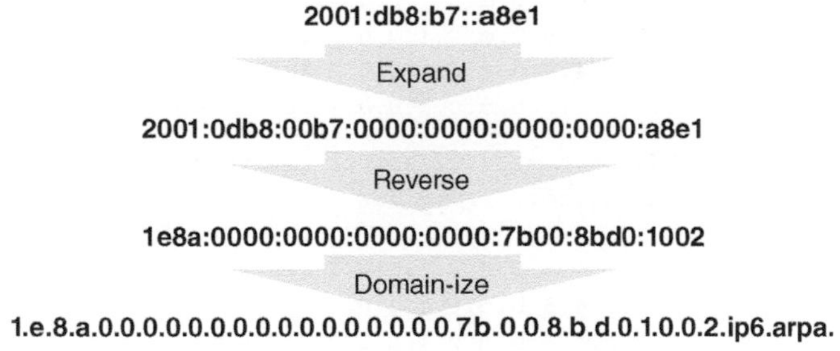

Figure 4.6   IPv6 address to reverse domain mapping.

2001:db8:b7::a8e1

Netwrok   Less detailed   More detailed   *Host*

1.e.8.a.0.0.0.0.0.0.0.0.0.0.0.0.0.0.0.0.0.0.0.7.b.0.0.8.b.d.0.1.0.0.2.ip6.arpa.

Individual IP leaf of tree   More detailed   Less detailed   *Root domain top of tree*

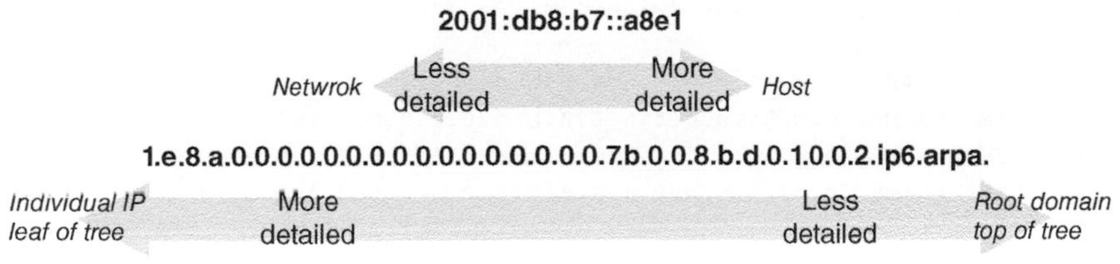

Figure 4.7   IPv6 reverse domain notation.

   Notation for reverse domains of IPv6 networks allocated on non-nibble boundaries
was not formally addressed in RFC 2317; however, the same techniques specified in the
RFC can be mapped to IPv6 reverse zones corresponding to non-nibble bounded IPv6
block allocations. Though we don't recommend allocated in non-nibble boundaries as
we'll discuss in Chapter 6, it is not prohibited, so let's illustrate this by example. Say the
North America team desires to allocate four /54 blocks from its 2001:db8:
4af0:8000::/52 block, namely: 2001:db8:4af0:8000::/54, 2001:db8:4af0:8400::/54,
2001:db8:4af0:8800::/54, and 2001:db8:4af0:8c00::/54. Using CNAME resource records
to refer queriers to servers responsible for these corresponding reverse zones, the
8.0.f.a.4.8.b.d.0.1.0.0.2.ip6.arpa zone file would look something like:

```
8.0.f.a.4.8.b.d.0.1.0.0.2.ip6.arpa. IN SOA dns.ipamworldwide.com.
admin.ipamworldwide.com. ( 1 2h 30m 1w 1d )
$ORIGIN 8.0.f.a.4.8.b.d.0.1.0.0.2.ip6.arpa. //implicit
0/54    IN NS dns.A1.ipamworldwide.com.    //authoritative servers
        IN NS dns.A2.ipamworldwide.com.    // for
2001:db8:4af0:8000::/54
0       IN  CNAME  0.0/54.8.0.f.a.4.8.b.d.0.1.0.0.2.ip6.arpa.
1       IN  CNAME  1.0/54.8.0.f.a.4.8.b.d.0.1.0.0.2.ip6.arpa.
2       IN  CNAME  2.0/54.8.0.f.a.4.8.b.d.0.1.0.0.2.ip6.arpa.
3       IN  CNAME  3.0/54.8.0.f.a.4.8.b.d.0.1.0.0.2.ip6.arpa.

4/54    IN NS dns.B1.ipamworldwide.com.    //authoritative servers
        IN NS dns.B2.ipamworldwide.com.    // for
2001:db8:4af0:8400::/54
4       IN  CNAME  4.4/54.8.0.f.a.4.8.b.d.0.1.0.0.2.ip6.arpa.
5       IN  CNAME  5.4/54.8.0.f.a.4.8.b.d.0.1.0.0.2.ip6.arpa.
6       IN  CNAME  6.4/54.8.0.f.a.4.8.b.d.0.1.0.0.2.ip6.arpa.
7       IN  CNAME  7.4/54.8.0.f.a.4.8.b.d.0.1.0.0.2.ip6.arpa.

8/54    IN NS dns.C1.ipamworldwide.com.    //authoritative servers
        IN NS dns.C2.ipamworldwide.com.    // for
2001:db8:4af0:8800::/54
8       IN  CNAME  8.8/54.8.0.f.a.4.8.b.d.0.1.0.0.2.ip6.arpa.
9       IN  CNAME  9.8/54.8.0.f.a.4.8.b.d.0.1.0.0.2.ip6.arpa.
a       IN  CNAME  a.8/54.8.0.f.a.4.8.b.d.0.1.0.0.2.ip6.arpa.
b       IN  CNAME  b.8/54.8.0.f.a.4.8.b.d.0.1.0.0.2.ip6.arpa.

c/54    IN NS dns.D1.ipamworldwide.com.    //authoritative servers
        IN NS dns.D2.ipamworldwide.com.    // for
2001:db8:4af0:8c00::/54
c       IN  CNAME  c.c/54.8.0.f.a.4.8.b.d.0.1.0.0.2.ip6.arpa.
d       IN  CNAME  d.c/54.8.0.f.a.4.8.b.d.0.1.0.0.2.ip6.arpa.
e       IN  CNAME  e.c/54.8.0.f.a.4.8.b.d.0.1.0.0.2.ip6.arpa.
f       IN  CNAME  f.c/54.8.0.f.a.4.8.b.d.0.1.0.0.2.ip6.arpa.
```

   Following standard domain tree traversal, when the querying NS queries the
DNS server authoritative for the `8.0.f.a.4.8.b.d.0.1.0.0.2.ip6.`

arpa. zone, the file above on the corresponding DNS server provides not a resolution, but a next step, pointing the desired IPv6 address answer to another FQDN via a CNAME record. So far in the process, a PTR query requesting the hostname for IP address 2001:db8:4af0:8d03::f6 results in a CNAME pointing to d.c/54.8.0.f. a.4.8.b.d.0.1.0.0.2.ip6.arpa. We also know who to ask to resolve this query because two NS records are listed as authoritative for this domain, namely dns. D1.ipamworldwide.com and dns.D2.ipamworldwide.com. The corresponding d.c/54.8.0.f.a.4.8.b.d.0.1.0.0.2.ip6.arpa. zone file on these servers would contain the following:

```
c/54.8.0.f.a.4.8.b.d.0.1.0.0.2.ip6.arpa. IN SOA dns.
D1.ipamworldwide.com.
admin.ipamworldwide.com. ( 1 2h 30m 1w 1d )
// Implicit $ORIGIN 128/25.2.0.192.in-addr.arpa.


        IN NS dns.D1.ipamworldwide.com.
        IN NS dns.D2.ipamworldwide.com.


1.0.b.0.0.0.0.0.0.0.0.0.0.0.0.3.0.c    IN  PTR  public1.ipamworldwide.com.
0.2.0.a.4.0.0.0.0.0.0.0.0.0.0.3.0.c    IN  PTR  public2.ipamworldwide.com.
f.c.0.0.0.0.0.0.0.0.0.0.0.0.0.3.0.d    IN  PTR  www.ipamworldwide.com.

. . .

6.f.0.0.0.0.0.0.0.0.0.0.0.0.0.3.0.d    IN  PTR  server-y.ipamworldwide.com.
```

Querying this zone file for this referenced CNAME alias, that is, 6.f.0.0.0.0.0.0.0.0.0.0.0.0.0.0.3.0.d.c/54.8.0.f.a.4.8. b.d.0.1.0.0.2.ip6.arpa., we find our PTR record pointing to the associated hostname server-y.ipamworldwide.com, completing the resolution.

Additional Zones

Root Hints

We mentioned a *hints file* during the overview of the resolution process. This file should provide DNS server names and addresses that the server should query if the resolver query cannot be resolved via authoritative, forwarded or cached data. The hints file will typically list the Internet root servers, which are authoritative for the root (.) of the domain tree. Querying a root server enables the querying server to start at the top to begin the traversal down the domain tree in order to locate an authoritative server to resolve the query. The contents of the hints file for Internet root servers may be obtained from www.internic.net/zones/named.root, though most DNS server implementations include this file with their distributions and/or support the ability to retrieve it automatically.

Some environments may require use of an internal set of root servers, where Internet access is restricted by organizational policy. In such cases, an internal version of the hints file can be used, listing names and addresses of internal root servers instead of the Internet root servers. The organization itself would need to maintain the listing of internal root servers, as well as their requisite root zone configurations.

Localhost Zones

Another zone that proves essential is the localhost zone. The localhost zone enables one to resolve "localhost" as a hostname on the given server. A corresponding in-addr.arpa. zone file resolves the 127.0.0.1 loopback address and an ip6.arpa resolves ::1. A single entry within the 0.0.127.in-addr.arpa zone maps address 1 to the host itself. This zone is required as there is no upstream authority for the 127. in-addr.arpa domain or subdomains. Likewise, the IPv6 equivalents need to be defined for the corresponding IPv6 loopback address, ::1. The localhost zone simply maps the localhost hostname to its 127.0.0.1 or ::1 IP address using an A and AAAA record, respectively.

DNS Update

DNS Update messages enable a client, DHCP server, or other source to perform an update (add, modify or delete) of one or more resource records within a zone. The DNS update message enables specification of a prerequisite that defines required conditions attached to the update. Prerequisite conditions include whether a set of resource records for a given lookup value (e.g. hostname) exists and matches (or doesn't exist) in the zone being updated. Such prerequisites can be used to minimize the overwriting of a given resource record by a dynamic client. For example, if "host-A" has a resource record within a given zone, a prerequisite can be used to prevent another host from using the name "host-A."

When a DHCP server performs dynamic updates of DNS data upon assigning an IP address, it can perform a DNS update with the hostname-IP address record (A or AAAA) along with an additional resource record, identifying the particular client to which the hostname is associated. This additional record, a DHCP Identifier (DHCID) or Text (TXT) record, includes a hash of the host's hardware address receiving the IP address to uniquely identify the host. The prerequisite condition for updating the address record provides a means to ensure that only the original holder of this A or AAAA record can modify it, minimizing naming duplication or hijacking. Please consult Chapter 19 for details about DNS update and other DNS messages.

5

IPAM Technology Applications

As we've discussed so far, IPAM technologies form the very foundation of your IP network for automating IP address assignment and humanizing network navigation. As we shall discuss in this chapter, these technologies have also proven indispensable in enabling and securing key network applications, from automated network bootstrapping and services location to mobility support.

DHCP Applications

The most fundamental application for DHCP is automated address assignment. We take DHCP for granted when we connect to an IP network. This basic function renders IP applications easier to use by automating initialization of the IP layer. End users need not contact the service desk to obtain and enter IP addresses into their devices. DHCP not only automates IP address assignments but it also enables network administrators to retain control of what IP addresses may be assigned to certain clients, even up to denying access.

In this section, we'll discuss technology applications that rely on DHCP, which are implicitly reliant on the consistency of DHCP configurations with the IP address plan. We'll cover those applications requiring special purpose DHCP configurations, including device-specific configuration and broadband provisioning. DHCP-based access control could also be grouped within this topic, but we'll cover that in the context of security in Chapter 11 instead.

A core capability in supporting various applications with DHCP is the ability of the DHCP server to classify a device requesting an address and to supply an appropriate IP address and additional configuration information. This classification of clients into client classes enables the DHCP administrator to identify a parameter value within a particular DHCP packet field or option to match on a

IP Address Management, Second Edition. Michael Dooley and Timothy Rooney.
© 2021 The Institute of Electrical and Electronics Engineers, Inc.
Published 2021 by John Wiley & Sons, Inc.

per-DHCP transaction basis. When a client is classified, the DHCP server may then determine:

- which IP address pool from which to assign an address to the client (if any)
- what additional or alternative option parameter values to provide to the client

Leading DHCP reference implementations from ISC and Microsoft support both the vendor class identifier (option 60 for IPv4 and 16 for IPv6) and the user class identifier (option 77 for IPv4 and 15 for IPv6) options as class parameters. When these options are included in the discover or solicit packet, the server can use this information to identify the type of device that is requesting its configuration.

Device Type Specific Configuration

The most common example device-type provisioning application is that of multi-media device initialization, such as VoIP devices. This application can be extended to any device requiring device type or application-specific provisioning, as long as the DHCP packet contains identifying information that your DHCP server is able to process. Most device manufacturers encode a given value within the vendor class identifier option which can be filtered by the DHCP server. Configuring the DHCP server to recognize this particular value enables the server to supply particular DHCP options required by the client and to assign an IP address from a specific address pool. Other application-specific DHCP clients requiring particular configuration parameters may likewise be identified and configured based on the value of the vendor class option.

The user class identifier option is another candidate for determining client configuration. However, since the user class identifier is typically end user settable, it is considered less reliable. Should a user outside of the user class group discover the value or setting, he or she could program his or her device accordingly. For example, using Microsoft's ipconfig utility with the /setclassid argument, it's quite easy to set the value of the user class identifier option.

Figure 5.1 illustrates a simple example of configuring an ISC DHCP server to identify clients of class "vendor-y" if a DHCP packet contains a vendor class identifier option value of "vendorY." If so classified as a vendor-y device, the client would be issued an address from the 10.16.129.20-10.16.129.250 pool on the subnet with corresponding routers and DNS server options. These option values are specified along with the allow members of "vendor-y" statement within this pool declaration.

Similarly, devices of class "vendor-x" will be identified by clients supplying a vendor class identifier option value of "vendorX." Such devices will be assigned from the 10.16.128.20-10.16.128.250 pool from the 10.16.128/23 subnet with the specified routers option values.

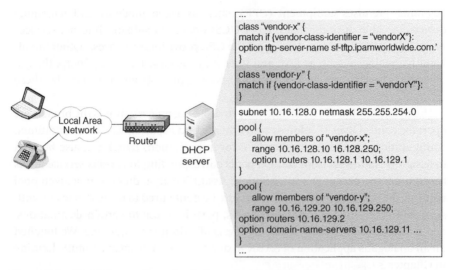

```
...
class "vendor-x" {
match if {vendor-class-identifier = "vendorX"}:
option tftp-server-name sf-tftp.ipamworldwide.com.'
}

class "vendor-y" {
match if {vendor-class-identifier = "vendorY"}:
}

subnet 10.16.128.0 netmask 255.255.254.0

pool {
    allow members of "vendor-x";
    range 10.16.128.10 16.128.250;
    option routers 10.16.128.1 10.16.129.1
}

pool {
    allow members of "vendor-y";
    range 10.16.129.20 10.16.129.250;
option routers 10.16.129.2
option domain-name-servers 10.16.129.11 ...
}
...
```

Figure 5.1 Specifying configuration information for DHCP clients by class.
Source: Based on [30].

Some DHCP servers support filtering on additional class parameters, in fact up to any packet parameter from MAC address, a subset of the MAC address, or any option value. This is convenient if a given MAC address (interface card) or MAC prefix (manufacturer) needs to be filtered and assigned certain parameters. As another example, some DHCP server products filter on the option request option or parameter request list option to "fingerprint" certain vendor and model devices based on requested options in particular order.

Depending on the DHCP product you deploy, there are various menu interfaces or text file editors that can be used for managing the configuration of address pools and server behavior as well as criteria you can specify to dictate address assignment logic. For example, Microsoft DHCP servers can be configured through a Windows graphical user interface (GUI), while ISC DHCP servers can be configured via text editor and ISC Kea via json files. For mixed ISC and Microsoft environments, the use of a centralized IPAM system can help abstract the individual vendor interfaces and enable configuration of both with a single user or API interface.

Broadband Subscriber Provisioning

The cable industry defined a standard for data transmission over cable, referred to as Data Over Cable Service Interface Specifications (DOCSIS®). The DOCSIS specifications, authored by CableLabs, require the use of DHCP for provisioning of customer premises equipment (CPE), such as cable modems and telephony devices. A cable operator that offers DOCSIS-based broadband Internet services must deploy DHCP servers to support the CPE provisioning process. Other broadband technologies such as DSL and fiber may also use DHCP or Bootp, though other techniques such as PPP (point-to-point protocol) are also used by these technologies.

The incorporation of DHCP into the provisioning process affords the broadband operator control over IP address assignments and capacity, as well as additional configuration parameters used by CPE for initialization. DHCP can also be used to assign IP addresses from address pools corresponding to various service levels based upon the customer's subscription. Assigning an address from a given pool requires the network routing infrastructure be configured to route IP packets with such addresses only to certain networks, permit access to certain destinations, and treat packets with corresponding levels of priority and queuing. We touched on an analogous application of SADR in our discussion of Internet multi-homing in Chapter 3.

Let's consider an example to illustrate these concepts. In Figure 5.2, three subscribers are connected to a common broadband gateway via the broadband access network. The figure depicts each subscriber with various levels of service as indicated by different shading, connected to individual ports on the broadband gateway. Depending on the broadband access technology, these may be physical ports or logical ports for shared network access.

Regardless of the broadband access technology, service providers using DHCP need to base address and parameter assignment on known or trusted information. Instead of relying on the client hardware address field of the DHCP packet,

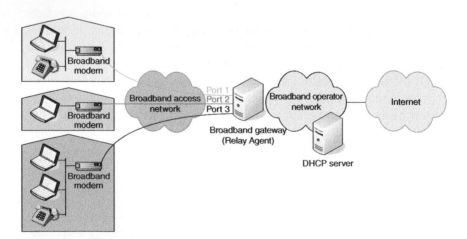

Figure 5.2 Broadband access scenario.

which can be spoofed, service providers rely on information from the broadband gateway, which resides in the service provider's network and is considered trustworthy.

The broadband gateway acting as a DHCP relay agent forwards the DHCP packet to the appropriate DHCP server(s). The gateway may be configured to insert the relay agent information option parameter as the last option before the null option terminator. The relay agent information option provides information such as the subscriber device hardware address or subscriber virtual circuit identifier to help the DHCP server identify the subscriber client that issued the Solicit or Discover packet.

This enables the DHCP server of either protocol to provide, based on its configuration, an appropriate number of IP addresses and/or option parameters for a given subscriber. The relay agent information option is comprised of the following IPv6 options and IPv4 relay agent sub-options (of the relay agent option, code 82), respectively.

IPv6 code	IPv4 code	Generalized option/sub-option name	Description	RFC References
18	1	Interface ID (v6)/ circuit ID (v4)	Encodes information about the connection to the subscriber. This consists of a virtual circuit identifier corresponding to the subscriber, typically corresponding to a layer 2 identifier such as a ATM virtual circuit ID, frame relay data link connection identifier (DLCI), or remote access server or switch port number	8415 [20] 3046 [31]
37	2	Remote ID	Encodes information about the remote client device such as its Ethernet address, modem identifier, or caller ID for a dial-up connection	4649 [32] 3046 [31]
N/A	4	DOCSIS device class	Encodes the DOCSIS device class of the cable CPE. This option is applicable to DOCSIS cable access networks and the CMTS (cable edge device) may include this sub-option based on the gathering of this information during the DOCSIS registration process	3256 [33]

IPv6 code	IPv4 code	Generalized option/sub-option name	Description	RFC References
N/A	5	Link selection	Encodes an IP address to be used in lieu of the GIAddr field by the DHCP server when selecting a subnet address for address assignment to the client. This would apply when shared subnets[a] are in use	3527 [34]
38	6	Subscriber ID	Encodes a subscriber identifier string to associate the Discover or Solicit with the given subscriber's client. This is useful if the subscriber can access the network over various media where use of the circuit identifier or remote identifier would only indicate the underlying access mechanism and not the subscriber association	4580 [35] 3993 [36]
81	7	RADIUS attributes	Encodes RADIUS attributes per the RADIUS protocol (RFC 2865) to use by the DHCP server in making parameter assignments. These attributes are encoded as a type-length-value octet stream and can include the user name, passwords, access server IP/port, and others	7037 [37] 4014 [38]
N/A[b]	8	Authentication	Encodes authentication information as a means to provide message integrity checking on relay agent information. This encoding is similar to that used for DHCP authentication, which is discussed in Chapter 10.	4030 [39]
N/A	9	Vendor-specific information	Encoded as one or more sets of vendor-specific information each consisting of a three-tuple: IANA-registered enterprise number, length, and data	4243 [40]
N/A	10	Relay agent flags	Extensible sub-option to flag conditions; one flag is currently defined to indicate that the relay agent received the DHCP packet via unicast (1) or broadcast (0)	5010 [41]

IPv6 code	IPv4 code	Generalized option/sub-option name	Description	RFC References
N/A	11	Server identifier override	Instructs the DHCP server to use this specified value in its Server Identifier field in its response to the client; this enables the relay agent to receive DHCPRENEW packets that it may not otherwise have visibility to, enabling the relay agent to insert other relay agent sub-option values associated with the client when forwarding the DHCPRENEW packet to the server	5107 [42]
N/A	12	Relay agent identifier	Identifies the relay agent from which this DHCP packet has been sent. The identifier should be a stable identifier configured in the relay agent. This option can be helpful to the DHCP server in assigning an appropriate IP address or as a filter when querying DHCP leases using bulk leasequery	6925 [43]
105	13	Access technology type	Denotes the access network technology type from which the relay agent received this DHCP packet. This is useful for the DHCP server when assigning a particular address for which corresponding routing treatment may be applied particularly in a mobility application for example	7839 [44]
106	14	Access network name	Conveys the name of the mobile access network from which this DHCP packet originated according to the relay agent. For example, if the access network is of type Wi-Fi, the network name would be the SSID	7839 [44]
107	15	Access point name	A unique device name of the access point from which the DHCP packet was sent	7839 [44]
108	16	Access point BSSID	The 48-bit Basic SSID (BSSID) of the access point to which the DHCP packet originating device is connected	7839 [44]

IPv6 code	IPv4 code	Generalized option/sub-option name	Description	RFC References
109	17	Operator identifier	The private enterprise number (PEN) of the operator of the mobile network to which this DHCP client is connected	7839 [44]
110	18	Operator Realm	The unique realm name of the operator of the mobile network to which this DHCP client is connected	7839 [44]
135	19	DHCP relay source port	UDP port the server should use in response to this relay agent. Some configurations do not use the well-known DHCP source port (67/547) for scalability reasons	8357 [45]
68	151	DHCP virtual subnet selection	Identifies the virtual private network (VPN) from which the client DHCP packet originated	6607 [46]
N/A	152	DHCP virtual subnet selection control	This valueless option is included with the virtual subnet selection option; if the DHCP server understands the VPN encoding presented in that option, this sub-option is removed from its response. Its inclusion in the response back to the relay indicates the server is merely echoing back the option and therefore did not understand the sub-option or the VPN encoding	6607 [46]

a Shared subnets refers to the provisioning of multiple logical subnets on a single physical subnet (router interface).
b DHCPv6 authentication is end-to-end using the authentication option (11).

An example configuration using ISC DHCP syntax [30] is shown following. This statement declares the class "broadband" which is based on matching the circuit ID suboption of the relay agent identification option. Here we define a single client class but provision subclasses to identify specific instances of the broadband class. In this case we simply define two subclasses for two corresponding values of the circuit ID suboption.

```
class "broadband" {
    match option agent.circuit-id;
}
```

```
subclass "modem" "45023"; {
    [ declarations and parameters for modem devices ]
}
subclass "phone" "67032"; {
    [ declarations and parameters for phone devices ]
}
```

A more scalable approach utilizes the class spawning feature of the ISC DHCP implementation. We'll illustrate this along with the ability to the limit the number of leases or IP addresses assignable to a subscriber. A basic level of service may promise a single IP address, while a higher level of service (and perhaps price) may include two or more. The lease limit statement enables this feature control within the ISC DHCP configuration file. This statement can be associated with a client class definition to specify the maximum number of leases that can be provided to clients matching this class.

Class spawning enables dynamic creation or spawning of client subclasses on the fly based on information in the DHCP packet. The spawn with declaration defines a spawning class with the parameter on which to base the spawn. For example, the DHCP server can be configured to spawn client classes based each unique circuit ID relay agent sub-option value. Thus, when a DHCPDISCOVER is received by the DHCP server, it analyzes the circuit ID sub-option. If a class exists (was previously spawned) for the given value, the corresponding parameters and declarations are analyzed for processing; if a class with that circuit ID does not exist, the DHCP server spawns a new subclass for the given value. The example below illustrates the definition of a broadband client class with a spawning subclass based on the circuit ID that limits outstanding subscriber leases to a maximum of 6 using ISC DHCP syntax [30].

```
class "broadband"; {
    spawn with option agent.circuit-id;
    lease limit 6;
}
```

Related Lease Assignment or Limitation Applications

The use of lease limiting and parameter setting based on relay agent information is not exclusive to broadband environments. Other applications may use the same technique assuming relay agents support the population of the relay agent information option. In such cases, use of the ISC DHCP server enables address and parameter assignment as well as lease limiting based on defined classes and relay agent information parameters. This technique may be employed to throttle address assignments on certain subnets or to provide configuration parameters to devices in factory or similar applications.

Pre-Boot Execution Environment (PXE) clients

Pre-boot execution environment (PXE) ("Pixie") clients are devices that boot up relying on network servers instead of a co-resident hard disk. Such diskless servers and other such devices typically use DHCP to obtain an IP address as well as boot parameters including boot server addresses and boot file names. DHCP provides a convenient mechanism to initialize these devices without manual intervention. Historically, DHCP servers had to be configured with the MAC address of each PXE client to provide configuration information specific to the device, even if multiple PXE clients of the same "type" could leverage exactly the same boot information.

RFC 4578 [47] is an informational RFC defining a means whereby a PXE client can identify its type or architecture to the server. This information can be used by the DHCP server to identify and provide appropriate device initialization parameters. The DHCP server would need to be configured to match on particular client-provided PXE option values, then map these results to a corresponding set of configuration parameters or options to return to the client. Naturally, this is accomplished using client class processing.

Options to be included between PXE clients and the DHCP server are:

- *Option 93* – client system architecture type – specifies the architecture type of the PXE device and must be included in all DHCP packets during the transaction
  - o Intel x86PC
  - o NEC/PC98
  - o EFI Itanium
  - o DEC Alpha
  - o Arc x86
  - o Intel Lean Client
  - o EFI IA32
  - o EFI BC
  - o EFI Xscale
  - o EFI x86-64
- *Option 94* – client network interface identifier – identifies the network interface type and version and must be included in all DHCP packets in the transaction. The only defined interface type is for universal network device interface (UNDI).
- *Option 97* – client machine identifier – identifies the type of machine booting. This option is encoded with a type and identifier. The only currently defined

type, 0, indicates the identifier is encoded as a 16-octet globally unique identifier (GUID).

- *Options 128–135* – these options are to be requested by PXE clients and are intended for use by downloaded bootstrap programs if needed, though they are not officially assigned for PXE use.

Be aware that PXE clients using options 128–135 may conflict with the alternative assigned meaning of these options as summarized in Chapter 18.

PPP/RADIUS Environments

The RADIUS (remote access dial in user service) protocol provides a means to authenticate end users attempting to connect to a network. RADIUS is a vital component of 802.1X, a popular layer 2 media access control protocol proposed within leading network admission control (NAC) solutions. RADIUS and its successor protocol, diameter, provides an authentication, authorization, and accounting (AAA) service for IP hosts attempting to access a network. The connection from a client to a RADIUS server is commonly performed via a PPP or extensible authentication protocol (EAP) connection, e.g. when the client is attempting to access a network edge device. The RADIUS server challenges the client to enter a user name and password, authenticates the entered information against its internal or external database, then provides access to the network by providing an IP address to the client.

This IP address assignment process can be performed by configuring an address pool directly on the server or by configuring the RADIUS server to obtain an address via a DHCP server. In the latter scenario, the RADIUS server functions as a DHCP proxy on behalf of the client. The RADIUS server initiates the DHCP process, issuing a Discover packet. One caveat with this approach is that the RADIUS server must generate a hardware address or client identifier on behalf of each client to uniquely identify each. Otherwise, by using the RADIUS server's hardware address, the DHCP server would assume that the same client is continually rebooting and assigns the same IP address on all requests!

The RADIUS server can spoof the client's hardware address using an internal mechanism but needs to map the derived address to the end client to process subsequent lease transactions like Renews and Releases. An alternative approach is to leverage the RADIUS Attributes sub-option of the Relay Agent Information option in order to uniquely identify each client.

While vastly simplifying the RADIUS protocol, the relevant concept here is that some RADIUS servers or even edge router devices can be configured with address pools from which individual IP address assignments can be made to authorized clients. In some cases, RADIUS servers can be configured to actually utilize the DHCP protocol to obtain an address from a DHCP server. In this case, the RADIUS server acts as a DHCP proxy to obtain an IP address on behalf of, and for assignment to, the requesting client.

Mobile IP

IP mobility support, or mobile IP, enables an IP node to communicate seamlessly while moving from link to link. This means that upper layer transport and application layer communications remain intact despite a changing underlying network, data link, and physical layer network. Certainly, when changing link attachment, e.g. when moving from a 5G wireless service to a local Wi-Fi network, which implies an IP prefix change, the mobile device must, by necessity, change its IP address. This changeable IP address which is associated with the current network attachment is referred to as the *care-of address*.

IP mobility support differs somewhat between IPv4 and IPv6 but both protocols leverage the concept of a mobile node possessing a home address, the node's address on the "home" network and a care-of address, its address on the visited network. Mobile IPv6 eliminates the need for "triangular routing" required under mobile IPv4.

When the mobile IPv6 device is "home" or not roaming, IPv6 traffic routes normally to and from the device using its home address. When the device roams, it obtains a care-of address using SLAAC or DHCP based on its then-current location and point of network attachment. The mobile node then registers its care-of address with its *home agent*, a mobile IPv6-configured router serving the link on which the mobile node's home address resides. When the mobile host is home, the home agent routes IPv6 packets to it just as would a normal router, on its serving link as shown in Figure 5.3. When the mobile host is roaming, the home agent intercepts IPv6 packets destined for the mobile host's home address and tunnels them to the mobile host using its care-of address.

Communications between the mobile host and another host (*correspondent node*) may ensue in one of two ways. Using the tunneling approach just mentioned, IPv6 packets may be communicated directly to the home address, where they will be intercepted by the home agent and tunneled to the mobile host; return traffic would follow the same route, reaching the correspondent node by way of the home agent. This is depicted on the upper half of Figure 5.4.

Figure 5.3 Mobile IPv6 with mobile at home.

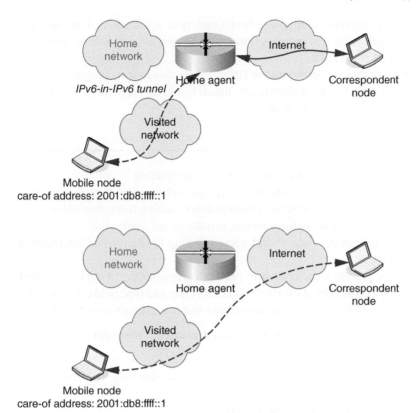

Figure 5.4 Mobile IPv6 with mobile roaming.

Generally, this "triangular routing" process is inefficient and can lead to resource overload on the home agent. A more efficient and direct communications mode between the mobile node and correspondent node is shown on the lower half of Figure 5.4. This more efficient routing process is available as long as the correspondent node supports the mobile IPv6 protocol, including the mobility extension header. The mobility header is used to carry messages between the mobile and correspondent nodes to verify care-of and home address association, direct routability and to communicate binding updates as the mobile host continues to move.

Popular DNS Applications

DNS inherently lends itself well to "translating" a given piece of information into another related piece of information. This resolution process is the very reason for DNS' invention, and it has been extended beyond resolving hostnames into IP addresses and vice versa to support a broad variety of applications. Virtually, any service or application that requires translation of one form of information into another can leverage DNS.

Each resource record configured in DNS enables this lookup function, returning a resolution answer for a given query. Recall the structure of a resource record is comprised of the following fields:

Owner	Time to live	Class	Type	RData

- *Owner* – this field contains the information being queried.
- *TTL* – the number of seconds for which the information contained in this resource record is valid for servers and resolvers caching this information.
- *Class* – the Class of the resource record, usually IN for Internet.
- *Type* – the type of resource record corresponding to the type of information being sought
- *RData* – the "record data" or answer portion corresponding to the information being sought by matching the Owner (Name), class and type field contents. The RData format varies by resource record type and may contain several subfields.

DNS queries contain a Question which specifies three of these fields for which a lookup is desired:

- *QNAME* – the queried name which maps to a matching resource record Owner field.
- *QCLASS* – the class of the resource record.
- *QTYPE* – the resource record type for which an answer is sought.

The DNS server parses these question attributes seeking a match within the corresponding domain's zone repository. The Rdata field of a matching record or records contains the corresponding answer to the query, while the TTL defines the time interval this record can be reliably cached. When multiple resource records match the queried name, type and class, all matching records, the resource record set (RRSet), are returned within the Answer section of the DNS response message.

Most but not all new applications require new resource record types to enable definition of application-specific information, and these new resource record types are standardized via the IETF RFC process. This section summarizes the most common lookup applications of DNS. A full reference is provided in Chapter 19.

Host Name and IP Address Resolution

The most common DNS application is host name resolution, looking up a host domain name and obtaining its corresponding IP address. Two resource record types are supported for IP address lookups, one for IPv4 and the other for IPv6 addresses. The corresponding reverse record utilizes a common record type for both IPv4 and IPv6, the PTR record type.

When managing a mixed IPv4–IPv6 network, note that DNS will strongly influence which protocol will be used to reach a given destination host. For example, if I wish to access a website, my resolver may return answers for addresses of one or both types. Based on host policies, most devices will attempt to connect to the resolved IPv6 address, then after a short delay, the IPv4 address, then connect based on the first response. We'll talk more about these nuances of connecting to dual stack servers in Chapter 7.

A – IPv4 Address Record

The A record is a common resource record type used to map a queried host domain name to an IPv4 address. The format follows the standard convention per the example below. Hosts may have multiple A records to provide load balancing or mapping of a hostname to multiple devices and/or interfaces.

```
www.ipamworldwide.com. 3600 IN A 10.100.0.99
```

AAAA – IPv6 address record

The AAAA ("quad-A") record provides an IPv6 address based on lookup of a host domain name. The RData field includes an IPv6 address which can be abbreviated using standard IPv6 abbreviation conventions.

```
www.ipamworldwide.com. 3600 IN AAAA 2001:db8:3a::a450:1
```

PTR – Pointer Record

The PTR resource record provides mapping from an IP address to a FQDN. The PTR record is used to map both IPv4 and IPv6 addresses. The IPv4 version of the PTR includes the IP address reversed and concatenated with "in-addr.arpa." within the owner field and the corresponding FQDN within the Rdata field. The IPv6 version is formed by expanding the IPv6 address in its hexadecimal colon format, with all zeroes included; that is, filling in leading zeroes and double colon shortcuts. Then drop the colons, reverse the digits, and concatenate with "ip6.arpa."

```
1.32.65.10.in-addr.arpa. 3600 IN PTR sf1.ipamworldwide.com.
1.0.0.1.0.0.0.0.0.0.0.0.0.0.0.0.0.0.0.0.0.0.0.8.b.d
.0.1.0.0.2.ip6.arpa.
3600   IN   PTR   sf1.ipamworldwide.com.
```

The IPv4 address in this example corresponds to 10.65.32.1, while the IPv6 address is 2001:0db8:0000:0000:0000:0000:0000:1001 or 2001:db8::1001 in abbreviated form.

Alias Host Name Resolutions

The CNAME resource record type enables lookup of a host domain name by alias name. CNAME lookups return not an IP address, but a host domain name that must then be queried for its IP address, though most DNS servers responding to a CNAME query will include the corresponding A and/or AAAA record within the Additional section of the DNS response message.

CNAME – Canonical Name Record

The CNAME record enables creation of alias names for hosts. The owner field contains the alias name being looked up, and the RData field yields the canonical host domain name. This host domain name would then need to be resolved to obtain the host's corresponding A and/or AAAA record.

`w3.ipamww.com. 3600 IN CNAME  www.ipamworldwide.com.`

Note that it is not legal to configure a CNAME Rdata field as pointing to another CNAME owner field in order to chain records. This Rdata field must point directly to an A/AAAA resource record owner name. The owner name of each CNAME record must also be unique; a single alias cannot resolve to multiple answers. CNAME records can also be used for mapping reverse domains as we discussed in Chapter 4.

Network Services Location

IP devices booting on a network often need to find specific services for device initialization. While DHCP provides some level of service location via specification of certain option values such as TFTP server IP addresses, DNS provides a services location mechanism using the services location resource record type (SRV). The SRV record provides a means for non-DHCP clients or for clients seeking services after initialization to locate servers providing requested services.

If you've worked with Microsoft clients and domain controllers since the introduction of Windows 2000, you're probably very familiar with SRV records. When Windows domain controllers boot up, they perform a dynamic DNS (DDNS) update to add their respective A and SRV records, enabling them to effectively advertise services availability.

The SRV record owner field is comprised of a concatenation of a particular service, which is available via a particular protocol (TCP or UDP), for a given domain.

The service name is prefixed with an underscore, as is the protocol value. The underscores were added to eliminate collisions with valid domain names. While technically not a valid host domain name character per the original DNS RFC 1035, Microsoft and BIND servers can be configured to tolerate the underscore character via the check-names option parameter.

SRV – Services Location Record

The SRV record is used to enable resolver clients to identify servers offering particular services such as lightweight directory access protocol (LDAP), Kerberos, and others. This record is critical for Microsoft Windows clients in locating Windows Domain Controllers though it has found widespread adoption among other applications.

```
_ldap._tcp.ipamww.com. 3600 IN SRV 10 0 389 ldap
.ipamww.com.
```

The owner field is comprised of a concatenation of a particular service, which is available via a particular protocol (TCP or UDP), for a given domain. The RData field includes a priority field, which instructs clients to use numerically lower priority targets when multiple SRV records are returned.

The weight field is used to further prioritize records with the same priority. The port is the TCP or UDP port number to use to access the given service and the target is the host domain name of the server running the specified service. A couple of examples follow.

```
    _ldap._tcp.ipamww.com. 86400 IN SRV 10 5 389
ldapeast1.ipamww.com.
    _ldap._tcp.ipamww.com. 86400 IN SRV 10 10 389
ldapeast2.ipamww.com.
    _ldap._tcp.ipamww.com. 86400 IN SRV 20 1 389
ldapeast3.ipamww.com.
```

In the three sample SRV records above, which advertise the location of LDAP services over TCP for the ipamww.com domain, the second record would be used first. It shares the lowest priority number (10) with the first record, but it has a higher priority field (10) than the first record (5). The third record would be used thirdly, as it has a larger priority value despite its lower weight.

The port, 389 in the examples above, is the TCP port number of the given service and the domain name of the server running the specified service follows the port. If not also returned in the additional section of the message from the DNS server, the client may request corresponding A or AAAA records for the server domain name to complete the resolution process.

Textual Information Lookup

The TXT record is one of the workhorse resource record types, often used as an interim resource record in support of specific applications pending standardization and implementation. The TXT record enables lookup of a generic reference name, e.g. a domain name, host domain name, or other owner values, and returning arbitrary textual information. Most recently, the TXT record has been used for interim support of DDNS update uniqueness checking (now officially the DHCID record type) and for spam reducing applications.

TXT – Text Record

The TXT record enables the association of up to 255 bytes of arbitrary binary data with a resource record owner. It has proven very versatile in providing interim support of new services.

```
txt.cfo.ipamww.com.  86400 IN     TXT    "CFO
Office (610) 555-1212"
```

Many More Applications

Numerous other applications and resource records are summarized in Chapter 18 including those supporting email server location, anti-spam, telephone number lookups, email authentication, DNS and network security and more.

Part II

IPAM Mechanics

Part II delves into the application of IPAM functions to various network types including traditional multi-service, multi-tiered IP networks, IPv6, the Internet of Things (IoT), and private and public cloud services.

6

IP Management Core Tasks

IPAM Is Foundational

Adept IPAM practice incorporates the effective management of the three foundational aspects of IP networking we covered in prior chapters:

1) *IP address subnetting and tracking (IPv4/IPv6 address planning)* – maintenance of a cohesive IP address plan that promotes route summarization, maintains accurate IP address inventory, streamlines operational practices, and provides an automated individual IP address assignment and tracking mechanism. This also requires tracking individual IP address assignments on each subnet, some assigned by hard-coding, e.g. routers or servers, and others assigned dynamically, e.g. laptops, IoT devices, cloud instances, VOIP phones.
2) *DHCP* – automated IP address and parameter assignment relevant to location and device type. This requires tracking the address assignments configured on devices and setting aside dynamically allocated address pools. These address pools can be configured on DHCP servers in order to enable devices to request an IP address and receive a location-relevant address in reply.
3) *DNS* – lookup or resolution of domain names to IP addresses, among other data resolution types. This third IPAM cornerstone deals with simplifying IP communications for humans as well as cloud service chains as we'll see in Chapter 9, through the use of names, not IP addresses, to establish IP communications.

Given the dynamic nature of IP address assignment for mobile and cloud devices, it follows that updating the DNS name for each dynamic address assignment is generally necessary. This enables those seeking to connect to my laptop to connect using its hostname, provided that DNS is updated to translate the name to the current IP address. This also enables each device to communicate using certain applications, such as VPNs, which typically require device names and their IP addresses to be retrievable from DNS.

IP Address Management, Second Edition. Michael Dooley and Timothy Rooney.
© 2021 The Institute of Electrical and Electronics Engineers, Inc.
Published 2021 by John Wiley & Sons, Inc.

Hence, when a device obtains an IP address from a DHCP server, whose address pools are provisioned based on corresponding subnets defined in the IP address plan, the DHCP server can update a DNS server via dynamic DNS (DDNS). DDNS provides the mechanism for updating DNS upon dynamic address assignment using DNS update messages. While DDNS provides a linkage between DHCP and DNS within the scope of IP management, "static" IP devices such as routers or servers on-premises or in the cloud generally require accessibility by name as well, so from the perspective of associating a host or domain name with an IP address, the linkage to static and dynamic IP address inventory also exists.

Recalling our IP networking overview in Chapter 1, possession of an IP address is a prerequisite for communicating on an IP network. Each IP address must be unique and relevant to each user's location within the network to effectively communicate using IP applications such as email, web browsing, and mobile apps. Those responsible for operating the IP network need to assure proper allocation of these valuable IP address resources to provide adequate address capacity while maintaining effective network operations.

You may be wondering: sure, it may be complicated to get the network setup in terms of IP address allocations, assignments, and DHCP and DNS server configurations; but once everything is setup, you're done, right? Depending on your business, this is rarely the case. Most IP networks grow, shrink, and morph with the demands of the business: new stores are opened, offices are closed or moved, containers are deployed, cloud virtual networks and instances are provisioned or changed, companies are acquired, and new devices and device types need IP addresses. These and other changes impacting the IP network can have major repercussions on the existing IP address plan. As the number of users and IP addresses increases, along with the number of subnets or sites, the task of tracking and managing IP address allocations, individual assignments, and associated DNS and DHCP server configurations grows in complexity. IPAM practice seeks to bring order and discipline to managing this complexity.

Impacts of Inadequate IPAM Practice

Network managers responsible for maintaining accessibility to an IP network need to keep IPAM information organized, accurate, and secure. The ramifications of not properly managing IP addresses include the inability of users to connect to the network due to

- Router subnet configuration misalignments with the IP topology and source address-dependent routing policies
- Inaccurate IP inventory inhibiting troubleshooting of issues related to particular IP addresses

- Duplicate assignment of IP addresses to multiple devices
- Improper or inaccurate configuration of DHCP servers resulting in an inability to properly assign addresses dynamically
- Elevated security vulnerabilities due to lack of adequate IP address and device inventory, forensics history or monitoring of IP assignments and DNS transactions
- Improper or inaccurate configuration of DNS services resulting in an inability to reach web servers, email servers, or other IP application servers by name
- Lack of availability of IP addresses due to fully assigned address pools
- Fragmented visibility of IP blocks, subnets, and assignments across sites, data centers, cloud, IoT networks, etc.
- Misalignments of inventory with actual IP network assignments due to "localized" address assignment ("Oh, I'll just connect my own printer to this Ethernet cable and assign it address X.")
- Lack of history tracking inhibiting change control, auditing, reporting, and troubleshooting

IPAM Is Core to Network Management

The discipline of network management has long offered technical and business benefits to organizations with the centralization of the monitoring, control, and provisioning of distributed network elements such as routers and application or services databases. These benefits include holistic management of the entire network from a centralized location where appropriate resources are concentrated for troubleshooting, resolution, and escalation. The centralized pan-network approach lends itself well to supporting structured network change control procedures and is even more crucial today with networks continually expanding into clouds, IoT subnetworks, and mobile networks.

It's a small leap to consider DNS and DHCP servers as network elements, as they provide critical IP services to clients on an IP network. While not in-band or on the data path for user IP traffic like traditional network elements, they provide necessary services required to make such in-band data paths possible and usable. From a telephony intelligent network analogy, DNS and DHCP are akin to Network Control Points within the control plane in providing look-up and addressing information. So it follows that centralized management of these servers is equally wise and beneficial. A blip on a network manager's screen could ultimately have been caused by an IP address misconfiguration, so equipping him or her with the corresponding capabilities for monitoring and control of DHCP and DNS services in the network can reduce overall troubleshooting and resolution time.

Because IP addresses and associated DHCP and DNS functions are so foundational to services and applications running over an IP network, these functions must be prudently managed, much as other critical network infrastructure elements are managed. The most commonly applied network management approach is that of the FCAPS model from a functional perspective and ITIL® from a service management perspective. We'll discuss common IPAM tasks within the context of the FCAPS model, then relate functional mapping of these tasks to ITIL® process areas toward the end of the chapter.

FCAPS Summary

FCAPS is defined in international telecommunications union (ITU) standard M.3400 as part of the telecommunications management network (TMN) framework for managing data networks. The FCAPS model covers the following key functions within the practice of network management:

- $F = fault\ management$ – involves monitoring and detection of network faults with the ability to diagnose, isolate, and resolve them. As network elements such as routers, servers, and switches are monitored to detect faults or outages, DHCP and DNS services should likewise be monitored. Appropriate workaround mechanisms such as providing for high availability services may also be implemented.
- $C = configuration\ management$ – entails accurate configuration and backups of network elements, including DHCP and DNS servers and IP address repositories. Accurate and timely configuration of network elements reduces provisioning errors and time intervals within change management windows.
- $A = accounting\ management$ – involves tracking and policing of usage of network resources with respect to business quotas or customer entitlements. Aspects of IP management regarding access control policies, address utilization with respect to business parameters, and monitoring service-level agreement (SLA) compliance fall within accounting management.
- $P = performance\ management$ – deals with tracking performance of network elements and services, along with resource utilization. Tracking of IP address utilization and DHCP/DNS server performance are key requirements for effective IPAM.
- $S = security\ management$ – includes the securing of information regarding the network and its users, defining access controls, as well as audit logging and security breach detection. IPAM security management includes IP address access policies, DNS and DHCP security, rogue or illicit device detection on the network and general network security measures that incorporate IPAM and DNS within a defense-in-depth security strategy.

Leveraging the FCAPS framework, we'll discuss the most common IP management tasks, starting with "configuration," then move on to the other categories. Some functions may likely require the use of multiple management systems depending on your IPAM system capabilities. For example, if your IPAM system consists of a spreadsheet, you'll need another tool to perform fault management functions. Likewise for commercial IPAM systems, varying subsets of functions and tasks will be available natively within the system, while others will require supplemental systems. We'll come back to this topic relating key functions and the associated costs of performing them in Chapter 15.

Configuration Management

When most people think of IPAM, they primarily consider it a configuration management mechanism. Early IPAM systems in fact focused solely on configuration management, though most have expanded into other FCAPS roles. Nevertheless, configuration management is a fundamental IPAM function. In this section, we'll discuss common tasks required when managing IP address space and DHCP/DNS server configurations. These tasks relate to the day-to-day activities of an IP address planner with respect to moves, adds, and changes for IP addresses, subnets, address pools, domains, and other aspects of DHCP and DNS configuration.

Configuration management within the context of IPAM entails the configuring of DHCP and DNS servers for lease and parameter assignment and name resolution, respectively, within the scope of the overall address plan. This involves at minimum, configuration of IPAM-related information, i.e. address pools and associated parameters and DNS configuration and zone repositories. The configuration process may also entail configuration of high availablilty deployments and server-level configuration parameters, for server-based, appliance-based, or cloud-based DHCP/DNS servers.

The configuration management function assures that each of the DHCP and DNS servers within the network is configured with the information necessary to perform its respective role in the network; e.g. primary DHCP server for a set of address pools, failover DHCP configuration, DNS zones, parameters, and options. From this perspective, the goal is to base each DHCP and DNS server's configuration on its type (e.g. ISC, NLNet Labs, PowerDNS, Knot, or Microsoft), its role in deployment, and the portion of the network it is serving. The portion of the network relates to the association of a set of DNS domains, subnets, and address pools assigned to each server and should align with the overall plan for address space and DNS domains.

Another function closely aligned with IPAM is configuration of routers with new, moved, or deleted subnets, as well as relay agent information regarding which DHCP servers to which to relay DHCP packets. Few IPAM systems on the market perform this level of router integration natively. Historically, the network or server teams were distinct from router teams, so inter-team automation was discouraged; after all, if a router ended up being misconfigured, it would come back to the router team. Some IPAM systems enable automation of this process nonetheless, natively or via an API call, which can "hook" the output of an IPAM system subnet allocation to the input of a router configuration tool. The brute force method likely entails sending an email to the router team after a subnet has been allocated in the IP address repository. We'll examine the automation approach in more detail in Chapter 9.

Address Allocation Considerations

As we've discussed in prior chapters, we stress the necessity of a solid IP address plan as the foundation upon which address assignments and DHCP and DNS services can be configured. Your IP address plan is fundamental to managing all other IPAM features and functions.

Address Capacity Considerations Starting at the top of the IPAM food chain, allocation of address space should be performed hierarchically from the top down. Planning address space allocations must consider business requirements with respect to address capacity for each application and user community at each site from the bottom up. Ultimately, each site will be served from the respective allocation, so capacity planning should incorporate addressing needs at each current and planned future site, including cloud and IoT networks.

If you don't have time or resources to conduct a full capacity analysis, one rule of thumb for enterprise organizations is to consider the number of employees at each location and multiply this number by five. This quantity provides a rough estimate and accounts for each employee's devices, occasional visitors, as well as infrastructure devices like routers and servers. On the other hand, if you have plentiful address space for the size of your organization, i.e. as is the case with IPv6 address space, you may just want to allocate uniformly.

Network Topology Considerations Once address capacity has been quantified per site, consider the routing topology and how to best model the addressing hierarchy. Besides analyzing and forwarding IP packets across your network, routers also communicate among themselves regarding reachability of destination networks and nodes. Use of a routing protocol like OSPF or BGP enables routers within a given network to identify optimal routes for IP packets across your network and to reroute around congestion or failure points.

Thus, routers need to communicate frequently to identify and reroute around network issues. In each such communication, routers generally communicate reachability metrics for each network to provide information to peer routers for making routing decisions. If your network is modestly sized with less than a few hundred subnets, routing performance may be of minor concern. However, for larger networks, the volume of "routes" communicated in each routing protocol exchange literally reduces the router cycles available to process user IP packets. In addition, processing of IP packets may require more cycles if routing tables updated by these routing protocols are correspondingly large. For such networks, your IP address plan can help improve routing efficiency by supporting hierarchical allocation.

Many modest to large networks are architected with a traditional three-layer model, with an access layer comprising routers directly serving end users, which feed into routers within a regional layer which handle primarily intra-regional routing with escalation to routers within a core layer, which interconnect regions. Cloud, IoT, partner, and related subnetworks must also be accounted for, typically at the core level. Using a core-regional-access router topology lends itself to a corresponding mapping of addressing hierarchy.

A hierarchical address plan allocates large blocks for each core router, while each regional router is allocated space from its respective core address block. Each access router is in turn allocated space from its respective regional address block. Such a topology features a backbone or core network feeding regional networks, which in turn feed access or local networks. Routers serve as topological interfaces and provide aggregation of networks and routers for their downstream networks.

This hierarchical allocation model enables your core routers to communicate just one route each in its routing updates. Each of your regional routers can likewise communicate a single route in its routing update. And finally, each access router communicates reachability to its allocated network. As you can imagine, the "roll up" of address space hierarchically leads to optimal efficiency in routing tables and routing protocol communications. We can now integrate the capacity data with the topology to identify the roll-up of address space at each hierarchy level.

Application Routing Considerations Routers leverage routing tables stored in memory to make routing decisions. Routers may also be configured to use additional information to make routing decisions, particularly based on information in the header of each IP packet it processes, including source and destination IP addresses. The router may drop packets from certain source IP addresses, may prioritize packets of with a given destination address or other header parameter values, or otherwise treat packets based on header parameter values.

For example, some organizations allocate separate address space to be assigned to VoIP devices as contrasted to data devices. An IP packet incoming to a router with a source IP address assigned from the VoIP space should be treated in accordance with the VoIP policy. Similarly, a packet with source IP address from the data space should be treated as configured for the data policy. In this scenario of configuring source address dependent routing (SADR) policy based on the source and destination IP addresses, your IP addressing plan will directly impact the simplicity or complexity of defining such policies.

Security Considerations   Another factor to consider is your reliance on IP addresses for securing your network. Much like the definition of SADR treatment policies, security policies can be scoped based on IP addresses. Filtering of packets based on source or destination IP addresses and perhaps other header information such as port number is common practice. Hence, your IP address plan will have an impact on the day-to-day manageability of configuring and updating security policies.

Configuring access control lists (ACLs) based on IP addresses can be simplified if the address plan is defined such that ACLs can be defined with just a few entries in the ACL configuration of the router, firewall, DNS server, or device in question. Ongoing security operations may require the need to redirect traffic, isolate, or quarantine a site known to have an active virus or bot, or to "zoom in" on a particular traffic flow for troubleshooting or analysis. For example, if each access router in our hierarchy was allocated a single block for each site, this allocation strategy facilitates the quarantining of a given site from a security perspective by blocking traffic into the regional routers from the site's network.

Address Allocation Tasks
Uniform Allocation Tactics

Who thought IP address planning considered such careful thought! But now let's get down to actually performing example address allocations. Let's say we'd like to model our routing topology in allocating address space; this should facilitate route aggregation as well as security policy enactment. Our top-level allocation will provision our address space into three core regions though we'd like to keep some spare address space for future expansion or acquisitions. Starting with a 10.0.0.0/8 private address block, the binary representation of this network is shown below to illustrate the allocation process and its impacts on network addresses. The network portion of the address, whose length is identified as the first eight bits by virtue of the /8 notation is highlighted as bold italics, while the local portion is in plain text.

Private network	10.0.0.0/8	***00001010***	00000000	00000000	00000000

Given our desire to save address space as unallocated for growth and possible acquisitions, let's slide our allocation size to the next four bits of our network address and allocate equal-sized /12 networks. This would provide $2^{(12-8)} = 16$

equal-sized allocations, while providing $2^{(32-12)} > 1$ million IP addresses per allocation. We enumerate these sixteen allocations, simply incrementing bits 9–12, counting in binary as shown below. We can then select our first six and denote them for specific purposes, leaving the 10 remaining blocks unallocated.

Before allocation

Private network	10.0.0.0/8	*00001010* 00000000 00000000 00000000

After allocation

Region 1	10.0.0.0/12	*00001010 0000*0000 00000000 00000000
Region 2	10.16.0.0/12	*00001010 0001*0000 00000000 00000000
Region 3	10.32.0.0/12	*00001010 0010*0000 00000000 00000000
Cloud service 1	10.48.0.0/12	*00001010 0011*0000 00000000 00000000
Cloud Service 2	10.64.0.0/12	*00001010 0100*0000 00000000 00000000
IoT networks	10.80.0.0/12	*00001010 0101*0000 00000000 00000000
Unallocated	10.96.0.0/12	*00001010 0110*0000 00000000 00000000
Unallocated	10.112.0.0/12	*00001010 0111*0000 00000000 00000000
Unallocated	10.128.0.0/12	*00001010 1000*0000 00000000 00000000
Unallocated	10.144.0.0/12	*00001010 1001*0000 00000000 00000000
Unallocated	10.160.0.0/12	*00001010 1010*0000 00000000 00000000
Unallocated	10.176.0.0/12	*00001010 1011*0000 00000000 00000000
Unallocated	10.192.0.0/12	*00001010 1100*0000 00000000 00000000
Unallocated	10.208.0.0/12	*00001010 1101*0000 00000000 00000000
Unallocated	10.224.0.0/12	*00001010 1110*0000 00000000 00000000
Unallocated	10.240.0.0/12	*00001010 1111*0000 00000000 00000000

We have thus transformed our 10.0.0.0/8 block into six allocated /12s and ten /12s which remain unallocated. Block sizing decisions for each allocation level depend largely on the relative scarcity of your address space. If address space is plentiful, e.g. you run a small to modest sized IP network, then applying uniform allocations as illustrated keeps things simple. But if you run a large enterprise or service provider network, an optimal allocation strategy may make more sense at least for IPv4 allocations.

Optimal Allocation   This optimal allocation strategy entails rolling up blocks into larger "chunks" which may be made available for variable sized allocations that may be required in the future. If you have ever endured a company merger, you may have encountered a situation like the following which illustrates the optimal allocation motivation. Let's say your company acquires another company and the network integration strategy requires an allocation of about four million IP addresses to the newly acquired division. To minimize confusion (and to exude networking mastery over the rival IT organization), you desire the allocation of a single /10 to support 4,194,304 addresses.

In order to keep unallocated blocks as large as possible, we can either perform uniform allocation as we illustrated above, then join unallocated blocks to form larger blocks. To join blocks, we need to decrease the CIDR mask size of two (or more) blocks such that they fall within a common larger block. Observing the bottom of our listing of unallocated blocks, the bottom two blocks share a common /11 prefix, 10.224.0.0/11 as we see here:

Unallocated   10.224.0.0/12   ***00001010 11***00000 00000000 00000000

Unallocated   10.240.0.0/12   ***00001010 11***10000 00000000 00000000

In fact, if we continue up the table to include the bottom four unallocated blocks, we find a common /10 prefix, 10.192.0.0/10, and the bottom eight blocks share the 10.128.0.0/9 prefix. Moving the CIDR size to /8, we have a mix of block states and cannot join all of these together, but we were able to join eight of our blocks into one /9. Restarting the join process above the /9, we can join the next two blocks to consolidate them into the 10.96.0.0/11 block. Thus, we've consolidated our 16 blocks into eight.

Before allocation

Private network 10.0.0.0/8   ***00001010*** 00000000 00000000 00000000
After allocation

Region 1   10.0.0.0/12   ***00001010 0000***0000 00000000 00000000

Region 2   10.16.0.0/12   ***00001010 0001***0000 00000000 00000000

Region 3   10.32.0.0/12   ***00001010 0010***0000 00000000 00000000

Cloud service 1	10.48.0.0/12	*00001010*	*0011*0000	00000000	00000000
Cloud service 2	10.64.0.0/12	*00001010*	*0100*0000	00000000	00000000
IoT networks	10.80.0.0/12	*00001010*	*0101*0000	00000000	00000000
Unallocated	10.96.0.0/11	*00001010*	*011*00000	00000000	00000000
Unallocated	10.128.0.0/9	*00001010*	*1*0000000	00000000	00000000

Another way to accomplish this instead of equally splitting then joining the unallocated blocks is to merely allocate in this manner in the first place by successively halving the address space down to the size required. If we start with our 10.0.0.0/8 block and halve it, we end up with two /9 blocks as illustrated below. Note that thanks to binary arithmetic, associating the next "host" bit with the network enables halving of the original network. Now the 10.0.0.0/8 network technically no longer exists, it has been split into our two /9 networks.

Original network	10.0.0.0/8	*00001010*	*00000*000	00000000	00000000
First half	10.0.0.0/9	*00001010*	*0*0000000	00000000	00000000
Second half	10.128.0.0/9	*00001010*	*1*0000000	00000000	00000000

Next, let's halve the "first half" above, leaving the 10.128.0.0/9 block available for future allocation growth (or acquisitions). We extend the network portion of the address now to the tenth bit to halve the 10.0.0.0/9 to yield two /10s as below. Note that as with the 10.0.0.0/8 network, the 10.0.0.0/9 network no longer exists as an entity. It has been split into the two /10s shown. However, the 10.128.0.0/9 network is available to the organization for further allocation as needed.

Original network	10.0.0.0/8	*00001010*	00000000	00000000	00000000
Original first half	10.0.0.0/9	*00001010*	*0*0000000	00000000	00000000
First /10	10.0.0.0/10	*00001010*	*00*000000	00000000	00000000
Second /10	10.64.0.0/10	*00001010*	*00*0000000	00000000	00000000
Second half	10.128.0.0/9	*00001010*	*0000*0000	00000000	00000000

One way to visualize this halving process from an overall allocation perspective is to view the address space as a pie chart as shown in Figure 6.1. If our entire pie represents the base network, 10.0.0.0/8, then we cut it in half to render two /9s as shown on left of the figure. We can then leave one of the /9s as "available" (left half) and slice the other /9 (right half) into two /10s as shown on the right of the figure.

Iterating this process with our "first" free block in each case, we get to having two /12s as shown below, along with unallocated /11, /10, and /9 blocks.

Original network	10.0.0.0/8	*00001010*	00000000	00000000	00000000
First half (/9)	10.0.0.0/9	*00001010*	*0*0000000	00000000	00000000
First /10	10.0.0.0/10	*00001010*	*00*000000	00000000	00000000
First /11	10.0.0.0/11	*00001010*	*000*00000	00000000	00000000
First /12	10.0.0.0/12	*00001010*	*0000*0000	00000000	00000000
Second /12	10.16.0.0/12	*00001010*	*0001*0000	00000000	00000000
Second /11	10.32.0.0/11	*00001010*	*001*00000	00000000	00000000
Second /10	10.64.0.0/10	*00001010*	*01*000000	00000000	00000000
Second half (/9)	10.128.0.0/9	*00001010*	*1*0000000	00000000	00000000

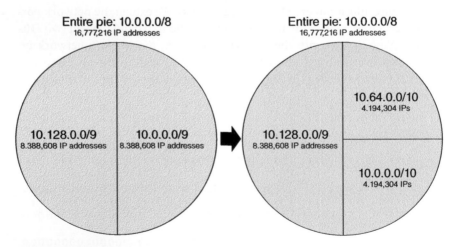

Figure 6.1 Pie chart view of address allocations.

As each "first" block is split, it creates two networks of network mask length of one bit longer than the original block. Now that we've performed this split, we have two of our required /12 networks: 10.0.0.0/12 and 10.16.0.0/12. To allocate our next /12, we take the smallest unallocated block (the rule is to maintain larger blocks for future availability), which is 10.32.0.0/11 and continue the process. The resulting pie chart is illustrated in Figure 6.2, with the allocated space highlighted.

This view clearly illustrates we have retained many large blocks which are available for further allocation or assignment. Only the darker shaded wedge of the pie comprising our six /12 networks has been assigned.

If we've optimally allocated our address space, we may happen to have a /10 readily available if needed. If we had taken a uniform approach of allocating /12s everywhere as illustrated above, we may readily have four contiguous /12s which we can combine into a single /10, but over time, other allocations may have been made, and we may be lucky to identify four contiguous /12s. If we cannot identify four contiguous /12s, we may have to assign four noncontiguous /12s; this adds four times the overhead to routing tables and routing protocol update entries.

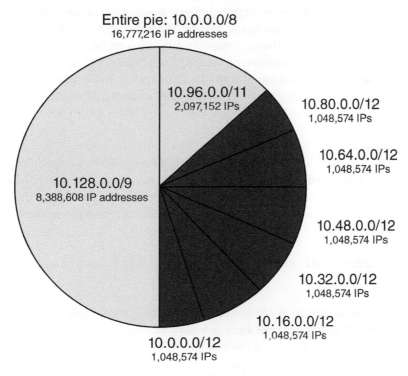

Figure 6.2 Allocation of 6 /12s from /8 space.

With optimal allocation, a /10 is less likely to be broken up for other allocations since we always choose the smallest available block and we're more likely to have address space readily available for assignment.

Second and Subsequent Level Allocations Now that we allocated our top block hierarchy tier, we can then allocate from each regional block to accommodate address allocations to our access or feeder routers in accordance with our topology. Each of our allocated /12s in this case would serve as fresh pies to be allocated within each corresponding region following the same process of successive halving. Third tier and subsequent levels follow a similar approach. We'll illustrate such a multitiered approach in our IPAM use case in Chapter 13.

IPv6 Block Allocation Though IPv6 addresses are represented differently than IPv4 addresses, the allocation process works essentially the same way. The main difference is in converting hexadecimal to binary and back instead of decimal to binary and back (or using an IPAM system to save you the trouble). The process of optimal assignment of the smallest available free block described above for IPv4 is an example of the best-fit allocation algorithm. Due to the vast difference in available address space, IPv6 space may be allocated not only with an analogous best-fit algorithm but also a sparse allocation method. We'll also discuss a random allocation method that can be used in lieu of simple subnet numbering starting from 1 and counting up given the plentiful address space and opportunity for obfuscation. We'll outline each of these algorithms in this section, using the example IPv6 network 2001:db8::/32.

Best Fit Allocation

Using a best fit approach, we'll follow the same basic bit-wise allocation algorithm we used for IPv4 described earlier. After converting the hexadecimal to binary, the process is identical in terms of successive halving by seizing the next bit for the network portion of the address. For example, consider our example network 2001:db8::/32 below.

__0010 0000 0000 0001 0000 1101 1011 1000__ 0000 0000 0000 0000 0000...

Let's say we'd like to allocate 6 /40 networks from this space. In following the analogous IPv4 allocation example from a binary perspective, by successively halving the address space down to a /40 size shown by the larger bold italic bits below, you should arrive at the following:

0010	*0000*	*0000*	*0001*	*0000*	*1101*	*1011*	*1000*	*1*000	0000	0000	0000	0000...
0010	*0000*	*0000*	*0001*	*0000*	*1101*	*1011*	*1000*	*0*100	0000	0000	0000	0000...
0010	*0000*	*0000*	*0001*	*0000*	*1101*	*1011*	*1000*	*00*10	0000	0000	0000	0000...
0010	*0000*	*0000*	*0001*	*0000*	*1101*	*1011*	*1000*	*0001*	0000	0000	0000	0000...
0010	*0000*	*0000*	*0001*	*0000*	*1101*	*1011*	*1000*	*0000*	*1*000	0000	0000	0000...
0010	*0000*	*0000*	*0001*	*0000*	*1101*	*1011*	*1000*	*0000*	*0*100	0000	0000	0000...
0010	*0000*	*0000*	*0001*	*0000*	*1101*	*1011*	*1000*	*0000*	*00*10	0000	0000	0000...
0010	*0000*	*0000*	*0001*	*0000*	*1101*	*1011*	*1000*	*0000*	*0001*	0000	0000	0000...
0010	*0000*	*0000*	*0001*	*0000*	*1101*	*1011*	*1000*	*0000*	*0000*	0000	0000	0000...

Here we readily have two /40 networks available (highlighted above), and translating these back into hex we have: 2001:db8:100::/40 and 2001:0db8:0000::/40 (i.e. 2001:db8::/40). After this allocation, we can split the block above the shaded area (2001:db8:200::/39) into two /40 blocks:

0010 0000 0000 0001 0000 1101 1011 1000 0000 0010 0000
0000 0000...
0010 0000 0000 0001 0000 1101 1011 1000 0000 0011 0000
0000 0000...

This yields 2001:db8:200::/40 and 2001db8:300::/40. We need two more /40s, so our next smallest unallocated block is now 2001:db8:400::/38, two networks above the shaded blocks in the hierarchy above. To derive two /40s from this /38, we split this into two /39s, then split one /39 to arrive at 2001:db8:400::/40 and 2001:db8:500::/40, leaving 2001:db8:600::/39 unallocated. Figure 6.3 illustrates this successive halving in a pie chart form.

After allocating these six /40 networks, highlighted in Figure 6.3, the remainder of the pie is available for allocation.

Sparse Allocation Method

You'll notice from the prior algorithm that by allocating a /40 from a /32, we incrementally extend the network length to the 40th bit as we did with IPv4 allocation. We then assign the network by assigning a 0 or 1 to the 40th bit as our first two /40 networks. In essence, we process each bit along the way, considering "1" the free block and "0" the allocated block. However, if we step back and consider the eight subnet ID bits that extend the /32 to a /40 as a whole, instead of incrementally halving the network, we observe that we've actually allocated our subnets by simply numbering or counting within the subnet ID field as denoted by the highlighted bold italic bits in this table:

```
0010 0000 0000 0001 0000 1101 1011 1000 0000 0000 0000
0000 0000...2001:db8::/40
0010 0000 0000 0001 0000 1101 1011 1000 0000 0001 0000
0000 0000...2001:db8:100::/40
0010 0000 0000 0001 0000 1101 1011 1000 0000 0010 0000
0000 0000...2001:db8:200::/40
0010 0000 0000 0001 0000 1101 1011 1000 0000 0011 0000
0000 0000...2001:db8:300::/40
0010 0000 0000 0001 0000 1101 1011 1000 0000 0100 0000
0000 0000...2001:db8:400::/40
0010 0000 0000 0001 0000 1101 1011 1000 0000 0101 0000
0000 0000...2001:db8:500::/40
```

Thus, if you knew in advance that the original /32 network would be carved uniformly into only /40-sized blocks, a simpler allocation method would be to

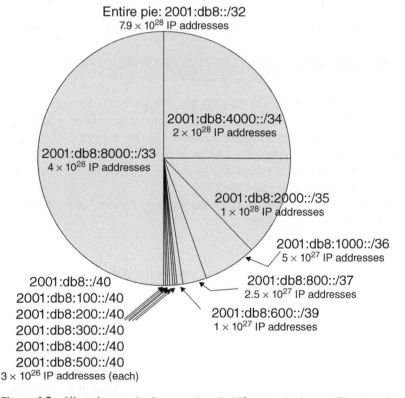

Figure 6.3 Allocation results from carving six /40 networks from a /32 network.

simply increment the subnet ID bits. The next allocation of /40s would use subnet ID values of `0000 0110`, `0000 0111`, `0000 1000`, and so on. In some networks, though in admittedly rare cases, this uniform policy of allocating /40 blocks may not apply, so the method of successive halving may be more appropriate.

On the other hand, if you are a Local Internet Registry or ISP, a sparse allocation method may be attractive. The sparse allocation method seeks to spread out allocations to provide room for growth by allocating blocks with the maximum space *between* each block. The sparse algorithm also features halving of the available address space, but instead of continuing this process down to the smallest size, it calls for allocating the next block on the edge of the new half. This results in allocations being spread out and not optimally allocated. Again, the philosophy is that this provides room for growth of allocated networks by leaving ample space between allocations within the plentiful IPv6 space. Considering an example, our allocation of three /40s from our 2001:db8::/32 space would look like:

0010 0000 0000 0001 0000 1101 1011 1000 `0000 0000` 0000
0000 0000...2001:db8::/40
0010 0000 0000 0001 0000 1101 1011 1000 `1000 0000` 0000
0000 0000...2001:db8:8000::/40
0010 0000 0000 0001 0000 1101 1011 1000 `0100 0000` 0000
0000 0000...2001:db8:4000::/40
0010 0000 0000 0001 0000 1101 1011 1000 `1100 0000` 0000
0000 0000...2001:db8:c000::/40
0010 0000 0000 0001 0000 1101 1011 1000 `0010 0000` 0000
0000 0000...2001:db8:2000::/40
0010 0000 0000 0001 0000 1101 1011 1000 `1010 0000` 0000
0000 0000...2001:db8:a000::/40

Note that our subnet ID bits are effectively counted from left-to-right, instead of the conventional right-to-left method used for "normal" counting, that is, the reverse of the bit values we saw in the monotonic case. This allocation method enables spreading out of address space as illustrated in Figure 6.4. Should the recipient of the 2001:db8:8000::/40 network require an additional allocation, we could allocate a contiguous or adjacent block, 2001:db8:8100::/40. This block will be among the last to be allocated under the sparse method, so there's a good chance it will be available. In such a case, the recipient of our two contiguous blocks could identify (and advertise) their address space as 2001:db8:8000::/39.

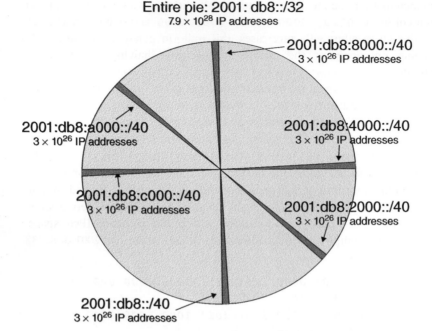

Figure 6.4 Sparse allocation example.

RFC 3531 [48] describes the sparse allocation methodology. Because network allocations are expected to follow a multilayered allocation hierarchy, several sets of successive network bits can be used by different entitles for successive allocation. For example, an Internet Registry may allocate the first macro block to a regional registry, who in turn will allocate from that space to a service provider, who may in turn allocate from that subspace to customers, who can further allocate across their networks. RFC 3531 recommends the higher-level allocations, e.g. from the registries, utilize the left most counting or sparse allocation, the lowest-level allocations use the rightmost or best-fit allocation, and others in the middle use either, or even a center-most allocation scheme.

Random Allocation

The random allocation method selects a random number within the sizing of the subnetwork bits to allocate subnetworks. Using our /40 allocations from a /32, a random number would be generated between 0 and $2^8 - 1$ or 255 and allocated assuming it's still available. This method provides a means for randomly spreading allocations across allocated entities and generally applies to uniform-sized allocations. Randomization provides a level of "privacy" in not ordering blocks and subnets monotonically starting with "1." Be aware that random allocation may render the identification of larger contiguous blocks per our earlier merger example more difficult as well as the freeing up contiguous space for renumbering purposes. So while it makes sense to allocate sparsely at the top layer of allocation, the random or best fit methods are more appropriate at the subnet allocation level.

Block Allocation Summary For base and subsequent address block allocations, updating the address plan is a necessary first step. But there's more to be done. To implement the plan, the allocated address space should be configured in each core router, respectively, to enable dynamic routing. Additional housekeeping tasks may be necessary to add the newly allocated address space to server ACLs at the network interface level and also at the DNS service level regarding "allow" options such as allow-query, allow-recursion as well as view definitions if appropriate. There is perhaps more to block allocation than it seems. In summary, the task of address block allocation includes the following subtasks:

- Enumerate your places of business and sites requiring IP space and associated quantities of users or IP devices required per site; this includes virtual networks within private and public cloud systems.
- Identify any nonintegrated IoT deployments, e.g. field-based deployments that require backhauling via a service provider or Internet connection, especially if IPv6 over low power and lossy networks technology is required; we'll address this technology in Chapter 8.
- Define the routing topology in terms of address aggregation requirements.
- Determine if allocation by application is warranted. If so, categorize your IP devices per site by application.
- Identify the minimum allocation at each level of the topology considering growth plans, and employ allocation policies such as a uniform or as-needed strategy.
- Identify free address space within the IP address inventory and allocate a block of the selected size, denoting the allocated block as such in the IP inventory repository.
- Update router configurations with the allocated network and relay agent information.
- Update router, firewall, other security systems, as well as DHCP and DNS ACL configurations as appropriate.
- Manage the overall allocation process to track locations and servers coming on line. Subnet allocations per location are covered next.

Subnet Allocation Subnets are allocated by applying the same allocation logic in terms of hierarchically subdividing the "IP address pie" down to a subnetwork that is allocated for individual IP address assignment. Even after this base allocation has been deployed, there will be occasions for performing subsequent allocations. Business initiatives will likely drive such occasions. Planned deployment to support several new sites and/or cloud subnets requiring IP addresses due to expansion of the business, plans for new service offerings, and even a merger or acquisition each can heavily impact the IP address plan. A similar process with respect to sizing up expected capacity requirements, mapping capacity rollups to the supporting routing topology, and consideration of free address capacity and allocation policies can be applied for subnet allocations.

This basic task of subnet allocation involves the identification of an unallocated address block of at least the size of the required subnet which rolls up within the address plan for the given location and application. Once identified, the subnet should be denoted as assigned in the IP address plan repository, and the remainder of the parent address block from which the subnet has been allocated should likewise be recorded. That is, if a /24 subnet is allocated from a /23 parent block, denote the subnet /24 address and the remainder unassigned /24 block.

In addition to identifying and recording the allocated block, the subnet allocation process requires provisioning of the allocated subnet on the appropriate router interface. Some addresses on the subnet need to be assigned to infrastructure devices like routers and servers. Defining and updating DHCP server configurations may also be needed to account for address pool(s) and corresponding DHCP options and/or client class parameters required for devices that will use DHCP on the allocated subnet.

Devices to be assigned addresses on the subnet now and in the future will likely require name resolution information in DNS. At a minimum, this information applies to a forward domain for domain name-to-IP address lookup and a reverse domain for the IP address-to-name lookup. This likely requires defining and updating DNS server configurations with domain updates (e.g. in-addr.arpa and ip6.arpa domain(s)) and resource record updates for name servers and statically assigned addresses.

Depending on your domain topology, adding a new subnet to an existing location may enable hosts on the subnet to fall within an existing domain, though this is certainly not necessarily the case. If a new domain is desired, the new domain may be defined and configured as a subdomain or as a new zone on the appropriate DNS servers. In the same way, the reverse domain corresponding to the subnet address may need to be added as well, unless a higher layer in-addr.arpa or ip6.arpa zone will host the corresponding PTR resource records.

The subnet allocation process illustrates one example of the tight interrelationship among address allocation, assignment, and DHCP and DNS server configuration tasks. Depending on your business processes, subnets may be allocated or reserved prior to address assignment and DHCP/DNS configuration. Nonetheless, this set of steps will typically be required to bring a subnet into production.

In summary, the task of subnet allocation includes the following subtasks:

- Identify free address space of the required size within the scope of the topology where the subnet is needed
- Allocate the chosen subnet of the required size from the appropriate address space and record the allocation and remaining unallocated space (if any) in the IP address inventory repository
- Update router configurations regarding the allocated network or provision the assigned subnet within your cloud services using a cloud orchestrator or API
- Assign and provision manually assigned addresses for routers, servers, virtual machines, or other statically assigned devices
- Design and configure DHCP address pools if necessary, to serve dynamic hosts on the subnet. This may require association of options, directives, and client classes based on requirements of devices planned for utilization of the address pool(s)
- Determine whether new DNS domains are required to serve hosts on the subnet and configure appropriate DNS servers accordingly
- Complete the allocation process by confirming provisioning and reachability of the subnet, as well as by verifying corresponding DHCP and DNS configurations.

IP Address Assignment

Assigning, deassigning, and reassigning IP addresses to individual hosts is usually the most frequent IP management activity in most organizations. This is typically associated with deployment, redeployment, or decommissioning of IP devices, including routers, servers, printers, virtual machines, and the like. In terms of manual address assignment, the IP address inventory database must be consulted to identify an available IP address. If possible, it would be useful to ping the IP address to be assigned just to verify accuracy of the inventory, though we'll discuss the process of overall inventory assurance as a separate management task. The IP address to be assigned should then be denoted as assigned to the given device within the IP inventory database.

The actual physical IP address assignment may be performed by manually (statically) configuring the device, by using DHCP (in this case, we'll assume Manual DHCP is used to assign the designated IP address to the corresponding host) or via IPv6 SLAAC. In the static assignment case, the assigned address must be configured directly on the device, so unless the IP address assigner is also responsible for the physical assignment, this process would entail an email or phone call to the device owner conveying the assigned IP address information to be entered.

When using manual DHCP (M-DHCP), an entry in the appropriate DHCP server's configuration file would be necessary to map the device's hardware address to the assigned IP address. Another approach entails booting up the device to obtain an IP address via D-DHCP, then converting the lease from D-DHCP to M-DHCP. This method enables the device to retain the same IP address over time. A SLACC-enabled device will construct its IPv6 address and verify its uniqueness through the duplicate address detection process automatically.

Assigning IP addresses to public cloud virtual machines follows a similar process as the public cloud provider is generally authoritative for IP address assignments to virtual machines or containers. As such, the cloud system tracks assigned and available IP addresses. The process in this case requires either querying the cloud API for an available IP address and using that IP address as a parameter for virtual machine instantiation, or creating the virtual machine with a request for a cloud-assigned IP address then polling the device's IP address via the cloud API after instantiation. We'll review these scenarios in more detail in Chapter 9.

Most devices with IP addresses will require corresponding DNS resource records to enable reachability by name. Using the DHCP method of address assignment, the DHCP server can be configured to update a DNS server upon assignment of the IP address. This update would affect the forward domain for domain name-to-IP address (A/AAAA) lookup and the reverse domain for the reverse (PTR) lookup. A similar DNS update task would be required if assigning the address manually or if a device autoconfigures. Updating DNS with this new host information may entail editing or updating the corresponding zone information on the server or by sending dynamic updates.

You may not want an autoconfigured device to update DNS on its own, at least on an enterprise network, though this may be suitable for a community or ad hoc network. Identifying the presence of a newly autoconfigured device to manually update DNS presents its own challenge. If such devices require resolution information in DNS, use of a router log or router neighbor table polling may be necessary to identify the IPv6 address. Policies would likely be needed to define how such discovered devices should be reflected in DNS if at all depending on your application requirements; for example, you may not desire DNS entries for name-access to IoT devices.

In summary, the task of IP address assignment includes the following subtasks:

- Define how the device will obtain its IP address: via manual configuration, DHCP, SLAAC, or cloud API
    o If manually configured on the device, identify a free IP address within the subnet where the device is located and assign the address to the device. Have the assigned static IP address configured on the device manually.
    o If enabling stateless autoconfiguration, periodically scan such subnets (i.e. neighbor tables) for new occupants.

- o If D-DHCP or A-DHCP, determine if current address pools, if any, on the subnet have capacity to support the device; if so, this task completes; if not, configure an address pool of the corresponding DHCP type on the DHCP server along with necessary option parameters. Typically, the address assignment itself occurs without intervention (at least that's the idea!) so periodic address pool utilization collection is useful to verify capacity.
  - o If M-DHCP, identify a free IP address within the subnet where the device is located and assign the address to the device by configuring DHCP to reserve or use M-DHCP for the device's MAC address.
  - o If cloud API, either query for a free IP address, then use for assignment during instantiation or instantiate the virtual machine, then query its IP address via the cloud API.
  - o In all cases update the IP address plan with the assigned address, whether a spreadsheet or other IPAM tool.
- Determine if DNS resource records need to be manually created and updated. This would generally be the case for statically assigned addresses and discovered autoconfigured devices. For DHCP-assigned devices, the DHCP server can be configured to perform dynamic updates, though in some cases where dynamic updates are not feasible or allowed by policy, manual updating of corresponding resource records may be required.

Verify completion of the address assignment process by pinging the address successfully and verifying its resource records in DNS. For devices assigned an address via an address pool, verification may not be needed; however, if it is, the address may not be known a priori. Locating the device's MAC address in the DHCP lease file, followed by a ping of the corresponding address confirms its assignment in this case.

Address Deletion Tasks

As we've illustrated, address allocation is a top–down process, with allocation of hierarchical blocks, from which subnets can be allocated, from which IP addresses can be assigned. Deletion of address space requires the inverse operation and is necessarily bottom-up. Deleting an address block before the underlying blocks, subnets, and IP addresses have been deleted would strand these underlying elements, so unless you enjoy mass chaos, a more controlled process is warranted.

Deleting IP Addresses   Deleting an IP address is relatively straightforward: delete or free up the IP address in the IP inventory, removing the M-DHCP entry from the DHCP server if appropriate along with releasing the lease, and removing associated DNS resource records. However, care must be taken to assure the address has been relinquished by the device and that DHCP and DNS updates have been completed before assigning the address to another device. Simply deleting a lease on a DHCP server does not force the client holding that lease to relinquish it. Denoting the address as in a state of "pending deletion" or something similar would alert other administrators not to assign that address to another device until confirmation is received of its availability. This pending deletion state is common on many public cloud systems, which hold IP addresses of destroyed virtual interfaces in such an unassignable state for a time. The confirmation process entails pinging the address directly or via cloud API, perhaps successively over several hours, and confirming the deletion of its associated data in DNS and DHCP servers.

Deleting Subnets Deleting a subnet may be required when closing a site or consolidating address space. Devices with IP addresses on the subnet to be deleted should be moved or decommissioned such that the subnet is free of address assignments (other than perhaps subnet-serving routers and switches). After all IP addresses have been verified as free, the subnet may be reclaimed into the free address space for future allocation. The subnet address may then be removed from corresponding router configurations.

Upon freeing up of a subnet, it may be possible to join the freed space with a contiguous free address block, creating a larger free block. For example, if I delete subnet 10.32.142.0/24, which is contiguous with the 10.32.143.0/24 block, which is also free, I could join these two blocks into a single free block, 10.32.142.0/23. Doing so now makes it clear that this "bigger block" /23 could be assigned for growth or a new location within the topology.

Additional housekeeping tasks related to DHCP and DNS ACL configurations should be considered too if impacted by the subnet deletion.

Deleting Blocks Address block deletion may result from the withdrawal from a major business market or cloud service provider or as a result of consolidation of sites or application address spaces, among other reasons. Generally, all downstream IP addresses, subnets, blocks, address pools, resource records and domains should first be decommissioned before the macro level block can be freed up for future assignment consideration. Thus, after the individual delete IP address tasks and delete subnet tasks within the target block have been completed, the block itself may be freed up. As with a modest to large allocation task, project planning resources may be required to verify deletions up the hierarchy. The deleted or freed block space may be joined with contiguous free space of an equal size in the same manner as in deleting subnets.

Address Renumbering or Movement Tasks

Moving or renumbering address blocks, subnets, or individual addresses combines the allocation process with the deletion process. The allocation process, as described above, should be performed from a top–down perspective to allocate space to which underlying subnets and IP addresses will be moved. The deletion process frees up address space from the bottom up as addresses are moved to the target allocated space. In essence, the size of the scope of the addresses to be moved must be allocated to accommodate the addresses to be moved, temporarily doubling the address space associated with this set of devices. As addresses are moved, the former address space can be freed up, returning address allocations to previous levels.

IP Address Moves   Moving an IP address can be considered a combination of assigning an IP address on the destination subnet and deleting the IP address on the current subnet. Depending on the method of address assignment and the type of move, different tactics can be employed. The type of move relates to physical movement of a device to a different subnet (flash move) vs. the reassignment of the IP address on the same or a different subnet (mobile move). A flash move is characterized by the physical movement of a nonmobile IP device like a server which will typically involve a "reboot" of the device.

Flash Moves

For nonmobile devices, "flash" moves imply powering down, moving, then powering up devices at the destination location or simply installing a new device at the new location and switching over to the new device. Once address blocks and subnets have been allocated and your IPAM repository updated, an appropriate device address can be assigned.

For D-DHCP and A-DHCP assigned devices, if an entire pool is being moved, the destination pool should be setup on a [same or different] DHCP server. Make sure the router(s) serving the destination subnet are configured to relay DHCP packets to the DHCP server configured with the new pool. When these devices power up, they will likely attempt to renew the most recent lease they possessed on the old subnet. Make sure that A-DHCP devices do issue renewals upon power up and don't just continue using their old IP lease; if they assume the old [infinite] lease is valid, manual intervention will be required to reset the device's address. Otherwise, the DHCP server will deny the renewal attempt. The client will then revert and issue a Discover/Solicit packet to request a new lease. The DHCP server obliges with a lease within the new destination pool.

Physical movement of an M-DHCP device entails creating the M-DHCP entry in the DHCP server serving the new subnet and deleting the entry on the former DHCP server. If the same DHCP server is being used, simply edit the IP address associated with the device's MAC address while the device is in transit. When the device powers up on the new subnet, it should follow a similar process to D-DHCP and A-DHCP, with a renewal attempt, which the DHCP server would deny, followed by reversion to restarting the address reassignment process under the standard DHCP process.

Moving a device that autoconfigures its IPv6 address will lead to the device detecting its new subnet via neighbor discovery, autoconfiguring its address, then verifying its uniqueness through duplicate address detection.

Updating of DNS resource records may be performed by the DHCP server or manually if dynamic updates are prohibited for these DHCP cases. DNS updates for autoconfigured devices present the same challenge as when adding such devices. Once all devices have physically moved, the pool serving the old subnet may be decommissioned.

Physical moves of manually configured devices requires assignment of an address from the IP inventory, and manually configuring the new IP address in the device as it powers up on the new subnet. At this point, the old address can be freed up. DNS resource records should be updated as well to reflect the device's new IP address.

Movement of cloud or manually addressed devices follows a similar process. An available destination IP address is identified from the IP inventory or cloud API, and that IP address is configured on the device. Once confirmed, the old address can be freed up, though the cloud system may delay full freedom of the address for a time. DNS resource records should be updated as well to reflect the device's new IP address.

In all of these cases, the IP inventory should be utilized to identify free address(es) on the destination subnet or pool and to free up addresses on the old subnet as device moves are confirmed.

Mobile Moves

Mobile moves typically involve DHCP, and an address pool containing the destination IP addresses should be configured or available on the [same or different] DHCP server. The lease time for the pool or device should be stepped down in advance of the move date. For example, if a normal lease time is one week, it should be lowered to one day, for example during the week leading up to the move and to two–six hours on the day of the move. A device may have renewed a weeklong lease just before you changed the lease time to days, so it will not attempt to renew until halfway through the week. Thus, if your nominal lease time is two weeks, ratchet down the lease time two weeks before the planned move. On the day of the move, set the lease time to a minimum time if it's important that all devices move at nearly the same time. Minimum time can be on the order of minutes or hours depending on network traffic and server performance considerations. The shorter the lease time, the more DHCP packets will be sent, but the more time-aligned, the move of DHCP clients can be orchestrated. If move coincidence is not critical, leaving lease times on the order of hours should yield a complete move within a few hours.

In this scenario, it is recommended that the DHCP server perform DNS updates if possible, to more closely map DNS information updates with actual address changes. Manual intervention of A-DHCP devices may be necessary unless they do adhere to lease renewal policies despite possessing infinite leases.

Mobility or logical movement of an autoconfigured device can be performed by configuring the router serving the corresponding subnet to ratchet down the preferred and valid address lifetime values it advertises via the neighbor discovery process. Shortening these timer values for the address prefix from which the device is being moved while introducing the new prefix with a "normal" address lifetime will enable autoconfigured devices to perform this logical move automatically. Once all devices have moved and the valid lifetime of the former prefix expires, the subnet prefix can be removed.

Subnet Moves   Moving a subnet could involve one of two tasks: movement of the subnet and its assigned IP addresses to another router interface (or cloud virtual network), preserving the current address assignment; or movement to another router interface, requiring a new subnet address. We'll include the subnet renumbering task also in this discussion with respect to the latter case as it too results in a new subnet address though without necessarily moving the subnet to another router interface. The first subnet move case requires consideration of address space rollup within the hierarchy but consists primarily of modifying and verifying router provisioning compliance with the plan, as well as updates to routing tables and DHCP relay addresses as necessary.

Flash movement of a subnet or subnet renumbering requires a bit more work; such a move of devices, e.g. when an office is moved, is inherently disruptive. The destination subnet may be allocated and provisioned on the destination router interface, along with the other tasks described above related to reserving static addresses and updating DHCP and DNS configurations in preparation for the move. When each moved device plugs in, it will need to be manually readdressed with the new address and/or obtain a DHCP lease on a pool relevant to the new subnet as described above for IP address moves. After all devices have been moved from the old subnet to the new subnet, the old subnet may be freed up using the delete subnet process.

Block Moves   Moving macro-level blocks with underlying subnets and IP addresses requires careful project planning and execution. The allocation of the destination block should follow those tasks outlined for block allocation. Assuming a move is for renumbering only, a like-sized destination block would likely be allocated. If the move is motivated by or otherwise spurs the opportunity for address consolidation or expansion, the destination allocation should be sized based on underlying capacity requirements and topology architecture as discussed in the Block Allocation section. Once the allocation has been made, suballocations and subnet allocations may begin. IP addresses and pools can then be moved following the process described for IP address and subnet moves. As IP addresses and subnets completely move from their old assignments, these can be decommissioned or freed up when moves have been confirmed.

Block/Subnet Splits Splitting an address block entails the creation of two or more smaller sized blocks from a given source block. Splits may be necessary to free up address space or even as a means of suballocation of address space. In the former case, the addresses within a subnet may be consolidated to the first half of the subnet, freeing up assignments in the second half. In this case, splitting the block yields an occupied subnet (first half) and a free subnet (second half). Some organizations have historically allocated regional blocks, then split them to assign subblocks and subnets lower in the address hierarchy. In some sense this is a form of block allocation.

Splitting a block need not be restricted to only splitting in half, say a /24 into two /25s. A split may be used to carve out a /23 from a /20, which yields a /23 and free space consisting of a /23, a /22 and a /21. In this example, we preserved large blocks following our optimal allocation strategy as we discussed in the Block Allocation section. Alternatively, we could have simply split our /20 into eight /23s, though this may be wasteful unless uniform (same-sized) allocations are used by policy.

In summary, the process of splitting a block is similar to that of allocating a block. The block to be split is successively divided until the desired block size is attained. Remaining free blocks are either retained or also split to the same size as the desired block to render a uniform block split.

Block/Subnet Joins A join combines two contiguous same-sized address blocks or subnets into a single block or subnet. We saw an example of joining blocks in the block deletion section. After freeing up the 10.32.142.0/24 block, we joined it to a contiguous free block, 10.32.143.0/24 to create a single 10.32.142.0/23 block. Successive joins may be performed to consolidate smaller chunks of contiguous address space. Joins are only valid for contiguous blocks of the same size. Joining a /25 and a /24 is not valid as the "other /25" not included in the join must remain uniquely identified. However, two /25s and a /24 can be joined to form a /23 assuming all blocks are contiguous. The two /25s would be joined first to form a /24; then this and the other /24 can be joined to create a /23.

Network Services Configuration
With a well-defined IP address plan in hand, derivative network services configurations can be defined and deployed. Basic DHCP and DNS configuration tasks are discussed in this section, while additional security configuration considerations are described in Chapter 10.

DHCP Configuration Tasks You should consider the following topics when preparing to configure your DHCP servers.

- Address pool sizing to meet capacity requirements for IPv4 and IPv6 clients by class is more of a challenge for IPv4 but requires identification of clients of each class by location, which hopefully fed into the original block allocation process such that subnet sizes per location accommodate capacity needs. From there, pools need to be sized and classes identified.
- Identifying class-specific configuration requirements leads to mapping these to client-identifying parameters (e.g. vendor class identifier option) and corresponding client configuration parameter requirements.
- High availability planning and management requires planning for pool redundancy or splitting across multiple DHCP servers for DHCP resiliency in the event of a DHCP server or partial network outage. We'll discuss various approaches for DHCP redundancy in Chapter 14.
- Configuring the appropriate DHCP server(s) with the allocated address pools, client class definitions, redundancy configuration, and associated general and class-specific pools and option values.
- Monitoring DHCP servers as well as address pool capacity to assure availability of DHCP services with adequate quantities of addresses for clients.

The actual server configuration syntax and interface will depend on the server type. For example, ISC DHCP servers can be configured by editing the dhcp.conf text file, ISC Kea uses json format, while Microsoft DHCP can be updated using a Windows Microsoft Management Console (MMC) interface. These and other DHCP vendors also provide command line interfaces or APIs to perform configuration updates.

DNS Configuration Tasks Major DNS configuration elements are summarized below:

- Identify and obtain a public domain name (or likely several) from your ISP or domain name registrar(s) depending on the TLDs beneath which you desire your domain to be available. For example, you will likely consider .com, but there are now thousands of TLDs, in the form of geographical (city names or country codes), subject area (e.g. food, jewelry, and tickets), brand name, and internationalized domain names.
- Define internal name space including subdomains and subzones; identify administrators and DNS servers to support subzone delegations.
- Enumerate hosts and corresponding resource record information to expose externally for resolution from external or Internet queries; configure corresponding external DNS servers.
- Enumerate hosts and corresponding resource record information to expose internally for resolution from internal queries; configure corresponding internal DNS servers.

- Define DNS update mechanisms and configure servers accordingly; in general, external DNS servers should not support dynamic updates.
- Configure DNS server parameters based on the server vendor attributes for security, scalability, master/slave configurations, etc.
- Configure DNS security parameters and features. Monitor DNS servers for status and query rates to detect outages, denial of service attacks, or query capacity issues. We'll explore this in more detail in Chapter 10.

The actual DNS server configuration syntax will depend on the server type. ISC BIND servers can be configured by editing the configuration file and associated zone files on the server. Some vendors store configuration and zone data in structured query language (SQL) databases. DNS servers that support DDNS may also support resource record updates in this manner. The use of nsupdate or similar DDNS mechanism provides a means to perform incremental updates without having to manually edit zone text files and reload respective zones.

Server Upgrades Management   New versions of DHCP and DNS server software are published periodically to address security vulnerabilities, provide bug fixes, or offer new features. The urgency to perform an upgrade is usually dictated by what's provided in the upgrade, with security vulnerabilities certainly being of highest urgency. The upgrade process is typically vendor-specific and may require alignment of which hardware platforms and operating systems the upgraded version has been certified to run on. Hopefully, the underlying operating system requirements would change only for new feature introductions and not security or bug fixes, but this is governed by vendor policy.

Most vendor DHCP/DNS hardware and virtual appliance upgrades roll in the operating system upgrades as necessary within an overall upgrade package. Because the appliance vendor typically provides the operating system with the hardware platform, they should publish compatibility upgrades as necessary for newer versions of their DHCP and DNS services. Most appliance solutions enable centralized staging of upgrade packages, with deployment to distributed appliances, vastly simplifying the upgrade process over a software-based upgrade process, where the planned software upgrade must be validated with current or planned operating system versions or patches.

If you're running ISC, Microsoft, or other vendor DHCP or DNS daemons on your own hardware, you'll need to keep apprised of not only DHCP/DNS security updates but also those affecting the corresponding operating system running on the hardware or virtual platform.

Fault Management

Fault management encompasses not only fault detection but also alert notification, trouble isolation capabilities, trouble tracking, and resolution processes. Monitoring of DHCP and DNS servers for faults and events enables a proactive means of minimizing services outages. In a well-designed network services architecture, clients should be able to obtain leases and resolve domain names despite a given DHCP or DNS server outage. Nevertheless, detection of such an outage is important as the outage reduces the number of servers that clients may use to obtain these services thereby raising the vulnerability to service outage in the event of an additional server failure. For example, in a DHCP failover deployment, failure of one server will leave just one server available to service DHCP clients. In such a scenario, detection of the failed server facilitates timely, though not panicked, resolution of the server outage.

Monitoring and Fault Detection

Fault detection may be performed using a variety of methods depending on the capabilities supported by deployed DHCP and DNS servers. These range from proprietary polling or notification, to syslog scanning and/or forwarding, to simple network management protocol (SNMP) polling and trap detection by SNMP-based network management systems. Some commercial IPAM systems offer intra-system or proprietary monitoring, particularly for hardware and virtual appliance-based products. Since appliances are fully self-contained solutions, incorporating not only DHCP and DNS services but also a hardware platform and operating system, the appliance vendor should have the ability to fully access fault information related to the appliance at the hardware, operating system and DHCP/DNS levels.

In addition to monitoring the state of DHCP and DNS servers, as reported by the servers, it's a good idea to monitor for hung services. This may occur if a service is running but is in a state where it is unable to perform its role in providing leases or resolving DNS queries. This can be detected by analyzing successive polls for lease or query transactions received and processed, and verifying differential counts greater than zero, assuming normal transaction rates at that particular time of day are nonzero.

An alternative, on-demand form of service testing involves sending the server a DNS query or Discover/Solicit packet and verifying receipt of a proper response. This tactic provides some assurance that the services are not only running, but are responding to clients. The bottom line is that some form of service functional fault detection can provide a truer mapping to what an end user may consider a fault or outage.

In addition to monitoring DHCP and DNS servers, monitoring of the IPAM system itself provides benefits of assuring access to IP address and DHCP and DNS server configuration information which may otherwise be prevented by an outage. At a minimum, backup or distribution of the data store provides a snapshot to reconstruct the information in the event of a site outage or disaster.

Monitoring of networking equipment and communications links is a common practice for general network monitoring and can provide insights into outages affecting the ability of clients to reach DHCP or DNS servers. This added information can be very helpful in troubleshooting a particular problem or fault.

Fault correlation is the analysis of individual faults received from multiple network elements or management systems to help isolate the root cause of a set of faults. For example, faults from a layer 2 switch, a router, and a WAN access device can be analyzed collectively to suggest that these three faults are related and the likely root cause is a link outage. Fault correlation is a common feature of large-scale network management systems, and if your IP management system provides alarm feeds, it may be able to feed into a higher level alert correlation function. Whether fault correlation is performed automatically by a network management system or manually by comparing information from multiple systems, this process exposes a broader set of data for fault analysis with the goal of isolating a fault to a given server, link, or network element.

Troubleshooting and Fault Resolution
DHCP/DNS Server Troubleshooting
Fault management capability is an important consideration for those responsible for managing an IP network, and critical DHCP and DNS network services should be among those elements monitored. Mitigation of the impacts of faults may be achieved through deployment of highly available configurations to minimize end-user impacts of an outage of any individual component. Once a fault has been detected, troubleshooting server faults requires network reachability to the server, secure login to view logs and to restart services or daemons as necessary. If the server is hung and needs to be rebooted, this may require local manual intervention.

Use of "lights out" management capabilities such as Intel's intelligent platform management interface (IPMI) or HP's integrated lights-out (iLO) technologies enable remote rebooting or power cycling of server or appliance hardware. These interfaces also enable monitoring of the boot process as if one was viewing the console interface locally. These interfaces are also helpful from a monitoring perspective in providing temperature, power, and other key indicator readings for the server.

IP Address Troubleshooting   A variety of tools are available to troubleshoot IP address assignments, some of which may be provided by your IPAM product. To verify or identify IP address assignments, intentional or otherwise, a variety of discovery techniques will prove beneficial. Ranging from a simple ICMP Echo request, ping, traceroute, nmap, SNMP, or cloud API, a variety of tools may be used to attempt to contact individual hosts or view router or switch ARP and neighbor tables. Many IPAM systems incorporate several forms of discovery to provide verification of IP address assignments or to assist in troubleshooting.

DNS Service Troubleshooting Beyond server reachability and server/service status checks, troubleshooting of DNS resolution is a key function required to diagnose and resolve DNS issues. Among the most popular DNS diagnostic tools are nslookup (name server lookup) and dig (domain information groper), both of which ship with the BIND software distribution. Nslookup also ships with the Microsoft Windows DNS distribution.

Nslookup

Nslookup [49] is a utility that enables querying of a DNS server. Today, many administrators prefer dig, which provides much more detail and control over the query formulation, resolver configuration override, output formatting, and more. To perform a single lookup using nslookup, simply type:

```
nslookup lookup-value [name server]
```

where `lookup-value` is the host domain name or IP address to lookup and the `name server` is the DNS server name or IP address to query. Additional options may be included preceding the `lookup-value` with each option name prefixed with a hyphen (e.g. `-timeout=5`). Interactive mode for nslookup may be invoked by either entering nslookup with no arguments or entering nslookup followed by a hyphen, space character, and name server hostname or IP address like:

```
nslookup - 172.18.71.105
```

Interactive mode enables entry of commands to formulate and perform queries.

Dig

Dig enables the formulation of a DNS query using standard DNS messages, emulating a resolver, or recursive server. Dig provides granular control of the format of a query which can be sent to a DNS server to analyze the results.

A common example usage of the dig command simply requests a resolution for a host name:

```
dig @ns1.ipamworldwide.com A ftp-sf.ipamworldwide.com
```

This example would result in the issuance of an A record query for ftp-sf.ipamworldwide.com to the DNS server ns1.ipamworldwide.com. Several additional arguments for the dig utility may be entered to focus the test query. For example –p enables specification of the UDP (or TCP) port number to query as the destination port, –6 issues the query over IPv6, and –x IP-address queries for the PTR record(s) for the entered IP-address. All dig options and parameters are discussed in the dig man page [50].

DHCP Service Troubleshooting DHCP transactions can be tested using DHCP client capabilities like ipconfig for Windows or ifconfig commands for Unix or Linux. These commands provide that ability to perform DHCP releases, renews, and set user class. For example, using `ipconfig` on a Microsoft Windows command line enables display of the IP configuration using the following arguments:

- /all – displays IP configuration information for each interface including
  - o IPv4 address and subnet mask
  - o   Additional IP addresses including IPv6 addresses
  - o MAC address
  - o Interface description
  - o DNS domain suffix
  - o Default gateway
  - o DHCP server from which the lease was obtained along with dates/times the lease was obtained and that the lease expires
  - o DNS servers for resolver configuration
  - o WINS servers to query for NetBIOS lookups if configured
- Omitting the /all argument displays the IP addresses, subnet mask, domain suffix, and default gateway only.
- /? – displays help in the form of a command summary
- `/displaydns` – displays contents of the resolver's cache
- `/showclassid` *adapter* – displays the user class configured for the specified interface adapter.

`ipconfig` also provides the following commands:

- `/release` [*adapter*]– issues a DHCPRELEASE to release the lease for all or the specified interface adapter
- `/renew` [*adapter*] – issues a DHCPRENEW to renew all leases or that for the specified interface adapter
- `/registerdns` – issues a DHCPRENEW to renew all leases and updates DNS A record(s) directly (client to DNS server, not DHCP server to DNS)

- /flushdns – clears the resolver cache
- /setclassid *adapter class* – sets the user class name for the specified interface adapter

Accounting Management

Accounting management is intent on keeping everyone honest. Are those assigned addresses still in use? Are any unassigned addresses actually being used? Did the new subnet get provisioned on the router or in the cloud yet? Thus, accounting management enables verification of successful configuration, as well as overall adherence to the IP addressing plan. Techniques for accounting management functions include discovery of IP addresses, provisioned router subnets, switch port mappings, DNS resource records, and DHCP lease repositories.

Analysis of discovered information is necessary in order to compare this information with the inventory "plan of record." Such discrepancy reporting and comparison can be difficult work if not automated, but it provides a level of assurance of IPAM inventory accuracy. Without such a function, rogue users could access free service or otherwise infiltrate the network. In addition, planned network changes yet unimplemented may cause downstream process delays and violation of internal or external SLA on provisioning intervals.

Inventory Assurance

Each of the common IPAM tasks we've covered so far relies on accurate IP address inventory to enable the allocation, deletion, and movement of blocks, subnets, IP addresses and DHCP and DNS server configurations. But accurate inventory is also essential for general troubleshooting. Should a remote site be unreachable due to a network outage, it may be necessary to identify IP addresses, resource records, or other IPAM related data for devices at the site. Only by maintaining an accurate IP inventory can such information be accessed when it may be needed most and when it cannot be obtained directly from the network.

In this section, we'll review steps you can take to assure the accuracy of your IP inventory. This includes controlling who can make certain changes to certain IPAM information, to discovering actual network data, reconciling the actuals with the inventory, and finally reclaiming address space.

Change Control and Administrator Accountability As we've seen in reviewing our IPAM tasks so far, a change in IP inventory often affects other network elements, including routers, DHCP servers, and DNS servers. If different individuals or teams manage these different elements, it's a good idea to convene a planning or change control meeting periodically or as needed to review and schedule upcoming planned addressing changes. A bit of rigor can add some discipline to the process and keep those potentially affected by changes in the loop.

One way to help assure accuracy of IP inventory itself is to limit write access to the inventory to those whom are authoritative for and keenly knowledgeable of the IP addressing plan. Using a single password-protected spreadsheet that the one and only IP planner can modify is one approach to protecting the IP inventory from inadvertent or erroneous changes. However, for even modestly sized organizations, this approach is unwieldy. With the organization reliant on a single individual for the entire IP address plan, the individual must work around the clock and should she or he leave the organization, recovery of access to the inventory may be very difficult unless a successor is groomed in advance.

Support of multiple simultaneous administrators is a key feature of most IPAM systems on the market, and most allow some level of scope control so that certain administrators can only perform certain functions on certain devices or portions of the network. Make sure your chosen system supports administrator logging should you need to investigate "who did what" on the system.

As important as disciplined multiadministrator scoped access to the IP inventory is to delegating accountability, arbitrary changes to IP address assignments, DNS resource records, and subnet addresses can be made outside of the scope of the IP inventory. For example, manual configurations can be mistyped, subnets can be provisioned on the wrong router interface, and client or DHCP updates to DNS can all contribute to IP inventory drift from reality. The IP inventory is a model of the IP address plan, and IPAM tasks rely on the accuracy of the plan. Therefore, additional "pulse readings" are required from the IP network itself. Periodically polling and comparing the actual assignments on the network with the inventory is key to assuring inventory accuracy.

Network Discovery   A variety of methods are available to gather network actuals data, from ping, to DNS lookups, port scans, cloud, or orchestrator API calls, router cache polls, to SNMP queries. Pinging enables detection of an occupant of an IP address and provides a basic method to determine which IP addresses are in use for comparison with the respective portion of the IP inventory. Ping is very useful but be aware that some routers or firewalls will drop ping packets and some devices can be configured to ignore pings. Setting up remote ping agents to perform local pinging on command can help avert the router/firewall traversal issue.

Nmap is a useful tool that combines several discovery mechanisms to gather a variety of information from devices connected to the IP network, including ping sweeps, DNS lookups, and port scanning. When sweeping a subnet, nmap can perform these tasks in one command, issue a ping to each address, looking up a corresponding PTR record in DNS, and attempting connections to various TCP and UDP ports to identify the device's operating system. From an IPAM perspective, ping results help identify IP address occupancy, DNS lookups help corroborate hostname-to-IP address mapping between DNS servers and the IP inventory and port scanning can provide additional information about the type of device occupying each IP address.

SNMP is another means of discovering IP inventory-related information. While most end devices like laptops or VoIP phones don't natively enable SNMP, most infrastructure elements such as routers, switches, and servers do. Of particular interest within router MIBs are the Interfaces, IpAddresses, Arp, and Neighbor (NetToMedia) tables. If your infrastructure devices support MIB-II, the interpretation of these tables *should* be consistent across different products. Just be aware of minor variations, even among different products from the same vendor. The information in these tables enables collection of the interfaces and subnets per interface provisioned as reported by the router. This provides useful validation of inventory in general, but can also be polled when in the process of allocating, moving, or deleting blocks and subnets.

Polling router ARP and neighbor cache tables can provide a mapping of MAC addresses to IP addresses on recent subnet communications. Even if a device refuses to respond to a ping, it must use ARP or neighbor discovery to formulate a layer 2 (e.g. Ethernet) frame in which to envelop its intended IPv4 or IPv6 packet, respectively. As implied by the fact that this is cached information, it is transient and may need to be polled frequently.

IP Inventory Reconciliation   Network discovery information provides a reality check on actual subnet allocations, IP address assignments, and associated resource records. By comparing discovered information with the IP pools and inventory database, discrepancies can be identified and investigated. While this comparison may require "eyeballing," the differences between the inventory spreadsheet and the discovery output, the effort can prove beneficial for several reasons. For example, database discrepancies can be identified that may be the result of

- Inaccurate router provisioning – incorrect subnet address, mask/prefix length, router interface, etc.
- Incomplete router provisioning – planned change not yet implemented
- Device reachability issue – if a device should be at a given IP address and no response is received. This could result from a device outage, a transient outage (reboot), address reassignment, or network unreachability
- Incorrect IP address assignment – SLAAC or manually configured address is incorrect or the device obtained a DHCP address from an unintended pool or address
- Physical IP address misassignment – in some decentralized scenarios, the installer of a device on the subnet may arbitrarily select an IP address; discovery can be used to update the IP inventory accordingly

- Incomplete IP address assignment – some or all aspects of the assignment process, whether manual or DHCP, are incomplete. This issue is particularly applicable to manually assigned addresses where manual effort is needed to configure the assigned IP address and to update DNS, though it could occur when SLAAC is used if DNS is not updated
- Rogue device presence – an unknown or unauthorized device has obtained an IP address

In addition to detecting these and other potential discrepancies, discovery information analysis can confirm completion of allocation or assignment tasks, as well as deletion tasks. Discovery data is indispensable when moving blocks, subnets, and IP addresses. Since moves require allocation of the new address(es), movement, then deletion of the old address(es), confirmation of move completion is essential prior to deleting the old address(es) from the IP inventory. These addresses should not be deleted before the move completes so they are not unknowingly reassigned to other devices or subnets prior to their actual relinquishment.

In summary, network discovery is essential to assuring the accuracy of the IP inventory. It is also beneficial to monitoring provisioning or assignment progress and time frames, managing the completion of tasks requiring multiple related subtasks, and detecting incorrect assignments as well as potentially rogue devices.

Address Reclamation   One of the benefits of network discovery and reconciliation just discussed is the detection of device reachability issues. If a physical or virtual server has been provisioned and has historically responded on a given IP address, but now no longer does so, for example such an event should stimulate further investigation. If there were no plans to move or decommission the device or there are no network problems reaching other devices on the subnet, the device may be suffering an outage, may be rebooting, may have been moved or disconnected or may have been re-addressed. If the server is providing critical services or applications, hopefully you're monitoring its status via a network management system (if the server is a DHCP or DNS server, it may be monitored via the IPAM system) which can corroborate the outage prognosis and trigger corrective actions.

If the IP address is discovered on the next attempt, perhaps it was simply rebooting. If it does not respond for the next *n* attempts, perhaps it is no longer virtually or physically (at least electrically) there. Unfortunately, people don't always inform the IP planning team that a device has been removed or moved elsewhere, even in the tightest of organizations. A quick phone call to the site to check on the device's status may prove fruitful, but it's often difficult and time-consuming to identify the device's "owner" to verify status.

Nevertheless, the key point to assessing the possible fate of the device is that it may take multiple discovery attempts to determine if a device was physical or virtually there and no longer is, suffered a transient outage or disconnect, or was borrowed and has now been returned. Tracking a succession of discovery attempts may be difficult. A running log or spreadsheet can be used to log discrepancies or "missing" IP addresses as they are [not] detected. Reviewing this log over time may help determine if an IP address recorded as in use actually isn't.

In reviewing such a log, if a given IP address had been successfully discovered until a month ago, when it was last reachable after so many attempts, e.g. 30, it may be confirmed as available for future assignment, or *reclaimable.* The concept of reclaim entails identifying IP addresses that are denoted as in use in the IP inventory, but are in reality not in use, nor have they been in use in recent history. Analyzing multiple discovery results provides a reasonably robust sample set on which to base a reclaim decision, essentially deleting the device from the inventory and freeing it up for assignment to another device.

Besides providing robust confirmation of a device deletion from the IP inventory, reclaim may likewise be applied to subnets. When deleting a subnet, it's generally advisable to verify that all IP address occupants have been deleted and are no longer using IP addresses on the subnet. Analyzing discovery results from all addresses on a given subnet can provide assurance that the subnet may be deleted. But like IP address reclaim, multiple sample sets provide more robust confirmation of the reclaimable disposition. Just keep in mind that you'll rarely see zero responses on a subnet, at least while it's still provisioned on a router interface, so you'll want to check successive discovery results ignoring routers, switches, and perhaps other device types.

Performance Management

Performance management entails monitoring functions of the IPAM system and the DHCP and DNS services operating in your network. It's useful to track basic server statistics such as central processing unit (CPU) utilization, memory, disk, and network interface input/output (I/O), especially for virtualized hosts. Such monitoring enables tracking of the hardware's ability to support the DHCP and DNS (and any other services) running on the server. Trending analysis in this regard is beneficial as well to enable proactive planning of future hardware procurements to enable load distribution among more servers.

Services Monitoring

Monitoring of the DNS service helps assure adequate DNS horsepower to meet the demands for name resolution and to help identify any exception conditions. BIND supports flexible logging of a variety of event types to a configurable set of output destinations or channels, including syslog, file, null, or stderr (the operating system's standard error output destination). Microsoft supports the DNS server event viewer with settable severity level reporting and counters for total queries/second received and responses/second sent. DHCP servers likewise provide logging to monitor overall service health and statistics, typically to a log file, syslog, or an event log. Components from the Elastic stack such as Metricbeat and Packetbeat also enable "logging" of server vitals and in and outbound DHCP/DNS packets.

These measures enable collection of performance data from the server's perspective. However, they don't convey the services' performance as experienced by DHCP clients and DNS resolvers. Measuring client performance requires the remote issuance of a DNS query or Discover/Solicit packet and measuring the response time for receipt of a proper response. As mentioned in the fault management section, the absence of a response may indicate a services outage and should be investigated if it persists. This remote issuance could originate from services probes deployed in various locations to generate these "synthetic transactions" and measure and store response time results. Analyzing historical data from different probes can provide keen insight into DNS/DHCP services and network performance.

Address Capacity Management

Overall, IP address capacity monitoring is another key IPAM performance management function. Along the lines of inventory assurance, tracking address utilization from devices manually addressed, autoconfigured, as well as those obtaining addresses via DHCP, enables proactive management of address space. Address allocations are initially based on estimated forecasts, which hopefully are accurate. Even when the forecast is perfect however, IP network dynamics due to employee movement, new services, cloud deployments, large events, subscriber growth, and unplanned address demands can consume the entire capacity of a subnet and its address pools. Periodic monitoring of utilization levels on pools, subnets, and shared subnets, with historical tracking and trending can provide forewarning of a capacity crunch to trigger a supplemental allocation to expand capacity before it exhausts.

Many DHCP server products enable monitoring of lease levels by command line, scripts or SNMP. Microsoft DHCP also provides a general 90% alerting threshold, providing notification should an address pool reach 90% capacity. Other servers and IP management systems provide similar or additional alert threshold definition and application. It's usually better to be notified by an IP management or network monitoring system than by irritated end users attempting to access the network.

Auditing and Reporting

Most management systems in general provide some level of auditing of "who did what when" and varying levels of reporting. These functions, which could just as easily be categorized under Accounting Management, enable administrators to track and troubleshoot activity and to convey status information in report format.

Auditing of IP address usage, that is, who had a given IP address at a certain point in time is valuable information when troubleshooting a network issue or investigating potential illicit activity. Likewise, if you are attempting to track the history of IP address occupancy for a given device, reporting by DUID and IAID or hardware address is also beneficial.

Performing such auditing without an IPAM system may be difficult except for the smallest of networks. Iterative dumps of DHCP lease data to track dynamically addressed clients over time are necessary. The ability to search for a given IP address requires access to a single (or two if failover or split scopes is in effect) DHCP server's lease history, while the search by hardware address necessitates searching across all DHCP servers, assuming the device is capable of mobility. If you have several DHCP servers, this may be a tedious task.

Common reports of interest for IP address planning include the following, though your system may provide different or additional reports.

- Address utilization report – by pool, subnet, block, rollups through hierarchy
- Address assignment report – summary of assigned addresses by subnet or block as current snapshot and/or history
- Address discrepancy report – highlights of discrepancies between the IP inventory and discovered IP address information
- DHCP performance report – summary and details of DHCP protocol messages by type and/or client and server key metrics summary
- DNS performance report – summary and details of queries by type, by querier, by question, and server key metrics summary
- Audit reports – administrator activity, by subnet, by IP address, by hardware address, by resource record, and by server

Security Management

Security is of such vital importance that we've dedicated three chapters to the subject, Chapters 10–12. These chapters cover strategies to secure IPAM components, to use IPAM technologies to improve overall network security, and to leverage IPAM in securing your Internet presence respectively. As server deployment strategies also play into both performance and security management, Chapter 14 covers these aspects.

ITIL® Process Mappings

ITIL, formerly known as the Information Technology Infrastructure Library, is a documented set of best practices for use by an IT organization desiring to manage, monitor, and continually improve IT services provided to the enterprise organization. ITIL was originally developed by the UK Office of Government and Commerce, and is now managed by Axelos, a joint venture company created by the Cabinet Office of Her Majesty's Government in the UK and Capita, plc. Its IT-service oriented approach has been deployed by a number of organizations. The most common drivers for ITIL implementation include the following:

- Cost reduction of IT services delivery to the organization
- IT service level consistency and improvements
- Risk management through disciplined planning and evaluation of potential service-affecting changes
- Efficiencies in utilizing documented processes and continual improvement

ITIL 4, the latest version, which was launched in February, 2019, is an evolution of version 3 [51]. There are many similarities between the two versions, but the major changes introduced in ITIL 4 include the following:

- The concept of "process" has been broadened to that of "practice," which defines a broader perspective and accounts for people, partners, technology, and processes.
- The service value chain concept has replaced the ITIL 3 service lifecycle in order to loosen the implication of an ordered serial process and to more accurately reflect the use of service value chain activities alone or in conjunction with others in no specific order to provide value.
- The concept of how value is created has evolved from that of being created by IT alone (service provider) to that of being jointly created by the service provider and the service consumer, which in turn comprises the *customer* or services definer, *user* of the service and *sponsor* or budget authorizer.

Many of the functions within these practice areas are identical or similar to those discussed earlier in the chapter, so we'll simply summarize these within their respective mappings to ITIL practice areas.

ITIL Practice Areas

ITIL practices are split into three areas: general management, service management, and technical management. General management practices focus on broad business and management areas. Service management practices relate to IT services management, while technical management deals with IT software development and infrastructure management. A brief summary of the practices that fall within each ITIL practice area and their relevance to IPAM is discussed next.

General Management Practices   *Architecture management* comprises inventorying all of the elements that comprise the organization and the interrelationships among them. Identification of such assets including people, technology, and processes enables an organization to manage complex change in an agile and controlled manner.

Tracking and managing IPAM assets including IPAM physical and virtual servers, IP address blocks, IP assignments, DHCP servers, pools and leases, and DNS servers, domains, and resource records fall under this area. An IPAM system that tracks the dynamics of this information is indispensible for accurate identification of assets that need to be redeployed, for example to address a business need.

Continual improvement focuses on understanding the current state of IT services, the desired state of such an assessment of how to progress to the desired state possibly through a number of steps. As business needs evolve and change, the desired state likely changes as well, ergo the use of the "continual" moniker.

An IPAM system can provide an accurate perspective on the current and predicted future state of IP address space, DHCP pool capacity, and DNS server performance, for example. Each of these items and others may require improvements to better meet the demands of the business, and understanding the current state helps to define incremental steps required to attain the desired state.

Information security management is focused on securing the information that the organization requires to conduct operations. This includes identifying risks, assessing the likelihood and cost of addressing each risk, and defining a plan to prevent, detect, and correct situations where such risks are exploited.

Part 3 of this book addresses various security measures that can be employed to protect, detect, and mitigate IPAM-related risks and vulnerabilities. Our *DNS Security Management* [52] book delves more deeply into DNS security in particular and applies the National Institute of Standards and Technology (NIST) Cybersecurity Framework Core to the practice of securing DNS.

Knowledge management entails assuring appropriate access to information and knowledge within the organization to improve efficiencies and decision-making. This practice implies providing simple access to information for those requiring such information without exposing it beyond the need to know in keeping with the security principle of least privilege. Your IPAM system should support administrator controls to define access by certain users to certain information for which they are responsible.

Measurement and reporting are critical to supplying the information necessary to detect fault or security incidents and to assure services availability and performance. You can't manage what you can't see. Monitoring IP address usage, DNS and DHCP server states and performance metrics, for example provides valuable input to assess service availability and assure operation.

Organization change management deals with managing organizational changes smoothly including managing human aspects of such changes as appropriate. Any changes affecting IPAM responsibilities of particular personnel should be reflected in system access permissions coincident with such changes.

Portfolio management practices are intended to assure the organization is supporting a solid mix of IT services, products, and solutions to meet its overall business objectives. As the scope of an organization's requirements for IT services expands to incorporate newer technologies such as IoT, cloud, artificial intelligence, etc., this practice would be responsible for managing IT services evolution to incorporate these requirements. IPAM impacts of these items in particular are covered in subsequent chapters.

Project management comprises the practice of efficiently planning, executing, and completing projects within time and budget constraints.

Relationship management focuses on the organization's stakeholders and manages these relationships with respect to maximizing stakeholder satisfaction through the understanding of stakeholder requirements, prioritization of IT projects, and effective delivery of products and services accordingly.

Risk management is broader than information security management in considering all of the risks and vulnerabilities to an organization, including risks to facilities, people, and business operations. Relevant details are covered in part 3 of this book.

Service financial management naturally includes accounting, similar to accounting management in the FCAPS model, though the financial management area addresses actual dollars and cents as well. This process area also deals with any chargebacks or cost allocations for certain departments under an IT funding or cost allocation model.

Some firms do implement cost chargebacks for IP address usage. In such a scenario, the financial management processes would need to account for tracking of IP address usage along with the corresponding user and chargeable entity (e.g. department). Depending on the billing or chargeback cycle, this IP address usage information will need to be stored for the current cycle and beyond to enable archiving or dispute resolution. Audits and history data in your IPAM system can be a big help with cost allocation.

Strategy management entails the enumeration of the goals of the organization and the allocation and management of resources necessary to achieve said goals. Each goal is distilled in terms of impacts on constituent organizations including IT, which must manage its resources to fulfill its role in meeting organizational goals.

Supplier management involves supplier contract management and the continual measuring of each supplier's performance with respect to meeting the objectives established upon contracting with each. Collaboration with key suppliers can facilitate improved value creation through joint enhancements or solutions.

Workforce and talent management practices involve assuring people resources are properly aligned with the organization's goals with respect to staffing and recruiting of people with appropriate skill sets for each job role, training and development, and succession planning.

Services Management Practices Availability management is a service delivery process area focused on making sure IT services are available to end users. High availability, a common goal for applications including DHCP and DNS, requires deployment of redundant configurations and the ability to leverage these configurations to provide continuous service in the face of a component outage.

Deployment of redundant DHCP and DNS server clusters, e.g. virtual or physical appliances, can provide localized clustering, while implementation of DHCP failover or split-scopes and multiserver DNS deployments provides an additional layer of redundancy. Redundant IPAM database deployments through LDAP, sharded clusters, or replicated relational databases can also assure availability of the IPAM application for managing IP space. Monitoring of the availability of each of these redundant components enables proactive detection of outages to facilitate rapid outage resolution (mean time to repair), while redundant components shoulder the load.

Business analysis is a key practice in understanding business requirements and fermenting these into IT requirements for technology, training, and operations processes needed to meet stated business goals.

Capacity and performance management simply involves assuring adequate IT resources of the proper type are available for the business to conduct its work. Considering the application of this concept to IPAM, certainly IP address capacity management springs to mind, but one should also consider DHCP and DNS server load capacity. In the former case, capacity management requires monitoring of addresses and address pools to provide enough IP addresses for employees to get an address and access the network. Monitoring for trends is helpful, and enabling alerting for low pools is also recommended for tightly allocated networks. Of course, given the magnitude of IPv6 address space, this will likely not be an issue for IPv6 space for most enterprise networks.

With respect to server capacity management, monitoring each physical and virtual server's network, memory and CPU utilization over time can provide insights into its load and performance. Such performance tasks may in fact be required as a linkage to service-level management in terms of percentage of transaction completion (lease or resolution) as well as response times. Regardless, excessive loads on servers can have detrimental impacts on the availability of DNS and DHCP services, so server monitoring and perhaps even probe-like transactional monitoring can provide effective measures of service levels and capacity.

Change control provides controls on the implementation of changes in the IT infrastructure. This involves assuring that all affected parties are in agreement with respect to the scope and implementation timing of the proposed change. In terms of IPAM, the scope of change management commonly affects IPAM components, such as the addition of an address pool, deployment of a new DHCP/DNS server in the network, or upgrading a server to a new software version. And some

IPAM changes require network changes, such as subnet provisioning or updating relay agent router configurations. Basically, anything affecting any part of the infrastructure, whether it's physical or software or even underlying appliance operating system, falls under the change management process, which seeks to assure all appropriate approvals are in place and corresponding back-out plans are available.

Incident management is a practice area which involves tracking and resolving incidents to restore normal services as efficiently as possible. Through incident management, IT can also detect and troubleshoot network issues proactively. Regardless of the means of detection for a given incident, access to IP inventory data is indispensible to troubleshooting and incident resolution. In addition, monitoring of server states with thresholds, alerts, logging information, and audits can provide a head start to incident detection and verification of incident resolution.

IT asset management involves managing the lifecycle of IT assets from purchasing decisions, allocation of assets as required, reuse, retirement, and disposal within the context of meeting organizational, contractual, and regulatory requirements while maximizing value, controlling costs, and managing risks. From an IPAM perspective, this practice must assure proper sizing of IPAM, DHCP, and DNS servers, trading off budget availability with performance requirements, among other criteria. Refreshes of hardware is also a critical component of this practice to assure hardware reliability.

Monitoring and event management entails surveilling all or at least core network components to verify appropriate performance and to detect state changes or events that may arise as they inevitably do. The goal is to identify events that could indicate potential or pending incidents or faults. Certainly, we recommend you monitor your IPAM, DHCP, and DNS services to identify performance degradation, communications errors, or other issues that could herald a server or service outage. This practice calls for initiating proactive measures to restore hampered servers while relying on redundant servers to compensate prior to and in an effort to prevent a full service outage.

Problem management calls for the tracking of known problems and resolutions in a problem forensics database. If someone calls into the service desk with an incident, for example it could get bumped over to problem management to identify whether this incident has been reported and addressed in the past. If so, the defined resolution path can be followed to quickly troubleshoot and resolve the issue.

While IPAM systems traditionally don't store problem histories with resolution annotations, some can provide a database of problem information through logging history, as well as inventory change audits. Some vendors enable access to general knowledge databases, available as part of their support services. Network management system integration through APIs can provide a holistic view of problem history by providing IPAM data through the API to a trouble ticketing system for example. IPAM is a key part of the overall network or IT service management approach, but it's not comprehensive; no system is. Having that integration is a key to garnering a holistic view of the problem management scope.

Release management is a practice area which provides controls on deployed releases for hardware and software versions, not only for operating systems but also for applications and appliances. This process area is responsible for making those versions available and accessible on the IT network and assuring there's an authorized set of releases and versions available that can be deployed appropriately.

Release planning, release management, dealing with upgrades, and patch management for DHCP and DNS services at remote sites and in the cloud from a central location can be a big timesaver. The alternative, requiring on-site upgrades of operating system, patches, and application software, is costly and time-consuming. Release management of the IPAM system also falls within this category.

Service catalogue management consists of maintaining a centralized repository of all services, solutions, products, and service components supported by IT for the organization. Such a catalogue documents the suite of IT services available to the user (customer) community as well as technical and organizational steps required for implementation of each to enable efficient and consistent service delivery.

Service configuration management is similar to the FCAPS configuration management functionality in terms of identifying, recording, and controlling configuration items (CIs) affecting IT services. And as we've discussed extensively in this chapter, configuration management functions are a core IPAM function. This includes configuring new address pools from a DHCP perspective, zones, and resource records in DNS, IP addresses for subnets on routers or cloud systems, etc. The IPAM database can be considered a configuration management database (CMDB) component of an IT's confederation of CMDBs for network configuration inventory.

Administrator controls need to be considered for organizations with more than one IPAM administrator to ensure that changes to DHCP and DNS configurations are performed within the appropriate scope and permissions. For instance, you may want administrators to be able to make changes, but not actually deploy them on the DHCP and DNS servers – restricting that function to a higher level of administrator. On the back end, audit information is key for accountability tracking and reporting.

Possessing accurate IP configuration information is necessary to provide a solid foundation on which future configuration changes can be planned. A corollary requirement leads to the necessity of validating that inventory against network actual data. IP inventory tracked on a spreadsheet is great, but requires constant manual updating. The ability to collect information from the network and compare it with the plan is crucial to automation and IP inventory assurance. Audits go hand in hand with inventory information collection. Arming the service desk with this information can provide a solid first line for addressing calls immediately, or to at least moving them through the resolution process more quickly.

Service continuity management is related to availability management in that it deals with providing continuous services. For example, in the event of a disaster, this process area would require a disaster recovery plan be in place. As discussed in the business continuity section earlier, a variety of strategies are available based on the criticality and scope requirements of the organization for particular DHCP/DNS servers and IPAM systems.

Service design is the practice area where technology solutions and products are integrated for the purpose of providing a given IT service to the organization. This practice requires creative skills for identifying service components, and associated suppliers, and potentially stitching together two or more components in a "service chain" to provide the overall desired service. Supplier management skills are required for the evaluation and testing of products as fit for purpose as well as integration capabilities in accordance with service requirements.

Service desk serves as the interface to the user community. The Service Desk filters input to the IT organization for incident reporting, change requests, and even new service requests. It serves to qualify and direct user requests or problems to any one of the other ITIL areas, providing end users with a helpdesk function.

The policies and culture of the organization will drive whether the Service Desk performs traditional "level 1" support only by logging troubles with subsequent follow-ups, or higher support levels, performing a thorough diagnosis. In the case of level 1 support, little more is needed than a ticketing system with the ability to assign tickets to those responsible for other process areas depending on the caller's issue. A service desk staffed to perform some trouble diagnosis will require access to status monitoring tools to try to "see what the caller sees" with respect to the issue.

For IP address or name resolution-related calls, providing service desk personnel access to IP inventory information may prove beneficial. For instance, if a person located in the headquarters office is not able to get an IP address, the service desk needs to know the address plan for headquarters in order to focus on the problem and trouble resolution process on that particular subnet, associated routers, or DHCP/DNS servers.

The service desk is the interface not only for trouble reports but also for change requests, such as IP subnet or address assignments. Providing service desk personnel with basic access to the IPAM system to request such changes, or better yet, enable end users themselves to register such service requests to an automated IT portal can increase end users' satisfaction with IT services through rapid fulfillment. As we'll discuss in Chapter 9, such a portal interface with linkages to your IPAM system can streamline the service request process.

Service-level management is a service delivery process area which encompasses the specification of service levels for various services provided by the IT organization. This is akin to a SLA. An example metric is the time frame within which an IP address will be assigned or a DNS resolution provisioned. Service-level management includes measurement of service delivery against these specifications to monitor adherence and measure the level of service that IT provides.

From an IPAM perspective, service-level management involves definition and measurement of the levels of service provided to those requesting IPAM related services, whether it be end users requesting an IP address or the business needing to open a new office. Treating end users of the business as customers, this process seeks to gauge whether service delivery is meeting defined service levels, such as timeliness of completion of these requests. Automating IPAM-related service delivery as we'll discuss further in Chapter 9, whether solely IPAM-impacting or involving IPAM as a component of a broader IT service such as VoIP deployment, facilitates timely and accurate services delivery.

Service request management comprises the handling of user requests for defined IT services, e.g. from the services catalogue. Establishment and measurement of SLAs for service requests enables the IT organization to provide a reliable service enabled in a timely manner.

Service validation and testing seeks to ensure the implementation of a new or modified IT service meets requirements set forth by the organization when commencing and deploying new development or modification of a service.

Technical Management Practices   *Deployment management* ultimately involves the "putting into production" new, updated, or modified software, hardware, processes, documentation, and operations-related practices. Prior to production rollout, this practice also entails lab testing and staging as warranted to improve the likelihood of a successful deployment.

Infrastructure and platform management consists of monitoring IT infrastructure and platform components with respect to industry offerings and solutions and how they could benefit the organization in terms of enhancing current services or otherwise improve the organization's operations. Such forward looking activities are required to maintain parity if not leadership with industry initiatives and trends.

Software development and management deals with design, specification, development, testing, delivery, and feedback/fixes/enhancements for software developed within the organization. Many IT organizations employ a DevOps approach given a well-scoped user community in general which can provide input and iterative feedback as software enhancements and fixes are released.

Conclusion

Designed as an evolutionary change, ITIL 4 seeks to broaden the perspective of IT services management to broader organizational goals and constituents, while building upon most of the foundational concepts and processes specified in prior ITIL versions. ITIL best practices serve as an industry benchmark against which you can measure the effectiveness of your IT practices and plan for improvements.

7

IPv6 Deployment

Given that IPv6 is *the Internet Protocol*, you may be wondering why we've dedicated a chapter to deploying IPv6. You may even believe that this book should have been written about IPv6 alone, without discussing the *legacy Internet Protocol*, IPv4. The reality is, despite these epithets, nearly every enterprise network as of today is comprised of IPv4 and about a third to one-half utilize IPv6 to varying degrees as well. IPv6 deployments continue to grow steadily as does the IPv6 density within the Internet, but why hasn't IPv6 achieved ubiquity?

Many organizations have deferred IPv6 deployment because the estimated effort to deploy and support IPv6 outweighs the perceived benefits. While IPv6 offers many advanced features, most of these have been added to IPv4 as well. Many organizations already possess sufficient IPv4 address space, obviating the need for expanded address space, which if needed, would most likely consist of IPv6 allocations; for all intents and purposes, IPv4 address space is no longer available for allocation. If you've been following along over the last decade or so, Dr. Geoff Huston of APNIC has published enlightening analysis updated daily at ipv4.potaroo.net [53] illustrating the rapidly diminishing IPv4 resource pool.

Recent estimates [54–56] agree that about 4.5 billion people have access to the Internet as of this writing. This tally accounts for residential users but does not consider corporations, governments, or other organizations. Given that several RIRs had exhausted IPv4 address space for years now, how has the Internet continued to expand beyond the theoretical maximum quantity of IPv4 addresses? Clearly, some proportion of these users use IPv6, while others share IPv4 addresses behind Carrier Gateway NATs (CGNs), which are massively scalable NATs that translate private IPv4 addresses into shared public IPv4 addresses. Some mobile and broadband service providers deploy CGNs to extend the lifetime of their IPv4 addresses. Each IPv4 address can be shared by thousands of individual subscriber devices by employing port translation as well. We'll discuss these and other IPv4–IPv6 technologies later

IP Address Management, Second Edition. Michael Dooley and Timothy Rooney.
© 2021 The Institute of Electrical and Electronics Engineers, Inc.
Published 2021 by John Wiley & Sons, Inc.

in this chapter. Ultimately, these "interim" technologies may max out in scalability, performance, and cost-effectiveness in the face of ongoing growth in Internet demand, creating a sudden swell in IPv6 traffic but time will tell.

IPv6 Deployment Process Overview

IP address planning is certainly among the critical functions required within the overall process of planning and executing an IPv6 deployment project. After all, one needs IPv6 address space in order to implement IPv6, and current IPv4 space must be managed in conjunction with the addition of IPv6 space. But the overall IPv6 deployment process requires not only IPv6 address space but an assurance that network and computing infrastructure is capable of processing and supporting IPv6 address space.

At a high level, the deployment process generally requires a computing and networking assessment, which entails the validation of IPv6 support for your network infrastructure, devices, and applications. Such validation starts with an accurate inventory of said infrastructure, devices, and applications. If you already maintain up-to-date network documentation including this information, you have already completed the first step. Otherwise, various forms of discovery may be required to identify and catalog these elements of your network. While you're performing device and application discovery, it's a good idea to also discover and document your current IPv4 address space as well which will come in handy later.

With an itemized network infrastructure document in hand, the next step in planning your deployment consists of identifying IPv6 capability. This step may rely on respective vendor statements of compatibility or support at least initially, but ultimately will require testing prior to production rollout. For each network and computing component, you'll need to validate IPv6 capability or determine mitigation steps required to bring the current state of a component to support IPv6. Such mitigation may entail a software upgrade, replacement, or supplementation, e.g. in the case of supplementing DHCPv4 servers with DHCPv6 servers.

Upon completion of your review and assessment of your computing inventory, you'll end up with two lists: one consisting of your IPv6-ready components and the other of your IPv6 "to do" list itemizing those elements requiring upgrade, replacement, or supplementation. IPv6 has been around for quite some time, at least as a set of specifications, so vendors have had time to implement IPv6 support and hopefully most if not all of your components are IPv6 capable today. If not, you may have to prioritize your "to do" list based on the magnitude of the list along with your available resources. This may require scoping of your deployment to a finite region of your network, which is probably a good idea in any case to deploy initially within a controlled scope.

You'll then be able to create a project plan based on your scope and "to do" list, including lab testing to validate IPv6 capability and to prepare operationally prior to production. Your plan also needs to include your strategy for allocating your IPv6 address space and for managing your IPv4–IPv6 network. Plan to obtain an IPv6 address block from your ISP or RIR.

With an IPv6 address block in hand, how should you carve this up to support your IPv6 deployment? Certainly, you'll need to allocate IPv6 space in a manner that provides IPv6 address availability to those infrastructure and computing devices requiring IPv6 communications. This is where your IPv4 address space documentation or discovery can help in identifying IP address capacity requirements. But before you carve up your IPv6 address space in a manner analogous to your IPv4 space, consider the many other implications of IP address allocation and network management, discussed next.

IPv6 Address Plan Objectives

As we discussed in Chapter 6, your IP address plan is vital not only to making sure network devices are uniquely addressed but also to facilitating ongoing management of your network. We'll walk through specific examples illustrating these concepts in more detail, but first let's review the objectives of an IP address plan.

- Provide address capacity
  The fundamental goal of an IP address plan is to provide IP addresses to infrastructure and end-user devices. Without an IP address, a device by definition cannot communicate on an IP network. Of course, you may want to control which devices obtain IP addresses and also structure your IP address space to streamline routing performance and ongoing operational tasks.
- Enable end nodes to communicate (or not)
  Not every device obtaining an IP address on your network should necessarily possess the capability to communicate with any other IP address on your network. Controlling access to sensitive systems and applications is a network management necessity and is typically based on IP addresses, e.g. controlling which source IP addresses can reach given destination IP addresses. And in the age of mobility and cloud, controlling access from end-user devices represents an opportunity for an additional layer of access controls.
- Enable Internet communications (or not)
  Most enterprises enable internal users to communicate to Internet hosts, though the set of destination hosts may also be constrained due to security or corporate policies implemented in Internet routers. User devices or visitors may be granted access only to Internet destinations.

Inbound communications from the Internet is generally controlled through the deployment of a "demilitarized zone" (DMZ) where external facing web, email, DNS, and other Internet servers are deployed "in front of" an enterprise network gateway which constrains access from Internet source addresses. Thus, these policies are likewise dependent on the IP address plan.

- Enable communications via supported applications
  IP networks supporting multimedia communications impose different traffic flow and response time requirements. Voice communications generally require low latency though occasional intermittent packet drops are tolerable; meanwhile, data communications are more tolerant to higher latency but less so to packet drops in general, though this also depends on the particular data application in question.

  Satisfying media-specific communications requirements generally involves configuration of routers to provide application specific treatment. And in many cases, the router is configured to recognize a given application for treatment based on the source and/or destination IP addresses in each IP packet it processes.
- Facilitate a visual mapping of IPv6 address to location, application, node, etc.
  If you've been managing your IPv4 network for a while, you can probably classify an IPv4 address by sight with respect to its respective location, application, or even node type (router, switch, server, etc.). A well-structured IP address plan promotes this ability to visually identify node properties from its IP address, as this can help improve manageability and reduce troubleshooting time.

  While it may seem simple to map the value of up to four decimal numbers within a dotted-decimal IPv4 address to a given property, mapping a much lengthier hexadecimal IPv6 address may seem intimidating. But as we'll see, a well-constructed address plan should enable such recognition at least based on a subset of the full address.

IPv6 Address Plan Examples

In this section, we will review and contrast two example allocation strategies to help convey the trade-offs in defining the order of allocation in terms of routing efficiency and simplified policy management.

Case 1

Let's start with a source IPv6 block, 2001:db8:1a::/48, as assigned by our ISP. We will allocate space successively for the following layers: application, location, business unit, and site. Let's perform our first-layer allocation by application: VoIP, video, data, wireless, etc. This will enable us to define one SADR policy across all of our routers for each application as appropriate. We have less than 16 allocations, so let's allocate the first nibble, bits 49–52 as follows, using the sparse allocation technique to allow room for growth.

Data	2001:db8:1a:**0**000::/52
Voice	2001:db8:1a:**8**000::/52
Video	2001:db8:1a:**4**000::/52
Wireless	2001:db8:1a:**c**000::/52
Management	2001:db8:1a:**2**000::/52

Our single video routing policy statement to be configured in all of my routers need only enumerate application to packets with source IPv6 address within the 2001:db8:1a:4000::/52 block.

Next, we'd like to allocate our second layer by region, taking the next nibble or four bits. These we will also allocate sparsely. For each application block defined above, we now need to allocate by region. Consideration our Voice block, our regions might be allocated as follows:

Voice – Eastern region	2001:db8:1a:8**000**::/56
Voice – Northern region	2001:db8:1a:8**800**::/56
Voice – Western region	2001:db8:1a:8**400**::/56
Voice – Southern region	2001:db8:1a:8**c00**::/56

We would repeat this allocation of four regions within each application block, assuming each application is supported in each region. With five blocks at my top layer and four in the second layer, we will have made up to 20 allocations so far.

Now, let's define a third layer, this one by business unit, and we'll use the next nibble, bits 57–60. Assuming each business unit requires representation in each region and for each application, we need to add each business unit to our 20 existing allocations. If we have five business units, that is 100 allocations! Let's look at the Voice – Southern region branch (2001:db8:1a:8c00::/56) and add our business unit allocations monotonically:

Voice – Southern region – Corporate	2001:db8:1a:8c**00**::/60
Voice – Southern region – Finance	2001:db8:1a:8c**10**::/60
Voice – Southern region – Marketing	2001:db8:1a:8c**20**::/60
Voice – Southern region – Engineering	2001:db8:1a:8c**30**::/60
Voice – Southern region – Customer Support	2001:db8:1a:8c**40**::/60

We have four bits remaining which we can allocate to specific subnets for each business unit with each region for each application. For example, if we have three subnets for my Marketing team for voice service in the southern region, I could allocate randomly:

Voice – Southern region – Marketing – Site 1	2001:db8:1a:8c**2a**::/64
Voice – Southern region – Marketing – Site 2	2001:db8:1a:8c**29**::/64
Voice – Southern region – Marketing – Site 3	2001:db8:1a:8c**2e**::/64

Observations

As you may have observed as we built out our example, successively drilling down, our subnet bits, particularly bits 49–64, do provide a visual mapping to a given subnet's application, region, business unit, and site. In our final allocation, you can see that the subnet "8c29" represents voice, southern, marketing, and site 2. If we've maintained uniformity in our allocations across parallel branches, we can also readily state that subnet "403e" applies to video (first nibble, "4"), east ("0"), engineering ("3"), and site 3 ("e") though with a random allocation my site number may not map analogously. But in general, the visual mapping goal has been achieved, and over time, you will recognize each by sight!

I could generally conclude that we should be able to achieve the goal of providing communications by our supported IP-based applications, given this criterion comprised our first layer. And my routing policy implementation and management is quite simple given one entry (IPv6 block) per application. Assuming I've identified my regions and sites according to my current network reach and capacity requirements, it's likely I can check off the goal of providing IP address capacity. In terms of route efficiency, assuming routers are conveyed at the region level, my core routers will require at least 20 routes in this example.

As for the goal of selectively enabling or disabling communications among nodes internally and to or from the Internet, my achievement of this goal is not so obvious. This is where you should consider those criteria that drive your filters and ACLs regarding constraining access by IP address. If you have a frequent need to throttle applications by policy or set security policies by application, then this allocation scheme achieves this with relative simplicity, with one block defined for each application across my network. Setting such policies for a given region will require five statements (a given region is defined in each of the five application blocks) in our example. In general, setting second-layer policies upon a single nibble first layer requires up to 16 entries. Setting such policies by business unit is more onerous, requiring setting of only 20 in our example but up to 65,536 (two nibbles' worth) of policies to define the business unit traffic per region and per application.

Case 2

Let's start over with our source IPv6 block, 2001:db8:1a::/48. This time, we will allocate space successively for the following layers: business unit, application, location, and site. Following similar logic to that discussed above, let's allocate as follows for our top layer, business unit:

Corporate	2001:db8:1a:**0**000::/52
Finance	2001:db8:1a:**1**000::/52
Marketing	2001:db8:1a:**2**000::/52
Engineering	2001:db8:1a:**3**000::/52
Customer Support	2001:db8:1a:**4**000::/52

Our next layer is application, so considering application allocations within our Engineering block:

Engineering – Data	2001:db8:1a:3**0**00::/56
Engineering – Voice	2001:db8:1a:3**8**00::/56
Engineering – Video	2001:db8:1a:3**4**00::/56
Engineering – Wireless	2001:db8:1a:3**c**00::/56
Engineering – Management	2001:db8:1a:3**2**00::/56

We allocate by region as our third layer, so drilling into Engineering – Data, we have:

Engineering – Data – Eastern region	2001:db8:1a:30**0**0::/60
Engineering – Data – Northern region	2001:db8:1a:30**8**0::/60
Engineering – Data – Western region	2001:db8:1a:30**4**0::/60
Engineering – Data – Southern region	2001:db8:1a:30**c**0::/60

And finally by site, considering our Engineering – Data – Northern region block:

Engineering – Data – Northern region – Site 0	2001:db8:1a:308**0**::/64
Engineering – Data – Northern region – Site 1	2001:db8:1a:308**1**::/64
Engineering – Data – Northern region – Site 2	2001:db8:1a:308**2**::/64

Observations

As in Case 1, our nibble-based allocation has again yielded a visually discernible classification of a subnet by business unit, application, region, and site, which should generally facilitate manageability. We may also surmise that our goals of providing for capacity and applications use have likewise been satisfied. Our route efficiency, again assuming a route is required at the core for each regional level, has suffered as we now have 100 unique region entries, one per application per business unit.

Regarding our routing and security policies, this case certainly simplifies setting of policies by business unit, with one block for each. This comes at the expense of increasing the effort to institute application-based policies and further complicates regional-based policies. In general, the number of policy entries at each level for a given criterion is calculated as the product of the number of allocations of each layer above in the allocation hierarchy.

General IPv6 Address Plan Guidelines

As you begin preparing your IPv6 address plan, keep in mind there is no "cookie-cutter" solution and each address planner must consider and trade-off several factors as illustrated above. Think about your router topology and relative importance of constraining router table sizes. Consider the applications supported by your network, particularly those utilizing IP-based routing treatment. Identify and prioritize your frequent management and security processes and requirements. Review the goals we discussed earlier and define those that are most important to you.

In terms of allocation layers and address block structure, you should consider your current IPv4 structure as a data point, not necessarily as a model. You may wish to allocate an IPv6 subnet for every IPv4 subnet you've allocated, but you may be able to consolidate subnet addresses given the vast size of a given /64 subnet with capacity for 1.8×10^{19} addresses.

Your current IPv4 address space also provides useful information regarding IP address capacity requirements at the host level, helping define how many addresses are required in given locations and by application or media type. In general, it's a good idea to baseline your IPv4 address plan as input to the IPv6 plan, again as a data point, not necessarily as a template.

The following is a summary of key guidelines when defining your IPv6 address plan.

- Baseline your IPv4 address space in terms of documenting your IP blocks, subnets, host assignments, and DHCP pools across your entire network, including cloud, IoT, partner networks and other adjunct networks. If you're using an IPAM system, this information should be readily available. Otherwise, you may need to run network discoveries to confirm and validate IP address allocations.
- Define all of your IPv6 address space(s) to be allocated. So far, we've talked about public space from your ISP or RIR and briefly mentioned ULA space.

Also consider if you use or plan to use any IPv4–IPv6 coexistence technologies besides dual stack including tunneling or translation techniques, most of which have implications on IP address assignment and formats. We'll discuss these later in the chapter. Your address plan should enumerate each use of IPv6 address space.

- Identify your network routing and switch infrastructure and document your network architecture, e.g. routing layers. Determine the level of importance of routing table sizes in your environment. The more critical for you to keep routes contained, the higher a router level allocation layer should be in your plan's layers.
- Enumerate IP address-based policies in use or planned for your network. This includes routing policies, packet treatment policies, filtering, ACLs, and other IP address-based configuration parameters within your infrastructure. Determine the rate of change or urgency to enact policies at a given level. If you plan to setup application-based policies once and plan no or minimal changes, then your application allocation, should you choose to include such a layer, may be deeper in your allocation plan. For those frequently changing policies or for potentially urgent requirements (e.g. to quarantine a site), consider placing allocations encapsulating the scope of these policies higher in your allocation plan.
- Define the homogeneity of your network. In our use cases, we assumed all applications were to be available at all locations for all business units. If this is not the case, then those more universal criteria should be higher than those more limited in scope in your allocation layers.
- Consider administrator delegation and responsibilities, especially if defined by IP addresses, and how frequently or urgently these are changed.
- Identify DNS configurations (zone files) recognizing that as you deploy IPv6, hosts will require IPv6 DNS resource records (AAAA and PTR among others). That is for a dual stack implementation a given hostname should have both A and AAAA records in the corresponding DNS zone. If you delegate DNS responsibilities within your organization, zone administrators may require training to properly configure DNS resource records and IPv6 reverse (ip6.arpa) zones.
- Evaluate alternative allocation techniques, uniform/monotonic, sparse, best-fit, and random, then define your approach for each layer.
- Plan to allocate on nibble boundaries to ease the allocation process, to provide visual address mapping, and to simplify DNS configurations especially for delegated zones corresponding to IPv6 allocations.

ULA Considerations

Most IP planners have become accustomed to the common IPv4 addressing strategy of utilizing private RFC 1918 space internally within their networks, and through the use of proxies and/or NATs, translating private address space to a smaller pool of public IP addresses for communication over the Internet. As such, NAT was an effective component in extending the lifetime of IPv4 as each enterprise required a smaller pool of public IPv4 addresses.

IPv6 does not suffer the scarcity issues of IPv4 and was designed to restore the endpoint-to-endpoint communications model originally intended for the Internet Protocol. Hence, use of NAT for end-to-end IPv6 communications is highly discouraged. While NAT functions may provide a sense of security by filtering and hiding internal addresses, IPv6 address footprinting is much more difficult, given the sheer size of IPv6 space. Privacy extensions to SLAAC also enable individual hosts to periodically change their addresses to further complicate the reconnaissance process for would-be snoopers. NAT devices also potentially interfere with end-to-end application performance and operation.

Public IPv6 addresses, otherwise known as global unicast addresses (GUAs), should be assigned to your devices. Filtering is recommended from a security perspective but not NAT. Hence, a model using ULA internally NAT'd to public IPv6 is discouraged. Nevertheless, ULA space has utility for assignment to devices that don't require Internet access or for use on private, partner, and VPN connections.

Note that you should still utilize a firewall to examine, filter, and potentially drop IPv6 packets, though it need not translate IP addresses.

Renumbering Impacts

Another goal of an IP address plan not stated above but certainly in the back of every IP planner's mind is to "get it right the first time," so you don't have to renumber your network. Renumbering of networks is generally a difficult and time-consuming project and should be avoided if at all possible. This is one reason we encourage you to take the time to develop your allocation plan, evaluate alternative strategies, and to understand the trade-offs made in your final strategy. Regardless, even with the best laid plans, unforeseen events occur and impact the network in such a way that a partial or complete renumbering is required.

An initiative as seemingly innocuous as changing ISPs may necessitate a complete renumbering of your network as discussed in Chapter 3. But if you've done the analysis in diligently preparing your IPv6 address plan, such a change in IPv6 prefix may be a simple prefix substitution (assuming the same prefix length) within the address plan, though actual device re-addressing must also ensue. The IETF recognizes renumbering to be a difficult problem to solve as indicated in the title of RFC 5887, *Renumbering Still Needs Work* [57]. This is due to the need to update devices with hard-coded IP addresses for communications, those for use within APIs and configuration files and those used by network management and security systems as well.

Note that these steps are required for your initial IPv6 "numbering" project, so we advise you to document your steps diligently so you can refer to them later should a renumbering become necessary. Though of incomplete consolation, IPv6 does support new helpful features in renumbering, namely router advertisements, SLAAC, and address lifetimes. Suffice it to say that you should think through your IPv6 address plan to derive to best possible address plan for your network, and document your process for possible future reference.

Take the time to carefully consider your IPv6 address structure and strategy to develop an address plan to facilitate your IPv6 deployment and management of your network in steady state.

IPv4–IPv6 Coexistence Technologies

Numerous technologies are available to facilitate the coexistence with and migration to IPv6 and/or to support IPv4 devices and applications within a network predominantly running IPv6. The approaches will be discussed according to the following basic categories:

- *Dual stack* – support of both IPv4 and IPv6 on network devices
- *Tunneling* – encapsulation of an IPv6 packet within an IPv4 packet for transmission over an IPv4 network or vice-versa
- *Translation* – IP header, address, and/or port translation such as that performed by gateway or NAT devices

Your selected strategy requires effective coordination of the following:

- IPv4 and IPv6 network and subnet allocations, existing and planned
- DHCP deployment for stateless or stateful IPv6 and/or IPv4 address assignments and configurations
- DNS resource record configuration corresponding to appropriate name resolution to address(es) for desired tunneling or translation
- Compatible client/host and router support of selected tunneling mode as appropriate
- Deployment of translation gateway(s) as appropriate

Dual Stack Approach

The dual stack approach consists of implementing both IPv4 and IPv6 protocol stacks on devices requiring access to both network layer technologies, including routers, other infrastructure devices, application servers, and end-user devices.

Such devices would be configured with both IPv4 and IPv6 addresses, and they may obtain these addresses via methods defined for the respective protocols as enabled by administrators. For example, an IPv4 address may be obtained via DHCPv4, while the IPv6 address may be autoconfigured.

Dual Stack Deployment

Deployment of dual-stacked devices sharing a common physical network interface implies the operation of both IPv4 and IPv6 over the same physical link. After all, Ethernet and other layer 2 technologies support either IPv4 or IPv6 payload thanks to protocol layering. Dual-stacked devices require routers supporting such links to be dual stacked as well. This overlay approach is fairly common in IPv6 deployments and is depicted in Figure 7.1. This diagram can be extended beyond a physical LAN to a multihop network where routers support IPv4 and IPv6 and route IPv4 packets among native IPv4 hosts and IPv6 packets among IPv6-capable hosts.

DNS Considerations

DNS plays a crucial role in proper operation of each transition technology. End users attempting to access a dual-stack device will query DNS, which can be configured by administrators with an A type resource record corresponding to the node's IPv4 address and a AAAA resource record type corresponding to its IPv6 address. The owner field of the resource record may have a common host name corresponding to the device per the following example.

```
dual-stack-host.ipamworldwide.com.  86400 IN  A     10.200.0.16
dual-stack-host.ipamworldwide.com.  86400 IN  AAAA  2001:db8:2200::a
```

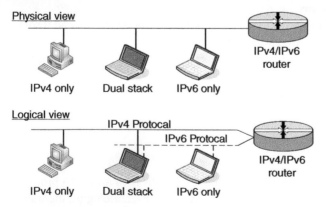

Figure 7.1 Dual-stacked network perspectives.

Resolution of IP-address-to-host name may also be configured in DNS within the appropriate .arpa domain:

```
16.0.200.10.in-addr.arpa. 86400 IN PTR dual-stack-host
.ipamworldwide.com.

a.0.0.0.0.0.0.0.0.0.0.0.0.0.0.0.0.0.0.0.0.0.0.0.2.2.8.b.d.0
.1.0.0.2.ip6.arpa.
86400     IN    PTR     dual-stack-host.ipamworldwide.com.
```

A dual-stack node itself must be able to support the querying and reception of A and AAAA records during its own DNS resolution processing, and communicate with the intended destination using the address and protocol corresponding to the returned record. Some resolver configurations may enable definition of the preferred network protocol when both an A and AAAA record are returned from the query, not to mention the protocol to use when issuing DNS queries themselves. In addition, as we shall see, some automatic tunneling technologies utilize specific IPv6 address formats, so addresses corresponding to one or more tunneled address formats may also be returned and may be used to the extent that the resolving host supports the corresponding tunneling technology.

The default preference is IPv6 transport if a device resolves a hostname with both IPv4 and IPv6 addresses. However, the recommended scheme per RFC 8305 [58] is to attempt to connect to the resolved host's IPv6 address, then to its IPv4 address a short time later, nominally 250 ms. If multiple IPv4 and IPv6 addresses are returned from DNS, the originating device should alternate IPv6 and IPv4 connection attempts down the list of addresses until a connection succeeds. The objective is to prefer IPv6 but to quickly fallback to IPv4 with minimal delay to the user. RFC 8305 also recommends issuing a query for the destination's IPv6 address (AAAA), then for it's IPv4 address (A).

In terms of IP version used in the transport of DNS queries and answers, RFC 3901 [59] (Internet best current practice 91) recommends that each recursive DNS server should support IPv4-only or dual-stack IPv4/IPv6. The RFC also recommends that every DNS zone should be served by at least one IPv4-reachable authoritative DNS server. These recommendations were set forth to provide backward compatibilty for IPv4-only resolvers which will be around for quite some time.

DHCP Considerations

The mechanism for using DHCP under a dual-stack implementation is simply that each stack use its version of DHCP. That is, to obtain an IPv4 address, use DHCPv4; to obtain an IPv6 address or prefix, use DHCPv6. Specifications have been defined for DHCPv4 over DHCPv6 or DHCP 4o6, which enables encapsulation of DHCPv4 messages within DHCPv6 packets to provide configuration of IPv4 information for devices behind an IPv4–IPv6 translator for example.

Configuration information beyond IP addresses is provided by both forms of DHCP, such as which DNS or NTP server to use. These server addresses are formatted within the same protocol version of the respective version of DHCP. The information obtained could lead to incorrect behavior on the client, depending on how the information from both servers is merged together. This remains an ongoing area of concern, as documented in RFC 4477 [60], but the current standard is to use a DHCP server for IPv4 and a DHCPv6 server for IPv6, possibly implemented on a common physical server.

Tunneling Approaches

A variety of technologies have been developed to support IPv4 over IPv6 and IPv6 over IPv4 tunneling. These technologies are generally categorized as *configured* or *automatic*. Configured tunnels are predefined, whereas automatic tunnels are created and torn down on the fly.

In general, tunneling of IPv6 packets over an IPv4 network entails prefixing an IPv6 packet with an IPv4 header or vice-versa. This enables the tunneled IPv6 packet to be routed over an IPv4 routing infrastructure for example; the IPv6 packet is simply considered payload within the IPv4 packet. The entry node of the tunnel, whether a host or router, performs the encapsulation. The source IPv4 address in the IPv4 header is populated with the originating node's IPv4 address and the destination address is that of the tunnel endpoint. The Protocol field of the IPv4 header is set to 41 (decimal) indicating an encapsulated IPv6 packet. The exit node or tunnel endpoint performs decapsulation to strip off the IPv4 header and routes the packet as appropriate to the ultimate destination via IPv6 (Figure 7.2).

Tunneling Scenarios for IPv6 Packets over IPv4 Networks

Using this basic tunneling approach, a variety of scenarios based on tunnel endpoints have been defined. These include router-to-router tunnel, depicted in Figure 7.3, host-to-router, and host-to-host.

In this figure, the originating IPv6 host on the left has IPv6 address of 2001:db8:f::1. A packet[1] destined for the host on the far end of the diagram with

---

[1]This packet is crudely identified in the figure as the solid-line rectangle beneath the originating host displaying the packet's IPv6 source address and destination address. The tunnel header is shown as the dotted-line rectangle in this figure.

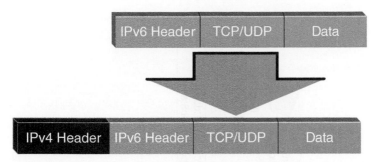

Figure 7.2 IPv6 over IPv4 tunneling.

IPv6 address of 2001:db8:a:ea is sent to a router serving the subnet. This router, with IPv6 address (on the interface facing the IPv6 network) of 2001:db8:f::2 and IPv4 address (on interface facing the IPv4 network) of 192.0.2.1, receives the IPv6 packet.

Configured to tunnel packets destined for the 2001:db8:a::/48 network on which the destination host resides, the router encapsulates the IPv6 packet with an IPv4 header. The router uses its IPv4 address, 192.0.2.1, as the source IPv4 address and the tunnel endpoint router, with IPv4 address of 192.0.2.254, as the destination address as depicted by the dashed rectangle beneath the IPv4 network in the centre of Figure 7.3.

The tunneled packets are routed like "regular" IPv4 packets to the destination tunnel endpoint router. This endpoint router decapsulates the packet, stripping off the IPv4 header and routes the original IPv6 packet to its intended destination, 2001:db8:a::ea. As mentioned, the tunnel endpoints may extend to hosts on either or both sides, using the same basic tunneling process.

Configured tunnels are predefined by administrators in advance of communications. In the scenarios described above, configuration of the respective tunnel endpoints is required to configure each device regarding when to tunnel IPv6 packets, i.e. based on destination, along with other tunnel configuration parameters that may be required by the tunnel implementation.

An automatic tunnel does not require tunnel preconfiguration, though enablement of tunneling configuration may be required. Tunnels are created based on information contained within the IPv6 packet, such as the source or destination IP address. Numerous tunneling approaches have been defined, so we'll summarize just a couple of the currently popular implementations.

Dual-Stack Lite

Dual-stack lite [61] is a technology that enables a service provider to deploy IPv6 within their network, while facilitating long-term support and efficient utilization

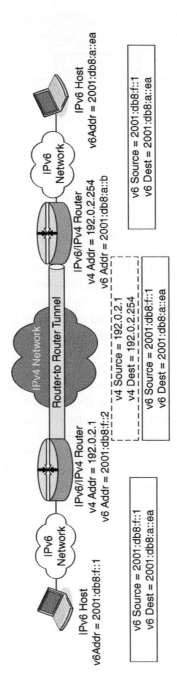

Figure 7.3 Router-to-router tunnel.

of IPv4 addresses assigned to customer network devices. Service providers typically assign an IP address to a customer router or gateway which interfaces directly to the broadband access network. The customer gateway performs DHCP server functions in assigning IP addresses to IP devices in the home network. The assumption is that such home network devices will support only IPv4 for quite some time. In this scenario, the tunneling features the encapsulation of an IPv4 packet with an IPv6 header.

The components comprising a dual-stack lite implementation include the following:

- *Basic Bridging BroadBand (B4) element* – bridges the IPv4 home network with an IPv6 network; the B4 function may reside on the customer gateway device or within the service provider network.
- *Softwire IPv4-in-IPv6 tunnel* – tunnels IPv4 traffic between the B4 and the AFTR over IPv6.
- *Address family translation router (AFTR)* – terminates the IPv4-in-IPv6 softwire tunnel with the B4 element and also performs IPv4-IPv4 NAT functionality.

Figure 7.4 illustrates the inter-relationship of these three components within an end-to-end IP connection. Starting on the left of the figure, the IPv4 host obtains an IPv4 address, 10.1.0.2, from the DHCP server function of the customer gateway. Let's say this IPv4 host desires to connect to a website, which has been resolved to IP address 192.0.2.21. The IPv4 host formulates an IP packet with source address 10.1.0.2 and source port of 1000 for example, and destination address 192.0.2.21 port 80. The host transmits this packet to its default route, the customer edge (CE) gateway.

The customer gateway in this example includes the B4 element, which sets up the softwire IPv4-in-IPv6 tunnel if it is not already established. The customer gateway has been assigned an IPv6 address on its WAN port (facing the service provider network), and it is over this connection that the tunnel is established. The customer gateway has also been configured with the AFTR IPv6 address manually or via DHCPv6 (option code 64). As shown in Figure 7.4, the B4 element encapsulates the original IPv4 packet with an IPv6 header and transmits it to the AFTR.

The AFTR terminates the tunnel and removes the IPv6 header. The AFTR then performs an IPv4–IPv4 network address and port translation (NAPT) function. NAPT leverages address plus port (A+P) addressing to effectively extend addressing bits beyond the IPv4 address field to all or a portion of the port field. The NAPT translates the original packet's private IPv4 source address into a public IPv4 address, which may be reused over multiple connections when used with a unique source port number. Thus, the service provider must provision a pool of public IPv4 addresses and corresponding ports which can be used as source IP

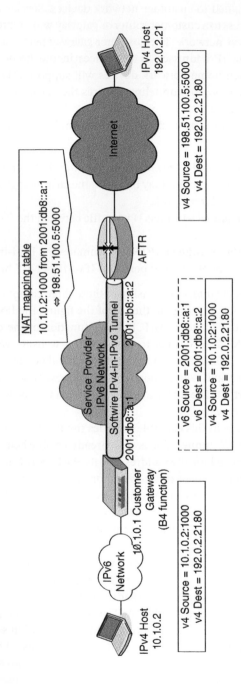

Figure 7.4 Dual-stack lite architecture.

addresses on packets destined for IPv4 destinations. The AFTR performs port translation as well and must track this mapping for each NAT operation in order to properly map IPv4 addresses and port numbers bi-directionally. This function is referred to as *stateful* mapping given the need to perform such bidirectional translation.

In Figure 7.4, the AFTR has mapped the customer's source IPv4 address and port, 10.1.0.2:1000 to 198.51.100.5:5000. Since customers generally utilize private address space where overlaps may occur, the NAT mapping table also tracks the tunnel over which the packet originated. The packet ultimately transmitted to the destination host utilizes this mapped IPv4 address and port, 198.51.100.5:5000. Return packets destined for this address/port are mapped to [destination] address 10.1.0.2:1000 and tunneled to 2001:db8::a:1.

Customers deploying native IPv6 or dual-stack hosts can have respective IPv6 addresses provided by DHCPv6 functionality implemented in the customer gateway or via autoconfiguration. IPv6 packets transmitted over the home network to the customer gateway would not utilize the softwire tunnel, but instead be routed natively over the IPv6 access network.

Lightweight 4over6

Lightweight 4over6 [62] is a variant of DS-Lite where the stateful NAPT function is shifted from the AFTR to the CE device. This decentralized approach obviates the need for a per IP flow stateful CGN function in the service provider network as necessitated by dual-stack lite. Under Lightweight 4over6 (lw4o6), the AFTR only performs tunnel decapsulation and IPv4 address and port (A+P) routing.

The "lightweight B4" (lwb4) devices at the edge performs the NAPT function and must be provisioned with its public IPv4 address and port set, the IPv6 address of the lwAFTR and its IPv6 binding prefix (tunnel endpoint address) e.g. via DHCPv6 or DHCP4o6. The lwAFTR implements a binding table mapping each customer's source IPv4 address and provisioned port set to its IPv6 binding prefix (tunnel endpoint address).

Mapping of Address and Port with Encapsulation (MAP-E)

Mapping of address and port with encapsulation (MAP-E) is comparable to a stateless (from the perspective of the network operator) version of lw4o6, where semantically the B4 device is replaced with a CE device and the AFTR with a border relay (BR). The CE first performs a stateful NAPT function, translating the original source IPv4 address and UDP/TCP port into a derived public IPv4 address and port; this translation information is derived from the

CE IPv6 prefix and basic mapping rule (BMR) provisioned for the CE. The BMR, comprised of an IPv6 prefix, IPv4 prefix, and embedded address (EA) field length, is the same for all CEs within a given MAP domain, meaning that all such CEs will be assigned IPv4 addresses from this common prefix, and many CEs will have common IPv4 addresses, but unique port sets. The CE-specific IPv4 address + port set identifier is defined in each CE's provisioned IPv6 prefix.

There are a lot of moving parts here, so let's consider an example [63]. Consider the following information provisioned for a CE:

CE IPv6 prefix:	CE's unique prefix	2001:db8:12:3400::/56
	Rule IPv6 prefix:	2001:db8::/40
Basic mapping rule:	Rule IPv4 prefix:	192.0.2.0/24
	Rule EA-bit length:	16
Port set ID length	EA-length − IPv4 suffix	$16 - (32 - 24) = 8$
Port set ID offset	Mask well-known ports	6

Each CE within this MAP domain shares the 2001:db8::/40 prefix. The bits between the rule prefix (/40 in this case) and the CE unique prefix length (/56) convey the EA information for the CE. For this particular CE, the 16 bits of the EA field within the CE IPv6 prefix that follow the rule IPv6 prefix bits comprise the 8-bit IPv4 suffix (in this case, $0 \times 12 = 18$, appended to the rule IPv4 prefix to derive the full IPv4 address 192.0.2.18) and an 8-bit port set identifier (0×34 PSID).

The port set ID offset indicated above with a default value of 6 indicates that $2^{(16-6)} = 2^{10}$ ports (0–1023) are reserved as the well-known port set, not for use in port sharing. In many cases, the port set ID offset is set to 4 to reserve ports 0–4095 from use by this MAP domain's port set configuration. In our example, with six of the eight PSID bits masked, each CE has a port range of four ports ($2^{(8-6)} = 2^2$), spread at consistent intervals across the port range, 1024–65535.

With a PSID of $0 \times 34 = 52$, the port intervals begin at $1024n + (52 \times 4)$, where $n = 1, ..., 63$. Thus, the available UDP/TCP source ports for use by the CE are 1232–1235, 2256–2259, ..., 64720–64723 (please see RFC 7597 [63] Appendix B for the details of the Generalized Modulus Algorithm used to derive these).

The CE's interface identifier is comprised of 16 zero bits, followed by its public IPv4 address, 32 bits in hex, and the PSID. Per the example above, the IID would be ::c000:212:34 and the CE's source IPv6 address, 2001:db8:12:3400::c000:212:34. The destination IPv6 address of the encapsulating IPv6 header is that of the BR, which will decapsulate the message and send along the resultant IPv4 packet to its destination.

Additional Tunneling Approaches

Several other automatic tunneling techniques have been contrived and are summarized following:

- *6to4* – 6to4 is an IPv6 over IPv4 tunneling technique that relies on a particular IPv6 address format to identify 6to4 packets and to tunnel them accordingly. The address format consists of a 6to4 prefix, 2002::/16, followed by a globally unique IPv4 address for the intended destination site. For example, a router with unique IPv4 address of 192.0.2.131 as a tunnel endpoint would advertise its reachability to the corresponding 2002:c000:283::/48 prefix. We converted our 192.0.2.131 address into hexadecimal, c0.00.02.83 and appended this to the 6to4 2002::/16 prefix.
- *ISATAP* – Intra-site automatic tunneling addressing protocol provides automatic host-to-router, router-to-host, or host-to-host tunneling; ISATAP IPv6 addresses are formed using an IPv4 address to define its interface ID. The Interface ID is comprised of ::5efe:w.x.y.z, where w.x.y.z is the dotted decimal IPv4 notation. So an ISATAP interface ID corresponding to 192.0.2.131 is denoted as ::5efe:192.0.2.131. The IPv4 notation provides a clear indication that the ISATAP address contains an IPv4 address without having to translate the IPv4 address into hexadecimal. This ISATAP interface ID can be used as a normal interface ID in appending it to advertised network prefixes to define IPv6 addresses.
- *6over4* – 6over4 is an automatic tunneling technique that leverages IPv4 multicast. IPv4 multicast is required and is considered a *virtual link layer* or *virtual Ethernet* by 6over4. Because of the virtual link layer perspective, IPv6 addresses are formed using a link local scope (fe80::/10 prefix). A host's IPv4 address comprises its 6over4 interface ID portion of its IPv6 address. For example, a 6over4 host with IPv4 address of 192.0.2.85 would formulate an IPv6 interface ID of ::c000:255, translating decimal to hex, and thus a 6over4 address of fe80::c000:255. 6over4 tunnels can be of the form host-to-host, host-to-router and router-to-host, where respective hosts and routers must be configured to support 6over4. IPv6 packets are tunneled in IPv4 headers using corresponding IPv4 multicast addresses. All members of the multicast group receive the tunneled packets, thus the analogy of virtual Ethernet, and the intended recipient strips off the IPv4 header and processes the IPv6 packet. As long as at least one IPv6 router also running 6over4 is reachable via the IPv4 multicast mechanism, the router can serve as a tunnel endpoint and route the packet via IPv6.
- *Tunnel brokers* – tunnel brokers automate tunnel setup by assigning tunnel gateway resources on behalf of hosts requiring tunneling of IPv4 packets over IPv6. The tunnel broker manages tunnel requests from dual-stack clients and tunnel broker servers, which connect to the intended IPv6 network. These

requests may result from an end user logging into the tunnel broker to connect to an IPv6 host. Upon successful authentication, the tunnel broker configures a tunnel server regarding the new tunnel, assigns an IPv6 address or prefix to the client, registers the client in DNS, and informs the client of this information.

- *Teredo* – automatic tunneling through NAT firewalls whereby IPv6 packets are tunneled over UDP over IPv4 for host-to-host automatic tunnels. Teredo incorporates an additional UDP header in order to facilitate NAT/firewall traversal. Many NAT/firewall devices will not allow traversal of IPv4 packets with the protocol field set to 41, which is the setting for tunneling of IPv6 packets as described previously. The additional UDP header further "buries" the tunnel to enable its traversal through NAT/firewall devices, most of which support UDP port translation.
- *Dual-stack transition mechanism* – DSTM provides a means to tunnel IPv4 packets over IPv6 networks, ultimately to the destination IPv4 network and host. The host on the IPv6 network intending to communicate to the IPv4 host would require a dual stack, as well as a DSTM client. Upon resolving the hostname of the intended destination host to only an IPv4 address, the client would initiate the DSTM process, which is very similar to the tunnel broker approach.

Translation Approaches

Translation techniques perform IPv4-to-IPv6 translation (and vice-versa) at a particular layer of the protocol stack, typically network, transport, or application. Unlike tunneling, which does not alter the tunneled data packet but merely appends a header or two, translation mechanisms do modify, i.e. translate, IP packets commutatively between IPv4 and IPv6. Translation approaches are generally recommended in an environment with IPv6-only nodes communicating with IPv4-only nodes. In dual-stack environments, native or tunneling mechanisms are preferable.

IPv4–IPv6 translation methods developed early on in the specification stages of IPv6 have proven inconsitent and in many scenarios insecure. Leveraging early "lessons learned," a new series of RFCs were published to define IPv4–IPv6 translation methods, addressing and consistent approaches. RFC 6144 [64] defines the framework for IPv4–IPv6 translation and defines internetworking scenarios for which such translation applies. These scenarios are instructive as they scope the applicability of translation approaches as summarized in the following table. Each scenario portrays the initiation of communications from a host on a private network or the global Internet of one protocol attempting to connect with a host on a network or the global Internet of the other protocol (Table 7.1).

Table 7.1 Viable translation approaches.

Scenario	Source network	Destination network	Applicability
1	IPv6 network	IPv4 Internet	Stateless translation approach is viable with DNS64
2	IPv4 Internet	IPv6 network	Stateless translation approach is viable with network-specific prefix
3	IPv6 Internet	IPv4 network	Stateful translation approach is viable with network-specific prefix and IPv4 translatable addresses or those defined in the translator's explicit address mapping table [65] published in DNS (AAAA records)
4	IPv4 network	IPv6 Internet	Translation NOT viable
5	IPv6 network	IPv4 network	Like scenario 1, viable
6	IPv4 network	IPv6 network	Like scenario 2, viable
7	IPv6 Internet	IPv4 Internet	Translation NOT viable
8	IPv4 Internet	IPv6 Internet	Translation NOT viable

Source: Based on Baker et al. 2011 [64].

Scenarios 4 and 8 are not viable, given the inability to uniquely translate an IPv6 address within the scope of the entire Internet into an IPv4 address representation. Unlike scenario 3 which is viable given the ability to constrain an IPv4 network's addresses within a single IPv4-translatable IPv6 address prefix, scenario 7 is not constrainable in such a way across the entire Internet address space.

IP/ICMP Translation

Now that we've introduced the scenarios under which IPv4–IPv6 translation is viable, let's explore the mechanics of translation. The algorithm for translating between IPv4 and IPv6 packets is the IP/ICMP translation algorithm specified in RFC 6145 [66], which is implemented on a host or gateway to convert outgoing IPv6 packet headers into IPv4 headers, and incoming IPv4 headers into IPv6 or vice versa. While the translation algorithm may be implemented on hosts (i.e. "Bump in the Host" [BIH] approach described later), we'll consider the case of a network translation gateway performing this function to simplify our discussion. The translation process involves consideration of address translation, packet fragmentation, ICMP mapping, and translation of IP header fields.

Address Translation

Address translation is defined in RFC 6052 [67] and applies to any entity needing to translate IPv4 and IPv6 addresses including not only translation gateways but also DNS64 services, for example. Semantically, an *IPv4-converted* IPv6 address is an IPv6 address used to represent an IPv4 node, while an *IPv4-translatable* IPv6 address is an IPv6 address assigned to an IPv6 node for use with stateless address translation. The former is essentially the output of a translation process, while the latter represents a premapped IPv6 address with an embedded IPv4 address.

Both have exactly the same format, which consists of an IPv6 prefix concatenated with the 32-bit IPv4 address, followed in most cases by a suffix. The only twist is that bits 64–71 (the first eight bits of the IID) are set to zero in all cases for compatibility with the IPv6 addressing architecture which specifies bit 70 as the universal/local ("u") bit and bit 71 is the individual/group ("g") bit, where zeroes in these bits indicate a locally administered unicast address. Depending on the length of the IPv6 prefix, the IPv4 address is inserted after the prefix and around this "U" byte as shown in Figure 7.5. Note that RFC 7136 [12] negated the significance of the "u" and "g" bits for IIDs not generated using the EUI-64 algorithm as in this scenario, but RFC 6052 predates this declaration and remains as specified here.

IPv6 prefix lengths must be defined as in Figure 7.5: 32, 40, 48, 56, 64, or 96 bits in length. A well-known 96-bit prefix has been assigned as 64:ff9b::/96, though this can only be used to represent unique public IPv4 addresses and generally only applies to organizations operating a translation service. Use of the 96-bit prefix must also assure zero bit values in the U field. For example, one could assign a /64

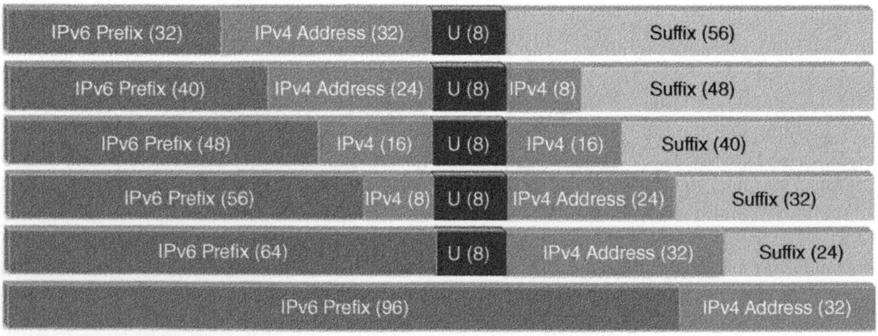

Figure 7.5 IPv4-translatable and IPv4-converted IPv6 address format.

prefix and append 32 zeroes to derive a compliant 96-bit prefix. But the concept is that an organization would allocate a prefix dedicated for use to represent IPv4-translatable addresses from their assigned address space, generally 8 bits longer than the total allocation (1/256 of allocated space, e.g. use a /56 if allocated a /48), and advertise this prefix if not already rolled up in an aggregated advertisement. The translation gateway would need to be configured to recognize this IPv4-translatable prefix and translate the IPv6 packet to IPv4, using the embedded IPv4 address as the destination address.

As an example, consider representing a host's IPv4 address of 198.51.100.49 as reachable through a translation gateway with configured IPv4-translatable IPv6 prefix 2001:db8:3a01:4f00::/56 prefix. Mapping the IPv4 address to hex, c633:6431, and appending it to the prefix while retaining the U zero bits, we arrive at 2001:db8:3a01:4fc6:33:6431:: as the IPv6-translatable address. In Figure 7.6, this is the host on the left, with only its IPv6 address represented. Its reachability in DNS could be published with a A record for 195.51.100.49 and a AAAA record for 2001:db8:3a01:4fc6:33:6431::. Likewise, the host on the right has IPv4 address 192.0.2.188 which can be represented as an IPv4-converted IPv6 address of 2001:db8:3a01:4fc0:0:2bc:: with corresponding A and AAAA records (or DNS64-generated AAAA records as we'll discuss later). Resolving this information for the IPv4 host, the host on the left sends a packet as shown in the figure destined for 2001:db8:3a01:4fc0:0:2bc::. Packets destined for 2001:db8:3a01:4f00::/56 are routed to the NAT64 gateway, which performs the IP/ICMP translation function described in this section, including mapping IPv6 addresses to corresponding IPv4 addresses as shown in the figure. If the host on the right was dual stacked and reachable directly via IPv6, the translation function would have been bypassed; it is only applied when no native protocol routes exist.

Packet Fragmentation Considerations

Packet fragmentation enables a large packet to be subdivided into two or more smaller packets to enable traversal of intermediate networks between the source and destination that have a smaller maximum transmission unit (MTU) than the

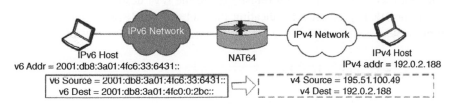

Figure 7.6 IP/ICMP translation example.

original packet size. With IPv4, routers along the path of a packet can fragment a packet if needed; in IPv6, fragmentation is performed solely by endpoints, not by routers. IPv6 hosts engage in MTU path discovery to ascertain the minimum path MTU to properly size packets prior to transmission. Hosts transmit packets to the intended destination initially assuming the path MTU is equal to that of the local link MTU; if an intermediate hop's MTU is less than the packet size, an ICMPv6 *packet too big* error message is returned to the host indicating the MTU of the offending link. The host may then begin retransmission adjusting the packet size to the indicated MTU size; this process may repeat if smaller MTUs further along the path are discovered.

IPv4 nodes may also perform MTU path discovery by sending a packet of the desired MTU to the destination, but because routers may automatically fragment large packets in IPv4, the host must set the Don't Fragment (DF) bit in the IPv4 header to disable intermediate fragmentation. Analogous to the IPv6 case, if the packet size exceeds the MTU along the way, an ICMP *fragmentation needed* error message is returned by the corresponding router detecting the issue.

When a translator receives an IPv4 packet with the DF bit set and the MTU of the next (or subsequent IPv6 hops upon receipt of an ICMPv6 *packet too big* message) is less than the IPv4 packet size + 20 (to account for the IPv6 header incremental size), then an ICMP *fragmentation needed* message is sent back to the source IPv4 address. If the DF bit is not set and the packet's size likewise exceeds the next and subsquent hops' MTU, the translator should fragment the packet. If the packet is smaller than the MTU, the translator may also be configured to add a fragment header merely to indicate fragmentation is permissible. The fragmentation header should never be included if DF was set despite ample MTU sizing for the packet.

When a translator translates an incoming IPv6 packet to IPv4, it sets the DF flag by default. If it then receives an ICMP *fragmentation needed* in reply, this in turn is translated to an ICMPv6 *packet too big* message and sent back to the originating IPv6 host. The originating host is not required to use a packet size smaller than the minimum IPv6 MTU of 1280 octets, but it will retransmit the packet with a fragment header from which the translator will map the IPv4 identification header value for each derived fragment transmitted to the IPv4 destination. In this scenario, the DF flag is not set indicating that subsequent IPv4 fragmentation is permissible.

IP Header Translation Algorithm

The IP header translation process applies the following field mapping on each packet. The field mapping is summarized below for both translation directions:

IPv4 -> IPv6 header translation

Version = 6

Traffic class = IPv4 header TOS bits or translator-configured value

Flow label = 0

Payload length = IPv4 header total length value – (IPv4 header length + IPv4 options length)

Next header = IPv4 header protocol field value (change ICMP (1) to ICMPv6 (58))

Hop limit = IPv4 TTL field value – 1

Source IP address = IPv4-translatable IPv6 address based on the associated IPv6 prefix and IPv4 source address

Destination IP address = IPv4-translatable IPv6 address derived from the destination IPv4 address (stateless) or a mapped IPv6 address based on the translator's stateful address maps (binding information base)

IPv6 -> IPv4 header translation

Version = 4

Header length = 5 (no IPv4 options)

Type of service = IPv6 header traffic class field or translator-configured value

Total length = IPv6 header payload length field + IPv4 header length

Identification = 0

Flags = Don't fragment = 1, more fragments = 0 (unless the IPv6 packet had a fragment header indicating fragmentation is permissible)

Fragment offset = 0

TTL = IPv6 hop limit field value – 1

Protocol = IPv6 next header field; ICMPv6 (58) is changed to ICMP (1) and IPv6 headers IPv6 hop-by-hop (0), IPv6-Route (43), IPv6-Frag, and IPv6-Opts (60) are skipped over as not applicable to IPv4

Header checksum = Computed over the newly formed IPv4 header

Source IP address = IPv4 address derived from the IPv4-translatable IPv6 address that falls within the IPv6 translatable prefix; or a mapped IPv6 address based on the translator's stateful address maps (binding information base) for the source IPv6 address

Destination IP address = IPv4 portion of the IPv4-converted IPv6 destination address

Options = None

Now let's look at some techniques that employ the IP/ICMP translation algorithm to translate IPv4 and IPv6 packets.

Bump in the Host (BIH)

BIH is a host-based IPv4–IPv6 translation technique that enables a host running IPv4 applications to communicate with IPv6-only hosts. The concept is to shield

IPv4 applications from any knowledge of the underlying IPv6 communications. The class of IPv4 applications for which BIH applies include those that use DNS for address resolution and that do not use IP address literals in application protocol payloads. Defined in RFC 6535 [68], BIH is not recommended for use in conjunction with NAT64, which would introduce double protocol translation, and is recommended only when native dual stack or tunneling cannot be used.

BIH is a successor combination of bump in the stack (BIS [69]) and bump in the API (BIA [70]) technologies. As such it incorporates a choice of either of these techniques where BIS translates IP packets in the IP stack (network) layer, while BIA translates at the API (application programming interface) or socket layer.

The API (socket) layer strategy, the recommended alternative among the two architectures, translates between IPv4 and IPv6 APIs and is implemented between the application and TCP/UDP layer of the stack on the host. The architecture of this approach comprises an API Translator, Address Mapper, Extension Name Resolver, and Function Mapper as depicted in Figure 7.7.

When the IPv4 application sends a DNS query to determine the IP address of a destination host, the Extension Name Resolver intercepts the query and creates an additional query requesting AAAA records. An affirmative DNS reply to the A record query will provide the answer to the API query with the given IPv4 address. Resolution of only a AAAA record stimulates the extension name resolver to request an IPv4 address from the Address Mapper to map to the returned IPv6 address. The Name Resolver utilizes the mapped IPv4 address to create an A record response to the application via the API. The Address Mapper maintains this mapping of IPv6 addresses to those IPv4 adddresses assigned from an internal address pool consisting of the private (RFC 1918) IPv4 address space. The Function Mapper intercepts API function calls and maps IPv4 API calls to IPv6 socket calls and returns results as in response to the IPv4 API call.

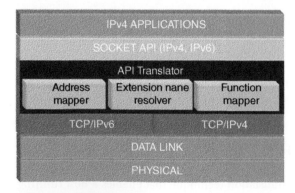

Figure 7.7 BIH socket based architecture.

The network layer approach snoops data flowing between the TCP/IPv4 module and link layer devices (e.g. network interface cards) and translates the IPv4 packet into IPv6. The components of the network layer approach are shown in Figure 7.8.

The Translator component translates the IPv4 header into an IPv6 header according to the IP/ICMP translation algorithm described in the prior section. The Extension Name Resolver snoops DNS queries for A record types; upon detecting such a query, the Extension Name Resolver component creates an additional query for the AAAA record type for the same host domain name (Qname) and class (Qclass). If no affirmative answer is received from the AAAA query, the communications ensues using IPv4; if both the A and AAAA queries are successfully resolved, the Extension Name Resolver instructs the Address Mapper component to associate the returned IPv4 address (A record) with the returned IPv6 address (AAAA record). If only a AAAA response is received, the Address Mapper assigns an IPv4 address from an internally configured pool of private IPv4 addresses.

The IPv4 address is needed in order to provide a response up the stack to the application requesting resolution to the A query. Thus, the Address Mapper maintains the association of the real or self-assigned IPv4 address with the IPv6 address of the destination. Any data packets destined to that IPv4 address are then translated by the Translator into IPv6 packets for transmission via IPv6.

Requests for PTR records that map a given IP address to a host domain name are handled by either form of BIH. The PTR call/query is intercepted and if the corresponding IP address has been mapped by the Address Mapper, a PTR query for the corresponding IPv6 address will be issued and the host domain name results mapped to the original request.

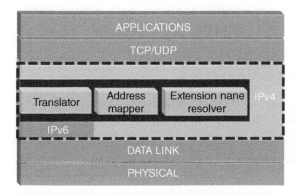

Figure 7.8   BIH network layer architecture.

DNS security extensions (DNSSEC) validation of DNS queries is natively supported in the socket version of BIH as socket calls simply request resolution and validation is handled at the resolver/network level. Support for the network layer approach requires configuration of the Extension Name Resolver with trusted keys to assure it can validate DNSSEC responses.

In the case of the BIH host receiving an IPv6 packet initiated from an external host that is not already mapped, the Address Mapper will assign an IPv4 address from its internal pool and translate the IPv6 header into IPv4 for communication up the stack.

Network Address Translation for IPv6–IPv4 (NAT64)

NAT64 is defined in RFC 6146 [71] and defines the functions of stateful operation. NAT64 enables IPv6 hosts to initiate connections to IPv4 hosts but not the reverse, barring an existing configuration of IPv4–IPv6 address mappings in the NAT64 gateway. NAT64 uses a NAPT approach which enables a single IPv4 address to map to multiple IPv6 addresses by virtue of A+P addressing, i.e. by differentiating the TCP/UDP source port number.

For example, a host initiating a UDP/IP packet with source IPv6 address 2001:db8::1 and port 4040 might be mapped outbound from the NAT64 gateway as having source IPv4 address 192.0.2.31 and port 2024, while another IPv6 host using 2001:db8::2 port 3701 might be mapped to 192.0.2.31 port 2025. This protocol mapping information is stored in a binding information base (BIB), of which three are dynamically maintained: one for TCP, one for UDP, and one for ICMP (ICMP identifiers are associated with addresses instead of port numbers). Likewise, three session tables, one for each of these upper layer protocols is maintained to track each session in terms of source and destination addresses and ports for the IPv4 leg and the IPv6 leg. In the example of Figure 7.9, a slightly modified reproduction of Figure 7.6, we've added port numbers, signified by the p=<port> notation shown within each data packet. If this was a TCP session, the TCP BIB would contain:

(2001:db8:3a01:4fc6:33:6431::, 1911) ⇔ (195.51.100.49, 3931)

And the TCP session base would track the entry:

(2001:db8:3a01:4fc6:33:6431::, 1911), (2001:db8:3a01:4fc0:0:2bc::, 80) ⇔ (195.51.100.49, 3931), (192.0.2.188, 80)

Thus, at a basic level, the NAT64 performs two main functions: IP/ICMP protocol translation in accordance with the discussion in the prior section and address translation to map inbound and outbound addresses. Address translation requires the NAT64 gateway to maintain two address pools: an IPv6 address

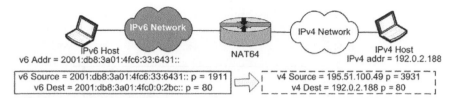

Figure 7.9 NAT64 protocol and address translation.

pool to represent IPv4 addresses within the IPv6 network and an IPv4 address pool to represent IPv6 addresses in the IPv4 network. The IPv6 address pool consists of the prefix allocated for the purpose of IP/ICMP translation we discussed earlier, e.g. 2001:db8:3a01:4f00::/56 per our prior example. The IPv4 address pool is an allocation of public IPv4 addresses for use in initiating IPv4 communications on behalf of IPv6 originating hosts, which in our preceding example was 195.51.100.0/24.

NAT64 and DNS64

As we just discussed, NAT64 translates IPv6 packets into IPv4 packets using the IP/ICMP translation process, with the optional addition of a stateful component, featuring an IPv4-IPv6 address mapping process independent of the IPv4 address being translated. Using either stateless or stateful translation enables an IPv6 host to communicate with IPv4 destinations.

Key to this strategy is the DNS64 component, which is a special recursive DNS server in that it processes queries for AAAA records normally and passes through valid responses for IPv6 addresses, but it additionally issues A record queries for failed AAAA responses in an attempt to identify an IPv4 destination address in the absence of an IPv6 address. If a valid A resource record set is received by the DNS64 server, it formulates a response to the resolver for the initial AAAA query comprised of the IPv4-converted IPv6 address in accordance with the IP/ICMP translation algorithm.

This process is illustrated in Figure 7.10, where our IPv6 host on the left queries the DNS64-configured recursive server for the IPv6 address of host.example.com. Failing the AAAA resolution, the recursive server queries for the IPv4 address of host.example.com, which resolves to 198.51.100.49. The DNS64 server is configured with the NAT64 prefix following our prior example, 2001:db8:3a01:4f00::/56, and synthesizes an AAAA response with the IPv4-converted address, 2001:db8:3a01:4fc6:33:6431::. The IPv6 host initiates an IPv6 connection to the resolved IPv6 address, which routes to the NAT64 gateway for translation.

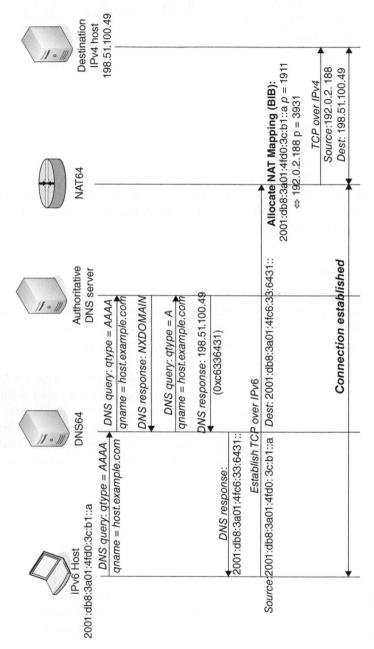

Figure 7.10 DNS64/NAT64 connectivity.

464XLAT

IPv4–IPv6–IPv4 Translation (464XLAT) offers an approach that concentrates a pair of translation gateways, an IPv4–IPv6 translator (NAT46) and a NAT64 gateway in order for two IPv4 hosts to communicate while traversing an IPv6 network. This approach applies in a wireless or broadband network, for example which is fully IPv6, but offers its customers to use IPv4 devices to access IPv4 hosts on the Internet. In the scenario, the NAT46 device, the customer translator (CLAT) function resides in the mobile device or customer premises access device.

Considering Figure 7.11, an IPv4 host with address 198.51.100.5 resolves its intended Internet destination to IPv4 address 192.0.2.21. Upon receipt of the IPv4 packet so addressed, the NAT46 function applies IP/ICMP translation, in this case using the well-known 64:ff9b::/96 prefix, to derive an IPv6 header encoding the respective IPv4 source and destination addresses. The NAT64 gateway at the edge of the service provider network translates the IPv6 packet into IPv4 for delivery to the intended destination.

Mapping of Address and Port with Translation (MAP-T)

Mapping of address and port with translation (MAP-T) applies the same IPv4 address and port mapping algorithm as MAP-E, but instead of tunneling the native IPv4 packet in IPv6, MAP-T translates the IPv4 header to IPv6. The source IPv6 address is derived in the same manner as with MAP-E. Another difference from MAP-E is that the destination IPv6 address is not that of the BR itself, but encapsulates the destination IPv4 address as an IPv4-translatable IPv6 address as discussed earlier in this section. The CE must be provisioned with a default mapping rule (DMR) in addition to the BMR to identify the "default route" to the MAP-T BR for stateless translation of the IPv6 packet to IPv4 for subsequent routing to its destination.

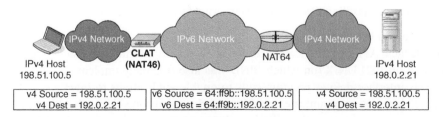

Figure 7.11 464XLAT translation example.

Other Translation Techniques

From a historical perspective, other techniques that translate IPv4 and IPv6 packets include the following:

- *SOCKS IPv6/IPv4 gateway* – SOCKS, defined in RFC 1928 [72], provides transport relay for applications traversing firewalls, effectively providing application proxy services. RFC 3089 [73] applies the SOCKS protocol for translating IPv4 and IPv6 communications. And like the other translation technologies already discussed, this approach includes special DNS treatment, termed *DNS name resolving delegation*, which delegates name resolution from the resolver client to the SOCKS IPv6/IPv4 gateway. An IPv4 or IPv6 application can be "socksified" to communicate with the SOCKS gateway proxy for ultimate connection to a host supporting the opposite protocol.
- *Transport relay translator (TRT)* – Much like the SOCKS configuration, TRT features a stateful gateway device that interlinks two "independent" connections over different networks. The TCP/UDP connection from a host terminates on the TRT, and the TRT creates a separate connection to the destination host and relays between the two connections. TRT requires a DNS-Application Layer Gateway, DNS–ALG, which acts as a DNS proxy. TRT is specified to enable IPv6 hosts to communicate with IPv4 destinations. As such, the primary function of the DNS–ALG is to perform an AAAA resource record query as requested by IPv6 resolvers; if an AAAA record is returned, the reply is passed on to the resolver and the data connection may ensue as an IPv6 connection. If no AAAA records are returned, the DNS–ALG performs an A record query, and if an answer is received, the DNS–ALG formulates an IPv6 address using the IPv4 address contained in the returned A record.
- *ALG* – ALGs perform protocol translation at the application layer and perform application proxy functions, similar to HTTP proxies. A client's application would typically need to be configured with the IP address of the proxy server, to which a connection would be made upon opening the application, e.g. web browser for the HTTP proxy case. An ALG may be useful for web or other application-specific access to the IPv4 Internet by hosts on an IPv6-only network.

Application Migration

The de facto API for TCP/IP applications is the *sockets* interface originally implemented on BSD UNIX (on which BIND was also originally implemented). The sockets interface defines program calls to enable applications to interface with TCP/IP layers to communicate over IP networks. Microsoft's Winsock API is also based on the sockets interface. Both sockets and Winsock interfaces have been modified to support IPv6's longer address size and additional features. In fact, most major operating system have implemented support for sockets or Winsock including Microsoft Windows, Solaris, Linux, Mac OS, AIX, and HP-UX. The updated sockets interface supports both IPv4 and IPv6 and provides the ability for IPv6 applications to interoperate with IPv4 applications by use of IPv4-mapped IPv6 addresses. Check with your application vendors for IPv6 compatibility and requirements.

If you are an application developer, you'll need to concern yourself not only with the TCP/IP API but also with the rendering, database storage, and user entry of IPv6 addresses. ARIN has published a useful guide [74] for application developers highlighting these and other issues to consider when developing IPv6 applications or porting current IPv4-only applications to support IPv6 as well.

Planning Your IPv6 Deployment Process

There's certainly no shortage of technology options when considering an IPv6 implementation approach. Having many options is good, but it can be intimidating. Selecting the right path will depend on your current environment in terms of end user devices and operating systems, router models and versions, as well as key applications, budget and resources, as well as time frames. Given the proliferation of dual-stack support in leading operating systems and networking products, a dual-stack approach will likely be the most common approach for enterprise networks.

For those who are skeptical about whether IPv6 deployment is necessary, we'd recommend at least scoping out an order of magnitude estimate of effort required to implement IPv6, should some Internet event or news inspire a call from the leaders of your organization to deploy IPv6 quickly. Deploying IPv6 requires analysis of your current IPv4 network, scoping IPv6 deployment, identifying upgrades or modifications to network equipment, applications or end-user devices, and managing the project to completion.

To begin the process, you'll likely need to justify the resource allocation. Capital outlay and expense payments to embark on an IPv6 deployment project or even the discovery and assessment phases of the project to fully define the expected costs to a high degree of confidence will need to be determined. Access to existing network and computing system documentation can help you estimate costs for discovery and assessment alone, or the entire deployment.

In terms of the upside, which is measured by increased revenue, lower costs and/or reduced lost sales, the following should be analyzed with respect to your business:

- Sustained or increased revenue growth especially if you are a service provider who relies on IP connectivity.
- Universal Internet presence if your organization offers products or services to consumers around the world. The opportunity cost of not deploying IPv6 is that

IPv6 "eyeballs" will never reach your site. As Internet growth is fueled over time by IPv6 users, these incremental prospects will be lost. Conversely, your internal users will be unable to access IPv6 Internet resources.

- Competitive advantage or parity, which can have amplified impacts if you're in a technology-related industry.
- As more employees bring their own devices to work, many current and future portable devices will be IPv6-ready. Many leading operating systems already support IPv6 by default. If you work with partners who have only IPv6 address space, you may need to support IPv6 at least for such connections.
- Network visibility to IPv6 traffic given end user device IPv6 support. Awareness and visibility to native or tunneled IPv6 traffic as well as external probes or attacks using IPv6 is necessary from a network security perspective.
- Supporting emerging applications that leverage unique IPv6 features for mobility and autoconfiguration.
- Creating an interesting and challenging work environment for IT or Operations teams. Managing an IPv4-IPv6 network is certainly more challenging than managing a single protocol network, but this can be rewarding for employees' knowledge and career growth.
- Supporting IPv6 due to regulatory or legal requirements.

You may want to qualify the opportunity cost based on the Internet's IPv6 density. For example, once the percentage of IPv6 users and websites on the Internet exceeds 40%, this may represent a sufficiently large population to justify IPv6 deployment to communicate with the full Internet including those among the 40%. This is a decision your organization needs to make. But whether that density is 51% or 99%, it behooves you to have in hand a plan to initiate the IPv6 deployment project at the appointed time.

The basic overall deployment process follows five basic steps as depicted in Figure 7.12. Assessing your network, identifying gaps, and creating a project plan are advisable for immediate or deferred execution based on your decision criteria. The authorization process seeks to secure internal resources primarily to perform the assessment typically based on a business case if needed, which requires a basic definition of the goals, scope, plan, costs, and benefits of IPv6 deployment.

The planning phase comprises four core planning aspects: network and computing infrastructure assessment and planning, IP address planning, security and network management planning. Effective planning leads to the deployment phase which includes an initial testing and verification process followed by production deployment.

Once in production, management of your IPv4/IPv6 network requires similar processes over managing IPv4 alone, though with a few modifications and additions. At some point perhaps in the distant future, IPv4 will be retired. It's hard to

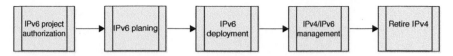

Figure 7.12 Basic overall process.

imagine this at this point in time, but some day it will happen, though probably not for another decade or two.

To delve deeper into IPv6 deployment strategies, we invite you to read our IPv6 Deployment and Management book [75].

8

IPAM for the Internet of Things

IoT refers to the extension of today's Internet beyond connectivity and interaction among traditional user-operated devices such as PCs, tablets, phones, and like types of devices into the realm of connectivity and interaction with nonuser operated devices such as sensors, monitors, and remotely controllable devices.

Internet-enabling such "unmanned" devices allows them to autonomously report updates, status changes, events, or to perform directed actions commanded by users or other devices via the Internet. The popularity of home assistants, security systems, video doorbells, thermostats, door locks, etc., evinces the expected continuing expansion of IoT devices within residences.

IoT also boasts exceptional growth prospects for organizations such as enterprises, educational institutions, government organizations, and others. While IoT applications such as remote surveillance and security monitoring systems for example apply to most types of organizations, particular IoT applications can provide expanded "eyes and ears" on buildings, factory floors, remote assets, etc., to help organizations improve efficiencies and reduce costs. Remotely accessible sensors or controls can increase the breadth and depth of an organization's visibility and control to achieve organizational objectives.

IoT Architectures

IoT devices by definition require Internet Protocol accessibility. Note that some types of remote sensors or "things" do not use IP protocols but can usually interface with an IP network through a border translation router, though full stack translation devices up to the application layer may be required in such cases. Fortunately, the IETF has published several RFCs defining an IPv6 adaptation layer to facilitate Internet protocol communications among IoT and non-IoT devices. The initial adaptation layer was focused on IEEE 802.15.4 networks but

IP Address Management, Second Edition. Michael Dooley and Timothy Rooney.
© 2021 The Institute of Electrical and Electronics Engineers, Inc.
Published 2021 by John Wiley & Sons, Inc.

has recently expanded to enable adaptation to other link and physical network technologies including Bluetooth.

From a network topology perspective, IoT devices could be considered typical IP hosts sprinkled across existing subnets as is the case with most residential deployments. Alternatively, one could allocate an independent IP block(s) to facilitate IoT application specific capacity, security, and manageability practices. Figure 8.1 illustrates a network partitioning approach for IoT subnetworks apart from the general enterprise network through a set of IoT border routers interfacing with the enterprise network. This figure shows an example where we've allocated two separate IoT subnetworks, perhaps to enable routing or control for different applications or security requirements.

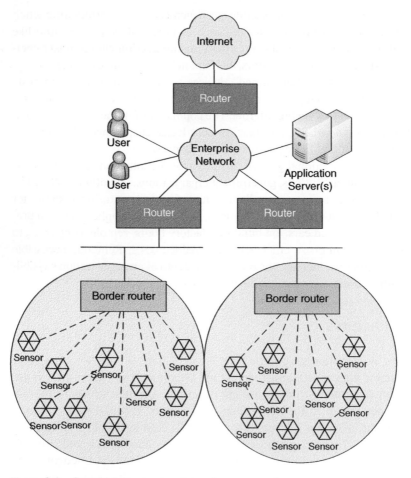

Figure 8.1 General IoT subnetwork topology approach.

Within this "self-contained" approach, IoT subnetworks are still interconnected to the internal enterprise network through one or more border routers without necessarily traversing public networks or the Internet. This architecture affords IT managers a deeper span of control with simpler IoT "containment" than they would have when connecting IoT devices deployed in remote locations over public or service provider links, as shown in Figure 8.2. In this scenario, IoT devices deployed "in the wild" interface typically via wireless with a wireline backhaul to a border router. One or more border routers in turn may communicate with the enterprise network via a VPN over the Internet or a carrier network.

6LoWPAN

Depending on your particular application, some or all IoT devices may need to be deployed in remote areas or harsh environments where communications services

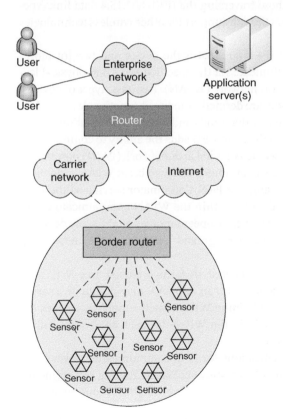

Figure 8.2 IoT remote subnetwork.

are minimal or unreliable. For example, pressure sensors may be deployed every so many miles along a pipeline spanning desolate territory to detect pressure variances which could indicate a fracture or break in the line. Such sensors provide the benefits of continual monitoring and early detection of such an event which could lead to detrimental consequences economically if not environmentally. Ideally, these sensors would be deployed and operated for years without requiring potentially costly on-site maintenance. This requirement necessitates conservation of battery power through low power consumption by limiting processing power and memory, as well as communications capabilities with short range wireless and frequent sleep intervals.

Devices sharing such characteristics are denoted "constrained" and the Internet community along with the IEEE have developed a set of protocols to enable full Internet protocol stack connectivity to such devices. The IETF's "IPv6 over low-power wireless personal area networks" (6LoWPANs) working group has produced several RFCs specifying Internet communications over lossy and low power wireless networks, specifically those traversing the IEEE 802.15.4 data link (specifically MAC) and physical layers though support for other wireless technologies has also been specified since.

The most basic component of IEEE 802.15.4 is the device and two [or more] devices which support and communicate via the specified MAC and physical layers comprise a wireless personal area network (WPAN). Two basic types of devices, reduced-function and full-function, are defined. A reduced-function device (RFD) serves as an endpoint such as a sensor that sends and receives information to only one full-function device (FFD) at a time. An FFD adds the ability to communicate with several devices and to serve as the personal area network (PAN) coordinator.

Each WPAN must include a PAN coordinator and two basic WPAN topologies are specified. The star topology features a PAN Coordinator serving as the focal point with which other RFDs and FFDs within the WPAN communicate exclusively in a hub and spoke fashion. The peer-to-peer topology enables any device to communicate with any other device in range and facilitates mesh networking topologies (Figure 8.3).

Peer-to-peer WPANs can be concatenated to form a cluster tree WPAN to broaden network reach. A PAN coordinator in one PAN may nominate another FFD as the PAN coordinator of an adjoining WPAN. Such a topology implies the likely potential for multiple hops within the WPAN to reach the border router, which brings us to the network layer.

RFC 4944 [76] defines the specifications for IPv6 communications over IEEE 802.15.4 networks and RFC 6606 [77] specifies 6LoWPAN routing requirements. Two forms of "routing" are defined in RFC 6606: layer three (IP) routing, termed "route-over" and link layer multihopping referred to as "mesh-under." The route-over approach could feature several routers within the IoT subnetwork, e.g. with

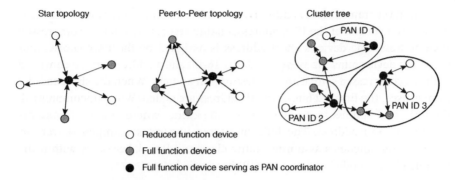

Star topology   Peer-to-Peer topology   Cluster tree

PAN ID 1

PAN ID 2   PAN ID 3

○ Reduced function device
◉ Full function device
● Full function device serving as PAN coordinator

Figure 8.3 IEEE 802.15.4 topologies.

devices communicating with PAN coordinators which perform basic routing functionality in routing packets perhaps via other routers to devices within the WPAN or to the border router to egress the WPAN. Unlike traditional routing, one or more IPv6 prefixes are shared across the multihop WPAN and does not necessitate a subnet allocation per constituent router/PAN coordinator. This multihop routing approach utilizes one or more IPv6 subnets applied across the entire WPAN. The mesh-under approach handles "routing" at the link layer within and across PANs within the overall 6LoWPAN and therefore appears to the IP layer as a composite broadcast domain or subnet.

Under either scenario, each IoT device within a subnet is assigned a unique IPv6 address, generally using standard IPv6 methods based on options conveyed in router advertisements, sent in response to a router solicitation from the device (periodic unsolicited transmissions of router advertisements are generally discouraged unless required by a particular application due to frequent sleeping intervals and to conserve precious bandwidth). When using SLAAC, the IID portion of the IPv6 address is formulated using the device's IEEE 802.15.4 64-bit EUI address or by concatenating the PAN ID, zero padding and the device's short (16-bit) WPAN address.

Given an IEEE 802.15.4 MAC layer frame comprises only 127 bytes, economizing protocol operations and required packet contents including the IP header, is warranted. Compression of the IPv6 header for 6LoWPAN was first specified in section 10 of RFC 4944 and later replaced by RFC 6282 [78]. The algorithm defined in RFC 6282 yields compression of the IPv6 header to as few as two octets for link local packets and effectively translates the IPv6 packet for communication over the WPAN between the IoT device and the border gateway.

6LoWPAN header compression algorithms rely on compressing an IPv6 address based on IPv6 prefixes registered with the 6LoWPAN via the border router. Such prefix contexts along with the deterministic relationship between the link layer frame (MAC) address or the WPAN short address with the EUI-derived IID portion of the IPv6 address, enable reconstruction of a compressed IPv6 address. The device's short address is assigned by the PAN coordinator when the device joins the WPAN and this 16-bit short address can be conveyed within a compressed source and/or destination address. When the short address form is used, the first 112 bits of the IP address are elided. When uncompressed, the link local address is `fe80::ff:fe00:xxxx` where "xxxx" represents the 16-bit short address. The following table illustrates examples of various compression outcomes assuming traffic class and flow label fields within the IPv6 header are elided and no next (IP) header is present.

Compression type	Non-address fields	Source prefix	Source IID	Destination prefix	Destination IID	Total header
Uncompressed IPv6 packet	8 bytes	8 bytes	8 bytes	8 bytes	8 bytes	40 bytes
Link local implied IIDs	2 bytes	0 bytes (fe80::/10)	0 bytes (derived from source MAC)	0 bytes (fe80::/10)	0 bytes (derived from dest. MAC)	2 bytes
Link local WPAN short addressing	2 bytes	0 bytes (fe80::/10)	2 bytes (WPAN short address)	0 bytes (fe80::/10)	2 bytes (WPAN short address)	6 bytes
Link local specified IIDs	2 bytes	0 bytes (fe80::/10)	8 bytes	0 bytes (fe80::/10)	8 bytes	18 bytes
Internet destination using context prefix and EUI-64 MAC	3 bytes	0 bytes IPv6 address decompressed as {context prefix}:: EUI-64 IID	0 bytes (derived from source MAC)	8 bytes	8 bytes	19 bytes
Internet destination WPAN short addressing	3 bytes	0 bytes IPv6 address decompressed as {context prefix}:: ff:fe00:xxxx	2 bytes (WPAN short address)	8 bytes	8 bytes	21 bytes
Internet destination full source IP	2 bytes	8 bytes	8 bytes	8 bytes	8 bytes	34 bytes

Though not an exhaustive enumeration of 6LoWPAN header compression combinations, it is clear that this compression technique offers multiple methods of IPv6 address compression with up to 55% header size reduction for communications with Internet (nonlink local) destinations.

DHCPv6 may also be used for device address assignment. If the 64-bit EUI-derived SLAAC or DHCPv6 assignment methods are used, DAD is not required. If other forms of assignment are used, e.g. through the generation of stable and opaque IID [24], a streamlined DAD process [79] must be performed.

The DAD process for 6LoWPAN networks uses a registration scheme whereby devices notify linked routers of respective autoconfigured IP address assignments. This obviates the need for multicast solicited node messages and accounts for the presence of frequently sleeping devices (for power conservation) by enabling devices to initiate the process. The address registration option (ARO) within the neighbor discovery packet enables a device to register its EUI-64 IID for the router to cache for delivery of packets to the device.

Another neighbor discovery option allows a router to convey one or more IPv6 context prefix(es), which can be used in conjunction with 6LoWPAN header compression. The use of a context prefix requires an additional 6LoWPAN header byte within the compression scheme to identify source and destination context prefix identifiers to apply to the associated communique (ergo the specification of three bytes instead of two for non-address fields in the previous table) when a context prefix is referenced. Any IPv6 context prefix may be specified in this option, enabling compression of non-6LoWPAN prefixes with which the device may frequently communicate.

The authoritative border router option (ABRO) is sent in Router Advertisements for 6LoWPANs and is comprised of multiple routers and/or prefixes. This option conveys the address(es) of the border router(s) that is authoritative for prefixes assigned to the 6LoWPAN, along with an advertisement version number to enable detection of changes in an environment of unreliable communications. This option serves to legitimize prefix changes, e.g. they can't be made under any other authority.

Figure 8.4 illustrates the neighbor discovery process in a multihop configuration. A device initializing will autoconfigure its link local IPv6 address based on its EUI-48 MAC address, and use this as the source address in multicasting a Router Solicitation including the source link layer address option (SLAAO) set to its EUI-64 address to the All_Routers multicast address. A recipient router would unicast a Router Advertisement response to the device and supply the following options:

- Prefix information option (PIO)
- IPv6 prefix context option (6CO)

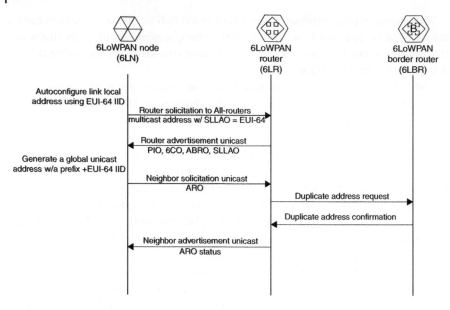

Figure 8.4 6LoWPAN neighbor discovery.

- ABRO
- SLLAO from the device's router solicitation

To communicate beyond the WPAN, the device must configure a global IPv6 address. It can configure a tentative address using an advertised prefix from the RA and an IID based on its EUI-64 or that constructed using its 16-bit short address to conserve overhead. The device then transmits a neighbor solicitation message with the tentative address within the address request option, as well as its SLLAO/EUI-64.

In a multihop topology the router receiving the Neighbor Solicitation issues a duplicate address request (DAR) ICMPv6 message to the border router. If the requested tentative address is unique, the border router replies with a duplicate address confirmation (DAC) affirming its availability and caches the address. The intervening router caches the confirmed address and associated device link layer address and replies with the NA accordingly. The device may then use the address for its registered lifetime, and may extend the lifetime by sending a NS with the ARO before the lifetime expires.

If the requested tentative address was not available, the border router indicates this in its DAC and the intervening router passes on the NA denying availability of the address. The device must not use the address and may form another tentative IPv6 address and restart the NA process.

As the authoritative source of IPv6 prefixes and routes within the WPAN, the border router translates 6LoWPAN-encoded IPv6 packets to standard IPv6 packets for communications with the Internet and/or internal IP networks. From an IPAM perspective, administrators need to assign an IPv6 subnet for each 6LoWPAN network using mesh-under routing and one or more subnets using route-over techniques. Individual IP assignments may be performed using SLAAC as discussed or via DHCPv6. Naming of IoT devices could be handled using DDNS updates from the DHCPv6 server to respective DNS servers if DHCPv6 is used. Otherwise, accessing 6LoWPAN router caches would be required to identify auto-configured IP addresses, and a method would be required to auto-generate corresponding host domain names.

Summary

IoT technologies enable organizations to extend their "eyes and ears" to on-premises or remote locations for monitoring, data collection, and controls. Performance of these functions necessitates appropriate IPAM configuration. In some scenarios, you may desire to allocate IP addresses to IoT devices as you would nonthing devices. In these cases, normal integrated IPAM processes would apply. Otherwise, the IPAM implications for segregated or field-based IoT devices include the following:

- Block/subnet allocation for IoT subnetworks
- DHCPv6 configuration if used though in most lossy environments, SLAAC would be more efficient for zero-touch bootstrapping
- IPv6 address tracking, particularly when SLAAC is in use. Periodic polling of border router neighbor tables can be useful
- DNS configuration as appropriate

9

IPAM in the Cloud

Cloud computing is transforming the means by which organizations offer and support computing and communications services to their users, constituents, and customers. The cloud enables IT or service provider operations teams to provide network, computing, and services capacity with flexibility, efficiency, and elasticity. These benefits are realized primarily through the cloud's characteristic use of virtualization technologies, which facilitates the rapid instantiation of additional capacity for a required service element within minutes. If capacity requirements fluctuate over time, capacity can just as quickly be withdrawn or allocated elsewhere. This elasticity affords organizations agility and cost efficiencies in offering network, computing, and services resources dynamically sized to changing capacity needs over time.

Enterprises can leverage public cloud services such as those offered by Amazon Web Services (AWS), Microsoft Azure, Google Cloud, and others. They can also build cloud functionality within their own data center infrastructure. Such "private cloud" configurations can be paired with one or more public cloud services in a hybrid implementation that enables the enterprise to support typical busy time services capacity while relying on the public cloud to support particular services and/or capacity overflow.

Service providers, inherently cloud providers by virtue of supporting networks and services external to their customers, can leverage cloud technologies not only for efficient services capacity management but also for rapid service deployment. Historically, service providers needed to acquire specialized hardware and software to perform functions required for new service offerings. Such capital-intensive investments were necessary to meet service providers' rigorous reliability, availability, and scalability requirements, among others. By virtualizing network functions (i.e. network functions virtualization, NFV), service providers seek to lower capital costs and accelerate time to market by focusing any specialized development to the software function only, while leveraging common robust hardware. Such software-defined networks (SDN) offer rapid, cost-effective, and flexible services delivery.

IPAM VNFs

Virtualizing IPAM functions themselves affords you the same benefits of elastically managing deployments for IPAM as for other network functions. Rapidly deploying a cloud DNS server, for example enables you to add flexible capacity to support a marketing event, bypass a server upgrade, or to manage a server transition.

Cloud IPAM Concepts

IP Initialization Process

As in traditional enterprise networks, network services are just as critical in cloud environments. Virtual machines (VMs) or cloud (e.g. Docker) containers (we'll refer to these virtualized platforms collectively as virtual network functions [VNFs]), require provisioning of basic IP network information upon instantiation as would any network device upon deployment on the network. As such, cloud-capable core network services are critical for virtual environments. Certainly, each VNF requiring network connectivity will require assignment of an IP address or in some instances, multiple IP addresses. In most cases, the VNF will be assigned a hostname such that it can be referenced by name as well as its IP address.

This name reference is necessary not only to simplify navigation by humans as mentioned earlier, being able to connect to a VNF using its name, but also potentially by other VNFs as necessitated by *service chaining*. For example, a series of VNFs may be required to provide a given service; if a predecessor VNF references its next VNF in the chain or series by name, this enables the provisioning of elastic capacity for the function provided by that VNF.

Consider the simple example in Figure 9.1. A given service requires in-band processing through two service components. The service provider[1] can manage the service capacity dynamically through the deployment of these service elements as VNFs within a private, public, or hybrid cloud deployment. A given user's data path may traverse any individual element as long as both functions are traversed. As demand grows or even spikes at a given time, dynamic instantiation

---

1 We're using the term "service provider" in a broad sense to include IT organizations providing networking services to their constituents.

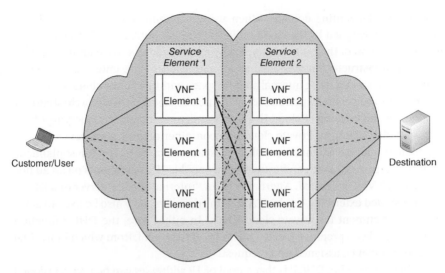

Figure 9.1 Example service serialization.

of supplemental VNFs enables deployment of additional service element capacity. When demand subsides, VNFs may then conversely be decommissioned.

In providing a service like the one in Figure 9.1, IP packets from each *service element 1* VNF must be routed to a *service element 2* VNF. Instead of configuring each assigned IP address of each downstream (*service element 2*) VNF into each precedent (*service element 1*) VNF, which adds effort, time, and the opportunity for error in the provisioning or decommissioning process, one can merely add or remove the created or destroyed VNF's IP address from a DNS entry for the given function. Thus, a "function" entry in DNS such as `service-element-2.example.com` can resolve to one, two, or any number of IP addresses, i.e. one per actively provisioned VNF's resource record set.

As capacity fluctuates based on demand, correspondingly active VNF IP addresses can simply be updated in DNS within the function's resource record set. For each new customer flow, the VNF need only query DNS to identify a successive node in the path. Of course, if a deterministic flow among VNFs is required for the service, each VNF's unique host domain name and IP address association may be published in DNS instead.

IP Initialization Implementation

Let's consider some approaches to configuring these key network parameters during the process of instantiating a VNF. Among other parameters, each VNF, technically each VNF interface, requires assignment of a unique IP address, unique at least within the routing domain. When using a public cloud service, public IP addresses are assigned by the cloud provider, while a public cloud customer may allocate a portion of their internal (typically private) address space for use for public cloud infrastructure provisioned as an extension of the enterprise network. However, even when using internal address space within a public cloud, IP address assignments are generally performed by the public cloud platform orchestrator or API; hence, the tracking of cloud IP address assignments requires querying of the corresponding platform. Private cloud and container orchestrators generally also automate IP address assignments within the space allocated by IP address planners.

In-house (private cloud) orchestrators may enable IP assignments on an ad hoc basis as each VNF is created. Alternatively, an "internal" DHCP server or a DHCP server operated externally, e.g. by IPAM administrators, may also be used to automate IP assignment for private cloud VNFs. In either case, the DHCP function needs to have been preprovisioned with an IP address pool, from which individual IP addresses can be assigned upon request.

The benefit of using DHCP is that a pool of IP addresses can be preprovisioned and assigned to VNFs on the fly as capacity needs dictate. Another benefit is that additional IP initialization parameters, such as a bootfile location, can be communicated to the requesting device via DHCP options included with the assigned IP address. The downside is that the DHCP pools must be monitored to assure IP address availability upon demand; if an address pool depletes of its IP addresses, additionally created VNFs will be unable to obtain an IP address and successfully initialize for network communications. Also, some cloud providers, namely Microsoft Azure explicitly block DHCP traffic. If DHCP is not used, then a means to assign a static IP address to each VNF upon instantiation is required. This may necessitate a manual lookup in a spreadsheet or an automated link to an IPAM system as we'll discuss later.

Using either method for IP address assignment, DHCP or static, an entry in DNS is also likely needed for reasons discussed previously. Updating DNS requires entry of the assigned IP address in association with the VNF hostname or function name within the DNS configuration. Such entry can be performed manually by editing the appropriate DNS zone file or by performing an update via a utility like nsupdate. Alternatively, if DHCP is used to assign the VNF IP address, it can automatically update DNS, though mapping the IP address to the individual VNF host name, not to a broader service name.

DHCP Method

Let's consider the process flow for initializing the IP configuration using DHCP as outlined in Figure 9.2. Along the top of the figure, our three basic macro-level steps entail preparation to instantiate the VNF, followed by the action of instantiation,

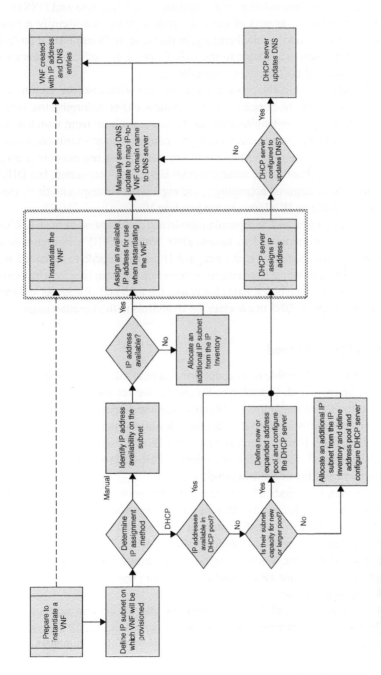

Figure 9.2 IP initialization using DHCP.

then by completion of instantiation with a unique valid IP address and DNS entry. Supporting this process, as part of the preparation phase, we identify *a priori* which assignment method we shall employ. In this case, we'll use DHCP, so there needs to be an IP address available in the DHCP pool with addresses relevant to the subnet on which the VNF is to be provisioned.

If an address is available, the process may continue; otherwise, we need to supplement the pool capacity. Supplementation entails either enlarging the size of the current address pool or by allocating an additional subnet from which a pool can be defined. A DHCP server can typically be configured with multiple subnets as "shared subnets," where multiple pools are considered common to a given physical or virtual subnet. Once adequate pool sizing has completed, the DHCP server needs to be configured according to the expansion strategy, and then it will be ready to distribute an IP address to the pending VNF.

The VNF can be created and configured to obtain an IP address(es) from DHCP. The DHCP server can be configured to update DNS with the VNF's hostname-to-IP address mapping automatically. If the assigned IP address needs to be added to a functional DNS resolution, e.g. `service-element2.example.com`, this entry may likely require manual entry. First, determine the assigned IP address and then create an entry to update DNS to associate the IP address to the function name.

Private Cloud Static Method

If use of DHCP is undesirable or not supported, a manual IP address assignment method may be employed. Considering Figure 9.3, we see the same three macro-level steps at the top of the figure. In this case, our assignment method is manual, so we must next identify an IP address for the relevant subnet that can be assigned to the pending VNF. If our inventory of subnet IP addresses indicates a free IP address, the chosen IP address should be denoted as used to prevent future erroneous assignment of the address in duplication.

It's a good idea to periodically validate your inventory by comparing it with actual IP assignments, discernable by pinging or otherwise communicating with each host on the subnet or ideally using an orchestrator API. This "discovery" process helps identify those host IP addresses that perhaps were inadvertently not recorded as in-use or those that were unilaterally assigned outside of the process. The assignment of the same IP address to two or more hosts will render neither of them able to communicate.

If an IP address is not available for assignment, allocation of an additional subnet may be required. This action too necessitates consulting the IP address space inventory to identify a free subnet that can be assigned. Once assigned and provisioned, an available IP address from the subnet may be recorded then assigned to the VNF pending instantiation. This IP address with hostname and/or function

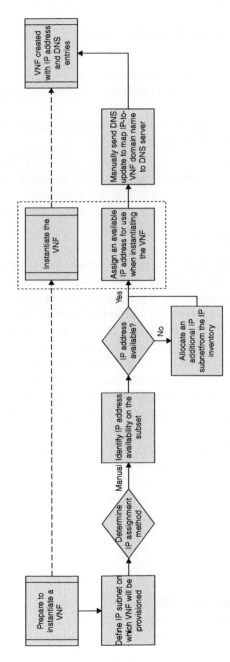

Figure 9.3 IP initialization using manual assignment.

name mapping should also be updated in DNS using *nsupdate*, an IPAM system, or similar utility.

Both the DHCP and manual IP approach have several potential issues, summarized as follows:

- For DHCP, pools must be monitored proactively so IP addresses are available on demand; configuration of multiple pools or discriminating option parameters can be error-prone and tedious.
- The manual approach requires a per-VNF manual step which is error-prone, time-consuming, and as such not very scalable.
- Both approaches require accurate tracking of IP address space to enable confident expansion of address pools, assignment of IP addresses, and allocation of additional subnets.

Public Cloud Static Method

As mentioned earlier, the assignment of IP addresses within a public cloud infrastructure will generally be controlled by the public cloud platform itself. Some public cloud services hold over an IP address for example, keeping the address unassignable for a time period after its corresponding VNF was destroyed to allow the address to "time out" of any systems in which it was being tracked.

In such a scenario, the IPAM integration process entails tracking the cloud-assigned IP and DNS information upon successful instantiation. Figure 9.4 shows a simple scenario, where the VNF is instantiated and the IPAM system is triggered to poll for the VNF's assigned IP address and domain name in order to update the IPAM repository. This cooperative method enables the centralized tracking of IP addresses and DNS names in a holistic database for public clouds where the cloud is authoritative for the address space as well as private clouds and internal networks where the IPAM system is generally authoritative.

As in the private cloud scenario, discovery of IP address assignments is recommended to align public cloud IP assignments with those tracked within your IPAM system. This is helpful in not only assigning unique IP addresses but also for monitoring IP address capacity to enable allocation of additional subnets as needed well before IP address capacity exhausts and VNF creation is rendered impossible.

Cloud Automation with APIs

Automation is among the key benefits of implementing an IPAM system. With ubiquitous adoption of Internet-based technologies and applications, the networking industry has promoted convergence of applications running on IP

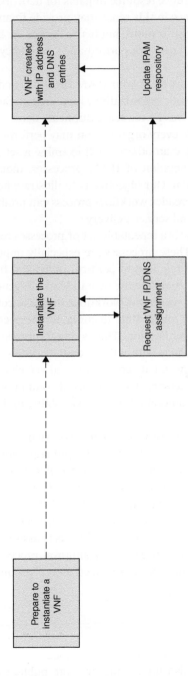

Figure 9.4 IP initialization within a public cloud.

networks to simplify and reduce resource impacts for networked applications and related support. Convergence in this sense may provide financial, efficiency, and productivity benefits for organizations, but it also "raises the bar" in terms of reliance on and visibility of IP network performance, resiliency, and incorporation into key business processes.

Automation of all or a portion of your IPAM functions and processes can provide lucrative benefits to your organization, including streamlining your IPAM process workflows themselves by reducing duplicate data entry and driving out inconsistency errors. While every organization may perform their processes and workflows a bit differently than others, we'll examine a set of common "primitives" with respect to automation of IPAM processes, then discuss additional opportunities for automation. Our objective is to illustrate how incorporation of IPAM functions within a broader workflow process can produce efficiency gains and streamline processes and service delivery.

An automation workflow is a repeatable set of processes required to perform a function or unit of work. These processes are especially important when several different organizations are required to perform individual functions in a structured sequence in order to complete the overall work. In general, the more tasks and organizations involved within the workflow, the more complex it is. Usually, this complexity results in a longer time to complete the overall workflow and a greater need for process coordination. This is due to process hand-offs between organizations or process owners within the overall workflow. These hand-offs are usually performed manually and are communicated via telephone, email, or process review meetings as necessary. These forms of communications are typically ad hoc in nature and add additional time and variability to the defined processes within the workflow.

Simply documenting current processes in terms of steps or tasks, groups responsible for each task, as well as task input and output requirements can be enlightening in defining processes and identifying possible improvements. Another benefit to documenting processes is that it proves helpful in identifying approval points in the process. Such points enable review of the proposed task output or change for approval, modification, or disapproval. Change control teams, for example are commonly inserted into key workflows to assure adequate communication and change approval. An expedited approval process can be defined to address cases of urgent change requests needed to resolve configuration or capacity issues.

Multi-Cloud IPAM

Many organizations deploy pockets of private cloud solutions within their data centers or networks and also utilize one or more public cloud solutions. You should consider applying your automation processes across noncloud, private cloud, public cloud, and hybrid cloud domains to streamline the flow to best accommodate the platform diversity of your network. You may be unable to define a single unified flow for a given process and may have separate workflows for different cloud systems for a given function. For example, when instantiating VM on AWS, you'll want to track the assigned IP address within your IPAM system. The order of events will likely differ from this AWS flow from one which incorporates VMware, for example where you can poll your IPAM system for an available IP address and assign to the VNF during instantiation.

Private Cloud Automation

Private cloud operation is typified by the use of an orchestrator which provides a graphical user interface from which VMs may be managed. When a VNF is created or destroyed, the orchestrator may be configured to invoke an IPAM system API call to either assign or free up the corresponding VNF IP address and DNS resource records. Figure 9.5 illustrates this process for a private cloud scenario where the IPAM system is authoritative for IP address assignment, as is typically the case in such an environment. The orchestrator calls the IPAM system API to request an IP address and DNS information from the centralized IPAM system repository. This provides a fully automated, hands-free mechanism for robust address assignment during the instantiation process.

From an IP address and pool capacity management perspective, the IPAM system should provide monitoring of IP address utilization. User-definable thresholds would enable alerting of administrators of the need to allocate more capacity or even the automated allocation of supplemental capacity without user intervention.

Figure 9.5 illustrates our basic three-step VNF instantiation process when used with an IPAM system. The preparation phase consists of IPAM periodically analyzing IP address capacity by monitoring DHCP pool occupancy if DHCP is used or by leveraging an orchestrator API. Impending address pool or subnet IP address capacity exhaustion detection enables automated IP capacity management so you can be confident an IP address will be available for assignment when required. Capacity thresholds would ideally provide a means to alert administrators with settable varying levels of warnings. Threshold triggers that can initiate subnet allocation fully automate the capacity management process.

The key point is that the IPAM system needs to track subnet allocations, IP address assignments, and remaining free IP space so successive allocations can be made easily and accurately with an API call. With the preparation phase ongoing in the background to monitor address availability, you can confidently create and destroy VNFs dynamically based on your services and capacity needs. Following

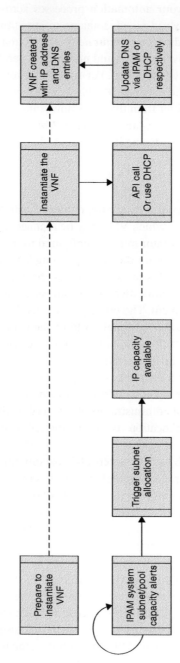

Figure 9.5 Orchestrator-IPAM instantiation process.

the flow, the actual VNF creation process obtains an available IP address from the IPAM system via an API call and the IPAM system retains the tracking of IP address assignments within a holistic repository. The IPAM system should also automate DNS resource record creation as well based on naming policies so that DNS too can be updated without human intervention. The overall process yields a virtually hands-free integration of critical network services initialization within the process of VNF instantiation. This saves time, eliminates errors, and scales well.

Public Cloud Automation

Ideally, your IPAM system should support public cloud interaction as well as private cloud to support private-only, public-only, or hybrid cloud environments. In the public cloud scenario, cloud functions are typically performed via an API but may also be performed using the cloud orchestrator function.

Within such an environment, a workflow incorporating the IPAM system API in conjunction with a cloud API may perform allocation or deallocation of subnets, instantiation or destruction of VNFs, and the discovery of subnets and IP assignments. Figure 9.4 illustrates this basic process flow for instantiating a public cloud VNF. Through a single "Create VNF Instance" API calls from an automation system, it may poll the cloud API for a free IP address, instantiate the VNF using the available IP address, then update the IPAM system with the IP address and name assignment made by the public cloud.

Discovery functions provide for the collection and comparison of IP addresses from both the cloud system and the IPAM system to update the IPAM system based on the cloud's status of IP address assignments. In this manner, IP address assignments may be detected and optionally synchronized with those tracked in the IPAM repository. This enables accurate tracking of IP address assignments within public cloud services, analogously to that provided for noncloud and private cloud networks.

IPAM Automation Benefits

Implementing a disciplined and automated IPAM foundation as a core component of your cloud deployment strategy enables you to achieve the following benefits:

- *Faster VNF provisioning* – Whether using DHCP, an orchestrator plug-in to automatically assign a VNF IP address, and/or a public cloud platform, the provisioning process need not pause to assign and IP address and update DNS. Automation facilitates rapid provisioning, amplifying the cloud's agility benefit to organizations.

- *Improved provisioning accuracy* – Automation via DHCP or the IPAM API enables more accurate provisioning. The requestor for an IP address need only issue the request for a free address for assignment whether in the IPAM system or within the public cloud platform, while updating the other.
- *Reduced manual effort* – Automation reduces manual effort, which can reduce time intervals, opportunities for erroneous manual entry, and staff costs.
- *Centralized IPAM for your entire network* – Depending on the expanse of your network, you likely have noncloud network components you need to manage, like subnets in remote offices for example. Such an IPAM deployment enables you to manage all of your IP space holistically, integrating the view of cloud IP space and noncloud IP space through a single pane of glass.
- *Simpler troubleshooting* – With all of your IP address information secured in a robust repository including all assignments and discoveries recorded, the IPAM database serves as the IP address plan of record which provides critical information during troubleshooting. Subnet and IP address templates also promote consistency of IP address assignments which further reduces confusion and aids in rapid troubleshooting.
- *Integrate IPAM processes* – IPAM automation functionally integrates IP address assignment, IP address-to-name association in DNS with IPAM repository updates to maintain accurate and timely network perspective.
- *Segment administrative authority* – Different administrators may be responsible for certain subsets of the network or subsets of functions like cloud and noncloud for example. Complementary administrative assignment functions within your IPAM system can help you manage administrator access to least privilege security principles.
- *Virtualized DHCP and DNS network functions* – Containers or virtual appliances for DHCP/DNS services, as well as the IPAM system itself provide the same elasticity and speed of service benefits to your IPAM services. As your need for elasticity for these core network services dictates, these systems can be instantiated and destroyed across your private and public cloud infrastructure.
- *Lower cost* – Automation can help you lower costs of cloud administration though reduced manual staff effort, fewer errors to troubleshoot, and higher customer or constituent satisfaction through rapid, accurate provisioning. This approach mirrors and supports those benefits of the cloud itself with agility, elasticity, and lower costs.

Unifying IPAM Automation

Use of a single holistic IPAM system spanning cloud and noncloud environments extends IPAM visibility across the entire enterprise. At the same time, it can offer consistent change control and approval points for common tasks that can be applied to public cloud, private cloud, and noncloud platforms. For example, an approval point may be warranted on the subnet allocation process whether performed within the traditional network or cloud.

Let's examine a sample workflow, considering Figure 9.6, which depicts a simple subnet allocation workflow. In this example, three different organizations or entities may initiate the workflow as shown at the left of the figure. For instance, the help desk or call center team may receive a complaint about an inability to obtain an IP address, the server team within Operations or IT may notice that a DHCP server is at full capacity for one or more address pools, and/or the network management team may receive an alert from a network management system (NMS) regarding a DHCP server capacity outage.

These initial notifications to the IP address team, which is responsible for IP address allocation, may be in the form of phone calls or emails. Upon receipt of the notification, the IP address team would need to locate the affected address pools and/or subnets, and identify available address space that could be assigned to the location to supplement the address capacity. Following the subnet allocation IPAM process we reviewed in Chapter 6, the IP address team would then allocate the identified address space, say 10.2.3.0/24, to the location. This necessitates updating of the IP address assignment database, spreadsheet, or IPAM tool. There will likely be additional information to be defined and tracked with the assigned subnet, such any DHCP address pools, as well as host and domain names.

Once the subnet has been allocated and recorded, its approval through a change control process may be necessary as highlighted by the approval point in the figure. Once requisite approvals have been granted, the subnet needs to be deployed on the IP network, either within the enterprise network or on a cloud virtual network. The deployment within an enterprise network shown in the figure typically involves adding the block or subnet to the router or edge device serving the affected location. Deployment within a cloud services provider network would likely require two or more API calls to the cloud platform to create the subnet and to update DNS. We'll review this process variation in the next section.

The router team is often an organization independent of the IP address team, so an interorganizational communiqué would typically be issued to request the assignment of the subnet to the appropriate router interface. In parallel with this router configuration step, the DHCP server(s) serving devices at the location must be configured with the corresponding address pools within the allocated subnet. For example, allocation of a/24 network with 254 usable IP addresses may comprise 43 static devices and 211 dynamic or pool addresses. The pool portion of the subnet must be configured in the DHCP server so it can service clients requesting space from the pool. The DHCP server team would perform this task based on an explicit communiqué from the IP address team with appropriate approvals.

Notice that a different set of information would be conveyed to the router team (add 10.2.3.0/24 to router X interface Y) than to the DHCP server team (add pool 10.2.3.44–10.2.3.254 to DHCP server W). Additional information may be required for complete DHCP server configuration, including associated DHCP options, policies, and client classes required for the address pool. Provisioning the subnet within a public cloud service typically necessitates logging into the cloud account to define the subnet within the appropriate private zone. DHCP is not typically provisioned within public cloud environments, so the DHCP provisioning steps would be unnecessary.

Meanwhile, a third communiqué containing a third set of information would be communicated to the DNS server team: create appropriate A records in the forward zone and create the 3.2.10.in-addr.arpa zone file and add PTR records to it on master DNS server Z for static addresses 10.2.3.1–10.2.3.43 each with enumerated fully qualified domain names. Again, additional information may be conveyed to completely configure the DNS server for the network, including prepopulation of resource records for the dynamic addresses and association of the subnet with a DNS view, for example.

Each of these three parallel processes must be completed to proceed to the next step, verification, or audit of completion by the network team and/or IP address team to close out the process. As the router team and DHCP and DNS server teams complete their respective work, notification must be provided to the network or IP team. Upon receiving confirmation from all three organizations, the network or IP team can verify proper configuration through reports, audit trails, or actual network testing and discovery. At this point, our sample workflow for allocating an address block is complete.

Streamlined Subnet Allocation Workflow

Our example subnet allocation workflow in Figure 9.6 is a relatively simple, high-level workflow. It's likely that each process illustrated in the figure itself involves several subprocesses. But even this high-level flow illustrates a key point: ad hoc communiqués among organizations are not usually efficient and generally introduce a delay in completion of the overall workflow. This delay stems from time lags in remembering to send and actually sending the communiqué from the source organization, and in receiving the communiqué (e.g. picking up emails and voicemails if not directly accessible) at the destination organization. Even if many of said "teams" are one person, there are always interruptions and distractions from completing all tasks across a variety of management systems.

Processes such as the network verification step in Figure 9.6 may require multiple parallel processes to complete and introduce an additional complexity in tracking acceptable input from each preceding process prior to beginning the next

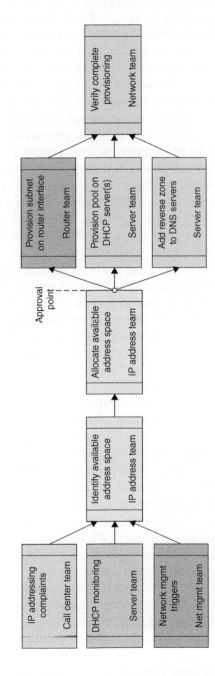

Figure 9.6 Subnet allocation workflow example.

step. Required change control approval steps may also introduce delays in conven-
ing approval meetings, presenting the case, and garnering the approval.

Let's examine one method of simplifying this workflow by introducing automated inter-process communiqués via electronic messages such as intersystem
API calls. Figure 9.7 illustrates the same process steps as in Figure 9.6, but through
the leveraging of APIs between processes, the overall workflow can be streamlined from an overall time perspective as well as manual effort standpoint.

In Figure 9.7, the same three input processes may kick-off the address identification and allocation processes. In this streamlined process example, however, the
help desk call or email to the IP address team is replaced by an API call from the
call center's trouble ticketing system to the IPAM system. This call may request
the IPAM system to automatically identify and preallocate or reserve an address
block. If the server team is utilizing a DHCP pool monitoring mechanism with
capacity alerts, or if the IPAM system supports such monitoring and alerts, these
alerts may trigger the IPAM system to take the next step in defining appropriate
address space. Likewise, electronic triggers from a NMS may invoke similar action.

Any of these triggers may stimulate the IPAM system to notify an administrator
or reserve or suggest an appropriate address block for allocation to the location in
need. Hence, the IP address team process may be configured for either notification only, for notification with reservation of address space pending team approval,
or notification and automated identification and allocation of appropriate address
space. The degree of such automation is dependent on organizational policies for
such automation and the capabilities of the IPAM system itself to perform these
steps as we'll discuss in the next section.

Whether the address space is allocated manually by the IP address team or automatically by the IPAM system, the IPAM system must communicate the allocated
subnet information to requisite downstream processes. A "pending approval"
state may be required to halt the process until the change control approval has
been granted. Once approved, communication of the allocation to the router team
may be in the form of an IPAM system-initiated email to the router team or by a
"callout" from the IPAM system to the router configuration management system
upon block allocation. In the former case, the router team must receive the email
and perform the corresponding process; in the latter case, the callout from the
IPAM system could call a script to create a work ticket or directly enter an API call
to a configuration management system or router.

The updating of associated DHCP and DNS servers traditionally falls into the
purview of the IPAM system itself. In this case, assuming configuration information at the level required for DNS and DHCP server updates is spawned during the
block allocation process, and that the IPAM system can automatically or periodically update DHCP and DNS servers, then these processes can be fully automated.
This level of automation saves time and effort in communicating the block

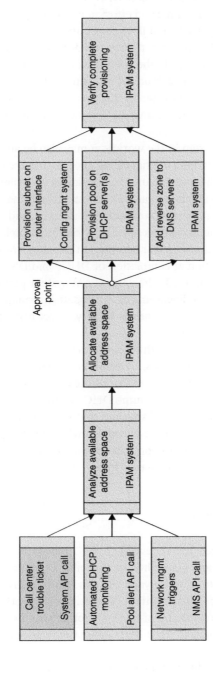

Figure 9.7 Fully automated workflow via APIs.

information and associated DHCP and DNS information to each server team, respectively, and this can save time and effort in otherwise performing these tasks by manually configuring DHCP and DNS configuration files via text editors. This "intra-IPAM" system efficiency can reduce the duration of these processes and thereby contribute time savings to the overall workflow for all such IPAM functions. This automation, of course, is one of key benefits of implementing an IPAM system, and as we'll discuss in Chapter 15, the system chosen for deployment should be selected based on the features that it provides to minimize your costliest IPAM functions.

The final confirmation step in the workflow may also be automated to a large degree depending on the router configuration process and the capabilities of the IPAM system in use. If the router team communicates via email after completing its process, there is little efficiency gain. However, if the router team uses a configuration management system to configure the routers, and the configuration management system enables callouts upon provisioning completion for example, the callout could be used to confirm completion to the IPAM system electronically. Likewise, confirmation of completion of DHCP and DNS server configuration updates can be streamlined when the IPAM system performs and records completion of these updates. Recording of the update information enables confirmation and audits of changes and change history. IP discovery provides an additional level of verification as well.

This subnet allocation process within a cloud service can likewise become fully automated as illustrated in Figure 9.8. This flow is very similar to that of the enterprise network, but through the integration of the cloud API, the subnet may be defined within the cloud. Here we assume DHCP is unnecessary and that step in omitted. Through the use of an IPAM system that supports a robust inbound and outbound API for automated subnet allocation with the ability to pass relevant allocation details downstream to configuration management systems or cloud APIs, etc., the process may be fully hands free.

Workflow Realization

As you've probably noticed, there are a lot of "ifs" in these workflow descriptions. This variability on one hand highlights the flexibility of defining numerous combinations of workflows to adapt to your policies and infrastructure capabilities, but on the other hand renders definition of cookie-cutter workflows rather difficult. The extent of your realization of these and other workflows and their corresponding benefits will depend upon the integration capabilities of your IPAM system, the mating capabilities of other systems with which integration is desired, and your policies, procedures, and desire to integrate. For example, in the

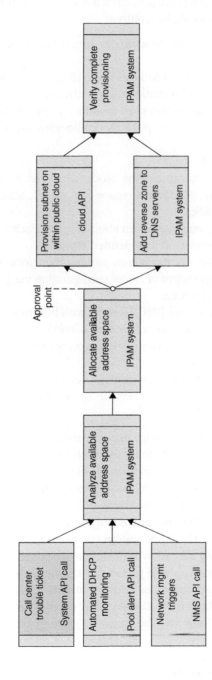

Figure 9.8 Fully automated subnet provisioning in the cloud.

streamlined block allocation process described above and outlined in Figure 9.7, the following capabilities would be required:

- Trouble ticketing system with the ability to automatically generate an API call to the IPAM system.
- NMS with the ability to issue an API call to the IPAM system based on definable events, such as address pool depletions; alternatively, if the IPAM system itself provides event triggers, the system must be able to initiate some action based on this trigger, namely the initiation of the block allocation process for the affected subnet or location.
- IPAM system with the ability to
  - o Receive API calls to initiate the block allocation process, which may entail reservation of address space or actual allocation based on organizational policies.
  - o Utilize addressing templates when allocating the block to assign addresses and address pools based on a predefined template.
  - o Trigger downstream events such as passing the allocated block information to a work order system or router configuration management system to enable router provisioning.
  - o Update relevant DNS and DHCP servers with information associated with the allocation automatically or based on administrator approval.
  - o Perform IP, subnet, or cloud network discovery in various forms to confirm successful deployment.
- A work order or configuration management system with the ability to receive API calls to create work order tickets or to automate router provisioning, respectively.

With these components in place with the required capabilities, this streamlined workflow can be implemented, reducing the time required and minimizing data entry errors along the path of the workflow. While component system capabilities are required to fully automate this process, organizational policies or methods of procedure may dictate a semiautomated flow with one or more approval points.

For example, let's discuss the change control approval point prior to deployment of the subnet allocation. If the IPAM system can reserve the subnet intended for allocation and this pending allocation information can be summarized for presentation to the change control approval parties,[2] inserting this approval point is easily accomplished. Once approved, an authorized administrator can modify the state of the allocated subnet from a reserved or pending state to a deployed or allocated state or simply "approve" the request. Assuming this state change could

---

2 In this context, we mean presentation *to* the parties involved in change control, not *at* parties to discuss change control, which certainly might make such meetings infinitely more enjoyable!

then trigger associated downstream events in the flow, automation may ensue to complete the workflow.

The bottom line is that you should consider the capabilities of your component systems and mask those with required policies and procedures. We'll provide examples of time-saving automated workflows later in this chapter, but keep in mind that these may need to be adapted to your systems' capabilities and organizational methods and politics.

Tips for Defining Workflows

First of all, you'll need to have a good handle on the capabilities of your IPAM system and those with which you'd like to integrate. We've also mentioned the impact of organizational policies, procedures, and politics in defining automation break points for approvals; the break points may also be necessary for inter-organizational (e.g. inter-business unit or department) hand-offs. Having such hand-offs occur behind the scenes electronically may not be acceptable, at least until the automation can be "trusted," meaning that it has been tested to the satisfaction of both ends of the hand-off. This highlights the fact that with any change in process, some resistance to change may naturally occur. Prove-in of benefits can go a long way to working through this resistance, though it may inevitably take some time.

Stepping back, the first thing to do is to understand your current processes, intra- and interorganizational, for performing certain tasks. You can start with the list of discrete tasks we described in Chapter 6 as well as the examples later in this chapter. These define common processes, though your team may perform these tasks in different ways or in differing order. Thus, steps may be omitted, inserted, or reordered in accordance with the way you do business.

Mapping out current processes provides a baseline from which process improvement or automation may be applied. Look for task transitions and dependencies. Can information between tasks be better conveyed electronically? Can other forms of automation, such as alerting, provide additional streamlining opportunities? When asking these questions, consider again the capabilities of your IPAM and associated systems. How can the automation of a particular task be implemented? If your vendor does not support a particular feature today, will they in the future? If so, when? Provide your input to the vendor, as this may help other customers of the same product attempting similar implementations.

It's a good idea to start small to prove in a workflow concept and obtain measurable productivity or process time saving metrics. Such hard data provides the ammunition needed to further automate other tasks, especially when attempting cross-organizational lines. Potential workflow scenarios you may find useful are discussed next.

Automation Scenarios

Recognizing that most organizations seek to continuously improve operational efficiencies and desire to integrate IPAM processes into broader IT and Operations workflows in general or as part of a broader initiative such as ITIL*, the use of an IPAM
system can facilitate automation of IPAM workflows. Many IPAM products provide
one or more interfaces for electronic communiqués for workflow automation, typically including command line interfaces (CLIs) and an API. These interface points
facilitate scripting of multiple tasks as well as integration with other management
systems needing to initiate actions or obtain information from the IP address management system. Some systems also provide downstream calls for actions taken
within the IPAM system itself. For example, when a device or subnet is created,
edited, or deleted, these systems enable the passing of relevant data fields to another
management system. In this manner, the IPAM system provides integration points to
externally initiate IPAM functions from an upstream system and to enable IPAM
system-initiated functions to commence further actions downstream in the workflow.

Intra-IPAM Automation

Before continuing with broad workflow examples involving multiple systems and
functions, let's consider automation of some of the IPAM process we discussed in
Chapter 6. For these scenarios, the input mechanism could simply be the IPAM
system native user interface, its CLI or API interfaces, an automation system such
as Ansible or Chef or even an in-house web-based IT portal. The IT or Operations
organization can create a web portal or expand an existing one for distributed
administrators or even end users to log requests for IP subnets, addresses, hostnames, IPAM-related information, and more. The benefits of creating such an IT
portal include the following:

- Offload the processing of common, more mundane tasks from the IT management team, enabling them to focus on issues requiring their higher level of
  expertise. This promotes resource efficiency and can improve job satisfaction for
  members of the IT management team by providing focus on more challenging work.
- Empower distributed administrators or end users with the ability to log IP
  address related requests and obtain immediate or deferred (e.g. upon approval)
  feedback and resolution. Empowerment and rapid feedback elevate end user
  satisfaction and productivity.
- Maintain IPAM data integrity with the ability to log requests and make changes
  using a variety of user interfaces, while enforcing end user access controls to
  viewing or modifying such data within the centralized repository.

- Enable the IT management team to retain overall control of the information in your IPAM system, while exposing only those parameters or functions that are required for distributed administrators. In other words, the IPAM team can minimize the ability of end users to enter "dangerous" data that could have ripple effects in the system by virtue of what features are exposed on the portal input screens. This abstract user interface layer on top of the IPAM system is also useful if the granularity of access controls is insufficient on the native IPAM system.

You can use your favorite web technology (e.g. nodeJS, Python, Perl, PHP) to activate your https portal screens or add to your existing IT portal if appropriate to process user requests and perform API calls into the IPAM system. You have full levity to define each request page to define input parameters that are germane to your conduct of business. A script can be processed upon submitting the web request page to parse the input parameters and interface to the IPAM system. For example, a web page that requests a user ID and password along with location, subnet size needed, description, and purpose would be appropriate for a subnet request screen. The script called from clicking the "submit" button can either pass entered information directly to the IPAM system, or it can be used to authenticate the requestor, then replaced by an employee ID that can be mapped to a "group" user ID in the IPAM system with permissions to make such requests. The other input fields can be mapped directly to the IPAM system API call to log the request. The workflow of Figures 9.7 or 9.8 may then ensue if desired to fully automate the assignment process, or workflow approval points can be leveraged for added scrutiny and control. Error processing on the API call also needs to be coded to provide direct user feedback regarding the status of the request such as entry error, rejection, success, pending approval.

Keep in mind that there are many other ways of handling the mapping of the information you need to collect on the web request page to what your IPAM system needs to process the request. This enables maximum flexibility to adapting the request information to your organization's policies.

DHCP Server Configuration

We consider this flow as intra-IPAM as it entails automated creation of a DHCP server configuration file or command set based on the IP address plan, and implementing this on a distributed DHCP server. Many IPAM systems include this inherently, but if you're using spreadsheets, an in-house system, or other less integrated IPAM systems, this workflow could save time and reduce configuration errors. A DHCP server's configuration consists of IP address pools, individual assignments for M-DHCP clients, associated option settings, potentially failover configuration, and other functional parameter settings. Certainly, the address pools and individual assignments must be linked tightly with the overall IP address plan. The other configuration aspects listed may also be definable within the IPAM system or a using a script that creates these configuration directives and transfers them to or executes them on the corresponding DHCP server.

A deployment approval point in the process may be appropriate, whereby delegated administrators make proposed changes in DHCP configuration using the IPAM system, but such changes are not deployed to respective DHCP servers without review and approval by a senior administrator or the change control team. A means of viewing proposed changes and even proposed configuration differences would be helpful in the review and approval process, whether provided natively by the IPAM system or by an external method. This workflow example could be considered a building block to our subnet allocation example illustrated in Figure 9.7, if such a subnet contained a DHCP pool or M-DHCP objects.

DNS Server Configuration

As with DHCP server configuration, the automated generation of configuration files or commands for DNS server updates can help save time. Leveraging linkages with the IP address plan can reduce entry errors and facilitate data consistency. As you assign IP addresses, you may in most cases also need to update corresponding forward and reverse DNS zones associated with the IP address and domain name. And as with the DHCP example, a deployment approval process may be desirable to control changes impacting DNS configuration. This workflow scenario can also be considered a building block to the prior subnet allocation workflow examples of Figures 9.7 and 9.8.

Subnet Assignment

Of course, our subnet allocation process is an intra-IPAM flow with the exception of the cloud API case which does necessitate an outbound cloud API capability of your IPAM system. We could take this flow to another level if we expand it to the opening of a new retail store or branch office which may require the allocation of several subnets, such as a subnet each for wireless, voice, LAN data, management. Such a flow is more complex as it (or your IPAM system) must process the allocation of multiple subnets, likely of differing sizes, with different DHCP pool sizes, and IP assignments. But imagine deploying your IP address space for a forthcoming retail store in one click! Automation is a beautiful thing.

IP Address Assignment Request

Another popular time-saving workflow features the logging and creation of individual IP address assignments. If your IT management team spends a lot of time responding to phone calls or emails requesting individual IP addresses, this flow can be very useful. Create a web portal page to enable end users to identify who and where they are, then simply request an IP address. Additional input criteria may be desired to declare the purpose of the request, to identify the particular device type, e.g. a printer, to enable entry of hostname information for creation of A/AAAA and PTR resource records, and even to define whether the device address will be manually (statically) configured or obtained via Manual DHCP (in this case, the MAC address will also be a required input field).

Extra-IPAM Workflow Examples

The intra-IPAM workflows defined above can be leveraged to enable their insertion into broader workflows involving additional systems beyond the IPAM system. We've already illustrated the subnet allocation flow with the IPAM system receiving input from an upstream trouble ticketing or NMS and providing output downstream to a public cloud, work order, or configuration management system. In this case, we essentially interchange the web portal input upstream with the ticketing or management system. Creation of such task routines, comprising discrete sets of tasks to perform a particular function enables reuse among many workflow variations. This in itself saves work in redefining flows, creating new ones, and executing flow updates and improvements. Therefore, it is conceivable that sets of example flows discussed in this chapter can be joined together to create larger macro flows. Again, we recommend you start small, but take heart in knowing that simple flows will likely be reusable when building larger ones.

Regional Internet Registry Reporting

Service providers and some enterprises obtain additional address space directly from RIRs such as ARIN or RIPE. These and other RIRs have defined policies and automated email interfaces to enable IP address consumers to notify them upon allocation of address space internally or to their customers. Hence, as an additional step added to the block allocation flow previously discussed, the allocation information could be automatically conveyed to the corresponding RIR in the format required, typically JSON via REST.

This process addition would require inclusion of the address block allocated, a network name, and additional contact information associated with the block. Therefore, this form of workflow would generally be a function of the IPAM system, postprocessing each block allocation, edit, or delete. In this manner, the RIR is informed of address space utilization over time. When additional address space is needed, the request process with the RIR can be expedited as the registry already has much of the supporting information. This ongoing reporting also saves the otherwise manual effort required to identify each block allocation and its respective utilization in order to justify the request for additional address space.

Router Configuration Provisioning

We hinted at this workflow as part of our earlier subnet allocation example. If you're inventorying router devices and associated subnet assignments, this workflow may come in handy. In some organizations, politics may disqualify such an automated provisioning workflow. Those responsible for router configurations may need to retain control and/or perform updates at specified times. In this situation, the work order creation flow may be a better choice. In either case, information pertaining to the block allocated and its association with a router and interface information would be passed to a router configuration management tool or to a work order creation system, respectively. This automation can help reduce manual transcription of IP subnet information for entry into a router command line or configuration tool, especially when considering IPv6 subnets!

Customer Provisioning

Service providers offering IP services from ISPs to broadband providers to managed services providers typically allocate an IP address, several IP addresses, or address blocks to their customers. The block or IP address assignment process applies, but most likely billing and support systems must also be provisioned. Entry of new customer information into a customer relationship management (CRM) or billing system would be ideally performed using one interface, with the associated external system interfaces enabling automation among systems, including the IPAM system. As billing systems would retain the plan of record for customer billing information, the IPAM system would need to be updated to maintain the plan of record for the IP address plan.

Asset Inventory Integration

Many organizations employ an asset management system to track valuable assets such as servers, laptops, printers, VoIP phones, and so on. Many of these systems are keyed by an asset identifier and not IP address. However, some IPAM systems can facilitate integration between asset and IP inventory systems with the use of its integration points and user defined fields. If a given asset ID is a field that can be entered for an IP address, your IPAM system may be able to pass this information downstream to the asset management system using its CLI/API. This workflow can eliminate the duplicate entry of information in two different systems. If desired, the converse flow can also be implemented.

Another form of asset-IP system linkage can be achieved with the use of URL-based data entry fields or even SQL or LDAP lookups. If the asset system provides URL, SQL or LDAP reachable access, such a linkage could be defined in your IPAM and/or asset system to eliminate duplication of information entry across systems. Thus, not only can the creation process be streamlined but also the inter-system navigation can be as well.

Trouble Ticket Creation

If your IPAM system tracks DHCP address utilization data from the DHCP servers running across your network, it may also provide fixed or user definable thresholds to trigger alerts. If these alerts enable triggering of downstream events, you may be able to leverage this automated trigger point. Should a threshold be triggered, you could utilize this mechanism to automatically create a trouble ticket or otherwise notify relevant personnel. This notification is very helpful in identifying pending address depletions before they actually occur. Once such a depletion occurs, end users will be affected and the help desk phones will ring.

Summary

Automation workflows provide substantial savings of time, money, and effort within your organization. Depending on your current business processes and the tools you use or plan to use, including IPAM tools, workflows can be defined and implemented to automate common functions to streamline IPAM-related and extra-IPAM processes across cloud and noncloud networks.

Part III

IPAM and Security

IPAM plays an increasing role in helping network managers secure their networks and their enterprises at large. This part covers security techniques for securing IPAM components, and approaches for the use of IPAM technologies as an additional layer within a defense in depth security approach to secure your network and your Internet presence.

10

IPAM Services Security

As the Internet transformed from a scientific and educational network experiment into a global commercial communications network over the last five decades, its widespread adoption by organizations and individuals fueled its explosive growth, which continues unabated to this day. Providing the ability to communicate, update bank accounts, access critical information remotely, and much more, the Internet serves as the prime vehicle for anytime, anywhere communications. As such it has also became an extremely attractive target for criminals seeking to disrupt an organization's web presence or email, infiltrate an enterprise's internal network, and steal valuable data, including personal, corporate, or government classified information, among other things.

Organizations have responded by implementing various security measures including intrusion protection mechanisms such as firewalls, authentication and encryption technologies, proactive security scanning, attack detection monitors, and security education to name a few. With defensive implementations deployed, attackers seek targets that are less well defended or that provide a generally free-flowing communications pathway like HTTP, simple mail transfer protocol (SMTP), or DNS.

While attacks on web traffic and email have been fairly well publicized, though they continue to evolve over time, attacks on DNS represent an emerging threat to organizations. Unlike HTTP, SNMP, and other application layer protocols, DNS is an "application helper" protocol that exists to facilitate application ease-of-use. DNS is not an end-user application, but without DNS end-user applications would largely be useless.

DHCP too provides a vital network service in supporting device network initialization. Attacks on DHCP can deny user access to networks or misconfigure devices. As foundational IP network services, an outage or exploitation of DNS or DHCP services would likely impact large numbers of users or subscribers, leaving them

IP Address Management, Second Edition. Michael Dooley and Timothy Rooney.
© 2021 The Institute of Electrical and Electronics Engineers, Inc.
Published 2021 by John Wiley & Sons, Inc.

unable to connect or communicate. As we'll see, even the seemingly innocuous use of IPAM technologies, particularly DNS, may lend itself to nefarious activities.

Securing DHCP

There are a number of security threats to DHCP information and in its communications with those requesting information. In addition, given the role of DHCP in disseminating IP addresses for access to the network, the DHCP service itself plays a key role in providing a basic level of network access control by virtue of its inherent admittance function. For example, will you configure DHCP to provide an IP address to any device that requests one or will you configure a more discriminating policy? We'll discuss this issue with respect to securing network access in the ensuing chapter.

DHCP Service Availability

Your users rely on DHCP for basic IP network initialization, so if DHCP services are unavailable or are performing inadequately, end users or subscribers may be unable to access the network. Risks associated with the availability of DHCP services include the following:

- Inadequate DHCP capacity due to too few servers deployed and/or servers deployed with inadequate processing or input/output specifications.
- Unavailability of DHCP services due to network unreachability, possibly due to poor or asymmetric routing or suboptimal network placement of DHCP servers.
- The failure of a DHCP server due to hardware failure, power failure, natural disaster, or human error can cause unreachability due to a server or subnetwork failure and can increase the load on a failover DHCP server that supports the failed server.

DHCP Server/OS Attacks

As with all network servers, vulnerabilities within the server operating system (OS) and applications may be exploited by attackers in order to severely hamper or crash the server. These attacks can be of the following forms:

- *Hardware* – Physical access to DHCP servers enables the attacker to unplug, disconnect, or physically remove the server, literally removing the server from service, thereby reducing the availability of the DHCP service and possible capture of configuration information. Physical removal of a server affords the attacker an opportunity to hack the server for IP address and associated configuration parameters that may relate to broader network details such as NTP, DNS, or file transfer protocol (FTP) server IP addresses.

- *Operating system attacks* – An attacker may attempt to gain local or remote console access to the server by hacking passwords or overflowing the code execution stack or buffer. In general, an attack may exploit a known vulnerability of the operating system or version of DHCP software running on the hardware server or virtualized platform.
- *DHCP service attacks* – An attacker may attempt to exploit a known vulnerability for a given vendor and version of DHCP server software running on the victim server to shut it down or otherwise corrupt and/or disrupt service.
- *API channel attack* – The DHCP server may support an API interface, which if exploited, could provide a convenient mechanism to remotely control or configure the DHCP server. Such power may entice an attacker to attempt to access the API channel to perform nefarious functions such as stopping the DHCP service thereby denying IP address assignment services to network clients.

DHCP Server/OS Attack Mitigation

The following approaches may be employed to defend against DHCP server attacks:

- DHCP server host access controls including ACLs, identity/password access, encrypted transport, and least privilege permissions.
- DHCP server operating system hardening to prevent access via unauthorized protocols.
- Monitor security advisories (e.g. computer emergency response team [CERT]) for operating system or DHCP service vulnerabilities and keep systems updated to prevent exploitation.
- Protect the DHCP service API channel using available controls such as ACLs, authentication, and encryption.
- Monitor DHCP server configuration for changes to detect unauthorized changes; this could consist of periodically checking configuration file checksums and to verify changed values with authorized changes.
- Physical access controls to constrain access to data centers or rooms housing DHCP servers.

DHCP Service Threats

Within enterprise environments, most threats to DHCP services are posed by internal (i.e. intraorganizational) clients. DHCP servers should not be reachable by external clients by simply not deploying DHCP servers on external subnets nor relaying DHCP packets from external sources. For service providers that initialize subscriber devices using DHCP, whether cell phones, cable or fiber routers, etc., threats to DHCP service can originate externally to the network by definition. In short, all organizations using DHCP are vulnerable. The degree of vulnerability and the impacts of compromise should drive the response in the form of securing DHCP to minimize such impacts.

Like all network services, DHCP is vulnerable to traffic sniffing and denial of service (DOS) attacks. Those with access to the data path over which DHCP packets traverse have the ability to sniff DHCP traffic for use in identifying network devices, their IP addresses, and other parameters. A DOS attack involves an attacker flooding a given server with requests too numerous for the server to handle, so the server spends all of its cycles attempting to deal with the flood and not on legitimate client requests; thus leaving these legitimate clients unserved, and thereby denying service.

Another type of DHCP attack involves a rogue client attempting to obtain a valid IP address and configuration to access the network. This could be malicious, e.g. theft of broadband service, or merely accidental, e.g. a visitor plugging into the wall jack in the conference room. But this relates to broader network security so we'll cover this in Chapter 11.

A third form of attack features a rogue DHCP server which responds to lease requests from clients with an invalid or inappropriate IP address and/or option parameter information. This "man in the middle" type of attack may attempt to set improper configuration parameters on the client, such as the default gateway or DNS server address(es) to use. Note that with IPv4, a rogue DHCP server attack is generally only applicable when the server is on the same subnet as the client; relay agents should be configured to relay DHCP packets to authorized DHCP servers. A remote rogue DHCPv6 server may be reachable via the DHCP servers well-known multicast address.

The client may receive Advertisements or Offers from both the legitimate DHCP server(s) and the rogue server. Many clients will select the first such offer that includes its requested parameters. If the rogue server is on the same subnet as the client, and legitimate servers are not, then it's likely the rogue server may be able to specify the IP configuration of the client.

DHCP Threat Mitigation

For an enterprise network, protection against DOS attacks could be implemented via packet rate limiting, e.g. via iptables albeit in a reactionary fashion, but DOS protection should be considered in a broader context comprising all key network services, not just DHCP. Other potential targets within an organization including

DNS servers or web servers imply that a gateway-based packet filtering approach be considered to protect all servers with a common solution. Such a solution typically involves packet analysis and predefined thresholds to limit the number of outstanding packets in process, though care must be taken with DHCP since most clients' transactions are funneled through DHCP relay agents, concentrating packets from a given set of source addresses.

Service providers may experience what appears to be a DHCP DOS attack when a power outage is restored and thousands of residential customers, i.e. DHCP clients, power back up, and request IP addresses. Many large service providers deploy carrier-class DHCP servers in a manner that load balances traffic across multiple servers in such a scenario.

Mitigation steps for the threat of unknown DHCP clients accessing the IP network by illicitly obtaining an IP address from DHCP requires identification of clients based on various access control techniques we'll address in Chapter 11.

Rogue DHCP servers may be difficult to detect, especially for clients on the same subnet as the rogue server. Periodic IP address sweeps or discoveries can help identify rogue devices including illicit DHCP servers. And both ISC and Microsoft implementations provide means to mitigate rogue servers. For ISC, use the `authoritative` directive, which configures the server to issue a negative acknowledgment if a client requests a lease for an address for which the server is authoritative yet for which the server has no record. Microsoft requires DHCP servers to be authorized within Active Directory; thus when a Windows DHCP server boots, it verifies its authorization in Active Directory before processing DHCP packets.

DHCP Authentication and Encryption

The DHCPv6 protocol supports authentication and encryption of DHCPv6 messages between relay agents and servers through the use of standard IP security (IPSec) architecture in accordance with RFC 8213 [80]. Encryption effectively combats traffic sniffing, while authentication prevents imposter relay agents from interfacing with a given DHCP server. RFC 8213 also applies to DHCPv4 as a means to secure relay agent-to-DHCP server communications.

In a nutshell, IPSec enables authentication and data integrity validation through the inclusion of an additional authentication header (AH), which enables a recipient to validate the identity of the sender and the message integrity. The encapsulating security protocol (ESP) also supports authentication and data integrity validation but adds the ability to encrypt data as well. Both AH and ESP process packet data using a pairwise shared secret key or key shared via a key exchange mechanism such as Internet key exchange (IKE).

RFC 8213 describes security for the relay-server link, though the IETF has also defined an end-to-end (client-server) DHCP authentication mechanism for IPv4 in RFC 3118 [81]. This scheme provides simple validation of the sender of DHCP packets via the use of shared tokens or keys. A token is simply a fixed value that is inserted into the DHCP Authentication option field. The receiver of the packet examines the token and if the token matches its configured token, the packet is accepted; otherwise it is dropped. This method provides weak endpoint authentication and no message verification. The use of shared keys can provide stronger endpoint authentication with message verification. However, shared keys must be configured on each client, with each client's key configured on each DHCP server through which the client obtains leases. The DHCP Authentication specification does not define the mechanism for key distribution. Mobile clients, for example would need to be configured with tokens for each DHCP server with which they may interact and vice versa.

The client creates a hashed message authentication code (HMAC)-MD5 hash of its Discover packet and signs it using the shared key. The resulting digest is placed in the DHCP Authentication option and transmitted within the Discover packet to the server. For the purposes of the hash computation, the hash portion of the DHCP Authentication option must be set to zero. The DHCP server would then compute a hash of the received message utilizing the shared key associated with the client (identified by the secret ID field of the DHCP Authentication option). The server zeroes out the hash value, hops, and GIAddr fields for the purposes of the hash computation. If the calculated hash matches that transmitted in the original DHCP Authentication option, the client and the contents of the packet are considered authenticated. The DHCP server utilizes the same shared key to compute the hash value of its DHCP Authentication option when it prepares its Offer and future packets to the client.

There have been very few implementations of DHCP Authentication. The challenges of key distribution and management as well as processing delays due to hash computation have been deemed too heavy a price to pay for the perceived benefits. Security of the DHCP service then typically falls on DHCP server administrators to monitor networks and servers and react to incidents as they occur.

DNS Infrastructure Risks and Attacks

Now we shall turn to DNS and vulnerabilities to your DNS infrastructure, which includes not only the DNS servers themselves but also the DNS resolvers which query for address lookups on behalf of user applications on end-user devices, the integrity of DNS information, and the collective DNS service of resolving host-names on behalf of resolvers.

DNS Service Availability

As with DHCP, DNS suffers from exposure to DNS services availability vulnerabilities due to

- Inadequate DNS capacity thanks to too few servers deployed and/or servers deployed with inadequate processing or memory.
- Unavailability of DNS services due to network unreachability, i.e. poor network placement of DNS servers.
- The failure of a DNS server due to hardware failure, power failure, natural disaster, or human error can cause unreachability due to a server or subnetwork failure and can increase the load on other DNS servers authoritative for the same zones.
- Failure to segment server deployments by "role" (i.e. authoritative vs. recursive) can overload servers and expose them to multiple attack vectors.

DNS Server/OS Attacks

As with DHCP servers, your DNS server hardware and OS are likewise vulnerable to attack. These attacks can be of the following forms:

- *Hardware* – Physical access to DNS servers enables the attacker to unplug, disconnect or physically remove the server, removing the server from service, thereby reducing the availability of the DNS service and possible capture of zone information, DNS infrastructure information and possibly private keys used for DNSSEC.
- *Operating system attacks* – Attaining local or remote console access to the server by brute force hacking, social engineering, or overflowing the code execution stack or buffer may leverage a known vulnerability of the operating system or version of DNS software running on the server.
- *DNS service attacks* – An attacker may attempt to exploit a known vulnerability for a given vendor and version of DNS server software running on the victim server to shut it down or otherwise corrupt and/or disrupt service.
- *DNS API attack* – The DNS server control channel or API interface provided in most implementations provides a convenient mechanism to remotely control the DNS server, such as stopping/halting the server's DNS software (e.g. "named," "nsd"), reloading a zone, and more. Such power may entice an attacker to attempt to access the control channel to perform nefarious functions such as stopping the DNS service thereby denying DNS service to querying servers and resolvers.

DNS Server/OS Attack Mitigation

Compromise of the DNS server or the DNS service running on a server can enable an attacker to reduce the availability of DNS service or to modify DNS configuration. Compromise may come in the form of host access, operating system, or DNS service disruption through exploitation of a known vulnerability, or access to the DNS control channel if equipped, which may enable an attacker to stop the DNS service, freeze dynamic updates, or other disruptive activities.

The following approaches may be employed to defend against DNS server attacks:

- DNS server host access controls including ACLs, identity/password access, encrypted transport, and least privilege permissions.
- DNS server operating system hardening to prevent access via unauthorized protocols.
- Monitor security advisories (e.g. CERT) for operating system or DNS service vulnerabilities and keep systems updated to prevent exploitation.
- Inhibit responses to "version" queries.
- Protect the DNS service control channel using available controls such as ACLs as well as authentication and encryption keys.
- Physical access controls to constrain access to data centers or rooms housing DNS servers.

DNS Service Denial

The types of DoS/DDoS attacks against DNS servers may be in the form of the following:

- *DNS query flood* – The attacker issues a large number of DNS queries beyond which it has capacity to resolve.
- *UDP packet flood* – An attacker may issue large numbers of UDP packets using random UDP destination port numbers, forcing the server to respond with an ICMP Destination Unreachable message for each.
- *TCP SYN attack* – While DNS typically utilizes UDP, TCP is permitted and the SYN attack involves the attacker opening a TCP connection by sending the TCP SYN message from varying source IP addresses and/or ports, then ignoring the SYN-ACK thereby not completing connection establishment with this third message of the three-way handshake. While awaiting each ACK, the server keeps the half-open TCP connection pending, and ultimately depletes its capacity for TCP connections.
- ICMP flood – The attacker issues a constant stream of ICMP packets to the server which uselessly occupies its processing capabilities.

Distributed Denial of Service

A variant of this type of attack is the use of multiple distributed attack points and is referred to as a DDoS attack. The intent is the same, though the scale is much larger, with multiple attack origination points. Attackers can enlist others to manually conduct an attack on a target simultaneously. However, in many cases, the use of bots installed on other computers within the enterprise or on the Internet can be enlisted to join in the attack.

Such an attack occurred on 21 October 2016, during the DDoS attack on DynDNS. Based on a statement about the attack from Dyn [82], DNS packets from tens of millions of IP addresses associated with the Mirai botnet barraged Dyn's DNS infrastructure. The Mirai malware had infected over 100 000 devices, predominantly nonperson entities (NPEs) otherwise known as IoT devices, and enlisted these devices in the attacks.

Bogus Domain Queries

This attack seeks service denial through the flooding of a recursive server with queries for bogus domain names. This causes the server to utilize resources to futilely locate the authoritative server within the domain tree (Figure 10.1).

In addition to processing a high volume of such queries as in a typical DoS attack, the recursive server expends resources iterating queries to name servers within the domain tree in an attempt to identify the authoritative servers for each bogus domain. Ultimately, query errors will be returned for lame delegations or NXDOMAIN responses but the sheer volume of such pending queries can inhibit its processing of legitimate queries.

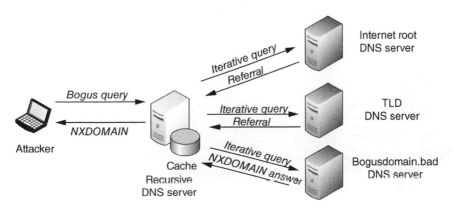

Figure 10.1 Bogus domain query attack.

Pseudorandom Subdomain Attacks

A variant of the generic bogus domain query attack focuses queries on a given domain served by a common set of authoritative servers. This attack vector has been shown to impact not only the authoritative servers but recursive servers awaiting responses from these authoritative servers. This attack, called a pseudorandom subdomain (PRSD) attack, features an attacker launching a large number of queries with PRSDs of a target domain, let's say example.com. Thus, an attacker queries for names like iopqewf.example.com, a84fj.example.com, etc., in large volumes. The large volume of queries can inundate the DNS servers authoritative for the example.com domain, thereby denying service.

Worse still, the ripple effect on the recursive server(s) to which the queries have been launched, e.g. the attacker's ISP's DNS servers, can be debilitating. Once the authoritative servers have essentially crashed, the recursive server continues processing queries. As the number of outstanding unanswered queries grows, the ability of the recursive servers to handle new legitimate queries diminishes, thereby reducing or even denying recursive DNS services for the ISP's customers.

Figure 10.2 shows the basic attack flow. An attacker may enlist a botnet formed from a collection of malware-infected residential devices of a given ISP. When the attack commences, attacker resolvers flood the ISP's recursive server with queries requesting resolution for PRSD names beneath the target domain as discussed above. As the queries mount against the authoritative DNS servers, legitimate queries are drowned out, and ultimately the authoritative servers may crash. Meanwhile, as the recursive DNS servers continue to launch queries, they may exhaust their resources awaiting responses on unanswered queries to the target authoritative DNS servers. This service denial not only impacts the target domain's DNS servers but also the recursive servers.

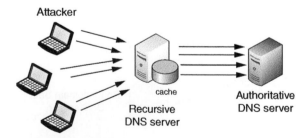

Figure 10.2 Pseudorandom subdomain attack.

Denial of Service Mitigation

Effective DoS mitigation requires limiting the level of server processing of attack packets such that legitimate packets are still handled properly. Methods to reduce the impact of D/DOS attacks include the following:

- Inbound ACLs at the server and DNS service level regarding from which IP networks or hosts the server will process queries.
- Inbound rate limiting of packets from specific sources and/or by type (TCP, UDP, DNS, etc.).
- DNS anycast deployment where multiple DNS servers use a common IP address. This approach was proven effective against a DDOS attack against Internet DNS root servers in February 2007.
- To protect against bogus query attacks, limit the number of outstanding queries per client.
- Implement outbound query quotas to constrain the quantity of outstanding queries for a given server or zone.

Reflector Style Attacks

The reflector form of attack attempts to use one or more DNS servers to send massive amounts of data to a particular target, thereby denying service for the target machine. Accomplishing this type of attack relies on leveraging DNS servers (or routes to DNS servers) which do not perform ingress IP filtering and on DNS servers configured to enable recursion. Typically, this form of attack features an attacker querying "open resolvers" or Internet-facing DNS servers configured to enable query recursion (Figure 10.3).

While recursion should be disabled for authoritative external DNS servers, unfortunately, there are millions of so configured servers operating on the Internet today according to the Open Resolver Project [83]. Upon receiving a query from a given IP address, each server will perform its recursion function and respond accordingly to the purported requesting IP address. This attack is analogous to a Smurf attack, initially observed in the 1990's whereby an attacker would spoof the target IP address within ICMP (used for "ping" and similar utilities) packets directed at numerous Internet servers to inundate the target with the spoofed IP address with ping responses.

- *Reflector attack* – The attacker issues numerous queries to one or more DNS servers using the target machine's IP address as the source IP address in each DNS query. This attack could be issued using authoritative or recursive DNS servers which will happily respond accordingly to the source IP address.

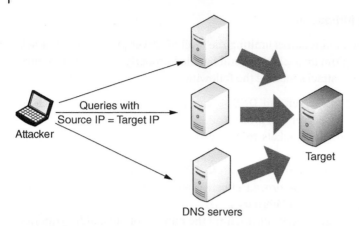

Figure 10.3 Reflector style attack.

If several servers are queried at the same time, the volume of DNS response packets can become very large.

- Amplification – Using the reflector approach while querying for resource record types with large quantities of data such as ANY queries, naming authority pointer (NAPTR), and DNSSEC-signed answers amplifies this attack by providing much larger response packets. Each responding server responds with the data to the "requestor" at the spoofed IP address to inundate this target with a large data flow, amplifying the attack volume with respect to typical query answers [84].

Reflector Attack Mitigation

Reflector and amplification attacks entail an attacker issuing a high volume of DNS queries using the source IP address of the intended target. To protect against this style of attack, the following techniques may be employed:

- Provision ingress filtering on routers to minimize the ability to spoof addresses.
- Implement response rate limiting to control the response flow to a reasonable level.

Authoritative Poisoning

Authoritative poisoning attacks attempt to corrupt DNS information published within authoritative DNS servers. Unlike cached information which eventually times out, corruption of authoritative information persists until detected and corrected. Poisoning of authoritative DNS server information enables an attacker to modify resolution data directly on the server resolving DNS queries. Authoritative DNS servers may be infiltrated with falsified resource record data by the following means.

- *Dynamic updates* – An attacker may attempt to inject or modify data in a DNS zone by attempting to issue a DNS Update message to the DNS server. This type of attack could manipulate resolution data, redirecting resolutions from clients for the intended destination to an attacker-specified destination.
- *Server configuration* – An attacker may attempt to gain access to the physical server running the DNS service. One of the many actions an attacker can take upon gaining access is to edit DNS files residing on the system to manipulate resolution data. Assuming the infiltrated server is a DNS master for its configured zones, modified DNS zone data will be automatically conveyed to zone secondaries to appear fully authoritative.
  Among other attacker steps beyond being able to manipulate configuration and zone information, an attack of this type could enable the use of the server as a stepping stone to other targets, especially if this server is trusted internally.
- *Configuration errors* – While typically not malicious (though most attacks are initiated from internal sources), misconfiguring the DNS service and/or zone information may lead to improper resolution or server behavior.

Authoritative Poisoning Mitigation

Zone editing requires either physical access to the server or the ability to transfer falsified data to the server using a file transfer protocol (FTP, TFTP), secure copy protocol (SCP), etc.) or via DNS zone transfer. If an administrator uses a separate configuration tool such as a DNS GUI or IPAM system, entry mistakes or uncaught errors could corrupt a zone's information. Mitigation of these forms of zone information corruption consists of the following techniques:

- Implement DNS server host access controls and monitor and audit access attempts and activities.
- DNS server operating system hardening to prevent access via unauthorized protocols.
- Limit DNS file permissions settings on a need to know basis and check for file changes, e.g. by detecting file checksum changes over time.
- Use of a robust DNS GUI or IPAM system or use of DNS configuration or zone checking utilities to maximize server information integrity.
- ACLs on hosts/networks from which the server will accept DDNS (and Notify) messages.
- Implement signatures on DDNS updates and zone transfers.

Resolver Redirection Attacks

The stub resolver on a client device must be initialized with at least one DNS server IP address to which DNS queries can be issued. This IP address is the destination address for all DNS queries originating from the client. Other resolver configuration information such as domains suffixes may also be defined. The resolver configuration may be performed manually or automatically via DHCP or PPP. If an attacker can redirect recursive queries to a server under their control, any and all resolution information can be corrupted at will.

- *Corruption through DHCP/PPP* – This type of attack seeks to redirect the resolver from the legitimate recursive DNS server to an attacker's DNS server to poison the resolver with malicious DNS query answers. Manipulation of client configuration obtained through DHCP or PPP would generally require the provision of a rogue DHCP or Radius server on the part of the attacker.
This attack vector was engaged via "Trojan.AndroidOS.Switcher" Android malware which attacks wireless access points [85]. When an infected device discovers its presence on a Wi-Fi network, it attempts to login to the wireless router administrative interface via user ID and password guessing. Once the malware accesses the wireless router, it modifies the DNS server parameters to point all the Wi-Fi network's DHCP clients to the attacker's DNS servers.
- *Device infiltration* – An attack to gain access to a device could provide the ability to edit the resolver configuration among other host information including installation of a root certificate signed by a rogue certificate authority (CA) operated by the attacker. This infiltration could be in the form of a brute force attempt to access the host resolver software or via malware.

Resolver redirection can be an effective means for an attacker to resolve seemingly attractive queries, e.g. to financial institutions, to direct the user to the attacker's site, which may proxy the session to the legitimate site to capture user information in transit as illustrated in Figure 10.4. The installation of the attacker's certificate enables seemingly legitimate transport layer security (TLS) connection to a malicious web server.

Individual client resolver attacks can severely impact the corresponding client device but generally have little impacts on other DNS components.

Resolver Attack Defenses

Attackers desiring to steer resolvers to illicit recursive servers may attempt to corrupt the "DNS servers" setting (among others) of the resolver accordingly. Protecting against this class of attack necessitates the following actions:

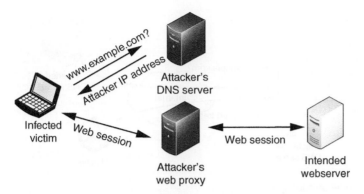

Figure 10.4 Resolver infiltration for man in the middle attack.

- Device access controls
- Verify proper provisioning of DHCP/PPP parameter settings
- Monitor for rogue DHCP servers which may be setting improper parameters
- Monitor to detect unauthorized resolver configuration changes and changes to DHCP server configurations

Securing DNS Transactions

Cache Poisoning Style Attacks

DNS resolvers and recursive caching servers maintain a cache of resolved resource records to improve resolution performance as described earlier. If an attacker succeeds in corrupting a recursive server's cache, the corrupted information may be provided to several users requesting the same or similar domain name information. Corrupting the cache requires an attacker to provide a seemingly legitimate query answer with falsified resolution information in part or in total.

These types of attacks are generally conducted as shown in Figure 10.5, where an attacker appears to the recursive server as the legitimate authoritative server to which it issued the query. In the various forms of this attack, ultimately the attacker attempts to corrupt the cache of the recursive server, e.g. by pointing the resolution of a legitimate and even popular web or server address to a server operated by the attacker. What's worse, the falsified resolution data is returned not only to the originator of the query but is also returned to other resolvers querying for this information while the corrupted information resides in cache, i.e. for the duration of the TTL. This has the effect of hijacking potentially several resolvers and hence applications to incorrect destinations, e.g. websites.

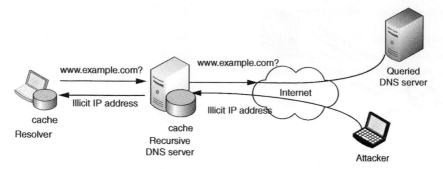

Figure 10.5 DNS cache poisoning.

To corrupt the cache, the DNS query response from the attacker must reach the querying recursive server before the legitimate response and must map to an outstanding query for which the recursive server is awaiting a response. The server will map a received answer to a previously issued query by matching the following fields in the response:

- The source IP address of the response maps to the destination IP address of the query and the destination IP address matches the address of this server.
- The destination port of the response matches the source port of the query and the responder's source port is 53.
- The DNS transaction ID within the DNS header matches on both the query and the response.
- The DNS question consisting of the queried name, class, and resource record type (RRtype) matches on both the query and the response.
- The domain names in the Authority and Additional sections of the response must fall within the same domain branch as the queried name. This is known as the bailiwick check.

Consider a recursive DNS server that receives two responses matching these criteria. The DNS server will generally accept the first matching answer it receives, cache it and respond to the stub resolver. If the attacker can match the parameters with a falsified answer that arrives before the legitimate answer from the authoritative name server, he or she will have succeeded in poisoning the cache with an answer that will be provided to other clients querying similar information.

Most cache poisoning attacks modify the answer itself, e.g., pointing www. example.com to an IP address operated by the attacker. The Kaminsky attack is a form of cache poisoning attack that actually manipulates the names or addresses with records of the Authority or Additional sections of the DNS message, and may even provide an accurate answer in the Answer section. Please refer to Chapter 19 for details regarding the DNS message structure.

Cache Poisoning Mitigation

The only definitive mitigation to cache poisoning is DNSSEC. DNSSEC eliminates the possibility of an attacker successfully poisoning the recursive server cache provided that the resolution data is DNSSEC-signed and the recursive server is configured to validate DNSSEC responses. DNSSEC provides origin authentication such that only the domain publisher can be authenticated, as well as data integrity checking to verify no data manipulation occurred in transit between the authoritative server and the recursive server. Authenticated denial of existence of resource record information is also provided by DNSSEC, so an attacker cannot indicate that an otherwise valid domain name does not exist.

DNSSEC Overview

DNSSEC uses digital signatures to enable the originator of a given set of data to sign the data using a private key, and a recipient to validate the data using a corresponding public key. Using asymmetric key cryptography, a private/public key pair is mathematically bonded such that data signed with the private key can be only be validated using the corresponding public key. This provides a means for holders of the public key to verify that data was signed using the private key, authenticating the data. Digital signatures also enable verification that the data received matches the data published and was not tampered with in transit.

Referring to Figure 10.6, the data originator, shown on the left of the figure, generates a private key/public key pair and utilizes the private key to sign the data. The first step in signing the data is to produce a hash of the data. Hashes are one-way functions[1] that scramble data into a fixed length string for simpler manipulation, and represent a "fingerprint" of the data. This means that it is very unlikely that another data input could produce the same hash value. Thus, hashes are

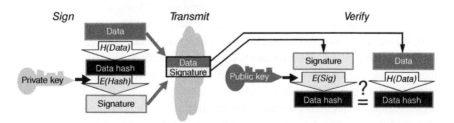

Figure 10.6   Digital signature creation and verification process.

---

[1] A one-way function means that the original data is not uniquely derivable from the hash. That is, one can apply an algorithm to create the hash, but there is no inverse algorithm to perform on the hash to arrive at the original data.

often used as checksums but don't provide any origin authentication (anyone knowing the hash algorithm can simply hash arbitrary data). The hash is processed using the private key to produce the signature.

Both the data and its associated signature are transmitted to or otherwise obtained by the recipient. Note that the data itself is not encrypted, merely signed. The recipient must have access to the public key that corresponds to the private key used to sign the data. In some cases, a secure (trusted) public key distribution system such as a public key infrastructure (PKI) is used to make public keys available. In the case of DNSSEC, public keys are published within DNS and signatures are included with query answers (i.e. the signed data).

The recipient computes a hash of the received resource record data, as did the data originator. The recipient applies the encryption algorithm to the received signature with the originator's public key. This operation is the inverse of the signature production process and produces the original data hash as its output. The result of this decryption, the original data hash, is compared with the recipient's computed hash of the data. If they match, the data has not been modified and the private key holder signed the data. If the private key holder can be trusted, the data is considered secure.

Any attempt to spoof or otherwise modify the resource record set (RRSet) data in route to the destination would be detectable by the recipient, i.e. the resolver or more typically, its recursive/caching DNS server on its behalf. This feature makes DNSSEC an effective mitigation strategy against man-in-the-middle and cache poisoning attacks.

The DNSSEC Resolution Process

The basic resolution process we reviewed in Chapter 4 still applies in terms of locating the DNS servers that are authoritative for the domain name in question by walking down the domain tree, then querying an authoritative server for an answer. If the recursive server is configured to validate and the resolution data is signed, the recursive server will perform the validation once the resolution data has been received. Thus, the validation process commences after the resolution process completes though much of the data required for validation can be gathered during the resolution process.

Let's assume the recursive server is configured with the DNS root zone trust anchor (public key). This trust anchor ultimately validates signed resolution data down the chain of trust, which mirrors the domain tree. Another way to think of this is given the resolution data and signatures received from the authoritative DNS server relevant to the query answer, we can trace the chain of trust up the DNS tree to the root zone to validate the signature. Figure 10.7 illustrates this basic process.

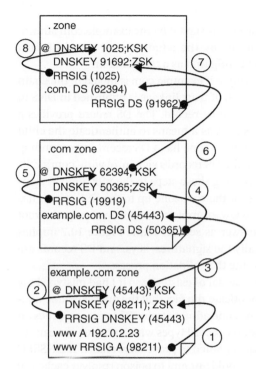

Figure 10.7 DNSSEC chain of trust traversal.

Let's say I've issued an A record query for www.example.com. My recursive server is configured to validate DNSSEC and has the trust anchor corresponding to key signing key (KSK) id 1025 configured. My recursive server issues iterative queries down the domain tree. The example.com administrator has signed the zone and the authoritative DNS server responds with the answer to my query and includes a signature for the www.example.com A resource record set in the form of an resource record set signature (RRSIG) resource record.

To validate this signature, I'll need the zone's public key(s) that correspond to the private key(s) used to sign the zone. Zones are usually signed with two keys, a zone signing key (ZSK) to sign all RRSets in the zone and a key signing key (KSK) a longer key which signs only the zone's public keys. We'll discuss the motivation for this approach later, but these public keys are published in the zone file in the form of the DNSKEY RRSet.

The recursive server first validates the query answer, the A record answer by hashing the answer and applying the ZSK to compare with the RRSIG signature. If these match, shown as step 1 in Figure 10.7, the recursive server shall repeat this process to validate the ZSK and KSK by verifying the signature on the DNSKEY RRset as step 2. Having performed these two validations, my recursive server can confirm that the query answer was signed by the example.com administrator and the answer was as published by the administrator. But do I trust example.com's key? No, this key is not configured as a trust anchor.

Thus, the recursive server must determine if example.com is linked in the chain of trust to its parent zone, .com. This chain of trust linkage is published in DNS in the form of a delegation signer (DS) resource record. The DS record provides a hash of the corresponding child zone's KSK as a means to authenticate the child KSK. Step 3 in our process verifies the parent zone has a DS record corresponding to example.com's KSK. Step 4 validates the DS record's signature with .com's ZSK while step 5 validates .com's keys. Repeating these steps to the root zone in steps 6–8, we arrive at validating signatures for the root zone up to the KSK which has linked down to our query answer for www.example.com. Since we trust the root zone public KSK, we consider this answer as secure. While Figure 10.7 implies querying "up" the domain tree, typically the signatures, keys, and DS records are cached by the recursive server to expedite the validation process.

DNSSEC also provides authenticated denial of existence so if I had mistyped my query, the recursive server could authenticate the fact that the queried name does not exist in the zone as published by the zone administrator. This process relies on the next secure (NSEC) or NSEC3 resource record types which provide a means of identifying the "gap" into which the query failed to prove answerable. If DNSSEC did not provide this feature, an attacker could attempt to poison resolver caches by sending nonexistent domain (NXDOMAIN) responses for otherwise valid data. Imagine an NXDOMAIN answer honored by caching servers for your www address. Fortunately, with DNSSEC this vulnerability can be mitigated.

Just as passwords should be changed periodically, signing keys should also be changed. We'll talk the specifics regarding the mechanics for changing (rolling) keys in Chapter 12, but the impact on recursive servers is that if the root zone key changes without updating the trust anchor configuration, DNSSEC validations will fail. Fortunately, RFC 5011 [86], defines a means for recursive servers to automatically detect trust anchor changes and to update corresponding trust anchor configuration. RFC 5011 defines the procedures for authenticating new and revoked trusted keys based on a manually configured initial trusted key. This "initial key" serves as the "initial condition" in rolling forward over time with new, revoked, and deleted root zone keys. All major recursive server vendors automatically provide the root public keys for validation by default and automatically detect and update this trust anchor as the root zone key rolls over.

Negative Trust Anchors

As DNS administrators initially implement DNSSEC, they sometimes make errors in properly aligning the keys, zone signing, timing, and linking the chain of trust.

After all, public key cryptography is not natively an area of expertise for DNS administrators. Nevertheless, such misconfigurations can cause errors in DNSSEC validation, breaking the chain of trust.

If you detect validation failures for a certain domain, contact the domain administrator to convey the issue and to confirm the issue is indeed an error condition and not an attack such as a key compromise. If confirmed to be user error, you can define the domain as a negative trust anchor, which temporarily suspends the domain from requiring DNSSEC validation for successful resolution. Your users will be able to resolve DNS information for this domain, albeit without DNSSEC validation.

Ask the domain administrator when they expect to repair the DNSSEC configuration. You can obtain the domain administrator's email address from the zone's SOA record or possibly from whois. Try to perform a DNSSEC query for a record in the domain at the appointed time. If the issue persists, notify the domain administrator. No one likes to be a nag, but if this domain is relatively popular, nagging may be the only means at your disposal to encourage resolution of the issue. Once resolved, you should remove the negative trust anchor to re-engage DNSSEC validation for the domain.

ISC BIND enables the setting of negative trust anchors via its remote name daemon controls (rndc) control channel. Use the rndc nta command to configure the specified domain as a negative trust anchor. You can configure the nta-lifetime and nta-recheck options within the named.conf options block to configure the default time until the negative trust anchor expires and DNSSEC validation is restored for the domain and the interval between automated DNSSEC enabled queries to the domain to detect resumption of proper DNSSEC validation, respectively. These options help automate the detection of resumption of zone signing without the necessity of nagging the zone administrator.

DNSSEC Deployment

In order to authenticate each DNS query answer, the answer must be signed. Thus, the authoritative server must publish signed zones and the recursive server must perform DNSSEC validation. Unfortunately, while 91% of the US government zones are signed, only 8% of university zones and 3% of industry zones are signed according to NIST estimates [87]. Thus, the majority of non-US government zones remains unsigned as of today. In terms of DNSSEC validating resolvers, APNIC measurements indicate about one-third of DNS resolvers support DNSSEC validation [88].

As mentioned, major DNS server vendors support DNSSEC validation by default, and we recommend you configure your recursive servers accordingly. However, given the modest deployment of signed zones, the additional measures of randomized Transaction IDs and UDP port numbers must be implemented to protect your DNS caches. Case randomization may also be used for added entropy if your server supports this.

Last Mile Protection

Since the recursive server typically performs DNSSEC validation, not the stub resolver, resolution data is only validated between the recursive server and the authoritative server. There is an implicit trust network between the stub resolver and the recursive server. However, this may not be the case and this link between the stub resolver and the recursive server, sometimes referred to as "the last mile," may not be secured. We discuss here some approaches to secure this link should it be of sufficient risk to your organization.

DNS Cookies

DNS cookies provide a lightweight authentication mechanism for DNS clients and servers without requiring configuration *a priori*. The client creates a cookie by hashing its IP address, server IP address, and a random quantity and passes this to the server. The server can respond with its own cookie which the client would use in subsequent queries, based on a hash of the querier's IP address, cookie, and random quantity.

The use of DNS cookies could be used as a weak form of authentication in this case. Alternatively, Microsoft requires an secure sockets layer (SSL) connection from Windows clients to Windows DNS servers to secure this link. Other forms of authentication and encryption using datagram transaction layer security (DTLS) could be used as well. Implementation may be challenging based on the quantities and types of clients you support in your network. This should be considered when assessing your risk of last mile corruption.

DNS Encryption

DNS Over TLS (DoT)

TLS is an Internet standards track protocol for securing Internet communications, providing authentication, integrity verification, and confidentiality/encryption [89]. TLS comprises two primary components:

- A handshake protocol to authenticate the entities establishing communications and to negotiate parameters of the communication.

- A record protocol which encrypts IP traffic using keys as parameters negotiated within the handshake protocol.

A client initiates a TCP connection to a server and begins the TLS handshake indicating its supported encryption capabilities and a random number. The server uses a private key to sign the random number and presents an ISO X.509 certificate which conveys the server domain name, issuing authority, the public key corresponding to the signing private key, and other information. If the client successfully decrypts the random number and is configured to trust the presented certificate, the client may then deem the server trustworthy. This is typically the case within a private network where a trusted certificate is preinstalled on the validating device. In the general case, the client needs to follow the certificate to a trusted certificate authority (CA) that has signed the servers' certificate. If the CA is trusted and verifies the certificate, the client then trusts the server and initiates the TLS connection.

TLS is designed to support any TCP application, and not surprisingly, the most popular application is http, which when encrypted via TLS becomes https. Http sessions are initiated on port 80 while https generally uses port 443. Other TCP applications leverage TLS as well, including internet message access protocol (IMAP), SMTP, FTP, Telnet, DNS, and others. DNS over TLS [90] requires establishment of a TCP session as opposed to the common use of UDP for DNS.[2]

A resolver desiring to query DNS over TLS (DoT) opens a TCP session with the corresponding DNS server on port 853 (or another pre-defined port but not 53). After establishing the TCP session, the TLS handshake ensues, then the client and server encrypt subsequent DNS communications.

DNS Over HTTPS (DoH)

While http over TLS provides secure web browsing, DNS over http over TLS provides a means for web browsers to initiate DNS queries and receive responses over https. DNS over https (DoH) [91] has stirred controversy within the Internet community for several reasons, chief among them the Mozilla-Cloudflare partnership which implements DoH by default without user opt-in. While encrypting DNS traffic protects user privacy, the autocratic funneling of all Mozilla browser-initiated DNS queries to a single DoH provider, Cloudflare, by default reduces the uninitiated user's freedom of choice regarding implementing DoH and with whom.

Figure 10.8 illustrates the basic DNS query architecture without DoH and with a DoH service provider. In the top portion of the figure, DNS queries from stub resolvers are directed to configured recursive DNS servers. Within an enterprise environment, these recursive servers typically reside within the enterprise network, affording IT managers visibility to DNS traffic for performance monitoring,

---

[2] It is also possible to operate DNS over datagram TLS [288] which supports TLS over UDP.

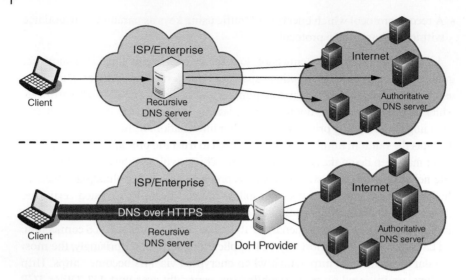

Figure 10.8 DNS query architecture without DoH (top) and with DoH (bottom).

query/response analytics, DNS firewalling, tunneling mitigation, and anomaly detection. ISPs have analogous access to DNS data within a residential or wireless environment where the broadband or wireless provider is the ISP. Many ISPs offer services that rely on real time DNS data such as parental control features and access for law enforcement in response to subpoenas or other regulatory requests.

With the implementation of DoH, illustrated in the bottom half of Figure 10.8, DNS queries are encrypted within an https session between the client (browser) and the DoH provider. The role of the DoH provider is to serve as the https endpoint and to proxy DNS queries to Internet-based authoritative DNS servers. The backend query resolution process between the DoH provider and authoritative DNS servers is not encrypted, so this is not an end-to-end solution in this scenario, but it does encrypt DNS data, occluding DNS traffic visibility to enterprise or ISP administrators.

In the non-DoH scenario, recursive DNS administrators gain visibility to all of your DNS queries. This affords them the ability to block malware-infected devices or otherwise analyze query and response traffic, which is key to IPAM performance management practices. Thus, such access is desirable for enterprise organizations certainly and ISPs can use this data for various purposes.

With DoH, DNS queries are indistinguishable from web traffic and traffic cannot reasonably be blocked nor analyzed for performance or security purposes. The DoH architecture also centralizes DNS query information. Without DoH, each ISP has DNS traffic visibility, though there are hundreds of diverse ISPs throughout the world; with DoH all query traffic is invisible to these ISPs but fully visible to the DoH provider, of which there exist a handful. This concentration of DNS query information affords the DoH provider DNS traffic details for a vastly larger set of resolvers than in the decentralized ISP architecture.

In summary, DoH remains controversial as of this writing for the following key reasons:

- Internet DNS centralization empowers DoH providers with vast DNS data including all DNS queries for each user, a glaring privacy concern.
- Loss of geographic-based resolution to steer a client to the "closest" destination.
- This architecture does not support end-to-end encryption as the second leg of queries originated by the DoH provider is unencrypted.
- Inhibits enterprise organizations' abilities to monitor or DNS traffic for performance management.
- Eliminates enterprise organizations' abilities to apply response policies, apply query limiting or quotas (DDoS protection), and other DNS-related security measures.
- Prevents ISPs from abiding by law enforcement requests for access to DNS information.
- Nonbrowser-initiated Internet sessions, e.g. via email POP clients, potentially introduce disparity in use of DoH.
- DoH is redundant to DoT.

To the extent that you as an IT administrator control user device configuration, you could impose configuration constraints to prohibit use of DoH. For field or remote workers, you could setup your own DoT or DoH proxy servers within your DMZ. This would enable your users to encrypt DNS queries to prevent snooping within coffee shops, airports, or other public places. Otherwise, for user-owned devices with DoH configured resolvers, you could deploy your own DoH proxy and instruct users on configuration steps for connecting to it.

Encryption Beyond the Last Mile

The DNS Privacy working group within the IETF has produced RFCs regarding DNS over TLS and DNS over DTLS, among other technologies.[3] The working group is currently working on specifications for incorporation of DoT and related techniques to secure communications between recursive servers and authoritative servers. The working group is striving to specify methods to protect privacy and encrypt DNS queries and responses beyond the stub resolver to recursive server to enable encryption of DNS queries and responses from recursive servers to the root, TLD, and subdomain authoritative DNS servers.

---

[3] Though not DoH, which was published by the DoH working group.

11

IPAM and Network Security

The prior chapter discussed the security of your vital IPAM network services in terms of securing servers providing such services as well as assuring the integrity of the services provided. This chapter covers the use of IPAM technologies to secure the integrity of your overall IP network: controlling network access, defending against malware, mitigating network disruptions, and preventing data theft.

Securing Network Access

Network access control or "(NAC)" is a broad term which comprises a set of technologies which seek to identify who is attempting to access your network prior to providing such access. Various techniques are available offering various levels of access control. We'll start by analyzing DHCP-based access control, which admittedly is among the weaker approaches to network access control. We'll then touch on more wide-reaching techniques.

Discriminatory Address Assignment with DHCP

Let's focus first on DHCP services and some approaches to implement discriminatory address assignment. There are several levels of policies or controls most DHCP solutions provide for discrimination of "who's asking" for an IP address via DHCP. The first is to simply filter requests by an available form of client identifier such as the MAC address of the client requesting an address. Recall that DHCPv6 device identifiers consist of the DUID and Identity Associations (IAs) which identify each client and interface, respectively, while the MAC address is found in the chaddr field of a DHCPv4 packet.

If the DHCP server has a list of acceptable (and/or unacceptable) device identifiers, it can be configured to provide a certain IP address and associated

IP Address Management, Second Edition. Michael Dooley and Timothy Rooney.
© 2021 The Institute of Electrical and Electronics Engineers, Inc.
Published 2021 by John Wiley & Sons, Inc.

parameters to those clients with an acceptable identifier, and either no IP address or a limited function IP address to those without an acceptable device identifier. By *limited function IP address*, we mean that the network routing infrastructure is preconfigured to route IP packets with such source IP addresses (source address dependent routing) to only certain networks, such as to the Internet only. An IP packet with source address A may be routable across the enterprise while one with source address B may be routable only to the Internet, for example.

This type of IP address and configuration assignment is similar to the filtering on the client class of the device requesting an IP address as discussed in Chapter 5. Certain clients, such as VoIP phones, provide additional information about themselves when requesting an IP address in the vendor class identifier field of the DHCP packet. The user class identifier field may also be used or even the option request option which some vendors refer to as a "DHCP fingerprint." If your DHCP server can be configured to recognize particular option values provided by the client, then you can selectively configure the client's IP address and configuration parameters. Addresses can be assigned from a certain pool and/or additional configuration parameters can be provided to the client via standard or vendor-specific DHCP options.

Another level of discriminating IP address assignment is possible by authenticating the user of the machine requesting an IP address. This function can be used in conjunction with discriminatory address assignment. For example, if a client with an unknown or unacceptable device identifier attempts to obtain an IP address, one option is to completely deny an address; another option is to require the user of the client to login via a secure access web portal page.

This enables easier capture of new device identifiers for legitimate users of your network. (Those users sometimes bring in new devices!) Solutions ranging from perl scripts such as NetReg [92], to sophisticated integrated software solutions are available to direct such users to a login/password requesting webpage. A simple lookup against a database of legitimate users then allows access or denial of the client to a production IP address. These systems typically work in accordance with the following packet flow as illustrated in Figure 11.1.

Walking through this flow, the process begins with a device connecting to the network, attempting to obtain an IP address via DHCP. The DHCP server, employing device identifier or client class type filtering, determines if the device is a known user device.[1] If the device is known or has otherwise already authenticated, the DHCP process may continue with an Offer/Advertise for a production IP address, followed by a Request and Ack/Reply. However, if the device is not known or is required to authenticate, the DHCP server can still provide an IP address though the IP address assigned in this case would be a *captive portal*, *walled garden*, or *quarantined* IP address.

---

1 In some cases, even known user devices may require periodic reauthentication as a security precaution.

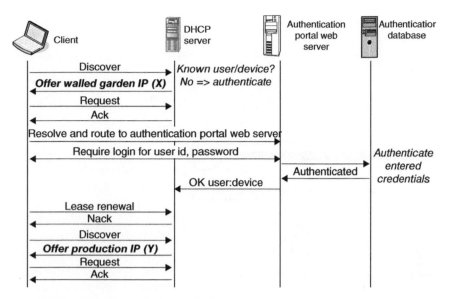

Figure 11.1 Basic DHCP captive portal flow.

These terms refer to the fact that the IP address assigned to the client will only be routed to the subnet or VLAN that has the authentication web server and associated servers running. This quarantined VLAN enables IP communications but only to this restricted set of devices. This approach seeks to cordon off the device from infiltrating the rest of the network until the corresponding user can be authenticated. The routing infrastructure must be configured to route packets with a source address from the quarantined address pool to the quarantined VLAN and/or the client must be configured with the classless static route option. Thus, walled garden address X as shown in Figure 11.1 is a member of the quarantined VLAN, on which only limited network resources are available. Figure 11.2 illustrates an example network topology of this captive portal configuration.

Now when the user opens up a web browser, he/she can type in any web address. A *limited configuration* DNS server is required on the quarantined VLAN; limited in the sense that it will resolve any and every query to the IP address of the authentication web server. Thus, no matter what website address is entered in the web browser, the web address is resolved to the captive portal web server. The authentication web server presents the login page. You may have seen something similar to this if you travel and use a hotel's broadband or wireless service. Once the requested credentials are entered, which for an enterprise environment, would typically comprise a user ID and password, the web page can pass the entered credentials to a back-end database for authentication.

Based upon the results of the authentication, the requesting device would then be deemed authorized or not, and if authorized, optionally at a particular service

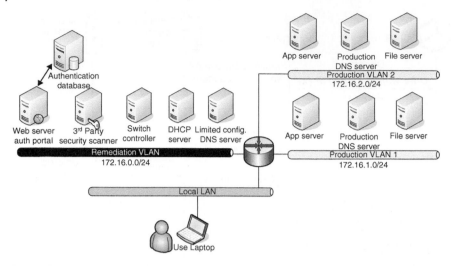

Figure 11.2 Captive portal network diagram.

class. The service class of authorization provides more granularity than a simple Boolean "authorized or not," where different authorized users can be assigned a different production IP address, which in turn can provide access to different network resources. For example, basic-level users may be granted access to a basic set of resources, while advanced-level users may be granted access to additional resources, e.g. IT resources. Once again this requires the routing topology be configured with multiple source-routed or VLAN segments, with these networks and corresponding routing plan mapped to DHCP server configurations in terms of associating address pools with service levels.

The manner in which the production IP address is assigned follows from expiration or denial of renewal of the quarantined IP address. The quarantined IP address lease time is generally configured as a short lease time (~1–5 minutes). This enables the device to attempt to renew quickly. Should the device still be in the process of authentication, its renewal attempt would be ACK'd, extending the lease. Once authentication is completed successfully, the authentication system updates the DHCP server to add the device identifier to the "known" or "allow" pool. The renewal attempt for the quarantined address would then be NAK'd, enabling a fresh DHCP process to provide a "production" IP address (address Y in Figure 11.1). Should the device fail authentication, the renewal can be NAK'd and subsequent address attempts denied; alternatively, the quarantined address renewal attempt can be granted in order to provide access only to resources on the quarantined network if desired.

Beyond these device and user identification measures based on device identifiers, this general flow can also provide additional validation on the machine requesting the IP address. The DHCP process can be used to invoke an external security scanning system like openVAS or another third-party application to scan the requesting client for viruses or to validate use of acceptable virus protection software. This device scanning step can be used alone or in conjunction with the device identification measures to provide a robust access security solution via DHCP.

Let's consider the network configuration for DHCP-based secure access is depicted in Figure 11.2. The DHCP server shown in the diagram would be configured with a number of client class sets. We refer to the client class as the matching criteria in the DHCP packet, which links to the associated network accessibility. For example, we would need a client class set for at least each of the following in our example:

- Captive portal network (Remediation VLAN)
- Production network 1 network
- Production network 2 network

Think of these client class sets as bins into which individual clients are placed based on the linking of their authentication state to the device's client class. Thus, client class members would be categorized by the DHCP server in accordance with defined client classes as they appear on the network and users authenticate. These client classes would generally map to pool definitions on the DHCP server as shown in the following simple example ISC server configuration [30]. Note that additional options can be defined for each of the pools to provide additional configuration granularity to clients falling into each set or pool.

```
subnet 172.16.0.0 netmask 255.255.252.0 {
# subnet level options here…
    pool{                                      #captive portal pool
        range 172.16.0.10 172.16.0.254;
        option domain-name-servers 172.16.0.5; #limited config DNS server
        default-lease-time 150;                #short lease time
        allow unknown clients;                 #clients not predefined.
    }
    pool {                                     #Prod Net 1
        range 172.16.1.10 172.16.1.254;
        option domain-name-servers 172.16.1.5; #production DNS server
        default-lease-time 14400;              #normal lease time
        deny unknown clients;                  #clients must be predefined.
        allow members of "net1";               #client class net1 allowed
    }
    pool {                                     #Prod Net 2
        range 172.16.2.10 172.16.2.254;
        option domain-name-servers 172.16.2.5; #production DNS server
        default-lease-time 14400;              #normal lease time
        deny unknown clients;                  #clients must be predefined.
        allow members of "net2";               #client class net2 allowed
    }
}
```

Based on the results of the authentication process, the authentication server must be able to update the DHCP configuration to place the client into the appropriate bin or class. Thus, if the device is successfully authenticated for access to production network 2, the authentication portal needs to add the specific device identifier to the client class group for production network 2 ("net2" class in the example above). This update may be performed, for example using the ISC DHCP server object management application programming interface (OMAPI) interface. This client class declaration can define class-specific options on the DHCP server to provide to the client, e.g. default gateway, DNS server, along with any other option.

The captive portal VLAN may consist only of "unknown clients," a designation configurable with the ISC DHCP server. The captive portal network (the remediation VLAN in the figure) is deployed including the limited configuration DNS server, web server as the authentication portal, with access to an authentication database, and optionally a security scanning server and any other required preaccess services.

More than one DHCP server may be deployed for high availability and/or for scaling for larger networks. This approach does complicate things, as the DHCP server configurations need to be consistent on both servers to route unknown clients or clients requiring authentication to the captive portal net. We'll explore this topic further in Chapter 14.

DHCP Lease Query

To verify alignment of authorized DHCP assignments with actual addresses attempting to initiate IP connections, DHCP lease query can be used. Given most or all addresses on a subnet are configured using DHCP by policy, each IP address *should* have a corresponding DHCP lease. The DHCP Lease Query is a DHCP protocol message that enables an edge router to query the DHCP server regarding the lease status of a particular device or set of devices. This provides some assurance that a device attempting to communicate via the router has not spoofed an address that should have been assigned by the DHCP server.

When the router receives IP traffic within a layer 2 frame from a particular device, for example it can issue a DHCPLeaseQuery message to its configured DHCP servers (i.e. in its role as relay agent) to determine the state of a DHCP lease, querying by IP address, DUID, or MAC address. If a DHCP server had previously provided a lease for the client, it will respond to the router, and the router will give the green light and route the device's packets. If not, the device does not have a lease and the router can drop the device's packets. The router can cache this information as well to constrain the Lease Query rate. Of course, this form of access control applies only when all clients on a subnet use DHCP such as in broadband access networks, not when other statically addressed devices communicate on the subnet.

Alternative Access Control Approaches

You may be thinking that the DHCP-based approach is fine for clients utilizing DHCP, but what about those "clever users" who figure out the subnet address, then manually encode a static IP address on their machines to access the network? These clever users may after all be those of most concern from a secure access perspective. In addition, for devices using SLAAC, no DHCP interaction is required for address assignment.

There are two basic alternative approaches for enabling detection and associated remediation action of devices without relying solely on the DHCP-based approach.

- Layer 2 switch alerting
- 802.1X

Layer 2 Switch Alerting

The layer 2 switch alerting approach leverages SNMP-enabled switches to issue an SNMP trap upon a link-up state on one of its ports and to accept port-level VLAN configurations. This alerting capability along with SNMP writeable configuration information can enable gatekeeper-like functionality by dynamically identifying devices attempting to access the network, and configuring the switch to provision the port to a particular VLAN. A third-party system or product would be needed to process traps, make decisions on appropriate VLAN assignments, and configure the switch accordingly.

Let's look at how this would work. If we consider the process of a device connecting to a network from the beginning, the device "boots up" on the network from layer 1 on up. Thus, the physical layer/electrical connectivity is first attained; then the data link layer is initialized whereby layer 2 frame synchronization occurs. Then layer 3 follows, with the issuing of a DHCP packet for example, or directly issuing IP packets if a static address is configured at layer 3. As the data link layer initializes (prior to layer 3), the switch to which the device is connected will deem the "link up" and issue a trap. Because the trap is sent prior to layer 3 initialization, this scheme can identify both statically addressed and yet-unassigned DHCP-addressed devices.

Traps would be directed to a system that can identify the link up state, ascertain the link layer (MAC) address of the newly connected device, then determine whether the device requires authentication or validation. This determination can be made via a MAC address database within the system that identifies known or acceptable MAC addresses and differentiates these from unknown or known unacceptable MAC addresses. The system would associate these two or perhaps more MAC address categorizations with corresponding VLAN assignments, which would then be programmed on the corresponding switch for the given port. The connected device would then be connected to the assigned VLAN. You can probably see the analogy to the DHCP scenario we discussed using client classes. In this case, the third-party system uses its database and configures the layer 2 switch using SNMP or other means instead of deferring to the IP address policies using DHCP.

For quarantined or captive portal access, the VLAN assignment would lead only to the authentication network. For those passing authentication and/or device validation, the system could reassign the MAC address to the acceptable list, then configure the switch accordingly to change the port's VLAN association. Depending on the authentication method, client software may or may not be required. For web-based login/password, it may not be necessary to configure each of your client computers with authentication clients. However, if Radius, or other challenge/response authentication strategies are employed, client software will be necessary.

802.1X

IEEE 802.1X is the foundation of most network access control systems, including those used for zero trust networks. 802.1X is a protocol specification enabling edge device capture of new access attempts, with the use of Radius authentication and dynamic switch port configuration. You may have used Radius in the days of pre-broadband Internet dial-up, which used the point-to-point protocol at layer 3. 802.1X, developed by the IEEE 802.1 working group focused on layer 2 protocols, is as you'd expect, a layer 2 protocol. 802.1X is based on standards, which theoretically enables use of different vendors' products as components within the overall solution.

As depicted in Figure 11.3, 802.1X requires a client or agent called a *supplicant*, which interacts with an *authentication server* by way of an *authenticator* (e.g. switch). Upon initial connection to a network, the supplicant utilizes Extensible Authentication Protocol (EAP) over 802.1x to initiate a connection request to the network access device. The switch can be configured to block all traffic by default except EAP packets from unauthenticated ports.

The access switch to which the device is connected at the data link layer, transmits the EAP traffic to the authentication (i.e. Radius) server. The Radius server, in turn, challenges the client for an ID and password. Upon successful authentication, the Radius server communicates to the edge device to enable access to the associated device's port. Certificate authentication via TLS is also supported by some vendors.

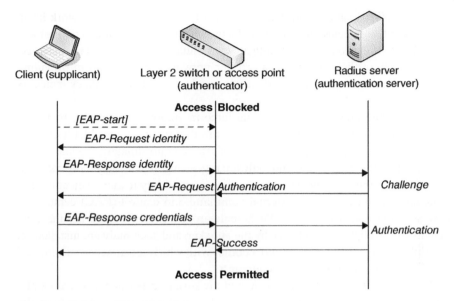

Figure 11.3 802.1X authentication.

Securing the Network Using IPAM

While useful in helping control access to your network, IPAM technologies can play an even stronger role in facilitating application of security policies, detecting malware, and in helping to prevent data exfiltration from your network.

IP-Based Security Policies (ACLs, etc.)

Effective address planning can help simplify application of IP address-based security policies such as ACLs, iptables or firewall rules, and for routing treatment preferences. As we discussed in Chapter 6 and particularly in Chapter 7, your IP address plan can facilitate enforcement of IP address-based security policies. You can sequence address allocation by application, region, site, etc., to enable creation of firewall or other filtering rules based on one or several address block entries, depending on ordering within your allocation process.

Malware Detection Using DNS

While DNS is the first step in IP communications, many enterprise security strategies trivialize or startlingly even ignore its role in communications and therefore its susceptibility to attacks on this vital network service or on the network itself. Most security strategies and solutions focus on filtering "in-band" communications flow in order to detect and mitigate cyber-attacks. However, as we shall see, filtering DNS traffic can support a broader network security plan in providing additional information for use in identifying and troubleshooting attack incidents such as malware infestation.

Malware continues to be a menacing force in enterprise networks. In earlier days, malware consisted of malicious software that stealthily installed itself on a device to perform a preprogrammed form of attack. Unfortunately, this static form of malware is the rarity today, and malware is growing increasingly more sophisticated in hiding itself on host systems, operating stealthily to avoid detection and remediation, and contacting external command and control (C&C) centers for new software and instructions. Such malware effectively transforms the host machine into a bot for remote use by the attacker, and such malware installed on multiple devices can be formed into a botnet with which the attacker may launch a variety of attacks from multiple endpoints.

Stealthy resilient malware is considered an advanced persistent threat (APT). The malware is advanced in its ability to adapt with software updates from the C&C center, persistent in the sense that it utilizes a variety of strategies to avoid detection and thus persist on the network, and a threat given the attack forms range from DDoS to data exfiltration.

Malware and APTs often utilize DNS to locate the attacker's C&C center. After all, if the malware used a hard-coded IP address, the malware could be shut down by simply blocking the corresponding IP address once the malware has been detected. Using DNS enables the malware operator to modify their IP address to avoid notice. They often modify their domain name as well to avoid detection, creating various forms of fast-flux networks using dynamically generated domain names.

Malware Proliferation Techniques

With the ubiquity of mobile devices which employees bring into the office and connect to your network, your control of endpoint security may be very constrained. Your perimeter defenses may be effective for protecting your network devices from attacks originating from the Internet, but if users bring infected devices physically into the confines of your network, you are susceptible to internal attacks instigated by malware unwittingly installed on user devices.

But malware can also be installed on residential or nonuser devices which may be less protected from Internet-based attacks. The September 2016 DDoS attack on Brian Krebs' security blog leveraging the Mirai malware installed on IoT devices highlights this vulnerability [94]. A similar attack was launched in October 2016 against DynDNS [82] weeks later where over 100 000 IoT devices infected with the Mirai malware launched a DDoS attack exceeding 1.2 Tbps. The botnet was formed by leveraging default user names and passwords installed on IoT devices such as surveillance cameras and home routers to gain access and install the malware.

Besides leveraging manufacturer default user IDs and passwords to access and install malware on devices, other methods for installing malware are widespread including the following tactics.

Phishing

Attackers may send generic emails enticing users to click a link that leads to their website for installation of their malware. Such emails may promise fortunes for the claiming or inform readers of a need to validate personal information or otherwise react to a pending dangerous situation, or any variety of means of enticement. The objective is to formulate an email that appears credible enough that several users will click the embedded link in order to download and quietly install the malware.

Spear Phishing

Spear phishing is a more focused phishing attack where the attacker targets a specific individual with the intent to appear "familiar" when contacting the target individual. By researching social media posts, public Internet information, or social engineering, the attacker may be able to send an email that garners a click from the target to download and install the attacker's malware.

Software Downloads

Who wouldn't want free software? Such offers of free stuff certainly attract attention and can be a useful tactic in phishing-related attacks. But any time users download software (even free malware removal software), music, games, etc., from Internet sites, they are susceptible to malware installation. Virus (malware) protection software can help to identify and prevent installation, but new malware may not yet be recognizable by current virus protection.

File Sharing

Any form of file sharing using shared media, network drives, or network protocols such as FTP, HTTP, or SCP exposes the recipient system to malware installation. At minimum, virus protection scanning of incoming files can help prevent installation of known malware. Such scanning should run periodically without user intervention.

Email Attachments

Clicking innocent looking email attachments may utilize embedded macros to install malware on the corresponding machine. Locky ransomware, for example typically arrives at a target machine via spam email in the form of a Microsoft Word (or Excel) attachment. When the attachment is opened and macros are permitted, the macro runs to download the malware and lock the files on the victim machine while displaying a ransom message.

A variant on this form of attack is subtler with the attacker embedding object linking and embedding (OLE) objects within a Microsoft document. When a user clicks on the embedded Word document for example, the document opens and runs a macro or embedded code to install malware.

Watering Hole Attack

A watering hole attack targets visitors of a given website. The website may function as a community of interest destination for users the attacker seeks to target. An attacker who can successfully infect the website to install his/her malware and entice visitors to the website to download it can successfully infect devices of such visitors.

Replication

Once installed on a device, some malware snoops your network and replicates itself, installing on other devices. Some malware can snoop IP traffic on the wire to identify potential targets to which to attempt to replicate.

Brute Force

The Mirai botnet, which attacked krebsonsecurity.com and DynDNS as mentioned previously, was formed when the attacker infiltrated a large number IoT devices such as surveillance cameras. For the most part, the attacker hacked into these IoT devices by merely logging in using vendor default user IDs and passwords. Having gained access, the malware was installed, establishing a huge botnet from which attacks could be launched. The attacker then published the source code of this Mirai malware online for free use by like-minded attackers to leverage this strategy.

Malware Examples

The following is merely a sampling of malware that has been identified and characterized. The complete list is much larger and continues to grow.

Backoff [95] – Malware targeting point-of-sale (POS) devices to capture credit card information to exfiltrate payment information to its C&C center. Backoff malware had infiltrated some high-profile retail companies.

Crytolocker [96] – Ransomware generally targeted at Windows machines via an email attachment typically appearing as a zip file containing a file with a .pdf extension which executes when opened.

Dridex [97] – P2P malware which seeks to infect computers, harvest credentials, and steal money from users' financial accounts, as well as participate in DDoS attacks and send spam.

Locky [98] – Ransomware which is typically installed by virtue of a user opening an email attachment which triggers the running of document macros.

Masque [99] – Malware installable on iOS devices that can steal login credentials, access sensitive data from local cache, and gain iOS root privileges.

Mirai [100] – Publicly published malware that installed itself on tens of thousands of IoT devices forming a botnet, launching high-profile attacks on Krebs Security and DynDNS.

Nivdort [101] – Malware that can delete Microsoft Windows system files, change security settings, and corrupt the Windows registry.

Simda [102] – Botnet with self-propagating capabilities which may reroute a user's Internet traffic to attacker websites, obtaining user credentials, installing additional malware, or performing other malicious activities.

Zeus or GameOverZeuS [96] – Trojan horse malware that runs on Microsoft Windows targets often used to gather keystrokes or form-captures to steal financial information.

Malware Mitigation

Up-to-date anti-malware software installed on all network-attached devices is recommended as a first line of detection at the device level to reject malware installation attempts. As malware producers develop new "strains" to outwit defenses, anti-malware vendors characterize behavior then develop remedies to quarantine or extricate the malware. Malware producers then seek new methods and the arms race spirals onward. Frequent changing of passwords is also recommended as is keeping kernel, operating system and application software patched and updated. Some firewalls and intrusion prevention systems can also be configured to block malware infiltration based on traffic patterns or signatures. Changing of vendor default user IDs and passwords, along with other host controls are necessary as well.

By analyzing your DNS query data, you may be able to identify the presence of malware within your network before your anti-virus software has remedied a block for it. While relying exclusively on DNS query data to detect malware is by no means recommended, DNS query analytics can serve as valuable input to your overall malware detection "eco-system" and mitigation strategy. Data from hosts, routers, firewalls, intrusion detection systems, and DNS can all help identify suspicious and malicious activity.

DNS Firewall

DNS itself can be used to block certain malware communications and identify infected hosts. DNS firewalls can block malware attempts to contact a known C&C center, as most such attempts begin with a DNS query. With multiple inspection points during device communications attempts, at the device, DNS and the connection/router levels, the chances for malware detection increase as recommended by a defense in depth security approach.

DNS firewall policies are configured on recursive DNS servers to apply policies to query responses to block, drop, or modify such responses matching response policy triggers, such as known bad actor domains. Response Policy Zones (RPZs), which provide the DNS firewall functionality, define triggers and corresponding policies to apply to matching query responses. RPZ information can be updated periodically using an RPZ data provider via signed zone transfers.

DNS firewall rules are defined in the language of DNS servers, that is, resource records within zone repositories. Specially coded resource records each indicate a trigger and a corresponding policy. In the example of Figure 11.4, the trigger is an IPv4 address (A record type) question (Qname) of *.bad-example.com, which interpreting the * wildcard, indicates any Qnames within the bad-example.com domain branch, i.e. any Qname suffixed with bad-example.com. The corresponding policy applied for responses matching this trigger indicate setting the answered IP address to 172.16.200.1. Thus, the DNS firewall modified the response from the authoritative server of 192.0.2.24 to an internal walled garden server on 172.16.200.1.

The currently defined trigger types are the following:

- *Qname match* – The queried domain name (or within a domain branch if specified with a wildcard prefix) matches the owner field of the RPZ resource record.

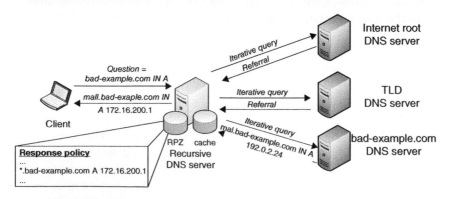

Figure 11.4 DNS firewall example.

Specifically, the owner name and resource record type fields corresponding to the question section of the query/response are matched.

- *RPZ-IP* – The IP address (or block) within the query response matches the IP address in the general format: <prefix length>.<reversed IP address>.rpz-ip. For example, to match an answer with an IP address from the 192.0.2.0/24 block, this would be encoded as `24.0.2.0.192.rpz-ip`. An IPv6 address can be similarly encoded with the abbreviation of "zz" for a double colon abbreviation; for example one could match an IPv6 address in the answer from the 2001:db8:4b30::f0/128 as `128.f0.zz.4b30.db8.2001.rpz-ip`.
- *RPZ-NSIP* – Authoritative name server IP address, encoded similarly as rpz-ip matches but with the `rpz.nsip` suffix.
- *RPZ-NSDNAME* – Authoritative name server domain name, e.g. `bad.example.com.rpz-nsdname`.
- *RPZ-CLIENT-IP* – Client IP address formatted as above with prefix length and reversed IP address and with the `rpz-client-ip` suffix.

Triggers are matched on a best fit basis. That is, all records with triggers matching the query or answer are sorted by the best fit (e.g. longest prefix match for IP addresses) or most granular match; the policy corresponding to such a best match trigger is then applied.

For each defined trigger, a policy can be defined to answer the query with either

- *NXDOMAIN* – Indicates an answer for the queried name was not found
- *NODATA* – Signified by a NOERROR response with no query answers (a zero "answer count"); this indicates a queried name was valid but no data for the queried type was found
- Pass-through – No alteration of the response
- Drop – Provide no answer to the query
- *TCP-only* – Respond with the truncated (TC) bit set in the DNS header to stimulate the client to requery over TCP
- Local policy such as redirecting the querier to portal or walled garden to initiate remediation or to display a web page indicating an invalid query or possible infection.

Each of these policies and corresponding triggers can be defined within RPZ files. The BIND response-policy statement enables association of these zones as RPZs and enables policy overrides per zone (e.g. disable all policies defined in the zone for troubleshooting). This statement also enables the specification of overriding parameters for RPZs including

- *Recursive-only* – This policy indicates PRZ processing shall only apply to recursive queries; this policy may be applied to an individual zone or all RPZs.

- *Max-policy-ttl* – This statement enables setting of the TTL of the response resource record. The TTL dictates how long the client should cache this response. Once the cache expires, the client will issue a query once again should the client request this information. This enables rapid refreshing of policies if desired. This policy may be applied to an individual zone or all RPZs.
- *Log* – This parameter applies only to individual zones and indicates whether RPZ policy hits should be logged. Logging must also be configured per the Logging Configuration section below.
- *Break-dnssec* – By default, RPZ is not applied to queries where DNSSEC validation has been requested. Given that DNSSEC authenticates the publisher and data integrity of the DNS response, any change to the response per RPZ policy would by definition destroy the message integrity and invalidate the DNSSEC signature. Setting this parameter to "yes" instructs the server to perform RPZ processing even on DNSSEC queries, permitting the server to "break DNSSEC."
- *Min-ns-dots* – This parameter applies globally and stipulates the number of "dots" in the queried domain name that must exist to apply RPZ processing (not counting the root zone "dot"). A value of "1," the default, would apply to example.com, for example.
- *Qname-wait-recurse* – Normally, the recursive server performs full recursion to ascertain the query answer prior to seeking a response policy action. Setting this parameter to "no" configures the server not to await recursion, since it receives the Qname with the query from the client, and to apply any defined response policy for the Qname immediately.
- *Nsip-wait-recurse* – Normally, the recursive server performs full recursion to ascertain the query answer prior to seeking a response policy action. Setting this parameter to "no" instructs the server to access its cache for the Qname and, if it exists, the corresponding answering DNS server IP address. If the IP address is defined as a RPZ-NSIP trigger, apply the corresponding policy immediately, bypassing full recursion.

DNS Firewall Policy Precedence

When an ISC DNS server loads a zone, including RPZs, it reorders the RRSets in canonical order. While a "longest prefix" style trigger match is applied to each query response, the first detected such longest match will dictate the corresponding policy to be applied. You may desire to block most records in a domain but define pass through records for known reputable records within that domain or a child domain.

While the ordering within a file is canonical and not the order in which you enter the data, you can specify multiple zones, up to 32, to which to apply response policies. The order in which you define these zones is honored such that the policy is applied corresponding to the longest match in the first file detected. Thus, you can list zones with pass through policies first, then list blocking policies in subsequent zones.

Logging Configuration

It's recommended to configure DNS logging to receive notification of RPZ policy triggers. Such notification can inform your security team of a potentially malware-infected device for rapid remediation. ISC BIND supports logging configuration by specifying a logging channel(s) and then directing predefined logging category events to respective channel(s). Logging channels may be in the form of server log files, syslog, standard error, or null. The "rpz" logging category applies to DNS queries that trigger an RPZ policy. Thus, configuring rpz category events to direct output to a syslog channel would provide the ability to collect RPZ policy event notifications via syslog. Log processing logic could optionally be applied using a third-party log collector such as Splunk to perform additional actions such as alerting.

Other Attacks that Leverage DNS

Several broader network attacks use the DNS itself to inflict damage on other network components or to exfiltrate sensitive information outside the network.

Network Reconnaissance

DNS by design houses a repository of hostname-to-IP address mapping among other things. If an attacker desired to glean information about particular hosts that may be more attractive to attack than others, he/she may start with DNS. Hosts named for the application or type of information contained therein (e.g. "payroll. example.com") may prove a desirable target. Query information could also expose broader privacy concerns given that pervasive monitoring in itself is an attack [103].

An attacker may also seek targets on which to install malware to enlist them under the control of the attacker within a botnet. Whether a device is attacked while inside the enterprise network or a user device is physically brought onto the network, if it is trusted within the confines of an enterprise network it may have access to sensitive information. The malware may perform data collection, locating internal resources using DNS reconnaissance. In addition, DNS could be used to identify the current IP address of the attacker's external destination for transmission of the information.

The following methods may be utilized by attackers to reconnoiter your namespace:

- *Query sniffing* – An attacker with access to the communications path to and from a given DNS server may log queries and answers in an attempt to identify potential targets.

- *Name guessing* – One brute force approach to such reconnaissance consists of guessing hostnames of interest and issuing standard DNS queries to obtain corresponding IP addresses if they exist.
- *Wildcard (ANY) queries* – An attacker may issue a query to your DNS server setting the QTYPE to '*' which is referred to as an ANY query. Servers configured to support this query, which most are by default, will typically respond with all of the resource records associated with the corresponding domain name (QNAME).
- *Zone transfers* – Impersonating a DNS slave server and attempting to perform a zone transfer from a master is a form of attack that attempts to map or footprint a zone to identify targets for direct attacks.
- *Next secure queries* – If a given zone is signed via DNSSEC with the use of NSEC resource records to support authenticated denial of resource record existence instead of the hashed NSEC3 version, an attacker may be able to identify hostnames in a zone by successively querying the zone for NSEC records to enumerate domain names.

Network Reconnaissance Defenses

The intent of DNS is to publish address information about hosts on the network. However, this information may be gathered and analyzed by an attacker to facilitate target identification for further attacks. Naming hosts intuitively certainly simplifies user accessibility though "attractive" names may tempt attackers, so this is a trade-off. However, limiting who can query for such information can help constrain the scope of access to this information for recursive or internal authoritative servers. Host information published in external DNS servers (where constraining query sources makes less sense) should be limited to those accessible via the Internet.

In summary, the following defense mechanisms may be put in place to protect against overt network reconnaissance:

- Implement ACLs limiting zone transfers to only other authorized authoritative DNS servers
- Implement ACLs limiting the scope of hosts that are permitted to query the server
- Constrain responses to ANY queries
- Enable Qname minimization to reduce the number of full Qname (FQDN) queries to the root, TLD, etc., presented on the Internet. This feature configures your recursive server to query for the next level down in the domain tree without repeatedly exposing the FQDN on each iterative query. Thus, for example when querying the root, just query for ".com"; when querying .com, query just for "ipamworldwide.com" then query the ipamworldwide authoritative servers for the FQDN, www.ipamworldwide.com.
- Enable DNS encryption using DoT (or DoH)

DNS Rebinding Attack

A DNS rebinding attack is so called because the resolution data for the same question is modified in the following manner. When a user browses to an attacker website, enticed by content, a phishing attack, social engineering, or other form of subtle coercion, the IP address resolved for the web address is the "legitimate" attacker web server IP address. The TTL for this RRSet is configured to a very short time interval. The corresponding web page contains malicious browser-side code such as flash or javascript.

When the browser code is executed, the code contains links to the website URL once again, which given the short TTL or the initial query, the resolver has already timed out of cache. Upon issuing a subsequent query to the attacker's DNS server as initiated by the browser-side code, the DNS server returns the IP address of an internal target, likely a private IP address. Thus, the IP address for the same domain name has been changed or rebound, to which the malicious browser code launches its attack, e.g. a DDoS or other attack. This type of attack has impacted residential users, for example where an attacker can modify settings on a smart home device (e.g. thermostat) by posting commands to its IP address after the rebinding of the resolved address.

This attack typically requires initial network reconnaissance using DNS or other form of discovery to identify the attack target. The target's IP address is used as the resolution data for the attacker's webserver during the rebinding phase. The querying of the attacker's domain repeatedly helps pass browser origin enforcement.

Data Exfiltration

Data exfiltration refers to the transmission of data originating from within one security domain, e.g. an enterprise network, to another entity or organization, i.e. the attacker's server. There are two basic forms of data exfiltration using DNS:

- The use of DNS as a data protocol to communicate between two endpoints through firewalls
- The use of DNS to locate external resources to which to convey information or obtain instructions for attack

Data Exfiltration Mitigation

Stealing data from sources within a network and transmitting it to an attacker's system externally may prove to be a very attractive attack vector. Use of DNS to identify external system domain names or to serve as the transmission protocol itself facilitates this style of attack. Steps you can take to mitigate these include the following:

- Implement a DNS firewall to prevent resolution of known "bad domains" to reduce resolution possibilities for external attacker systems.
- Monitor DNS transactions to identify potential tunnels by seeking pairwise "sessions" to a given name server over time, particularly with large and high-entropy query names and responses.

DNS as Data Transport (Tunneling)

DNS tunneling entails the use of the DNS protocol as a data communications channel. This approach leverages the fact that DNS traffic is generally permitted through firewalls. This technique enables a user or a device within the network to communicate with an external destination, easily traversing any intervening firewalls. Initially developed as a means to enable devices to communicate via a for-pay Wifi network, the technology has also been used by malware to exfiltrate information from enterprise networks.

Utilizing the DNS protocol to tunnel data packets entails the client tunnel endpoint behaving as a resolver to issue a query to an "authoritative DNS server." The Question section of the query contains end-user data encoded as a domain name. The domain suffix corresponds to the domain for which the server-side tunnel endpoint is "authoritative." Let's say an attacker sets up a server endpoint using the domain: tunnel-example.net. When registering the domain, the NS and glue records supplied to the parent domain (.net in this case) consist of the tunnel endpoint servers themselves.

A query to ns1.tunnel-endpoint.net, for example will be directed to the tunnel endpoint server, as will link-to-my-email-or-website.tunnel-endpoint.net, a facetious expression of how client data would be transmitted to the server. The recursive server, root and TLD servers, not shown in Figure 11.5, process the DNS query like any other, locating the name servers authoritative for tunnel-endpoint.net and directing the "query" to the server. The queried record type is usually TXT but NULL has also been used, though this RRType has been deprecated.

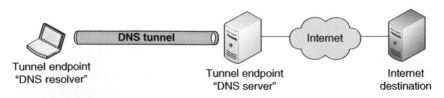

Tunnel endpoint
"DNS resolver"

Tunnel endpoint
"DNS server"

Internet
destination

Figure 11.5 DNS tunneling.

Even an A or AAAA type can be used with return data in the form of a CNAME response.

The tunnel server decodes the query name and passes on the application request to the intended destination. Some level of fragmentation and reassembly may be required over the tunnel given DNS label length restrictions (63 octets) and full name length (255 octets). The client may post several A record queries to get full file across for example, while the DNS server tunnel endpoint may reply with CNAME records with response data encoded within the record data portion.

Use of EDNS0 (DNS extensions) enables much longer responses, perhaps obviating the need for fragmentation and reassembly based on MTU support of the intervening infrastructure. The tunneling server processes responses from the Internet destination and encodes the response for transmission to the resolver. Typically, base32 encoding of the data is used on outbound tunnel transactions and base64 in responses to support case sensitivity in the response octets, which the client tunnel endpoint decodes and presents back to the application software.

Advanced Persistent Threats

APTs are organized, stealthy forms of network intrusion where an attacker attains access within a target network to steal data, disrupt communications, or otherwise infiltrate network components. APTs are persistent in that the intent is to retain access to the network for a lengthy time frame, if not indefinitely, so they require continual evasion techniques to avoid detection.

Attackers may deploy malware within a network via a variety of means as discussed earlier in this chapter. The attacker who successfully infiltrates a number of devices can instruct the malicious code to perform operations on behalf of the attacker. While attempting to avoid detection through stealthy activities, the attacker's bots typically need to communicate to the attacker's C&C center. The C&C center is typically a server to which each bot connects to receive updates and commands to instigate attacks, update malware code, or collect information from the network in which a given bot resides. Typically, this process involves DNS queries to identify the IP address of the C&C center since it needs to be an Internet-accessible server for bot access.

If an IT administrator identifies the presence of APTs within his or her network and can discern the C&C IP address based on DNS queries, he or she may block the IP address via a network or DNS firewall. To avoid such "easy" detection, many botnet administrators leverage the power of DNS to modulate the IP address and domain name of the C&C center to evade detection.

Advanced Persistent Threats Mitigation

The following mitigation strategies should be considered to combat APTs:

- A DNS firewall can help disable DNS resolution of APT malware bots that use DNS to resolve external command and control centers for instructions.
- DNS tunneling detection provides notification of possible data exfiltration.
- DNS query analytics provide not only useful information about DNS transactions across your network but can facilitate detection of anomalies or unusual activity which could indicate APT operations.

12

IPAM and Your Internet Presence

If you do business on the Internet, whether that entails full-on e-commerce sales or as a vehicle for information dissemination or lead generation, your Internet presence projects your organization's image with which you generally desire to make a positive impression. Certainly, first impressions mean a lot! Our final chapter related specifically to security covers the use of IPAM technologies to help protect your Internet presence from compromises to the integrity of your public IP address space, DNS namespace, email servers and domains, and even website security.

IP Address Space Integrity

First and foremost, your Internet presence necessitates IP addresses for servers representing your presence. BGP is the standard Internet exterior routing protocol to communicate IP reachability to your presence. Each holder of IP address space advertises reachability to hosts within that address space to the global Internet using BGP. Many organizations obtain IP address space from ISPs and each ISP can advertise reachability to its address space, within which your space resides. In this way, Internet users desiring to connect to your website, will have their IP packets routed to you via your ISP. But many organizations use provider independent (PI) address space or otherwise desire to advertise their address space using BGP.

You can readily imagine the impact if the BGP route to your address space was altered maliciously or otherwise. Consider the inadvertent BGP route leak that occurred in June, 2019, where a small ISP advertised a portion of Cloudflare's IP space, a more specific set of blocks than Cloudflare advertised. This leak caused a

IP Address Management, Second Edition. Michael Dooley and Timothy Rooney.
© 2021 The Institute of Electrical and Electronics Engineers, Inc.
Published 2021 by John Wiley & Sons, Inc.

portion of Cloudflare's traffic corresponding to the more specific route, to route through the ISP which was ill equipped for the IP packet deluge.

The ISP had implemented a route optimizer, which seeks to advertise the minimum block size; the ISP advertised the smaller block to one of its customers, who in turn advertised to another ISP in its multihoming configuration, and the other ISP advertised this reachability globally, manifesting the leak. ISPs can implement the following policies to reduce the likelihood of such an occurrence:

- Accept a fixed number of prefixes from a given customer
- Accept a minimum size prefix to further advertise
- Implement Internet Routing Registry (IRR) filtering to corroborate advertised routes with network information maintained by RIRs
- Implement Resource Public Key Infrastructure (RPKI) which applies certificate authentication and encryption to IRR updates and data access.

While BGP has performed and scaled well over the years, it does rely on prudent participation from a variety of organizations. Since not all organizations implement these BGP checks, it's important to monitor your IP traffic and investigate any unusual traffic fluctuations.

Publicizing Your Public Namespace

Certainly, user location of your Internet presence requires DNS, so the integrity of your DNS namespace, your zones, and resource records, is paramount. The main objective of attackers attempting to manipulate your namespace data include modification of resolution data. With such power, the attacker can essentially make your domain disappear or he/she could repoint your resolution data such that traffic is steered toward attacker resources for personal or financial data collection. Manipulation of resolution data can be affected by modifying resource record data on the authoritative server itself or by falsifying the answer to a given query for the zone for which the server is authoritative. To protect your namespace, consider the approaches described in this chapter and the authoritative poisoning mitigation strategies discussed in Chapter 10.

Domain Registries and Registrars

Another vulnerability to resolvers' ability to locate your domain information relates to the integrity of your parent and any other ancestor domains. An attacker modifying your name server information effectively hijacks your domain by changing the pointers down the domain tree to the attacker's name servers instead of yours. Typically, an organization will register a second-level domain with a domain registrar for the desired TLD. For example, I could register example.com with a .com registrar.

The domain registrar is authorized by the domain registry to uniquely assign subdomains (for .com in this case). Said another way, the domain registry technically manages the domain and is responsible for the data within and access policies for the repository containing domain registrations for immediate child domains. The registry publishes the domain zone file. A domain registrar is accredited by the corresponding registry and manages reservations of domain names within the registry repository.

There are over 1500 TLDs available to choose from, given the recent "new gTLD" program conducted by the Internet Corporation for Assigned Names and Numbers (ICANN). You can view the current list of TLDs, including the country code TLDs, internationalized TLDs, and new gTLDs on the IANA website [104]. Contact a registrar for the TLD for which you are interested in registering.

Consider the security practices of your domain registrar including the authentication and authorization technologies used for updating domain information and the use of DNSSEC. Registrars that lock domains require you to access your account to unlock the domain, then submit the update using an Authorization Code, and then relock the domain. This process is more secure than merely submitting a change via email with just an auth code; an attacker that can glean your auth code, e.g. via hacking your email account, could submit seemingly authorized changes (be sure to secure your email account as well). Such a two-factor change authorization process at the registry level is also critical to securing updates to your domain information. Such an authorization assumes a secure account access process as well, including a notification process should the registrar detect a breach or better yet, whenever a change is made.

All new gTLDs support DNSSEC as mandated by ICANN and most other TLDs do as well, with 90% of all TLDs presently being DNSSEC-signed [105]. You'll need to understand the DNSSEC update process as well, as your registrar will need to update your downstream pointing DNSSEC records (Delegation Signer, DS) when you roll your key signing key. We'll discuss this process later in the chapter.

One more thing to consider is whether you'd like your personal contact information published in the globally accessible whois database, which is in the process of being supplanted by RDAP. This database enables people to query information for a given domain, including contact name, address, email, and telephone number. Most registrars offer an option to anonymize this information by using a "hostmaster" or similar generic label for the contact name and the registrar's address, email, and telephone number. This may be of particular interest if you operate a multi-national network amid various regulations relating to the international transfer of personal information.

If your domain information related to your name servers is compromised, you will notice a precipitous drop in inbound query traffic. Recursive servers seeking your domain from the root servers down the domain tree will be pointed elsewhere thanks to the attacker's change of your NS, glue, and DS information in your parent domain. You should login to your registrar account to view the current configuration. If it has indeed been modified, correct the information, change your password, and notify the registrar of the breach.

Any falsified resource records provided to queries at your expense for your domain information will have been served by the attacker's servers and will be cached by recursive servers for the duration of the TTL, which could generally be up to a week. You will need to contact your subscribers or customers to inform them of the issue and how to rectify the situation by flushing relevant cache information.

DNS Hosting Providers

If you publish your external DNS namespace utilizing a third-party DNS provider instead of or in addition to operating external DNS servers in-house, you should consider similar precautions as you should with your domain registrar. Verify appropriate security practices for your provider including authentication and authorization methods, transaction encryption, and support of DNSSEC to secure your namespace's integrity.

Unlike registry or registrar compromise, an attacker with access to your external namespace can perform more surgical modifications. While an attacker can still resteer your domain (and therefore subdomains) to his or her own servers, he or she can also simply update a record or two such as your www or mail records to divert certain transactions. In fact, the attacker could merely add their records to your existing RRSet in an attempt to siphon off a portion of your traffic while attempting to avoid detection through a severe drop in resolution traffic.

In such cases, monitoring traffic by RRType may be useful but drops within an expected variance would not likely trigger an alarm. A better approach to detect such an attack is to simply confirm your zone information contains only that which you intend. You can detect zone changes through notification from your service provider and/or by retrieving the zone periodically and scanning it for changes to determine if the changes were authorized. This "diff" approach requires fairly regular polling since this will define your window of exposure before detection.

Just querying the serial number for each zone is certainly a simpler approach, but if the attacker can modify the zone with being forced to update the serial number, this method may not detect such an attack.

Depending on the form of the attack, you may see similar symptoms as with a registry or registrar compromise if the attacker modifies or deletes zone information. If you see a vacuum of DNS traffic, you should access your domain account to verify. If the attacker changed your credentials, while you work with your domain provider to reauthenticate yourself to regain access, you can issue queries for records you had configured in the zone. This assumes you have a record or a copy of your external zone. In this regard, you may want to setup a DNS server as a slave to your service provider DNS servers, so you can receive zone-level notifications of changes as they occur unless the attacker is clever enough to change this too.

Validating your zone contents through zone transfers if you have a valid server on the "allow-transfer" list of the master enables a straightforward means of viewing how the world views your zone. Short of this, issuing queries periodically for resolution data you've published rather frequently and alerting upon detection of changes provides another method to detect changes. You can ignore authorized changes of course, but this can supply warning of an unauthorized change. If your domain account has been compromised, notify your service provider and reset your credentials immediately.

Defenses against domain registry, registrar, or hosting provider attacks lie predominantly on the respective provider of these corresponding services. Proactive periodic checks on what your namespace looks like on the Internet is important for detecting unusual conditions that could indicate breach of integrity.

Signing Your Public Namespace

Users attempting to resolve your Internet namespace may unwittingly be redirected by an attacker's modification of not only your authoritative data but also of your namespace data during the resolution process, i.e. via cache poisoning. The solution to cache poisoning attacks requires the authentication of each DNS query answer as having been published by the authoritative domain owner. As we introduced in Chapter 10, DNSSEC specifications provide for query answer authentication as well as data integrity validation to assure no manipulation of query answers in route to the validating resolver. DNSSEC also provides authentication of information that does not exist in the domain's zone, or "authenticated denial of existence." DNSSEC provides these features by digitally signing DNS data.

DNSSEC Zone Signing

Signing a zone requires the generation of a key pair. The IETF's DNSSEC operational practices document [106] recommends (but does not require) two key pairs. A ZSK which is a shorter key to lessen computational complexity and time for signing all of the zone RRSets. Typically a longer key, the KSK is used only to sign

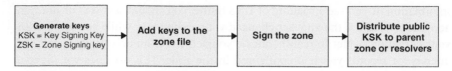

Figure 12.1   Basic DNSSEC implementation steps.

the DNSKEY RRSet, that is the RRSet that identifies the public keys, ZSKs and KSKs, used (or to be or have been used) within the zone.

Figure 12.1 illustrates the basic process of signing a zone. Step 1 consists of generating two key pairs, a private and public pair as a ZSK and a KSK. For both pairs of keys for each zone, the public keys are published within the zone in the form of DNSKEY resource records as step 2. The third step utilizes the private keys to sign the RRSets in the zone. Again, the KSK signs only the DNSKEY RRSet and the ZSK signs all RRSets.

The fourth step entails linking the KSK into the chain of trust by having the corresponding DS record provisioned in the parent zone. In the event that the KSK is a trust anchor for any resolvers, e.g. if you've deployed an internal signed root or if your domain is not fully linked in a chain of trust to the Internet root, such resolvers must be updated to reflect the new trust anchor key.

Key Rollover

Once your zones are signed, keys must be changed or rolled over occasionally. The fact that keys are rolled "occasionally" can lead to errors as is sometimes the case when performing complex tasks infrequently. Fortunately, most of these functions including key rollover can be automated thanks to leading vendor implementations. Note that vendor implementations also enable you to manually manage zone signing and maintenance if you prefer that level of control. We will review the automated procedures here but offer references to further information for detailed manual implementation steps and troubleshooting tips.

The ZSK can be changed more frequently, e.g. every 30–90 days, and such change has no impact on other DNS domains in the domain tree. The KSK however is represented in the parent zone in the form of a DS record which links the chain of trust up the domain tree. You can publish your updated DNSKEY RRSet and corresponding parent DS RRset in the form of CDNSKEY and child delegation signer (CDS) resource records, respectively, if your parent zone supports these. These resource records can be periodically polled by the parent zone administrators to identify changes in these RRSets in order to incorporate such changes in its own zone. These records must be signed, of course to secure the update process. Nevertheless, the multiple administrator domain coordination of key changes serves as the motivation for the KSK being a more secure (longer) key that may be changed less frequently.

The process for key rollover mimics that of initial zone signing with the generation of a new key pair for the key being rolled, publication of the public key within respective zone file, re-signing of the zone, and for KSK rollovers, linking into the chain of trust. There is some added complexity however in that you cannot simply replace your current keys and re-sign the zone. Since validating resolvers cache not only resolution data but also signatures and keys, we must account for the fact that a resolver may utilize a cached public key to validate signatures on a fresh resolution.

For example, if my recursive server queried for mail.example.com yesterday, which was signed, my recursive server will query for the zone's public key to validate the RRSet's signature. Let's assume the TTL on my public key (DNSKEY) record is two days. If I then query today for www.example.com, which also is signed, my recursive server must once again validate this RRSet's signature. Given it possesses a DNSKEY record for the zone in cache as the TTL has not yet expired, it shall attempt to use the cached key to perform validation. If I had signed the www RRSet today with a new key, the validation would fail and the resolution considered bogus. Recursive servers may possess the resolution data with signature or the public key or both within cache. The rollover process needs to account for a resolver possessing one or the other but not both to enable validation of the cached data based on what is currently published in the zone.

Thus, when rolling keys, you'll need to publish two keys for a given period of time, either signing with just one or signing with both. In the former case, the "pre-publish" rollover method, two keys are included in the zone file, the incumbent key used to sign the zone and the new key which is published but not used in signing. Recursive servers seeking to validate signatures will obtain both keys within the DNSKEY RRSet and will try both during the validation process; in this case, the incumbent key validates. If the new key had also been used to sign the zone, each RRSet in the zone would have two signatures, corresponding to the two keys. This double signature approach would vastly increase the size of your zone files and resolution data payload given two signatures per RRSet. Thus, the pre-publish method is typically recommended to roll ZSKs so that each RRSet has one signature. And because the KSK signs only the DNSKEY RRSet and because the parent zone's corresponding DS rollover must coincide, the dual-signature approach is typically used to rollover KSKs.

Prepublish Rollover

Let's dig deeper into these two rollover strategies by first considering the prepublish rollover method of Figure 12.2. Our initial condition features our zone signed with a ZSK with key id 14522 and KSK key id 6082. Both of these keys are used to sign the zone as indicated by the pen icon adjacent to the corresponding keys in

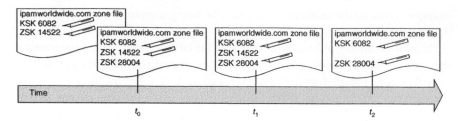

Figure 12.2   Pre-publish rollover.

the figure. Let's initiate the rollover process at time t_0, by publishing a second ZSK DNSKEY resource record with key id 28004 into the zone file. Our DNSKEY RRSet now consists of these three keys. With this change, we re-sign the zone with KSK 6082 and ZSK 14522.

The new ZSK (28004) is not currently signing the zone, but the key is made available for resolver and recursive server caching. As such we need to wait an interval of time approximately equal to the amount of time required to distribute zone updates from the master server to all of its secondaries (upper bounded by the zone expiration time) plus the TTL of the DNSKEY RRSet. When this time elapses, we reach time t_1, and now we can re-sign the zone, keeping all three keys in the DNSKEY RRSet, but now signing with KSK 6082 and ZSK 28004.

We need to retain the old ZSK in the zone for a time so that resolvers possessing resolution data with signatures from the old key, e.g. fetched right before time t_1, can still be considered valid. Thus, we should keep the formerly signing ZSK in the zone file for an interval of the time required to distribute zone updates from the master to the slaves plus the maximum TTL value of zone data. When this time elapses, we reach time t_2, and we can remove ZSK 14522 and re-sign the zone.

In some instances, it may be simpler from an operations perspective to always publish two ZSKs, one active and one either being staged or pending departure. Thus, at time t_2, we could introduce a third ZSK which would eventually be used to sign the zone upon the next rollover. This third ZSK would remain published until the next rollover time (e.g. 30–90 days usually) which maps to time t_1 when the new ZSK will be used to sign the zone. The $t_2 - t_1$ interval should retain the same time period as above and at t_2, the old ZSK can be replaced by a new ZSK to be used to sign the zone upon the next rollover.

Dual Signature Rollover

The dual signature method is typically recommended for KSK rollovers, and the basic process is illustrated in Figure 12.3. Because the parent zone's DS record must reference a valid KSK in this zone to link the chain of trust, we'll illustrate the state of the parent zone DS record in this figure. Our initial condition is as

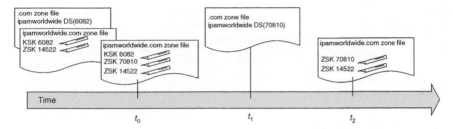

Figure 12.3   Dual-signature KSK rollover.

before with a KSK with key id 6082 and ZSK with key id 14522. The parent zone DS properly references the active KSK 6082.

We begin the rollover process by creating a new KSK key pair and publishing the public key in the zone file. Sign the zone with both KSKs (and the ZSK of course). Next, we need to inform our parent domain administrator that we're rolling our KSK and the corresponding DS record in the parent zone must be updated to reflect this. The method(s) of performing this update will be dictated by your parent zone administrator's policies. You may need to securely login to a web portal and upload your DNSKEY or the corresponding DS RRSet. Or you may be able to upload it directly. Another mechanism defined by the IETF in RFC 7344 [107] calls for publication of the change in your DNS zone through the publication of a CDS and/or CDNSKEY resource record in your zone. The parent zone may periodically poll its children zones for the existence of one or both of these records as a signal to update its corresponding DS record(s). An out of band notification mechanism defined by the parent zone administrator may also be used to initiate the DS record update.

Once you've confirmed the parent zone has published the DS record corresponding to your new KSK and the longest zone TTL has expired since signing with both KSKs, the old KSK (14522 in our example) may be removed from the zone and the zone re-signed. Note that if your KSK is configured as a trust anchor within recursive resolvers which utilize RFC 5011 [86] for automated trust anchor management, you'll need to set the "revoke" bit on the outgoing KSK to signal its outgoing state to such resolvers. Figure 12.4 would be modified in this case at time t_2, where both KSKs would remain published and signing the zone, but the KSK 6082 would be published with its Revoke bit set for a period of time equal to the maximum zone TTL, after which KSK 6082 may be removed.

Algorithm Rollover

As cryptography technology evolves and new signature algorithms are introduced into DNSSEC standards, you may desire to add and/or remove algorithms used for

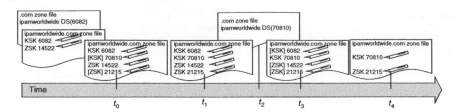

Figure 12.4 Algorithm rollover.

signing your zones. Note that validating resolvers will also need to support one or more algorithms that you've implemented to enable proper validation.

The algorithm rollover process entails prepublication of the signatures of a new set of keys using the new algorithm prior to publication of the keys themselves. The reason for this stems from the requirement that every RRSet have a valid signature for every algorithm represented in the zone's DNSKEYs. Considering Figure 12.4, we start with KSK 6082 and ZSK 14522, with our parent DS properly referencing our KSK.

At time t_0, we begin by signing the zone with the private keys utilizing the new algorithm and publishing the corresponding signatures but not the public keys. We denote this in Figure 12.4 as enclosing the KSK or ZSK text within square brackets with the pen indicating publication of respective signatures. Thus, the private keys sign the zone data, but the public keys are not published as yet. This enables resolver caches to obtain signatures with the current and new keys. If the keys had also been published at this time, resolvers could fetch the DNSKEYs and previously cached resolution data would not have signatures yet for the new keys, violating the requirement.

Once the zone master–slave propagation time plus zone TTL time has transpired, the corresponding DNSKEY records may be added to the zone at time t_1. By now, new resolution data with both sets of signatures should be cached. At time t_2, after the DNSKEY TTL expires, the parent zone administrator may replace the DS record to reference the new KSK 70810. Once this DS (70810) is published in the parent zone, the keys using the former algorithm may be removed once the DS TTL expires at time t_3. Note that the signatures for the removed keys should remain in the zone until once again the zone propagation plus TTL time is reached. At this time, t_4, the signatures generated with the old keys may be removed. If your KSK is a trust anchor, insert step $t_{2.5}$ after the DS record is updated to revoke the outgoing KSK for a DNSKEY TTL time period before removing the KSK.

You can use this algorithm rollover process to rollover from NSEC to NSEC3 authenticated denial of existence. These records authenticate the nonexistence of queries to a signed zone with NSEC publishing the "next secure" record in the zone, while NSEC3 publishes hashed next records to hinder simple zone footprinting.

Key Security

The private keys corresponding to your published public keys must be secured from theft. Should an attacker obtain a private key currently in use for signing one of your zones, he or she could sign arbitrary DNS resource records and sign them with your private key, successfully poisoning validating resolver caches. Hardware security modules (HSMs) may be deployed to securely store private keys and to perform zone signing using a cryptographic token interface [108].

Emergency rollover procedures should be devised and documented in the event of compromise of a private key corresponding to an active KSK or ZSK. Should an attacker obtain the private key, he/she could forge zone data and sign it with the private key. Resolvers and recursive servers would authenticate the falsified data based on the published corresponding public key. As we've seen, the ZSK can be changed autonomously and should be changed immediately. This may cause validation issues due to conflicting cached data. Note that your zone is still vulnerable until the TTL of the signatures generated by the compromised key(s) expire.

Changing the KSK, however, does require broader involvement and coordination. We recommend documenting a process for emergency rollovers that includes the parent zone administrator, as well as a means to communicate to users who have configured the KSK as a trust anchor. This could be via a registered email list or secure website posting. There are three ways you can perform an emergency KSK rollover, each with its corresponding risks.

1) Maintain the chain of trust
   a) Generate a new KSK and add the corresponding DNSKEY record to the DNSKEY RRSet, keeping the compromised key published. Lower the DNSKEYs' TTL value to promote rapid expiration during this rollover.
   b) Sign the DNSKEY with both the new and compromised KSKs. The reason we continue publishing and signing with the compromised KSK is due to the fact that the parent zone still references the compromised KSK via a DS record. Set the signature validity interval to the time until the parent zone can publish the DS corresponding to the new KSK plus the DS TTL value.
   c) Upload the DS record corresponding to the new KSK to the parent zone administrator and request removal of the DS record pointing to the compromised KSK.
   d) After the new DS record appears in the parent zone and the old DS expires from caches based on its TTL, remove the compromised KSK from the DNSKEY RRSet and re-sign. Note you may have to repeat step b to refresh signatures if this DS publication process is delayed.
2) Break the chain of trust
   a) Publish a new KSK and remove the old KSK from the DNSKEY RRSet and re-sign the zone. Note that the parent zone still points to the compromised

KSK and not your new KSK, enabling the attacker and not you to validate up the chain of trust.

b) Upload the DS record corresponding to the new KSK to the parent zone administrator and request removal of the DS record pointing to the compromised KSK.

c) Once the DS for the new key is published, the chain of trust will have been repaired, though the compromised key will likewise still validate while the old DS remains cached.

3) Render the zone insecure

a) Request removal of the (all) DS records from the parent zone. This will break the chain of trust and render your zone insecure, as it will the attacker's zone which uses the compromised KSK.

b) After the DS TTL expires, generate a new KSK and add the corresponding DNSKEY record to the RRSet and sign the zone.

c) Upload the DS record corresponding to a new KSK to the parent zone administrator.

Enhancing Internet Application Encryption Integrity

As we've seen the DNS is fundamental to the proper operation of virtually all Internet applications, from web browsing to email, multimedia applications, and more. A given web page may require several DNS lookups. If you view the source of a random web page for example, count the number of link, hypertext reference (href), and source (src) tags that contain a unique domain name. Each of these stimulate your browser to perform a DNS lookup to fetch the referenced image, file, or script, and perhaps prefetch links. And each time you click a link to navigate to a new page, the process repeats with successive DNS lookups required to fully render the destination page.

Email too relies on DNS for email delivery, enabling you to send email using the familiar user@destination syntax, where DNS identifies the destination's IP address for transmission of the email. And DNS goes well beyond web or email address resolution. Virtually, every application on your mobile, computer, tablet, security cameras, thermostats, and other "things" that access the Internet require DNS for proper operation. Without DNS, navigating and accessing Internet applications would be all but impossible.

DNS can facilitate safer web browsing by enabling website publishers to post information about their TLS credentials, used to authenticate and encrypt secure HTTP traffic. The DNS-based Authentication of Named Entities (DANE) protocol [109, 110] enables access to a website publisher's certificate or CA information to protect against spoofed certificates or CAs, which can lead to website hijacking unbeknownst to the user/browser.

DNS-Based Authentication of Named Entities (DANE)

Before we dive into DANE, let's review how TLS works to illustrate the vulnerabilities that DANE mitigates. TLS (formerly, SSL) enables the authentication and encryption of IP traffic as well as data integrity verification. TLS leverages a PKI trust model. Consider Figure 12.5. The client identifies the web server address using DNS in step 1 as labeled in the figure. In step 2, the client initiates the connection to the server and begins the TLS handshake indicating its supported encryption capabilities and a random number.

The web server uses a private key to sign the random number, passes along the corresponding public key, and presents an ISO X.509 certificate which conveys the server domain name, issuing authority, a public key, and other information. If the client (browser) successfully decrypts the random number, it needs to follow the certificate to a trusted CA that has signed the servers' certificate. If the CA verifies the certificate per step 3 in Figure 12.5, then the browser trusts the web server and initiates the HTTPS connection.

The link to a trusted root CA, the CA chain of trust, may span multiple layers from the original server to an intermediate authority to a trusted root CA. Each operating system and browser vendor provides a set of several trusted CAs by default. Should the client successfully validate the certificate, it may then commence the secure web session using the server's public key for ensuing communications.

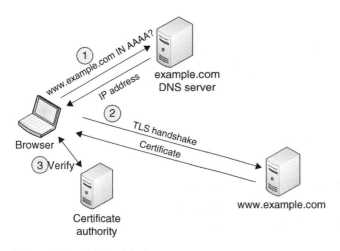

Figure 12.5 TLS handshake.

A major vulnerability of this PKI system arises due to the acceptance of a certificate as valid as long as it is confirmed by a configured (trusted) root CA. Since a CA can sign certificates for any child domain, a compromised trusted CA could sign arbitrary certificates for valid server domain names which can lead to false trust in a validated certificate. This can lead to a man-in-the-middle attack where a browser connects to an imposter website with which the user may willingly supply personal or financial data. CA compromise has occurred on a few occasions, such as the Comodo [111], DigiNotar [112], and Symantec [113] attacks and others.

Unfortunately, website administrators have no control over the integrity of CAs nor of the list of trusted root CAs installed in browsers. DANE enables website administrators to protect the integrity of their certificate authentication using DNS, and DNSSEC in particular. DANE introduces the TLSA resource record type, which enables a domain administrator to publish in DNS the association of a certificate or public key information with an end-entity, e.g. the domain name, or trusted issuing authority for the connection endpoint, e.g. webserver.

Referring to Figure 12.6, a browser connecting to a website, after having obtained its IP address from DNS (step 1 not shown in the figure) and a certificate from the associated webserver (step 2), verifies the certificate against the compromised CA (step 3), can query for a TLSA resource record for the domain name of the webserver in step 4. The TLSA record enables the DNS administrator to corroborate their webservers' certificates to enable direct validation of each certificate, its public key, or associated root CA. DANE requires DNSSEC validation to assure authentication and data integrity verification of this information.

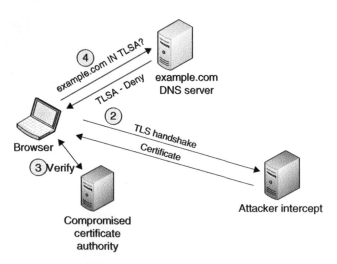

Figure 12.6 Certificate verification using DANE.

Securing Email with DNS

DANE technology has also found deployment success in securing TLS for email. An email client may authenticate an email server and encrypt communications between the client and server. This process works analogously to that just described for HTTPS. An email client may query for the mail domain's TLSA record for information about the domain's public keys and certificates, which it can leverage to establish a TLS connection.

Some might view spam email or unsolicited bulk email as a form of attack, and it has been a nuisance since the dawn of the Internet. A variety of techniques exist to combat spam, many of which involve the use of DNS.

Beyond antispam initiatives, the very security of your users' email transactions is likewise at risk of interception, redirection, and corruption where attackers can disrupt communications and gather sensitive information. Several attack vectors are initiated via email to induce users to click a link or attachment to initiate malware installation for example.

The National Cybersecurity Center or Excellence (NCCoE) published an excellent practice guide [114] which provides use cases, configuration examples, and testing outcomes for a variety of email transaction scenarios that leverage much of the technology discussed in this section. Before we delve into this technology, let's first look at the anatomy of an email transmission including the role of DNS in email delivery.

Email and DNS

An email typically originates from one person and is sent to one or more recipients. Each email address is formatted as follows: mailbox@maildomain. The mailbox commonly refers to the name of the person or owner of a mailbox or email account, while the maildomain, typically the company or Internet provider name, is the destination domain for delivery to the corresponding mailbox or Mail Exchange (MX). Emails are composed using an email client, such as Microsoft Outlook, Eudora, or web-based clients like Yahoo and Google. Regardless, when sent by the originator, the client connects to a SMTP server (using the SMTP protocol) to send the email. Acting like a default router for email, the SMTP server is responsible for forwarding the email to its destination.

The SMTP server must resolve the maildomain to an IP address for transmission of the message. Naturally, this is done using DNS with a lookup for the MX record type, as well as the corresponding A or AAAA record types.

Upon resolving the destination mail server, the SMTP server sends the message to the destination using the SMTP protocol. The ultimate destination server, to which recipient email clients connect, must support post office protocol (POP) or IMAP to enable client retrieval of the email message. Thus, when your email client performs a "send/receive," it utilizes SMTP to send outgoing messages to its configured SMTP server and POP or IMAP to retrieve incoming email messages from the configured POP/IMAP server.

TLS extensions have been defined for SMTP in RFC 3207 [115] and the server authentication portion was updated in RFC 7817 [116]. RFC 3207 enables an SMTP server to request a TLS connection with a client using the STARTTLS directive; if the client complies, it may then request the servers' certificate to authenticate and initiate encryption of ensuing packets. While advantageous, RFC 3207 points out vulnerabilities of this mechanism to man-in-the-middle attacks where an attacker can manipulate a client's acceptance of the TLS capability to keep the connection unencrypted or can insert its own certificate to the client to merely encrypt the connection to the attacker server. DANE addresses these vulnerabilities though the publication of the mail domain's certificate information in DNS with DNSSEC validation.

DNS Block Listing

The use of block listing [117] provides a simple means for the recipient email server to lookup a sender's IP address via DNS and to validate its legitimacy. Block list providers track IP addresses known to originate spam email and publish this information in DNS to facilitate a simple DNS lookup upon email receipt to determine if the email should progress to its recipient or be discarded. This lookup is typically formed by reversing the IP address of the source IP address of the email message, just as is done in forming PTR records. Note that the source IP address being analyzed is that from which the email was received directly, perhaps an email gateway, which may or may not be the original transmitter. However, the intent of such listing is to identify such senders of email by IP address as legitimate or not.

In this scenario, the reversed IP address is appended with a given domain name, typically that of the block list provider. The "host domain name" thus formed by this concatenation comprises the Qname which is queried in DNS using the A resource record query type, not PTR. The query answer is interpreted based on whether the record was found, in which case often an IP address within the 127/8 IPv4 block is returned, and on whether the list publishes known spammers (block list) or known non-spammers (allow list).

For example, upon receiving an email message with a source IP address of 192.0.2.95, my email server formulates an A record query for hostname 95.2.0.192.spamblocklist.org, assuming my chosen block list provider publishes lookups within the spamblocklist.org domain. Upon receiving a reply with answer (IP address) 127.0.0.5, my email server classifies the email as spam and rejects it. On the other hand, if NXDOMAIN is returned for the query, the email may be permitted. A allow list service, publishing known genuine email server addresses would render the opposite interpretation based on the DNS lookup.

Sender Policy Framework (SPF)

The sender policy framework (SPF) is defined in RFC 7208 [118]. SPF enables an organization to publish its own list of authorized outgoing email server addresses, a self-published allow list, though with substantially more sophistication. Under SPF, the received email message's envelope information is examined, and a TXT DNS query from the email recipient is based upon the sender, the sender's domain, as well as the sender's source IP address.

The sender policy framework attempts to provide validation of what hosts are configured to send email for a given domain. That is, SPF seeks to eliminate spam emails from spoofed domains purporting to be from the SPF publisher's domain. A recipient email host can look up the TXT record for the sender's domain to verify that the sending email host matches those authorized by the sender.

As mentioned, SPF utilizes the TXT RRType with a particular syntax for SPF interpretation per RFC 7208. The TXT record is encoded as a string of "mechanisms" that are used to process the source IP address from which the email originated, the domain portion of the MAIL FROM or HELO identity, and the sender parameter from the MAIL FROM or HELO identity. The TXT record syntax includes a version string (v=spf1) followed by a space, then one or more terms that define qualifiers on resource record types or IP network addresses, modifiers, and even macros. Please refer to Chapter 19 for these details.

Domain Keys Identified Mail (DKIM)

Domain Keys Identified Mail (DKIM) specifies a means for a sender to cryptographically sign an email message such that recipients may validate it upon receipt via retrieval and application of the sender's domain key. DKIM supports data origin authentication and data integrity verification through the use of digital signatures. This enables the originator of a given set of data (an email message in this case) to sign the data such that those receiving the data and the signature, along with a corresponding public key can decipher the signature. As with DNSSEC, DKIM employs an asymmetric key pair (private key/public key) model to provide email origin authentication and data integrity verification without encrypting the email.

A signature is created by signing a hash of the information (email message and selected header fields) with a private key by the sender. The signature can be validated by the recipient by decrypting the data with the corresponding public key and comparing with a hash of the data which should match. This provides authentication that the data verified was indeed signed by the holder of the private key. Digital signatures also enable verification that the data received matches the data published and was not manipulated in transit.

The email originator signs the message with its private key and the message and its associated signature are transmitted to the recipient. A new email header, dkim-signature, has been defined to transmit the signature with information on retrieving the public key. DKIM offers a "simple" or strict form of canonicalization and a "relaxed" form of signature validation. The simple form tolerates very little modification while the relaxed form permits white space replacement and header line rewrapping which may occur during email transmission, without impacting the signature validity.

Domain-Based Message Authentication, Reporting, and Conformance (DMARC)

Domain-based message authentication, reporting, and conformance (DMARC) builds upon and works in conjunction with SPF and DKIM. DMARC seeks to improve the information exchange between an email sender and receiver beyond that provided by SPF and DKIM in order to provide validation, message disposition, and sender feedback. Documented in RFC 7489 [119] DMARC enables domain owners to publish email policy assertions about their domains via DNS, while enabling email receivers to authenticate senders, determine email disposition, and report feedback to the sender.

DMARC policies are published in the DNS in the form of, you guessed it, TXT records. Upon receipt of emails from the domain, the receiver can query for TXT records for the sender's domain. Figure 12.7 illustrates how these policies are applied. The sender on the left creates an email and sends it. The sender email system inserts a DKIM header and transmits the email via SMTP to the recipient email system. The recipient system may perform standard blocklisting, rate limiting, etc., as a first line of defense. Next, the sender policy TXT records are retrieved for the sending domain which publishes SPF and DMARC policies in DNS. The receiving email system then validates the DKIM sending domain, the sender policies of the sender, then applies the DMARC policy based on the results of these prior validation steps.

If validation passes, the email is passed on to the recipient. If the DKIM and/or SPF validation fails, the DMARC policy shall dictate the desired action, whether

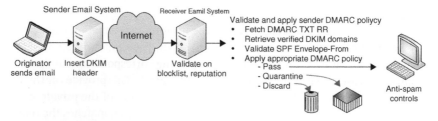

Figure 12.7 DMARC email policies.

to quarantine or discard the email. In this failed validation scenario, the receiving email system should store this disposition for future reporting to the sender according to the DMARC reporting policy. This process reduces ambiguity in handling emails failing validation and enables a feedback loop to the sender regarding the malformed or potential imposter email.

Part IV

IPAM in Practice

Part IV seeks to provide a practical example of the application of IPAM techniques within a fictitious network. We'll evaluate mapping business needs to IPAM planning in terms of address space, DHCP, and DNS deployment strategies and financial trade-offs when considering various IPAM implementation approaches. We conclude this part with our vision of how IPAM affects or is affected by emerging and future Internet technologies and trends.

13

IPAM Use Case

Introduction

We feel it's helpful to illustrate the application of IPAM principles by way of example. We'll apply each IPAM concept successively to a fictitious organization called International Processing and Materials (IPAM) Worldwide (play on words intended!). IPAM Worldwide's basic organization consists of a global headquarters in Philadelphia with three major geographic headquarters spanning the world, with a presence in Europe hubbed in Dublin, North America hubbed in Philadelphia, and Asia hubbed in Tokyo. Each regional headquarters houses a modest data center with support from two public cloud providers, such as AWS, Microsoft Azure, Google Cloud, for compute capacity elasticity as well as support for some new applications deployed in a cloud-native microservices architecture.

IPAM Worldwide has about 17 000 employees and 24 distribution centers which also serve as branch offices, and an additional 37 offices functioning solely as branch offices. Table 13.1 illustrates a basic location spreadsheet, highlighting each continental headquarters, and corresponding distribution centers and branch offices.

The deployment of the IP network is primarily driven by where the users (and "things") of the IP network are located per the sites listed in Table 13.1, by how many there are at each location, by a variety of user requirements for access to information resources such as internal applications and the Internet, by a variety of administration requirements for managing the IP network from security to auditing, and finally by infrastructure requirements to fulfill all of the above. Because of the variety of inputs related to individual business needs, one organization's IP network generally looks a little (or a lot!) different from another's. However, the techniques we discuss should be broadly applicable across a wide variety of networks, including yours.

IP Address Management, Second Edition. Michael Dooley and Timothy Rooney.
© 2021 The Institute of Electrical and Electronics Engineers, Inc.
Published 2021 by John Wiley & Sons, Inc.

Table 13.1 IPAM Worldwide locations and offices.

IPAM Worldwide global locations				
Core sites	Region	Regional site	Distribution centers	Branch offices
Philadelphia	HQ – Corporate	Philadelphia		
Philadelphia	HQ – North America	Philadelphia Public Cloud A Public Cloud B		
	N.A. – East	Norristown	Toronto Nashua Newark Baltimore Pittsburgh Charlotte Atlanta	Providence Quincy Albany Manhattan Ocean City Reston Richmond Charleston Montgomery
	N.A. – Central	Kansas City	Chicago Des Moines Memphis New Orleans Mexico City	Lisle Indianapolis Topeka Houston
	N.A. – West	San Francisco	Denver Vancouver Phoenix	Calgary Albuquerque Salt Lake City Boulder Edmonton Sacramento Anaheim
Dublin	HQ – Europe	Dublin Public Cloud A Public Cloud B		
	Europe - West	London	Amsterdam Paris	Manchester Madrid

(Continued)

Table 13.1 (Continued)

| | | | **IPAM Worldwide global locations** | |
Core sites	Region	Regional site	Distribution centers	Branch offices
				Lyon
				Lisbon
	Europe – South	Rome	Rome	Nice
				Milan
				Athens
	Europe – East	Berlin	Munich	Vienna
			Moscow	Prague
				Budapest
				Kiev
Tokyo	HQ-Asia	Tokyo	Tokyo	Seoul
		AWS Cloud		
		Azure Cloud		
		Public Cloud A	Beijing	Osaka
		Public Cloud B	Singapore	Singapore
		.	Auckland	Manila
				New Delhi
				Sydney

The IT team at IPAM Worldwide has decided to deploy a software defined wide area network or core network among the organizational and geographic headquarters. Emanating from each regional headquarters office is an intra-continental wide area network interconnecting each of the region's retail, distribution, and branch offices. Building on this basic two-layer hierarchy of core and regional networks, each branch network is furthered divided by geographic region. For example, within North America, they've divided the administration into three subregions: east, central, and west, and then further by major distribution center and branch office site. Likewise, the Europe region has been subdivided into west, south, and east regions

Connections to the Internet, the two public cloud providers, and an IoT set of networks are provisioned from each regional headquarters to provide routing redundancy as well as secured points of interfacing between the corporate network and these public networks.

Following this topology, the IT team has decided to mimic this structure with respect to address space to conserve route aggregation, as we'll see next. Hence, the core network interconnects the regional headquarters sites, and each regional headquarters serves as an intermediary between its corresponding regional network and the core network. Each regional network interconnects its respective distribution centers and branch offices within the region. From an organizational perspective, each region has its own IT team that would like to manage its own space and associated DHCP and DNS server configuration. Figure 13.1 depicts the high-level IPAM Worldwide network topology design.

In terms of IP address space allocation, IPAM Worldwide will deploy a 10.0.0.0/8 IPv4 private network internally and a global unicast 2001:db8:4af0::/48 network. Public IPv4 address space, 192.0.2.0/24, has been obtained from an ISP. This public space will be allocated for Internet facing devices such as web servers, email gateways, and VPN gateways for partner connections and remote employees. In addition, a portion of the public address space is reserved for deployment as a public address pool on a NAT firewall facing the ISP.

IPv4 Address Allocation

IPAM Worldwide supports legacy IPv4 addressing across its network including its cloud locations, as well as IPv6 to represent a fully dual stacked network, except

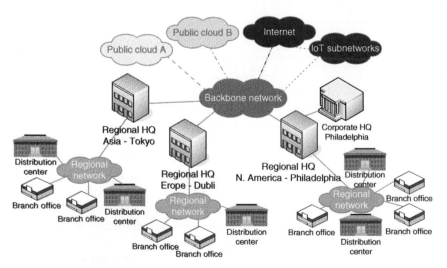

Figure 13.1 IPAM Worldwide Network Topology.

for the IoT subnetwork which is exclusively IPv6. Let's apply our IP allocation strategy to IPAM Worldwide's private address block, 10.0.0.0/8. When performing top-level allocations such as this, keep in mind not only the capacity required in terms of IP addresses but also the number of subdivisions or hierarchy layers that may be ultimately necessary. In the case of IPAM Worldwide, we will define our address hierarchy layers as follows:

- by application to facilitate routing treatment
- continental or core layer to support route aggregation
- campus or regional level to enable regional security controls
- sites or buildings to provide partitioned end user access

Our top-level allocation will divide our address space by application. Each application-specific allocation will then be allocated at the core router or continental level, then by region and finally by office. Since we have four layers of allocation hierarchy, we're going to have to allocate along nonoctet boundaries. So let's look at this from both a CIDR network notation and the corresponding binary notation.

First-Level Allocation

The binary representation of this network is shown below. The network portion of the address, whose length is identified by the /8 notation is highlighted as bold italics, while the local portion is in plain text.

Private network   10.0.0.0/8   ***00001010*** 00000000 00000000 00000000

Given IPAM Worldwide's desire to allocate by application at the top level, we can allocate the first four bits of our network address to allocate equal-sized /12 networks. This provides $2^{(12-8)} = 16$ potential high-level allocations, while providing $2^{(32-12)} > 1$ million IP addresses per allocation. Thus, we'll allocate a /12 each for the infrastructure address space, a /12 each for the VoIP, data and multimedia spaces. Given we only need four allocations of 16 possible networks, we'll "skip" a block and use every other block to provide room for growth, a simplified form of sparse allocation.

This allocation strategy is illustrated below with the bold italic bits once again representing the network (network + subnet) portion and normally formatted bits representing host bits.

Private network 10.0.0.0/8   ***00001010*** 00000000 00000000 00000000

Infrastructure   10.0.0.0/12   ***00001010 0000***0000 00000000 00000000

Voice   10.32.0.0/12 ***00001010 0010***0000 00000000 00000000

Data	10.64.0.0/12	*00001010*	*0100*0000	00000000	00000000
Multimedia	10.96.0.0/12	*00001010*	*0110*0000	00000000	00000000

After these allocations, we are left with the following unassigned or free address blocks from our original 10.0.0.0/8 block: 10.128.0.0/9, 10.0.16.0/12, 10.0.48.0/12, 10.0.80.0/12, and 10.112.0.0/12.

Second-Layer Allocation

This initial application level allocation yields four /12 spaces aligned per application. The decision to use /12 at this level is a trade-off between the number of first-level allocations and the number of addresses available per allocation. Given our sparse allocation strategy, we effectively allocated /11s, so if a particular allocation becomes exhausted, we can allocate the vacant adjoining /12 block. For example, we can expand the data allocation from 10.64.0.0/12 to include the next block, 10.80.0.0/12 to yield 10.64.0.0/11. This step merely changes an entry in routing tables without adding an additional entry which might otherwise be required when allocating a noncontiguous block. In addition, we have retained a /9 of free application space should the future require address-specific policies and allocations.

Block sizing decisions for second and subsequent level allocations may employ the same or different logic. For example, instead of trading off allocation size with the number of equal-sized allocations, an optimal allocation strategy could be used. This optimal strategy entails successively halving the address space down to the size required as we described in Chapter 6. The key reason for this approach is that it enables you to retain larger blocks of unallocated address space as available for larger requests and alternative allocations.

If we examine our first-layer infrastructure block, for example, 10.0.0.0/12, we can allocate up to sixteen /16 blocks for our next layer. In our case, if we need to allocate three such blocks, one for each region, we can break this down as illustrated in Figure 13.2.

Notice that we still have many large blocks available for further allocation or assignment. Only the darker shaded wedge of the pie comprising our three /16 networks has been assigned. In relating the successive splits in the table above to the pie chart, while each "first" half block was either assigned or divided into further allocations, it yielded a corresponding "second" half block which is still free or available. Thus, the resulting address allocations for IPAM Worldwide based on this initial allocation is as follows:

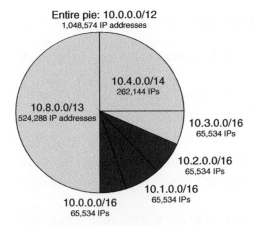

Figure 13.2   Allocation of 3 /16s from /12 space.

Original infra-structure (IS) block	10.0.0.0/12	*00001010*	*0000*0000	00000000	00000000
Free IS block	10.8.0.0/13	*00001010*	*00001*000	00000000	00000000
Free IS block	10.4.0.0/14	*00001010*	*000001*00	00000000	00000000
N.A. IS block	**10.0.0.0/16**	*00001010*	*00000000*	00000000	00000000
Europe IS block	**10.1.0.0/16**	*00001010*	*00000001*	00000000	00000000
Asia IS block	**10.2.0.0/16**	*00001010*	*00000010*	00000000	00000000
Free IS block	10.3.0.0/16	*00001010*	*00000011*	00000000	00000000

Following similar logic with the data, voice, and two cloud provider top-level address allocations, we can derive the following allocations:

Voice block	10.32.0.0/12	*00001010*	*0010*0000	00000000	00000000
Free voice block	10.40.0.0/13	*00001010*	*00101*000	00000000	00000000
Free voice block	10.36.0.0/14	*00001010*	*001001*00	00000000	00000000
N.A. voice block	**10.32.0.0/16**	*00001010*	*00100000*	00000000	00000000
Europe voice block	**10.33.0.0/16**	*00001010*	*00100001*	00000000	00000000

Asia voice block	10.34.0.0/16	*00001010*	*00100010*	00000000	00000000
Free voice block	10.35.0.0/16	*00001010*	*00100011*	00000000	00000000
Data block	10.64.0.0/12	*00001010*	*0100*0000	00000000	00000000
Free data block	10.72.0.0/13	*00001010*	*01001*000	00000000	00000000
Free data block	10.68.0.0/14	*00001010*	*010001*00	00000000	00000000
N.A. data block	10.64.0.0/16	*00001010*	*01000000*	00000000	00000000
Europe data block	10.65.0.0/16	*00001010*	*01000001*	00000000	00000000
Asia data block	10.66.0.0/16	*00001010*	*01000010*	00000000	00000000
Free data block	10.67.0.0/16	*00001010*	*01000011*	00000000	00000000
Multimedia block	10.96.0.0/12	*00001010*	*01100000*	*00000000*	*00000000*
Free multimedia block	10.104.0.0/13	*00001010*	*01101000*	*00000000*	*00000000*
Free multimedia block	10.100.0.0/14	*00001010*	*01100100*	*00000000*	*00000000*
N.A. multimedia block	10.96.0.0/16	*00001010*	*01100000*	*00000000*	*00000000*
Europe multimedia block	10.97.0.0/16	*00001010*	*01100001*	*00000000*	*00000000*
Asia multimedia block	10.98.0.0/16	*00001010*	*01100010*	*00000000*	*00000000*
Free multimedia block	10.99.0.0/16	*00001010*	*01100011*	*00000000*	*00000000*

Address Allocation Layer 3

Now that we've allocated address space at the top level, e.g. by application then at the core network level, each of these allocations can be subdivided further to serve requisite distribution center and branch office needs. In essence, these allocations serve as the block or pool of addresses that may be distributed for the given application within the respective region. This technique of top-down allocation ensures subsequent allocations from these initial allocations will roll-up hierarchically.

Thus, our core routers can simply advertise their /16 allocations to the other core routers. Also, any special per-service packet handling treatment can also be easily configured. For example, if we'd like to handle voice packets with highest priority treatment, we can configure our routers to provide such treatment for packets with source address from the respective voice space, e.g. 10.33.0.0/16 for Europe voice traffic (or 10.32.0.0/12 for all voice traffic). From this initial definition, further allocations can now be made further down geographical lines without affecting this treatment logic.

Let's drill into our North American voice space, 10.32.0.0/16. From our location table presented earlier in Figure 13.1, we see that North American sites are organized in three regions: east, central, and west. We'd also like to allocate independent space for headquarters. Assuming our routing topology aligns with this geographical organization, we will allocate address space accordingly. Thus, a WAN may interconnect North American regional sites of Philadelphia, Kansas City, and San Francisco with headquarters. This regional interconnection represents a "sub-core" network, and similar allocation logic can be applied as was at the top level.

Let's carve up our 10.32.0.0/16 block into four regional blocks. To allocate equally, we need to divide this space into four blocks, so we need to allocate the next 2 bits ($2^2 = 4$) in the North America data space, highlighted as larger font bold italic bits in the binary representation below.

N.A. voice	10.32.0.0/16	***00001010***	***00010000***	00000000	00000000
N.A. HQ voice	10.32.0.0/18	***00001010***	***00010010***	**00**000000	00000000
N.A. East voice	10.32.64.0/18	***00001010***	***00010010***	**01**000000	00000000
N.A. West voice	10.32.128.0/18	***00001010***	***00010010***	**10**000000	00000000
N.A. Central voice	10.32.192.0/18	***00001010***	***00010010***	**11**000000	00000000

We don't necessarily have to allocate the same sized blocks as we're showing, though this results in equal-sized allocations. We could just as easily have allocated a larger portion to the east, since it contains the most sites: 10.32.0.0/17 (East), 10.32.160.0.0/19 (Central), 10.32.192.0/19 (West), and 10.32.220.0/19 (HQ). But this introduces complexity and is discouraged unless you need to tightly conserve address space.

From this point, we can allocate from each region's space to its respective sites for addressing needs. Considering the North America West Voice space, 10.32.128.0/18, we can now allocate space for data applications in each of our distribution centers and branch offices. The simplest strategy for such allocation is one of *uniform* distribution, e.g. each site is allocated the same sized block as we performed at the top allocation level. However, one needs to consider the number of users and data devices per site, projected growth at each site, planned new sites within the region, and application networking requirements. In the case of IPAM Worldwide, distribution centers typically house 65 employees with additional automation machinery and infrastructure requiring IP addresses totaling around 200–250. Branch offices require only about 150–200 IP devices, including associate laptops, tablets, mobiles, and other data devices serving an average employee population of 40.

In such a scenario, it makes sense to allocate at least a /23 for distribution centers, providing 510 usable IP addresses and /24 for branch offices, providing 254 IP addresses. However, each site should be analyzed individually regarding its respective addressing requirements. In our case, we'll first allocate a /23 per distribution center, then a /24 per branch office. The following table illustrates this allocation, along with the remaining free space from the original 10.32.128.0/18 network available for future allocation.

Site	Network	Binary			
N.A. West voice	10.32.128.0/18	*00001010*	*00100000*	*10*000000	00000000
San Fran. site	10.32.128.0/23	*00001010*	*00100000*	*1000000*0	00000000
Denver site	10.32.130.0/23	*00001010*	*00100000*	*1000001*0	00000000
Vancouver site	10.32.132.0/23	*00001010*	*00100000*	*1000010*0	00000000
Phoenix site	10.32.134.0/23	*00001010*	*00100000*	*1000011*0	00000000
Calgary site	10.32.136.0/24	*00001010*	*00100000*	*10001000*	00000000
Albuquerque site	10.32.137.0/24	*00001010*	*00100000*	*10001001*	00000000
Salt Lake City site	10.32.138.0/24	*00001010*	*00100000*	*10001010*	00000000
Boulder site	10.32.139.0/24	*00001010*	*00100000*	*10001011*	00000000
Edmonton site	10.32.140.0/24	*00001010*	*00100000*	*10001100*	00000000
Sacramento site	10.32.141.0/24	*00001010*	*00100000*	*10001101*	00000000
Anaheim site	10.32.142.0/24	*00001010*	*00100000*	*10001110*	00000000
Free space	10.32.143.0/24	*00001010*	*00100000*	*10001111*	00000000
Free space	10.32.144.0/20	*00001010*	*00100000*	*1001*0000	00000000
Free space	10.32.160.0/19	*00001010*	*00100000*	*101*00000	00000000

For our headquarters location, we'll allocate /22 networks for each of the major corporate divisions. These allocations may be further subnetted based on networking deployments.

Core Address Space

The only remaining step at this core level is to allocate infrastructure space for the core routers themselves. The core network is after all a network requiring an IP subnet address and it lies "above" our intercontinental allocations. For this subnet, we'll carve out a /26 subnet. This sized subnet provides 62 host addresses, which provides sufficient capacity for growth. Let's allocate this from the smallest free infrastructure block, 10.3.0.0/16. Following similar logic we've just applied, we allocate the 10.3.0.0/26 network to our core backbone network. We have several free blocks available for future allocation:

Free IS block	10.3.0.0/16	*00001010*	*00000011*	00000000	00000000
Free IS block	10.3.128.0/17	*00001010*	*00000011*	*1*0000000	00000000
Free IS block	10.3.64.0/18	*00001010*	*00000011*	*01*000000	00000000
Free IS block	10.3.32.0/19	*00001010*	*00000011*	*001*00000	00000000
Free IS block	10.3.16.0/20	*00001010*	*00000011*	*0001*0000	00000000
Free IS block	10.3.8.0/21	*00001010*	*00000011*	*00001*000	00000000
Free IS block	10.3.4.0/22	*00001010*	*00000011*	*000001*00	00000000
Free IS block	10.3.2.0/23	*00001010*	*00000011*	*0000001*0	00000000
Free IS block	10.3.1.0/24	*00001010*	*00000011*	*00000001*	00000000
Free IS block	10.3.0.128/25	*00001010*	*00000011*	*00000000*	*1*0000000
Free IS block	10.3.0.64/26	*00001010*	*00000011*	*00000000*	*01*000000
Core Network Infrastructure Block	10.3.0.0/26	*00001010*	*00000011*	*00000000*	*00*000000

External Extensions of Address Space

IPAM Worldwide considers their public cloud infrastructure an extension of their enterprise network. We have configured a VPN to each public cloud provider and desire to provision a /16 for each provider, which in turn can be allocated further for each virtual private cloud. Drawing from other 10.4.0.0/14 free infrastructure block, we allocate 10.4.0.0/16 to our private network within cloud provider A and

10.5.0.0/16 for cloud provider B. Given the predominance of cloud addresses within our US cloud locations, we decide to allocate a /18 from each respective /16 for the US and a pair of /19s for Europe and Asia, respectively, leaving a /17 for each provider free as follows:

Cloud Provider A	10.4.0.0/16	*00001010*	*00000100*	00000000	00000000
N.A. Cloud A	10.4.0.0/18	*00001010*	*00000100*	*00*000000	00000000
Europe Cloud A	10.4.64.0/19	*00001010*	*00000100*	*01*000000	00000000
Asia Cloud A	10.4.96.0/19	*00001010*	*00000100*	*011*00000	00000000
Free Cloud A	10.4.128.0/17	*00001010*	*00000100*	*10*000000	00000000
Cloud Provider B	10.5.0.0/16	*00001010*	*00000101*	00000000	00000000
N.A. Cloud B	10.5.0.0/18	*00001010*	*00000101*	*00*000000	00000000
Europe Cloud B	10.5.64.0/19	*00001010*	*00000101*	*01*000000	00000000
Asia Cloud B	10.5.96.0/19	*00001010*	*00000101*	*011*00000	00000000
Free Cloud B	10.5.128.0/17	*00001010*	*00000101*	*10*000000	00000000

A similar philosophy of private space extension applies to their "external" IoT space, which they consider encompassing distribution vehicles, which typically communicate with the enterprise network through a wireless carrier and the Internet. However, they are using IPv6 exclusively for this space given the mobility aspects of the application for which 6LoWPAN technologies are used. Note that some IoT address assignments are feathered into their core/region/campus IPv4 address space like other infrastructure devices. This approach offers the convenience of using the same address space to provide access to local site IoT devices providing surveillance, security, and facilities monitoring and control which are connected via reliable wired or wireless links.

Allocation Trade-Offs and Tracking

As you add layers in the address allocation hierarchy, the network portion of the address grows, shrinking the number of host bits assignable to IP devices. Each of the sites listed in the table of the prior section were assigned /24 or /23 address space, leaving 8 or 9 host bits available providing capacity for 254 or 510 individual IP hosts per site, respectively.

Individual IP address capacity requirements per subnet will help you derive the endpoint allocation size. Many organizations plan for allocating 254 hosts in a /24 allocation per end subnet. Multiple subnets could be allocated if needed and available. Using this octet boundary helps simplify translation from binary to decimal as you can see in the summary above, but it may not be feasible for your organization due to address capacity requirements. If you're required to allocate outside octet boundaries, use of an IP address management tool can probably help assure accuracy of allocations without overlaps while conserving address hierarchy.

Whether you decide to use an IPAM system or not, you must track address allocations. This of course is the foundation of IPAM. To illustrate one simple tracking method, we've recast our spreadsheet presented at the beginning of this chapter listing IPAM Worldwide's network locations to reflect respective block allocations. In the updated version shown below in Table 13.2, we've listed distribution centers and branch offices together under a common Sites column.

Our top-level hierarchical blocks which comprise the address supply at each hierarchy level, are shown for each region, to differentiate them from subnets. We followed a common allocation approach to keep things simple, allocating a /23 for each distribution center and a /24 for each branch office. We're only illustrating a small subset of the spreadsheet, but the same methodology is used for Europe and Asia sites and for voice and data applications.

A convenient side effect of this form of allocation yields the ability to easily associate an address with a location. For example, knowing that 10.0.79.0/24 is the infrastructure subnet for Quincy, one could deduce that 10.32.79.0/24 is the VoIP subnet and 10.64.79.0/24 is the data subnet for Quincy. This octet pattern of 10.X.Y.0 networks maps the application (octet X) and the location (octet Y) by sight. In our example octet X is 0 for infrastructure, 32 for VoIP and 64 for data. Octet Y is 79 for Quincy in this example (Table 13.2).

IPAM Worldwide's Public IPv4 Address Space

Now let's look at IPAM Worldwide's public address space, 192.0.2.0/24, obtained from our ISP. IPAM Worldwide has an Internet connection to their chosen ISP from the Philadelphia headquarters office. While two diverse-routed local loops provide a level of access redundancy, future plans call for supporting a multi-homed connection from another location. For the time being, the 254 public IP addresses available within the /24 will be used to address Internet (externally) reachable hosts such as web, email, and external DNS servers, and a shared address pool to enable internal clients to access the Internet. A pair of NAT devices has been installed to enable load sharing and address translation for access by internal clients to the Internet. In reality, this /24 will likely need to be itself subnetted to partition Internet-reachable hosts from NAT addresses and perhaps employ A+P routing.

IPAM Worldwide's IPv6 Allocations

IPAM Worldwide has obtained the 2001:db8:4af0::/48 block for allocation. This address block will be allocated hierarchically in accordance with IPAM Worldwide's geographic structure. We'll also allocate these networks using common subnet ID numbers for each location as in our earlier 10.X.Y.0 example, for pattern consistency and easier visual correlation (don't worry, it'll become second nature soon enough!).

We'll use the same allocation approach as with IPv4, allocating first by application, then by region. In IPAM Worldwide's case, let's use sparse allocation at the top layer. From this allocation, we can further sparsely allocate to our regions, then use a best-fit approach for our distribution centers and branch offices. While we're only running data applications over IPv6 for the time being, we should still perform an application-level allocation for application expansion or growth.

We will adhere to our recommended approach and allocate on nibble boundaries. Each nibble affords 16 possible allocations, so we'll simply allocate our four blocks to represent our application-layer allocation, while tracking the remaining 12 blocks as unallocated (not shown in the table below). Using the sparse, method, we arrive at the following allocations:

Application allocation	Bits 49–52				Public space allocation
Infrastructure	0	0	0	0	2001:db8:4af0::/52
Voice	1	0	0	0	2001:db8:4af0:8000::/52
Data	0	1	0	0	2001:db8:4af0:4000::/52
Multimedia	1	1	0	0	2001:db8:4af0:c000::/52

Applying a similar approach, using our next nibble, bits 53–56 for our next level allocations, we arrive at the following suballocations for the Voice space:

Application allocation	Bits 53–56				Public space allocation
N.A. voice	0	0	0	0	2001:db8:4af0:8000::/56
Europe voice	1	0	0	0	2001:db8:4af0:8800::/56
Asia voice	0	1	0	0	2001:db8:4af0:84000::/56

And if we further allocate the North America Voice block, taking our third nibble, again allocating sparsely.

Table 13.2 IPAM Worldwide's IPv4 block allocations (partial).

Core sites	Region	Regional site	Sites	Infrastructure networks	VoIP networks	Data networks	Media networks
Philadelphia	HQ – Corp.	Philadelphia		**10.0.0.0/12**	**10.32.0.0/12**	**10.64.0.0/12**	**10.96.0.0/12**
Philadelphia	HQ – N.A.	Philadelphia		**10.0.0.0/16**	**10.32.0.0/16**	**10.64.0.0/16**	**10.96.0.0/16**
			Core Net	10.3.0.0/26			
			Cloud A	10.4.0.0/18			
			Cloud B	10.5.0.0/18			
			Philadelphia – Exec	10.0.0.0/22	10.32.0.0/22	10.64.0.0/22	10.96.0.0/22
			Philadelphia – Fin.	10.0.4.0/22	10.32.4.0/22	10.64.4.0/22	10.96.4.0/22
			Philadelphia – Ops	10.0.8.0/22	10.32.8.0/22	10.64.8.0/22	10.96.8.0/22
			Philadelphia – Tech	10.0.12.0/22	10.32.12.0/22	10.64.12.0/22	10.96.12.0/22
			Philadelphia – Mktg	10.0.16.0/22	10.32.16.0/22	10.64.16.0/22	10.96.16.0/22
			Philadelphia – R&D	10.0.20.0/22	10.32.20.0/22	10.64.20.0/22	10.96.20.0/22
	N.A.-East	Norris-town		**10.0.64.0/18**	**10.32.64.0/18**	**10.64.64.0/18**	**10.96.64.0/18**
			Norristown	10.0.64.0/23	10.32.64.0/23	10.64.64.0/23	10.96.64.0/23
			Toronto	10.0.66.0/23	10.32.66.0/23	10.64.66.0/23	10.96.66.0/23
			Nashua	10.0.68.0/23	10.32.68.0/23	10.64.68.0/23	10.96.68.0/23
			Newark	10.0.70.0/23	10.32.70.0/23	10.64.70.0/23	10.96.70.0/23
			Baltimore	10.0.72.0/23	10.32.72.0/23	10.64.72.0/23	10.96.72.0/23
			Pittsburgh	10.0.74.0/23	10.32.74.0/23	10.64.74.0/23	10.96.74.0/23

(Continued)

Table 13.2 (Continued)

Core sites	Region	Regional site	Sites	Infrastructure networks	VoIP networks	Data networks	Media networks
			Charlotte	10.0.76.0/24	10.32.76.0/24	10.64.76.0/24	10.96.76.0/24
			Atlanta	10.0.77.0/24	10.32.77.0/24	10.64.77.0/24	10.96.77.0/24
			Providence	10.0.78.0/24	10.32.78.0/24	10.64.78.0/24	10.96.78.0/24
			Quincy	10.0.79.0/24	10.32.79.0/24	10.64.79.0/24	10.96.79.0/24
			Albany	10.0.80.0/24	10.32.80.0/24	10.64.80.0/24	10.96.80.0/24
			Manhattan	10.0.81.0/24	10.32.81.0/24	10.64.81.0/24	10.96.81.0/24
			Ocean City	10.0.82.0/24	10.32.82.0/24	10.64.82.0/24	10.96.82.0/24
			Reston	10.0.83.0/24	10.32.83.0/24	10.64.83.0/24	10.96.83.0/24
			Richmond	10.0.84.0/24	10.32.84.0/24	10.64.84.0/24	10.96.84.0/24
			Charleston	10.0.85.0/24	10.32.85.0/24	10.64.85.0/24	10.96.85.0/24
			Montgomery	10.0.86.0/24	10.32.86.0/24	10.64.86.0/24	10.96.86.0/24
			...				
	N.A. – Central	Kansas City		**10.0.192.0/18**	**10.32.192.0/18**	**10.64.192.0/18**	**10.96.192.0/18**
			Kansas City	10.0.192.0/23	10.32.192.0/23	10.64.192.0/23	10.96.192.0/23
			Chicago	10.0.194.0/23	10.32.194.0/23	10.64.194.0/23	10.96.194.0/23
			Des Moines	10.0.196.0/23	10.32.196.0/23	10.64.196.0/23	10.96.196.0/23
			Memphis	10.0.198.0/23	10.32.198.0/23	10.64.198.0/23	10.96.198.0/23
			New Orleans	10.0.200.0/23	10.32.200.0/23	10.64.200.0/23	10.96.200.0/23
			...		...	...	...

Subvoice allocation	Bits 57–60	Public space allocation
N.A. voice – HQ	0 0 0 0	2001:db8:4af0:8000::/60
N.A. voice – East.	1 0 0 0	2001:db8:4af0:8080::/60
N.A. voice – Cent.	0 1 0 0	2001:db8:4af0:8040::/60
N.A. voice – West	1 1 0 0	2001:db8:4af0:80c0::/60

Within each of these /60 allocations, we can further allocate individual /64 subnet addresses for each distribution center and branch office. We'll perform this allocation using a monotonic approach and summarize a subset of our allocations in our expanded address allocation spreadsheet on the next page. IPv6 subnets in general should be allocated with /64 network prefixes. Many IPv6 features such as Neighbor Discovery assume (rely on) this prefix size.

As mentioned, allocation on a single nibble boundary affords 16 children blocks. But in our North America East region, we actually need 17. Given our sparse allocation, we can increase the allocation to North America East by allocating the adjoining /60 block to effectively assign a /59. For example, North America Voice – East in the preceding table would be allocated the 2001:db8:4af0:8080::/59 block, comprising the 2001:db8:4af0:8080::/60 and 2001:db8:4af0:8090::/60 blocks. You could track these as two /60s if it's easier for you to keep things consistent but from a network configuration standpoint, you should use the /59 network to minimize superfluous routes or policies.

For router point-to-point or back-to-back links, you may assign a /127 subnet, analogous to a /31 in IPv4 providing two host addresses. The /128 prefix denotes a single IP address, analogous to /32 in IPv4.

External Extensions Address Space

Most organizations allocate one protocol or another to their cloud provider virtual networks, but we'll illustrate a dual stack environment as many cloud providers now support IPv6. We shall then allocate to each cloud using the same numerical identifier (four for cloud provider A and five for B) plus our IoT space:

- Cloud provider A: 2001:db8:4af0:4::/64
- Cloud provider B: 2001:db8:4af0:5::/64
- Field IoT space: 2001:db8:4af0:6::/64

Let's add these IPv6 allocations to IPAM Worldwide's IP address spreadsheet, as shown (partially) on the following page:

Core sites	Region	Regional site	Sites	Infra. IPv4 nets	Infra. IPv6 nets	VoIP IPv4 nets	VoIP IPv6 nets	Data IPv4 nets	Data IPv6 nets
Philadelphia	HQ – Corp.	Philadelphia		**10.0.0.0/12**	**2001:db8:4af0::/56**	**10.32.0.0/12**	**2001:db8:4af0:8000::/56**	**10.64.0.0/12**	**2001:db8:4af0:4000::/52**
Philadelphia	HQ – N.A.	Philadelphia		**10.0.0.0/16**	**2001:db8:4af0::/60**	**10.32.0.0/16**	**2001:db8:4af0:8000::/60**	**10.64.0.0/16**	**2001:db8:4af0:4000::/56**
			Backbone net	10.3.0.0/26	2001:db8:4af0::/64				
			Cloud provider A	10.4.0.0/18	2001:db8:4af0:4::/64				
			Cloud provider B	10.5.0.0/18	2001:db8:4af0:5::/64				
			Field IoT		2001:db8:4af0:6::/64				
			Philadelphia – Exec	10.0.0.0/22	2001:db8:4af0:7::/64	10.32.0.0/22	2001:db8:4af0:8004::/64	10.64.0.0/22	2001:db8:4af0:4004::/64
			Philadelphia – Finan.	10.0.4.0/22	2001:db8:4af0:8::/64	10.32.4.0/22	2001:db8:4af0:8005::/64	10.64.4.0/22	2001:db8:4af0:4005::/64
			Philadelphia – Ops	10.0.8.0/22	2001:db8:4af0:9::/64	10.32.8.0/22	2001:db8:4af0:8006::/64	10.64.8.0/22	2001:db8:4af0:4006::/64
			Philadelphia – Tech	10.0.12.0/22	2001:db8:4af0:a::/64	10.32.12.0/22	2001:db8:4af0:8007::/64	10.64.12.0/22	2001:db8:4af0:4007::/64
			Philadelphia – Mktg	10.0.16.0/22	2001:db8:4af0:b::/64	10.32.16.0/22	2001:db8:4af0:8008::/64	10.64.16.0/22	2001:db8:4af0:4008::/64
			Philadelphia – R&D	10.0.20.0/22	2001:db8:4af0:c::/64	10.32.20.0/22	2001:db8:4af0:8009::/64	10.64.20.0/22	2001:db8:4af0:4009::/64
	N. A. – East	Norristown		**10.0.64.0/18**	**2001:db8:4af0:80::/59**	**10.32.64.0/18**	**2001:db8:4af0:8080::/59**	**10.64.64.0/18**	**2001:db8:4af0:4080::/59**
			Norristown	10.0.64.0/23	2001:db8:4af0:80::/64	10.32.64.0/23	2001:db8:4af0:8080::/64	10.64.64.0/23	2001:db8:4af0:4080::/64

Toronto	10.0.66.0/23	2001:db8:4af0:81::/64	10.32.66.0/23	2001:db8:4af0:8081::/64	10.64.66.0/23	2001:db8:4af0:4081::/64
Nashua	10.0.68.0/23	2001:db8:4af0:82::/64	10.32.68.0/23	2001:db8:4af0:8082::/64	10.64.68.0/23	2001:db8:4af0:4082::/64
Newark	10.0.70.0/23	2001:db8:4af0:83::/64	10.32.70.0/23	2001:db8:4af0:8083::/64	10.64.70.0/23	2001:db8:4af0:4083::/64
Baltimore	10.0.72.0/23	2001:db8:4af0:84::/64	10.32.72.0/23	2001:db8:4af0:8084::/64	10.64.72.0/23	2001:db8:4af0:4084::/64
Pittsburgh	10.0.74.0/23	2001:db8:4af0:85::/64	10.32.74.0/23	2001:db8:4af0:8085::/64	10.64.74.0/23	2001:db8:4af0:4085::/64
Charlotte	10.0.76.0/24	2001:db8:4af0:86::/64	10.32.76.0/24	2001:db8:4af0:8086::/64	10.64.76.0/24	2001:db8:4af0:4086::/64
Atlanta	10.0.77.0/24	2001:db8:4af0:87::/64	10.32.77.0/24	2001:db8:4af0:8087::/64	10.64.77.0/24	2001:db8:4af0:4087::/64
Providence	10.0.78.0/24	2001:db8:4af0:88::/64	10.32.78.0/24	2001:db8:4af0:8088::/64	10.64.78.0/24	2001:db8:4af0:4088::/64
Quincy	10.0.79.0/24	2001:db8:4af0:89::/64	10.32.79.0/24	2001:db8:4af0:8089::/64	10.64.79.0/24	2001:db8:4af0:4089::/64
Albany	10.0.80.0/24	2001:db8:4af0:8a::/64	10.32.80.0/24	2001:db8:4af0:808a::/64	10.64.80.0/24	2001:db8:4af0:408a::/64
Manhattan	10.0.81.0/24	2001:db8:4af0:8b::/64	10.32.81.0/24	2001:db8:4af0:808b::/64	10.64.81.0/24	2001:db8:4af0:408b::/64
Ocean City	10.0.82.0/24	2001:db8:4af0:8c::/64	10.32.82.0/24	2001:db8:4af0:808c::/64	10.64.82.0/24	2001:db8:4af0:408c::/64
Reston	10.0.83.0/24	2001:db8:4af0:8d::/64	10.32.83.0/24	2001:db8:4af0:808d::/64	10.64.83.0/24	2001:db8:4af0:408d::/64
Richmond	10.0.84.0/24	2001:db8:4af0:8e::/64	10.32.84.0/24	2001:db8:4af0:808e::/64	10.64.84.0/24	2001:db8:4af0:408e::/64
Charleston	10.0.85.0/24	2001:db8:4af0:8f::/64	10.32.85.0/24	2001:db8:4af0:808f::/64	10.64.85.0/24	2001:db8:4af0:408f::/64
Montgomery	10.0.86.0/24	2001:db8:4af0:90::/64	10.32.86.0/24	2001:db8:4af0:8090::/64	10.64.86.0/24	2001:db8:4af0:4090::/64
N.A. – Cent. KC	**10.0.192.0/18**	**2001:db8:4af0: 40::/60**	**10.32.192.0/18**	**2001:db8:4af0: 8040::/60**	**10.64.192.0/18**	**2001:db8:4af0: 4040::/60**
Kansas City	10.0.192.0/23	2001:db8:4af0:40::/64	10.32.192.0/23	2001:db8:4af0:8040::/64	10.64.192.0/23	2001:db8:4af0:4040::/64
Chicago	10.0.194.0/23	2001:db8:4af0:41::/64	10.32.194.0/23	2001:db8:4af0:8041::/64	10.64.194.0/23	2001:db8:4af0:4041::/64
Des Moines	10.0.196.0/23	2001:db8:4af0:42::/64	10.32.196.0/23	2001:db8:4af0:8042::/64	10.64.196.0/23	2001:db8:4af0:4042::/64
Memphis	10.0.198.0/23	2001:db8:4af0:43::/64	10.32.198.0/23	2001:db8:4af0:8043::/64	10.64.198.0/23	2001:db8:4af0:4043::/64
New Orleans	10.0.200.0/23	2001:db8:4af0:44::/64	10.32.200.0/23	2001:db8:4af0:8044::/64	10.64.200.0/23	2001:db8:4af0:4044::/64

As we noted with the IPv4 allocations where Pittsburgh, for example uses "site number" 74 (third octet), and we can identify its IPv6 site number as x085, the fourth hextet, where x = encoded application (0 = infrastructure, 4 = data, 8 = voice, c = multimedia). That is, this fourth hextet encodes our allocations consistently, using example hextet value 4085:

Fourth hextet nibble	Example value	Interpretation
1	4	Data application
2	0	North America
3	8	Eastern region
4	5	Pittsburgh

We'll make one more allocation from our IPv6 space for our externally (Internet) accessible servers within our DMZ, such as DNS, web, file transfer, and email servers, 2001:db8:4af0:a::./64 from our Infrastructure space. Our IPv4 space was allocated using two different address spaces: private space for internal allocations and public space for external. For IPv6, we've used our global unicast address allocation for all IPv6 allocations, so we could have omitted the "2001:db8:4af0" prefix from each spreadsheet entry to reduce "clutter."

IP Address Tracking

Now we have completed our initial allocation planning for IPAM Worldwide and we have recorded each allocation in our spreadsheet. The next tier of IP address tracking comprises tracking individual IP assignments within each subnet, a critical process to assure address uniqueness. A good approach entails enumerating the available IP addresses, well at least for IPv4, and indicating whether each address is assigned, unassigned, or part of a DHCP pool within which a DHCP server manages assignments. Enumerating each IPv6 address within a /64 subnet isn't feasible nor worthwhile, so it's probably best to track what addresses have been assigned statically, via SLAAC or DHCPv6 and to assure uniqueness when making further assignments over time.

While tracking individual DHCP leases using a spreadsheet is not suitable, allocation of address pools within the spreadsheet or database should be performed at the least to mask off these addresses from static assignment.

This consolidated address assignment data store provides the known level of IP address inventory. The IPAM Worldwide team has assigned a consistent set of IP addresses on each subnet for static devices such as routers, switches, and servers. The team has also defined a number of Manual DHCP addresses for printers and address pools for sharing among DHCP client devices like laptops and VoIP phones. We've created a new tab for each site (this spreadsheet is getting quite large!) to inventory individual address as well as address pool assignments. Additional "comment" information is useful to track as well for certain devices, such as vendor contact, support information, asset information, and the like.

We've organized the table ascending by IPv4 address, and we track the corresponding IPv6 interface ID for the device (Figure 13.3).

Location and subnet addresses	IPv4 address/IPv6 IID	Address and device type	Comments
Charleston 10.32.85.0/23 2001:db8:4af0:808f::/64	10.32.85.1 482:f10a:87b9:2aa	Static - Router	Charleston VoIP subnet router 1
	10.32.85.2 e9:23ac:cca1:c80b	Static - Router	Charleston VoIP subnet router 2
	10.32.85.3 83dd:7e9a:bce4:90	Static - Router	Charleston VoIP subnet router HSRP address
	10.32.85.4 cb7b:83ec:9e1:550e	Static - DNS Server	Contact Fred Jones for support
	10.32.85.5 3fc:846a:8070:effc	Static - FTP Server	
	10.32.85.6 e24e:89:75f5:2aaa	Static - File Server	San Fran secondary
	10.32.85.7 bae3:8f39:d6ea:bc44	Static - File Server	Backup for Atlanta
	10.32.85.8 7eda:ef81:a6a6:abc3	Static - File Server	Backup for Pittsburgh
	10.32.85.9		
	10.32.85.10 c73e:930a:750c:4d98	Static - IP PBX	IP PBX-CS1
	10.32.85.11 bb65:9830:73d7:2e3	Static - IP PBX	IP PBX-CS2
	. . .		
	10.32.85.20 516d:d87e:4acc:e630	Engineering Lab Server	Contact Engineering for assistance
	10.32.8521 a966:a6e9:b87:388c	Engineering Lab Server	Contact Engineering for assistance
	10.32.85.22 1144:4bcc:84d2:9881	Engineering Lab Server	Contact Engineering for assistance
	. . .		
	10.32.85.50- 10.32.86.240	VoIP DHCP Pool	Contact Mary Smith for support
	::ffff:ffff:0:0/96	VoIP DHCP Pool	Contact Mary Smith for support
	. . .		

Figure 13.3 Sample inventory table for IP Addresses.

In addition to tracking IP address assignments, configuration of the corresponding DHCP server(s) must be performed to enable DHCP clients to obtain addresses. Configuration of the DHCP server entails configuring it with the address ranges corresponding to those assigned within the address plan. In Figure 13.3, we've allocated addresses 10.32.85.50–10.32.85.240 and 2001:db8:4af0:808f:ffff:ffff::/96 as DHCP pools, so these ranges must be defined on a DHCP server(s). In addition, any client class information, options, and other configuration parameters need to be configured on the DHCP server to properly configure different types of clients. A major advantage of using an IPAM tool is that IP inventory information readily enables definition of DHCP pools and much of the DHCP server configuration information can be defined in the IPAM system and then applied across multiple DHCP servers, instead of defining this iteratively on multiple servers.

DNS and IP Address Management

Now that we've defined our IP block and individual- or pool-level IP address assignments, we need to consider linking these IP addresses to user-accessible domain names. From an IPAM perspective, clearly reverse DNS domains have a direct association with IP address block and subnet allocations. These domains are derived directly from their corresponding IP addresses. IPAM Worldwide has secured the ipamworldwide.com domain name from its ISP or domain registry. In so doing, IPAM Worldwide supplied three DNS server addresses to which iterative queries seeking resolution for ipamworldwide.com suffixes can be directed. Assigning web, email, and related Internet-facing servers this domain suffix can help IPAM Worldwide create a global Internet presence.

Within the organization, this domain name is also used on the intranet. Subdomains are be defined for the Corporate, Sales, Engineering, and Logistics team. The Engineering subdomain (eng.ipamworldwide.com) has been delegated to Engineering team DNS administrators, while the remaining subdomains will be centrally administered within the IT group. The Engineering team may further create subdomains below eng.ipamworldwide.com without impacting the IT team's administration effort. By delegating the eng subdomain, the IT team is empowering the Engineering team to manage the resolution of all eng subdomain hosts as well as its subdomains.

In keeping with the philosophy of centralizing IP address inventory, it follows that tracking hostnames and resource records associated with each IP address should be performed. Building on our IP inventory spreadsheet we just reviewed for IPAM Worldwide's Charleston office, we can track this information for individual devices by simply inserting an FQDN column in our spreadsheet as shown in Figure 13.4.

Location and subnet addresses	IPv4 address/IPv6 IID	FQDN	Comments
Charleston 10.32.850/23 2001:db8:4af0:808f::/6 4	10.32.85.1 482:f10a:87b9:2aa	router cs01.ipamworldwide.com.	Charleston VoIP subnet router 1
	10.32.85.2 e9:23ac:cca1:c80b	router-cs10.ipamworldwide.com.	Charleston VoIP subnet router 2
	10.32.85.3 83dd:7e9a:bce4:90	router-cs11.ipamworldwide.com.	Charleston VoIP subnet router HSRP address
	10.32.85.4 cb7b:83ec:9e1:550e	ns-cs01.ipamworldwide.com.	Contact Fred Jones for support
	10.32.85.5 3fc:846a:8070:effc	ftp-cs.ipamworldwide.com.	
	10.32.85.6 e24e:89:75f5:2aaa	filecab-cs.ipamworldwide.com.	San Fran secondary
	10.32.85.7 bae3:8f39:d6ea:bc4 4	file-atl.ipamworldwide.com.	Backup for Atlanta
	10.32.85.8 7eda:ef81:a6a6:abc 3	file-pit.ipamworldwide.com.	Backup for Pittsburgh
	10.32.85.9		
	10.32.85.10 c73e:930a:750c:4d9 8	denalo1.corp.ipamworldwide.com.	IP PBX-CS1
	10.32.85.11 bb65:9830:73d7:2e 3	denalo2.corp.ipamworldwide.com.	IP PBX-CS2
	. . .		
	10.32.85.20 516d:d87e:4acc:e63 0	eng-cs1.eng.ipamworldwide.com.	Contact Engineering for assistance
	10.32.85.21 a966:a6e9:b87:388c	eng-cs2.eng.ipamworldwide.com.	Contact Engineering for assistance
	10.32.85.22 1144:4bcc:84d2:988 1	eng-cs3.eng.ipamworldwide.com.	Contact Engineering for assistance
	. . .		
	10.32.85.50-10.32.86240		Contact Mary Smith for support
	::ffff:ffff:0:0/96		Contact Mary Smith for support
	. . .		

Figure 13.4 Sample inventory table with FQDNs.

In the example above, we're tracking only the FQDN for each statically defined host. Hosts obtaining leases from the DHCP address pools can have their hostname information updated in DNS via Dynamic DNS. We need to assure that we properly transcribe this inventory information into the DNS server configurations. From this "database," we can derive the A, AAAA, and PTR records corresponding to each host. We could expand the columns on the spreadsheet to track additional resource records associated with given hosts such as CNAME, SRV, MX, etc.

14

IPAM Deployment Strategies

General Deployment Principles for DHCP/DNS

As a critical component underpinning the operation of your network as well as your Internet presence, IPAM Worldwide acknowledges the need to plan for redundancy for DNS and DHCP services. An outage from the perspective of our constituents will inhibit business productivity and could pose major threats to the business including loss of revenue, integrity, and competitive standing. We provide specific deployment guidelines for DHCP and DNS in this chapter, but the core principles to account for when planning or assessing your deployments include the following:

- *Resiliency* – Plan for redundant deployments such that clients have multiple means to perform a given function, e.g. obtain an IP address or resolve a hostname. This includes deploying multiple servers with duplicate or complementary address pools and with duplicate zone information as well as supporting diverse networking paths to each.
- *Scale* – Size your hardware and virtualization resource availability to support configuration loads (pools, leases, zones, resource records, etc.), input/output (lease and query performance), and replication requirements (DHCP failover communications, zone transfers).
- *Scope* Deploy servers, particularly for DNS, with specific roles and provision network protections to constrain accessibility to clients requiring access. For example, deploy a separate set of DNS servers solely to resolve your Internet facing external name space and define server ACLs and firewall filters to prevent external queries from traversing interior portions of your network. This approach aligns with the security zones concept and to a lesser degree, least privilege access.

IP Address Management, Second Edition. Michael Dooley and Timothy Rooney.
© 2021 The Institute of Electrical and Electronics Engineers, Inc.
Published 2021 by John Wiley & Sons, Inc.

- *Monitor and adapt* – Define contingencies for outage recovery or capacity expansion such as repository sharding, triggered instantiation, or cloud bursting.

Disaster Recovery/Business Continuity

Business continuity practices seek to maintain the operation of the enterprise in the face of a major outage. A major outage or "disaster," implies that the sheer magnitude of the outage goes beyond a handful of servers or network devices. Automated and manual procedures must be documented in advance to reconfigure or redeploy resources to maintain operation of the network and applications, or at least the critical services and applications.

Business continuity of IPAM operations will likely require deployment of multiple IPAM repositories. Deployment of multiple active databases or primary/backup configurations will depend on your selected vendor. Vendors implement a wide variety of approaches to facilitate redundancy such as full database copies and transfer, multimaster databases that require some level of network partitioning, to deployment of database replication technologies using storage area networks or SQL or LDAP replication capabilities. Operations tasks required to perform a disaster recovery will likewise vary per vendor.

Evaluation of vendor disaster recovery capabilities will depend on your business objectives, budget, and polices, but three key questions should be considered:

1) Is the IPAM database involved in name resolution or address assignment? For example, some systems route dynamic updates from DHCP to the IPAM database for uniqueness checks prior to routing to DNS. If the IPAM database is in such a "critical path," redundancy and high availability are paramount.
2) How frequently do your administrators make changes to IPAM data? The more frequent the rate of change, the more data changes may be lost between data synchronizations between the primary and backup database(s). A daily database backup may be acceptable in cases where changes are made infrequently whereas a subdaily or transactional replication process may be required for high rate-of-change environments.
3) What is the process to perform invocation of the backup system? Some vendors provide a relatively simple recovery procedure, while others require more manual intervention. Hopefully disasters occur infrequently if never, but when needed, the failover process should be executable by staff on hand within time constraints defined by policy.

These basic questions are interdependent. If the answers to questions 1 and 2 are "yes" and "frequently," respectively, then the answer to question 3 should probably be "single step" or at least "very streamlined."

DHCP and DNS server redundancy features should provide network services continuity in the event of a single server outage as we'll discuss next.

DHCP Deployment

Most DHCP server deployment strategies face the omnipresent trade-off of budget dollars against quantities of servers. A reasonable approach entails deploying DHCP servers where end users will always be able to obtain these services in a timely manner, while minimizing the total dollars spent on servers deployed and associated server lifecycle expenses. Budget amounts must account not only for server purchases, but for ongoing support and maintenance, which includes server hardware upgrades, operating system (OS) patches, and upgrades, as well as DHCP upgrades for new features, bug fixes, or security measures.

DHCP Server Platforms

DHCP servers can be deployed in a variety of platforms from physical hardware servers or appliances, or as virtual servers on a virtual machine platform. When we discuss deployment options, we'll generically use the term "platform," which can generally be interpreted as either one of these options in each case.

DHCP Servers
The traditional model for deploying DHCP servers entails deploying a physical server supporting the recommended processing components and operating systems supported by the corresponding DHCP vendor. Often, other applications are installed on such servers to maximize hardware utilization.

Virtualized DHCP Deployment
Deployment of virtualized DHCP servers enables organizations to instantiate and destroy DHCP services on demand for supported platforms. Deployment on virtual machines or containers also saves on hardware costs, rack space, and cooling/power draw, while enabling better segregation than in installing a DHCP daemon on a generic hardware server. Major appliance vendors also offer their appliance products as virtual machines, combining the benefits of VNFs with the benefits of appliances.

DHCP Appliances
DHCP appliances are preinstalled DHCP services on secure hardware platforms, typically Intel-based platforms with a hardened Linux operating system. Like routers, which were initially deployed as software running on general purpose

hardware and evolved to special purpose hardware platforms, DHCP appliances offer an evolutionary path to self-contained hardware platforms for DHCP services. Appliances are "hardened" in that the base Linux kernel installed on the platform has been stripped of any unnecessary services. This results in a customized kernel and OS that supports only DHCP services (and other services supported by the vendor such as DNS). Underlying file system, users, permissions, and network ports should also be pared down accordingly by the appliance vendor to limit the attack surface.

Appliances offer simplified deployment with one-stop shopping, instead of having to coordinate and acquire server hardware, install the proper OS version and patch levels, then install DHCP services software. Appliances can simplify the ongoing upgrade process by prepackaging upgrades with compliant OS and services versions with corresponding hardware platforms. Depending on your vendor, these upgrades may be applied from a single centralized console, eliminating the need to physically deploy staff to perform upgrades. In addition, most vendors support centralized monitoring of deployed appliances, enabling proactive detection of outages or degradations.

Of course, appliances generally cost more than general purpose server hardware, and most incorporate open source DHCP services, which are freely available for most leading OSs. Next, we'll focus on deployment strategies for DHCP services, regardless of implementation on general hardware, appliances, or virtualized platforms or a mix thereof.

DHCP Deployment Approaches

Centralized DHCP Server Deployment

The deployment of DHCP servers generally comes down to a trade-off between wide distribution of a large number of servers "closer" to clients vs. narrow distribution of a fewer number of DHCP servers serving clients from a variety of locations. The extremes of this trade-off consist of a DHCP server on every subnet vs. one or more DHCP servers centrally located serving all of the organization's clients. The key is to balance availability and reasonable performance of the DHCP service between clients and servers while remaining within budget constraints for servers and ongoing management thereof. Your deployment will likely fall between these two extremes.

Figure 14.1 illustrates the fully centralized deployment approach scenario for IPAM Worldwide. Overlaying the high-level network diagram from Figure 13.1, this scenario features the deployment of a pair of DHCP servers per region, one functioning as the primary and the other as failover or backup. All DHCP traffic must be funneled to the regional headquarters sites, imposing higher reliance on robust network connectivity to these sites from the respective regions. This

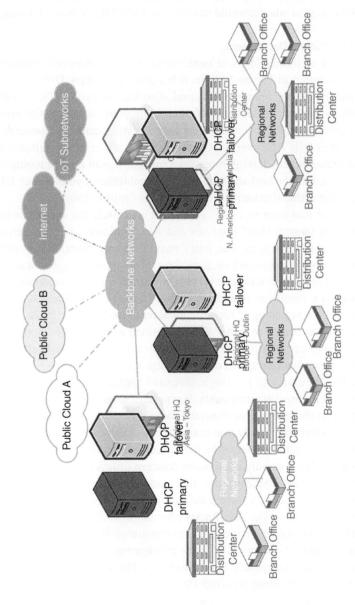

Figure 14.1 Centralized DHCP server deployment for IPAM worldwide.

architecture also implies the DHCP server hardware is sufficiently sized to meet performance and capacity requirements. Note that DHCP primary and failover servers should generally be deployed in separate physical locations for disaster resilience. An outage at one site would not interrupt all DHCP services for a region.

Distributed DHCP Server Deployment

At the other end of the deployment continuum, the decentralized deployment approach is illustrated in Figure 14.2. In this figure, a primary DHCP server is located at [nearly] every branch office and distribution center. This localizes DHCP traffic, affording deployment of less stringently sized DHCP servers. Network connectivity to the regional headquarters is still required however due to the deployment of DHCP failover servers there. These servers act as failover servers for the regional servers, though more than one per region may be required for load sharing. Consider the load and redundancy capabilities of your chosen DHCP vendor to identify viable alternative architectures for your network.

Contrasting the two extremes of Figures 14.1 and 14.2, the former requires fewer, albeit more powerful DHCP servers and rock solid network connectivity to the regional headquarters sites. The latter requires many more DHCP servers, though of more modest specifications, providing localized services with a network reachable shared backup. You may be wondering, if the network link to a site goes down, what good is having an IP address from a DHCP server? Without a redundant link, other than providing IP access to local network resources in the absence of local Internet breakout, it may indeed be of limited value. As always, the trade-off must be considered and generally a mixed approach of centralized with at least partial distribution often minimizes overall outage risk.

While the ISC DHCP server is a single-threaded application, its performance is usually sufficient for most environments. If you have several thousand DHCP clients attempting to obtain leases at about the same time however, some delays will be likely. If this occurs frequently, you may want to consider deploying additional servers and partitioning finer networks-per-server granularity to reduce the load per server. Again, this is usually not a major concern unless you are a service provider utilizing DHCP to initialize devices like customer premises modems for paying subscribers. After recovery from a neighborhood power outage, devices will come back up and inundate the DHCP server for addresses. In such environments, we recommend you consider a commercial performance-oriented DHCP server.

Prepare your routers to support DHCP by configuring the IP addresses of your DHCP servers within your routers' relay agent lists. These lists within each router enable the router to terminate received Discover/Solicit packet broadcasts, then retransmit them as unicast packets to each configured DHCP sever IP address on its relay agent list. If you partition your network such that address pools for certain subnets are served by a given DHCP server, while those for other subnets are

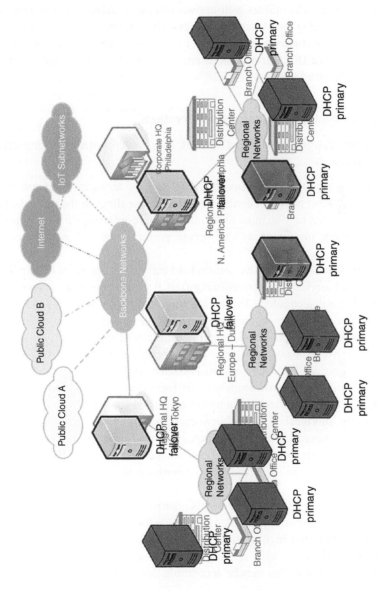

Figure 14.2 Distributed DHCP server deployment for IPAM worldwide.

served by another DHCP server, make sure you configure routers serving those subnets accordingly. You could add all DHCP servers to all routers, but this will result in needless relay agent traffic, especially if you have several DHCP servers. DHCP for IPv6 networks utilizes well-known multicast addresses, obviating the need to configure relay agent lists on routers, though such configuration may alternatively be performed on the relay agent to control which DHCPv6 servers are to process relayed DHCP transactions and not just any DHCPv6 server listening on this multicast address.

DHCP Services Deployment Design Considerations

Key considerations when formulating the DHCP server deployment design including the following:

- *Response time requirements* – Do your clients have stringent response time requirements? Most popular clients tolerate response times in the seconds, but certain applications may be more demanding. The more stringent your requirements, the more important will be server performance and perhaps client proximity.
- *Load requirements* – Do you have certain load conditions that must be handled? For broadband service providers utilizing DHCP as a customer premises equipment initialization technology, load spikes may occur upon recovery from a residential power outage or equipment installation or reboot. For enterprise environments, such a spike could occur at the start of the work day if several associates arrive at or near the same time, though many devices will simply attempt to renew an IP address previously used by default.
- *Traffic expectations* – Do you employ short lease times to minimize overbooking, which causes more frequent renewal attempts? Generally, the shorter the lease time, the shorter the interval between obtaining the lease and subsequent lease renewal attempts. This drives increasing traffic on the network to and from the DHCP server(s) and must be considered when designing to the aforementioned response time and load requirements for server quantities and associated bandwidth.
- *Availability requirements* – Do your clients positively have to be able to obtain an IP address or configuration via DHCP 24 × 7 or is the service "best effort" based? Most will answer that high availability is critical, but with devices growing increasingly multinetworked, as long as one network's address assignment mechanism is available this may be acceptable.[1] Mean time to repair (MTTR) is

---

1 Of course, this statement assumes different DHCP services serve these different interfaces which may not be the case.

another consideration in meeting DHCP services availability objectives. Having a spare server locally or the ability to instantiate a virtual instance can shorten MTTR (though lease information may not be available) while having to order a replacement will delay this process.

The first three considerations above relate to deploying sufficient quantities of servers of given lease distribution rate to meet respective performance objectives. A good starting point is to identify the number of expected DHCP clients at each site on your network. This number should account for all devices requiring DHCP, including data devices, voice devices, and all IP devices requiring DHCP at each site. Don't forget to account for "peak" quantities of users and devices so that everyone, even associates visiting on temporary basis, may obtain a valid lease.

After accounting for peak quantities of DHCP clients, consider the frequency of DHCP transactions. This will be dependent on your lease times, as well as client lease release configuration. Most clients will "remember" a prior lease and attempt to request it upon power-up, e.g. when an employee returns to work the next day, though this is not always the case.

The fourth consideration listed above relates to providing high availability DHCP services for DHCP clients. Once you've designed your deployment based on performance requirements, total or selective high availability may be planned. Based on server technologies you plan to deploy, implementation of high availability will impact not only the number of servers required, but potentially your address space plan.

Most DHCP servers support a DHCP redundancy or failover protocol such that for a given address pool, one DHCP server will act as the primary, while a second DHCP server will act as the backup or failover server. This basic configuration is illustrated in Figure 14.3.

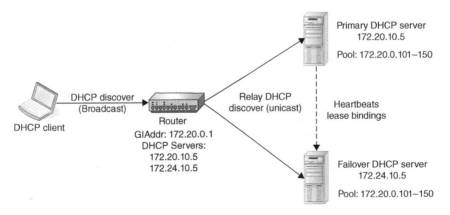

Figure 14.3 DHCP failover configuration.

Each relay agent must be configured to unicast received DHCP (for IPv4) broadcast packets to both the primary and failover DHCP servers, 172.20.10.5 and 172.24.10.5 in Figure 14.3. Recall that DHCPv6 relay agents can likewise be configured with DHCPv6 server addresses or may utilize the well-known multicast address, ff05::1:3. The DHCP servers utilize a failover protocol such that the primary sends heartbeat messages as well as lease binding information to the failover server. The failover server utilizes user-settable parameters to determine that the primary is down and begins processing the unicast DHCP packets from the relay agent(s). Thus, clients are able to continue receiving IP address and parameter assignments despite the primary server being down. Upon recovery, the primary server obtains the current lease database from the failover server, then assumes its role as primary once again.

Another technique is referred to as a *split scopes* approach, which entails deploying two DHCP servers with complementary address pools, *not the same address pools*. In this way, either server can process DHCP transactions without worry of duplicate assignment. In Figure 14.4, we illustrate the splitting of 50-address pool 172.20.0.101–150 into two non-overlapping pools and deploy each on two different DHCP servers, respectively. Like the failover configuration in Figure 14.3, each relay agent needs to be configured with both DHCP server addresses on which the split scopes are provisioned. Both DHCP servers should receive all DHCP transactions within the given subnet and provide a lease if capacity exists. Thus, clients on the subnet should have access to the same address pool, albeit split across two DHCP servers in this case.

Since both servers are required to meet the capacity needs, you may end up with an inability to meet IP address demands should one fail. Another alternative is to allocate double the number of addresses such that each DHCP server is

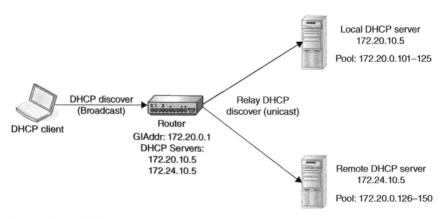

Figure 14.4 Split scopes configuration.

configured with 100% of the required capacity. In this manner, each server can handle the capacity needs should one fail. Referring to Figure 14.4 for this scenario, one DHCP server would be configured with address pool 172.20.0.101–150 and other server with 172.20.0.151–200 to provide the full pool capacity, 50 IP addresses, on each server. This solution provides full redundancy at the expense of doubling the required address space.

DHCP Deployment on Edge Devices

Most router and access point products provide a DHCP service as a component of their router platforms. This may lead one to question whether a separate server is needed to support DHCP services. As with most design questions, the answer is, "it depends." Small environments with a few sites with local routers serving up to 100 or so monolithic clients each may be well served by configuring the router to provide DHCP services. However, larger organizations or those requiring more advanced DHCP services, e.g. for discriminating voice vs. data clients for address and option parameter assignment, would be better served deploying discrete (non-router-integrated) DHCP servers.

The advantages of running DHCP on a router device include:

- *Lower hardware cost* – No need to procure a server or set of servers.
- *Single user interface* – The same command line interface can be used to configure the router and the DHCP server, and no relay agent configuration is needed.
- *"Fewer moving parts"* – One less communication link and server required to perform DHCP functions, which in general can increase the overall solution reliability.

The main disadvantages of running DHCP on a router are:

- *Options support* – Most router based DHCP servers are primitive, supporting address assignment but little in the way of options support.
- *Client class support* – Major vendors do not support client classes, which is required for discriminatory address/option assignment to different devices, e.g. VoIP vs. data devices.
- *No failover* – If a router fails, you've probably lost connectivity in any case but if there are two routers serving a subnet for redundancy a split scopes approach would have to be employed, increasing management complexity.
- *No centralized management* – Router-based DHCP services are configured via command line and unless a centralized tool is employed, each router DHCP server must be configured manually with respect to the IP addressing plan; less likely support is possible if multiple router vendor products are in use.

DNS Deployment

The core objectives of your DNS infrastructure are to enable resolution of your users' queries for internal or external destinations and to enable resolution of your external namespace by global Internet users. Deploying DNS servers along functional lines helps to minimize overhead and contain security breaches to the given set of servers, minimizing impacts on other DNS servers performing other functions. We'll describe deployment strategies that effectively partition DNS information and communications in order to contain vulnerabilities and attacks within these respective *trust zones* or *microsegments* if you prefer zero trust security parlance (actually, we'll use the term "trust sector" for DNS given the potential ambiguity of the term "zone" when talking DNS). We'll discuss basic network firewall policy settings that serve as a focal point to partitioning these trust sectors from a networking perspective and DNS filtering tactics at the DNS protocol level that are supported by various DNS server products.

Generally, DNS deployment designs should account for high availability, performance, scalability, human intervention and of course, security. Using a trust sector approach to DNS server deployment allows you to segment namespace and resolution responsibility which provides a solid foundation for achieving these objectives. Keep in mind that there is no "one size fits all" cookie cutter deployment architecture. However, by defining role-based server configurations as trust sectors, you can select which are applicable based on your environment's scale and policies.

Some general deployment principles to keep in mind include the following.

- Deploy a master DNS server and at least two secondaries as authoritative for any given zone or set of zones. If you perform relatively infrequent zone changes, a multi-master implementation may be used though it could be more trouble than it's worth as the rate of zone changes rises. Look for an implementation that specifically supports multi-master capabilities given the complexity of synchronizing zone information while receiving updates from multiple sources such as DHCP servers.
- For non-multi-master implementations, consider deploying a redundant hardware for the master to minimize impacts of a master server outage. Should a master server become unavailable, secondaries can still resolve queries authoritatively at least until the zone expires (as defined in the zone's start of authority [SOA] record). An alternative master could be promoted in order to effect any zone changes with replication to secondary servers.
- Deploy servers that are authoritative for a set of zones each on different subnets and ideally, different locations for site-diverse high availability. Should a subnet or router become unreachable, DNS services should be available from alternative sites.

- Deploy authoritative servers "close" to clients/resolvers for better performance and less network overhead. For external servers, deploy close to Internet connections; for internal servers, deploy nearer to higher density employee areas.
- Consider anycast deployment to provide redundancy as well as potentially improved resolution performance. Consider load balancing deployment as well to optimize performance.
- To provide functional separation, different DNS servers should be deployed to handle external queries vs. internal queries and for handling recursive vs. authoritative queries. This principle is critical to deployment of DNS trust sectors, to maintain network-level separation and granular access controls.
- Deploy dedicated recursive servers to support client/stub resolver resolution. You may want to consider a tiered recursion model as we'll discuss later in this chapter.

DNS Trust Sectors

We define four major trust sectors based on:

- *Query source* – From where a query originates.
- *Query scope* – The scope of information being queried.

We define the query source as either external queries originating from outside your organization, e.g. the public Internet, Internet of things (IoT) network, etc., which generally has low to no trustworthiness, or internal queries originating from within your organization, which may possess moderate trust. The query scope also follows an analogous breakdown, with external scope dealing with Internet-reachable resolution data and internal encompassing resolution information for destinations within your organization. The following table summarizes this categorization (Figure 14.5).

You may also overlay a DNS management trust sector which may correspond to a physically or virtually separate network or VLAN used to configure and manage each DNS server. A summary of each of these trust sectors follows.

- *External DNS sector* – This sector consists of DNS servers deployed to resolve queries originating from the Internet for your public resolution information, i.e. your external namespace. If you have an Internet connection for a website, email or for other publically available Internet applications, this category must be addressed in your deployment strategy.
- *Extranet DNS sector* – This sector includes queries from specific sources outside the organization seeking resolution for internal hosts and resources. Such resolution should generally be forbidden, but organizational partners may require secure access to certain servers that aren't available publicly. You may also

		Query scope	
		External	Internal
Query source	External	External DNS	Extranet DNS
	Internal	Recursive DNS	Internal DNS

Figure 14.5 Basic DNS trust sectors.

consider queries originating from public cloud services within this category. With the provision of such partners access to a subset of "internal" resolution information, this sector is marginally of higher trust than the external sector. DNS server deployment for this category (for partner access) should mimic the external DNS scenario, though possibly deployed as a parallel per-partner implementation.

- *Recursive DNS sector* – This sector consists of queries originating from within your organization requesting external/Internet resource resolution.
- *Internal DNS sector* – This sector deals with internally originated queries seeking internal resolution information.

You should always deploy an external set of DNS servers (or use an external DNS provider), a set of internal authoritative servers, and a set of recursive servers. This is the minimum trust sector deployment configuration, though in smaller networks you could consolidate recursive and internal authoritative functions within a common set of servers. Larger or more sophisticated deployments may feature tiered approaches and possibly extranet DNS. Let's explore each of these sectors in more detail in the context of network deployment.

External DNS Trust Sector

The external DNS trust sector relates to your Internet presence, servicing DNS queries originating outside or external to the organization. Resolution services must be provided for your Internet presence, i.e. your organization's website, email, and other applications. But care must be taken to secure the information integrity of these external servers, given their inherent exposure and potential vulnerability in serving external clients.

The recommended approach for the External DNS trust sector calls for two or more secondary DNS servers to resolve external requests, and to configure these servers with IPv4 and IPv6 addresses. These servers should never be queried by any stub resolver directly; only by recursive name servers resolving on behalf of stub resolvers. As such, external DNS servers should never be configured to support recursion.

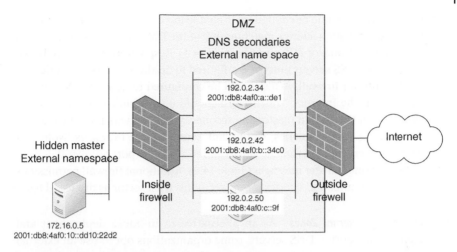

Figure 14.6 External DNS trust sector deployment.

These secondary servers may be deployed directly on an external DMZ exposed to the Internet, behind a "first line" firewall, as shown in Figure 14.6. Note that the inside and outside firewalls depicted in Figure 14.6 may physically be a single firewall device, but we'll use this logical view for clarity. If you have multiple ISP access links, you should deploy at least one secondary DNS server at each DMZ.

In this example, we've configured each DNS server as dual-stack (IPv4 and IPv6) to enable reachability via either protocol. We've placed each external DNS server on its own physical subnet and ideally router/interface with public IP addresses as shown, though internally reachable IP addresses must also be assigned for server management and zone transfers from the master.

Figure 14.6 illustrates a *hidden master* DNS server deployed behind a DMZ internal firewall and should not be directly query-able from external clients. Since this master server maintains the "master configuration" from which the secondary servers transfer, its information integrity must be safeguarded. For this reason, this master DNS server should be configured as hidden, meaning that it cannot be identified by querying other DNS servers.

The mechanics of hiding a master name server entail excluding publication of NS and glue records corresponding to the hidden server in this and the parent zone and modifying the master server name ("mname") field of the SOA record in each zone. The mname field typically enables an entity desiring to update the zone to locate the DNS server to which to direct the update. External facing zones are static zones, disallowing dynamic updates, so modifying the mname field should have no repercussions.

This External DNS trust sector should be isolated by setting appropriate firewall rules on both inside and outside firewalls. With respect to enabling DNS traffic, the outside firewall should be configured to enable incoming DNS queries from any source with a destination address matching any of the DMZ secondary DNS servers on destination UDP and/or TCP port 53 (Table 14.1). Responses likewise need to be permitted. These DNS servers must be configured to disallow recursive queries.

As for the interior firewall, ACLs should be configured to deny all DNS queries originating from the Internet. This firewall should only permit DNS queries and answers between the hidden master and secondary DNS servers for zone maintenance, including refresh queries, Notify and zone transfer messages. Note that major DNS implementations enable you to define a specific port number if desired for Notify and zone transfer messages (Table 14.2). Additional firewall permissions need to be set for outbound queries for the recursive trust sector as discussed later.

DNS Hosting of External Zones As an alternative to in-house deployment and management of external DNS servers, some organizations opt to use an external DNS service provider, which provides a web user interface for the entry of externally resolvable resource records. DNS hosting providers typically offer site-diverse anycast-addressed DNS servers to host customer zone information. A third-party provider offers the convenience of offloading internal resources otherwise required to manage external DNS servers with expertise in configuring, monitoring and troubleshooting them.

You can also deploy a hybrid configuration where your hosting provider provides added redundancy by hosting secondary servers to your in-house master(s) or conversely hosting masters and secondaries, in conjunction with in-house secondary servers. Be sure to follow similar guidelines as discussed above, when configuring your in-house DNS servers to securely interact with your hosting provider's DNS servers and the Internet at large.

When selecting an external DNS hosting provider, keep in mind the following security requirements:

- Unique per user login/password access.
- Encrypted connection for administrator access.
- Administrator access logs which can be reviewed and audited.
- DNSSEC signing with planned and emergency key rollover support.
- Other DNS security features including ACLs (i.e. no recursion, allow-transfer, etc.), geographic resolution, and response rate limiting (which we'll cover in later chapters).
- DNS availability support and SLA.
- Notification of configuration changes.
- DNS denial of service mitigation.
- Parent domain (typically TLD) security controls and vulnerability/breach notification process.

Table 14.1 Example external firewall rules for DNS messages.

Message/direction	Control	Source address	Source port	Destination address	Destination port
DNS queries from the Internet	Allow	Any	>1023	192.0.2.34, 192.0.2.42, 192.0.2.50, 2001:db8:4af0:a::de1, 2001:db8:4af0:b::34c0, 2001:db8:4af0:c::9f	53
Responses to DNS queries	Allow	192.0.2.34, 192.0.2.42, 192.0.2.50, 2001:db8:4af0:a::de1, 2001:db8:4af0:b::34c0, 2001:db8:4af0:c::9f	53	Any	>1023
All others	Deny	Any	Any	Any	Any

Table 14.2 Example internal firewall rules for DNS messages.

Message/direction	Control	Source address	Source port	Destination address	Destination port
Queries from secondaries to master for zone maintenance	Allow	DMZ DNS server IPv6 and private IPv4 addresses	>1023	172 .16.0.5, 2001:db8:4af0:10::dd10:22d2	53 or configured
Responses from master to secondaries from zone maintenance	Allow	172.16.0.5, 2001:db8:4af0:10::dd10:22d2	53 or configured	DMZ DNS server IPv6 and private IPv4 addresses	>1023
All others	Deny	Any	Any	Any	Any

External DNS Diversity Supporting a web presence requires a robust infrastructure including external DNS. If your organization relies on the web for commerce, collaboration, or communications, deploying a robust external DNS infrastructure is paramount. We've mentioned the requirement to deploy multiple DNS servers dedicated to the external DNS trust sector. But you may want to consider adding further diversity to provide high availability and robustness in the face of attacks or other vulnerabilities such as human error or natural disasters. Consider implementing the following diverse components:

- Deploy multiple DNS servers deployed in different geographic locations.
- Implement multiple DNS server vendor implementations to protect against attacks on a given vendor's vulnerabilities.
- Use multiple external DNS providers or supplement your in-house implementation with an external service provider.

While managing a diverse external DNS infrastructure may cost more and require incrementally higher management effort, this approach can help your External DNS trust sector withstand a variety of attacks.

Extranet DNS Trust Sector

The Extranet DNS trust sector comprises external partner hosts querying information regarding partner-related (non-public) resolution information. In general, divulging information about internal hosts is undesirable and a potential security risk particularly within the realm of hostname reconnaissance. Even interconnected partners should only have access to guarded information, certainly not the entire internal namespace. Thus, the extranet trust sector is only incrementally less restrictive than the external trust sector.

Depending on your trust in public cloud providers, you may consider links from your cloud providers within this trust sector as well. But if you're confident with their security practices, you may just consider the public cloud an extension of your internal network. Just be cognizant that compromise of your cloud provider could enable virtualized malware instances to attain presence within your internal network.

Inter-partner and cloud provider connections are typically configured as VPN connections over the Internet or private network and typically involve a "partner DMZ" or firewall between the partner space and the internal network, similar to the external design. Thus, the DNS deployment architecture for this category, shown in Figure 14.7, mimics that of the External DNS deployment though the resolution data configuration is somewhat different. Depending on what resolution data may be divulged to a given partner, the DNS server queried by partner clients must be configured accordingly with such data. Only systems to which each partner is authorized access should be published in DNS. Thus, the concept

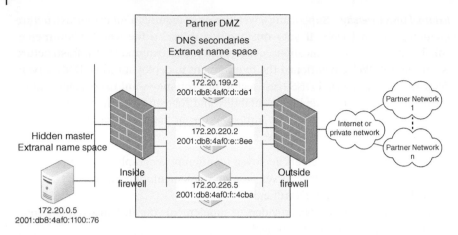

Figure 14.7 Extranet DNS trust sector.

of a hidden master with visible secondaries supporting no recursion per the external sector applies.

The partner-specific resource record information may be defined within an "extranet" namespace, as defined within respective zones configured on these DNS servers. Additionally, implementing views on the DNS servers serving the partner link enables per-partner resolution information if multiple partners access a common set of DNS servers. DNS views allow the DNS server to answer queries depending on "who's asking" in the match-clients statement and "whom they're asking" with the match-destinations statement. In this manner, resolving a given hostname for a Partner A client may differ from that query of the same hostname from a Partner B client.

One caveat relates to partners' use of common VPN termination hardware or address space, as the use of views requires the mapping of separate IP address space for each partner. DNS views are supported on ISC's BIND but not on NSD or PowerDNS authoritative products, though separate server instances may be run for each partner if desired.

Your extranet DNS servers should only be configured to resolve information that you wish to divulge to your partners about your network. The Extranet DNS trust sector is isolated in a manner similar to the External DNS trust sector. The outside firewall serves as your VPN termination point. The inside firewall should be configured from a DNS standpoint to enable DNS transactions only between the master and secondaries.

With respect to your Extranet DNS server configuration, parameters specified for the External DNS sector apply with the addition of ACLs limiting the query source IP address space to known partners or public cloud providers (which is typically derived from your private address space).

Recursive DNS Trust Sector

This trust sector comprises internal stub resolvers querying internal DNS recursive servers, which in turn query either other internal recursive DNS servers or external DNS servers directly to resolve client queries. Servers within this sector are generally not authoritative for any zone information and are configured solely to resolve queries on behalf of resolvers. Queries for internal namespace should be directed and/or forwarded to the internal authoritative servers, while all other queries should leverage cache or the servers' hints files to query Internet root servers down the domain tree to resolve queries, building up a cache of resolved data. Intervening DNS forwarder servers may also be deployed, providing a tiered caching architecture.

Tiered Caching Servers Deployment of DNS servers dedicated to recursion and caching is a recommended approach to provide functional, physical, and administrative separation from servers in other trust sectors. Caching servers deployed near client populations can facilitate rapid resolution performance once cache has been primed. However, on the flip side, if several such servers are deployed throughout your network, each issuing DNS queries through your firewalls to Internet DNS servers, the task of controlling and monitoring query traffic could quickly grow cumbersome.

Internet name resolution requires IP (DNS) traffic outbound from the organization to the Internet, which may increase exposure from a security policy perspective. And many servers in different locations may issue redundant queries for the same resolution information, reducing efficiencies. One approach to alleviate these concerns entails the use of a set of tiered caching servers as a second layer through which all outbound queries can be issued. The first tier comprises local recursive servers to which local stub resolver's direct queries. These local recursive servers can be configured to forward all or certain queries to the second-tier servers, which comprise a set of what we'll call "Internet caching" servers. These Internet caching servers then query DNS servers on the Internet to resolve queries and cache answers. Similar queries from different local recursive servers can leverage the broader cache accumulated by the Internet caching tier without requiring Internet DNS lookup, thereby improving performance and reducing the volume and origination points of Internet DNS transactions.

Internet caching servers serve as funnel points to resolve queries from local recursive servers for information outside of the internal name space. The deployment of Internet caching servers not only helps constrain the sources of outbound queries, but simplifies configuration of firewalls for Internet DNS queries from internal sources by reducing the number of valid querying IP address sources. Other name servers within the organization will forward queries to these caching name servers when they are unable to resolve directly from authoritative configuration or their own cache.

Internet caching servers should be deployed in a high availability configuration, due to the reliance on these servers for resolving Internet queries on behalf of internal hosts. Since these caching servers will frequently send and receive Internet traffic, they should be deployed close to Internet connections. Adding this to our previous External DNS trust sector figure to illustrate bi-directionally originated queries, Figure 14.8 illustrates deployment of a high availability pair within the internal network but relatively close to the Internet connection. If you have two diverse Internet connections, as with external DNS servers, it's a good idea to deploy a server or pair near each connection.

While the external servers resolve queries for your public information for external queries, the Internet caching servers resolve external information on behalf of your internal clients. The Internet caching name servers' public IP addresses need to be added to the firewall permit lists to enable resolution of Internet host names for internal clients. The use of one or a small number of such name servers enables specification of only these few addresses instead of every DNS server address within the organization that would otherwise execute iterative queries. This policy to permit outbound queries and responses from/to Internet caching servers needs to be applied to both inside and outside firewalls (Table 14.3). Configuring IP address filtering using reverse path forwarding on your (and hopefully your ISP's) routers in accordance with BCP 38 [17] can help reduce the success of spoofing.

This configuration applies when Internet access is serviced to a small number of locations, and an analogous configuration applies to your Extranet DNS trust sector as well. For organizations with several independent Internet and cloud access points, e.g. Internet breakout within an SD-WAN deployment, you may achieve superior DNS resolution performance both in time and resolution quality, by deploying caching servers locally to each Internet accessible location. Many cloud providers customize DNS resolution based on the DNS query origination point, thereby pointing resolvers to local cloud points of presence.

Caching server configuration for DNS processing is relatively trivial in the sense that there are no zones or resource records to configure. However, you will need to configure root hints, localhost related zones, forwarding to internal authoritative servers, and forwarding to upper layered caching servers if deployed. But configuration for security purposes and monitoring of query activity over time are critical to effectively managing DNS and network security. The following settings should be configured for servers within your recursive DNS trust sector:

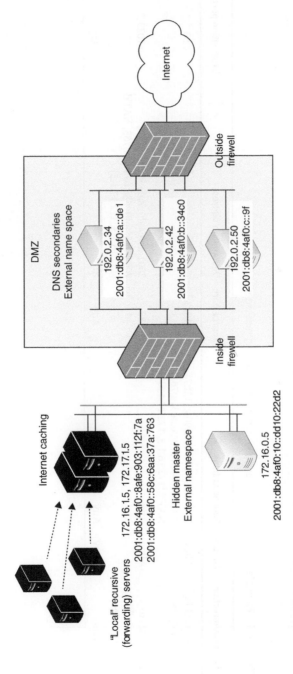

Figure 14.8 Addition of caching servers for external resolution.

Table 14.3 Example external firewall configuration for DNS caching messages.

Message/direction	Control	Source address	Source port	Destination address	Destination port
Internet caching server queries	Allow	2001:db8:4af0::8afe:903:112f:7a, 2001:db8:4af0::58c:6aa:37a:763, NAT'd {172.16.1.5, 172.17.1.5}	>1023	Any	53
Responses to Internet caching server queries	Allow	Any	53	2001:db8:4af0::8afe:903:112f:7a, 2001:db8:4af0::58c:6aa:37a:763, NAT'd {172.16.1.5, 172.17.1.5}	>1023
All others	Deny	Any	Any	Any	Any

- Allow recursive queries only from lower tier forwarder DNS servers (local recursive servers) and/or internal clients using your allocated internal (e.g. private) address space.
- Allow query access to cache to lower tier forwarders and/or internal clients.
- Allow recursion, queries, and access to cache only on the server interface connected to your internal IP address space. This will help prevent spoofed queries received on other server interfaces (e.g. DMZ-facing).
- Prevent externally spoofed query packets by configuring router/firewall IP address filtering using reverse path filtering.
- Disallow dynamic updates and zone transfers.
- Prevent administrative access except from the "management" (i.e. internal) IP address space.
- Inhibit exposure to server implementation details to the extent possible, e.g. disable vendor and version information, e.g. via dig @<dns_server_ip_address> version.bind chaos txt.
- Secure the DNS server using server and operating system controls.
- Define query rate limits.
- Configure DNSSEC validation.
- Configure a DNS firewall (response policy zones).

Internal DNS Trust Sector

DNS servers are required to resolve queries for internal destinations from internal hosts. These DNS servers are configured with authoritative information for the internal name space. As with external master DNS servers, internal master DNS servers should be "hidden" for added security and information integrity. For larger organizations, some business units, or entities may desire to run their own name subspace within the organization's name space through delegation.

Some highly secure networks disallow Internet access and manage the entirety of their resolvable namespace interiorly. Internal root servers can be configured as the authoritative root of the internal name space for resolution of such internal queries. The intent of an internal root is to eliminate queries from internal sources from reaching the Internet root servers or Internet DNS servers in general. This type of deployment helps secure DNS resolution by constraining all internal queries within the internal network but only enables resolution of domain names provisioned within subdomains of the internal root.

When configuring Internal DNS trust sector servers, consider the following measures to secure your servers and DNS transactions.

- Allow queries only from IP addresses within your allocated internal address space.

- Prevent externally spoofed query packets by configuring router/firewall IP address filtering using reverse path forwarding.
- Allow recursion, queries, and access to cache only on the server interface possessing the internal IP address. This will help prevent spoofed queries received on other server interfaces.
- Disallow dynamic updates and zone transfers from any source other than explicitly defined, e.g. from your DHCP servers, other DNS servers as appropriate and your IPAM system.
- Sign updates and zone transfers to authenticate message origin and assure information transfer integrity.
- Prevent administrative access except from the "management" (i.e. internal) IP address space.
- Inhibit exposure to server implementation details to the extent possible.
- Secure the DNS server using server and operating system controls.
- Define query rate limits.
- Consider DNSSEC signing of your internal zones.

Deploying DNS Servers with Anycast Addresses

Configuring DNS servers with anycast addresses enables multiple DNS servers to utilize a common IP address. Recall that an anycast address is an address assigned to multiple interfaces, typically on different nodes. Anycast is used when attempting to reach any one of the anycast addressable hosts without caring which host is reached. The routing infrastructure handles routing metric updates to track reachability and routing to the nearest host configured with the destination anycast address. Figure 14.9 illustrates an example with three DNS servers configured with anycast address 10.4.23.1.

As depicted in Figure 14.9, Router 1 has three routes to anycast address 10.4.23.1/32, corresponding to our three DNS servers. The closest server is that homed on Router 2 and is two hops from Router 1. The next closest server is homed on Router 5 and is reachable in three hops via Router 4. Lastly, the server connected to Router 6 is reachable in four hops via either Router 2 or 4. The logical view from Router 1's perspective is illustrated in Figure 14.10, where the anycast IP address is considered a single destination, reachable via multiple paths.

Anycast Addressing Benefits

Deploying anycast addressing offers a number of benefits:

- Simplified resolver configuration to singular DNS anycast address
- Improved resolution performance due to routing to the closest server

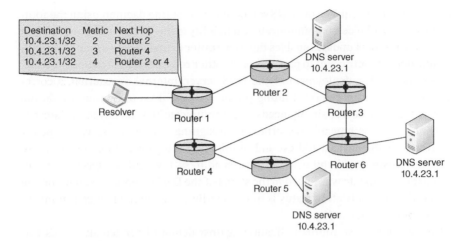

Figure 14.9   Anycast routing table example.

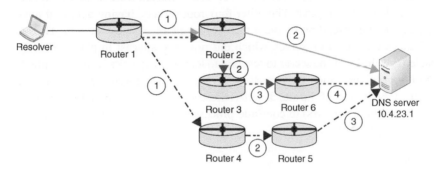

Figure 14.10   Logical routing perspective from Router 1 showing hop counts.

- High availability DNS services with dynamic routing
- Resilience from DNS denial of service attacks by spreading attacks upon one IP address across several servers

Resolvers configured with the DNS servers' anycast address have their queries routed to the nearest (routing-wise) DNS server configured with that anycast address. Thus, regardless of where the resolver host connects to the network, the same anycast IP address may be used by the resolver to locate a DNS server. This localized query process improves performance of the resolution process. A query to a DNS anycast address is routed to the closest DNS server, thereby reducing the round-trip delay portion of the overall query transaction.

The outage of a DNS server can be communicated (by the absence of communication) to the routing infrastructure in order to propagate via routing updates accordingly. This requires the DNS server to run a routing daemon using the routing protocol of choice to communicate reachability to the local router. Participation in routing protocol updates enables the local router to update its routing table with an appropriate metric and to pass this on to other routers via the routing protocol. Depending on the deployment of the DNS server, internal or external, a corresponding interior or exterior routing protocol would need to be running on the DNS server. The server simply needs to communicate that its anycast address is reachable. This is typically performed by assigning one of the server loopback addresses[2] as the anycast address and running a routing daemon on one or more ports advertising reachability to the anycast address. It would be especially useful if this routing update was linked to the status of the DNS daemon or service on the server, though application status is not generally considered when communicating IP address reachability.

Deploying anycast affords mitigation against denial of service attacks as evidenced by the DDoS attack on multiple root servers on 6 February 2007 [120]. Of the six root servers targeted, the two most severely affected were those which had not yet implemented anycast. The other four root servers, having deployed anycast, enabled the spreading of the attack across more physical servers. Thus a DDoS attack on the I-root server, which did not have anycast in place, severely impacted the ability of the server to respond to legitimate queries, while the attack on the F-root server, which had over 40 servers sharing the F-root anycast address, distributed the impact of the attack across these servers. This form of load sharing enabled the F-root server(s) to continue processing legitimate queries while suffering a barrage of attack requests.

Anycast Caveats

While anycast provides many benefits, consider the constraints and caveats of deploying anycast. Because resolvers may query any DNS server configured with the anycast address at a given time, it's important that the resolution information configured on each server be consistent. For example, the implementation on Internet root servers consists of a set of master servers which rarely changes. These root servers do not accept dynamic updates. If anycast is desired for dynamic zones, then each server must have a unicast address in addition to its anycast address. Every anycast server will require a unicast address for administration, but to support dynamic zones, the unicast address is required to provide an interface for updates, notifies and zone transfers. This enables updates to be directed to the

---

[2]The term "loopback address" here refers to the software loopback address commonly implemented in routers and servers as the "box address" reachable on any of its interfaces.

master's unicast address, which may in turn notify its secondaries via their respective unicast addresses.

Another consideration is the requirement to run a route daemon on your DNS servers configured with anycast addresses. While routing of packets to anycast addresses is primarily a routing function, the unreachability of a DNS server host may result in lost query attempts. Such would be the case if static routes are used to configure routers with fixed metrics for the DNS servers configured with a common anycast address. Should a server become unavailable, the serving router has no way to detect this and would not reroute packets destined for the anycast address. Therefore, incorporating a routing daemon on the DNS server improves overall robustness. Should a server fail, the local router will determine that it is no longer reachable and will update its routing table and those of other routers via routing protocol updates. Internet root servers support BGP, given their deployment on the global Internet, though deployment within organizations will likely require support for OSPF, interior gateway routing protocol (IGRP), or the interior routing protocol of choice.

Lastly, troubleshooting can be a little more challenging when using anycast addresses. Debugging a bogus response from a server's anycast address is difficult given the server ambiguity. To identify which anycast-addressed server is troublesome, it's a good idea to configure the server identification with the server-id option if your vendor supports it.

Configuring Anycast Addressing

Participation in routing protocol updates is key to maximizing the benefits of your DNS anycast implementation. The first step is to assign your chosen anycast address to your set of DNS servers sharing the address. This address is commonly assigned to the server loopback address. On Linux or Unix systems, this can be performed using the ipconfig command such as follows:

```
ifconfig lo:0 10.4.23.1 netmask 255.255.255.255
```

The simplest form of routing participation is to apply static routes which merely tells the local router to route the anycast address to the interface connected to the DNS server, and then to redistribute this static route among its peer routers.

```
ip route 10.4.23.1 255.255.255.255 172.20.23.1
```

But the use of static routes offers no benefits of rerouting based on routing protocol metrics such as network load, not to mention server reachability as just discussed. Use of a route daemon on the DNS server itself will enable the server to provide reachability information dynamically such that performance from a routing perspective among all anycast servers is optimized.

The open source routing package, quagga is commonly used for this purpose. Quagga supports a variety of routing protocols including RIP, RIPng, OSFPv2 and v3, and BGP. Configuration of quagga is relatively simple and entails configuring the zebra kernel routing manager component of quagga to configure it to include the server's network interfaces such as:

```
interface eth0
ip address 172.20.23.1/24
interface lo
line vty
```

The virtual teletype (vty) interface enables interactive access to the configuration while zebra is running. With zebra running as the interface to the kernel, configure the corresponding routing protocol configuration. For example, to run OSPF, the ospfd.conf file should include interface and OSFP declarations:

```
interface eth0
interface lo
router ospf
   ospf router-id 172.20.23.1
   log-adjacency-changes detail
   redistribute connnected
   network 172.20.23.0/24 area 0.0.0.100
line vty
```

After configuring quagga's zebra component and the routing component for your routing protocol, you then need to update the connected router configuration to associate the router interface with the assigned OSPF area, 100 in this case.

IPAM Deployment Summary

High Availability

We've implicitly addressed this already throughout this chapter, but it bears repeating. Deploy multiple servers within each trust sector and size the servers such that the query load can be handled by a subset of the total number of servers should one or more become unavailable.

Multiple Vendors

Deploying multiple DNS and DHCP servers running software from diverse vendors can help protect against the widespread impact of an attack exploiting a given vendor's implementation. For example, within your recursive DNS trust sector, you may choose to deploy one set of DNS servers running ISC BIND and another set running Unbound. This complicates your server management processes, but this diversification approach can help deflect vendor-specific targeted attacks.

Sizing and Scalability

Within each trust sector or DHCP deployment, you must also size the quantities, locations, and server specifications required to achieve high availability and resiliency. One logical location deployment approach is to place servers in more densely populated regions of your network to provide performance by proximity. However, sufficiently sized network links with redundancy enables a more centralized approach if preferred.

Server specifications need to be based on expected query load and resiliency requires the addition of one to a few servers to a design that fully meets the query load; the intent is to ease the load per server while enable the outage of a server or two (or links thereto) to not hinder overall query performance. Monitor and measure your servers' performance from a query rate, CPU, memory, and I/O perspective to track and assure adequate performance; monitoring is also critical for detecting threat events as well.

Load Balancers

Load balancers may be deployed in front of a set of DNS servers to enable the processing of DNS queries across a number of DNS servers. DNS queries would be addressed to the load balancer IP address and the load balancer would be responsible for forwarding the query to an available DNS server for resolution. Load balancers introduce an additional element within your network and DNS flow, but can be instrumental in providing improved performance and resiliency.

Note that the load balancer should pass through the query source IP address from the original query instead of NATing this address. This will prevent bypassing of your address-based ACL configurations on your DNS servers, unless you configure comparable ACLs on your load balancers.

Lab Deployment

A laboratory network should be deployed if feasible that is physically and networking-wise separate from your production network. While full replication of your production network within a lab is likely unrealistic, a subset of your deployment in terms of modeling each IPAM, DHCP, and DNS server vendor and version as well as role can help you test network changes in a controlled environment without affecting the production network should a test configuration fail.

15

The Business Case for IPAM

IPAM Business Benefits

No two enterprise IP networks are exactly the same. And the corresponding management approaches likewise differ. Throughout this book, we've mentioned the use of spreadsheets and text editors as vehicles for IP management. These primitive "brute force" methods are certainly valid for any size organization, but they offer none of the benefits one can attain by deploying an IPAM system, such as automation, integration, reporting, and scalability. In this chapter, we'll discuss IPAM business aspects, highlighting key areas where its implementation can provide a return on an investment in an IPAM tool.

Many of the IPAM business benefits relate to automation, thereby *reducing time* and *reducing errors* in performing certain tasks. If you run your network like a service provider, whether offering commercial services to customers or providing services to internal or external constituents using an ITIL® approach, time reduction in provisioning and trouble resolution can translate into actual dollars saved. In addition to such efficiency savings, your organization's overall reputation may be enhanced by promoting constituent goodwill through rapid provisioning and resolution of issues. While not hard dollar savings, solid organizational standing offers intangible benefits that could further improve intraorganizational efficiencies.

Other business benefits relate to readiness and accuracy of information. Fundamental to good security practice is an accurate inventory of all organizational assets including network-reachable assets via IP addresses. Regulatory requirements may dictate tracking of IP address assignments over time. Network audits may require tracking of who made certain changes in key network elements including DHCP and DNS servers. And reports for external authorities such as industry oversight organizations or Internet registries for example may be

IP Address Management, Second Edition. Michael Dooley and Timothy Rooney.
© 2021 The Institute of Electrical and Electronics Engineers, Inc.
Published 2021 by John Wiley & Sons, Inc.

required on an ad hoc or periodic basis. And certainly with access to this required information readily available, including IP address allocations and assignments as well as DHCP/DNS server configurations, you can save time in satisfying these requirements as well as reducing troubleshooting time. These and other key business benefits are summarized below.

Automation

First and foremost, IPAM leverages the close interrelationships among IP addressing, DHCP, and DNS to share common information across these key elements. This information reuse can reduce data entry requirements by multiple across multiple systems otherwise required with a discrete approach. Automation reduces manual effort and associated data entry errors and can reduce the time required to perform certain tasks. Automation benefits may also extend beyond IPAM functions, particularly into multi-cloud environments.

Outage Reduction

As we've seen throughout this book, IPAM services are foundational to the very operation of the IP network supporting all of your IP applications, yet are rendered in such a manner that offers little visibility, leading most end users to take them for granted. Of course, once an outage occurs due to IP address misassignments, or DHCP to DNS services failure, the visibility can become blinding. If an end user cannot obtain a relevant IP address that is unique, or cannot resolve host names, he or she will likely consider the network down and contact the help desk. This event is effectively an outage since there is at least one end user attempting to use the network that cannot.

A considerable business benefit of effective IPAM is the reduction of these outages. Forrester Research [121] estimated that up to 15% of network outages are related to DHCP and DNS issues. Hence, employing IPAM discipline can help reduce network outages, thereby reducing fire-fighting and associated costs while improving end user satisfaction with increased network uptime.

Rapid Trouble Resolution

Should a site or portion of the network become unreachable for direct diagnosis, a centralized IP database may prove indispensible in identifying occupied and available IP addresses, perhaps to configure a "back door" to the isolated site. The very moment the information is needed may be when it may not be directly attainable from the source; hence, a centralized IP address database is critical to facilitating rapid trouble resolution.

Accurate IPAM Inventory and Reporting

Maintaining a centralized repository of IP address information eases the process of tracking inventory for configuration, management, and reporting. Of course, accuracy of the information is key, so mechanisms to periodically reconcile inventory information with the network are recommended. Audit tracking concerning who had which IP address and who made particular network changes are also important to meet accountability, forensics, and possibly regulatory requirements.

Expanded IP Services

Historically, most organizations implemented IP in order to support an external web site. IP implementations are expanded to internal IP network deployments in the form of intranets and ultimately to support other IP data applications. Today, with the proliferation of wireless networks, private and public, as well as voice and multimedia over IP technologies, your IP network is now indispensible for your business or organization. Given these and other advanced IP services rollouts, a solid foundation of accurate and effective IP address inventory and planning as well as accurate DHCP and DNS server configuration is paramount.

Distributed Administration

While centralized management is a common network management approach, the ability to delegate responsibility for certain functions and/or subportions of the network is important as well. Enabling other administrators to manage subsets of the network enables the centralized team to handle issues requiring a higher level of expertise such as troubleshooting escalation. Even empowering end users for simple tasks such as requesting an IP address can reduce staff time requirements and improve responsiveness through self-service.

Enhanced Security

Implementing an IPAM system and management procedures enables you to maintain and secure IP network information and related user information. As mentioned, tracking asset inventory including those connected to your network is a key security function. Auditing of network access attempts and access control mechanisms also contribute to your overall network security plan. Securing access to your IP network as well as securing DNS and DHCP information and communications need also be considered.

Business Case Overview

The exercise of creating a business case can not only help you identify the key aspects of IP management that may be lacking in your organization, and therefore inflicting high costs, but it can help you target your search among the multitude of IPAM system vendors in the marketplace. Knowing whether you need a complete overhaul or simply an improvement in a subset of key functions is important when considering alternative solutions. But it's up to you to investigate which solutions can best help you based on your particular environment. Note that while we use US Dollars in the sample business case in this chapter, merely apply your own currency units and prices as applicable to your organization.

We'll start our business case analysis by considering key cost saving opportunities when implementing an IPAM system. As with any system you purchase, the intent is to reap savings of time as well as reduced errors and rework. These savings represent the "income" portion of the business case. The costs of a tool and its implementation, support, and ongoing management represent the expense side of the equation. In most cases, investment in an IP management tool requires an up-front purchase payment. This initial outlay will be "paid back" over time as savings mount. Note that managed IPAM services, either in the form of consultants operating your IPAM system of choice or actual managed services from an IPAM service provider offer an additional vehicle for managing IPAM within an organization. The expense side of our business case example is applicable in these cases, but the savings and "investment" side will depend on capital requirements and ongoing services charges.

As we walk through the income and expense sides of the return on investment (ROI) equation, we'll walk through our IPAM Worldwide example to illustrate this payback. The base assumptions for our example are as follows. Again, every network is different and only your input parameters will map the relevance to your network.

Macro IP address blocks:	40	DHCP servers:	16
IP subnets:	380	DNS servers:	24
Assigned IP addresses:	75,000	Routers:	48

The general observed or estimated parameters of IPAM operation are as follows.

For blocks, 10% are allocated and assigned per year and 5% are deleted and 5% are changed.
20% of subnets and IP addresses are allocated and assigned on average per year.
15% of subnets and IP addresses are deleted on average per year.

10% of subnets and IP addresses are changed on average per year.
Of changes, about 75% are parameter changes, 25% moves.
Of IP address assignments, 75% manual, 25% MDHCP.
Router and IP discoveries are run once a week.

Business Case Cost Basis

To derive an accurate cost estimate, you will need to analyze the manual labor costs of performing IP address management tasks over a few days or so to sample how much IPAM is costing your organization on a daily or weekly basis. If this sounds like a time and motion analysis, it is! And this practice from the field of industrial engineering has been helping maximize the efficiency of manufacturing and other process-oriented workflows for decades. Certainly, if you are comfortable making rough estimates you may do so to save time. People often remark that labor savings are "soft costs," and thus it's difficult to justify the investment in IP management tools. If this argument had deterred Henry Ford, perhaps we might still be riding horses. Service providers will typically have additional income components to the business case with the very necessity of IPAM-related functions in providing services to paying customers. This revenue may be for broadband or WAN service or for a managed IPAM service and render investment in an IP management tool easier to justify.

If you desire to quantify these labor costs for your environment, record the time spent on every IP management task (in a spreadsheet if desired!), from block allocation, to address assignment to configuring DHCP and DNS servers. We covered the details of these tasks throughout this book, though we'll summarize them here and group common sets of tasks. When considering each task, don't just record the time it takes to type in the information. Consider the "think time" required to select an appropriate subnet or IP address, to define the DHCP address pool parameters, to create the zone file or make changes, and so on. After all, the think time is the hard part, where mistakes can be made creating future rework and hence even more time.

If a resource is unavailable, such as a server requiring an update or a spreadsheet in use by another, record this wait time as well; it adds into the lost productivity of the administrator doing the waiting, and perhaps the end user(s) also awaiting the requested change. Help desk calls referred to the IP team should also be recorded in terms of duration, impact on the end user community if outage-related, and time taken for help desk staff logging of the trouble, referral to the server or networking team, problem isolation and resolution, and closure of the trouble with feedback to the help desk. This type of information is usually readily available from your help desk phone system or trouble ticketing system.

We refer to an "outage" in this chapter as a situation where a client is unable to obtain an IP address (fully booked address pool, duplicate address, server outage, incorrect DHCP configuration, etc.) or resolve an IP address (server or network down, incorrect DNS configuration, etc.) Such outages themselves may provide sufficient justification to implement a more rigorous IPAM process and tool.

Outages represent one form of an exception condition, where work is generated that requires an interrupt level prioritization to complete, at the expense of whatever else was being worked on. Other forms of exception conditions might include periodic auditing requirements for internal, legal, or regulatory controls, major project planning and execution, such as expanding the network or opening a new store, and performing upgrades of DHCP and DNS servers. These tasks are beyond the day-to-day moves, adds, and changes and usually require concentrated resources for bursts of time. The length of time and resources required for each burst depends on the scope of the work.

The following discussion breaks down common IPAM tasks including exception conditions. For each event, determine the amount of time spent per resource type, assuming different pay scales. Normalize the time, including exceptions to a common time of a month or year. Multiply the time by the cost per unit time and sum to derive your costs for your current IP management methodology. Review the areas that are high cost runners for your organization. This will be helpful when searching for an IP management system, to focus your search on reducing those particular cost areas.

Address Block Management

If your network address plan accurately reflects your production addressing hierarchy, you may think there's no need to focus on address block allocations. In this context, we're referring to "blocks" as those allocated above the subnet level in the address space hierarchy, e.g. recall the application, continental and regional allocations we discussed in Chapter 13. As long as you have your plan well documented, the underlying subnets and address assignments align with the plan, and the rate of change of network allocation is low, you're probably right. However, should one of these three conditions not hold, you should consider the cost of documenting the plan, renumbering your network to attain alignment, and updating your allocation process to prevent "misaligned" allocations in the future and to accommodate even occasional moves, adds, and changes. Stabilizing this information and the processes that influence it provide a solid foundation for the more frequent downstream subnet and IP allocation tasks, which in turn will be performed with fewer costly errors.

Another problem with minimizing the address block allocation function is that the allocation plan feeds not only downstream allocations, including subnet allocations, cloud and/or router provisioning, and corresponding router protocol updates and tables, but also subnet-resident static address assignments, DHCP pool configuration, and DNS domains and resource records updates. Another point to consider is that business initiatives may impact the address block allocation plan. Planned deployment of many new sites requiring IP addresses due to expansion of the business, plans for new service offerings and even a merger or acquisition each can heavily impact the IP address plan.

Planning address space allocations for any of these business initiatives begins with understanding the business requirements with respect to address capacity for each application at each site. This in itself can be a tedious process. Once this capacity has been quantified, this should be folded into the overall IP allocation plan. For example, if we embarked on an expansion into Latin America, the IP planners may decide to deploy a core level router to participate at the top level of the corporate backbone. Allocating address space for each suballocation "beneath" this router in the topology requires updating of the spreadsheet or database, enumerating the locations and capacity requirements. Aggregating these capacity requirements and adding some additional space for growth, the allocation may be sized. From this allocation, suballocations to each set of locations by application may commence.

The key steps involved in address block allocation include identification of address capacity needs based on the defined block hierarchy, rollup of capacity requirements within the hierarchy, sizing up the proper allocation based on the capacity requirements, recording allocations and suballocations, and updating corresponding core routers. If a new allocation is driven by a major business initiative, such as our expansion into Latin America, it's likely that additional DHCP and DNS servers will be required to service the end users within the region. Thus, we've included tasks for DHCP and DNS server sizing (how many servers of a given size of each type are needed where), procurement of the servers, then base level server configuration. This base configuration would include basic policy definition, as well as zones corresponding to the domain plan for the addition. A project manager resource or team would also likely be required to coordinate and manage the deployment process to completion.

Table 15.1 illustrates an example block allocation cost analysis for this scenario. Note that additional costs for DHCP and DNS server hardware, shipping, travel, and expenses to have them installed are not shown in the example below but need to be considered in the overall ROI analysis. Note also that these costs, as well as sizing, procurement, and installation, will likely be incurred whether an IPAM system is used or not.

The largest cost component of block allocation relates to analyzing capacity requirements to determine the need for a new allocation or carving up of an existing one. This task likely involves multiple team members, e.g. from facilities

Table 15.1 Block allocation cost analysis.

Block allocation	Resource type	Average staff-time required (hours)	Resource hourly cost	Cost per event	Events per year	Annualized cost
Identify capacity requirements	Business team	20.00	$30	$600	4	$2,400
Design Rollup to address capacity (new)	Engineering	40.00	$50	$2,000	1	$2,000
Design Rollup to address capacity (build on existing)	Engineering	10.00	$50	$500	3	$1,500
Address plan update	Engineering	4.00	$50	$200	4	$800
Router (or cloud) provisioning of new network(s) and relay agents	Router Ops	8.00	$40	$320	4	$1,280
DHCP and DNS server sizing	Engineering	4.00	$50	$200	4	$800
DHCP and DNS server procurement	Engineering & purchasing	24.00	$50	$1,200	1	$1,200
Basic DHCP and DNS server configuration	Server Ops	16.00	$40	$640	4	$2,560
Total annual block allocation costs						$12,540

Table 15.2 Block deletion cost analysis.

Block deletion	Resource type	Average staff-time required (hours)	Resource hourly cost	Cost per event	Events per year	Annualized cost
Identify block and downstream blocks and subnets	Engineering	0.10	$50	$5	2	$10
Verify downstream blocks and subnets are free	Engineering	1.00	$50	$50	2	$100
Delete block and verify	Engineering	0.10	$50	$5	2	$10
Join newly freed block with contiguous free block	Engineering	0.25	$50	$13	2	$25
Total annual block deletion costs						**$145**

planning, human resources, and related business functions, or from product management and marketing for a service provider organization. As such, five staff members for a 4-hour meeting amounts to 20 hours for each of our four allocations per year. Assuming only one of these quarterly meetings involves a new allocation, about a week of rollup planning and block design is assumed. Recall that multiple parallel allocations may be needed to maintain allocation consistency. For example, we may allocate five blocks per location for various applications, so adequate allocations must be designed.

For all allocations, the block inventory database must be updated and corresponding routers and/or cloud systems provisioned. DHCP and DNS services requirements must be assessed, and if needed, additional servers procured and configured. Address block management also entails deletion of address blocks as well as moving blocks. Block deletions may result from the withdrawal from a major business market or consolidation of sites for example. The deleting of an address block within the hierarchy is a bottom-up process, the converse of the top-down allocation process. All downstream IP addresses, subnets, address pools, resource records, and domains must first be decommissioned before the macro level block can be freed up for future assignment consideration.

The process of deleting a top or intermediate level block requires iterative execution of IP address and block deletion tasks, once for each address and subnet, respectively. As with a modest to large allocation task, project planning resources may be required to verify deletions up the hierarchy. Table 15.2 highlights the relatively insignificant block deletion costs taken in isolation, which occurs only once a quarter in our case given our judicious up front planning.

Moving, or renumbering address blocks combines the allocation process, which should be performed from a top down allocation to move (reassign) underlying subnets and IP addresses to the newly allocated block, and the deletion process, which frees up address space from the bottom up as addresses are moved away. In Table 15.3, we've combined the block modification task, which comprises four of the six annual block change tasks and the block move task. Modifying most block attributes is typically only a database update and is therefore trivial.

Movement of blocks however is a bit more involved. In our scenario, with one annual block move on average, a destination block needs to be identified and allocated, affected routers and DHCP/DNS servers provisioned, and the move executed. As the move progresses, monitoring and verification of successive IP address moves within downstream subnets enables deletion of the former addresses. A final audit validation, requiring ten staff-hours, is conducted prior to the final deletion of the block and completion of the move. In all moves or changes, the IP inventory must be updated to reflect changes.

Considering what we've discussed so far, our total costs for block management are $14 185, most of which is comprised of block allocations for expansions.

Table 15.3 Block change cost analysis.

Block changes	Resource type	Average staff-time required (hours)	Resource hourly cost	Cost per event	Events per year	Annualized cost
Identify block to move/change and downstream blocks and subnets	Engineering	0.50	$50	$25	4	$100
Modify block attributes	Engineering	0.25	$50	$13	4	$50
Identify destination block to which to move block	Engineering	0.50	$50	$25	2	$50
Address plan update	Engineering	0.50	$50	$25	4	$100
Router or cloud provisioning of new network(s)	Router Ops	0.25	$40	$10	2	$20
Basic DHCP and DNS server configuration	Server Ops	1.00	$40	$40	2	$80
Verify rolling move of IP subnets and blocks, and decommission moved blocks	Engineering	10.00	$50	$500	2	$1,000
Verify completion of all moved subnets and deleted former subnets	Engineering	1.00	$50	$50	2	$100
Total annual block change costs						**$1,500**

Table 15.4 Subnet allocation cost analysis.

Subnet allocation	Resource type	Average staff-time required (hours)	Resource hourly cost	Cost per event	Events per year	Annualized cost
Define and allocate subnet	Engineering	0.20	$50	$10	76	$760
Router or cloud provisioning of new subnet	Router Ops	0.25	$40	$10	76	$760
DHCP pool definitions – define range, apply options and client classes	Engineering	0.50	$50	$25	76	$1,900
DHCP server configuration	Server Ops	0.50	$40	$20	76	$1,520
DNS server config updates for allocated subnets	DNS Eng	0.25	$50	$13	76	$950
Allocation deployment verification	Net Ops	0.50	$50	$25	76	$1,900
Total subnet allocation costs						**$7,790**

Subnet Management

This basic task of subnet allocation involves the identification of a subnet that is available that rolls up within the address allocation plan for the given location or cloud network and application, then assignment of the subnet in the IP address plan database. In addition, this task requires provisioning of the subnet on the appropriate router interface or cloud virtual network, defining and updating DHCP server address pool configurations with corresponding options and/or client class parameters for expected devices on the allocated subnet, defining and updating DNS server configurations with domain updates (e.g. in-addr.arpa and ip6.arpa domains) and resource record updates for name servers and statically assigned addresses.

The subnet allocation process illustrates the tight interrelationship among address allocation, assignment, and DHCP and DNS server configuration tasks. Depending on your business processes, subnets may be allocated or reserved prior to address assignment and DHCP/DNS configuration. Nonetheless, this set of steps will typically be required to bring a subnet into production.

Devices to be assigned addresses on the subnet now and in the future will likely require name resolution information in DNS. At a minimum, this information applies to a forward domain for domain name-to-IP address lookup and a reverse domain for the reverse lookup. Of course, these domains must exist and be configured on the DNS server. Depending on your domain topology, adding a new subnet to an existing location will likely utilize an existing domain, though this is not necessarily the case. Likewise, adding a new subnet to a new location may or may not require a new domain definition. In either case, a new domain may need to be defined and configured as a subdomain or a new zone on the appropriate DNS server. In the same way, the reverse domain corresponding to the subnet address may need to be added as well, unless a higher layer in-addr.arpa or ip6.arpa zone will contain these resource records.

In our environment, 76 subnets will be allocated this year, based on the assumption of 20% of their current 380 subnets. The allocation process involves six basic tasks as shown in Table 15.4, each requiring a half hour or less.

Deleting a subnet may be required when closing a site or consolidating address space. Based on our initial assumptions, we expect to delete 57 subnets in the coming year. Devices with IP addresses on each subnet to be deleted must first be moved or decommissioned such that the subnet is free of address assignments (other than perhaps subnet-serving routers). After all IP addresses have been verified as free, the subnet may be reclaimed into the free address space for future allocation. Annualized costs for deleting subnets are tallied in Table 15.5.

Moving a subnet could involve one of two results: movement of the subnet and its assigned IP addresses to another router or interface, preserving the current

Table 15.5 Subnet deletion cost analysis.

Subnet deletion	Resource type	Average staff-time required (hours)	Resource hourly cost	Cost per event	Events per year	Annualized cost
Identify subnet and associated IP addresses	Engineering	0.10	$50	$5	57	$285
Verify subnet IP addresses are free	Engineering	0.25	$50	$13	57	$713
Delete subnet and verify	Engineering	0.10	$50	$5	57	$285
Join newly freed subnet with contiguous free block	Engineering	0.25	$50	$13	57	$713
Total annual subnet deletion costs						**$1,995**

address assignment or movement to another router or interface, requiring a new subnet address. The first case requires consideration of address space rollup within the hierarchy but generally consists of modifying and verifying router provisioning compliance with the plan, as well as updates to routing tables and DHCP relay addresses as necessary.

Movement of a subnet which requires an address change due to a physical move, e.g. when an office is moved, is inherently disruptive. The destination subnet may be allocated and provisioned on the destination router interface, along with the other tasks described above related to reserving static addresses and updating DHCP and DNS configurations. When each moved device "plugs in," it will need to be manually re-addressed with the new address, autoconfigure an IPv6 address or obtain a DHCP lease on a pool relevant to the subnet.

In our case, of the 38 subnet changes this year, 29 will involve simple subnet attribute updates and 9 will involve disruptive moves. The corresponding tasks and costs are so numbered by occurrences per year in Table 15.6.

IP Address Assignment – Moves, Adds, and Changes

Assigning, deleting, and reassigning IP addresses to individual hosts is usually the most frequent IP management activity in most organizations. This is typically associated with deployment, redeployment, or decommissioning of new physical or virtual devices, including routers, servers, printers, containers, virtual machines, and the like. The IP address inventory database should be consulted to identify an available IP address. If possible, it would be useful to ping the IP address to be assigned or verify it as available per the respective cloud API just to verify accuracy of the inventory, though we'll discuss inventory assurance as a separate task. The IP address to be assigned should then be noted as assigned to the given device.

The actual physical IP address assignment may be performed by relying on your cloud provider via API, manually configuring the device, or by using DHCP. Note that an autoconfiguring device requires no effort on the part of the IPAM team, at least until network discovery time. In the DHCP case, we assume M-DHCP would be used to assign the designated IP address to the corresponding host. This requires an entry in the appropriate DHCP server's configuration to map the device's hardware address to the assigned IP address. In the manual assignment case, the address must be entered directly on the device, so unless the IP address assigner is also responsible for the physical assignment, this process would entail an email or phone call to the device owner conveying the assigned IP address to be entered.

Most devices with IP addresses will require corresponding DNS resource records to enable their name resolution. Using the DHCP method of address assignment,

Table 15.6 Subnet change cost analysis.

Subnet changes	Resource type	Average staff-time required (hours)	Resource hourly cost	Cost per event	Events per year	Annualized cost
Identify subnet to move/change and affected IP addresses	Engineering	0.50	$50	$25	38	$950
Modify subnet attributes	Engineering	0.25	$50	$13	29	$363
Identify destination subnet to which to move subnet	Engineering	0.25	$50	$13	9	$113
Address plan update	Engineering	0.25	$50	$13	9	$113
Router provisioning of new network(s)	Router Ops	0.25	$40	$10	9	$90
DHCP pool definitions for new subnet	Engineering	0.50	$50	$25	9	$225
DHCP server configuration	Server Ops	0.50	$40	$20	9	$180
DNS server configuration for destination subnet	DNS Eng	2.00	$50	$100	9	$900
Verify rolling move of IP addresses and decommission moved IP addresses	Engineering	2.00	$50	$100	9	$900
Verify completion of change with all IP addresses moved and old ones deleted	Engineering	0.50	$50	$25	9	$225
Total annual subnet change costs						**$4,058**

Table 15.7 IP address assignment cost analysis.

IP address assignment	Resource type	Average staff-time required (hours)	Resource hourly cost	Cost per event	Events per year	Annualized cost
Identify available IP address	Engineering	0.05	$50	$3	15,000	$37,500
Update device configuration in DHCP server (M-DHCP)	Server Ops	0.10	$40	$4	3,750	$15,000
Static address assignment – email to owner then manual config	Engineering	0.10	$50	$5	11,250	$56,250
Update DNS for manually configured IP addresses	Server Ops	0.05	$40	$2	11,250	$22,500
Address assignment verification	Net Ops	0.05	$50	$3	15,000	$37,500
Total annual IP address assignment costs						**$168,750**

the DHCP server can be configured to update a master DNS server upon assignment of the IP address. This update would affect the forward domain for domain name-to-IP address lookup and the reverse domain for the reverse lookup. A similar DNS update would be required if assigning the address manually. Updating DNS with this new host information may entail editing or updating the corresponding zone files on the server or by sending dynamic updates. We expect to perform 15 000 IP address assignments this year, with 3750 of these performed via Manual DHCP and the remaining 11 250 requiring manual configuration. IP address assignment costs in our example are summarized in Table 15.7.

De-assigning or deleting an IP address is relatively straightforward: delete the IP address in the IP inventory, freeing up the virtualized network function via cloud API, removing the M-DHCP entry from DHCP if appropriate, and removing associated DNS resource records. Care must be taken to assure the address has been relinquished by the device before assigning it to another device. Thus, assigning the IP address a state of "pending deletion" or something similar as do public cloud systems, would alert other administrators not to assign that address to another device until confirmation is received of its availability. We expect 11 250 IP address deletions on average per year, so our costs amount to $56 250 as summarized in Table 15.8.

As with blocks and subnets, changes for IP addresses could involve simple attribute changes within the inventory or a more demanding move process. Of 7500 IP addresses requiring change, 5,6253 (75%) will involve attribute updates. Of the remaining 937 addresses requiring movement, 469 will utilize Manual DHCP and 1406 will require manual or cloud API configuration. Moving the IP address is a combination of assigning an IP address on the destination subnet then deleting the current IP address on the current subnet after the move. Inventory assurance strategies can be employed to track the address move and to maintain database accuracy.

While each address change task may take just minutes, this task is performed thousands of times throughout the year, yielding a rather astonishing total cost. as tabulated in Table 15.9.

Inventory Assurance

The inventory assurance task seeks to maintain IP inventory database accuracy. Like any "inventory system," the IP inventory should reflect the block, subnet, and address assignments on the actual network. This information is relied upon for future planning, troubleshooting, and auditing. Inventory assurance also provides an opportunity to analyze why a discovered discrepancy exists and can be critical in detecting autoconfigured devices, violations in network access policies, change control procedures, or provisioning and service level agreements. Finally, inventory assurance processes can help identify reclaimable address space to make the best use of address space and accurately model actual use in the inventory database.

The process of inventory assurance involves discovering network information, comparing discovered results with the inventory database or "plan of record," then following up by updating the database or otherwise investigating the discrepancy. Any changes to the inventory could also affect associated DHCP and/or DNS server configurations, as with subnet or address adds or deletes, especially with DNS updates necessitated by the appearance of autoconfigured devices.

In our case, summarized in Table 15.10, we'll poll via our cloud APIs and run SNMP sweeps of our routers once a week (2496 times per year total), and subnet ping sweeps once a week (19 760 subnet sweeps per year). The results are then visually compared with the corresponding subnet and IP address in our spreadsheets. We're assuming about 15 minutes to compare each cloud virtual network's or router's data and about 6 minutes per subnet inventory update. Each "discrepancy" requires the analyst to think and decide whether to accept the discrepancy, e.g. as an autoconfigured address vs. a rogue device address, and update the database and associated DNS and DHCP configurations, or denote the IP address as an open issue that must be further investigated. Such investigation may involve analyzing discovery history of the IP address, identifying the owner of the discovered device, or even physically locating and inspecting the device.

Address Capacity Management

Inventory assurance discovery tasks provide enumeration of occupied IP addresses within a subnet. This information is helpful not only in maintaining IP inventory accuracy but in determining the overall IP address utilization across our subnets considering assigned vs. total (assigned + available) IP addresses. Recall that addresses on a subnet can be assigned manually, automatically via autoconfiguration, by a cloud system, or by DHCP. Ping sweeps, cloud API calls, or similar host discovery methods enable detection of manual or autoconfigured addresses, while collection of DHCP lease information supplements these discovery methods, providing the added perspective of the DHCP server. Monitoring address pools in particular helps assure such pools are adequately sized to meet the IP address demands of each site.

The first step in the process for the DHCP case is to collect DHCP lease information. We collect address assignments from each of our 16 DHCP servers once each business day (270/year). This amounts to 4320 lease files per year. These files are collected primarily for address utilization monitoring, but this information can also be used to validate the pool sizing parameters on each subnet within the IP inventory database. These two tasks, comparison of pool size and analysis of addresses assigned are combined as shown in Table 15.11. Analysis of the results indicates that on average 5% of these lease files (216 occurrences) indicate additional capacity is required. These capacity enhancements can be provided by supplementing existing pools or adding new ones on existing subnets. The addition of

Table 15.8 IP address deletion cost analysis.

IP address deletion	Resource type	Average staff-time required (hours)	Resource hourly cost	Cost per event	Events per Year	Annualized cost
Identify IP address to delete	Engineering	0.05	$50	$3	11,250	$28,125
Delete subnet and verify	Engineering	0.05	$50	$3	11,250	$28,125
Total annual IP address deletion costs						**$56,250**

Table 15.9 IP address change cost analysis.

IP address changes	Resource type	Average staff-time required (hours)	Resource hourly cost	Cost per event	Events per year	Annualized cost
Identify IP address to move/change	Engineering	0.05	$50	$3	7,500	$18,750
Modify IP address attributes	Engineering	0.10	$50	$5	5,625	$28,125
Identify destination IP address	Engineering	0.10	$50	$5	1,875	$9,375
Update device configuration in DHCP server (M-DHCP)	Server Ops	0.10	$40	$4	469	$1,876
Static address assignment – email to owner then manual config	Engineering	0.10	$50	$5	1,406	$7,030
Update DNS for manually configured IP addresses	Server Ops	0.10	$40	$4	1,406	$5,624
Address move verification	Net Ops	0.10	$50	$5	1,875	$9,375
Total annual IP address change costs						**$80,155**

Table 15.10 Inventory assurance cost analysis.

Inventory assurance	Resource type	Average staff-time required (hours)	Resource hourly cost	Cost per event	Events per year	Annualized cost
Query routers via SNMP or cloud via API for subnets	Router Ops	0.05	$40	$2	2,496	$4,992
Compare discovery results with router-subnet inventory	Engineering	0.25	$50	$13	2,496	$31,200
Call cloud API per run ping sweep or other discovery method on a given subnet	Engineering	0.10	$50	$5	19,760	$98,800
Compare discovery results with IP address inventory	Engineering	0.05	$50	$3	19,760	$49,400
Assess discrepancies and update inventory or investigate cause	Engineering	0.25	$50	$13	1,113	$13,910
Update the inventory with accepted changes; make associated changes to DHCP and DNS if necessary	Engineering	0.10	$50	$5	890	$4,450
Total annual inventory assurance costs						$202,752

Table 15.11 Address capacity management cost analysis.

Address capacity management	Resource type	Average staff-time required (hours)	Resource hourly cost	Cost per event	Events per year	Annualized cost
Collect DHCP lease and IP assignments, e.g. via cloud API	Server/Cloud Ops	0.10	$40	$4	4,320	$17,280
Analyze IP assignments to identify discrepancies in pools or assignments vs. IP inventory as well as capacity utilization	Engineering	0.25	$50	$5	4,320	$54,000
Trigger block or pool allocation process for any pools at or nearing exhaustion	Engineering	0.10	$50	$5	216	$1,080
Update DHCP server configurations or expand subnet capacity via API	Server/Cloud Ops	0.25	$40	$10	216	$2,160
Analyze trends in utilization to initiate plans for address expansion or contraction	Engineering	2.00	$50	$100	12	$1,200
Total annual IP address capacity management costs						$75,720

pools requiring subnet allocation will be assumed a contributor to the 38 subnet allocations performed each year.

The last subtask within address capacity management involves analyzing several of these lease file "snapshots" to identify address utilization trends. Slated for once a month, our staff analyze the last three months' counts per pool to identify pools where address demands are growing or shrinking. This can be helpful in identifying those pools requiring closer attention in the analysis of daily lease file collections in the coming month to minimize address depletions.

Auditing and Reporting

Auditing and reporting are key functions of any management system and are absolute requirements for an IPAM system. In fact, as we look at the costs for manual audit tracking and reporting, we'll see that automating such tasks provides financial benefits as well. With that said, the intensity of auditing and reporting requirements varies across organizations, based upon organizational reporting policies and industry and government compliance laws and regulations. At minimum, organizations need to be able to research which administrator performed a certain IP management function for troubleshooting, training, feedback, or accountability tracking. It's also very useful to track which device occupied a given IP address at a certain point in time. If a firewall log scan indicates that a particular IP address potentially violated an internal policy for example, the ability to map the suspect IP address to a device or user within the given time frame of the incident can save a tremendous amount of time.

For our example network, the auditing process entails updating a consolidated audit log with detected IP address assignments and associated MAC addresses for each DHCP lease file collected. In addition, an audit log for tracking administrator moves/adds/changes of IP blocks, subnets, addresses, and DHCP and DNS server configurations and upgrades should be maintained. Unless one person makes all such changes, this information is difficult to maintain manually. It generally relies on every person making such a change to remember to log the change manually or send an email to a centralized person or team for consolidated logging. If this information is consolidated, the running of reports is theoretically simple. Auditing and reporting costs for our example are portrayed in Table 15.12.

Server Upgrade Management

Upgrades may be required for DHCP and DNS servers due to security vulnerability fixes, bug fixes, or new feature enhancements. Let's assume we perform upgrades for each server three times a year on average, or a total of 120 total upgrades as shown in Table 15.13. Of these, 5% require a coincident operating system upgrade or patch for compliance with the DHCP/DNS upgrade. Upgrades should be installed and tested in a lab environment to verify expected behavior prior to upgrading production servers. This lab test and soak time varies depending on policies, but we'll assume eight hours for installation and testing per upgrade.

Outage and Security Recovery Costs

IP address depletions, DHCP or DNS server outages, and errors in IP moves/adds/changes or DHCP/DNS server configuration can lead to the unavailability of these critical network services to end users, as can malware infestation or other forms of IPAM directed attacks.

Configuration errors at any level of the IPAM process can create outage conditions resulting in the same trouble flow from end user to the help desk to Engineering and Operations. A miscalculated block or subnet allocation could result in overlapping allocations, which can create routing loops or routing issues. Deleting a subnet or IP address prior to its relinquishment would stimulate complaints from affected end users. Likewise, erroneous DHCP and DNS server configurations can lead to improper name resolution with DNS, incorrect device initialization with DHCP or failure to load configuration files, which renders the DNS or DHCP service unavailable.

If address pools are diligently monitored, IP address depletions should be rare, though a few may occur due to planned or coincidental meetings in a given location causing a spike in demand. We'll assume that we experience no such outages due to our astute investment in proactive pool monitoring. If such an outage were to occur, however, those users attempting to obtain IP addresses after the pool becomes fully utilized will fail to do so. Unable to connect to the network, some may call the help desk complaining about the network being down. After collecting some information about the issue, the help desk staff would escalate to Engineering and Operations for troubleshooting and resolution.

Security issues such as a malware attack could affect a broad set of users within the organization depending on the nature of the attack. Some malware tunnels sensitive information into the attackers' hands, and such incidents can cost an organization millions of dollars in lost revenue, company reputation, compensation, or other costs.

In our scenario, we expect no capacity-related outages. Configuration errors are assumed to affect 1 in 200 (0.5%) IP management related changes. Malware attacks affect 0.1% of the user population per year. This amounts to 186 configuration errors of the total 37000+ IP management changes made within a year (based on all of the preceding tasks we've reviewed in this chapter) and 75 users attacked by malware. Each configuration outage is expected to last about half an hour, and malware outages one hour, though in reality, malware may remain undetected for days. This outage duration includes the initiation of the outage, the detection by administrators or end users, reporting back to those responsible for resolution, isolation of the problem, and finally closure with those reporting the issue. Thus,

Table 15.12 Auditing and reporting cost analysis.

Auditing and reporting	Resource type	Average staff-time required (hours)	Resource hourly cost	Cost per event	Events per year	Annualized cost
Analyze DHCP leases, IP assignments, cloud assignments, and log history of IP-MAC/DUID/VM ID assignments	Engineering	0.25	$50	$25	4,320	$54,000
Log all IPAM related changes made by staff	Engineering	0.02	$50	$1	37,271	$37,271
Run reports on demand	Engineering	1.00	$50	$50	100	$5,000
Total annual auditing and reporting costs						**$96,271**

Table 15.13 Server upgrades cost analysis.

Server upgrades	Resource type	Average staff-time required (hours)	Resource hourly cost	Cost per event	Events per year	Annualized cost
Assess OS, DHCP, DNS version compatibility	Engineering	0.50	$50	$25	120	$3,000
Install upgrade on lab server	Engineering	8.00	$50	$400	3	$1,200
Obtain OS patch for compliance	Engineering	0.10	$50	$5	6	$30
Install OS patch	Server Ops	2.00	$40	$80	6	$480
Install DHCP/DNS upgrade	Server Ops	4.00	$50	$200	120	$24,000
Verify successful installation and reachability	Engineering	1.00	$50	$50	120	$6,000
Update the inventory with current versions on the upgraded server	Engineering	0.50	$50	$25	120	$3,000
Total annual server upgrade costs						**$37,710**

about 93 hours of outages ("outage-hours") are expected due to a configuration error and 75 hours due to malware or related security incidents.

DHCP and DNS server outages may occur due to server failure, power outage, or from an end user perspective, network reachability issues. Targeted at four nines availability (99.99%), we anticipate that each server will suffer up to 0.01% downtime or 0.88 hours per server or about 35 hours for all servers.

With about 40 servers servicing 17 000 employees, the average server outage will impact about 425 end users. However, due to redundancy, we'll assume only half are impacted, plus we'll apply a simple proportional probability of occurrence during working hours as about 24% (annual working hours/annual total hours). The net impact is 51 end users/outage-hour. Each server outage will affect some Help Desk staff as well as a pair of Engineering and Operations staff members who will identify and resolve the outage on average within half an hour.

Based on the calculations at the top of Table 15.14, each hour of outage on average costs the organization $1882.50. Thus, outages due to configuration errors cost the organization $175 073 ($1882.50 × 93) while security attacks cost $141 188 per year and server outages $65 888.

IPAM System Administration Costs

System administration tasks generally entail backing up IP inventory data, DHCP and DNS server configurations, audit history, and related IP information. Depending on the system currently in use, such as an in-house developed system, ongoing development, testing and support costs need to be considered. New features may be required periodically in support of new DHCP or DNS features, for IPv6 support, or other enhancements. Even absent new development, support of the system to address bugs encountered or upgrade incompatibilities must be accounted for.

For a commercial off the shelf system, annual maintenance, training, support, and feature upgrade costs need to be considered. If considering a release upgrade, any costs associated with an upgrade should be considered. We've already addressed server upgrades, so in this context, upgrades refer to the product costs, associated software, hardware and staffing required to perform the upgrade of the management system. Some systems can be upgraded very quickly and easily while others are more cumbersome. The size and distribution of IPAM components on your network also plays strongly into the upgrade costs. If possible, annualize this cost by determining how many such upgrades are planned over the next three years and averaging the total cost (divide total cost by three years) or map out costs on an annual basis for three years or the length of your planning horizon.

Assuming we currently use spreadsheets, the only system administration cost is the weekly backup of the spreadsheet and all DHCP and DNS server configurations to an off-site server, which takes about an hour a week and costs just over

Table 15.14 Outages and security cost analysis.

Outages and recovery	Affected resource cost/hr	Resources impacted per outage	Cost per outage-hour	Outages	Outage hours	Annualized cost
Customer care/help desk	$30	0.25	$7.50			
Eng/Ops	$45	2	$90.00			
End users	$35	51	$1,785.00			
Total cost per outage-hour			*$1,882.50*			
Configuration errors				*186*	*93*	$175,073
Address pool depletions				*0*	*0*	$0
Malware incidents				*75*	*75*	$141,188
Total incidents				*261*		
Server outages (unavailability)					*35*	$65,888
Total outage hours per year					*203*	
Total annual outage and security costs						**$382,148**

Table 15.15 IPAM system administration costs.

System administration	Resource type	Average staff-time required (hours)	Resource hourly cost	Cost per event	Events per year	annualized cost
Data repository backup	Server Ops	1.00	$40	$40	52	$2,080
Other system administration costs	Server Ops	0.00	$40	$0	52	$0
In-house system analyst staff	Analyst	0.00	$0	$0	0	$0
In-house system development staff	Dev.	0.00	$0	$0	0	$0
In-house system testing staff	Testing	0.00	$0	$0	0	$0
In-house system help desk	Help Desk	0.00	$0	$0	0	$0
Commercial system admin	Server Ops	0.00	$0	$0	0	$0
Commercial system support costs	Dev.	0.00	$0	$0	0	$0
Commercial system upgrade costs	Dev.	0.00	$0	$0	0	$0
TOTAL						$2,080

$2k annually. We've listed other cost components discussed above in Table 15.15 for completeness if you are using a spreadsheet alternative, either an in-house system or a commercial system.

Cost Basis Summary

As summarized in Table 15.16, the total annual costs for execution of our IPAM tasks are $1 129 865. Seemingly minor daily tasks certainly add up! The scope of IPAM tasks is very broad so the total cost of IPAM operations is substantial. If an IPAM system can help automate tasks and reduce costs, particularly in the high expense areas of IP address assignment, IP inventory assurance, auditing and reporting in our example scenario, it may prove worthy as we'll investigate next. The following table summarizes the cost areas described so far.

We've grouped our IP management tasks into five task groups: Block Moves/ Adds/Changes, Subnet Moves/Adds/Changes, IP Address Moves/Adds/Changes, Management Functions, and Outage Recovery. For each function listed, the pair of columns listed under *Cost By Task* indicates the annual cost of each task and its relative cost contribution as a percentage of total cost. For example, IP Address Assignments cost $168 750 annually, representing 14.9% of the total IP management costs.

The next pair of columns highlights cost and cost contribution *By Task Group*. Thus, the *Subnet Moves/Adds/Changes* group totals $13 843 annually, which is comprised of the sum of Subnet Allocation, Subnet Deletion, and Subnet Changes tasks. Viewing your costs in this manner provides immediate insight into what IPAM functions are candidates for the largest cost reductions. It's interesting to note that in our scenario, the traditional IP management functional costs for block, subnet, and IP address moves, adds and changes amounts to around one-third of total IPAM costs at 29.5%. Management functions come in just over one-third at 36.7% of the total, and outages and security comprise the other third at 33.8% of costs.

To reduce these overall costs, we should seek an IPAM solution that provides strong IPAM features particularly IP address assignment, overall management functions with strong inventory assurance, and outage and security incident reduction. In ranking individual tasks by cost, these six-figure tasks account for over half of the total cost. Thus, computing your costs can help prioritize feature sets that can bring the greatest cost reduction in your environment.

Savings with IPAM Deployment

Now that we've enumerated the major IPAM tasks with our example set of costs, let's consider the upside of the business case as how much we can reduce these

Table 15.16   IPAM costs basis summary.

IPAM function	By task		By task group	
	Annual cost	% of total cost	Annual cost	% of total cost
Block moves/adds/changes			$14,185	1.3%
Block allocation	$12,540	1.1%		
Block deletion	$145	0.0%		
Block changes	$1,500	0.1%		
Subnet moves/adds/changes			$13,843	1.2%
Subnet allocation	$7,790	0.7%		
Subnet deletion	$1,995	0.2%		
Subnet changes	$4,058	0.4%		
IP address moves/adds/changes			$305,155	27.0%
IP address assignments	$168,750	14.9%		
IP address deletes	$56,250	5.0%		
IP address changes	$80,155	7.1%		
Management function costs			$414,533	36.7%
Inventory assurance	$202,752	17.9%		
Capacity management	$75,720	6.7%		
Auditing and reporting	$96,271	8.5%		
Server upgrades	$37,710	3.3%		
System administration	$2,080	0.2%		
Outage recovery costs			$382,149	33.8%
Configuration errors	$175,073			
Pool depletions	$0	15.5%		
Security incidents	$141,188	0.0%		
Server outages	$65,888	12.5%		
Total IPAM costs	**$1,129,865**	100.0%	**$1,129,865**	100.0%

costs. In general, these costs will not be completely eliminated, as implementing an IPAM tool will not necessarily drive these costs to zero. Some level of oversight, control and therefore manual effort will still likely be required, though the objective is to minimize this effort, especially for your high cost functions.

The interesting though somewhat speculative part of the business case is determining how much lingering manual effort will be required on an ongoing basis. Depending on the level of automation of the IPAM tool you may be considering, the average time per resource can be vastly diminished by 30–80%. For modest networks, a minimal investment in a point solution may be warranted to reduce 40% of key expense areas for a modest investment. On the other hand, for larger networks, a more integrated, multi-function system may be worth the investment to reduce manual expenses by 75% or more.

If you can evaluate a vendor's product, you can measure the relative time savings to perform certain tasks. Table 15.17 illustrates a post-IPAM implementation cost for the IP address assignment function for example. Contrast Table 15.17 with Table 15.7, which illustrates the analogous pre-IPAM implementation costs, $168 750 per year without IPAM and $131 250 with IPAM. Use of an IPAM system can trim 22% of the cost of assigning IP addresses in this case, where the key savings are realized in the automated update of DHCP and DNS servers. It's likely that the "identify available IP address" and "verification" tasks could be reduced further given most modern solutions enable one-click allocation of the address without researching, but we'll leave this unchanged to be conservative. You should consider the new time requirement and associated cost in a post-IPAM environment for each of the tables described earlier.

Armed with your priority list of features, evaluate various tools' strengths and weaknesses relative to automating your high-cost functions. Some IPAM systems for example can provide a level of automation with the IP address assignment task. Let's assume that a tool under evaluation enables automated DHCP and DNS configuration based on parameters entered during address assignment. The task still involves identifying an available IP address, but once selected, the tool can create a corresponding DNS record update.

Implementation of this system would eliminate the need for Server Operations to update DNS for manually configured devices. This saves us $11 250 per this corresponding row in Table 15.7. If the tool also automates Manual DHCP entry in DHCP servers, this automation can save an additional $3750. We've already contributed $15 000 to cost savings!

In our case, saving $15 000 would amount to a 1.3% cost savings, but this is only the first of the many IP management tasks that should be analyzed. The other tasks we discussed in this chapter should be considered with respect to savings that could be realized based on automation provided by the IPAM system in question.

Be diligent in considering every task. Certain tasks, such as system administration, may actually cost more after implementing an IPAM solution. Add in the additional administration staff costs including the annual support costs from the vendor. Just as we arrived at $1 129 865 as our base cost, consider each

Table 15.17 Post IPAM implementation IP address assignment cost analysis.

IP address assignment	Resource type	Average staff-time required (hours)	Resource hourly cost	Cost per event	Events per year	Annualized cost
Identify available IP address	Engineering	0.05	$50	$3	15,000	$37,500
Update device configuration in DHCP server (M-DHCP)	Server Ops	0.00	$40	$0	3,750	$0
Static address assignment – email to owner then manual config	Engineering	0.10	$50	$5	11,250	$56,250
Update DNS for manually configured IP addresses	Server Ops	0.00	$40	$0	11,250	$0
Address assignment verification	Net Ops	0.05	$50	$3	15,000	$37,500
Total annual IP address assignment costs using IPAM						**$131,250**

task with the new system in mind, and ideally in hand. A hands-on evaluation can facilitate a more accurate estimate of how the system would integrate with and automate related tasks. The Table 15.18 summarizes our analysis of IPAM "System A" in terms of current method costs, shown under the *Current Annual Costs* column against *Annual Costs* when using System A and the corresponding *Savings.*

Notice that system administration costs jump due to additional administrative tasks as well as annual support and training costs that are required with the system. Nevertheless, the total net savings if System A is deployed is estimated to be about $400k. This represents the annual savings of 35% should we invest in System A.

Business Case Expenses

As we just calculated our savings with IPAM System A, we also derived our residual annual expenses required to continue performing IPAM tasks with the new system in place. Next consider the investment required to implement System A, including licensing, hardware, and implementation and training costs. Any IPAM vendor you consider will provide you a price quote upon request for these expense items. Be sure to clarify whether new feature upgrades are included with support or cost an additional fee. This additional cost, if any, needs to be added to the expense side of the equation. As mentioned above, each tool is quite different in terms of feature set, so be sure to align the income (savings) side of the equation with the cost and features provided by the tool you're comparing on the expense side. After all, while using spreadsheets and manual DNS and DHCP configuration costs nothing in capital, the staffing costs to support required IP management tasks total over $1.1 million!

Continuing with our example, we determined we could reduce our net IP management task costs by $400k to $730k annually by deploying System A. Let's assume System A costs about $150k, with implementation costs of $40k. Recall that we already accounted for the annual support costs for System A shown by the increased system administration costs per Table 15.18. Our first-year investment then amounts to $190k. The next step is to calculate the return on this investment.

Netting it Out: Business Case Results

Now let's calculate the return on the $190k investment. In year 1, our return is double our investment, yielding a payback within six months. The payback period

Table 15.18 Example IPAM savings analysis.

IPAM function	Current annual costs	Costs with IPAM system A	
		Annual costs	Savings
Block moves/adds/changes			
Block allocation	$12,540	$9,400	$3,140
Block deletion	$145	$145	$0
Block changes	$1,500	$637	$864
Subnet moves/adds/changes			
Subnet allocation	$7,790	$4,104	$3,686
Subnet deletion	$1,995	$1,995	$0
Subnet changes	$4,058	$1,726	$2,333
IP address moves/adds/changes			
IP address assignment	$168,750	$131,250	$37,500
IP address deletes	$56,250	$56,250	$0
IP address changes	$80,155	$59,531	$20,625
Management function costs			
Inventory assurance	$202,752	$78,992	$123,760
Capacity management	$75,720	$42,024	$33,696
Auditing and reporting	$96,271	$59,000	$37.271
Server upgrades	$37,710	$37,710	$0
System administration	$2,080	$79,160	($77,080)
Outage recovery costs			
Configuration errors	$175,073	$34,179	$140,894
Pool depletions	$0	$0	$0
Security incidents	$141,188	$69,281	$71,906
Server outages	$65,888	$64,736	$1,152
Total IPAM costs	**$1,129,865**	**$730,119**	**$399,746**

is calculated by dividing our investment into our cash flow per unit time. For example, our investment ($190k) divided by savings ($400k/yr) results in a payback of less than half a year, as shown in the following equation.

$$\text{Payback Period} = \frac{\text{Investment}}{\text{Savings per unit time}} = \frac{\$190\,000}{\left(\dfrac{\$399\,746}{12}\right)\text{per month}} = 5.7\,\text{months}$$

This relatively rapid payback may make this investment decision quite simple. The other metric to consider is of course the ROI value itself, which is simply the cumulative savings over a given time span, typically three years, less the initial investment, divided by the investment amount.

$$\text{ROI} = \frac{\text{Savings} - \text{Investment}}{\text{Investment}} = \frac{(\$399\,746 \times 3 - \$190\,000)}{\$190\,000} = 5.31 \times 100\% = 531\%$$

Our three-year savings total nearly $1.2 million (one-year ROI is 110%). The net return is derived by subtracting the initial investment, $1.2 million − $190k = $1.0 million. This net return, divided by our $190k investment yields 531%. Many organizations consider the time value of money and apply a discount rate to account for tomorrow's dollars being worth less than todays. Using a 15% rate, our three-year ROI is 438%. Different organizations have different investment criteria, so be cognizant of your standard policies for decision making.

Conclusion

A rigorous business case analysis can help you financially justify investment in an IPAM product. In our hypothetical example, IPAM Worldwide can achieve a three-year ROI of over 500% by deploying an IPAM system. Quantifying your expenses under your current IPAM methodology using these techniques can also help you identify high cost areas. Knowledge of your high-cost functions enables you to focus your search for an IPAM solution to one that can lower the cost of these functions, thereby maximizing your return on IPAM system investment.

16

IPAM Evolution/Trends

In this chapter, we'll review current technology trends that are in various stages of maturity with respect to how IPAM affects or can be affected by each.

Security Advancements

With ever escalating frequency of infiltration attempts and variety of attack vectors, enterprises must constantly remain vigilant and proactive in developing monitoring and detection solutions. As we've discussed in prior chapters, IPAM fulfills a major role within your overall network security strategy, from tracking IP inventory to address space allocation methods, to the use of network access controls, and to DNS security. As the sophistication of attacks continues to rise, defensive strategies likewise evolve in an attempt to keep pace if not outpace exploitation of network vulnerabilities.

The concept of zero trust networks, originally posited by Forrester Research a decade ago, is rising in prominence as a fundamental network security approach [122]. As the name implies, zero trust networks begin with the assumption that no user or device is implicitly trusted. Contrast this with the castle-and-moat philosophy where users and devices within a network were implicitly trusted and defenses focused on detecting and repelling attacks originating externally to the network. Users' demand for access to networks from a growing diversity of computing devices with high mobility has raised your network's vulnerability to attacks originating within the network, maliciously or otherwise.

Implementing zero trust requires the identification of your most critical or sensitive data and enveloping it within a *protect sector*, like a micro-trust sector. Having identified your most important data, map how that data flows within and through your network to users, administrators, or other systems. This step

IP Address Management, Second Edition. Michael Dooley and Timothy Rooney.
© 2021 The Institute of Electrical and Electronics Engineers, Inc.
Published 2021 by John Wiley & Sons, Inc.

facilitates a tight scoping on the permissibility of such data across your network into micro-perimeters, comprised of the data sources, destinations, and network paths.

Admittance of users within the micro-perimeter requires employment of the principles of user authentication, device authorization, and minimal privilege access to allow users with approved devices to access only portions of the data required for their respective responsibilities. After you've implemented your micro-perimeters within your network via these admittance strategies as well as network access and flow controls, continual monitoring and analysis of data flows enables detection of anomalies as well as attempted or successful perimeter violations to initiate response and recovery actions. Automating the detection, characterization, and deterministic actions based on certain events is also recommended to reduce the window of attack exposure and to quickly remediate infringements and to shore up defenses.

IPAM serves a key role in zero trust networks deployment. Recall how your address plan and allocation strategy facilitates implementation of address-based security policies. Once you've defined your critical data and general network flows, you'll need to define its micro-perimeter, which would largely entail constraining what network endpoints (IP subnets or individual IP addresses) can access repositories housing the data by IP address and perhaps even defining access lists on the path along the way between them. An IPAM system affords quick and easy access to such information by inventorying IP address-to-host associations.

In terms of user authentication and device authorization, we discussed the premise of NAC systems in Chapter 11. However, the boolean allow/deny all-or-nothing outcome of NAC systems renders too coarse a disposition. Zero trust requires authentication and authorization of a given user and device respectively to not only access the network at large but also to access a particular set of data on a destination device. As such NAC systems could provide a first layer coarse assessment, but a finer grained modern solution obviates the need for NAC. Nevertheless, DHCP-initiated, autoconfigured, and cloud system IP address assignments must be tracked to detect devices present on the network with respect to authorized devices. Thus, many zero trust authentication solutions incorporate not only 802.1X and certificate-based authentication but various forms of discovery to identify potential unauthenticated devices and users.

Not surprisingly, DNS also plays a key role within zero trust networks. As the first step in establishing an IP connection, DNS can be configured to respond differently to the same query from different resolvers using DNS views, a feature which enables a DNS server to respond with differing answers based on certain criteria including query source IP address. For example, two views for an internal zone can be established, one which includes resolution to a server housing sensitive data and other that does not resolve the corresponding domain name. Views define match criteria to view a particular version of a zone via address match lists.

When a device becomes authorized, its corresponding IP address can be added to the address match list corresponding to the view that resolves the destination hosting the sensitive data. The only hitch is that the DNS configuration typically needs to be reloaded. You could alternatively soften the per host authorization access to such DNS resolutions and perhaps just match on addresses within a given subnet or set of addresses if authorized devices are known *a priori* to emanate from a given address pool or set of subnets and pools. A device would be assigned an address from such a pool upon authorization. This would enable static definition of your view statements though require integrated DHCP address assignment based on external inputs (device authorization).

Intent-Based Networking

The philosophy of intent-based networking entails enabling your business to express goals and objectives (i.e. intent) which are applied to your network as policies. For example, a business goal may be to provide high quality voice communications on 99% of calls over the network. This goal is translated into a set of network policies to reduce network latency for VoIP sessions to less than 80 ms 99% of the time. Intent-based networking then activates the policies through orchestration across various physical and virtual network components, e.g. routers, switches, network interface units, etc. as depicted in Figure 16.1. Recall that an IP address block allocation strategy that assigns VoIP space higher within the layers of allocation would simplify implementation of VoIP traffic-specific treatment to the extent that such treatment is keyed on IP addresses.

The Activation function of intent-based networking may involve orchestration of elastic capacity as needed to maintain the policy objectives. This could involve instantiation of virtual routers and switches to supplement capacity during peak calling times, and relinquishing such virtualized network functions as demand eases. Meanwhile, the network performance must be measured to verify successful policy implementation. This typically involves some form of machine learning systems which analyze call packet flows over time to predict rising demand before it overflows capacity. Such feedback would flow back to the policy level to enable its adaptation to predicted network conditions in order to expand capacity before limits are reached.

As the machine learning Assurance component continues to analyze VoIP traffic, it may predict a downturn in capacity needs and feed this back to the policy stage, which in turn can ultimately reduce elastic capacity based on current and

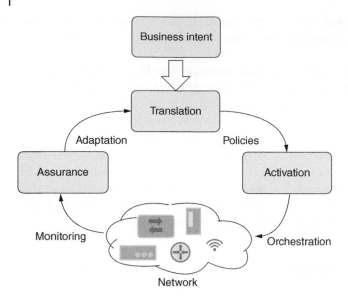

Figure 16.1   Intent-based networking concept.

predicted traffic. Of course, the increasing of capacity can lead and hopefully out-pace the demand based on predictions while the reducing of capacity must trail actual demand, e.g. based on actual usage and less so on predictions such that current traffic is not underserved even as it is diminishing in volume.

This simple example demonstrates the application of intent-based network on VoIP performance but countless other intentions may be expressed and implemented. IPAM is likely required at least in part for most "intents" as illustrated in the VoIP case, though one could enact IPAM "intents" as well such as resolving DNS queries within 10 ms 99% of the time for example. Intent based networking is but one application of machine learning to IP networking. Its application to security and other network management functions is continually expanding.

Artificial Intelligence Applied to IPAM

Artificial intelligence (AI) offers a growing expanse of IPAM benefits for automating the analysis of large amounts of data and for predicting outcomes based on data inputs. Machine learning (ML) is a discipline within the AI field that features a classification model that adapts, or learns, based on the quality of its outputs or "decisions." Dispositions are fed back through the model to enable adjustments to model parameters. Many machine learning models seek to emulate the human brain through the formation of a network of interconnected nodes, much like the synapses in our brains. These artificial neural networks (ANNs) process various inputs to arrive at a disposition and can feed back results to adjust node parameter weightings to modulate the "thought process" so to speak.

In their simplest forms, ANNs may comprise an input "layer" or set of nodes to which input data is fed. The input layer performs a given transformation of the input data and passes the output to another layer of nodes, each of which may apply weights to its respective input values received from the input layer. This layer applies a transform to the input and passes the output in the form of a quantity that can be interpreted based on decision criteria. While all ANN models comprise such an input layer and an output layer, often additional layers are modeled between the input and output layers, these "hidden layers" as illustrated in Figure 16.2, comprise nodes which likewise perform transforms on input parameters, apply weighting and sometimes even output discriminators.

Supervised ML utilizes a training data set to train the model by feeding data into the model while evaluating the accuracy of each machine outcome. Back propagation is the mechanism to feedback estimated outcomes and actual values in order to adjust model parameters. As more training data is processed through the model, it automatically adjusts due to back propagation until ultimately the resultant model is able to predict outcomes with reasonable accuracy. The trained model may then be deployed to process actual inputs to detect or predict relevant outcomes.

Besides supervised ML, other major ML approaches which do not train on data include unsupervised learning which lends itself to cluster analysis and can facilitate pattern recognition and reinforcement learning, which also does not train and attempts to evolve the model to maximize a given "cumulative reward."

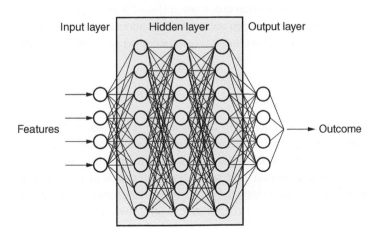

Figure 16.2 Artificial neural network model.

While development of accurate ML models currently requires considerable expertise and effort, once defined, each model must be refreshed with current data characteristics in order to adapt. Model update frequency will depend on the variability of the data you're analyzing. Despite the development and maintenance effort, ML promises to automate detection and prediction of outcomes based on data inputs, which can provide early warning of security events, capacity shortages, traffic anomalies, and other events that may require action prior to the occurrence of an undesirable event. The following are examples of where ML can be applied to managing your IP address space.

IP Address Capacity Management

Linear regression analysis is itself a ML model, which can be applied to analysis of DHCP address pool capacity. In analyzing active leases with respect to pool capacity over time, regression of such data points can be extended in time to predict potential pool exhaustion. This type of model can be applied to subnets in general, particularly those deployed within a cloud service, where instantiation of virtualized network functions can quickly exhaust deployed IP addresses.

Active address monitoring for address pools and subnets along with respective capacities serve as input to the model which can process history data to refine exhaustion predictions, and inform administrators proactively. If your IPAM system supports an API trigger based on such a detected event as a pending pool or subnet exhaustion, it can trigger the automated expansion of capacity by modify pool sizes, allocating additional pools, and/or allocating a subnet to supplement IP address capacity. Conversely, a declining trend could trigger the freeing up of pool space or subnets to return IP space to the allocation pool for future needs. As with intent-based networking, allocation automation should lead capacity predictions such that it is available when needed and trail on de-allocation, freeing up of capacity on after the pool or subnet is completely unoccupied so as not to disrupt active IP sessions.

DNS Query and Response Analytics

Many organizations have little visibility to DNS queries, responses, and general trends in DNS traffic. Unfortunately, one cannot improve or even secure what one cannot see. The sheer volume of DNS transactions traversing your network is likely very large and thereby intimidating to analyze. But this is just the sort of "big data" analytics that ML can provide to "pre-process" voluminous DNS query data and extract key trends in query performance, chatty resolvers, top queried domains, and even illicit queries such as those destined for malware command and control centers.

Attaining such a diverse set of outcomes may require different models for each. Query volume trending could perhaps employ a linear regression model, while detecting chatty resolvers and top queried domains may rely on a clustering model, and malware query detection may necessitate a deep (more than one hidden layer) learning model analyzing several features (i.e. model inputs) beyond raw query data.

DNS Malware Detection

Detecting a DNS query destined for a malware command and control center is very challenging, and numerous approaches are possible. The ultimate goal is to identify a malware query during the resolution process in order to block or perform other actions prior to the response being sent to the resolver of the infected host. Response policy zones (RPZs) can be used for this very purpose: to apply response policies on a resolution based on various attributes of the query and/or response.

We discussed RPZs, also known as DNS firewalling, in Chapter 11. RPZs provide an effective means of manipulating DNS responses prior to delivery to the querying resolver. However, the corresponding trigger must be provisioned in advance of the query. Should a new form of malware arise, which is highly likely, given that 350 000 new malicious programs and potentially unwanted applications are registered every day by the AV-Test Institute [123], it will likely utilize a unique domain name (that has not yet been seen), and it could be registered on DNS servers that fall outside of suspicious server names or IP addresses configured within RPZ policies. Such a query and response will likely bypass pre-defined RPZ filters.

In order to detect a malware-initiated DNS transaction during the resolution process, the DNS server must analyze the query, ideally using a ML model while the resolution ensues in parallel. In addition, the model should be derived from a large sample set, ideally from across the Internet to appropriate large data sets required for model generation, then deployed to recursive servers on or near customer premises. Centralized model derivation would also facilitate processing of additional features such as domain age, resolving name server names, addresses, and corresponding address autonomous system number and approximate geolocation.

Network Address Intrusions

Analytics focused on anomaly detection could prove helpful in detecting "unusual" IP address occupancy on a given subnet within the enterprise network or cloud. Analysis of "normal" IP address occupancy serving as a baseline enables rapid detection of anything that diverges from it. While such IP assignments may or may not prove malicious or erroneous in any way, rapid notification of such an event could be an initial indicator of trouble.

A first step to consider upon receiving such an indication would entail identifying any new yet unseen device, e.g. if viewing MAC address history. One can then quickly dismiss the new device as the mobile of a visiting professional or as something requiring deeper investigation.

IPAM Administration Activity Analysis

Auditing the activities of IPAM administrators, whether manual or automated, is a general security practice to assure adherence to system policies and procedures and to confirm administrator privileges are not overstepped. Manually poring through administrator logs for even modest sized organizations may be onerous. Such a task is well suited for application of ML to identify unusual activity and to raise a flag upon occurrence for further investigation. Illicit activities can result from malice or ignorance, but either cause must be remedied to assure system integrity.

AI Summary

ML technology is currently used in some IPAM systems to perform some of the tasks discussed in this section and promises to continue to support improved responsiveness and decision-making. Neural networking research continues to evolve toward more closely modeling human brain operation, which in turn promises more efficient use of computing resources. This branch of research, collectively referred to as *neuromorphic computing*, seeks to model biological neurons as complex dynamic systems whose intercommunications feature impulses or "spikes." Information is conveyed between nodes within such spiking neural networks (SNNs) by virtue of inter-impulse timing intervals and not weighted node parameter values. As neural network technology evolves, it will certainly become more deeply ingrained into our networks, our devices, and our lives.

Edge Computing

The concept of edge computing distributes AI from a centralized to a distributed (i.e. closer to the network edge) model. Since development of robust ML models requires large data sets, centralization of model development makes sense. On the other hand, exercise of the model with actual data to classify or predict may best

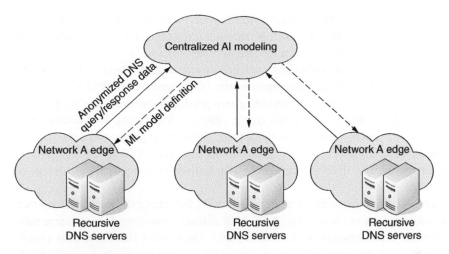

Figure 16.3 DNS edge computing example.

be performed locally, closer to the point where model output may play a role in local processing.

For example, in the malware detection scenario discussed earlier in this chapter, the centralized formulation of the DNS ML model implies not only a requisite large data set but also one drawn from a diverse set of resolvers. Such diversity is important in presenting to the model a more representative set of query information to process and "learn" from. The distribution of the ML model to distributed DNS servers would then enable faster application of query analytics, based on a broader query set than the server would see in isolation. This model of DNS edge computing is illustrated in Figure 16.3.

The ultimate goal is to process the query through the ML model within the window of DNS resolution time, serving as a real-time response policy for the query and response, to enable pass-through or to otherwise alter the response. This approach leverages an ML model honed by large sets of query data, larger and more diverse than any one recursive server may observe, presumably available within a cloud-based centralized model. The model's logic and parameters would be distributed to recursive DNS servers, closer to actual DNS query sources for more rapid application of the model's logic during the resolution process.

Identifier/Locator Networking

Several protocols have been specified within Internet standards and research bodies seeking an architecture evolution offering improved Internet scalability.

These protocols seek to separate the location of a node from the identification of the node itself, unlike the current Internet Protocol which overloads the IP address with both network location and host identifier information. These protocols were developed within the Internet Research Task Force (IRTF), which serves as the research and development arm of the Internet Activities Board. The IRTF Host Identity Protocol working group produced the host identity protocol (HIP) and the Routing Research Group (RRG) produced the identifier/locator networking protocol (ILNP). Both of these protocols separate the network and host portions of "addressability" though both rely on DNS for resolution of these components. The IRTF working groups for both of these approaches have been concluded.

The location/identifier separation protocol (LISP) seeks similar objectives as a developing protocol within the IETF. LISP defines a two-tiered architecture with a control plane separate from the data plane. The control plane performs a mapping function between endpoint identifiers (EIDs) and routing locators (RLOCs). RLOCs identify the node location while EIDs identify the connection endpoint within the specified RLOC domain. An end device uses DNS as it does normally to resolve the desired destination, which corresponds to its EID.

When the device sends its data to its LISP-enabled gateway router, the router performs a mapping look up to identify the RLOC serving the EID corresponding to the destination IP address; the router then encapsulates the IP packet with a LISP header which itself includes an IP header containing the router's RLOC as the source address and the resolved destination RLOC as the destination. In this manner, LISP "routers" tunnel packets to intended destinations in a manner that seeks to improve inter-domain routing scalability. LISP is positioned as an evolutionary protocol from the current IP-centric Internet toward a purely information centric Internet, which serves as the next evolutionary phase.

Information Centric Networking

Information centric network (ICN) is a proposed framework for further evolving the Internet from the current host-centric model, e.g. *on what server is the information I desire?* to one of information or content centricity where expressions of interest by content name lead to access to such content directly. This framework requires tracking of the availability of content and a forwarding information base within each "router" which directs interest packets to the "next hop" toward the content source or caches thereof. Speaking of which, the architecture features caching of content along the way from the source to the requestor, facilitating access by distributing the content to better handle multiple requests, work around network outages, or minimize excessive latency.

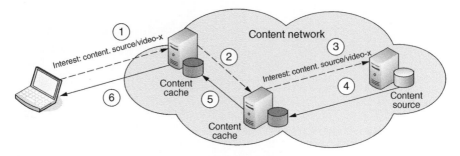

Figure 16.4 Information centric networking concept.

This process is illustrated in Figure 16.4. A user seeking to view video content on the left of the figure issues an Interest packet indicating the desired content, "video-x" in this case from a given content source. As the Interest packet proceeds toward the content source thanks to forwarding information bases within interconnected ICN "routers," each router tracks the request and awaits a reply. Upon receiving the notification of interest for the given content and perhaps after authentication and authorization, the content source sends the content back toward the originator. Along the path back, each "router" caches the content such that if another user requests the same content within a given time to live, the router may serve it directly without needing to re-query the content source.

Network protocols that route by content name instead of IP addresses would certainly seem to obviate the need for IPAM systems and DNS in particular. Without a need to locate a host to which to direct a request for content, there's no need for DNS. It's not clear to us exactly how management tasks such as configuration and monitoring of content servers would be performed, but it would seem some sort of IP addressing for host management would still be required.

Like IPv6 and DNSSEC, ICN could take years if not decades to reach critical mass deployment once fully specified. While uptake for streaming type content services should be rapid with ever increasing bandwidth offered by broadband and 5G in particular, other "legacy" client/server style applications could see less motivation to migrate to the new addressing and routing scheme.

Part V

IPAM Reference

The final part of this book provides a technical reference for each IPAM component: IP addressing, DHCP, and DNS. Protocol details with associated parameters are summarized along with a categorized RFC reference.

17

IP Addressing Reference

IP Version 4

The IPv4 Header

The IP layer within the TCP/IP suite adds an IP header to the data it receives from the TCP or UDP transport layer. This IP header is analyzed by routers along the path to the final destination to ultimately deliver each IP packet to its final destination, identified by the destination IP address in the header. RFC 791 defined the IP address structure as consisting of 32 bits comprised of a network number followed by a local address. The address is conveyed in the header of every IP packet. Figure 17.1 illustrates the fields of the IP header. Every IP packet contains an IP header, followed by the data contents within the packet, including higher layer protocol control information.

Version – The Internet protocol version, 4 in this case.

Header length – (Internet header length, IHL) – Length of the IP header in 32-bit units called "words." For example, the minimum header length is 5, highlighted in Figure 17.1, as the lightly shaded fields, which consists of 5 words × 32 bits/word = 160 bits.

Type of service – Parameters related to the packet's quality of service (QoS). Initially defined as ToS (Type of Service), this field consisted of a 3-bit precedence field to enable specification of the relative importance of a particular packet, and another three bits to request low delay, high throughput, or high reliability respectively.

The original ToS field has been redefined via RFC 2474 [124] as the differentiated services or DS field. The DS field provides a 6-bit codepoint (DSCP – differentiated services codepoint) field with the two remaining bits unused. The codepoint maps

IP Address Management, Second Edition. Michael Dooley and Timothy Rooney.
© 2021 The Institute of Electrical and Electronics Engineers, Inc.
Published 2021 by John Wiley & Sons, Inc.

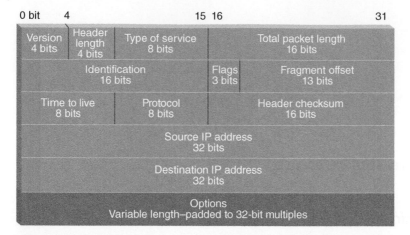

Figure 17.1   IPv4 header fields. Source: Modified from RFC 760 [3].

to a pre-defined service which in turn is associated with a level of service provided by the network. As new codepoints are defined with respective services treatment by the Internet authorities, IP routers can apply the routing treatment corresponding to the defined codepoint to apply higher priority handling for latency-sensitive applications for example.

Total length – Length of the entire IP packet in bytes (octets).

Identification – Value assigned to each packet by the sender to facilitate reassembly of packet fragments at the receiving end.

Flags – This 3-bit field is defined as follows:

- Bit 0 – reserved and must be 0
- Bit 1 – don't fragment – indicates that this packet should not be fragmented
- Bit 2 – more fragments – indicates this packet is a fragment, though this is not the last fragment

Fragment offset – Identifies the location of this fragment relative to the beginning of the original packet in units of 64-bit "double-words."

Time to live (TTL) – A counter decremented upon each routing hop; once the TTL reaches zero, the packet is discarded. This parameter prevents packets from aimlessly circulating on the Internet forever.

Protocol – The upper layer protocol that shall receive this packet after IP processing, e.g. TCP or UDP.

Header checksum – A checksum value calculated over the header bits to verify that the header is not corrupted.

Source IP address – The IP address of the sender of this packet.

Destination IP address – The IP address of the intended recipient of this packet.

Options – Optional field containing zero or more optional parameters which enable routing control (source routing), diagnostics (trace route, MTU discovery), and more.

IP Version 6

The IPv6 Header

The IPv6 header layout is shown in Figure 17.2. While the size of both the source and destination IP address fields quadrupled, the overall IP header size only doubled. The fields in the IPv6 header are as follows:

Version – The Internet protocol version, 6 in this case.

Traffic class – This field is analogous to the IPv4 ToS/DS header field and indicates the type or priority of traffic in order to request routing treatment.

Flow label – Identifies the "flow" of traffic between a source and destination to which this packet belongs as set by the source. This is intended to enable

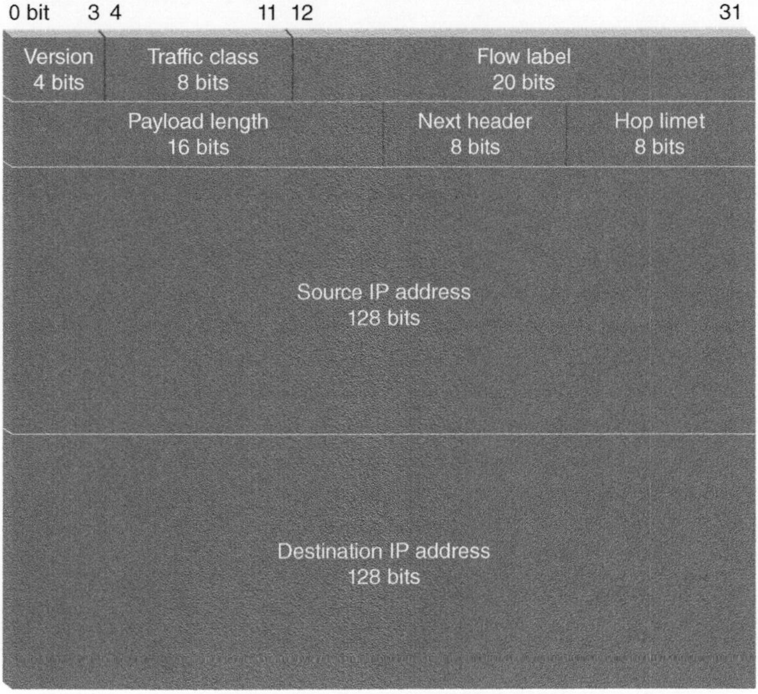

Figure 17.2 IPv6 header. Source: Based on RFC 8200 [264].

efficient and consistent routing treatment for packets within a given communications session, such as those within a real time transmission vs. a best-effort data transmission.

Payload length – Indicates the length of the IPv6 payload, that is the portion of the packet after the base IPv6 header, in octets. Extension headers, if included, are considered part of the payload and are counted within this length parameter.

Next header – This field indicates the type of header that follows this IP header. This may be an upper layer protocol header (e.g. TCP, ICMPv6, etc.) or an extension header. The extension header concept enables specification of source routing, fragmentation, options, and other parameters associated with the packet only when they are necessary, not as overhead on all packets as in IPv4.

Hop limit – Analogous to the IPv4 TTL field, this field specifies the number of hops over which this packet may traverse before being discarded. Each router decrements the value of this header field upon forwarding of the packet.

Source IP address – The IPv6 address of the sender of this packet

Destination IP address – The IPv6 address of the intended recipient(s) of this packet

IPv6 Multicast Addressing

Multicast addresses identify a group of interfaces typically on different nodes. Think of multicast addresses as a scoped broadcast. All multicast group members share the same group ID and hence all members will accept packets destined for the multicast group. An interface may have multiple multicast addresses; i.e. it may belong to multiple multicast groups. The basic format of IPv6 multicast addresses is illustrated in Figure 17.3.

The prefix ff00::/8 identifies a multicast address. The next field is a 4-bit field called "Flags." The format of the multicast address is dependent on the value of the Flags field. The Scope (also affectionately referred to as "scop") field indicates the breadth of the multicast scope, whether per node, link, global, or other scope values defined below. The value of the flags and scope fields can fortunately be easily discerned by looking at the address as the third and fourth hex digit within the address respectively as we'll summarize a bit later.

Figure 17.3 Multicast address format. Source: Based on RFC 4291 [11].

Flags

The Flags field is comprised of four bits, which we'll discuss starting from right to left [11, 125]:

X	R	P	T

- The **T** bit indicates whether the multicast address is of transient nature or is a well-known address assigned by IANA. The T bit is defined as follows.
  - ○ T = 0 – this is an IANA-assigned well-known multicast address. In this case, the 112-bit multicast address is a 112-bit Group ID field (Figure 17.4): IANA has assigned numerous Group IDs thus far.[1] For example, Group ID = 1 means all nodes within the associated scope (defined by the Scope field), Group ID = 2 refers to all routers within the scope, etc. The scope field is defined below, but example well-known multicast addresses are:
    - ff01::1 = all nodes on this link
    - ff02::2 = all routers on this link
    - ff05::1 = all nodes on this site
    - ff05::2 = all routers on this site
    - ff0e::2 = all routers on the Internet
  - ○ T = 1 – this is a temporarily assigned or transient multicast address. This can be an address assigned for a specific multicast session or application. An example might be ff12::3:f:10.
- The **P** bit indicates whether the multicast address is comprised partly of a corresponding unicast network prefix or not. The P bit is defined[2] as follows:
  - ○ P = 0 – this multicast address *is not* assigned based on the network prefix. The format of a multicast packet with P = 0 is as described above (i.e. when T = 0), with the 112-bit Group ID field.
  - ○ P = 1 – this multicast address *is* assigned based on the network prefix of the unicast subnet address "owning" the multicast address allocation. This enables allocation of multicast space associated with allocated unicast space for simpler administration. If P = 1, the T bit must also be set to 1. The corresponding format of a multicast packet is as shown in Figure 17.5.

    When P = 1, the Flags field is interpreted as "flag field 1," followed by the Scope field and in turn by a 4-bit "flag field 2" and by 4 zero bits (Reserved), an 8-bit prefix length field, 64-bit Network Prefix field, and a 32-bit Group ID field. The prefix length field represents the prefix length

---

1 Please refer to http://www.iana.org/assignments/ipv6-multicast-addresses for the latest assignments.
2 The definition of the P bit is documented in RFC 3306 [265].

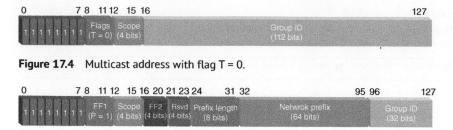

Figure 17.4   Multicast address with flag T = 0.

Figure 17.5   Multicast address with flag P = 1.

of the associated unicast network address. The Network Prefix field contains the corresponding unicast network prefix, while the Group ID is the associated multicast group ID.

For example, if a unicast address of 2001:db8:b7::/48 is allocated to a subnet, a corresponding unicast-based multicast address would be of the form: ff3*s*:0030:2001:db8:b7::g, where

- ff = multicast prefix
- 3 = $[0011]_2$, i.e. X = 0, R = 0, P = 1 and T = 1
- *s* = a valid scope as we'll define in the next section
- 00 = reserved bits
- 30 = prefix length in hex = [0011 0000]2 = 48 in decimal, the prefix length in our example
- 2001:db8:b7:0 = 2001:0db8:00b7:0000 = 48 bit network prefix in the 64-bit Network Prefix field.
- and *g* = a 32-bit Group ID.

A special case of this format occurs with P = T = 1 when the prefix length field = ff and $s \leq 2$. In this case, instead of the Network Prefix field consisting of the unicast network address, this field will be comprised of the Interface ID of the respective interface. The Interface ID used must have passed the duplicate address detection process, which is discussed later in this chapter, to assure its uniqueness. In this special case, the scope field must be 0, 1, or 2, meaning of interface-local or of link-local scope. This *link-scoped multicast address* format is defined as an extension of the IPv6 addressing architecture via RFC 4489 [126].

- The **R** bit within the Flags field enables specification of a multicast rendezvous point (RP) which enables multicast group would-be subscribers to link in temporarily prior to joining the group permanently. If the R bit is set to 1, the P and T bits must also be set to 1. When R = 1, the multicast address is based on a unicast prefix, but the RP Interface ID is also specified. The format of the

```
0              7 8  11 12  15 16 19 20 23 24      31 32                    95 96          127
┌─┬─┬─┬─┬─┬─┬─┬─┬────────┬──────┬─────┬─────┬──────────┬─────────────────────┬────────────┐
│1│1│1│1│1│1│1│1│ Flags  │Scope │Rsvd │RIID │Prefix    │  Netwrok prefix     │ Group ID   │
│ │ │ │ │ │ │ │ │(R = 1) │(4bits)│(0s)│(4bits)│length  │    (64 bits)        │ (32 bits)  │
│ │ │ │ │ │ │ │ │        │      │(4bits)│    │(8 bits)  │                     │            │
└─┴─┴─┴─┴─┴─┴─┴─┴────────┴──────┴─────┴─────┴──────────┴─────────────────────┴────────────┘
```

Figure 17.6 Multicast address with flag R = 1.

multicast address when R = 1 is identical to the case when R = 0 and P = 1 with the exception that the Reserved field is split into a 4-bit Reserved field and a 4-bit Rendezvous Point Interface ID (RIID) field is portrayed in Figure 17.6.

   o The IP address of the RP is identified by concatenating the Network Prefix of corresponding prefix length with the value of the RIID field. For example if an RP on the [unicast] network is 2001:db8:b7::6, the associated multicast address would be ff7s:0630:2001:db8:b7::g, where s = a valid scope defined below and g = a 32-bit Group ID.

   o The explicit breakdown of this address is as follows:

- ff = multicast prefix
- 7 = [0111]2, i.e. Y = 1, P = 1 and T = 1
- s = a valid scope defined below
- 0 = reserved bits
- 6 = RIID field, to be appended to the Network Prefix field.
- 30 = prefix length in hex = [0011 0000]2 = 48 in decimal, the prefix length in our example
- 2001:db8:b7:0 = 2001:0db8:00b7:0000 = 48 bit network prefix in the 64-bit Network Prefix field.
- and g = a 32-bit Group ID.

- The first Flag bit (X) is reserved and is set to 0.

Multicast Flags Summary Who thought multicast addressing could be so complicated? But as is typically the case, with complexity comes flexibility! To summarize, the net result of the above bit stipulations yields the following valid values of the Flags field as currently defined. Since the Flags field immediately follows the first eight "1" bits, we denote the "effective prefix" of these first eight bits followed by the valid 4-bit Flags field. We also illustrate prefixes should the X bit (the most significant bit of flag field 1) be assigned in the future (Table 17.1).

Scope The Scope field identifies, naturally enough, the scope or "reach" of the multicast address. This is used by routers along the multicast path to constrain the reach of the multicast communications with the corresponding scope. Note that scopes other than interface-local, link local, and global must be administratively defined within the routers serving the given scope in order to enforce the corresponding reach constraint (Table 17.2).

Table 17.1   Multicast flag field 1 summary.

Flags field 1 values (binary)	Effective prefix	Interpretation
0000 1000	ff00::/12 ff80::/12	Permanently assigned 112-bit group ID scoped by 4-bit Scope field
0001 1001	ff10::/12 ff90::/12	Temporarily assigned 112-bit group ID scoped by 4-bit Scope field
0011 1011	ff30::/12 fb0::/12	Temporarily assigned unicast prefix based multicast address
0111 1111	ff70::/12 fff0::/12	Temporarily assigned unicast prefix based multicast address with Rendezvous Point Interface ID
All other flags values	—	Currently undefined

Table 17.2   Multicast scope field interpretation.

Scope field			
Binary	**Hex**	**Meaning (scope)**	**Description**
0000	0	Reserved	Reserved
0001	1	Interface-local	Scope consists of a single interface on a node and is useful only for loopback transmission
0010	2	Link-local	Scope is only the link on which the multicast packet is transmitted
0011	3	Realm-local	Scope is the link layer realm as in IP-over-foo; e.g. as applied to all interfaces connected to a personal area network (PAN) ID for IoT
0100	4	Admin-local	Scope is limited to the smallest scope administratively configured. This is not based on physical connectivity or other multicast related configuration
0101	5	Site-local	Scope is limited to the site as administratively defined
0110–0111	6–7	Unassigned	N/A
1000	8	Organization-local	Scope consists of multiple sites within one organizational entity as administratively defined
1001–1101	9-d	Unassigned	N/A
1110	e	Global scope	Scope is unlimited
1111	f	Reserved	Reserved

Special Case Multicast Addresses

Solicited Node Multicast Address

One form of multicast address that each node must support is the solicited node multicast address. This address is used during the duplicate address detection phase of address auto-configuration and for the neighbor discovery protocol, which enables identification of IPv6 nodes on a link. The solicited node multicast address is formed by appending the low-order (rightmost) 24 bits of the solicited node's Interface ID to the well-known ff02::1:ff00:0/104 prefix.

For example, let's say a node wishes to resolve the link layer address of the device (interface) with IP address: 2001:db8:4e:2a:3001:fa81:95d0:2cd1. Using the low-order 24-bits, d02cd1 in hex, the device would address its request to ff02::1:ffd0:2cd1. (Figure 17.7).

Node Information Query Address

The node information query address is a multicast address enabling solicitation of hostname and IPv6 and IPv4 address information from an IPv6 host. If you think this sounds like an overlap with what DNS already provides, you're correct. However, according to RFC 4620 [127], this mode of resolution "is currently limited to diagnostic and debugging tools and network management." And instead of querying a DNS server for this information, a query is issued to the node information query address.

Use of this multicast address format enables an IPv6 address to be formed based only on the hostname of the intended recipient; if the IPv6 address is already known and hostname information is requested, the IPv6 address itself may be used as the destination address. When IP address information is being requested for a known hostname, the canonical hostname[3] is hashed using the 128-bit MD-5 algorithm, and the first 24-bits resulting from the hash are appended to the ff02::2:ff00:0/104 prefix. Each node receiving a message addressed to this node

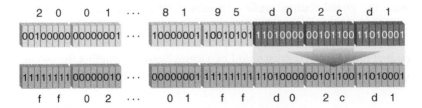

Figure 17.7 Solicited node multicast address derivation.

---

3 The "canonical hostname" is technically the first "label" in the fully qualified domain name in lowercase characters. This terminology is described in detail in Chapter 19 but suffice it to say that this generally is the intended destination hostname.

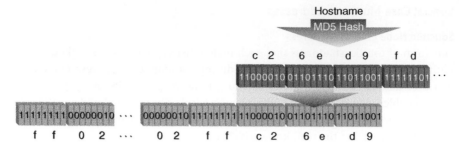

Figure 17.8 Solicited node information query address.

information query address compares the last 24 bits in the address with the first 24 bits of a hash of its own hostname; if it matches, the recipient will reply with the requested information. (Figure 17.8).

IPv6 Addresses with Embedded IPv4 Addresses
This type of address is not routable on the Internet and is used solely by some translation schemes, and should not generally be used within an IPv6 packet on a communications link. This address format consists of 80 zero bits, followed by 16 one bits, followed by the 32-bit IPv4 address (Figure 17.9).

This address notation combines the familiar IPv4 dotted decimal format appended to the specified IPv6 prefix. Thus, an IPv4-mapped IPv6 address for 172.16.20.5 would be represented as ::ffff:172.16.20.5.

Reserved Subnet Anycast Addresses
RFC 2526 [128] defines the format for reserved subnet anycast addresses. These addresses are used by IPv6 devices to route packets to the nearest device of a particular type on a specified subnet. For example, a reserved subnet anycast address can be used to send packets to the nearest mobile IPv6 home agent on a specified subnet. Since the global routing prefix and subnet ID are specified within this address type, it enables a node to locate the nearest node of the desired type on that subnet.

The format of the address takes on one of two forms based on whether the subnet prefix requires formulation of the interface ID field in modified EUI-64 format.

Figure 17.9 IPv4-mapped IPv6 address. Source: Based on Carpenter and Jiang 2014 [12].

Figure 17.10 Reserved subnet anycast address format when EUI-64 is required. Source: Based on Mrugalski et al. 2018 [20].

Figure 17.11 Reserved subnet anycast address format when EUI-64 is not required. Source: Based on Mrugalski et al. 2018 [20].

Recall that all global unicast addresses other than those beginning with $[000]_2$ must utilize 64-bit interface IDs.

4) If the EUI-64 algorithm is required, the reserved subnet anycast address is formulated by concatenating the following fields:
   o 64-bit global routing prefix and subnet ID
   o 57 bits of all 1s except the seventh bit in this sequence (the 71st bit from the beginning, counting left-to-right), which is 0. This seventh bit corresponds to the "u" bit (universal/local bit) of the company identifier field in the hardware address when applying the EUI-64 algorithm. This bit is always zero in this particular scenario to represent the "local" setting of the bit.
   o 7-bit anycast ID. RFC 2526 defines a single anycast ID of hex 7E for mobile IPv6 home agent anycast. Other anycast ID values are reserved, though IANA may assign additional anycast IDs based on future IETF RFC publications (Figure 17.10).
5) If EUI-64 is *not* required based on the global routing prefix and subnet ID, then the network prefix length is arbitrary at *n* bits, followed by 121-*n* 1 bits, followed by the 7-bit anycast ID (Figure 17.11).

18

DHCP Reference

DHCPv6 Protocol

DHCPv6 Packet Format

The DHCPv6 packet format is very simple. It consists of an 8-bit message type, 24-bit transaction ID, and a variable length options field as shown in Figure 18.1. That's it! Information regarding identification and configuration of the client is placed within the options field.

However, when a relay agent is in the path between the client and server, the relay agent modifies the message, yielding a common format for both forwarded and reply messages as shown in Figure 18.2:

- 8-bit message type.
- 8-bit hop count or the number of relay agents that have relayed this message, incremented by each along the path.
- 128-bit link-address – The IPv6 address that is used by the server to identify the link on which the client is located (similar to the DHCPv4 giaddr concept).
- 128-bit peer address – The IPv6 address of the client or relay agent from which the message to be relayed was received.
- Variable length options field, including the relay message option which includes the DHCPv6 message being relayed between the client and server.

DHCPv6 Message Types

The following message types have been defined for DHCPv6:

IP Address Management, Second Edition. Michael Dooley and Timothy Rooney.
© 2021 The Institute of Electrical and Electronics Engineers, Inc.
Published 2021 by John Wiley & Sons, Inc.

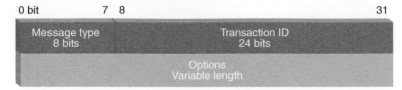

Figure 18.1 DHCPv6 packet format. Source: From RFC 8415 [20].

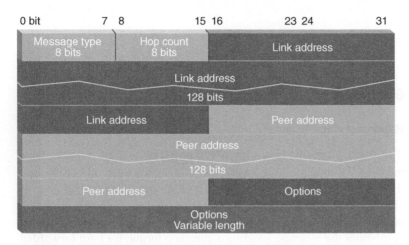

Figure 18.2 DHCP relay packet format.

Message type	Message	Purpose
1	SOLICIT	Issued by a DHCPv6 client to locate DHCPv6 server.
2	ADVERTISE	Issued by a server in response to a Solicit message to indicate availability of the server for DHCP service.
3	REQUEST	Issued by the client to request IP addresses and configuration parameters from a particular DHCPv6 server.
4	CONFIRM	Issued by a client to any available server to verify that the addresses assigned to it are still appropriate to its current subnet location.
5	RENEW	Issued by a client to the server from which it received its IP address to extend or renew its IP address lifetime and to update other parameters.
6	REBIND	Issued by a client to all available servers to extend its IP address lifetime and to update other parameters. This is sent after receiving no response from a prior RENEW message.

Message type	Message	Purpose
7	REPLY	Issued by a server to supply IP address and/or configuration parameters to a client in response to Solicit, Request, Renew or Rebind messages. The server also issues this message type to clients desiring to confirm their configurations via the Confirm message and to acknowledge receipt of Release and Decline messages from clients.
8	RELEASE	Issued by a client to the server from which it received its IP address to relinquish the IP address. The client must then cease use of the IP address.
9	DECLINE	Issued by a client to inform a server that one or more addresses assigned by the server are already in use on the link on which the client resides.
10	RECONFIGURE	Issued by a server to instruct a client to reinitialize as the server has new or updated configuration parameters for the client. The client must then issue a Renew or Information-Request as instructed by the server to obtain the updated or new information.
11	INFORMATION-REQUEST	Issued by the client to obtain configuration parameters other than IP addresses from a server.
12	RELAY-FORW	Issued by a relay agent to a server or set of servers directly or via another agent to encapsulate a client-initiated or relay agent-initiated message.
13	RELAYREPL	Issued by a server in reply to RELAY-FORW to a relay agent encapsulating a message destined for a client, which is encoded as an option within the RELAYREPL message. The relay agent may pass the message directly or via other relay agents to the client.
14	LEASEQUERY	Issued by a device such as an access concentrator or relay agent to request lease binding information from the DHCP server for a particular client IPv6 address, DUID, relay agent, link address or remote identifier. The IPv6 client DUID queries are for individual device lease queries whereas the other query types facilitate bulk lease query of multiple client lease states.
15	LEASEQUERY-REPLY	Issued by a server to the querying device in response to a LEASEQUERY message with the lease binding information relevant to the query.
16	LEASEQUERY-DONE	Issued by a server to the querying device indicating the end of results of a Bulk LeaseQuery.
17	LEASEQUERY-DATA	Issued by a server to the querying device to encapsulate a single DHCPv6 client's lease information when more than one client's data is provided in such results.

Message type	Message	Purpose
18	RECONFIGURE-REQUEST	Issued by a relay agent to a DHCP server to indicate a change of client configuration is warranted, e.g. during a Change-of-Authorization exchange with a Radius server; upon receipt of this request from the relay agent, the server may instruct the DHCP client to reconfigure.
19	RECONFIGURE-REPLY	Issued by a DHCP server to a relay agent to indicate status of the corresponding request.
20	DHCPV4-QUERY	Issued by a DHCP 4o6 client (DHCPv4 over DHCPv6) to a DHCP 4o6 server containing a DHCPv4 message.
21	DHCPV4-RESPONSE	Issued by a DHCP 4o6 server to a DHCP 4o6 client containing a DHCPv4 message.
22	ACTIVELEASE QUERY	Issued to a DHCP server to request some or all DHCPv6 lease binding to enable an external system to track lease bindings over time.
23	STARTTLS	An external system uses this message to establish a TLS connection to a DHCPv6 server, e.g. for an active lease query session.
24	BNDUPD	Issued by a DHCP server to send binding lease changes to its partner in a failover configuration.
25	BNDREPLY	Issued to acknowledge receipt and processing of a BNDUPD message.
26	POOLREQ	Issued by a secondary server to the primary to request an allocation of delegable prefixes in a manner that maintains balance between the two servers.
27	POOLRESP	Issued by a primary server to acknowledge receipt of the POOLREQ message.
28	UPDREQ	Issued by either server in a failover configuration to request its partner send all binding database changes that have not yet been confirmed; the partner responds with zero or more BNDUPD messages.
29	UPDREQALL	Issued by either server in a failover configuration to request its partner send all binding database information; the partner responds with zero or more BNDUPD messages.
30	UPDDONE	Issued by a server to indicated that all binding updates requested via UPDREQ or UPDREQALL have been sent and acknowledged.
31	CONNECT	Issued by the primary server to establish a failover connection with the secondary server and to transmit configuration attributes.
32	CONNECTREPLY	Issued by a secondary server to respond to a CONNECT message.

Message type	Message	Purpose
33	DISCONNECT	Issued by either server in a failover configuration when closing a connection and shutting down.
34	STATE	Issued by either server in a failover configuration to communicate a change in failover state or its current state after a connection is established in the COMMUNICATIONS-INTERRUPTED or PARTNER-DOWN states.
35	CONTACT	Issued by either server in a failover configuration to ensure that its partner considers the connection operational.

DHCPv6 Failover Overview

Deploying pairs of DHCP servers in a failover configuration provides an active/standby redundancy scheme to maximize availability of DHCP services to clients. Should one DHCP server fail, its partner can be configured to assume the primary role in managing address and prefix leases. Two modes are supported. Under the Independent Allocation scheme, supported for address but not prefix allocation, you configure a pair of DHCP servers with common IPv6 pools, but the primary server allocates "even" addresses (least significant address bit = 0) and the secondary allocates "odd" addresses (least significant bit = 1). This approach is a form of "split scopes" as neither server will distribute addresses from the other's set, even if its partner is down, though it may extend existing leases seeking renewal from the other's prefix. Independent Allocation also simplifies administration as there is no balancing required between the partner servers.

The Proportional Allocation method applies to both address and prefix allocation. Each partner has its own set of pools, referred to as delegable prefixes. Initially, the primary server "owns" all of the delegable prefixes and it delegates a portion of these to its secondary server upon request. Each server then delegates prefixes and assigns addresses from its own set of prefixes. In a PARTNER-DOWN state, in which a server has determined or has been configured that its partner server is down, the active server should allocate from its own delegable prefixes first, but may then allocate from its partner's prefixes.

Addresses that were last known to be leased by the downed partner can only be assigned to another client after a waiting period, which consists of the sum of a configurable parameter, the minimum client lead time (MCLT) and the maximum of the following:

- *Expiration-time* – The lease expiration time
- *Partner-lifetime* – The time after which the partner may consider the lease expired
- *Acked-partner-lifetime* – The partner-lifetime acknowledged by the partner

The reason for this seeming complexity in deciding when to reassign a previously partner-leased address or prefix stems from the fact that failover partners perform lazy updates. When a server assigns a lease, it updates its own lease repository prior to confirming with the client. The server does not attempt to update the partner in real time prior to client confirmation in order to retain reasonable lease assignment performance. The assigning server does update its partner at some point in the near future but not immediately. Hence, this delay or laziness increases the exposure to loss of server lease status synchronization. A lease may have been granted to a client by a server but not communicated to its partner moments before the server fails. As far as the partner is concerned, the prefix or address is available; thus, the rather complex handling process. Let's walk through an example of how this works.

Consider the timing diagram in Figure 18.3. The DHCP servers are configured with an MCLT of one hour and a desired lease time of three days. A DHCP client issues a SOLICIT to all DHCP servers. Since the client has no existing lease, the DHCP server calculates the lease time as the minimum of the desired lease time (three days) and the acked-partner-lifetime + MCLT (0 + 1 hour = 1 hour), or one hour. After assigning the client a lease time of one hour, at point A in the figure, the server subsequently updates its failover partner using the formula,

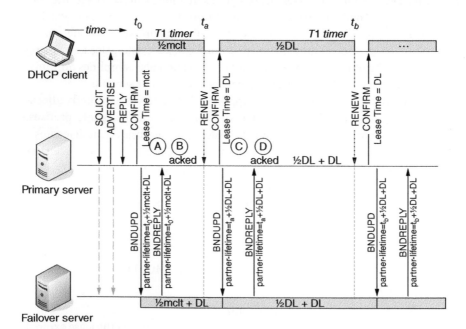

Figure 18.3 DHCP FailoverMessages.

$\frac{1}{2} \times$ lease time + desired lease time, which in this case is $\frac{1}{2} \times 1$ hour + 3 days = 3 days + $\frac{1}{2}$ hour. (The $\frac{1}{2} \times$ lease time coincides with the default T1 time upon which the client seeks a renewal.) The failover server acknowledges this lease time at point B, and the primary server denotes the acked-partner-lifetime value of 3 days + $\frac{1}{2}$ hour.

After $\frac{1}{2}$ hour, the client's T1 time, the client issues a RENEW message to the DHCP server to renew its lease prior to expiration. Now the minimum of the desired lease time (three days) and the acked-partner-lifetime + MCLT (3 days + $\frac{1}{2}$ hour ($-\frac{1}{2}$ hour elapsed time) + 1 hour) is 3 days < 3 days + 1 hour. The client lease is renewed with a lease time of three days, but the partner is provided a partner-lifetime of $\frac{1}{2} \times$ lease time + desired lease time = 1.5 days + 3 days = 4.5 days. The failover server acknowledges this at point D and the new acked-partner-lifetime becomes 4.5 days.

After a day and a half, at time t_b the client renews once again. The lease is renewed again for three days and the BNDUPD message to the partner indicates a partner-lifetime of 4.5 days. If the primary server failed at any point, the failover server would consider the lease duration longer than was actually assigned, reducing the likelihood of it reassigning the address to another client. Upon failure to achieve renewal from the primary server at T1 time, the client would multicast a REBIND message at time T2. If the active partner receives a REBIND message for an address its partner assigned, it will renew the current lease. DHCPv6 failover, and DHCPv4 failover for that matter which is similar in operation, is very complex, but its complexity stems from seeking to address several possible error states to provide a robust redundancy protocol for resilient DHCP services.

DHCPv6 Options

DHCPv6 options convey information relevant to the associated DHCP message, including DUIDs and IAs. Options are listed within the DHCPv6 message and have the general format shown in Figure 18.4.

The currently defined set of DHCPv6 options are defined in Table 18.1. Note that certain options may be nested, such as those associated with an IA.

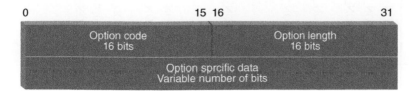

Figure 18.4 DHCPv6 options format. Source: From RFC 8415 [20].

Table 18.1 DHCPv6 options.

Code	Name	Meaning	References
1	OPTION_CLIENTID	Client Identifier (DUID of client)	RFC 8415 [20]
2	OPTION_SERVERID	Server Identifier (DUID of server)	RFC 8415 [20]
3	OPTION_IA_NA	Identity Association for non-temporary addresses – includes the IAID, T1 time, T2 time, and additional options for the IA for non-temporary addresses.	RFC 8415 [20]
4	OPTION_IA_TA	Identity Association for Temporary addresses – includes the IAID and additional options for this IA for temporary addresses.	RFC 8415 [20]
5	OPTION_IAADDR	IA Address option – specifies IPv6 addresses and associated preferred lifetime, valid lifetime, and options associated with an IA_NA or IA_TA. As such, this option may only appear as an option to the DHCPv6 message option OPTION_IA_TA or OPTION_IA_NA.	RFC 8415 [20]
6	OPTION_ORO	Option Request Option – used by clients to list option codes for which values are requested or by servers in a Reconfigure message to indicate which options the client should request in its subsequent Renew or Information-Request message.	RFC 8415 [20]
7	OPTION_PREFERENCE	Preference setting by the server to facilitate client selection of DHCP server.	RFC 8415 [20]
8	OPTION_ELAPSED_TIME	The amount of time since the client began the current DHCP transaction in hundredths of a second. Clients are required to use this option.	RFC 8415 [20]
9	OPTION_RELAY_MSG	The DHCP message being relayed by a relay agent.	RFC 8415 [20]
10	Unassigned		
11	OPTION_AUTH	Authentication information for use in reliably identifying the source of a DHCP message and to verify message integrity.	RFC 8415 [20]

Code	Name	Meaning	References
12	OPTION_UNICAST	Server unicast option indicates the IP address to which the client may unicast messages to this server.	RFC 8415 [20]
13	OPTION_STATUS_CODE	Status code option indicates a 2-byte status code and variable length status message. This option may be used as a DHCP message option or as an option within another DHCP message option.	RFC 8415 [20]
14	OPTION_RAPID_COMMIT	Rapid commit option – enables a client to request a direct Reply message from the server with an IP address and parameters, bypassing the Advertise and Request messages.	RFC 8415 [20]
15	OPTION_USER_CLASS	User class option – analogous to user class in DHCPv4 in assisting the server in making address assignment decisions.	RFC 8415 [20]
16	OPTION_VENDOR_CLASS	Vendor class option – analogous to vendor class in DHCPv4 in conveying the vendor or manufacturer of the device or interface to assist the server in making address assignment decisions. The vendor class option includes the IANA-assigned Enterprise Number for the vendor.	RFC 8415 [20]
17	OPTION_VENDOR_OPTS	Vendor specific information – this option includes the IANA-assigned Enterprise Number as well as one or more options, each defined with option code, length, and value.	RFC 8415 [20]
18	OPTION_INTERFACE_ID	Interface ID option – used by relay agents to convey the agent's interface ID on which the client message was received. This option may only appear in RELAY-FORW messages, and when it does, it is copied by the server to the RELAYREPL message.	RFC 8415 [20]
19	OPTION_RECONF_MSG	Reconfigure Message option – for use in the Reconfigure message to inform the client which message to use to reconfigure: either Renew or Information-Request.	RFC 8415 [20]

(Continued)

Table 18.1 (Continued)

Code	Name	Meaning	References
20	OPTION_RECONF_ACCEPT	Reconfigure Accept option – the client populates this option if it is willing to accept Reconfigure messages from the server.	RFC 8415 [20]
21	OPTION_SIP_SERVER_D	SIP Servers Domain Names option – lists domain names of the SIP outbound proxy servers that the client can use.	RFC 3319 [130]
22	OPTION_SIP_SERVER_A	SIP Servers IPv6 Address List option – lists the IPv6 addresses of the SIP outbound proxy servers that the client can use.	RFC 3319 [130]
23	OPTION_DNS_SERVERS	DNS Recursive Name Server Option – lists IPv6 address(es) of DNS recursive name servers to which DNS queries may be sent by the client resolver in order of preference.	RFC 3646 [131]
24	OPTION_DOMAIN_LIST	Domain Search List option – provides a domain search list for client use when resolving hostnames via DNS.	RFC 3646 [131]
25	OPTION_IA_PD	Identity Association for Prefix Delegation – includes the IAID, T1 time, T2 time and additional options for the IA_PD, including the associated prefix(es) defined within option code 26.	RFC 3633 [132]
26	OPTION_IAPREFIX	IA_PD Prefix option – specifies the IPv6 prefixes associated with the IA_PD, along with associated options and preferred and valid lifetimes. This option may only appear as an option to the DHCPv6 message option OPTION_IA_PD. The prefix is specified with an 8-bit prefix length and a 128-bit IPv6 prefix.	RFC 3633 [132]
27	OPTION_NIS_SERVERS	Network Information Service (NIS) Servers – ordered list of NIS servers by IPv6 address available to the client.	RFC 3898 [133]
28	OPTION_NISP_SERVERS	Network Information Service v2 (NIS+) Servers – ordered list of NIS+ servers by IPv6 address available to the client.	RFC 3898 [133]

Code	Name	Meaning	References
29	OPTION_NIS_DOMAIN_NAME	Network Information Service (NIS) domain name – NIS domain name to be used by the client.	RFC 3898 [133]
30	OPTION_NISP_DOMAIN_NAME	Network Information Service v2 (NIS+) domain name – NIS+ domain name to be used by the client.	RFC 3898 [133]
31	OPTION_SNTP_SERVERS	Simple Network Time Protocol (SNTP) servers – ordered list of SNTP servers by IPv6 address available to the client.	RFC 4075 [134]
32	OPTION_INFORMATION_REFRESH_TIME	Information Refresh Option – specifies the upper bound of the number or seconds from the current time that a client should wait before refreshing information received from the DHCPv6 server, particularly for stateless DHCPv6 scenarios.	RFC 4242 [135]
33	OPTION_BCMCS_SERVER_D	Broadcast and Multicast Service (BCMCS) Domain Name List – list of one or more FQDNs corresponding to BCMCS server(s). (BCMCS is used in 3G wireless networks to enable mobiles to receive broadcast and multicast services).	RFC 4280 [136]
34	OPTION_BCMCS_SERVER_A	Broadcast and Multicast Service (BCMCS) IPv6 Address List – list of one or more IPv6 address(es) corresponding to BCMCS server(s). (BCMCS is used in 3G wireless networks to enable mobiles to receive broadcast and multicast services).	RFC 4280 [136]
35	Unassigned		
36	OPTION_GEOCONF_CIVIC	Geographical location in civic (e.g. postal) format. This option can be provided by the server to relate the location of the server, the closest network element (e.g. router) to the client or the client itself. The location information includes an ISO 3166 country code (US, DE, JP, etc.) and country-specific location information such as state, province, county, city, block, group of streets and more.	RFC 4776 [137]

(Continued)

Table 18.1 (Continued)

Code	Name	Meaning	References
37	OPTION_REMOTE_ID	Relay Agent Remote ID option – remote identity inserted by the relay agent in RELAY-FORW message to the DHCPv6 server. This is useful in service provider environments where the "edge" device facing the subscriber device, inserts an identifier for the subscriber connection prior to relaying to the DHCPv6 server.	RFC 4649 [32]
38	OPTION_SUBSCRIBER_ID	Relay Agent Subscriber ID option – subscriber identity inserted by the relay agent in RELAY-FORW message to the DHCPv6 server. This is useful in service provider environments where the "edge" device facing the subscriber device, inserts an identifier for the subscriber from which the message originated, prior to relaying to the DHCPv6 server.	RFC 4580 [35]
39	OPTION_CLIENT_FQDN	Client FQDN option – indicates whether the client or the DHCP server should update DNS with the AAAA record corresponding to the assigned IPv6 address and the FQDN provided in this option. The DHCP server always updates the PTR record.	RFC 4704 [138]
40	OPTION_PANA_AGENT	This option provides one or more IPv6 address(es) associated with PANA (Protocol for carrying Authentication for Network Access) Authentication Agents that a client can use.	RFC 5192 [139]
41	OPTION_NEW_POSIX_TIMEZONE	Time zone to be used by the client in IEEE 1003.1 format (POSIX – portable operating system interface). This format enables textual representation of time zone and daylight savings time information.	RFC 4833 [140]
42	OPTION_NEW_TZDB_TIMEZONE	Time zone (TZ) database entry referred to by entry name. The client must have a copy of the TZ database, which it queries for the corresponding entry to determine its time zone.	RFC 4833 [140]

Code	Name	Meaning	References
43	OPTION_ERO	Relay Agent Echo Request option – used by relay agents in the RELAY_FORW message to request that the DHCPv6 sever echo back certain requested relay agent options, even if not supported on the sever. (DHCPv4 servers always echo back relay agent option [80] information but this is not required in DHCPv6, hence this option for relay agents requiring such echo back).	RFC 4994 [141]
44	OPTION_LQ_QUERY	The Query option is used in the LEASEQUERY message to identify the query information being requested. This option includes the Query type (by IA address or client ID option), link address to which the query applies and query options.	RFC 5007 [142]
45	OPTION_CLIENT_DATA	Client Data – this option contains the query response information for the requested client data within a LEASEQUERY-REPLY message. At a minimum this option includes the client identifier (OPTION_CLIENTID), the IA address or prefix (OPTION_IAADDR and/or OPTION_IAPREFIX) and client last transaction time (OPTION_CLT_TIME).	RFC 5007 [142]
46	OPTION_CLT_TIME	Client Last Transaction Time – indicates the number of seconds since the server last communicated with the client referenced by the lease query. This option is encapsulated within the OPTION_CLIENT_DATA option within a LEASEQUERY-REPLY message.	RFC 5007 [142]
47	OPTION_LQ_RELAY_DATA	Relay data – used in a LEASEQUERY-REPLY message to provide the relay agent information associated with the client information requested. This option includes the relay agent address from which the client's relay information was received along with the complete relayed message.	RFC 5007 [142]
48	OPTION_LQ_CLIENT_LINK	Client link – identifies one or more links on which the queried client has DHCPv6 bindings. The queried client can be identified by address or client ID.	RFC 5007 [142]

(Continued)

Table 18.1 (Continued)

Code	Name	Meaning	References
49	OPTION_MIP6_HNINF	Mobile IPv6 Home Network Information – used by the client to identify its target home network to the server (in an Information Request message).	RFC 6610 [143]
50	OPTION_MIP6_RELAY	Mobile IPv6 Relay Agent – used by a relay agent to identify home network information via a RELAY-FORW message).	RFC 6610 [143]
51	OPTION_V6_LOST	Location to Service Translation (LoST) server domain name; LoST protocol maps service identifiers and location information to service URLs.	RFC 5223 [144]
52	OPTION_CAPWAP_AC_V6	Control and Provisioning of Wireless Access Points (CAPWAP) Access Controller IPv6 address(es) to which the client may connect.	RFC 5417 [145]
53	OPTION_RELAY_ID	DHCPv6 Bulk LeaseQuery – requests lease and prefix delegation bindings for a specified relay agent identified by its DUID in this option.	RFC 5460 [146]
54	OPTION-IPv6_Addresss-MoS	List of IPv6 address(es) for servers providing particular types of IEEE 802.21 Mobility Service (MoS).	RFC 5678 [147]
55	OPTION-IPv6_FQDN-MoS	List of FQDN(s) for servers providing particular types of IEEE 802.21 Mobility Service (MoS).	RFC 5678 [147]
56	OPTION_NTP_SERVER	Network Time Protocol (NTP) server option.	RFC 5908 [148]
57	OPTION_V6_ACCESS_DOMAIN	Local Location Information Server (LIS) discovery.	RFC 5986 [149]
58	OPTION_SIP_UA_CS_LIST	DHCP SIP user agent configuration service domains.	RFC 6011 [150]
59	OPT_BOOTFILE_URL	URLto a boot file.	RFC 5970 [151]

Code	Name	Meaning	References
60	OPT_BOOTFILE_PARAM	Boot file parameter list, similar to command line arguments in modern operating systems.	RFC 5970 [151]
61	OPTION_CLIENT_ARCH_TYPE	Client system architecture type for network boot.	RFC 5970 [151]
62	OPTION_NII	Client universal network device interface (UNDI) identifier for network boot.	RFC 5970 [151]
63	OPTION_GEOLOCATION	Geographic location (latitude, longitude, and altitude) of the client as provided by the DHCP server.	RFC 6225 [152]
64	OPTION_AFTR_NAME	FQDN of the Address Family Transition Router (AFTR) used for Dual-Stack Lite.	RFC 6334 [153]
65	OPTION_ERP_LOCAL_DOMAIN_NAME	Extensible Authentication Protocol (EAP) Re-authentication Protocol (ERP) local domain.	RFC 6440 [154]
66	OPTION_RSOO	Relay agent-supplied DHCP options.	RFC 6422 [155]
67	OPTION_PD_EXCLUDE	Prefix exclusion from a prefix set.	RFC 6603 [156]
68	OPTION_VSS	Virtual subnet selection.	RFC 6607 [46]
69	OPTION_MIP6_IDINF	Mobile IPv6 Identified home network information pertaining to a specific realm.	RFC 6610 [157]
70	OPTION_MIP6_UDINIF	Mobile IPv6 unrestricted home network information.	RFC 6610 [157]
71	OPTION_MIP6_HNP	Mobile IPv6 home network IPv6 prefix.	RFC 6610 [157]
72	OPTION_MIP6_HAA	Mobile IPv6 home network home agent IP address.	RFC 6610 [157]
73	OPTION_MIP6_HAF	Mobile IPv6 home network home agent FQDN.	RFC 6610 [157]

(Continued)

Table 18.1 (Continued)

Code	Name	Meaning	References
74	OPTION_RDNSS_SELECTION	Recursive DNS Server selection for multi-interfaced nodes.	RFC 6731 [158]
75	OPTION_KRB_PRINCIPAL_NAME	Kerberos principal name.	RFC 6784 [159]
76	OPTION_KRB_REALM_NAME	Kerberos realm name.	RFC 6784 [159]
77	OPTION_KRB_DEFAULT_REALM_NAME	Kerberos default realm name.	RFC 6784 [159]
78	OPTION_KRB_KDC	Kerberos Key Distribution Center (KDC) configuration information (IPv6 address, etc.)	RFC 6784 [159]
79	OPTION_CLIENT_LINKLAYER_ADDR	Client's link layer address provided by an on-link relay agent.	RFC 6939 [160]
80	OPTION_LINK_ADDRESS	IPv6 address of the DHCP client for which a reconfigure command is requested by the relay agent.	RFC 6977 [161]
81	OPTION_RADIUS	Encodes RADIUS attributes from the relay agent/network access server for use by the DHCP server in making parameter assignments.	RFC 7037 [37]
82	OPTION_SOL_MAX_RT	Provided by the server to override the client default value of SOL_MAX_RT (maximum Solicit timeout).	RFC 8415 [20]
83	OPTION_INF_MAX_RT	Provided by the server to override the client default value of INF_MAX_RT (maximum Information-Request timeout).	RFC 8415 [20]
84	OPTION_ADDRSEL	Provides the address selection policy table to the client.	RFC 7078 [162]

Code	Name	Meaning	References
85	OPTION_ADDRSEL_TABLE	Provides address selection policy table options to the client.	RFC 7078 [162]
86	OPTION_V6_PCP_SERVER	Port Control Protocol (PCP) server IP address(es).	RFC 7291 [163]
87	OPTION_DHCPV4_MSG	DHCPv4 message encoded within a DHCPv6 message (DHCPv4 over DHCPv6, DHCP 4o6).	RFC 7341 [21]
88	OPTION_DHCP4_O_DHCP6_SERVER	DHCP 4o6 server IPv6 address(es).	RFC 7341 [21]
89	OPTION_S46_RULE	IPv4-IPv6 mapping options for Softwire46 customer edge (CE) devices to provide IPv4 connectivity over the service provider IPv6 access network.	RFC 7598 [164]
90	OPTION_S46_BR	IPv6 address of the border relay which borders the service provider IPv6 network with IPv4 destinations.	RFC 7598 [164]
91	OPTION_S46_DMR	IPv4-IPv6 default mapping rule for Softwire46 customer edge (CE) devices.	RFC 7598 [164]
92	OPTION_S46_V4V6BIND	Full or shared IPv4 address of a Softwire46 customer edge (CE) device.	RFC 7598 [164]
93	OPTION_S46_PORTPARAMS	Port set information for Softwire46 customer edge (CE) devices.	RFC 7598 [164]
94	OPTION_S46_CONT_MAPE	Softwire46 MAP-E (Mapping of Address and Port with Encapsulation) container option.	RFC 7598 [164]
95	OPTION_S46_CONT_MAPT	Softwire46 MAP-T (Mapping of Address and Port using Translation) container option.	RFC 7598 [164]
96	OPTION_S46_CONT_LW	Softwire46 Lightweight 4over6 container option.	RFC 7598 [164]
97	OPTION_4RD	Rule options for IPv4 residual deployment (4rd), which supports IPv4 tunneled over an IPv6 access network.	RFC 7600 [165]

(Continued)

Table 18.1 (Continued)

Code	Name	Meaning	References
98	OPTION_4RD_MAP_RULE	Address mapping rule for IPv4 residual deployment (4rd), which supports IPv4 tunneling over an IPv6 access network.	RFC 7600 [165]
99	OPTION_4RD_NON_MAP_RULE	Non-address mapping rule for IPv4 residual deployment (4rd), which supports IPv4 tunneling over an IPv6 access network.	RFC 7600 [165]
100	OPTION_LQ_BASE_TIME	Current absolute time of the DHCPv6 server for use in Lease Query transactions.	RFC 7653 [166]
101	OPTION_LQ_START_TIME	Query start time after which lease bindings are requested during Lease Query transactions.	RFC 7653 [166]
102	OPTION_LQ_END_TIME	Query end time before which lease bindings are requested during Lease Query transactions.	RFC 7653 [166]
103	DHCP Captive-Portal	Informs a client that it is behind a captive portal device and provides a URI to access an authentication page.	RFC 8910 [167]
104	OPTION_MPL_PARAMETERS	Parameter settings governing the Multicast Protocol for Low-Power and Lossy Networks (MPL).	RFC 7774 [168]
105	OPTION_ANI_ATT	Denotes the access network technology type from which the relay agent received this DHCP packet.	RFC 7839 [44]
106	OPTION_ANI_NETWORK_NAME	Conveys the name of the mobile access network from which this DHCP packet originated according to the relay agent.	RFC 7839 [44]
107	OPTION_ANI_AP_NAME	A unique device name of the access point from which the DHCP packet was sent.	RFC 7839 [44]
108	OPTION_ANI_AP_BSSID	The 48-bit Basic SSID (BSSID) of the access point to which the DHCP packet originating device is connected.	RFC 7839 [44]
109	OPTION_ANI_OPERATOR_ID	The private enterprise number (PEN) of the operator of the mobile network to which this DHCP client is connected.	RFC 7839 [44]

Code	Name	Meaning	References
110	OPTION_ANI_OPERATOR_REALM	The unique realm name of the operator of the mobile network to which this DHCP client is connected.	RFC 7839 [44]
111	OPTION_S46_PRIORITY	Priority list of supported Softwire46 mechanisms, e.g., from among DS-Lite, DHCP 4o6, MAP-E, etc.	RFC 8026 [169]
112	OPTION_MUD_URL_V6	Manufacturer Usage Description (MUD) URL provided by a device to identify device and manufacturer information.	RFC 8520 [170]
113	OPTION_V6_PREVIX64	IPv6 prefix list to be used for constructing IPv4-embedded IPv6 addresses of various types.	RFC 8115 [171]
114	OPTION_F_BINDING_STATUS	IPv6 address or prefix lease status/state for DHCPv6 failover.	RFC 8156 [172]
115	OPTION_F_CONNECT_FLAGS	Attributes of a connecting DHCP server for DHCPv6 failover.	RFC 8156 [172]
116	OPTION_F_DNS_REMOVAL_INFO	Information used to remove a DNS name that was entered by the failover partner.	RFC 8156 [172]
117	OPTION_F_DNS_HOST_NAME	Hostname that was entered into DNS by the failover partner.	RFC 8156 [172]
118	OPTION_F_DNS_ZONE_NAME	Zone name that was entered into DNS by the failover partner.	RFC 8156 [172]
119	OPTION_F_DNS_FLAGS	Information regarding the removal of the DNS name in question for DHCPv6 failover.	RFC 8156 [172]
120	OPTION_F_EXPIRATION_TIME	The longest lifetime in absolute time that this server has acknowledged to its partner in a BNDREPLY message for a given IP or prefix lease.	RFC 8156 [172]
121	OPTION_F_MAX_UNACKED_BNDUPD	The maximum number of BNDUPD messages that this server will accept over this TCP connection for DHCPv6 failover.	RFC 8156 [172]

(Continued)

Table 18.1 (Continued)

Code	Name	Meaning	References
122	OPTION_F_MCLT	The Maximum Client Lead Time (MCLT) in seconds, which is the upper bound on the difference allowed between the valid lifetime provided to a client and the valid lifetime known by this server's failover partner.	RFC 8156 [172]
123	OPTION_F_PARTNER_LIFETIME	The absolute time after which the partner may consider an IPv6 address expired and available for reuse for DHCPv6 failover.	RFC 8156 [172]
124	OPTION_F_PARTNER_LIFETIME_SENT	The absolute time echoed back from a received OPTION_F_PARTNER_LIFETIME option for DHCPv6 failover.	RFC 8156 [172]
125	OPTION_F_PARTNER_DOWN_TIME	The absolute time that the server most recently lost communications with its failover partner.	RFC 8156 [172]
126	OPTION_F_PARTNER_RAW_CLT_TIME	The absolute time when the partner most recently interacted with the client associated with the given address or prefix.	RFC 8156 [172]
127	OPTION_F_PROTOCOL_VERSION	The major and minor versions of the failover protocol this server is using.	RFC 8156 [172]
128	OPTION_F_KEEPALIVE_TIME	The number of seconds before which the server must receive a message from its partner before considering communications with the partner not "OK".	RFC 8156 [172]
129	OPTION_F_RECONFIGURE_DATA	The reconfigure-key created on the failover partner which this server may use.	RFC 8156 [172]
130	OPTION_F_RELATIONSHIP_NAME	A name for this failover relationship, used to distinguish among multiple failover relationships between two failover servers.	RFC 8156 [172]
131	OPTION_F_SERVER_FLAGS	Communications status parameters of a given server for DHCPv6 failover.	RFC 8156 [172]
132	OPTION_F_SERVER_STATE	Failover state of a given server for DHCPv6 failover.	RFC 8156 [172]

Code	Name	Meaning	References
133	OPTION_F_START_TIME_OF_STATE	The absolute time at which the server attained its current endpoint state or binding state depending on context.	RFC 8156 [172]
134	OPTION_F_STATE_EXPIRATION_TIME	The absolute time at which the current lease state will expire using with DHCPv6 failover.	RFC 8156 [172]
135	OPTION_RELAY_PORT	UDP port the server should use in response to this relay agent. Some configurations do not use the well-known DHCP source port (547) for scalability reasons.	RFC 8357 [45]
136	OPTION_V6_SZTP_REDIRECT	Secure Zero Touch Provisioning (SZTP) bootstrap server list.	RFC 8572 [196]
137	OPTION_S46_BIND_IPV6_PREFIX	IPv6 address assigned via DHCPv4 over DHCPv6.	RFC 8539 [173]
138–142	Unassigned		
143	OPTION-IPv6-Address-ANDSF	IP address of the Access Network Discovery and Selection Function (ANDSF).	RFC 6153 [174]
144–65535	Unassigned		

DHCP for IPv4

DHCP Packet Format

Let's examine the fields in the DHCP for IPv4 packet and how they relate to the overall DHCP process. Figure 18.5 illustrates the field layout.

DHCP packet field descriptions:

- *Operation code* – Leveraging the BootP predecessor, the values for this field are
  o 1 = BootRequest
  o 2 = BootReply
- Note that the type of DHCP message (Discover, Offer, Request, etc.) is actually defined in the options field with option number 53, DHCP Message Type, with the following valid values:
  o 1 = DHCPDISCOVER
  o 2 = DHCPOFFER
  o 3 = DHCPREQUEST
  o 4 = DHCPDECLINE

0 bit	7	8	15	16	23	24	31
Operation code (op) 8 bits		HW address type 8 bits		HW address length 8 bits		Hops 8 bits	
Transaction ID (xid) 32 bits							
Secs 16 bits				Flags 16 bits			
Client IP Address (ciaddr) 32 bits							
"Your" (Client) IP Address (yiaddr) 32 bits							
Next server IP Address (siaddr) 32 bits							
Relay agent (Gateway) IP Address (giaddr) 32 bits							
Client hardware Address (chaddr) 128 bits							
Server Host Name (sname) 512 bits							
Bootfile name (file) 1024 bits							
Options Variable length							

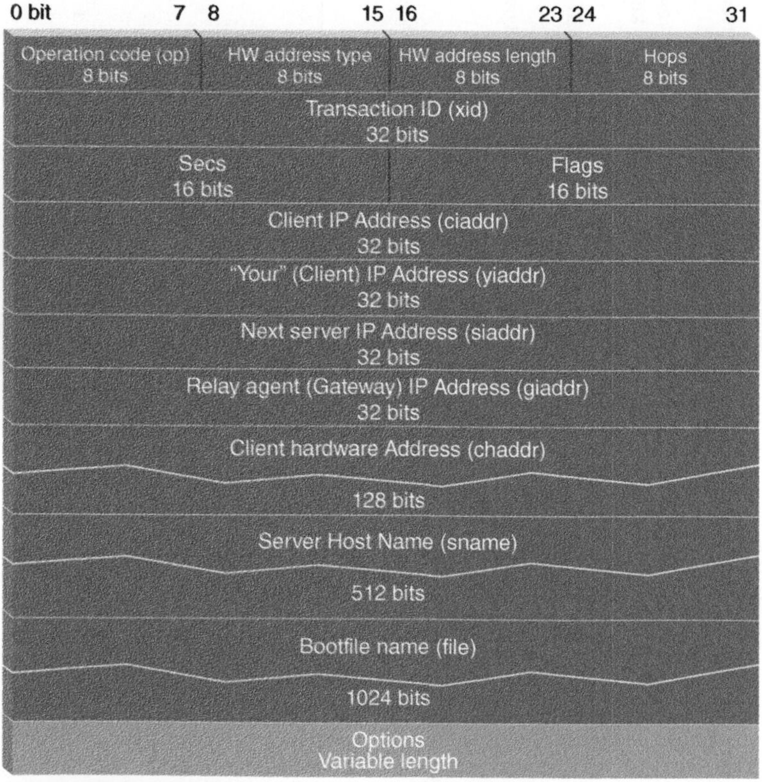

Figure 18.5 DHCP packet fields. Source: Based on Droms 1997 [175].

- o 5 = DHCPACK
- o 6 = DHCPNAK
- o 7 = DHCPRELEASE
- o 8 = DHCPINFORM
- o 9 = DHCPFORCERENEW
- o 10 = DHCPLEASEQUERY
- o 11 = DHCPLEASEUNASSIGNED
- o 12 = DHCPLEASEUNKNOWN
- o 13 = DHCPLEASEACTIVE
- o 14 = DHCPBULKLEASEQUERY
- o 15 = DHCPLEASEQUERYDONE
- o 16 = DHCPACTIVELEASEQUERY
- o 17 = DHCPLEASEQUERYSTATUS
- o 18 = DHCPTLS
- *Hardware address type* – The type of hardware or MAC address, such as Ethernet, 802, etc.
- *Hardware address length* – Defines the length of the MAC address in octets
- *Hops* – set to zero by clients, this field can be incremented by each router between the client and server
- *Transaction ID (xid)* – A random number chosen by the client to correlate messages and responses between the client and server
- *Seconds (secs)* – The number of seconds that have elapsed since the client began the process of obtaining an IP address or renewal
- *Flags* – This field is used by DHCP clients that cannot receive unicast IP packets until its IP protocol software has been configured. For such cases, the client sets the first bit in this field to 1, and sets the remainingbits to 0. When set to 1, the server (if locally connected) or the relay agent will broadcast the Offer and Ack messages to the client; otherwise, the server or relay agent will send them to the unicast address specified in the yiaddr field. This bit is sometimes referred to as the broadcast bit within the Flags field.
- *Client IP address (ciaddr)* – The IP address of the client used when known by the client, e.g. when in the BOUND, RENEWING, or REBINDING state
- *Your IP address (yiaddr)* – The IP address assigned by the DHCP server for use by the client
- *Server IP address (siaddr)* – The IP address of the "next" server to use for bootstrapping as provided by the DHCP server
- *Gateway interface address (giaddr)* – IP address of the interface on which the DHCP broadcast was received as populated by the relay agent
- *Client hardware address (chaddr)* – The link layer or hardware address of the client provided by the client
- *Server name (sname)* – DHCP server host name
- *File* – Boot file name, null or fully qualified directory pathname

Options – Additional IP parameters such as lease time, domain name, default gateway, and subnet mask (see next section for complete list). The first four octets of the options field is always the magic cookie of value (in hex): 63825363. This is a carry over from the original BootP specification in RFC 951 that was intended to provide a means to interpret the options, e.g. for vendor-specific purposes.

DHCPv4 Message Types

We've introduced the four basic DHCP message types, so let's expand on this and review the complete set of DHCP messages and their respective meanings. We often omit the "DHCP" prefix on these messages and just capitalize the first letter, but here's how they're officially defined:

- DHCPDISCOVER – Issued from the client to the server to solicit DHCP address assignment; the DHCPDISCOVER may include parameters or options required by the client.
- DHCPOFFER – Issued from the server to the client indicating an IP address offer including its corresponding lease time (and other configuration parameters) to the client in response to a DHCPDISCOVER.
- DHCPREQUEST – Issued from the client to a server in response to a DHCPOFFER to accept or reject the offered IP address, along with desired or additional parameter settings. The DHCPREQUEST is also used by clients desiring to extend or renew their existing IP address lease.
- DHCPACK – Issued from the server to the client to positively acknowledge the grant of the IP address lease and associated parameter settings. The client may now begin using the IP address and parameter values.
- DHCPNAK – Issued from the server to the client to negatively acknowledge the DHCP transaction. The client must cease use of the IP address and reinitiate the process if necessary.
- DHCPDECLINE – Issued from the client to the server, to indicate that the IP address offered by the server is already in use by another client. The DHCP server will then typically mark the IP address as unavailable.
- DHCPRELEASE – Issued from the client to the server to inform the server that the client is relinquishing the IP address. The client must cease use of the IP address thereafter.
- DHCPINFORM – Issued from the client to the server to request non IP address configuration parameters from the server. The server will formulate a DHCPACK reply with the associated values as appropriate.
- DHCPFORCERENEW – Issued from the server to the client to force a client into the INIT state[1] in order to obtain a new (different) IP address. Few clients have implemented support of this message.

---

1 We'll discuss DHCP states next.

- DHCPLEASEQUERY – Issued from a relay agent or other device to a server to determine if a given MAC address, IP address or client-identifier value has an active lease and its associated lease parameter values according to the DHCP server (used primarily by broadband access concentrators or edge devices).
- DHCPLEASEUNASSIGNED – Issued from a server to a relay agent in response to a DHCPLEASEQUERY informing the relay agent that this server supports that address but there is no active lease.
- DHCPLEASEUNKNOWN – Issued from a server to a relay agent in response to a DHCPLEASEQUERY informing the relay agent that the server has no knowledge of the client specified in the query.
- DHCPLEASEACTIVE – Issued from a server to a relay agent in response to a DHCPLEASEQUERY with the endpoint location and remaining lease time.
- DHCPBULKLEASEQUERY – Issued by a device such as a relay agent to request lease binding information matching specified criteria.
- DHCPLEASEQUERYDONE – Issued by a DHCP server to indicated the end of results for a Bulk LeaseQuery.
- DHCPACTIVELEASEQUERY – Issued by a device to request notification of lease updates from a DHCP server.
- DHCPLEASEQUERYSTATUS – Issued by a DHCP server as a "keep-alive" during an active LeaseQuery session.
- DHCPTLS – Issued to a DHCP server to initiate a TLS connection for transfer of active LeaseQuery bindings.

RFC 2131 defines a number of states in which the client may exist with respect to its IP address configuration using DHCP. The following states are defined:

- INIT – Initialization, meaning the client has no IP address nor any prior configuration information
- INIT-REBOOT – The client initializes though it has prior IP address information and desires to confirm its settings
- BOUND – The client and server are bound in their IP lease agreement
- RENEWING – The client is attempting the renew the lease
- REBINDING – The client is approaching lease expiration and is attempting to renew the lease
- SELECTING – Intermediate state where the client is awaiting and evaluating DHCPOFFERs from DHCP server(s)
- REQUESTING – Intermediate state where the client has selected an Offer and wishes to accept or has identified an Offer for an IP address that is already in use, in which case it sends a DHCPDECLINE to the server
- REBOOTING – Client is attempting to rebind after a reboot

The distinction between renewing and rebinding boils down to the urgency of the renewal request, with rebinding being of higher urgency, and to transport mode, with renewals being unicast and rebinding, broadcast. When a lease is initially obtained, the client sets two timers:

- T1 = 50% of the lease time by default
- T2 = 87.5% of the lease time by default

These timer values may be modified upon agreement between the DHCP client and server by specifying values within corresponding options within the DHCP packet exchange. Upon expiration of the T1 timer, the client enters the renewing state and attempts to renew the lease by unicasting a DHCPRENEW message to the DHCP server from which it obtained the lease. If a DHCPACK is received, the client re-enters the Bound state. If a DHCPNAK is received, the client ceases use of the IP address and enters the INIT state. Otherwise, having not received a response, the client awaits the expiration of the T2 timer, then broadcasts a DHCPRENEW in an attempt to renew the lease. The broadcast is issued in case the original server from which the lease was obtained is down and a failover DHCP server is available to renew the lease.

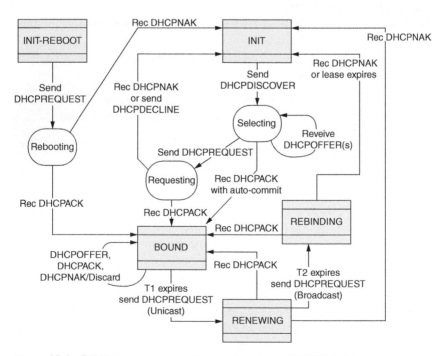

Figure 18.6 DHCP state transitions. Source: Based on RFC 2131 [175].

Table 18.2 DHCP options.

Code	Name	Len	Meaning	References
0	Pad	0	None	RFC 2132 [176]
1	Subnet Mask	4	Subnet Mask in "IP address" format	RFC 2132 [176]
2	Time Offset	4	Time Offset in Seconds from UTC (Deprecated by RFC 4833 which specifies use of options 100 & 101)	RFC 2132 [176]
3	Router	N	N/4[a] Router (default gateway) addresses	RFC 2132 [176]
4	Time Server	N	N/4 Timeserver addresses	RFC 2132 [176]
5	Name Server	N	N/4 IEN-116[b] name server addresses	RFC 2132 [176]
6	Domain Server	N	N/4 DNS server addresses	RFC 2132 [176]
7	Log Server	N	N/4 MIT Laboratory for Computer Science (LCS) UDP log server addresses	RFC 2132 [176]
8	Quotes Server	N	N/4 "Quote of the day" server addresses	RFC 2132 [176]
9	LPR Server	N	N/4 Line Printer server addresses	RFC 2132 [176]
10	Impress Server	N	N/4 Imagen Impress server addresses	RFC 2132 [176]
11	RLP Server	N	N/4 Resource Location Protocol server addresses	RFC 2132 [176]
12	Hostname	N	Client hostname string	RFC 2132 [176]
13	Boot File Size	2	Size of boot file in 512 byte blocks	RFC 2132 [176]
14	Merit Dump File	N	File pathname to which the client should dump its core image in the event of a client crash	RFC 2132 [176]
15	Domain Name	N	The DNS domain name of the client	RFC 2132 [176]

(Continued)

Table 18.2 (Continued)

Code	Name	Len	Meaning	References
16	Swap Server	N	Swap server address	RFC 2132 [176]
17	Root Path	N	Path name for the client's root disk	RFC 2132 [176]
18	Extension File	N	Path name of a file containing vendor-extension information retrievable via TFTP	RFC 2132 [176]
19	Forward On/Off	1	Enable/Disable IP packet forwarding	RFC 2132 [176]
20	Source Routing On/Off	1	Enable/Disable IP packet forwarding for packets specifying non-local source routes	RFC 2132 [176]
21	Policy Filter	N	Specifies acceptable non-local next hops to which IP packets may be forwarded for packets specifying non-local source routes	RFC 2132 [176]
22	Max Datagram Reassembly Size	2	The maximum size datagram the client should be ready to reassemble specified as a 16-bit unsigned integer	RFC 2132 [176]
23	Default IP TTL	1	Default IP time to live value for use in outgoing packet IP header TTL field	RFC 2132 [176]
24	Path MTU Aging Timeout	4	The timeout in seconds when performing path maximum transmission unit (MTU) discovery in accordance with RFC 1191; MTU discovery helps minimize packet fragmentation along the path	RFC 2132 [176]
25	Path MTU Plateau Table	N	A table listing maximum transmission unit (MTU) sizes to use when performing path MTU discovery per RFC 1191	RFC 2132 [176]
26	Interface MTU	2	The value of the maximum transmission unit (MTU) for this device interface	RFC 2132 [176]
27	All Subnets are Local	1	Indicates whether all subnets within the client's network use the same maximum transmission unit (MTU) as the local subnet to which the client is connected	RFC 2132 [176]

Code	Name	Len	Meaning	References
28	Broadcast Address	4	Specifies the broadcast IP address for the client's subnet	RFC 2132 [176]
29	Mask Discovery	1	Specifies whether the client should perform subnet mask discovery or not	RFC 2132 [176]
30	Mask Supplier	1	Specifies whether the client should respond to other clients performing mask discovery	RFC 2132 [176]
31	Router Discovery	1	Specifies whether the client should perform router discovery or not	RFC 2132 [176]
32	Router Solicitation Address	4	Specifies the IP address to which the client should direct router solicitation requests	RFC 2132 [176]
33	Static Route	N	Specifies a set of static routes the client should install in its routing cache; listed as "destination network – next hop router" pairings (Obsoleted by RFC 3442 defining the Classless static route option, 121).	RFC 3442 [177]
34	Trailer Encapsulation	1	Specifies whether the client should attempt to negotiate the use of layer 2 frame trailers (like headers but at the end of the frame payload) in ARP messages	RFC 2132 [176]
35	ARP Timeout	4	ARP cache timeout in seconds	RFC 2132 [176]
36	Ethernet Encapsulation	1	Specifies whether the client should use Ethernet II or IEEE 802.3 on an Ethernet interface	RFC 2132 [176]
37	Default TCP TTL	1	Default TCP time to live value	RFC 2132 [176]
38	TCP Keepalive Time	4	TCP keepalive interval in seconds	RFC 2132 [176]
39	TCP Keepalive Garbage	1	Specifies whether the client should send an octet of "garbage" within TCP keepalive messages for compatibility with older implementations	RFC 2132 [176]

(Continued)

Table 18.2 (Continued)

Code	Name	Len	Meaning	References
40	NIS Domain	N	Network Information Services domain	RFC 2132 [176]
41	NIS Servers	N	N/4 Network Information Services server addresses	RFC 2132 [176]
42	NTP Servers	N	N/4 Network Time Protocol server addresses	RFC 2132 [176]
43	Vendor Specific	N	Vendor specific information	RFC 2132 [176]
44	NETBIOS Name Server	N	N/4 NETBIOS Name server (aka WINS server) addresses	RFC 2132 [176]
45	NBDD Server	N	N/4 NETBIOS Datagram Distribution (NBDD) server addresses	RFC 2132 [176]
46	NETBIOS Node Type	1	Specifies the client as a specific NETBIOS Node Type	RFC 2132 [176]
47	NETBIOS Scope	N	Specifies the NETBIOS scope for the client	RFC 2132 [176]
48	X Window Font Server	N	N/4 X Window Font server addresses	RFC 2132 [176]
49	X Window Display Manager	N	N/4 X Window display manager addresses	RFC 2132 [176]
50	Address Request	4	IP address requested by the client (within a Discover message)	RFC 2132 [176]
51	Address Time	4	IP address lease time requested by the client (within a Discover or Request message)	RFC 2132 [176]
52	Option Overload	1	Indicates that the "sname" and/or "file" DHCP header fields contain additional DHCP option information if options to return to the client exceed the normal option space in the message	RFC 2132 [176]
53	DHCP Message Type	1	DHCP message type as we discussed earlier in this chapter (Discover, Offer, etc.)	RFC 2132 [176]

Code	Name	Len	Meaning	References
54	DHCP Server Identifier	4	DHCP server identification provided in the Offer (and Request and optionally ACK, NAK) to identify the server; e.g. to distinguish among multiple offers	RFC 2132 [176]
55	Parameter List	N	List of DHCP option code numbers for parameters requested by the client	RFC 2132 [176]
56	DHCP Error Message Text	N	Text containing an error message; can be used by the server in a Nak message to the client or by the client in a Decline message; e.g. this text could be included in logging details	RFC 2132 [176]
57	Maximum DHCP Message Size	2	The maximum DHCP message length the client is willing to accept	RFC 2132 [176]
58	Renewal (T1) Time	4	Interval from address assignment time to the time the client enters the Renewing state	RFC 2132 [176]
59	Rebinding (T2) Time	4	Interval from address assignment time to the time the client enters the Rebinding state	RFC 2132 [176]
60	Vendor Class Identifier	N	Used by clients to specify a vendor-specific identifier	RFC 2132 [176]
61	Client Id	N	Client Identifier	RFC 2132 [176]
62	Netware/IP Domain	N	Netware/IP Domain Name	RFC 2242 [178]
63	Netware/IP Option	N	Netware/IP sub Options	RFC 2242 [178]
64	NIS+ Domain	N	Network Information Services+ (NIS+) client domain name	RFC 2132 [176]
65	NIS+ Servers	N	N/4 Network Information Services+ (NIS+) server addresses	RFC 2132 [176]

(Continued)

Table 18.2 (Continued)

Code	Name	Len	Meaning	References
66	TFTP Server Name	N	TFTP server name; can be used when the "sname" DHCP header field has been overloaded with other options	RFC 2132 [176]
67	Bootfile Name	N	Boot file name; can be used when the "file" DHCP header field has been overloaded with other options	RFC 2132 [176]
68	Home Agent	N	N/4 Mobile IP home agent addresses	RFC 2132 [176]
69	SMTP Server	N	N/4 Simple Mail Transfer Protocol (SMTP) server addresses for outgoing e-mail	RFC 2132 [176]
70	POP3 Server	N	N/4 Post Office Protocol v3 (POP3) server addresses for incoming e-mail retrieval	RFC 2132 [176]
71	NNTP Server	N	N/4 Network News Transport Protocol (NNTP) server addresses	RFC 2132 [176]
72	WWW Server	N	N/4 World Wide Web (WWW) server addresses	RFC 2132 [176]
73	Finger Server	N	N/4 Finger server addresses; finger servers enable retrieval of host user information regarding login name, login duration, and more	RFC 2132 [176]
74	IRC Server	N	N/4 Internet Relay Chat (IRC) server addresses	RFC 2132 [176]
75	StreetTalk Server	N	N/4 StreetTalk server addresses; StreetTalk was a Banyan Vines user and resource directory	RFC 2132 [176]
76	STDA Server	N	N/4 StreetTalk Directory Assistance (STDA) server addresses; StreetTalk was a Banyan Vines user and resource directory	RFC 2132 [176]
77	User-Class	N	User Class Identifier	RFC 3004 [179]
78	SLP Directory Agent	N+1	N/4 Service Location Protocol (SLP) Directory Agent IP address(es)	RFC 2610 [180]
79	SLP Service Scope	N	Service Location Protocol (SLP) service scope the SLP agent is configured to use	RFC 2610 [180]

Code	Name	Len	Meaning	References
80	Rapid Commit	0	Rapid Commit – requests a two-packet DHCP transaction instead of the normal four packet DORA process for mobility or overhead-constrained applications	RFC 4039 [181]
81	Client FQDN	N	Fully Qualified Domain Name – defines the client's FQDN and whether the client or DHCP server should update DNS	RFC 4702 [182]
82	Relay Agent Information	N	Relay Agent Information – additional client information supplied by the intervening relay agent	RFC 3046 [31]
83	Internet Storage Name Service	N	Internet Storage Name Service (iSNS) server addresses and iSNS application information	RFC 4174 [183]
84	Unassigned	--	--	RFC 3679 [184]
85	NDS Servers	N	N/4 Novell Directory Services (NDS) Server IP addresses to contact for NDS client authentication and access the NDS directory repository	RFC 2241 [185]
86	NDS Tree Name	N	Novell Directory Services (NDS) tree name of the NDS repository the client should contact	RFC 2241 [185]
87	NDS Context	N	Novell Directory Services (NDS) initial context within the NDS repository the NDS client should use	RFC 2241 [185]
88	BCMCS Controller Domain Name	N	Broadcast and Multicast Server domain name (FQDN) list, used to construct follow-up SRV query(ies) (BCMCS is used in 3G wireless networks to receive broadcast and multicast services)	RFC 4280 [136]
89	BCMCS Controller IPv4 address	N	N/4 Broadcast and Multicast Server (BCMCS) Controller IP address(es) (BCMCS is used in 3G wireless networks to enable mobiles to receive broadcast and multicast services)	RFC 4280 [136]

(Continued)

Table 18.2 (Continued)

Code	Name	Len	Meaning	References
90	Authentication	N	Authentication option used to communicate authentication information between the client and server in accordance with the DHCP authentication protocol	RFC3118 [81]
91	Client-last-transaction-time option	4	Seconds since the last DHCP transaction with the client on this lease as queried in a DHCP Lease Query message	RFC 4388 [186]
92	Associated-ip option	N	List of IP addresses associated with the client as queried in a DHCP Lease Query message	RFC 4388 [186]
93	PXE Client System	N	PXE client system architecture type(s) each encoded as 16-bit code, e.g. Intel x86PC, DEC Alpha, EFI x86-64, etc.	RFC 4578 [47]
94	PXE Client Network Interface	3	PXE client network interface identifier with individual octets encoded for interface type, interface major version number, and interface minor version number	RFC 4578 [47]
95	LDAP	N	Lightweight Directory Access Protocol servers; this option is used by Apple Computer though no governing RFC has been published	RFC 3679 [184]
96	Unassigned	—	—	RFC 3679 [184]
97	PXE Client Machine Identifier	N	PXE client machine identifier with encoded type and identifier value	RFC 4578 [47]
98	User Authentication Protocol	N	List of locations (URLs) for services capable of processing authentication requests encapsulated using Open Group's User Authentication Protocol (UAP)	RFC 2485 [187]

Code	Name	Len	Meaning	References
99	Civic Location	—	Location of the server, network element closest to the client or the client itself as provided by the server encoded in country-specific civic (e.g. postal) format	RFC 4776 [137]
100	Time Zone	N	Time Zone encoded as IEEE 1003.1 TZ (POSIX)	RFC 4833 [140]
101	Time Zone database	N	Reference to a local (on the client) TZ database for lookup of time zone	RFC 4833 [140]
102-108	Unassigned	—	—	RFC 3679 [184]
109	Softwire Address	N	IPv6 address assigned via DHCPv4 over DHCPv6	RFC 8539 [173]
110-111	Unassigned	—	—	RFC 3679 [184]
112	Netinfo Address	N	NetInfo Parent Server Address; this option is used by Apple Computer though no governing RFC has been published; NetInfo is a distributed database user and resource information for Apple devices.	RFC 3679 [184]
113	Netinfo Tag	N	NetInfo Parent Server Tag; this option is used by Apple Computer though no governing RFC has been published. NetInfo is distributed database user and resource information for Apple devices.	RFC 3679 [184]
114	DHCP Captive Portal	N	Informs the client that they are behind a captive portal with a URI to an authentication function	RFC 8910 [167]
115	Unassigned	—	—	RFC 3679 [184]
116	Auto-Configure	1	Instructs the client to auto-configure a link local address (69.254.0.0/16) or not. This can be used by the DHCP server to inform the client that it has no IP addresses to assign and that the client may or may not auto-configure	RFC 2563 [188]
117	Name Service Search	N	Lists one or more name services in priority order that the client should use for name resolution: DNS, NIS, NIS+, or WINS	RFC 2937 [189]

(Continued)

Table 18.2 (Continued)

Code	Name	Len	Meaning	References
118	Subnet Selection	4	Identifies an IP subnet (address) from which to allocate an IP address to this client – overrides the GIAddr setting or DHCP server interface on which a broadcast Discover was received	RFC 3011 [190]
119	Domain Search	N	List of one or more domains for configuration of the client's resolver. If the application requests a resolution for a non-FQDN hostname, these domain(s) will successively be appended to the hostname prior to querying	RFC 3397 [191]
120	SIP Servers	N	A listing of one or more of either Session Initiation Protocol (SIP) server FQDN(s) or of SIP server IP address(es). SIP is a control protocol for management of multimedia calls or sessions.	RFC 3361 [192]
121	Classless Static Route	N	Specifies a set of static routes the client should install in its routing cache; listed as "<CIDR mask length>.<destination network> – next hop router" pairings. The destination network is enumerated only to significant octets, dropping local (non-subnet) portions; for example, 172.16.0.0/12 would be encoded as 12.172.16 and 10.0.0/18 as 18.10.0.0	RFC 3442 [193]
122	CableLabs Client Configuration	N	Specifies resource (e.g. provisioning server, DHCP server, etc.) locations and parameters for use by cable multimedia terminal adapters (MTAs), which are customer premises devices operating over a DOCSIS cable network, providing VoIP and related multimedia services	RFC 3495 [194]
123	Location Configuration Information	16	Provides the client its Location Configuration Information (LCI), including latitude, longitude, altitude and resolution of each coordinate	RFC 6225 [152]

Code	Name	Len	Meaning	References
124	Vendor-Identifying Vendor Class	N	Enables specification of multiple vendor classes, each identified by IANA-assigned Enterprise Number (EN); this is useful to identify the hardware vendor, software vendor, application vendor, etc. supporting the device	RFC 3925 [195]
125	Vendor-Identifying Vendor-Specific Information	N	Set of DHCP options grouped by vendor as identified by IANA-assigned Enterprise Number (EN);	RFC 3925 [195]
126-127	Unassigned	—	—	RFC 3679 [184]
128	PXE – undefined (vendor specific)			RFC 4578 [47]
Over-loaded			Etherboot signature. 6 bytes: E4:45:74:68:00:00	
			DOCSIS "full security" server IP address	
			TFTP Server IP address (for IP Phone software load)	
129	PXE – undefined (vendor specific)			RFC 4578 [47]
Over-loaded			Kernel options. Variable length string	
			Call Server IP address	
130	PXE – undefined (vendor specific)			RFC 4578 [47]
Over-loaded			Ethernet interface. Variable length string.	
			Discrimination string (to identify vendor)	

(Continued)

Table 18.2 (Continued)

Code	Name	Len	Meaning	References
131	PXE – undefined (vendor specific)			RFC 4578 [47]
Over-loaded	Remote statistics server IP address			
132	PXE – undefined (vendor specific)			RFC 4578 [47]
Over-loaded	802.1Q VLAN ID			
133	PXE – undefined (vendor specific)			RFC 4578 [47]
Over-loaded	802.1D/p Layer 2 Priority			
134	PXE – undefined (vendor specific)			RFC 4578 [47]
Over-loaded	Diffserv Code Point for VoIP signaling and media streams			
135	PXE – undefined (vendor specific)			RFC 4578 [47]
Over-loaded	HTTP Proxy for phone-specific applications			
136	PANA Agent	N	Identifies one or more IPv4 addresses of PANA (Protocol for carrying Authentication for Network Access) Authentication Agents for use by the client for authentication and authorization for network access service	RFC 5192 [139]
137	OPTION_V4_LOST	N	Location to Service Translation (LoST) server domain name; LoST protocol maps service identifiers and location information to service URLs	RFC 5223 [144]

Code	Name	Len	Meaning	References
138	CAPWAP Access Controller	N	Control and Provisioning of Wireless Access Points (CAPWAP) Access Controller IP address(es) to which the client may connect	RFC 5417 [145]
139	MoS Service IP addresses	N	IPv4 address(es) for servers providing particular types of IEEE 802.21 Mobility Service (MoS)	RFC 5678 [147]
140	MoS Service FQDNs	N	FQDN(s) for servers providing particular types of IEEE 802.21 Mobility Service (MoS)	RFC 5678 [147]
141	SIP UA Configuration Service Domains	N	DHCP SIP user agent configuration service domains	RFC 6011 [150]
142	ANDSF IPv4 address	N	IP address of the Access Network Discovery and Selection Function (ANDSF)	RFC 6153 [174]
143	SZTP bootstrap server URIs	N	Secure Zero Touch Provisioning (SZTP) bootstrap server list	RFC 8572 [196]
144	Geospatial Location	N	Geographic location (latitude, longitude and altitude) of the client as provided by the DHCP server	RFC 6225 [152]
145	ForceRenew Nonce Capable	N	Nonce value sent from the server to the client for authentication of possible future ForceRenew messages	RFC 6704 [197]
146	RDNSS selection	N	Recursive DNS Server selection for multi-interfaced nodes	RFC 6731 [158]
147-149	Unassigned			
150	TFTP server address (Tentatively Assigned – 23 June 2005) Etherboot GRUB configuration path name			RFC 5859 [293]
151	DHCP Bulk LeaseQuery status code			RFC 6926 [199]

(Continued)

Table 18.2 (Continued)

Code	Name	Len	Meaning	References
152	DHCP Bulk LeaseQuery base-time at which the LeaseQuery was created			RFC 6926 [199]
153	DHCP Bulk LeaseQuery elapsed time since the given IP address entered its current state			RFC 6926 [199]
154	DHCP Bulk LeaseQuery filters results by the time after which lease binding changes are requested			RFC 6926 [199]
155	DHCP Bulk LeaseQuery filters results by the time before which lease binding changes are requested			RFC 6926 [199]
156	DHCP Bulk LeaseQuery dhcp lease state			RFC 6926 [199]
157	DHCP Bulk LeaseQuery data source when two or more servers have information about the IP address binding			RFC 6926 [199]
158	Port Control Protocol (PCP) server IP address(es)			RFC 7291 [163]
159	Shared IPv4 address space port parameters			RFC 7618 [200]
160	Unassigned.			
161	Manufacturer Usage Description (MUD) URL provided by a device to identify device and manufacturer information			RFC 8520 [170]
162–174	Unassigned			RFC 3942 [198]
175	Etherboot (Tentatively Assigned – 23 June 2005)			
176	IP Telephone (Tentatively Assigned – 23 June 2005)			
177	Etherboot (Tentatively Assigned – 23 June 2005)			
178–207	Unassigned			RFC 3942 [198]
208	PXE Magic (deprecated)	4	F1:00:74:7E	RFC 5071 [201]

Code	Name	Len	Meaning	References
209	PXE Configuration File	N	Configuration filename or file pathname for second stage PXE boot loading	RFC 5071 [201]
210	PXE Path Prefix	N	Configuration file path prefix to the filename specified in the PXE configuration file option [204]	RFC 5071 [201]
211	PXE Reboot Time	4	Number of seconds to wait to "reboot if TFTP server is unreachable	RFC 5071 [201]
212	6rd Configuration	18 + N	Service provider's 6rd prefix and 6rd border relay IPv4 address(es)	RFC 5969 [202]
213	Access network domain name		Local Location Information Server (LIS) discovery	RFC 5986 [149]
214-219	Unassigned			
220	Subnet Allocation Option (Tentatively Assigned – 23 June 2005)			RFC 6656 [294]
221	Virtual Subnet Selection Option (Tentatively Assigned – 23 June 2005)			RFC 6607 [46]
222-223	Unassigned			RFC 3942 [198]
224-254	Reserved (Private Use)			
255	End	0	None	RFC 2132 [176]

[a] The N/4 notation refers to the use of "N" bytes to represent one or more IPv4 addresses, each of which is comprised of four bytes; thus, for a length of N, the field would contain N/4 complete IPv4 addresses. This implies of course that N is a multiple of 4 in cases where the data type is IP address.

[b] IEN-116 = Internet Experiment Note 116; IENs were eventually merged with RFCs as TCP/IP went into production across ARPANET.

Figure 18.6 depicts the state transition diagram among these DHCP client states and the respective state transition mechanisms. Note that the DHCPINFORM message is not included in the figure as this relates to non-IP address parameters. A client already configured with an IP address issues the DHCPINFORM to request additional parameter settings and the server replies with a DHCPACK indicating the requested values.

DHCP Options

Table 18.2 lists the current set of defined DHCP options. The Code column indicates the option code or number, and the name column lists the corresponding option name. Note that the Len (Length) column indicates the value of the Length field within the option. The total option length is this value plus two bytes, one byte for the code and one for the length field itself.

19

DNS Reference

DNS Message Format

Encoding of Domain Names

Chapter 4 discussed the organization of DNS information in the form of a domain hierarchy as well as the basics of how a client or resolver performs resolution by issuing a query to a recursive DNS server which in turn iterates the query in accordance with the domain hierarchy to obtain the answer to the query. In this chapter, we'll dig deeper into the DNS process and message format, but first we'll discuss the representation of domain names within DNS messages.

Domain names are formatted as a series of *labels*. Labels consist of a one-byte field specifying the length of the label, followed by that number of bytes/ASCII characters representing the label itself. This sequence of labels is terminated by a length field of zero indicating the root " . " domain. For example, the series of labels for www.ipamworldwide.com. would look like the depiction in Figure 19.1 in ASCII format.

Starting at the upper left of Figure 19.1, the value '3' of the first length byte indicates that the following three bytes comprise first label, 'www'. The fifth or next byte after this is our next length byte, which has a value of '13' (0xD), which is the length of 'ipamworldwide'. After this label, the following byte of value '3' is the length of 'com'. Finally, the zero value byte indicates the root ' . ' domain, fully qualifying the domain name. Note that the darker shaded bytes in the figure are encoded as length bytes to differentiate them from host or domain name characters containing numbers. The first byte in a name will

IP Address Management, Second Edition. Michael Dooley and Timothy Rooney.
© 2021 The Institute of Electrical and Electronics Engineers, Inc.
Published 2021 by John Wiley & Sons, Inc.

almost always[1] be a length byte followed by that number of bytes representing the first label, immediately followed by another length byte to eliminate ambiguity.

Name Compression

A given DNS message may contain multiple domain names, and many of these may have repetitive information, the `ipamworldwide.com.` suffix for example. The DNS specification enables message compression in order to reduce repetitive information and thereby reduce the size of the DNS message. This works by using *pointers* to other locations within the DNS message that specify a common domain suffix. This domain suffix is then appended at the point of location referenced by the pointer.

Let's say for example, that our query for `www.ipamworldwide.com.` returns a pair of DNS servers that can be queried for more information: `ns1 .ipamworldwide.com.`, and `ns2.isp.com`. The `ipamworldwide.com.` portion of these domain names is common to the query and one of the answers, while only the `.com` portion is common to the question, first answer and the second answer. Thus, the message is formulated by fully specifying the domain name `www.ipamworldwide.com.` as illustrated in Figure 19.1. Then when specifying `ns1`, instead of fully specifying `ns1.ipamworldwide.com`, only `ns1` is specified, followed by a pointer to the `ipamworldwide.com.` suffix earlier in the message. When identifying `ns2.isp.com`, the `ns2.isp` labels are specified, followed by a pointer to the `.com` suffix within the message.

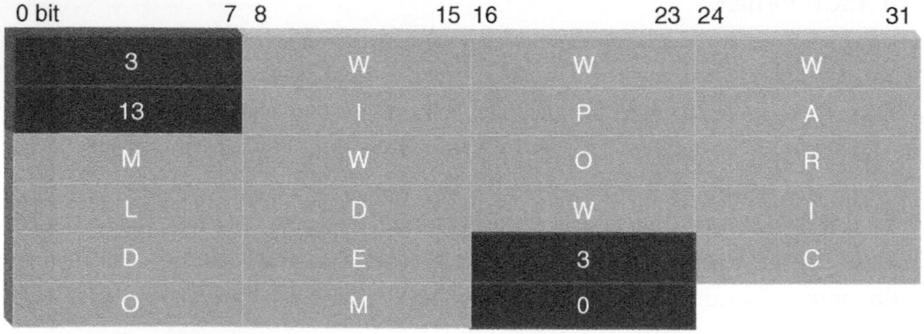

0 bit	7	8	15	16	23	24	31
3		W		W		W	
13		I		P		A	
M		W		O		R	
L		D		W		I	
D		E		3		C	
O		M		0			

Figure 19.1 DNS labels for www.ipamworldwide.com.

---

[1]As we'll discuss next, the length byte may alternatively consist of a two-byte pointer or a DNS extensions label.

How do DNS resolvers and servers differentiate a pointer from a standard label length byte? The DNS standard stipulates that each label may be of length 0–63 bytes. In binary, this is 000000000 to 00111111. Thus, the first two bits, 00 in this case, identify the byte as a standard length byte, indicating the length of the following label. A pointer is identified by setting the first two bits to $[11]_2$, and is comprised of two bytes, where the $[11]_2$ bits are followed by 14 bits identifying the offset in bytes from beginning of the DNS header. The first byte of the DNS message header is considered byte 0, and as the message is created, pointers are defined pointing to byte offsets from this point.

Let's look at how this maps out from our prior example. Let's say that beginning 12 bytes from the DNS header, we've included the domain name, www .ipamworldwide.com. Now, later in the message, beginning at byte 56 from the beginning of the header, we would like to encode responses ns1 .ipamworldwide.com and ns2.isp.com.

Figure 19.2 indicates how this would look. The first portion is as we discussed earlier, with length bytes (dark shading) followed by the respective number of label bytes (light shading). At byte position 56 in our example, the ns1 portion of the name is encoded normally, using a label length of '3', followed by ns1. However, the next byte is not a standard length byte but a pointer "double-byte" as it begins with $[11]_2$ and is shown as shaded black in the figure. The value encoded in the 14-bit offset field of the pointer is '16,' indicating that the portion of the domain name starting at an offset of 16 bytes from the start of the DNS header should be appended to the ns1 label already specified. The first row of bytes in Figure 19.2 below enumerates the individual byte offsets (italics), and byte 16 is the length byte of value '13,' followed by encoding for ipamworldwide, followed by a length byte of value '3,' then com, then . (length byte of value '0'). Concatenating this together, we arrive at the result: ns1.ipamworldwide.com.

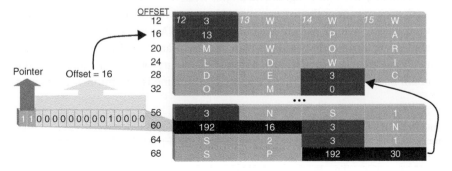

Figure 19.2 Name compression with pointers.

Returning to the next domain name after processing the pointer, we find encoding for ns2.isp followed by a pointer to byte offset 30[2], which points to the length byte of '3,' followed by com., completing the domain name as ns2.isp .com. Considering just these three example domain names, the number of bytes in the message occupied by domain names can be compressed from 59 to 39 bytes.

Internationalized Domain Names

DNS resolvers and servers communicate hostname queries and responses in ASCII-formatted messages. Configuration information is stored in ASCII text files or databases. Unfortunately, while ASCII characters have been defined to effectively represent the English language, they do not enable formatting of characters from other languages, especially those using a non-Latin based alphabet. This limitation certainly impacts the ease-of-use of IP applications in countries where people do not use the English language. RFC 5891 [203] is a standards track RFC that addresses this limitation.

RFC 5891 is one of six (5890–5895) RFCs addressing Internationalizing Domain Names in Applications (IDNA). The "in applications" qualifier in the title insinuates the involvement of applications in this process. Indeed, the onus is placed on the application, such as a web browser or email client, to convert the user's native language entry into an ASCII-based string that can be communicated to a DNS server for resolution. This ingenious approach enables application level support of international character sets for end users without affecting the DNS protocol (or other ASCII based IP protocols like simple mail transfer protocol (SMTP) either). Existing DNS servers can be configured to resolve these ASCII-encoded domain names as they would for native ASCII-based domain names.

International character sets are encoded as Unicode characters. The Unicode standard "provides a unique number for every character, no matter what the platform, no matter what the program, no matter what the language," according to the Unicode Consortium website (www.unicode.org). Every character is represented as a unique 2–3 byte hexadecimal number. The IDNA RFCs describe the process of converting a unicode-based domain name to an ASCII-formatted domain name. Note that technically, the domain labels are each converted, not the "domain name." As we just discussed, a domain name is communicated using a

---

[2]Note that pointer double bytes shown above in black are displayed with their byte-wise decimal number representation, which in our example conveniently displays the offset in decimal in the second byte. But just to state the obvious, don't rely on just this second byte when parsing a pointer, as a pointer value can range from 0 to 214= 16,384, which at this maximum value the decimal representation would be 255-255.

series of domain labels, one for each domain level or text string between the dots, each encoded with a length byte beginning with $[00]_2$.

To resolve international domain names, a DNS server must be configured with resource records encoded in ASCII format, specifically unicode-mapped ASCII characters referred to as *punycode*. The output of the punycode algorithm results in an ASCII string, which is then prefixed with the ASCII Compatible Encoding (ACE) header, xn--. Thus, within the DNS infrastructure, domains denoted as xn--<additional ASCII characters> are likely punycode representations of an international domain name. The application, e.g. web browser, is responsible for converting the user-entered URL into unicode format, then into punycode. The punycode domain name is passed to the resolver on the client for resolution via DNS using ASCII characters. The punycode algorithm is specified in RFC 3492 and several websites are available for performing conversions for entry in to DNS.

Consider an example [204]: let's consider a web server host address in the źdźbło.com domain. as www.źdźbło.com. The domain name contains diacritics and has characters outside of the ASCII character set. The web browser in which this URL is entered would convert this to ASCII characters or punycode as www.xn--dbo-iwa1zb.com. A corresponding A or AAAA record entry in DNS for the www.xn--dbo-iwa1zb.com. host would enable the end user to enter a native language URL while utilizing the existing base of DNS servers deployed throughout the world to identify and connect via the IP address of the destination web server. The net result is that these DNS messages sent on the wire are encoded in ASCII characters.

DNS Message Format

Now let's look more closely at the format of DNS messages used to perform this overall resolution function, incorporating the label formatted domain names we discussed earlier. DNS messages are transmitted over UDP by default, using port 53. TCP can also be used on port 53. The basic format of a DNS message is illustrated in Figure 19.3.

- The message header contains fields that define the type of message and associated information, including the number of records for each of the following fields.
- The Question section specifies the information being sought via this message.
- The Answer section contains zero or more resource records that answer the query specified in the Question section.
- The Authority section contains zero or more resource records referring to NSs authoritative for the given answer or pointing to delegated NSs down the domain tree to which a successive iterative query may be issued.

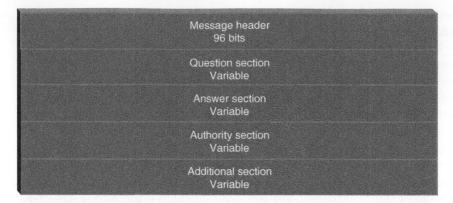

Figure 19.3   DNS message fields. Source: Based on RFC 1035 [28].

- The Additional section contains zero or more resource records that contain supplemental information related to the Question but are not strictly answers to the Question.

Message Header

The DNS message header is included with every DNS message and conveys what type of message is enclosed as well as associated parameters as illustrated in Figure 19.4.

The message header is comprised of six 16-bit fields:

- *Message ID* – Also referred to as transaction ID, an identifier assigned by the resolver and copied in replies from the DNS server to enable resolver correlation of responses with queries.
- *Codes* – Message codes germane to this message. We'll examine these code fields next.

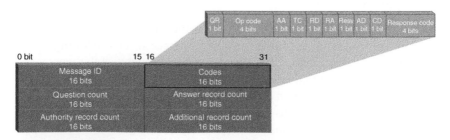

Figure 19.4   DNS message header. Source: Based on RFC 1035 [28].

- *Question count (QDCOUNT)* – The number of questions contained in the Question section of the DNS message.
- *Answer record count (ANCOUNT)* – The number of resource records contained in the Answer section of the DNS message
- *Authority record count (NSCOUNT)* – The number of resource records contained in the Authority section of the DNS message.
- *Additional record count (ARCOUNT)* – The number of resource records contained in the Additional section of the DNS message.

The following Codes bits have been defined:

- Query/Response (*QR*) – This flag indicates that this message is a query (0) or a response (1).
- Opcode – The operation code for this message. Presently, the following values have been defined:
  - o 0 = Query
  - o 1 = Reserved (formerly inverse query, now retired)
  - o 2 = Server status request
  - o 3 = Reserved
  - o 4 = Notify – enables a master zone server to inform a secondary server with the same zone (and for a secondary to acknowledge) that a change has been made to the zone data. For Notify messages, the Authority and Additional sections are not used and respective record counts in the DNS header should be set to 0.
  - o 5 = Update – enables a client or DHCP server to update zone data on a DNS server. For Update messages, the interpretation of DNS message fields and corresponding header fields differs from that described above. The message format for Update messages is described in the DNS Update Messages section.
  - o 6 = DNS Stateful Operations (*DSO*) for persistent stateful sessions with a DNS server
  - o 7–15 = Unassigned
- *Authoritative Answer (AA)* – When set, this message contains an authoritative answer to the question. This means the response was derived from a DNS server that was configured with the zone's information. If it is not set, the answer was derived from a non-authoritative DNS server, likely cached information from a prior query. Where multiple answers are provided, this flag pertains to the first record in the answers section. When set by the client on the query, this indicates that an authoritative answer (not cached) is required.
- *Truncated Response (TC)* – This code indicates that this message was truncated for transmission. This is generally due to the packet length restriction of UDP packets, the default transport layer protocol used by DNS.

- *Recursion Desired (RD)* – This flag indicates that the querier would like the DNS server to iteratively resolve the query, traversing the domain tree as necessary. Most resolvers set this flag to indicate a query as a recursive query, while a DNS server will not generally not set this flag when querying other servers.
- *Recursion Available (RA)* – This flag indicates that recursive query support is available from this DNS server.
- Reserved or Z bit – Reserved (0).
- *Authentic Data (AD)* – Used within the context of DNS security extensions, this bit is set by a name server to indicate that information within the answer and authority sections is authentic, meaning it has been authenticated.
- *Checking Disabled (CD)* – Used within the context of DNSSEC, this bit enables a DNSSEC resolver to disable signature validation in a DNSSEC name server's processing of this particular query.
- *Response Code (RCODE)* – Provides result status to the client. The currently defined response codes are summarized in Table 19.1. Note that given the four-bit RCODE field, decimal values 1–15 are encoded within the DNS header RCODE field.

The DNS extensions (EDNS0, discussed later in this chapter) OPT resource record adds a capacity for 8 additional RCODE bits, bringing the total to 12 bits (up to decimal value 4095) when used in combination with the header RCODE bits. Transaction key (*TKEY*) and Transaction signature (*TSIG*) recrods have a 16-bit error field supporting encoding values up to 65 535.

You'll notice two interpretations of the decimal value 16. BADVERS is the interpretation when encoded within the OPT resource record while BADSIG is the result when encoded within a TKEY or TSIG resource record.

Question Section

The Question section within the DNS message format contains, as you might have guessed, the question that is being asked for this query. This section can contain more than one question, as identified by the number referenced in the QDCOUNT header field. Each of these questions has the following format (Figure 19.5).

The QNAME field contains the domain name, formatted as a series of labels. The QTYPE field indicates the query type, or for what purpose is this question being asked. Any resource record type may be included, which we will cover in detail later in the chapter. However, there are some QTYPE values that are unique to requesting zone transfers for example that are presently defined including those listed in Table 19.2.

Table 19.1 DNS message response Codes.[a]

RCODE				
Decimal	**Hex**	**Name**	**Description**	**References**
0	0	NoError	No errors	RFC 1035 [28]
1	1	FormErr	Format error – server unable to interpret the query	RFC 1035 [28]
2	2	ServFail	Server failure – server problem has prevented processing of this query	RFC 1035 [28]
3	3	NXDomain	Non-existent domain – domain name does not exist	RFC 1035 [28]
4	4	NotImp	Not implemented – query type not supported by this server	RFC 1035 [28]
5	5	Refused	Query refused – server refused the requested query; e.g. refusal of a zone transfer request	RFC 1035 [28]
6	6	YXDomain	Name exists when it should not as determined during DNS update pre-requisite processing; DNAME substitution renders name too long	RFC 2136 [205], RFC 6672 [206]
7	7	YXRRSet	RR Set exists when it should not as determined during DNS update pre-requisite processing	RFC 2136 [205]
8	8	NXRRSet	RR Set that should exist does not as determined during DNS update pre-requisite processing	RFC 2136 [205]
9	9	NotAuth	Server is not authoritative for the zone listed in the zone section of the DNS update message; TSIG error	RFC 2136 [205], RFC 2845 [207]
10	A	NotZone	Name used in the pre-requisite or update section of a DNS Update message is not contained in zone denoted by the zone section of the message	RFC 2136 [205]

(Continued)

Table 19.1   (Continued)

RCODE				
Decimal	**Hex**	**Name**	**Description**	**References**
11	B	DSOTYPENI	Server supports DNS Stateful Operation but not the DSO-TYPE of the primary type-length-value (TLV) in the DSO request message	RFC 8490 [208]
12–15	C–F	Available for assignment		
16	10	BADVERS	Unsupported (bad) OPT RR version	RFC 2671 [209]
16	10	BADSIG	TSIG Signature Failure	RFC 2845 [207]
17	11	BADKEY	Key not recognized	RFC 2845 [207]
18	12	BADTIME	Signature out of the valid server signature time window	RFC 2845 [207]
19	13	BADMODE	Invalid TKEY Mode – requested mode not supported by this server	RFC 2930 [210]
20	14	BADNAME	Non-existent or duplicate key name	RFC 2930 [210]
21	15	BADALG	Algorithm not supported	RFC 2930 [210]
22	16	BADTRUNC	Bad truncation – Message Authentication Code (MAC) too short	RFC 4635 [211]
23	17	BADCOOKIE	Bad or missing server DNS cookie	RFC 7873 [212]
24-3840	18-F00	Available for assignment		
3841-4095	F01-FFF	Reserved for Private Use		RFC 5395 [213]
4096-65534	1000-FFFE	Unassigned		
65535	FFFF	Reserved		

[a] If you consult the IANA web site (www.iana.org/assignments/dns-parameters), you'll notice values above 4095. Technically these are not RCODEs but reflect the 16-bit error field within the the TSIG and TKEY meta resource record types, providing a capacity up to 65535 for these two resource record types.

The QCLASS field indicates for which class this query is being made; e.g. IN for Internet class, the most common class. Classes essentially enable management of parallel namespaces. Currently defined QCLASSes (and DNS CLASSes) in general are defined in Table 19.3.

Table 19.2   DNS QTYPEs [214].

QTypes only	Query purpose	QType ID (decimal)	IETF status	Defining document
*	All resource records	255	Standard	RFC 1035
MAILA	Mail agent resource records	254	Obsolete	RFC 1035
MAILB	Mailbox resource records	253	Obsolete	RFC 1035
AXFR	Absolute zone transfer (entire zone)	252	Standard	RFC 1035
IXFR	Incremental zone transfer (changes only)	251	Proposed Standard	RFC 1995

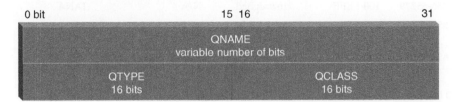

Figure 19.5   Question section format. Source: Based on RFC 1035 [28].

Answer Section

The Answer Section contains zero or more answers in the form of resource records. The number of answers is specified in the ANCOUNT header field. We'll discuss the different types of resource records later in this chapter, and they all share a common generic format as defined in Figure 19.6 and described below.

- The Name field, also called the Owner name field, is the lookup name corresponding to this resource record (corresponding to the lookup value or QNAME in the original question).
- The Type field indicates the type of information that is provided for this name. For example, a type of A means that this resource record provides IPv4 address information for the given name. Resource record types are summarized later in this chapter.
- The Class field represents the namespace class, such as IN for Internet. Valid classes are displayed in Table 19.3.
- The TTL or Time-to-live field provides a time value in seconds with respect to the valid lifetime of the resource record. The receiver of this information may

Table 19.3 DNS classes [214].

CLASS				
Decimal	**Hexadecimal**	**Name**	**Description**	**References**
0	0	Reserved	Reserved	RFC 5395
1	1	IN	Internet	RFC 1035
2	2	Unassigned	N/A	IANA
3	3	CH	Chaos	RFC 1035
4	4	HS	Hesiod	RFC 1035
5-253	5-FD	Unassigned	N/A	IANA
254	FE	None	None	RFC 2136
255	FF	Any	Any class (valid as QCLASS but not on resource records)	RFC 1035
256-65279	100-FEFF	Unassigned	N/A	IANA
65280-65534	FF00-FFFE	Reserved for Private Use	—	RFC 5395
65535	FFFF	Reserved	Reserved	RFC 5395

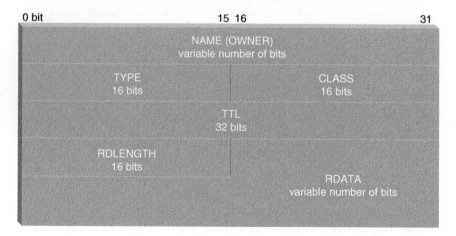

Figure 19.6 Answer section format. Source: Based on RFC 1035 [28].

cache this information for *TTL* seconds and may use it reliably. However, upon expiration of the TTL, the cached information should be discarded and a new query issued.

- The RDLength field indicates the length in bytes of the results field, RData.

- The RData field contains the corresponding information of the specified Type in the identified Class, for the given Owner. The RData field has a variable format as we shall see when examining the wide variety of resource record types.

Authority Section

The Authority Section contains NSCOUNT number of answers in the form of resource records of the same format as discussed in the Answer section. Generally only NS (name server) resource records are valid within the Authority section, though most name servers return a SOA record in this section if the queried name server is authoritative but the answer section is empty. This section also contains information about other name servers that are authoritative for the queried information. This information is used by the querying resolver or more likely, recursive name server, to determine the next name server to query in traversing the domain tree to find the ultimate answer.

Additional Section

The Additional Section contains ASCOUNT number of answers in the form of resource records, which provide additional or related information to the query, in the same format as discussed in the Answer section.

DNS Update Messages

Update messages enable a client, DHCP server, or other source to perform an update (add, modify, or delete) of one or more resource records within a zone. While Update messages utilize the same basic format as DNS messages just described, the interpretation of some of the fields varies. Update messages, denoted with Op Code = 5 in the DNS message header, are encoded as follows (Figure 19.7).

Contrast this format with that for non-Update DNS messages depicted in Figure 19.3. The message header is of the same format as that of "normal" DNS messages, though the interpretation differs.

The Zone section identifies the DNS zone to be updated by this Update message. The Prerequisite section enables the specification of conditions that must be satisfied in order to perform the update successfully. The condition and type of condition are determined by the value of each resource record-encoded parameter within the Prerequisite section. Table 19.4 defines how DNS Update prerequisites are interpreted based on the values of the owner, class, type and rdata fields within the Prerequisites section.

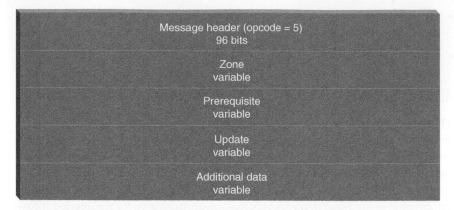

Figure 19.7 DNS update message format. Source: From RFC 2136 [205].

Table 19.4 DNS update prerequisite encoding.

OWNER	CLASS	TYPE	RDATA	Prerequisite interpretation
Match	ANY [250]	ANY	Empty	The matching owner name is in use in this zone
Match	ANY [250]	Match	Empty	An RRSet with matching owner and type exists (value independent, i.e. any Rdata match)
Match	NONE [249]	ANY	Empty	The matching owner name is not in use in this zone
Match	NONE [249]	Match	Empty	An RRSet with matching owner and type does not exist in this zone
Match	Same as Zone Class	Match	Match	An RRSet with matching owner, type and Rdata exists in this zone (value dependent, i.e. Rdata match)

The Update section contains the resource records to be added to or deleted from the zone using a similar encoding as used in the Prerequisite section as follows (Table 19.5).

The Additional Data section contains resource records related to this update; e.g. out of zone glue records.

Table 19.5 DNS update action encoding.

OWNER	CLASS	TYPE	RDATA	Update interpretation
Owner to add	Same as Zone Class	RR type	RR Rdata	Add this resource record(s) of the specified owner, type and Rdata to the zone's RRSet
Owner to delete	ANY [250]	RR type	Empty	Delete the resource records of the specified owner and type
Owner to delete	ANY [250]	ANY	Empty	Delete all resource records of the specified owner name
Owner to delete	NONE [249]	RR type	RR Rdata	Delete the resource record(s) of the specified owner, type and Rdata from the zone

Consider an example of an Update message received with the prerequisite and update fields encoded as follows:

Field	OWNER	CLASS	TYPE	RDATA
Prerequisite	host.ipamworldwide.com.	IN	DHCID	H8349a+)3jELeA==ES1
Update	host.ipamworldwide.com.	IN	A	10.0.0.200

The Update section contents will only be considered if the prerequisite condition is met. In this case, the prerequisite condition is that the `host.ipamworldwide .com. IN DHCID H8349a+)3jELeA==ES1` record exists in the zone, i.e. prerequisite type RRSet with matching owner, type and Rdata (value dependent). If it does exist, then the `host.ipamworldwide.com. IN A 10.0.0.200` resource record from the Update section will be added to the zone. If not, the update will not be performed.

This particular example illustrates how a DHCP server may perform dynamic updates of DNS data upon assigning an IP address, in this case 10.0.0.200 to host. ipamworldwide.com. The DHCID record provides a hash of the host's hardware address receiving the IP address to uniquely identify the host. The prerequisite condition for updating the address record provides a means to assure that only the original holder of this A record can modify it, minimizing naming duplication.

DNS Extensions (EDNS0)

Thus far in our discussion of the DNS message header, one may observe that all header code bits are assigned but one, and additional response code assignments have been required by necessity. In addition, many hosts can process larger multi-part UDP packets than the originally specified size limit of 512 bytes. As a result of these

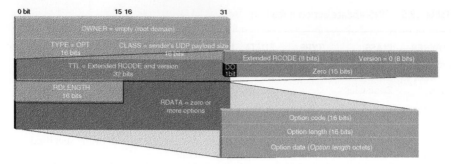

Figure 19.8   EDNS0 format. Source: Based on Vixie 1999 [209].

limitations, as well as the desire to add additional domain name label types, DNS extensions were defined in RFC 2671 [209] which was superseded by RFC 6891 [215].

The notation EDNS0 denotes extension mechanisms for DNS version 0. The EDNS RFCs address the constraints just mentioned by defining the following extensions:

- A new domain label type is defined to denote DNS extensions. As we discussed, the first two bits of the domain label uniquely identify the label as a length byte (first two bits = 00) or as a pointer (first two bits = 11). The extended label type has been assigned 01 as its first two bits.
- EDNS0 defines a pseudo-resource record, the OPT record (i.e. RRType = OPT). The OPT record is placed in the Additional Section by the resolver or server to advertise its respective capabilities. The OPT resource record is used to advertise capabilities of the sender (client or server) to the recipient, and only one OPT record should be present.

The OPT pseudo-resource record is encoded as per Figure 19.8, enabling specification of the senders' UDP packet size and additional response code bits.

As a pseudo-resource record, the OPT record should never appear in a zone file. Thus, while the OPT record utilizes the same wire format as other resource records, the definition of standard fields has been modified to provide extension information. The NAME (aka Owner) field is zero for the OPT record. The TYPE is OPT, and the CLASS field indicates the maximum size of the sender's UDP payload. The 32-bit TTL field is divided into three fields:

- *Extended response code* – adds 8 bits to the 4-bit RCODE in the DNS message header to provide 12 bits total.
- EDNS version number
- *Extended header flags* – bit 0 is currently defined as "DNSSEC Answer OK" meaning that the querying server is capable of processing DNSSEC resource records. The remaining 15 bits of the extended header are currently reserved.

The RDLENGTH field indicates the length of the RDATA field, which consists of a set of zero or more options, each encoded with an option code, option length, and option value. The following EDNS0 options have so far been allocated by IANA (Table 19.6):

The Long-lived query[3] (LLQ; option code = 1) option has recently been ratified. The Update Lease Life[4] (UL; option code = 2) option is currently on-hold and has not been officially published.

The name server identifier (NSID) option, defined with option code = 3, enables a resolver to request and a server to provide its identity as defined by the server administrator as its name, IP address, pseudo-random number, or other character string (configurable in BIND or PowerDNS using the `server-id` statement and in NSD and Knot using the `identity` parameter). This EDNS0 option is useful for debugging in environments where many servers share a common IP address, such as in deployments of anycast addressing or with load balancers.

Option codes 5–7 provide signaling of DNSSEC cryptographic algorithm support by a resolver. These options are only included in queries to inform the authoritative server of algorithm understanding, though they do not cause any change in server formulation of the response. Inclusion of the DNSSEC algorithm understood (DAU) option signals support of the specified digital signing algorithms. The DNSSEC hash understood (DHU) option indicates which delegation signer (DS) hash algorithms are supported. And the NSEC3 hash understood (N3U) option signals support for NSEC3 hash algorithms

Option 8, edns-client-subnet enables a stub resolver to indicate its IP subnet address. Some authoritative DNS servers supply or order resource records within a resulting resource record set based on the source IP address of the query in order to suggest a "closer" destination based on the IP address. However, with tiered resolvers where a stub resolver may query a recursive server which forwards to a centralized caching server, the source IP address may be far removed from the stub resolver. This option enables the stub resolver to convey its IP subnet address to influence the response.

The EDNS EXPIRE option provides a means for a slave server querying another slave server to convey the correct zone expiry time. In some deployments, a set of slave servers may query a master server, while other slaves query one of these first-tier slaves. The expire time field of the SOA record is a relative time value and it can be erroneously interpreted as extended by each slave query tier.

---

[3]A long-lived query is a mechanism for a resolver to request receipt of notification of zone information changes; something like a DNSNOTIFY for clients.
[4]The Update Lease Life mechanism would enable a DHCP server to inform the DNS server within a DNS Update message of the corresponding client's lease length in seconds for new and renewed leases.

Table 19.6 Currently assigned EDNS0 options.

OPTION CODE					
Decimal	Hex	Name	Description	Status	References
0	0	Reserved	Reserved		RFC 6891 [215]
1	1	LLQ	Long-lived query	Optional	RFC 8764 [295]
2	2	UL	Update lease life	On-hold	http://files.dns-sd.org/draft-sekar-dns-llq.txt
3	3	NSID	Name server identifier	Standard	RFC 5001 [216]
4	4	Reserved	Reserved		http://www.iana.org/go/draft-cheshire-edns0-owner-option
5	5	DAU	DNSSEC algorithm understood	Standard	RFC 6975 [217]
6	6	DHU	DNSSEC hash understood	Standard	RFC 6975 [217]
7	7	N3U	NSEC3 hash understood	Standard	RFC 6975 [217]
8	8	edns-client-subnet	Stub resolver subnet address	Optional	RFC 7871 [218]
9	9	EDNS EXPIRE	SOA zone expiry	Optional	RFC 7314 [219]
10	A	COOKIE	DNS transaction security	Standard	RFC 7873 [212]
11	B	edns-tcp-keepalive	Idle timeout for TCP connections	Standard	RFC 7828 [220]

12	C	Artificial message size increase to hamper size-based correlation of encrypted DNS transactions	Standard	RFC 7830 [221]
13	D	CHAIN	Request DNSSEC validation chain	Standard	RFC 7901 [222]
14	E	edns-key-tag	DNSKEY tag IDs resolver will use for validation	Optional	RFC 8145 [223]
15	F	Unassigned			
16	10	EDNS-Client-Tag	Opaque data field from a DNS client	Optional	draft-bellis-dnsop-edns-tags-01.txt [224]
17	11	EDNS-Server-Tag	Opaque data field from a DNS server	Opotional	draft-bellis-dnsop-edns-tags-01.txt [224]
18-26945	12-7111	Unassigned			
26946	7112	DeviceID	Stub resolver device identifier	Optional	https://docs.umbrella.com/umbrella-api/docs/identifying-dns-traffic2
65001-65534	FDE9-FFFE	Reserved	Reserved for local or experimental use		RFC 6891 [215]
65535	FFFF	Reserved	Reserved		RFC 6891 [215]

The COOKIE option enables a lightweight transaction security mechanism as discussed in Chapter 10. The EDNS keepalive option signals willingness to keep an idle TCP connection open to reduce the overhead of connection re-establishment for subsequent transactions. Option 13, CHAIN, requests the complete DNSSEC validation path to a specified point in the domain tree to eliminate the resolver from having to subsequently issue queries for this information. Option code 14, edns-key-tag signals which DNSSEC key id's the resolver will use for DNSSEC validation.

The DNS Resolution Process Revisited

Now that we've explored the details of the DNS protocol, let's take a deeper dive into the DNS resolution process to illustrate the query processing with respect to particular DNS protocol parameters. Considering Figure 19.9, the recursive server accepts recursive queries directly from client (stub) resolvers and performs the following steps to obtain the answer to the query on behalf of the resolver.

1) The stub resolver initiates a query to the recursive DNS server. The resolver knows which DNS server to query based on configuration via manual entry, router advertisement or via DHCP.

Figure 19.10 illustrates an example DNS packet issued by the resolver client. The client's IP address is 10.10.0.23 while the IP address of the recursive server is 10.20.5.100. The resolver uses a random source UDP port, 12510 in this case, and the standard DNS destination port, 53. The resolver also sets the transaction ID field to a random value as well, 37321 here. Flag settings indicate this as a standard query where recursion services are desired, requesting the recursive server

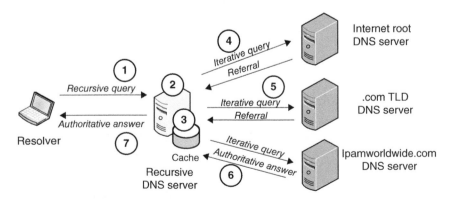

Figure 19.9 Recursive and iterative queries in name resolution.

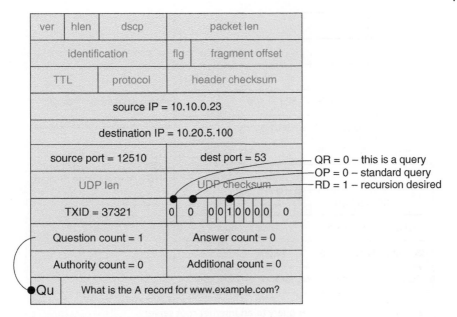

Figure 19.10   Resolver-issued DNS query packet example.

perform all queries necessary to resolve the query. Finally, the single question, here worded as a question, though in an actual packet would contain just the Qname (www.example.com), Qclass (IN), and Qtype (A).

2) The queried recursive DNS server will first search its configured data files. That is, the DNS server is typically configured with configuration and resource record information for which it is authoritative. If the answer is found, it is returned to the resolver and the process stops. If not and the server is configured to forward queries for this zone or for all queries, it does so and awaits a response.

3) If the queried recursive DNS server is not authoritative for the queried domain nor configured to forward this query, it will access its cache to seek the answer to the query.

4) If the queried recursive DNS server cannot locate the full query name information in cache, it will then attempt to locate the information via another DNS server using any cached partial domain information or by accessing its configured root hints file to begin traversing down the domain hierarchy to a DNS server that can provide an answer to the query.

In our example depicted in Figure 19.11, a root name server is selected from the root hints file, d.root-servers.net with IP address 199.7.91.13. The query is issued

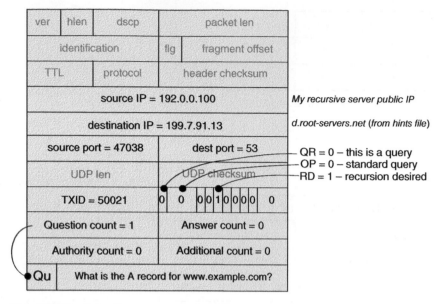

Figure 19.11 Recursive server query to an Internet root server.

using the DNS server's public IP address, 192.0.0.100, as its source address for proper Internet routing on well-known DNS destination UDP port 53. A random source UDP port and transaction ID are populated along with header bits indicating this is a query of the standard variety. Some recursive servers will set the recursion desired bit in the header, but this will be ignored by the root and TLD servers, and should be ignored by all external name servers including yours (by disabling recursion).

The root name server response refers the querying recursive DNS server to the name servers that are authoritative for the com domain as illustrated in Figure 19.12. The referral response is directed to the recursive server IP address and the UDP port it used in its query. The transaction ID is copied as well. The DNS header indicates no answer is provided to the query, but in this example, two records each are included in the Authority and Additional sections. The authority records provide the name server (NS) records of the servers authoritative for the .com domain. The additional section contains corresponding A (and/or AAAA) records that map the name server names to IP addresses. These additional records are the "glue" records to map the child domain's name server domain names to IP addresses to which further queries can be directed.

5) Having received this referral response, the recursive server selects one of the .com name server IP addresses and issues a query such as that shown in Figure 19.13. The answer received will also be a referral to the name server that

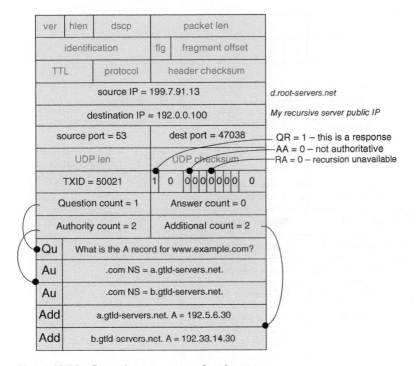

Figure 19.12   Example root server referral response.

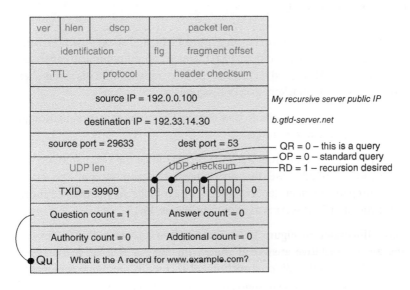

Figure 19.13   Recursive server iterative query to a .com name server.

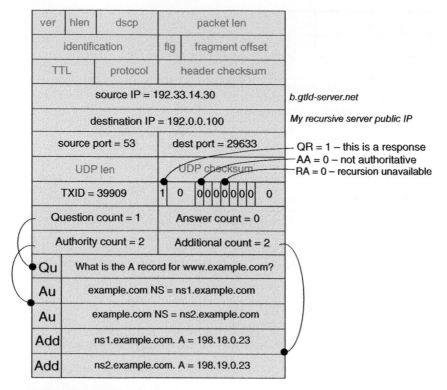

Figure 19.14 TLD server referral.

is authoritative for example.com. per Figure 19.14, and so on down the tree. Note each query should use random TXID values and monotonically increasing values should NOT be used for each successive transaction. This just makes it that much easier for attackers to spoof responses.

This referral response is very similar to that received from the root servers though for one layer down in the domain tree.

6) Upon receipt of the referral from the TLD server indicating two name servers and corresponding IP addresses that are delegated to example.com, the recursive server prepares its next iterative query, which looks very similar to those sent to the root and TLD servers as shown in Figure 19.15.

The response, illustrated in Figure 19.16, includes the answer with one answer record, and an authoritative answer at that, with the AA flag set in the DNS header. The authority and additional sections also contain the name server and address records for those servers authoritative for the example.com zone.

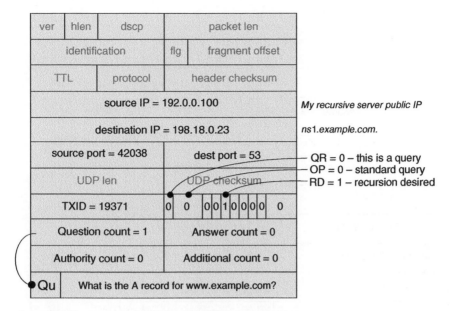

Figure 19.15 Recursive query to an example.com name server.

The recursive server updates its cache generally not only with the ultimate answer for the specific query, but for the contents of the authority and additional sections for the answer and referral messages received in the process. When the same or another stub resolver queries for another domain with the .com domain subtree, the recursive server can utilize its cache to query one of the .com NSs directly without needing to query the root server. If an answer cannot be found, the recursive server will also cache this "negative" information as well for use in responding to similar queries. Such negative cache entries expire from cache based on the zone's negative cache TTL parameter within its SOA record.

7) When the answer is received, the recursive DNS server will provide the answer to the stub resolver per Figure 19.17 and also update its cache and the process ends. Notice that the query answer maps the UDP ports and DNS transaction ID initially provided by the stub resolver upon its initial query.

The stub resolver may be configured to cache this information as well. In this case only the answer is cached, not other domain tree nodes, because the stub resolver always queries its configured name servers. But for users frequently visiting common sites, the stub resolver cache can greatly improve application response time.

The key parameters used by the recursive server to match responses with outstanding queries consist of the following.

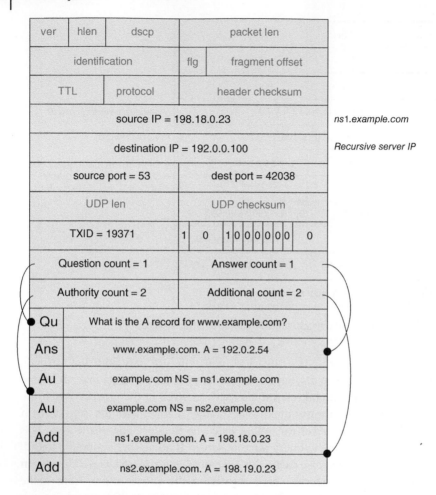

ver	hlen	dscp	packet len	
identification			flg	fragment offset
TTL		protocol	header checksum	
source IP = 198.18.0.23				ns1.example.com
destination IP = 192.0.0.100				Recursive server IP
source port = 53			dest port = 42038	
UDP len			UDP checksum	
TXID = 19371		1 0 1 0 0 0 0 0 0 0		
Question count = 1			Answer count = 1	
Authority count = 2			Additional count = 2	
Qu	What is the A record for www.example.com?			
Ans	www.example.com. A = 192.0.2.54			
Au	example.com NS = ns1.example.com			
Au	example.com NS = ns2.example.com			
Add	ns1.example.com. A = 198.18.0.23			
Add	ns2.example.com. A = 198.19.0.23			

Figure 19.16 Authoritative answer.

- Source IP address matches the IP address to which the query was sent and the destination IP address matches the address that was used as the outbound source address.
- Destination UDP (or TCP) port matches the source port number used on the outbound query. The source port should also match the outbound destination port, though this is almost always port 53, the well-known DNS port.
- The DNS header transaction identifier matches that used in the outbound query
- The question (name, class, and type) match that posed in the outbound query and the answer name matches. If character case matching is supported, the case of the Qname must match the Answer in the response.

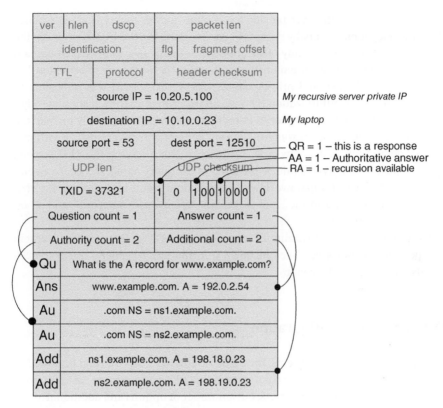

Figure 19.17 Query answer example.

- The Authority [name server] name falls within a common domain branch (e.g. example.com) as the Answer section name.

Should all of these parameters match, the recursive server will consider the answer valid and will continue processing by adding the record to cache and providing the answer to the resolver and future resolver queries for the duration of the answer record's time to live (TTL).

DNS Resolution Privacy Extension

In the prior resolution example, note how the question section always contained the FQDN of the query name for which an answer was sought. In our example, three separate packets traversed the Internet with this query FQDN from the recursive server IP address. Someone snooping query traffic or server cache may be able to infer information about clients based on what they are querying. The root and

TLD name servers will never provide a complete answer to a typical query since they are delegation servers by design. Thus, querying for the FQDN provides the root and TLD servers (and any other ancestor domains in a long-labeled domain name) with this query information, which in reality is "too much information."

To address this potential privacy concern, RFC 7816 [225] was published to specify query name minimization. Though an experimental RFC, it stipulates that the query name specified in queries to root name servers should only include the TLD for which a referral is sought. The root servers will never answer with any further detail than that in any case. Likewise, when querying the TLD servers, only the next layer down should be included as the query name. Hence for an end user query for pc52.dev.ipamworldwide.com, would result in a query to the root server for "com." And to the .com server for "ipamworldwide.com." and so on down the domain tree.

The intended effect is to minimize provision of "TMI" for Internet name servers and possible eavesdroppers seeking query information for general use or to classify user browsing or behavior.

DNS Resolver Configuration

On Unix or Linux based systems, the /etc/resolv.conf file can be edited to configure the resolver. The key parameter in this file is one or more nameserver statements pointing to DNS servers, but a number of options and additional directives enable further configuration refinement as described below. The italicized text should be replaced by actual data referenced; e.g. *domain* should be replaced with a DNS domain name.

- nameserver *IP_address* – The IP address of a recursive DNS server to query for name resolution; multiple nameserver entries are allowed and encouraged. The nameserver entry instructs the resolver where to direct DNS queries.
- domain *domain* – The DNS domain where this host (on which this resolver is installed) resides. This is used when resolving relative hostnames, as opposed to fully qualified host domain names.
- search *domain(s)* – The search list of up to six domains in which to search the entered hostname for resolution. Thus if we type in www for resolution, the resolver will successively append domains configured in this parameter in an attempt to resolve the query. If the entry search ipamworldwide.com. exists in resolv.conf, entry of www will result in a resolution attempt for www.ipamworldwide.com.

- `sortlist` *address/mask list* – Enables sorting of resolved IP addresses in accordance with the specified list of address/mask combinations. This enables the resolver to choose a "closer" destination if multiple IP addresses are returned for a query.
- `options` – Keyword preceding the following which enables specification of corresponding resolver parameters including the following:
  - `debug` – Turns on debugging
  - `ndots` *n* – Defines a threshold for the number of dots within the entered name required before the resolver will consider the entered name simply a hostname or a qualified domain name. When considered a hostname, the hostname will be queried as appended with domain names specified within the `domain` or `search` parameter.
  - `timeout` *n* – Number of seconds to wait before timing out a query to a DNS server.
  - `attempts` *n* – Number of query attempts before considering the query a failure.
  - `rotate` – Enables round robin querying among DNS servers configured within the `nameserver` directives. Queries will be sent to a different server each time and cycled through.
  - `no-check-names` – Turns off name checking of entered host names for resolution. Normally, underscore characters are not permitted for example, so setting this option enables query processing to proceed without validation of the entered hostname.
  - `inet6` – Causes the resolver to issue a query for a AAAA record to resolve the entered hostname before attempting an A record query.
  - `ip6-bytestring` – Causes reverse IPv6 lookups to use the now obsoleted bit-label format
  - `ip6-dotint` – Initiates IPv6 reverse lookups using the deprecated ip6.int domain; no-ip6-dotint initiates lookups in the ip6.arpa domain.
  - `edns0` – Enables EDNS0 queries
  - `single-request` – Forces the resolver to query for the domain for IPv6 and IPv4 in succession instead of in parallel.
  - `single-request-reopen` – The resolver uses the same socket for both IPv6 and IPv4 queries. If the hardware mistakenly sends back just one response, this option enables an override where the resolver will close the socket and reopen it to issue the second query.

`search` and `options` settings can also be overridden on a per process basis via corresponding environment variable settings.

DNS Applications and Resource Records

DNS inherently "translates" a given piece of information into another related piece of information. This resolution process is the very reason for DNS' invention, and it has been extended beyond resolving hostnames into IP addresses and vice versa to support a broad variety of applications. Virtually any service or application that requires translation of one form of information into another can leverage DNS.

Each resource record configured in DNS enables this lookup function, returning a resolution answer for a given query. The DNS server parses the query from the Question section of the DNS message, seeking a match within the corresponding domain's zone file for the query's QNAME, QCLASS, and QTYPE. Each resource record has a Name (aka Owner) field, Class (Internet class is assumed if not specified) and Type field. The Rdata field contains the corresponding answer to the query. The resource record type defines the type and format of the question (owner/name field) and corresponding answer (Rdata field). In some instances, multiple resource records may match the queried name, type, and class. In such cases, all matching records, a RRSet, are returned in the Answer section of the response message.

Most but not all new applications require new resource record types to enable definition of application-specific information, and these new resource record types are standardized via the IETF RFC process. This section describes the various forms of information that are stored in DNS along with the applications they support. A resource record summary is provided at the end of the chapter for reference.

Resource Record Format

When responding to a query for information, a DNS server will place the resource record information in the Answer section of a DNS message. The "on-the-wire format" dictated by the DNS protocol is depicted in Figure 19.18.

When representing resource records in zone files, all of these fields may be entered except the RDLength field, which is inserted when the resource record information is placed in a DNS message by the DNS server. The textual representation of a resource record generally follows a common convention shown below. Most resource records are defined with the following general fields, though many have subfields within the RData field.

Owner	Time to Live	Class	Type	RData

Owner (Name) – this field contains the information being queried.

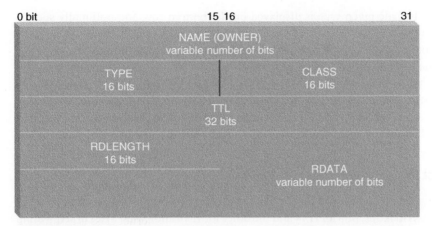

Figure 19.18   DNS resource record wire format. Source: Based on RFC 1035 [28].

Time to Live (TTL) – the number of seconds for which the information contained in this resource record is valid for servers and resolvers caching this information. After the TTL expires, the resource record information must be removed from the name server and resolver cache. The TTL can be specified on a per resource record basis or if omitted, a zone level default TTL value is used ($TTL).

Class – the Class of the resource record, usually IN for Internet.

Type – the type of resource record corresponding to the type of information being sought.

RData – the "record data" or answer portion corresponding to the information being sought by matching the Owner (Name), class and type field contents.

Now that we've covered the basic format, we're ready to jump into specific applications and the resource records that support them. As we review these resource record types, we'll review the interpretation of each type and provide an example. We'll cover those that have been "officially" accepted by the IETF, i.e. they've been published in an RFC; however, publication as an RFC does not guarantee universal implementation of the resource record type across all resolvers and servers. We'll point out some of those that may be new or experimental vs. those ol' reliables that have been around for years.

For each record type we'll discuss in this chapter, the resource record fields and examples are displayed using a common format. The header row specifies the base fields defined above for each record type. The next row displays the interpretation of these base fields for the particular type in question. An example resource record of the given type is displayed on the bottom row and optionally successive rows.

Note that we will use the term "domain name" to refer to the name of a DNS domain, while the term "host domain name" will refer to the DNS name of a host. The host domain name may be defined with the zone file as FQDN or simply a hostname interpreted in the context of the "current domain." The current domain in the case of ISC BIND DNS servers, is that defined in the zone declaration of the named.conf file which refers to this zone file.

Host Name and IP Address Resolution

As we know all too well by now, two resource record types are supported for IP address lookups, one for IPv4 and the other for IPv6 addresses. The corresponding reverse record utilizes a common record type for both IPv4 and IPv6, the Pointer (PTR) record type.

A – IPv4 Address Record

The A record is a common resource record type used to map a queried host domain name to an IPv4 address. The format follows the standard convention per the example below. Hosts may have multiple A records to provide load balancing or mapping of a hostname to multiple devices and/or interfaces.

Owner	TTL	Class	Type	RData
Host domain name	TTL	IN	A	IPv4 address
www.ipamworldwide.com.	86400	IN	A	10.100.0.99

AAAA – IPv6 Address Record

The AAAA ("quad-A") record provides an IPv6 address based on lookup of a host domain name. Formatted and processed similarly as the A record for host name to IPv4 address lookup, the RData field includes an IPv6 address which can be abbreviated using standard IPv6 abbreviation conventions.

Owner	TTL	Class	Type	RData
Host domain name	TTL	IN	AAAA	IPv6 address
www.ipamworldwide.com.	86400	IN	AAAA	2001:db8:3a::21:a450:1

PTR – Pointer Record

The PTR resource record provides mapping from an IP address to a FQDN. The PTR record is used to map both IPv4 and IPv6 addresses. The IPv4 version of the PTR includes the IP address reversed and concatenated with "in-addr.arpa." as the owner field and the corresponding FQDN as the Rdata field. The IPv6 version is formed by writing out the IPv6 address in its hexadecimal colon format, with all zeroes included; that is, fill in leading zeroes and double colon shortcuts. Then drop the colons, reverse the digits, then concatenate with "ip6.arpa."

Owner	TTL	Class	Type	RData
IP address in reverse domain format	TTL	IN	PTR	Host domain name
1.32.65.10.in-addr.arpa.	3600	IN	PTR	sf1.ipamworldwide.com.
1.0.0.1.0.0.0.0.0.0.0.0.0.0.0.0. 0.0.0.0.0.0.8.b.d.0.1.0.0.2.ip6.arpa.	3600	IN	PTR	sf1.ipamworldwide.com.

The IPv4 address in this example corresponds to 10.65.32.1, while the IPv6 address is 2001:0db8:0000:0000:0000:0000:0000:1001 or 2001:db8::1001 in abbreviated form.

Alias Host and Domain Name Resolutions

The CNAME resource record type enables lookup of a host domain name by an alias name. CNAME lookups return not an IP address, but a host domain name that must then be queried for its IP address, though most DNS servers responding to a CNAME query will include the corresponding A and/or AAAA record within the Additional section of the DNS response message if it falls within the same zone. Meanwhile, the DNAME record provides a similar aliasing function for domains. The DNAME record can be useful in migrating domain names.

CNAME – Canonical Name Record

The CNAME record enables creation of alias names for hosts. The owner field contains the alias name being looked up, and the RData field yields the canonical host domain name. This host domain name would then need to be resolved to obtain the host's corresponding A and/or AAAA record.

Owner	TTL	Class	Type	RData
Alias host domain name	TTL	IN	CNAME	Canonical host domain name
w3.ipamww.com.	86400	IN	CNAME	www.ipamww.com.

Note that it is not legal to configure a CNAME Rdata field as pointing to another CNAME owner field in order to chain records. This Rdata field must point directly to an A/AAAA resource record owner name. The owner name of each CNAME record must also be unique; a single alias cannot resolve to multiple answers. CNAME records can also be used for mapping reverse domains as we discussed in Chapter 4.

DNAME – Domain Alias Record

The DNAME resource record, defined in RFC 6672 [206] enables mapping of an entire subtree of the domain name space to another domain. The major motivation for developing the DNAME record was to simplify DNS impacts of IP network renumbering. For example, if the company running the ipamww.com domain was acquired by acquired.com, the ipamww.com namespace could conceivably be "moved" beneath acquired.com with the addition of a DNAME record illustrated below.

Owner	TTL	Class	Type	RData
Alias domain name	TTL	IN	DNAME	Target domain name
ipamww.com.	86 400	IN	DNAME	ipamww.acquired.com.

Resolvers seeking hosts within the ipamww.com domain subtree would be directed to seek the same hostnames under ipamww.acquired.com domain. DNAME records can also be used for mapping reverse domains as we discussed in Chapter 4. Note that the example above requires the resource records and subdomains of ipamww.com to be ported to their corresponding zones within the acquired.com domain subtree. RFC 6672 stipulates that the DNAME owner (ipamww.com. in this case) zone must not have any subdomains nor contain any resource records besides the DNAME and possibly CNAME resource records.

Network Services Location

IP devices booting on a network often need to find specific services for device initialization. While DHCP provides some level of service location via specification of certain option values such as TFTP server IP addresses, DNS provides a services location mechanism using the services location resource record type (SRV). The SRV record provides a means for clients seeking services after initialization to locate servers providing desired services.

SRV – Services Location Record

The SRV record is used to enable resolver clients to identify servers offering particular services such as LDAP, Kerberos, and others. This record is critical for

Microsoft Windows clients in locating Windows Domain Controllers though it has not found widespread adoption among other applications.

Owner	TTL	Class	Type				RData
Service encoding	TTL	IN	SRV	Priority	Weight	Port	Target host domain name
_ldap._tcp. ipamww.com.	3600	IN	SRV	10	0	389	ldap.ipamww.com.

The owner field is comprised of a concatenation of a particular service, which is available via a particular protocol (TCP or UDP), for a given domain. The RData field includes a priority field, which instructs clients to use numerically lower priority targets when multiple SRV records are returned.

The weight field is used to further prioritize records with the same priority. The port is the TCP or UDP port number to use to access the given service and the target is the host domain name of the server running the specified service.

If not also returned as additional information by the DNS server, the client may request corresponding A or AAAA records for hosts specified as targets to complete the resolution process.

AFSDB – DCE or AFS Server Record (Experimental)

The AFSDB record was defined in RFC 1183 [226] and was intended to enable location of a server, particularly for AFS (a registered trademark of Transarc Corp. and originally Andrew File System) and for the Open Software Foundation's distributed computing environment (DCE).

Owner	TTL	Class	Type		RData
Cell domain name	TTL	IN	AFSDB	Subtype	Host domain name
ipamworldwide.com.	86400	IN	AFSDB	1	afsdb1.ipamworldwide.com.

The RData field consists of:

- Subtype field, which identifies the AFS 3.0 volume location server for the cell domain name (subtype = 1) or the DCE directory services server for the given cell domain name (subtype = 2).
- Host domain name field identifies the server hostname.

The AFSDB resource record is not widely used, as the SRV resource record type provides generic server location functionality within DNS.

WKS – Well Known Service Record (Historic)
This resource record type identifies the well-known services such as FTP, telnet, and others that are available on a particular IP address using a particular protocol (TCP or UDP) for a host. This record is not generally used, as the SRV record provides similar functionality.

Owner	TTL	Class	Type		RData	
Host domain name	TTL	IN	WKS	IPv4 address	Protocol	Services
server.ipamww.com.	86400	IN	WKS	10.0.199.35	TCP	SMTP FTP

Host and Textual Information Lookup
The TXT record is one of the workhorse resource record types, often used as an interim resource record in support of specific applications pending standardization and implementation. The TXT record enables lookup of a generic reference name, e.g. a domain name, host domain name, or other owner values, and returning arbitrary textual information. Most recently, the TXT record has been used for interim support of DDNS update uniqueness checking (now the DHCID record type) and for spam reducing applications (the SPF record type), both covered later in this chapter.

TXT – Text Record
The text record enables the association of up to 255 bytes of arbitrary binary data with a resource record. It has proven very versatile in providing interim support of new services.

Owner	TTL	Class	Type	RData
Reference name	TTL	IN	TXT	Arbitrary text data
txt.cfo.ipamww.com.	86400	IN	TXT	"CFO Office (610) 555-1212"

HINFO – Host Information Record
The RDATA field of the HINFO resource record enables lookup of a host's processor and operating system.

Owner	TTL	Class	Type		RData
Host domain name	TTL	IN	HINFO	CPU	Operating System
sf1.ipamww.com.	86400	IN	HINFO	VAX 770/11	UNIX

HIP – Host Identity Protocol Record (Experimental)

The HIP resource record type supports the experimental host identity protocol (HIP), which essentially abstracts the association of a hostname with an IP address by inserting a "host identity" layer in the resolution process. This enables association of a domain name with a host identity, which is then associated with one or more IP addresses. An application or upper layer protocol can look up a host via the HIP resource record and obtain the host identifier (in the form of a public key) and other host identity information, including the IP address of the host or of a rendezvous server through which to connect to mobile devices.

Owner	TTL	Class	Type	RData					
Host domain name	TTL	IN	HIP	HIT Len.	PK Alg.	PK Len.	HIT	Public Key	RVS
hiphost. ipamww.com.	3600	IN	HIP	16	2	24	Iil...	8L9d...	rs.ipamww.com.

- The RData fields are defined as:
  - *HIT Len.* – Length in bytes of the host identity tag (HIT); this field is inserted by the server for wire transmission and is not displayed within a zone file.
  - *PK Alg.* – The algorithm used to generate the Public Key
    - 0 = no key is present
    - 1 = DSA formatted key
    - 2 = RSA formatted key
  - *PK Len.* – Length in bytes of the public key; this field is inserted by the server for wire transmission and is not displayed within a zone file.
  - *HIT* – The host identity tag, a 128-bit hash of the Host Identifier
  - *Public Key* – The public key associated with the host which can be used to validate signed messages from the host
  - *RVS* – (optional) – One or more rendezvous server host domain name(s) for connecting with mobile devices

RP – Responsible Person record

The RP resource record enables association of an email address and other text information with a node in the domain tree, whether an end host or domain. The RData field contains an email address, formatted without the @ sign; instead, a dot is substituted for the @ sign. The second field of the RData field indicates a record for which additional text information can be found as an additional lookup.

Owner	TTL	Class	Type	RData	
Host domain name	TTL	IN	RP	Email Address	TXT Pointer
payroll.ipamww.com.	86400	IN	RP	cfo.ipamww.com.	cfo-contactinfo. ipamww.com.

In this example above, we've used an RP record to associate the payroll server with our CFO, reachable at cfo@ipamww.com (substitute "." for "@" in email address field). The TXT pointer field points to a resource record containing additional information, such as the following example:

cfo-contactinfo.ipamww.com. 86400 IN TXT "CFO Office (610)-555-1212"

DNS Protocol Operational Record Types

Two "administrative" resource record types enable specification of zone authority information (the SOA record) and delegation name servers for this and child domains (NS). These record types are instrumental to the efficient operation of keeping DNS data in synch within a zone and of keeping delegation chains in effect down the domain tree.

SOA – Start of Authority Record

One and only one SOA record is required for each zone and follows the initial default TTL ($TTL) statement within the zone file. The SOA record defines the domain name for which this zone is authoritative, along with additional zone maintenance information. The SOA record is composed of the following fields.

Owner	TTL	Class	Type	RData					
				mname	contact	serial number	refresh interval	retry interval	expire interval	negative cache
Domain name	TTL	IN	SOA						
ipamww. com.	3600	IN	SOA	ns1. ipamww. com.	admin. ipam ww.com.	3945	2h	30m	1w	1d

- Domain name for which this zone file contains authoritative information
- TTL, time to live
- Record class (IN for Internet)
- Record type (SOA)

- *Master DNS server name (MNAME)* – The name of the DNS server that is master for this domain (zone).
- Domain contact email address (replace "@" with "." so that admin@ipamworldwide .com is written admin.ipamworldwide.com. Note that email addresses with dots prior to the @ sign should be prefixed with a backslash. Thus, super.admin @ipamww.com would be encoded as super\.admin.ipamww.com.
- *Serial number of the zone* – Incremented with every change to zone data – enables secondary servers to identify changes to zone data
- *Refresh interval* – Time period for secondaries to query the master for zone updates
- *Retry time* – If unable to reach the master, the secondary will wait this amount of time to retry to reach the master
- *Expire time* – If unable to reach the master after this amount of time expires, the secondaries will delete the zone information and no longer consider itself authoritative, thereby expiring its authority for the zone.
- *Negative caching TTL* – Time duration to maintain cache of negative responses from other servers; e.g. a specified domain or record doesn't exist.

An example SOA record for our ipamww.com zone file might look like:
ipamww.com. IN SOA dns1.ipamww.com dnsadmin.ipamww.com (

1	; serial number
2h	; refresh interval of 2 hours
30m	; retry after 30 minutes
1w	; expire after 1 week
1d)	; negative caching TTL of 1 day

NS – Name Server Record

The NS record enables lookup of an authoritative name server for a given zone. NS records are the key to distributing the DNS database. In delegating a child domain to another administrative authority, the child domain administrator must be running at least two name servers for redundancy. While traversing the domain tree, these NS records enable the queried name server along the resolution path in the domain tree to respond with a referral to another name server further down the tree which has more information about the intended destination. Each zone must also declare at least two NS records for its authoritative name servers as well.

Owner	TTL	Class	Type	RData
Domain name	TTL	IN	NS	Name server domain name
ipamworldwide.com.	86400	IN	NS	ns1.ipamworldwide.com.

Note that the name server hostname in the RData field must have a corresponding A or AAAA record to complete the required resolution to a reachable IP address. This is referred to as a "glue" record in that it "glues" the resolution of the authoritative name server hostname for the desired domain to the IP address of that name server.

Dynamic DNS Update Uniqueness Validation

DHCID – Dynamic Host Configuration Identifier Record

Dynamic DNS enables the updating of DNS information with DHCP clients' assigned IP address information. Thus, a DHCP server on behalf of the client or the client itself can update DNS with the client's IP address and hostname association via A/AAAA and PTR records. It is quite possible that the same hostname/FQDN may be claimed by multiple DHCP clients, or that a client may claim a hostname already assigned to a pre-defined (e.g. statically addressed) device.

The DHCID record provides client identification information in DNS to uniquely associate the particular DHCP client with the hostname/FQDN being updated by the DHCP server. The DHCID record would be defined in the Pre-requisite section of the DNS Update message to verify the record "owner" for updating. Please refer to the DNS Update section earlier in this chapter for more details and an example of this pre-requisite processing.

The DHCID record uses the same owner field as the corresponding A or AAAA record. The RData portion of the record is formed by performing a one-way secure hash using the SHA-256 algorithm over the following concatenated fields:

- *Identifier Type code (2 bytes)* – Identifies the information within the DHCP packet that was used in creating this hash. Possibilities include client hardware address, client identifier option, or DUID.
- *Digest Type code (1 byte)* – Identifies the hash algorithm. The RFC defines values of 0 (reserved) or 1 (SHA-256) though IANA maintains a registry for future value assignments.
- Digest of the data from the DHCP packet as identified by the Identifier value concatenated by the client's FQDN.

Owner	TTL	Class	Type	RData		
Host domain name	TTL	IN	DHCID	Identifier type	Digest type	SHA-256 hash of {identifier type, fqdn}
w3.ipamww.com.	86400	IN	DHCID	A1B87Y2/AuCcg8e93aQcjl...		

Telephone Number Resolution

DNS has proven very versatile and can even be used to map telephone numbers into IP addresses, which is useful for VoIP applications or related telephony over IP applications. The ENUM (E.164 telephone number mapping) service has been defined to support such resolution. ENUM supports the mapping of telephone numbers, in ITU E.164 format, into uniform resource identifiers (URIs)[5]. This mapping is performed primarily using the NAPTR resource record type.

Note that most enterprise IP PBX systems provide their own directories to map intra-PBX phone numbers to destination phones' IP addresses, so ENUM is not commonly implemented in such environments. However, VoIP service providers have a vested interest in assuring calls remain on their or their partners' IP and access networks to the maximum extent, to reduce call handling costs paid to non-partner network providers, or worse, competitors. And ENUM is key to enabling such call routing by virtue of telephone number mapping or resolution. That is not to say that you won't see ENUM within enterprise networks. ENUM provides resolution to multiple destinations with preference settings, which may find use within reachability or contact management type applications.

As just mentioned, the NAPTR resource record provides translation of telephone number information into destination URIs. Currently defined in RFC 3403 [227], NAPTR records were initially defined to provide a means to iteratively resolve an arbitrary string into a URI for the Dynamic Delegation Discovery System (DDDS). Some background on DDDS is provided in RFC 3402 [228], but it initially stemmed from the desire to define a resolution process that could enter with a resource name (e.g. a particular application or piece of data) which in itself, contains no network location information, and resolve it to a destination resource identifier by applying a series of iterative rules from a database. This separation of the specification of the resource name from the process to locate or resolve it facilitates the making of changes and re-delegations of resources without impacting the end user application's naming convention.

This effort expanded beyond resolving resource names to supporting resolution of generic lookup strings, and evolved into the DDDS, using DNS as one form of the rules database. The NAPTR record enables the specification of such rules within DNS, sometimes using multiple NAPTR records to fully complete the resolution process. Each NAPTR record translates a given entry string, i.e. a valid DNS domain name, into a rule that can be applied to the string to derive the next string

---

[5]A URI is an Internet identifier consisting of a uniform resource name (URN) and a uniform resource locator (URL). A simple example: for URL http://ipamworldwide.com, and URN file. txt, the corresponding URI is http://ipamworldwide.com/file.txt.

to lookup. This process iterates until a terminal rule is reached and the final result is returned to the requesting application.

NAPTR records are the building blocks of E.164 telephone number mapping service for service provider voice over IP services. RFC 3761 [229] provides the "application specific" interpretation of NAPTR fields for the ENUM application. A NAPTR record can be used to lookup a destination telephone number, and resolve the number to a destination, e.g. a session initiation protocol (SIP) server, email address, or other URI-formatted destination. NAPTR records also support the ability to define regular expressions, which supply logical rules as "next steps" for the resolver to locate the intended destination.

E.164 is an ITU standard for formatting telephone numbers. "Fully qualified" telephone numbers, meaning they are globally unique given the country code prefix followed by a country-specific telephone number format, are represented with a plus sign prefix, such as +16105551234. Much like reverse domains for IP addresses, formatting a telephone number requires a similar convention of reading the resource record from left to right as more specific to less specific. This convention requires reversal of the fully qualified telephone number (dropping the plus sign) and separating each digit with "dots" as illustrated in Figure 19.19.

Note the use of the .arpa top level domain. Similar to ip6.arpa and in-addr.arpa domain structures, the e164.arpa domain is a "reverse" domain in that it enables lookup of structured numerical value, a phone number. Like other .arpa lookups, the domain structure is organized top-to-bottom as generalized-to-specific, or country code-to-telephone line number. Thus, the fully formatted E.164 telephone number is reversed, each digit is separated with dots, and the e164.arpa. domain suffix is appended as illustrated in Figure 19.19.

This structure lends itself well to segmentation of telephone number space. For example, the domain 1.e164.arpa refers to all country code 1 telephone numbers and could be delegated to such a number authority. Likewise 44.e164.arpa could be delegated to the UK telephone numbering authority. Within each of these domains, further delegation may be accomplished in accordance with the numbering plan for

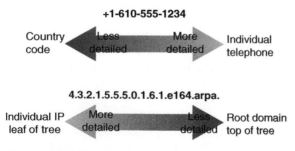

Figure 19.19 Telephone number mapping to domain structure.

the country. For example, within the United States, an area code represents the next logical administrative delegation point, followed by exchange. Thus the administrators for 1.e164.arpa may delegate the 0.1.6.1.e164.arpa zone to the numbering administrator for the 610 area code, who may in turn delegate 5.5.5.0.1.6.1.e164.arpa to those responsible for the 555 exchange within the 610 area code.

NAPTR – Naming Authority Pointer Record

The NAPTR record provides translation of a string[6] or telephone number information into destination URIs. The NAPTR record utilizes the e164.arpa. domain naming convention described above within its owner field to serve as the lookup format for telephone numbers. Unfortunately, this so far is only the easy part! The NAPTR record contains a number of additional subfields with its Rdata field. The additional subfields are described below, with examples provided for the ENUM application of NAPTR records.

- *Order field* – Specifies the order in which multiple records within the RRSet are to be processed; lower numbered order records are processed first
- *Preference field* – Specifies the order in which records with equal "order" values are to be processed; lower numbered preference records are processed first
- *Flags* – Provides information about the "next lookup" in the resolution process. Thus far, four flag values have been defined, though the Flag field can be empty:
  - o "u" – the output of the Regular Expression field of this record is a URI; i.e. this is a terminal resolution.
  - o "s" – next lookup should be for SRV records
  - o "a" – next lookup should be for A, A6, or AAAA records
  - o "p" – next lookup is protocol specific according to the protocol secified in the Services field.
- *Services* – This field encodes the services that are available based on the application in question. This field includes the type of resolution provided, a "+" sign or colon, followed by the protocol value, e.g. http, sip, mailto, ftp, tel, among others[7]. Examples of types or resolution include
  - o I2L – URI to URL
  - o N2L – Uniform Resource Name (URN) to URL
  - o E2U – ENUM service to URI
- *Regular expression* – An encoded expression that is to be evaluated. The syntax of this field is a sed-style expression.
- *Replacement* – An alternative "next lookup" fully qualified domain name in the absence of a regular expression.

---

[6]"Strings" refer to text or data strings. Fortunately, this is not the "string theory" of DNS!
[7]Please consult http://www.iana.org/assignments/enum-services for the currently assigned services values for ENUM.

Owner	TTL	Class	Type				RData		
Domain name	TTL	IN	NAPTR	Order	Pref	Flags	Services	Regexp	Replacement
me .ipamww .com.	86400	IN	NAPTR	10	5	"s"	"N2L+ http"	" "	www.ipamww .com.
4.3.2.1.5.5. 5.0.1.6.1. e164.arpa.	86400	IN	NAPTR	10	20	"u"	"E2U+ sip"	"!^.*$!sip:me@ipamww .com.!"	

Let's look more closely at the two example NAPTR records above. The first example provides a rule for resolution of me.ipamww.com. The Flags field value of "s" indicates to the resolver that the next lookup should be a query for SRV resource records. The Services field indicates a URN-to-URL service using HTTP protocol. Since the regular expression field is blank, the replacement field is used as the result of the resolution process.

The second example highlights an ENUM application example, where a lookup of a telephone number can be resolved. The "u" flag indicates that the result of the regular expression provided will be a URI, which can then be resolved to an IP address. The Services field indicates ENUM services using the SIP protocol. The regular expression field is comprised of two subfields, encapsulated with the "!" character. The first field contains "^.*$" and is interpreted as "match from the start of the line (^) to the end of the line ($), zero or more (*) characters (.)"; that is, match the entire Owner field. The second portion of the regular expression contains "sip:me@ipamworldwide.com" which is returned as the result of our regular expression. The Replacement field is not used in this case.

The resulting URI, sip:me@ipamworldwide.com would then initiate a DNS query for an address (A or AAAA) record for ipamworldwide.com. Note that some DNS servers may return relevant A or AAAA records as additional information in the query response containing the NAPTR records. The resulting IP address would be used as the destination address to initiate the sip session to the "me" user.

Email and Anti-spam Management

A variety of techniques exist to combat spam, many of which involve the use of DNS. To understand how DNS can help reduce spam, we'll first look at the anatomy of an email transmission including the role of DNS in email delivery, then review the use of DNS in various anti-spamming solutions.

Email and DNS

An email typically originates from one person and is sent to one or more recipients. Each email address is formatted as a mailbox@maildomain. The mailbox commonly refers to the name of the person or owner of a mailbox or email account, while the maildomain, typically the company or Internet provider name, is the destination domain for delivery to the corresponding mailbox or mail exchanger. Emails are composed using an email client, such as Microsoft Outlook, Eudora, or web-based clients like yahoo and google. Regardless, when sent by the originator, the client connects to a SMTP server (using the SMTP protocol) to send the email. Like a default router for email, the SMTP server is responsible for forwarding the email to its destination.

The SMTP server must resolve the maildomain to an IP address for transmission of the message. Naturally this is done using DNS with a lookup for the Mail Exchanger (MX) record type, as well as the corresponding A or AAAA record types.

MX – Mail Exchanger Record

The mail exchanger record is used to locate an email server or servers for a particular domain. If I send an email destined to tim@ipamworldwide.com, my SMTP server will use DNS to find the host(s) that can receive emails for users in the ipamworldwide.com domain. More than one MX record may be created per domain, and each can be defined with a different preference value. Use of the preference field enables the sending SMTP server to prioritize the destination host to which it will forward the email for the given domain, and if unavailable to a second (and third, etc.) choice destination. The lower the preference value, the more preferred the listed destination. In the example below, we have two MX records for the ipamworldwide.com domain. The destination smtp1 is preferred (lower preference) over smtp2. However, if smtp1 is unavailable, this mechanism provides a backup server for email delivery.

Owner	TTL	Class	Type		RData
Email destination domain	TTL	IN	MX	Preference	Mail server host domain name
ipamworldwide.com.	86400	IN	MX	10	smtp1.ipamworldwide.com.
ipamworldwide.com.	86400	IN	MX	20	smtp2.ipamworldwide.com.

Note that the mail server host domain name within the RData field must have a corresponding A or AAAA record to complete the required resolution to a reachable IP address. Many DNS servers supply these address records within the Additional section of the MX query response.

Upon resolving the destination mail server, the SMTP server sends the message to the destination using the SMTP protocol. The ultimate destination server, to which recipient email clients connect, must support POP or IMAP to enable client retrieval of the email message. Thus, when your email client performs a "send/ receive," it utilizes SMTP to send outgoing messages to its configured SMTP server and POP or IMAP to retrieve incoming email messages from the configured POP/ IMAP server.

Figure 19.20 highlights a very simple SMTP transaction between two servers, when my friend Mike sends me an email. On the left of the figure, Mike composes an email to tim@ipamworldwide.com using his email client and sends it. His configured SMTP server forwards the message to the destination server, as resolved by the MX record(s) for ipamworldwide.com. His SMTP server initiates a TCP connection on port 25 with the resolved destination server.

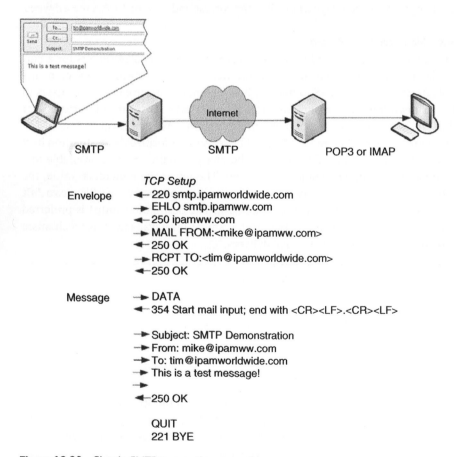

Figure 19.20   Simple SMTP transaction example.

Once the TCP session is established, the SMTP application utilizes the session to handshake then process the message. The envelope portion of the message begins with the HELO (or EHLO, enhanced HELO) which conveys the sending entity's identity. The MAIL FROM statement indicates the source of the message, followed by the RCPT TO statement indicating the destination mailbox. At this point in the exchange, the recipient server may refuse to accept the message and close the connection if the destination mailbox is unknown or blocked, or if the "from address" is prohibited. Otherwise, the transaction continues and the data or message portion[8] is transmitted. The receiving mail exchanger stores the email message or forwards it to the server on which the destination mailbox resides.

The store-and-forward approach used by the received email server may also be used by intermediate email gateways (aka message transfer agents) to provide multi-hopped email delivery. As mentioned above, the resolution of a destination mailbox domain to multiple MX records implies this ability to identify a "destination" mail server which may or may not be the final destination from which the intended recipient retrieves the email. The MX record preference field provides control over the relative preference of incoming mail servers or gateways, while providing selection from among multiple choices based on availability and performance.

Figure 19.21 illustrates a two-step email delivery scenario using SMTP. In this scenario, I'm sending the same email as shown in Figure 19.20. However, in this case, perhaps the intended destination server, smtp.ipamworldwide.com is busy and refuses a direct connection. Having resolved both the ipamworldwide.com server and an mta-gateway.com server via a DNS MX query, my outgoing mail server will attempt to send the email to the second choice, mta-gateway.com.

In accepting the SMTP transmission from my mail server, the mta-gateway.com server effectively agrees to forward the email to the ultimate destination on my behalf. The transaction between my mail server and the mta-gateway.com server completes before the second leg of transmission is attempted. SMTP uses a store-and-forward approach, not synchronous relaying of each message.

The first leg of the transmission looks very similar to that of Figure 19.20, except for the difference in the SMTP server. The second leg of the connection is also similar, except once again for the SMTP endpoints. The other difference is the insertion of the **Received:** line within the header portion of the data section of the mail. Each intermediate SMTP server which forwards the message prefixes a "Received" line indicating its domain name and corresponding time stamp. This enables tracing of the email from the destination back to its path. The RCPT TO line remains the same in both segments, indicating the mailbox to which errors in delivery should be sent.

---

[8]Note that the message portion of an email consists of a header and the body. As a point of reference, RFC 5391 [291] defines the SMTP specification, while RFC 5392 [292] defines the Internet message format for email, defining valid header and data syntax.

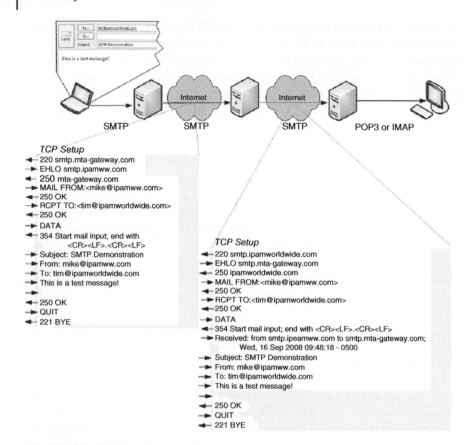

Figure 19.21 Email relay.

As footnoted above, the message portion of an email consists of a header and the body. Each header field consists of a label followed by a colon and a value. The header contains a variety of data including the following:

- originator fields: from, sender, reply-to, orig-date
- destination fields: to, cc, bcc
- identification fields: message-id, in-reply-to, references, msg-id, id-left, id-right, no-fold-quote, no-fold-literal
- informational fields: subject, comments, keywords
- resent fields (informational fields relating to the reintroduction[9] of a message into the Internet, e.g. by a e-mailing service): resent-date, resent-from, resent-sender, resent-to, resent-cc, resent-bcc, resent-msg-id

---

[9]Reintroduction is not forwarding. The transmission of an email with the *original sender* information instead of that of the transmitter is considered reintroduction. Forwarding uses the mailbox doing the forwarding as the sender.

- source trace information: trace, return, path received, name-val-list, name-val-pair, item-name, item-value

We have summarized the basic email process and types of information that may be included in a given email message because different anti-spam techniques utilize different information sources in validating the sender as a legitimate or acceptable sender of emails. We'll discuss those techniques that utilize DNS to perform this validation next.

Allow or Block Listing

The use of allow or block listing [230] provides a simple means for the recipient email server to lookup a sender's IP address via DNS and to validate its legitimacy. This lookup is typically formed by reversing the IP address of the source IP address of the email message, just as is done in forming PTR records. Note that the source IP address being analyzed is that from which the email was received directly, perhaps an email gateway, which may or may not be the original transmitter. However, the intent of such listing is to identify such senders of email by IP address as legitimate or not.

In this scenario, the reversed IP address is appended with a given domain name, typically that of the block list provider. The "host domain name" thus formed by this concatenation is queried in DNS using the A resource record query type, not PTR. The query answer is interpreted based on whether the record was found, in which case often an IP address within the 127/8 block is returned, and on whether the list publishes known spammers (block list) or known non-spammers (allow list).

For example, upon receiving an email message with a source IP address of 192.0.2.95, my email server formulates an A record query for hostname 95.2.0.192. spamblocklist.org, assuming my chosen block list provider publishes lookups within the spamblocklist.org domain. Upon receiving a reply with answer (IP address) 127.0.0.5, my email server classifies the email as spam and rejects it. On the other hand if NXDOMAIN is returned for the query, the email may be permitted. An allowlist service, publishing known genuine email server addresses would render the opposite interpretation based on the DNS lookup.

Sender Policy Framework (SPF)

SPF is defined in RFC 7208 [118]. SPF enables an organization to publish its own list of authorized outgoing email server addresses, a self-published allow list, though with substantially more sophistication. Under SPF, the received email message's envelope information is examined, and a TXT DNS query from the email recipient is issued to the sender's domain to request their particular sender policy.

Upon receipt of an email message, the recipient email server would issue a query for a TXT resource record for the source domain name. A TXT record is used instead of but with same format as the originally defined SPF record is which encoded as a string of "mechanisms" that are used to process the source IP address from which the email originated, the domain portion of the MAIL FROM or HELO identity, and the sender from the MAIL FROM or HELO identity.

SPF – Sender Policy Framework Formatting for a TXT Record

SPF attempts to provide validation of what hosts are configured to send email for a given domain. That is, SPF seeks to eliminate spam emails from spoofed domains. A recipient email host can look up the SPF records for the sender's domain to verify that the sending email host matches those authorized by the sender. SPF version 1 or SPF classic as it is also called, is documented in RFC 4408 and originally utilized the SPF resource record. Domain administrators can configure DNS with email hosts mapping to each host's mailfrom and SMTP HELO identities. SenderID is a related albeit historical spam detection technique that also used the SPF resource record type though it analyzed different information from an incoming email message. We'll cover SenderID a bit later.

Note that due to actual implementations of SPF using TXT records prior to IETF publication of RFC 4408, most implementations will use both SPF and TXT records for backward compatibility, though an SPF compliant resolver will discard the TXT records if both TXT and SPF records are returned. The format of the SPF record is identical to that of the TXT record; however, a particular syntax is employed for SPF applications instead of arbitrary text. The syntax includes a version string (v=spf1 for SPF, spf2.0 for SenderID covered later) followed by a space, then one or more terms that define qualifiers on resource record types or IP network addresses, modifiers, and even macros.

Owner	TTL	Class	Type	RData
Domain name	TTL	IN	SPF	version, directives and/or modifiers
smtp.ipamww.com.	86400	IN	SPF	v=spf1 +ip4:192.0.2.32/30 –all
smtp.ipamww.com.	86400	IN	SPF	spf2.0 pra +ip4:192.0.2.32/30 –all

Mechanisms

Mechanisms enable specification of the match criteria within the SPF (or TXT) record which a receiving email server can query to validate the sender of a given email message. Mechanisms are defined within the SPF record's Rdata field after specification of the SPF version, currently version 1, "v=spf1." Mechanisms are evaluated left to right. If a mechanism passes based on evaluation of the mechanism, the verification passes; otherwise, the next mechanism is tested until a pass or fail is found or no further mechanisms are defined.

Each mechanism can be defined with a qualifier, a prefix which instructs the mail or spam filter server how to interpret a given "match":

- + = pass (default) – consider this mechanism a pass if this mechanism matches
- − = fail – consider this mechanism a fail if the mechanism matches
- ~ = soft-fail – consider this mechanism somewhere between neutral and fail if this mechanism matches; this interpretation would not fail this check outright if it matched, but would hold it for closer scrutiny
- ? = neutral – consider this mechanism neutral if this mechanism matches

Qualifiers may be used with the following resource record check-based mechanisms to define the interpretation of a given mechanism as shown in the examples following:

- a = lookup the A record for the source domain (from the MAIL FROM or HELO identity); if it matches the source IP address of the message, this mechanism matches. This can be scoped to a specific domain and/or number of CIDR bits to compare in the addresses as illustrated in the following examples:
  - +a = pass if the A record query for the source domain matches the source IP address
  - −a:ipamworldwide.com = fail if an A record query for ipamworldwide.com matches the source IP address
  - ~a/24 – soft-fail if the first 24 bits of the IP address retrieved via A record lookup of the source domain matches the first 24 bits of the source IP address
- mx = lookup the MX record for the source domain (from the MAIL FROM or HELO identity); for each MX lookup resolved, look up the corresponding A record; if it matches the source IP address of the message, this mechanism passes. As with the "a" mechanism, the mx mechanism can be scoped to a specific domain and/or number of CIDR bits to compare in the addresses as illustrated in the following example:
  - +mx:ipamworldwide.com/28 = pass if an A record associated with a MX record lookup is returned where the first 28 bits match the first 28 bits of the source IP address of the message.
- ptr = lookup the PTR record (up to 10) corresponding to the source IP address of the email message; then compare two things with each domain name returned in the PTR lookup:
  - Check that the domain name returned matches the source domain of the email message

> o Check that the corresponding A or AAAA record returns an IP address matching the source IP address

If both conditions hold, this mechanism passes. This mechanism can be further scoped by a domain name, which can be used to filter multiple returned PTR-lookup domain names as illustrated in the following examples:

> o −ptr – fail if a domain name returned during the PTR lookup of the source IP address matches the source domain and if the A/AAAA domain name corresponding to the domain name returned during the PTR lookup matches the source IP address of the email
>
> o +ptr:ipamworldwide.com – pass if a domain name returned during the PTR lookup of the source IP address matches the source domain while falling within the ipamworldwide.com domain and if the A/AAAA domain name corresponding to the domain name returned during the PTR lookup matches the source IP address of the email

- ip4 = verify that the source IP address matches the IPv4 address specified; this mechanism may be qualified by CIDR length as illustrated in the following example:

> o ?ip4:192.0.2.32/30 – neutral if the source IP address of the message falls within 192.0.2.32–192.0.2.35

- ip6 = verify that the source IP address matches the IPv6 address specified; this mechanism may be qualified by prefix length as illustrated in the following example:

> o +ip6:2001:db8:f02b:2a::/64 – pass if the source IP address of the message falls within the 2001:db8:f02b:2a::/64 network.

- exists:*domain_name* = lookup the A record (not AAAA) corresponding to the *domain_name*; this mechanism matches if any answer (IP address) is provided (this mechanism must be scoped with a domain name to match as illustrated in the following example).

> o exists:ipamworldwide.com – matches if an A record lookup for the ipamworldwise.com domain returns an IP address

- include:*domain_name* = recursively evaluate the *domain_name* to leverage its SPF policies, e.g. to utilize the policy of a domain from multiple ISPs or from other domains from which you send email.
- all = matches everything; often used as the final parameter e.g., "-all" to fail if no prior mechanism matches

Modifiers

Modifiers may be specified within SPF records to provide additional information. Modifiers are name-value pairs, two of which have yet been defined:

- redirect=*domain_name* – enables "aliasing" of SPF records, e.g. to apply a common SPF processing record to multiple domains. This provides a convenience for ongoing change management: change the processing in one record, minimizing errors and maximizing consistency. In the following example, the MX record check for the ipamworldwide.com domain would apply to the hq and euro subdomains as well.

hq.ipamworldwide.com. IN SPF "v=spf1 redirect=_spf.ipamworldwide.com"
euro.ipamworldwide.com. IN SPF "v=spf1 redirect=_spf.ipamworldwide.com"
_spf.ipamworldwide.com. IN SPF "v=spf1 +mx:ipamworldwide.com –all"

The redirect can be used explicitly as in the above example, or as a "last resort", e.g. listed as the rightmost mechanism.

- exp=*domain_name* – explanation, which defines the domain for which a TXT record lookup must be done to identify the string to be presented as results upon a mechanism match failure.

Macros

Technically, the *domain_name* for any of the above mechanisms and modifiers need not be an explicitly defined (hard coded) domain, but one that can be defined using macros to dynamically formulate a domain name based on the message envelope under evaluation. Even the TXT record fetched by processing an exp modifier may be populated with macros. Macros are identified using the percent sign (%). The following macros have been defined:

- %{s} = the sender's email address
- %{l} = the local part of the sender's email address
- %{o} = the domain of the sender's email address
- %{d} = the current domain, usually the same as the sender's domain but may also have been processed, e.g. via the include mechanism
- %{i} = the source IP address of the message sender
- %{p} = the validated domain name via PTR lookup of the source IP address of the message sender.
- %{v} = the literal string "in-addr" if the source IP address is an IPv4 address and "ip6" if the source IP address is IPv6.
- %{h} = the domain part of the HELO/EHLO identity
- %% = the literal %
- %_ = space " "
- %- = a URL-encoded space, e.g. "%20"

The following macros are available for use in the TXT record referenced by an exp mechanism and may not be used elsewhere:

- %{c} = the SMTP client IP address
- %{r} = the domain name of the host performing the SPF check
- %{t} = the current timestamp.

Macro transformers enable use of a subset of the results of a macro, e.g. by specifying an integer quantity of domain name labels, or the reversal of the results of a macro, e.g. reversing an IP address. Reversal is performed by adding an r into the macro curly brackets.

Macro Examples

Consider the example of Figure 19.20, where Mike (mike@ipamww.com) sends me an email to tim@ipamworldwide.com from my SMTP host on IP addresses 192.0.2.32. Using this and other information from the figure, we can define the macro values for this email transmission as:

- %{s} = mike@ipamww.com
- %{l} = mike
- %{o} = ipamww.com
- %{d} = ipamww.com
- %{d3} = ipamww.com
- %{d2} = ipamww.com
- %{d1} = com
- %{i} = 192.0.2.32
- %{ir} = 32.2.0.192
- %{v} = in-addr
- %{h} = ipamww.com
- %{ir}.%{v}._spf.%{d} = 32.2.0.192.in-addr._spf.ipamww.com

SPF provides a powerful macro language to granularly articulate email policies for your organization.

Sender ID (Historical)

Another now historical mechanism for identifying potential spam email is called Sender ID. The Sender ID algorithm seeks to identify whether a given email from a given SMTP client at the given source IP address is authorized to send the email. Like SPF, Sender ID can examine the sender, sender domain and source IP address of the email message based on the MAIL FROM field. Unlike SPF, Sender ID can also or alternatively verify the sender and sender domain based on message header information. Sender ID, like SPF, utilizes the SPF resource record type, as defined in the previous section with a few modifications:

- the version string ("v=spf1") is replaced with "spf2.0"
- Sender ID includes a scope for the record: "mfrom" indicates the mailfrom entity as in SPF, and/or "pra" the *purported responsible address*, discussed next.
- modifiers are extended from the SPF definition to enable positional context as an alternative to the SPF-defined global context. That is, a modifier can affect

a preceding mechanism, unlike SPF where a modifier is always applied globally.

The scope field is used to derive the sender and sender domain for validation (i.e. the MAIL FROM entity and/or the PRA). The purported responsible address, PRA, scope relates to the identity of the sender closest to the receiving email system. The PRA algorithm examines the message header, not the envelope, and seeks a sender address by examining the following headers in order, taking the first address found:

- Resent-Sender header
- Resent-From header
- Sender header
- From header

A single valid sender mailbox address (i.e. of the form mailbox@maildomain) found in one of these headers is the PRA. In the simple cases illustrated in Figures 19.20 and 19.21, the purported responsible address would be mike@ ipamww.com as derived from the "From" header value. In the case where a third party is used to transmit email on behalf of a legitimate sender, the "Resent-From" or other header value would be used. The term "purported" is used since the algorithm relies on information supplied in the message header, which is supplied by the sender.

Domain Keys Identified Mail (DKIM)

DKIM specifies a means for a sender of email to cryptographically sign an email message such that recipients may validate it upon receipt via retrieval and application of the sender's domain key. DKIM utilizes digital signatures, which enable the originator of a given set of data (an email message in this case) to sign the data such that those receiving the data and the signature, along with a corresponding public key for deciphering the signature, can perform data origin and integrity verification. DKIM employs an asymmetric key pair (private key/public key) model. In such a model, the email message and selected header fields are encrypted with a private key and can be validated by decrypting the data with the corresponding public key. The private key and public key form a key pair. The mathematical details are very complex but conceptually, the private/public key pairs provide a means for holders of the public key to verify that data was signed using the corresponding private key. This provides authentication that the data verified was indeed signed by the holder of the private key. Digital signatures also enable verification that the data received matches the data published and was not tampered with in transit.

Referring to Figure 19.22, the data originator, shown on the left of the figure, generates a private key/public key pair and utilizes the private key to sign the data. The first step in signing the data is to produce a hash of the data, sometimes also referred to as a digest. Hashes are one-way functions[10] to scramble data into a fixed length string for simpler manipulation, and represent a "fingerprint" of the data. This means that it is very unlikely that another data input could produce the same hash value. Thus hashes are often used as checksums but don't provide any origin authentication (anyone knowing the hash algorithm can simply hash arbitrary data). Common hash algorithms include HMAC-MD5, RSA SHA-1, and RSA SHA-256. DKIM uses RSA SHA-256 by default but also supports RSA SHA-1. The hash is encrypted using the private key to produce the signature. The encryption algorithm is fed the hash and the private key to produce the signature.

Both the message and its associated signature are transmitted to the recipient. A new email header, dkim-signature, has been defined to store the DKIM signature with information on retrieving the public key. Based on our prior review of how SMTP works, you may be wondering how modification of envelope data and insertion of headers affect the signature. DKIM offers a "simple" or strict form of canonicalization and a "relaxed" form. The simple form tolerates very little modification while the relaxed form permits white space replacement and header line rewrapping without impacting the signature validity.

DKIM Signature Email Header Field

The recipient must extract the signature from the dkim-signature header field. The dkim-signature field also contains:

- the DKIM version (e.g. v=1)
- the algorithm used to generate the signature (e.g. a=rsa-sha256)

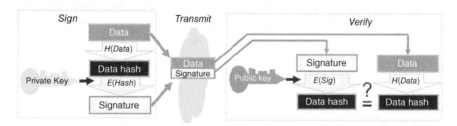

Figure 19.22   Digital signature creation and verification process.

---

[10]A one-way function means that the original data is not uniquely derivable from the hash. One can apply an algorithm to create the hash, but there is no inverse algorithm to perform on the hash to arrive at the original data.

- signature (e.g. b=dqdVx0fAK9...)
- hash of the canonicalized message body (bh=7Dkw0eE35Jlkjexcmpol...)
- canonicalization method (c=relaxed)
- the signing domain identifer – the domain of the signing entity (e.g. d=ipamworldwide.com)
- user or agent on whose behalf the message is signed (i=rooney@ipamworldwide.com)
- the selector or key reference within the domain (allows multiple keys per domain which aids in key rollover and more granular signatures) (e.g. s=europe)
- enumeration of the header fields that were signed (e.g. h=from:to:subject:date)
- additional optional information, including query methods to use to retrieve the public key. The default (and currently only) query method, q=dns/txt, instructs the recipient to perform a DNS query of querytype "txt" to retrieve the public key that corresponds with the private key that was used to sign the message. Another optional field of interest, the i = tag provides the identity of the user or agent on whose behalf this message was signed.

DKIM TXT Record

Using the query method q=dns/txt, the recipient performs a DNS query for a TXT record for the signing domain. The question section of the query is formulated by concatenating the selector value (s = value), the string "_domainkey" and the specified signing domain (d = value). Using the example where s=europe and d=ipamworldwide.com as specified in the dkim-signature field of an incoming email, a TXT query for europe._domainkey.ipamworldwide.com would be issued. The Rdata portion of the corresponding TXT record includes one or more tags similar to the dkim-signature field:

- DKIM version (v=DKIM1)
- Granularity of the key, which if specified, must match the local part of the identify flag in the dkim-signature header (g=*)
- Hash algorithm(s) accepted (e.g. h=sha256)
- Key type (k=rsa)
- Notes for human consumption (n=updated_key)
- The public key (p=Dkjeijf8d98Kz...)
- Service type (s=email)
- Flags indicating such things as the compliance rules among the i=tag in the dkim-signature header and the d=domain tag (encoded in the TXT record as t=s), as well as whether this domain is testing DKIM (t=y).

The only required tag is the p tag, the public key. An example TXT record follows:

europe._domainkey.ipamworldwide.com IN TXT ("v=DKIM1;p=Dkjeijf98Kz...")

Upon retrieving the public key, the recipient computes a hash of the received message body and signed header fields, as did the originator. The recipient applies the hash algorithm to the received signature using the originator's public key. The output of this decryption, the original data hash, is compared with the recipient's computed hash of the data. If they match, the data has not been modified and the private key holder signed the data.

If an incoming email message contains a dkim-signature header field, it's clear that the sender is using DKIM and has signed the message. But if an incoming email message does not contain a dkim-signature header field, does this mean the sender does not sign messages? This in fact could create an opening for a SPAM attacker issuing unsigned email messages from a spoofed source domain. DKIM relies on publication of author domain signing practices (ADSP), which enables a recipient email server to determine whether the message from a given domain by policy should be signed and if so, by whom and with what signature(s).

A recipient determines the sending domain's signing practices by issuing a query for Qtype=TXT and Qname = _adsp._domainkey.*signing-domain-identifier*, where *signing-domain-identifier* is again the d = value. The corresponding TXT record indicates whether email from this domain is always signed, may be signed, and is always signed and any unsigned email should be discarded. Please refer to RFC 5617 [231] for details.

DMARC TXT Record

Building on SPF and DKIM, the DMARC TXT record defines monitoring and disposition policies for incoming emails. The owner field of the TXT record is the organizational domain (email originator) prefixed with a "_dmarc" label. So for ipamworldwide.com, the owner name is _dmarc.ipamworldwide.com. The Rdata portion of the record contains a concatenated string of DMARC policies [119].

The following parameters may be defined within a DMARC record:

- v – protocol version; example: v=DMARC1
- pct – percentage of messages to monitor; example: pct=15
- ruf – reporting URI for forensics; example: ruf=mailto:antispam@ipamworldwide.com
- rua – reporting URI for aggregated reports; example: rua= mailto:antispam@ipamworldwide.com

- p – policy for the organizational domain (none, quarantine, reject); example: p=quanrantine
- sp – policy for subdomains of the domain (none, quarantine, reject); example: sp=reject
- adkim – alignment mode for DKIM, strict (s) or relaxed (r); example: adkim=r
- aspf – alignment mode for SPF, strict (s) or relaxed (r); example: aspf=s
- fo – failure reporting options, values include:
    o 0 – generate a DMARC failure report if all authentication mechanisms failt to produce an aligned "pass" result
    o 1 – generate a DMARC failure report if any authentication mechanisms failt to produce an aligned "pass" result
    o d – generate a DKIM failure report if the DKIM signature failed to validate
    o s – generate an SPF failure report if the message failed SPF evaluation
- r – reporting format, a list of plain-text report
- ri – reporting interval between aggregated reports

Historic Email Resource Record Types

These resource record types discussed in this section were defined in the early days of DNS and are no longer used. We list them here purely for historical significance.

MR – Mail Rename Record

The MR resource record type translates email to an alias or list into an individual (or multiple, one per MR record). In the simplest sense, it provides an alias for a mailbox name.

Owner	TTL	Class	Type	RData
Emailbox alias name	TTL	IN	MR	Emailbox name
cfo	86400	IN	MR	finance

MB – Mailbox Record

The MB record is defined in RFC 1035 and enables association of a user ID with the desired host containing the user's email box.

Owner	TTL	Class	Type	RData
Email ID	TTL	IN	MB	Mailbox hostname
joe	86400	IN	MB	smtp.ipamworldwide.com

MG – Mail Group Member Record

RFC 1035 defined the MG resource record to enable association of email users with a user group.

Owner	TTL	Class	Type	RData
Email group name	TTL	IN	MG	Email ID
finance	86400	IN	MG	joe

MINFO – Mailbox/Mailing List Information

The MINFO record was also defined in RFC 1035 and was intended to provide mailbox and mailing list information. It provides two email box addresses: one to request addition to the mailing list and another to report errors.

Owner	TTL	Class	Type	RData	
Mailbox name	TTL	IN	MINFO	Requests mailbox	Errors mailbox
newsalerts	86400	IN	MINFO	hostmaster	majordomo

Security Applications

Securing Name Resolution – DNSSEC Resource Record Types

We discussed DNSSEC zone signing in Chapter 12. This section discusses the resource records that provide DNSSEC signature, key, chain of trust delegation, and authenticated denial of existence functions.

DNSKEY – DNS Key Record

The DNSKEY resource record is used in DNSSEC to publish public keys used for validating signatures on zone information. The server signs its authoritative RRSets within a zone using a private key and the corresponding public key is published in the zone file in the form of the DNSKEY record. Two types of keys are published: a ZSK which signs resource record data and a KSK which signs the ZSK. The resolver can use this public key to validate the RRSet's signature.

Owner	TTL	Class	Type	Rdata				
Key name	TTL	IN	DNSKEY	Flags	Protocol	Algorithm	Key	
.ipamww. com.	86400	IN	DNSKEY	256	3	5	AweE8F(le...	

In this example, the RData fields are interpreted as follows:

- The Flags field provides information on the type and status of the key. Currently defined values for the Flags field are as follows.
  - Bit 7 – This key is a Zone Signing Key (Decimal = 256)
  - Bit 8 – Revoke this Key
  - Bit 15 – This key is a KSK (Decimal = 1)
  - Other bits – Unassigned
- The Protocol field must have a value of "3" indicating DNSSEC (this is the only value currently defined).
- The Algorithm has a value of "5" in the example above, indicating the RSA-SHA1 algorithm. Algorithms currently supported are encoded as follows:
  - Value = 1 – RSA/MD5, which is not recommended according to RFC 4034
  - Value = 2 – Diffie-Hellman
  - Value = 3 – DSA[11]/SHA-1
  - Value = 4 – Elliptic Curve
  - Value = 5 – RSA/SHA-1, which is mandatory according to RFC 4034.
  - Value = 6 – DSA-NSEC3-SHA1 – an alias for algorithm 3, but with the qualifier that NSEC3 records instead of NSEC records are used in signing this zone (causes NSEC-only aware resolvers to consider this zone insecure)
  - Value = 7 – RSASHA1-NSEC3-SHA1 – an alias for algorithm 5, but with the qualifier that NSEC3 records instead of NSEC records are used in signing this zone (causes NSEC-only aware resolvers to consider this zone insecure)
  - Value = 8 – RSA/SHA-512
  - Value = 9 – Reserved
  - Value = 10 – RSHA/SHA-512
  - Value = 11 – Reserved
  - Value = 12 – GOST R 34.10-2001
  - Value = 13 – ECDSA Curve P-256 with SHA-256
  - Value = 14 – ECDSA Curve P-384 with SHA-384
  - Value = 15 – Ed25518
  - Value = 16 – Ed448
  - Value = 17 – 122 – Unassigned
  - Value = 123 – 251 – Reserved
  - Value = 252 – Reserved for Indirect Keys
  - Values = 253–254 – Private algorithm
  - Values = 0, 255 – Reserved
- The Key is the public key.

---

[11]DSA = US Government Digital Signature Algorithm

Note that the Child DNSKEY (CDNSKEY) record type is of the same format as the DNSKEY record. The CDNSKEY record can be published by a zone administrator to signal the parent zone administrator to update the DS record corresponding to the new KSK defined by this DNSKEY in this [child] zone.

DS – Delegation Signer Record

RFC 4034 [232] defines the DS resource record type, which essentially extends the chain of trust to a delegated domain (zone). The DS resource record enables a parent zone to authenticate one of its child zone's public KSKs (DNSKEY record for the KSK). As such, it refers to a DNSKEY resource record in the delegated child zone. Authenticating the DS record enables clients to authenticate the child zone's DNSKEY.

Owner	TTL	Class	Type	RData			
Delegated domain	TTL	IN	DS	Key tag	Alg.	Type	Digest
child.ipamww.com	86400	IN	DS	32284	5	1	75CF28D3OQ35....

The Key tag field contains a reference to the corresponding DNSKEY record, and the Algorithm field identifies the algorithm field on the corresponding DNSKEY record. The DS record refers to a DNSKEY record by including a digest of the DNSKEY RR in the Digest field; the Digest Type field indicates the algorithm utilized to construct the digest.

Note that the CDS record type is of the same format as the DS record. The CDS record can be published by a zone administrator to signal the parent zone administrator to update the DS record corresponding to this [child] zone.

NSEC – Next Secure Record

The NSEC resource record type provides two sets of information. The set of NSEC RRs in a zone forms a chain of authoritative owner names in the zone and indicates which authoritative RRSets exist in the zone. The NSEC resource record contains the next owner name that identifies associated authoritative owner names within the chain, as well as the set of RR types present at the NSEC resource record's owner name.

Owner	TTL	Class	Type	RData	
RRSet Owner	TTL	IN	NSEC	Next RRSet Owner	Type Bit Maps
ns1.ipamww.com	86400	IN	NSEC	ns2.ipamww.com	A NS RRSIG NSEC

The Next RRSet Owner field contains the next owner name in the canonical ordering of the zone that has authoritative data or contains an RRSet of type NS defining a delegation point. This provides authenticated denial of existence of resource records between the RRSet identified within the NSEC Owner field and the Next RRSet Owner Rdata field. The Type Bit Maps field identifies the resource record types that exist at this NSEC resource record's owner name. Within this field, if a bit = 1, then the RRType corresponding to this bit number exists. Thus if bit 1 is 1, corresponding to RR Type = 1 or A record, then an A RRSet is present. Fortunately, the text representation of this is in the familiar resource record type code.

NSEC3 – NSEC3 Record

The NSEC resource record provides authenticated denial of existence for RRSets, but it also enables easy enumeration of RRSets in the zone, which can be considered an information security risk. In other words, a curious or malicious querier could attempt to resolve a bogus name and receive the pair of resource record owner names surrounding the queried host name.

Like NSEC, the NSEC3 record provides authenticated RRSet denial of existence, but obfuscates the chain of RRSets in the zone. This obfuscation renders the footprinting of a zone's contents much more computationally intensive. Instead of pointing to the new owner name field, NSEC3 points to the next hashed owner name field in hash order. And the salt value which is appended to each owner name prior to hash generation further complicates the generation of hashed owner names by someone attempting to footprint the zone.

For each RRSet in the zone, the owner field is hashed using the specified hash algorithm applied to the owner name concatenated with the salt field iteratively <Iterations> + 1 times. The following pseudo code states this in another way:

```
x = { RRSet owner field concatenated with Salt value }
y = H ( x )     a hash of x as defined in the prior
statement
    for ( i = Iterations value; i > 0; i--) {
        y = H ( y )
    }
```

Owner	TTL	Class	Type	RData							
Hashed RRSet Owner	TTL	IN	NSEC3	Hash Alg.	Flags	Iterations	Salt Len.	Salt	Hash Len.	Next Hashed Owner Name	Type Bit Maps
jAdfJE;...	800	IN	NSEC3	1	0	2	8	a808f6ce 1a950b1c	18	k0Lse7...	A RRSIG NSEC3

The RData fields for the NSEC3 record are defined as follows.

- *Hash Algorithm* – The algorithm used to construct the hash value; valid values are:
  - o 0 – Reserved
  - o 1 = RSA SHA-1
  - o 2–255 – Unassigned
- *Flags* – Consisting of a set of eight Boolean flags, the Flags field has currently a single flag defined (bit 0). If bit 0 is set, this indicates that this record covers one or more unsigned delegation records. This Opt-Out flag enables "opting out" of securing delegations to unsigned zones, another nuisance required when using the NSEC record.
- *Iterations* – Specifies the number of additional applications of the hash function
- *Salt length* – Included in the wire format but not presented in the resource record text format, this field indicates the length in bytes of the Salt field (valid values = 0–255)
- *Salt* – The value of the Salt field is appended to the RRSet owner prior to application of the hash function and is represented in case-insensitive hexadecimal.
- *Hash length* – The length in octets of the next hashed owner name field, included on the wire but not represented in resource record text format
- *Next Hashed Owner Name* – hash of the next RRSet owner name in this zone
- *Type bit maps* – This field defines the resource record types defined for this owner within the zone and is encoded in the same manner as the corresponding field in the NSEC record

NSEC3PARAM – NSEC3 Parameters Record

The NSEC3PARAM record type defines the parameters needed to compute hashed owner names and hence the corresponding NSEC3 records within the zone upon signing. The NSEC3PARAM record is used by the server on which the zone is configured to identify negative answers in response to a query and is not used by signature validating resolvers or servers. In other words, when a query arrives for a non-existent RRSet within the zone, the server applies the NSEC3PARAM parameters to hash the queried owner name in order to provide an appropriate NSEC3 response, i.e. between which two hashed RRSets does this queried owner name fall? Only one NSEC3PARAM record should be present within the zone. The NSEC3PARAM record is also used by the server when signing new or changed RRSets automatically.

The Rdata fields have identical meanings as corresponding fields within the NSEC3 Rdata fields.

Owner	TTL	Class	Type	RData				
				Hash		Itera-	Salt	
Domain name	TTL	IN	NSEC3PARAM	Alg.	Flags	tions	Len.	Salt
ipamww.com.	86400	IN	NSEC3PARAM	1	0	2	8	a808f6ce 1a950b1c

RRSIG – Resource Record Set Signature Record

The RRSet Signature resource record contains the digital signature associated with a given RRSet. This signature, along with the zone's public [zone signing] key are used to authenticate the corresponding RRSet's integrity and origin.

Owner	TTL	Class	Type	RData								
RRSet Owner	TTL	IN	RRSIG	Type Covered	Algorithm	Labels	Original TTL	Expire	Inception	Key tag	Signer	Signature
ftp1 .ipamww .com.	86400	IN	RRSIG	A	5	3	8640	20200 51513 3509	2020 8011 5133 509	27783	ipamww. com	N78E...

The RData fields within the RRSIG record are defined as follows.

- *Type covered* – The resource record type of the corresponding owner and class signed by this signature. This field is the standard resource record type discussed for resource records throughout this chapter. In the example above, the A (address) resource record type indicates that A records with name ftp1. ipamww.com (Owner field) of class IN are signed.
- *Algorithm* – The algorithm used in generating the data hash for comparison with the received signature. This field is encoded in the same manner as the Algorithm field of the DNSKEY resource record type.
- *Labels* – Indicates the number labels. Recall that labels refer to the text representation of domain names, with a label for each name "between the dots." Thus www.ipamworldwide.com has three labels. This field is used to reconstruct the original owner name used to create the signature in the case where the owner name returned by the server has a wildcard label (*).

- *Original TTL* – The TTL of the signed RRSet as defined in the authoritative zone, used to validate a signature. This field is needed because the TTL field returned in the original response is normally decremented by a caching resolver and use of that TTL value may lead to erroneous calculations.
- *Signature expiration* – The date and time of the expiration of this signature expressed as either the number of seconds since 1 January 1970 00:00:00 UTC or in the form of YYYMMDDHHmmSS where
  - o YYYY is the year
  - o MM is the month, 01–12
  - o DD is the day of the month, 01–31
  - o HH is the hour in 24-hour notation, 00–23
  - o mm is the minute, 00–59
  - o SS is the second, 00–59

- Signatures are not valid after this date/time.
- *Signature inception* – The date and time of the inception of this signature formatted in the same manner as the Signature Expiration field. Signatures are not valid before this date/time.
- *Key tag* – Provides an association with the corresponding DNSKEY resource record that can be used to validate this signature.
- *Signer's name* – Identifies the owner name of the DNSKEY resource record (i.e. the domain name) that is to be used to validate this signature.
- *Signature* – The cryptographic signature covering the resource record set defined by this RRSIG owner, class and covered type fields and this RRSIG RData fields (excluding this Signature field).

Other Security-oriented DNS Resource Record Types

TA – Trust Authority Record
While an RFC does not exist defining the TA resource record, IANA has assigned it a value, so we'll mention it here. The TA resource record is identical in format to the DS record type including RData fields for key tag, algorithm, digest type and digest. Use of the TA record enables a resolver to have a resource record signature validated by a known trust authority even if the root zone has not been signed. This functionality is now provided using the DLV record.

CERT – Certificate Record
RFC 4398 [233] defines the CERT record as a means to store certificates and certificate revocation lists (CRLs) in DNS. Certificates provide a means to identify an

organization, server, individual, or other entity and associate a public key with that identity. The public key can be used to authenticate the sender's identity and to encrypt and decrypt communications and validate message integrity. Certificates are hierarchical and can be used to validate up to a known trusted entity (Certificate Authority). CRLs are lists of certificates which have been revoked due to expiration or manual revocation.

CERT records containing certificates are stored in DNS to enable resolvers to obtain certificates via DNS instead of from a destination certificate server. The CERT resource record has the following format.

Owner	TTL	Class	Type	RData		
Domain name	TTL	IN	CERT	Certificate Type	Key Tag	Algorithm	Certificate or CRL
ipamww .com	900	IN	CERT	PGP	436	3	A4df480DFC9lLa....

The owner field identifies the entity to which the certificate applies when a certificate is included in the RData portion of the record. If a CRL is included in the RData section, the owner name should contain the domain name related to the issuing authority. The RData portion contains the following subfields:

- Certificate Type such as X.509/PKIX, PGP, and others
- Key Tag, which is used to streamline the identification of relevant certificates to those of matching key tags
- Algorithm – the algorithm used in generating the key, which is encoded in the same manner as the Algorithm field of the DNSKEY resource record type.
- The certificate or CRL

IPSECKEY – Public Key for IPSec Record

The IPSECKEY resource record type, defined in RFC 4025 [234], provides a means to store a public key in DNS for use with IPSec. This resource record enables a client seeking to establish an IPSec tunnel to a remote host to identify a means to authenticate the remote host and to determine whether to connect directly to the host or connect via another node acting as a gateway. IPSECKEY resource records are associated with the intended remote host's IP address or host domain name. IP addresses are stored in the .arpa. reverse domain space. The format of the IPSECKEY resource record is as follows.

Owner	TTL	Class	Type	RData					
IP address in .arpa. domain or host domain name	TTL	IN	IPSECKEY	Precedence	Gateway type	Algorithm	Gateway	Public key
1.0.12.10.in-addr. arpa.	86400	IN	IPSECKEY	10	1	2	10.100.1.2	Adf4C9lL....

The RData field contains the following fields:

- *Precedence* – Used to prioritize multiple records within a common RRSet, using the lowest precedence first.
- *Gateway type* – Indicates the format of the Gateway field
    - o 0 = no gateway is present
    - o 1 = IPv4 address
    - o 2 = IPv6 address
    - o 3 = FQDN

- *Algorithm* – The format of the Public Key field
    - o 0 = no key is present
    - o 1 = DSA formatted key
    - o 2 = RSA formatted key

- *Gateway* – Identifies a gateway to which an IPSec tunnel can be established to reach the remote host (identified by the owner field). The interpretation of this field is governed by the Gateway Type field.
- *Public key* – The key generated using the algorithm specified in the Algorithm field

KEY – Key Record

The KEY record was defined with the initial incarnation of DNSSEC, but was superseded by the DNSKEY resource record. However, prior to the release of DNSSECbis, the KEY record was also utilized to store public keys associated with the SIG(0) record. The KEY record has the same format as the DNSKEY record.

Owner	TTL	Class	Type	RData			
Key name	TTL	IN	KEY	Flags	Protocol	Algorithm	Key
K3941. ipamww.com	86400	IN	KEY	256	3	1	12S9X- weE8F(le...

KX – Key Exchanger Record

The KX record enables specification of an intermediary that can supply a key on behalf of another host. In other words, if intending to perform key negotiation with x.ipamworldwide.com, the KX record could point to the y.ipamworldwide.com host domain name with whom key exchange negotiation should ensue. A preference field enables specification of multiple alternate domains of varying preference for key negotiation.

Owner	TTL	Class	Type		Rdata
Host domain name	TTL	IN	KX	Preference	Key exchanger host domain name
x.ipamworldwide.com.	86 400	IN	KX	10	y.ipamworldwide.com.
x.ipamworldwide.com.	86 400	IN	KX	20	z.ipamworldwide.com.

SIG – Signature Record

The SIG resource record has been superseded by the RRSIG record within the scope of DNSSEC, though the SIG record is still in use for digitally signing DNS updates and zone transfers outside the scope of DNSSEC. That is, you don't need to deploy DNSSEC to enable transaction signatures of updates and zone transfers. Such transactions can be signed using shared secret keys via TSIG records or by using private/ public key pairs via SIG(0), where corresponding public keys are stored as KEY records. The notation SIG(0) refers to the use of the SIG resource record with an empty (0) Type Covered field. In such cases, RFC 2931 [235] recommends setting the owner field to root, the TTL to 0, and class to ANY as shown in the example below.

The SIG record is formatted identically to the RRSIG record, with the exception of the formatting of the Expiration Date and Inception Date fields; for the SIG record, these fields are not formatted by date per the RRSIG record and are instead formatted as an incremental integer, enumerated as the number of seconds since 1 January 1970 00:00:00 UTC. This counter will rollover to 0 and continue counting after the counter exceeds 4.29 billion seconds (a little over 136 years).

Owner	TTL	Class	Type									RData
RRSet Domain	TTL	IN	SIG	Type Covered	Alg.	Labels	Orig. TTL	Expire	Inception	Key tag	Signer	Signature
	0	ANY	SIG	0	3	3	600	1602 0819 77	1604 7603 77	26421	ipamww. com.	Zx9v...

SSHFP – Secure Shell Fingerprint Record

The Secure Shell (SSH) protocol enables secure login from a client to a server and other secure network services over an insecure IP network. The security of the connection relies upon the user authenticating him- or herself to the server as well as the server authenticating itself to the client via Diffie–Hellman key exchange. If the public key is not already known by the client, a fingerprint of the key is provided by the server for verification by the user. Storage of this key fingerprint in DNS provides a means for the client to lookup and verify the fingerprint out of band via a "third party." The lookup requires use of DNSSEC to secure the lookup process and assure message integrity. The SSHFP resource record is the record type used to store these SSH fingerprints.

Owner	TTL	Class	Type	RData		
Host domain name	TTL	IN	SSHFP	Algorithm	Fingerprint type	Fingerprint
srv21. ipamww.com	3600	IN	SSHFP	2	1	8Fd7q90D+fd...

The RData portion of the SSHFP record includes the following fields:

- *Algorithm* – currently defined values are
    - o 0 = Reserved
    - o 1 = RSA
    - o 2 = DSA
- *Fingerprint type* – currently defined values are:
    - o 0 = Reserved
    - o 1 = SHA-1
    - o Key fingerprint

Geographical Location Lookup

GPOS – Geographical Position Record

The GPOS resource record type, originally defined in RFC 1712 [236], has been superseded by the LOC resource record type. GPOS encoded the longitude, latitude and altitude of a host as shown below.

Owner	TTL	Class	Type	RData		
Host domain name	TTL	IN	GPOS	Longitude	Latitude	Altitude
srv1.ipamww.com	3600	IN	GPOS	39.582	−75.801	128.2

LOC – Location Resource Record

This type of resource record enables encoding of latitude, longitude, and altitude information about the respective host. RFC 1876 [237] defines the LOC record, which obsoletes the GPOS resource record type. The RData field for the LOC record presents each coordinate in the three dimensions:

- *Latitude* – degrees [minutes [seconds]] "N" or "S"
- *Longitude* – degrees [minutes [seconds]] "E" or "W"
- *Altitude* – altitude in meters
- Precision of each measure as diameter of "sphere (or circle) of error" in meters

Owner	TTL	Class	Type	RData			
Host domain name	TTL	IN	LOC	Latitude	Longitude	Altitude	Precision
srv-97.ipamww.com	86 400	IN	LOC	39°58′ N	75°38′ W	128°	50 m

In the example above, the host named srv-97.ipamww.com is located at 39°58′ N latitude, 75°38′ W longitude, is 128 m above sea level, all within a sphere of error with diameter 50 m.

Non-IP Host-Address Lookups

ISDN – Integrated Services Digital Network Record (Experimental)

The ISDN type enables association of an ISDN address to a host. The ISDN address is the form of a telephone number, as defined by the ITU standard E.164. The subaddress field is optional.

Owner	TTL	Class	Type	RData	
Host domain name	TTL	IN	ISDN	ISDN Address	Subaddress
isdnhost.ipamww.com	86400	IN	ISDN	16105551298	318

NSAP – Network Service Access Point Record

The network service access point (NSAP) resource record enables translation of a hostname or FQDN to an NSAP address. NSAP is the notation for a network device that supports the ISO connectionless network protocol (CLNP). Without getting into the details of NSAP addresses, which never really caught on, the NSAP resource record functions equivalently to an A record for IPv4 and AAAA for IPv6. It provides a destination address for a queried hostname.

Owner	TTL	Class	Type	RData
Host domain name	TTL	IN	NSAP	NSAP Address
nsap-host.ipamww.com	86400	IN	NSAP	47.0005.09. d78d01.1010.0ffe.0011...00

NSAP-PTR – Network Service Access Point Reverse Record

The NSAP-PTR record type performs the equivalent pointer record functionality for NSAP addresses, linking an NSAP address suffix to a host domain name. The nsap.int domain serves as the corresponding reverse TLD. As with IP address based pointer records, the NSAP address must be reversed, and dots inserted between each digit. Finally the nsap.int. suffix is added.

Owner	TTL	Class	Type	RData
NSAP Address Reversed	TTL	IN	NSAP-PTR	Host domain name
0.0...1.1.0.0.e.f.f.0.0.1.0 .1.1.0.d.8.7.d.9.0.5.0.0. 0.7.4.nsap.int.	86400	IN	NSAP-PTR	nsap-host. ipamww.com

PX – Pointer for X.400

The PX resource record is defined in RFC 2163 [238] and is intended to provide a mapping between DNS domain names and an X.400 address for email address mapping. X.400 is an ITU standard for messaging or email, though today most systems use SMTP. This resource record type is useful for networks containing SMTP-to-x.400 email gateways, referred to as MIXER (MIME Internet X.400 Enhanced Relay) gateways. The X.400 address is formatted using the Originator/Recipient (O/R) convention.

Owner	TTL	Class	Type	RData		
				Preference	DNS Domain	X.400 mapping
Domain name	TTL	IN	PX	Preference	Domain	X.400 mapping
ipamww.com	86400	IN	PX	10	ipamww. com	O=company.PRMD-netx.ADMD.C=tv..

X25 – X.25 PSDN Address Record (Experimental)

This is an experimental Resource Record and is not widely used, as X.25 packet switched data networks (PSDNs) are not widely in-use today. It has a number of possible applications:

- document the addresses to use in static configurations of IP-to-X.25 and SMTP-to-X.25;
- automatically associate an IP address to PSDN address;
- configure names to X.25 PSDN addresses.

It also provides a function similar to ARP for wide area non-broadcast networks.

Owner	TTL	Class	Type	RData
Host domain name	TTL	IN	X25	PDSN address
x25-host.ipamww.com	86400	IN	X25	31161700956

RT – Route Through

The Route Through resource record was defined in RFC 1183 [226] and is used to denote a proxy or alternative destination to which to route traffic for hosts without a direct network link. Multiple route through hosts can be identified, each with associated preference values, much like the MX resource record.

Owner	TTL	Class	Type		RData
				Preference	Proxy Hostname
Host domain name	TTL	IN	RT		
host.ipamww.com	86400	IN	RT	10	proxy.ipamww.com

The Null Record Type

NULL

The NULL resource record type is experimental and enables specification of up to 65535 bytes of "anything." It is usually ignored and not widely used.

Owner	TTL	Class	Type	RData
Host domain name	TTL	IN	NULL	Up to 65535 bytes of "anything"
host.ipamww.com	86400	IN	NULL	"Ignore this NULL resource record!"

Experimental Name-Address Lookup Records

IPv6 Address Chaining – The A6 Record (Experimental)

Given the sheer length of IPv6 addresses, the IETF had considered an iterative approach to resolving hostnames to IPv6 addresses. The A6 record, defined in RFC 2874 [239], intended to map a host domain name to a portion (or all) of an IPv6 address, with pointers for the resolver to iteratively resolve the remainder of the IPv6 address to its full 128 bits. This enabled resolution of the host domain name by starting most commonly with the interface ID, then adding in the appropriate subnet ID, and global routing prefix, essentially resolving the hostname address moving from right to left. The intent was to simplify renumbering of IPv6 networks that may be necessary due to network maintenance, changing of ISPs, or other reasons. Changing the subnet ID for a number of hosts was as simple as changing one record, instead of each host's record.

However, due to the complexity in accurately configuring DNS with the appropriate linkages (and preventing open linkages), this resource record type was changed to experimental status. To illustrate this, the example below illustrates the A6 resource record and how three successive queries would be used to fully resolve. Note that more or fewer linkages could be defined based on individual preference.

Owner	TTL	Class	Type	RData		
Host domain name	TTL	IN	A6	Prefix length	Address suffix	Prefix name
ftp-sf.ipamww.com	3600	IN	A6	64	::a05f:0:0:2001	sf-net.ipamww.com
sf-net.ipamww.com	3600	IN	A6	48	0:0:0:8400::	na-west.ipamwwe.com
na-west.ipamww.com	3600	IN	A6	0	2001:db8:4af0::	

Note that the RData portion of the A6 resource record contains three subfields. The prefix length indicates the number of offset bits from the start of the address to begin inserting the address suffix bits. Thus the first listed A6 record with owner field "ftp-sf.ipamww.com." indicates a prefix length of 64 bits, specifying the interface identifier of ::a05f:0:0:2001.

The prefix name field provides a linkage to a second look up to continue building the entire 128-bit address. In this case, we are linked to the "sf-net.ipamww.com." prefix name, which points to an A6 record with owner field, "sf-net.ipamww.com." The corresponding A6 record indicates a 48-bit prefix length with IPv6 address, 0:0:0:8400::. Note that the full IPv6 address notation is used, including the restriction of a single double colon. This record then points to the na-west.ipamww .com. A6 record, which completes our formulation of the IPv6 address for resolution with its zero offset. The following diagram illustrates this process:

APL – Address Prefix List Record (Experimental)

While A and AAAA records are used to resolve host IP addresses, the address prefix list (APL) record seeks to resolve address prefixes or subnet addresses. The following example illustrates a scenario of advertising a set of address ranges

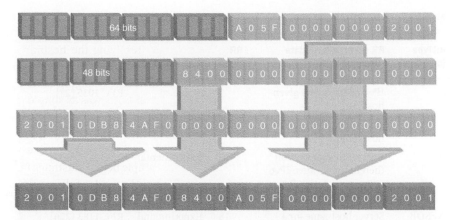

Figure 19.23 Iterative derivation of an IPv6 address using A6 records.

associated with a domain or host. The RData portion of the APL record consists of an optional negation character (!), the address family as defined by IANA[12] followed by a colon, then the address in CIDR notation (network/prefix length).

Owner	TTL	Class	Type	RData
Host domain name	TTL	IN	APL	Address Family:Address/Prefix
sf-ftp.ipamww.com.	86400	IN	APL	1:10.0.128/18, !10.16.128.0/18 2:2001:db8:4af0:8400::/56

In the above example, address prefixes associated with sf-ftp.ipamww.com.com are 10.0.128.0/18 for IPv4, not 10.16.128.0/18 for IPv4 and the prefix 2:2001:db8:4af0:8400::/56 for IPv6.

DNS Resource Record Summary

Table 19.7 summarizes the currently defined set of resource records in alphabetical order by resource record type (RRType – also corresponds to valid QType when a querier seeks this type of information from DNS, i.e. within the Question section of a DNS message). While not all resource records are IETF standards or even defined within the IETF, those that have been assigned an RR Type ID number by IANA are listed here. Current IETF status is provided along with the defining document which can be accessed for more details.

---

[12]Address family values are maintained by IANA – see http://www.iana.org/assignments/address-family-numbers. Relevant to our example, IANA has assigned family number 1 to IPv4 and 2 to IPv6.

Table 19.7   Resource record and query type summary.

RRType (or QType)	RR purpose (i.e. Rdata contents)	RR type ID	IETF status	Defining document
A	IPv4 address for a given hostname	1	Standard	RFC 1035 [28]
AAAA	IPv6 address for a given hostname	28	Draft Standard	RFC 3596 [240]
A6	IPv6 address or portion thereof for iterative IPv6 address resolution for a given hostname	38	Experimental	RFC 2874 [239]
AFSDB	Server hostname for a given AFS and DCE domain	18	Experimental	RFC 1183 [226]
APL	Address prefix lists for a given domain	42	Experimental	RFC 3123 [241]
ATMA	Asynchronous transfer mode (ATM) address for a host	34	Not Submitted	ATM Name System Specification by the ATM Forum [242]
CAA	List of certification authorities (CAs) authorized to issue certificates for this domain name		Standards Track	RFC 8659 [243]
CDS	Signal to a parent zone of updated Delegation Signer RRSet	59	Informational	RFC 7344 [107]
CDNSKEY	Signal to a parent zone of updated DNSKEY RRSet	60	Informational	RFC 7344 [107]
CERT	Certificate or Certificate Revocation List	37	Standards Track	RFC 4398 [233]
CNAME	Alias host name for a host	5	Standard	RFC 1035 [28]
CSYNC	Signal to parent zone of update NS and/or glue (A/ AAAA) RRsets	62	Standards Track	RFC 7477 [244]
DHCID	Associates a DHCP client's identity with a DNS name	49	Standards Track	RFC 4701 [245]
DLV	Authoritative zone signature for a trust anchor (Obsolete)	32769	Informational (DNSSEC)	RFC 4431 [246]

RRType (or QType)	RR purpose (i.e. Rdata contents)	RR type ID	IETF status	Defining document
DNAME	Alias domain name	39	Proposed Standard	RFC 6672 [206]
DNSKEY	Authoritative zone signature within a chain of trust	48	Standards Track (DNSSEC)	RFC 4034 [232]
DS	Signature for delegated child zone	43	Standards Track (DNSSEC)	RFC 4034 [232]
EUI48	48-bit extended unique identifier (link layer address – for use in private networks)	108	Informational	RFC 7043 [247]
EUI64	64-bit extended unique identifier (link layer address – for use in private networks)	109	Informational	RFC 7043 [247]
GID	Group ID	102	RESERVED	IANA-Reserved
GPOS	Lat/long/altitude for a given host – superseded by LOC	27	Experimental	RFC 1712 [236]
HINFO	CPU and OS information for a host	13	Standard	RFC 1035 [28]
HIP	Host identity protocol	55	Experimental	RFC 5205 [248]
IPSECKEY	Public key for a given DNS name for use with IPSec	45	Proposed Standard	RFC 4025 [234]
ISDN	Integrated Services Digital Network (ISDN) address and subaddress for a given host	20	Experimental	RFC 1183 [226]
KEY	Superseded by DNSKEY within DNSSEC but still used by SIG(0) and TKEY	25	Proposed Standard	RFC 2536 [249]
KX	Intermediary domain to obtain a key for a host in given domain	36	Informational	RFC 2230 [250]
L32	Network Locator to locate a 32-bit (IPv4) network for use in identifier/locator network protocol (ILNP)	105	Experimental	RFC 6742 [251]

(Continued)

Table 19.7 (Continued)

RRType (or QType)	RR purpose (i.e. Rdata contents)	RR type ID	IETF status	Defining document
L64	Network locator to locate a 64-bit (IPv6) network for use in identifier/locator network protocol (ILNP)	106	Experimental	RFC 6742 [251]
LOC	Lat/long/altitude and precision for a given host	29	Uncommon	RFC 1876 [237]
LP	Subnetwork name for use to identify L32 and L64 records for lookup in identifier/locator network protocol (ILNP)	107	Experimental	RFC 6742 [251]
MB	Mailbox name for a given email ID	7	Experimental	RFC 1035 [28]
MD	Mail delivery host for a given domain	3	Obsolete	RFC 1035 [28]
MF	Host that will accept mail for forwarding to a given domain	4	Obsolete	RFC 1035 [28]
MG	Mail group mailbox name for a given email ID	8	Experimental	RFC 1035 [28]
MINFO	Mailbox names for sending account requests or error reports for a given mailbox name	14	Experimental	RFC 1035 [28]
MR	Alias for a mailbox name	9	Experimental	RFC 1035 [28]
MX	Mail Exchanger for email host resolution	15	Standard	RFC 1035 [28]
NAPTR	Uniform resource identifier for a generic string – used for DDDS, ENUM applications	35	Standards Track	RFC 3761 [229]
NID	Node identifier for use in identifier/locator network protocol (ILNP)	104	Experimental	RFC 6742 [251]
NS	Name server for a given domain name	2	Standard	RFC 1035 [28]
NSAP	Network services access point address for a host	22	Uncommon	RFC 1706 [252]

RRType (or QType)	RR purpose (i.e. Rdata contents)	RR type ID	IETF status	Defining document
NSAP-PTR	Hostname for a given NSAP address	23	Uncommon	RFC 1706 [252]
NSEC	Authenticated confirmation or denial of existence of a resource record set for DNSSEC	47	Standards Track (DNSSEC)	RFC 4034 [232]
NSEC3	Authenticated denial of existence of a resource record set for DNSSEC (without trivial zone enumeration obtainable with NSEC)	50	Standards Track (DNSSEC)	RFC 5155 [253]
NSEC3 PARAM	NSEC3 parameters used to calculate hashed owner names	51	Standards Track (DNSSEC)	RFC 5155 [253]
NULL	Up to 65535 bytes of anything for a given host	10	Experimental	RFC 1035 [28]
NXT	Superseded by NSEC	30	Obsolete (DNSSEC)	RFC 3755 [254]
OPENPGP	OpenPGP key publication in DNS in accordance with DANE	61	Experimental	RFC 7929 [255]
PTR	Hostname for a given IPv4 or IPv6 address	12	Standard	RFC 1035 [28]
PX	X.400 mapping for a given domain name	26	Uncommon	RFC 2163 [238]
RP	Email address and TXT record pointer for more info for a host	17	Experimental	RFC 1183 [226]
RRSIG	Signature for a resource record set of a given domain name, class and RR Type	46	Standards Track (DNSSEC)	RFC 4034 [232]
RT	Proxy hostname for a given host that is not always connected	21	Experimental	RFC 1183 [226]
SIG	Superseded by RRSIG within DNSSEC; used by SIG(0) and TKEY	24	Proposed Standard	RFC 2536 [249]

(Continued)

Table 19.7   (Continued)

RRType (or QType)	RR purpose (i.e. Rdata contents)	RR type ID	IETF status	Defining document
SMIMEA	Certificate or public key information to help secure email (S/MIME) connection establishment	53	Experimental	RFC 8162 [256]
SOA	Authority information for a zone	6	Standard	RFC 1035 [28]
SPF	Sender policy framework – enables a domain owner to identify hosts authorized to send emails from the domain	99	Experimental	RFC 7208 [118]
SRV	Host providing specified services in a domain	33	Standards Track	RFC 2782 [259]
SSHFP	Secure Shell Fingerprints – enables verification of SSH host keys using DNSSEC	44	Standards Track	RFC 4255 [260]
TLSA	Certificate or public key information to help secure TLS connection establishment (DANE)	52	Standards Track	RFC 6698 [109]
TXT	Arbitrary text associated with a host	16	Standard	RFC 1035 [28]
UID	User ID	101	RESERVED	IANA-Reserved
UINFO	User Info	100	RESERVED	IANA-Reserved
UNSPEC	Unspecified	103	RESERVED	IANA-Reserved
URI	Provides the equivalent of more targeted NAPTR queries	256	Informational	RFC 7553 [261]
WKS	Services available via a given protocol at a specified IP address for a host – SRV RR more commonly used today	11	Standard	RFC 1035 [28]
X25	X.25 Packet Switched Data Network (PSDN)	19	Experimental	RFC 1183 [226]

20

RFC Reference

This chapter lists the major IPAM-relevant Request for Comments (RFCs) documents as published by the Internet Engineering Task Force (IETF). RFC documents may be retrieved from www.ietf.org/rfc. Obsoleted RFCs are not listed. RFCs 3789–3796 are surveys of deployed IPv4 addresses and are not listed in the tables below but provide interesting insight to the mention and definition of IPv4 addresses for specific applications.

The Status column indicates the RFC status as Informational, Experimental, Standards Track, Draft Standard, Proposed Standard, Standard, and Historic. RFCs that have been adopted as Best Current Practices (BCP) are enumerated by BCP number.

IPv4 Protocol RFCs		
RFC	**Status**	**Title**
791	Standard	Internet Protocol
1042	Standard	Standard for transmission of IP datagrams over IEEE 802 networks
1546	Informational	Host Anycasting Service
1878	Historic	Variable Length Subnet Table for IPv4
2101	Informational	IPv4 Address Behavior Today
2365	BCP 23	Administratively Scoped IP Multicast
3927	Proposed Standard	Dynamic Configuration of IPv4 Link-Local Addresses
4116	Informational	IPv4 Multihoming Practices and Limitations
4632	BCP 122	Classless Inter-domain Routing (CIDR): The Internet Address Assignment and Aggregation Plan
7335	Proposed Standard	IPv4 Service Continuity Prefix

IP Address Management, Second Edition. Michael Dooley and Timothy Rooney.
© 2021 The Institute of Electrical and Electronics Engineers, Inc.
Published 2021 by John Wiley & Sons, Inc.

IPv6 Protocol RFCs

RFC	Status	Title
1752	Proposed Standard	The Recommendation for the IP Next Generation Protocol
1881	Informational	IPv6 Address Allocation Management
1887	Informational	An Architecture for IPv6 Unicast Address Allocation
2375	Informational	IPv6 Multicast Address Assignments
2526	Proposed Standard	Reserved IPv6 Subnet Anycast Addresses
2894	Proposed Standard	Router Renumbering for IPv6
3582	Informational	Goals for IPv6 Site-Multihoming Architectures
3587	Informational	IPv6 Global Unicast Address Format
3627	Informational	Use of /127 Prefix Length Between Routers Considered Harmful
3701	Informational	6bone (IPv6 Testing Address Allocation) Phaseout
3879	Proposed Standard	Deprecating Site Local Addresses
3956	Proposed Standard	Embedding the Rendezvous Point (RP) Address in an IPv6 Multicast Address
4007	Proposed Standard	IPv6 Scoped Address Architecture
4076	Informational	Renumbering Requirements for Stateless Dynamic Host Configuration Protocol for IPv6 (DHCPv6)
4177	Informational	Architectural Approaches to Multi-homing for IPv6
4193	Proposed Standard	Unique Local IPv6 Unicast Addresses
4218	Informational	Threats Relating to IPv6 Multihoming Solutions
4291	Draft Standard	IP Version 6 Addressing Architecture
4294	Informational	IPv6 Node Requirements
4339	Informational	IPv6 Host Configuration of DNS Server Information Approaches
4489	Proposed Standard	A Method for Generating Link-Scoped IPv6 Multicast Addresses
4843	Experimental	An IPv6 Prefix for Overlay Routable Cryptographic Hash Identifiers (ORCHID)
4861	Draft Standard	Neighbor Discovery for IP version 6 (IPv6)
4862	Draft Standard	IPv6 Stateless Address Autoconfiguration
4941	Draft Standard	Privacy Extensions for Stateless Address Autoconfiguration in IPv6

IPv6 Protocol RFCs

RFC	Status	Title
4968	Informational	Analysis of IPv6 Link Models for 802.16 Based Networks
5006	Experimental	IPv6 Router Advertisement Option for DNS Configuration
5156	Informational	Special-Use IPv6 Addresses
5157	Informational	IPv6 Implications for Network Scanning
5375	Informational	IPv6 Unicast Address Assignment Considerations
5453	Standards Track	Reserved IPv6 Interface Identifiers
5902	Informational	IAB Thoughts on IPv6 Network Address Translation
5952	Proposed Standard	A Recommendation for IPv6 Address Text Representation
5963	Informational	IPv6 Deployment in Internet Exchange Points (IXPs)
6059	Proposed Standard	Simple Procedures for Detecting Network Attachment in IPv6
6164	Proposed Standard	Using 127-Bit IPv6 Prefixes on Inter-Router Links
6296	Experimental	IPv6-to-IPv6 Network Prefix Translation
6540	BCP 177	IPv6 Support Required for All IP-Capable Nodes
6543	Proposed Standard	Reserved IPv6 Interface Identifier for Proxy Mobile IPV6
6666	Informational	A Discard Prefix for IPv6
6724	Proposed Standard	Default Address Selection for Internet Protocol Version 6 (IPv6)
6782	Informational	Wireline Incremental IPv6
6791	Proposed Standard	Stateless Source Address Mapping for ICMPv6 Packets
6866	Informational	Problem Statement for Renumbering IPv6 Hosts with Static Addresses in Enterprise Networks
6879	Informational	IPv6 Enterprise Network Renumbering Scenarios, Considerations, and Methods
6883	Informational	IPv6 Guidance for Internet Content Providers and Application Service Providers
7010	Informational	IPv6 Site Renumbering Gap Analysis
7040	Informational	Public IPv4-over-IPv6 Access Network

IPv6 Protocol RFCs		
RFC	**Status**	**Title**
7050	Proposed Standard	Discovery of the IPv6 Prefix Used for IPv6 Address Synthesis
7051	Informational	Analysis of Solution Proposals for Hosts to Learn NAT64 Prefix
7066	Informational	IPv6 for Third Generation Partnership Project (3GPP) Cellular Hosts
7084	Informational	Basic Requirements for IPv6 Customer Edge Routers
7123	Informational	Security Implications of IPv6 on IPv4 Networks
7136	Proposed Standard	Significance of IPv6 Interface Identifiers
7217	Proposed Standard	A Method for Generating Semantically Opaque Interface Identifiers with IPv6 Stateless Address Autoconfiguration (SLAAC)
7343	Proposed Standard	An IPv6 Prefix for Overlay Routable Cryptographic Hash Identifiers Version 2 (ORCHIDv2)
7346	Proposed Standard	IPv6 Multicast Address Scopes
7368	Informational	IPv6 Home Networking Architecture Principles
7371	Proposed Standard	Updates to the IPv6 Multicast Addressing Architecture
7381	Informational	Enterprise IPv6 Deployment Guidelines
7404	Informational	Using Only Link-local Addressing inside an IPv6 Network
7421	Informational	Analysis of the 64-bit Boundary in IPv6 Addressing
7439	Informational	Gap Analysis for Operating IPv6-Only MPLS Networks
7527	Proposed Standard	Enhanced Duplicate Address Detection
7599	Proposed Standard	Mapping of Address and Port using Translation (MAP-T)
7608	BCP 198	IPv6 Prefix Length Recommendation for Forwarding
7707	Informational	Network Reconnaissance in IPv6 Networks
7721	Informational	Security and Privacy Considerations for IPv6 Address Generation Mechanisms
8064	Proposed Standard	Recommendation on Stable IPv6 Interface Identifiers

IPv6 Protocol RFCs

RFC	Status	Title
8065	Informational	Privacy Considerations for IPv6 Adaptation-Layer Mechanisms
8191	Proposed Standard	Home Network Prefix Renumbering in Proxy Mobile IPv6 (PMIPv6)
8200	STD 86	Internet Protocol, Version 6 (IPv6) Specification
8273	Informational	Unique IPv6 Prefix per Host
8425	Proposed Standard	IANA Considerations for IPv6 Neighbor Discovery Prefix Information Option Flags
8501	Informational	Reverse DNS in IPv6 for Internet Service Providers
8504	BCP 220	IPv6 Node Requirements
8585	Informational	Requirements for IPv6 Customer Edge Routers to Support IPv4-as-a-Service

IPv4/IPv6 Co-Existence RFCs

RFC	Status	Title
2185	Informational	Routing Aspects of IPv6 Transition
2529	Proposed Standard	Transmission of IPv6 over IPv4 Domains without Explicit Tunnels
2765	Proposed Standard	Stateless IP/ICMP Translation Algorithm (SIIT)
2767	Informational	Dual Stack Hosts using the "Bump-in-the-Stack" Technique(BIS)
3053	Informational	IPv6 Tunnel Broker
3056	Proposed Standard	Connection of IPv6 Domains via IPv4 Clouds [6to4]
3068	Proposed Standard	An Anycast Prefix for 6to4 Relay Routers
3089	Informational	A SOCKS-based IPv6/IPv4 Gateway Mechanism
3142	Informational	An IPv6-to-IPv4 Transport Relay Translator
3338	Experimental	Dual Stack Hosts Using "Bump-in-the-API" (BIA)
3574	Informational	Transition Scenarios for 3GPP Networks
3750	Informational	Unmanaged Networks IPv6 Transition Scenarios
3904	Informational	Evaluation of IPv6 Transition Mechanisms for Unmanaged Networks

IPv4/IPv6 Co-Existence RFCs

RFC	Status	Title
3964	Informational	Security Considerations for 6to4
3974	Informational	SMTP Operational Experience in Mixed IPv4/IPv6 Environments
4029	Informational	Scenarios and Analysis for Introducing IPv6 into ISP Networks
4038	Informational	Application Aspects of IPv6 Transition
4057	Informational	IPv6 Enterprise Network Scenarios
4213	Proposed Standard	Basic Transition Mechanisms for IPv6 Hosts and Routers
4215	Informational	Analysis of IPv6 Transition in Third Generation Partnership Project (3GPP) Networks
4241	Informational	A Model of IPv6/IPv4 Dual Stack Internet Access Service
4361	Proposed Standard	Node-specific Client Identifiers for Dynamic Host Configuration Protocol Version Four (DHCPv4)
4380	Proposed Standard	Teredo: Tunneling IPv6 over UDP through Network Address Translations (NATs)
4477	Informational	Dynamic Host Configuration Protocol (DHCP): IPv4 and IPv6 Dual-Stack Issues
4554	Informational	Use of VLANs for IPv4-IPv6 Coexistence in Enterprise Networks
4798	Proposed Standard	Connecting IPv6 Islands over IPv4 MPLS Using IPv6 Provider Edge Routers (6PE)
4852	Informational	IPv6 Enterprise Network Analysis – IP Layer 3 Focus
4942	Informational	IPv6 Transition/Co-existence Security Considerations
4966	Informational	Reasons to Move the Network Address Translator – Protocol Translator (NAT-PT) to Historic Status
4977	Informational	Problem Statement: Dual Stack Mobility
5181	Informational	IPv6 Deployment Scenarios in 802.16 Networks
5211	Informational	An Internet Transition Plan
5214	Informational	Intra-Site Automatic Tunnel Addressing Protocol (ISATAP)
5969	Proposed Standard	IPv6 Rapid Deployment on IPv4 Infrastructures (6rd)

IPv4/IPv6 Co-Existence RFCs

RFC	Status	Title
5991	Proposed Standard	Teredo Security Updates
6036	Informational	Emerging Service Provider Scenarios for IPv6 Deployment
6052	Proposed Standard	IPv6 Addressing of IPv4/IPv6 Translators
6081	Proposed Standard	Teredo Extensions
6127	Informational	IPv4 Run-Out and IPv4-IPv6 Co-Existence Scenarios
6144	Informational	Framework for IPv4/IPv6 Translation
6146	Proposed Standard	Stateful NAT64: Network Address and Protocol Translation from IPv6 Clients to IPv4 Servers
6147	Proposed Standard	DNS64: DNS Extensions for Network Address Translation from IPv6 Clients to IPv4 Servers
6180	Informational	Guidelines for Using IPv6 Transition Mechanisms during IPv6 Deployment
6333	Proposed Standard	Dual-Stack Lite Broadband Deployments Following IPv4 Exhaustion
6343	Informational	Advisory Guidelines for 6to4 Deployment
6346	Experimental	The Address plus Port (A+P) Approach to the IPv4 Address Shortage
6384	Proposed Standard	An FTP Application Layer Gateway (ALG) for IPv6-to-IPv4 Translation
6535	Proposed Standard	Dual-Stack Hosts Using "Bump-in-the-Host" (BIH)
6589	Informational	Considerations for Transitioning Content to IPv6
6654	Informational	Gateway-Initiated IPv6 Rapid Deployment on IPv4 Infrastructures (GI 6rd)
6674	Proposed Standard	Gateway-Initiated Dual-Stack Lite Deployment
6732	Historic	6to4 Provider Managed Tunnels
6751	Experimental	Native IPv6 behind IPv4-to-IPv4 NAT Customer Premises Equipment (6a44)
6877	Informational	464XLAT: Combination of Stateful and Stateless Translation
6908	Informational	Deployment Considerations for Dual-Stack Lite
6964	Informational	Operational Guidance for IPv6 Deployment in IPv4 Sites Using the Intra-Site Automatic Tunnel Addressing Protocol (ISATAP)

IPv4/IPv6 Co-Existence RFCs

RFC	Status	Title
7059	Informational	A Comparison of IPv6-over-IPv4 Tunnel Mechanisms
7269	Informational	NAT64 Deployment Options and Experience
7526	BCP 196	Deprecating the Anycast Prefix for 6to4 Relay Routers
7596	Proposed Standard	Lightweight 4over6: An Extension to the Dual-Stack Lite Architecture
7600	Experimental	IPv4 Residual Deployment via IPv6 – A Stateless Solution (4rd)
7755	Informational	SIIT-DC: Stateless IP/ICMP Translation for IPv6 Data Center Environments
7756	Proposed Standard	Stateless IP/ICMP Translation for IPv6 Internet Data Center Environments (SIIT-DC): Dual Translation Mode
7757	Proposed Standard	Explicit Address Mappings for Stateless IP/ICMP Translation
7785	Informational	Recommendations for Prefix Binding in the Context of Softwire Dual-Stack Lite
7915	Proposed Standard	IP/ICMP Translation Algorithm
8215	Proposed Standard	Local-Use IPv4/IPv6 Translation Prefix
8219	Informational	Benchmarking Methodology for IPv6 Transition Technologies
8305	Proposed Standard	Happy Eyeballs Version 2: Better Connectivity Using Concurrency
8421	BCP 217	Guidelines for Multihomed and IPv4/IPv6 Dual-Stack Interactive Connectivity Establishment (ICE)

IP Address Management RFCs

RFC	Status	Title
1219	Informational	On the assignment of subnet numbers
1518	Historic	An Architecture for IP Address Allocation with CIDR
1900	Informational	Renumbering Needs Work
1715	Informational	The H Ratio for Address Assignment Efficiency

IP Address Management RFCs

RFC	Status	Title
1918	BCP 5	Address Allocation for Private Internets
2008	BCP 7	Implications of Various Address Allocation Policies for Internet Routing
2050	BCP 12	Internet Registry IP Allocation Guidelines
2071	Informational	Network Renumbering Overview: Why would I want it and what is it anyway?
2908	Informational	The Internet Multicast Address Allocation Architecture
3171	BCP 51	IANA Guidelines for IPv4 Multicast Address Assignments
3194	Informational	The H-Density Ratio for Address Assignment Efficiency – An Update on the H ratio
3330	Informational	Special-Use IPv4 Addresses
3531	Informational	A Flexible Method for Managing the Assignment of Bits of an IPv6 Address Block
3819	BCP 89	Advice for Internet Subnetwork Designers
3849	Informational	IPv6 Address Prefix Reserved for Documentation
4147	Informational	Proposed Changes to the Format of the IANA IPv6 Registry
4192	Informational	Procedures for Renumbering an IPv6 Network without a Flag Day
4779	Informational	ISP IPv6 Deployment Scenarios in Broadband Access Networks
4786	BCP 126	Operation of Anycast Services
5505	Informational	Principles of Internet Host Configuration
5942	Proposed Standard	IPv6 Subnet Model: The Relationship between Links and Subnet Prefixes
6177	BCP 157	IPv6 Address Assignment to End Sites
6306	Experimental	Hierarchical IPv4 Framework
6319	Informational	Issues Associated with Designating Additional Private IPv4 Address Space
6342	Informational	Mobile Networks Considerations for IPv6 Deployment
6459	Informational	IPv6 in 3rd Generation Partnership Project (3GPP) Evolved Packet System (EPS)
6598	BCP 153	IANA-Reserved IPv4 Prefix for Shared Address Space

IP Address Management RFCs

RFC	Status	Title
6629	Informational	Considerations on the Application of the Level 3 Multihoming Shim Protocol for IPv6 (Shim6)
6752	Informational	Issues with Private IP Addressing in the Internet
6889	Informational	Analysis of Stateful 64 Translation
6890	BCP 153	Special-Purpose IP Address Registries
7020	Informational	The Internet Numbers Registry System
7157	Informational	IPv6 Multihoming without Network Address Translation
7249	Informational	Internet Numbers Registries
7695	Proposed Standard	Distributed Prefix Assignment Algorithm
7723	Proposed Standard	Port Control Protocol (PCP) Anycast Addresses
7793	BCP 163	Adding 100.64.0.0/10 Prefixes to the IPv4 Locally Served DNS Zones Registry
8190	BCP 153	Updates to the Special-Purpose IP Address Registries

DHCP Protocol RFCs

RFC	Status	Title
1534	Draft Standard	Interoperation Between DHCP and BOOTP
2131	Draft Standard	Dynamic Host Configuration Protocol
2132	Draft Standard	DHCP Options and BOOTP Vendor Extensions
2241	Proposed Standard	DHCP Options for Novell Directory Services
2242	Proposed Standard	NetWare/IP Domain Name and Information
2485	Proposed Standard	DHCP Option for The Open Group's User Authentication Protocol
2563	Proposed Standard	DHCP Option to Disable Stateless Auto-Configuration in IPv4 Clients
2610	Proposed Standard	DHCP Options for Service Location Protocol
2855	Proposed Standard	DHCP for IEEE 1394
2937	Proposed Standard	The Name Service Search Option for DHCP
3004	Proposed Standard	The User Class Option for DHCP
3011	Proposed Standard	The IPv4 Subnet Selection Option for DHCP

DHCP Protocol RFCs

RFC	Status	Title
3046	Proposed Standard	DHCP Relay Agent Information Option
3074	Proposed Standard	DHC Load Balancing Algorithm
3118	Proposed Standard	Authentication for DHCP Messages
3203	Proposed Standard	DHCP reconfigure extension
3256	Proposed Standard	The DOCSIS Device Class DHCP Relay Agent Information Sub-option
3361	Proposed Standard	Dynamic Host Configuration Protocol (DHCP-for-IPv4) Option for Session Initiation Protocol (SIP) Servers
3396	Proposed Standard	Encoding Long Options in the Dynamic Host Configuration Protocol (DHCPv4)
3397	Proposed Standard	Dynamic Host Configuration Protocol (DHCP) Domain Search Option
3442	Proposed Standard	The Classless Static Route Option for Dynamic Host Configuration Protocol (DHCP) version 4
3456	Proposed Standard	Dynamic Host Configuration Protocol (DHCPv4) Configuration of IPsec Tunnel Mode
3495	Proposed Standard	Dynamic Host Configuration Protocol (DHCP) Option for CableLabs Client Configuration
3527	Proposed Standard	Link Selection sub-option for the Relay Agent Information Option for DHCPv4
3634	Proposed Standard	Key Distribution Center (KDC) Server Address Sub-option for the Dynamic Host Configuration Protocol (DHCP) CableLabs Client Configuration (CCC) Option
3679	Informational	Unused Dynamic Host Configuration Protocol (DHCP) Option Codes
3925	Proposed Standard	Vendor-Identifying Vendor Options for Dynamic Host Configuration Protocol version 4 (DHCPv4)
3942	Proposed Standard	Reclassifying Dynamic Host Configuration Protocol version 4 (DHCPv4) Options
3993	Proposed Standard	Subscriber-ID Suboption for the Dynamic Host Configuration Protocol (DHCP) Relay Agent Option
4030	Proposed Standard	The Authentication Suboption for the Dynamic Host Configuration Protocol (DHCP Relay Agent Option)
4039	Proposed Standard	Rapid Commit Option for the Dynamic Host Configuration Protocol version 4 (DHCPv4)

	DHCP Protocol RFCs	
RFC	**Status**	**Title**
4174	Proposed Standard	The IPv4 Dynamic Host Configuration Protocol (DHCP) Option for the Internet Storage Name Service
4243	Proposed Standard	Vendor-Specific Information Suboption for the Dynamic Host Configuration Protocol (DHCP) Relay Agent Option
4280	Proposed Standard	Dynamic Host Configuration Protocol (DHCP) Options for Broadcast and Multicast Control Servers
4361	Proposed Standard	Node-specific Client Identifiers for Dynamic Host Configuration Protocol Version Four (DHCPv4)
4388	Proposed Standard	Dynamic Host Configuration Protocol (DHCP) Leasequery
4390	Proposed Standard	Dynamic Host Configuration Protocol (DHCP) over InfiniBand
4578	Informational	Dynamic Host Configuration Protocol (DHCP) Options for the Intel Preboot eXecution Environment (PXE)
4702	Proposed Standard	The Dynamic Host Configuration Protocol (DHCP) Client Fully Qualified Domain Name (FQDN) Option
4703	Proposed Standard	Resolution of Fully Qualified Domain Name (FQDN) Conflicts among Dynamic Host Configuration Protocol (DHCP) Clients
4776	Proposed Standard	Dynamic Host Configuration Protocol (DHCPv4 and DHCPv6) Option for Civic Addresses Configuration Information
4833	Proposed Standard	Timezone Options for DHCP
5010	Proposed Standard	The Dynamic Host Configuration Protocol Version 4 (DHCPv4) Relay Agent Flags Suboption
5071	Informational	Dynamic Host Configuration Protocol Options Used by PXELINUX
5107	Proposed Standard	DHCP Server Identifier Override Suboption
5192	Proposed Standard	DHCP Options for Protocol for Carrying Authentication for Network Access (PANAP) Authentication Agents
5223	Proposed Standard	Discovering Location-to-Service Translation (LoST) Servers Using the Dynamic Host Configuration Protocol (DHCP)

DHCP Protocol RFCs

RFC	Status	Title
5417	Proposed Standard	Control and Provisioning of Wireless Access Points (CAPWAP) Access Controller DHCP Option
6148	Proposed Standard	DHCPv4 Lease Query by Relay Agent Remote ID
6153	Proposed Standard	DHCPv4 and DHCPv6 Options for Access Network Discovery and Selection Function (ANDSF) Discovery
6225	Proposed Standard	Dynamic Host Configuration Protocol Options for Coordinate-Based Location Configuration Information
6607	Proposed Standard	Virtual Subnet Selection Options for DHCPv4 and DHCPv6
6656	Informational	Description of Cisco Systems' Subnet Allocation Option for DHCPv4
6704	Proposed Standard	Forcerenew Nonce Authentication
6731	Proposed Standard	Improved Recursive DNS Server Selection for Multi-Interfaced Nodes
6842	Proposed Standard	Client Identifier Option in DHCP Server Replies
6925	Proposed Standard	The DHCPv4 Relay Agent Identifier Sub-Option
6926	Proposed Standard	DHCPv4 Bulk Leasequery
7291	Proposed Standard	DHCP Options for the Port Control Protocol (PCP)
7710	Proposed Standard	Captive-Portal Identification Using DHCP or Router Advertisements (RAs)
7724	Proposed Standard	Active DHCPv4 Lease Query
7819	Informational	Privacy Considerations for DHCP
7839	Proposed Standard	Access-Network-Identifier Option in DHCP
7844	Proposed Standard	Anonymity Profiles for DHCP Clients
7969	Informational	Customizing DHCP Configuration on the Basis of Network Topology
8357	Proposed Standard	Generalized UDP Source Port for DHCP Relay
7341	Proposed Standard	DHCPv4-over-DHCPv6 (DHCP 4o6) Transport
7618	Proposed Standard	Dynamic Allocation of Shared IPv4 Addresses

DHCPv6 Protocol RFCs

RFC	Status	Title
3319	Proposed Standard	Dynamic Host Configuration Protocol (DHCPv6) Options for Session Initiation Protocol (SIP) Servers
3646	Proposed Standard	DNS Configuration options for Dynamic Host Configuration Protocol for IPv6 (DHCPv6)
3769	Informational	Requirements for IPv6 Prefix Delegation
3898	Proposed Standard	Network Information Service (NIS) Configuration Options for Dynamic Host Configuration Protocol for IPv6 (DHCPv6)
4075	Proposed Standard	Simple Network Time Protocol (SNTP) Configuration Option for DHCPv6
4580	Proposed Standard	Dynamic Host Configuration Protocol for IPv6 (DHCPv6) Relay Agent Subscriber-ID Option
4649	Proposed Standard	Dynamic Host Configuration Protocol for IPv6 (DHCPv6) Relay Agent Remote-ID Option
4703	Proposed Standard	Resolution of Fully Qualified Domain Name (FQDN) Conflicts among Dynamic Host Configuration Protocol (DHCP) Clients
4704	Proposed Standard	The Dynamic Host Configuration Protocol for IPv6 (DHCPv6) Client Fully Qualified Domain Name (FQDN) Option
4776	Proposed Standard	Dynamic Host Configuration Protocol (DHCPv4 and DHCPv6) Option for Civic Addresses Configuration Information
4833	Proposed Standard	Timezone Options for DHCP
4994	Proposed Standard	DHCPv6 Relay Agent Echo Request Option
5007	Proposed Standard	DHCPv6 Leasequery
5192	Proposed Standard	DHCP Options for Protocol for Carrying Authentication for Network Access (PANA) Authentication Agents
5223	Proposed Standard	Discovering Location-to-Service Translation (LoST) Servers Using the Dynamic Host Configuration Protocol (DHCP)
5460	Proposed Standard	DHCPv6 Bulk Leasequery
5970	Proposed Standard	DHCPv6 Options for Network Boot
6153	Proposed Standard	DHCPv4 and DHCPv6 Options for Access Network Discovery and Selection Function (ANDSF) Discovery
6221	Proposed Standard	Lightweight DHCPv6 Relay Agent

DHCPv6 Protocol RFCs

RFC	Status	Title
6276	Proposed Standard	DHCPv6 Prefix Delegation for Network Mobility (NEMO)
6334	Proposed Standard	Dynamic Host Configuration Protocol for IPv6 (DHCPv6) Option for Dual-Stack Lite
6355	Proposed Standard	Definition of the UUID-Based DHCPv6 Unique Identifier (DUID-UUID)
6603	Proposed Standard	Prefix Exclude Option for DHCPv6-based Prefix Delegation
6607	Proposed Standard	Virtual Subnet Selection Options for DHCPv4 and DHCPv6
6610	Proposed Standard	DHCP Options for Home Information Discovery in Mobile IPv6 (MIPv6)
6644	Proposed Standard	Rebind Capability in DHCPv6 Reconfigure Messages
6653	Informational	DHCPv6 Prefix Delegation in Long-Term Evolution (LTE) Networks
6731	Proposed Standard	Improved Recursive DNS Server Selection for Multi-Interfaced Nodes
6784	Proposed Standard	Kerberos Options for DHCPv6
6853	BCP 180	DHCPv6 Redundancy Deployment Considerations
6939	Proposed Standard	Client Link-Layer Address Option in DHCPv6
6977	Proposed Standard	Triggering DHCPv6 Reconfiguration from Relay Agents
7031	Informational	DHCPv6 Failover Requirements
7037	Proposed Standard	RADIUS Option for the DHCPv6 Relay Agent
7078	Proposed Standard	Distributing Address Selection Policy Using DHCPv6
7148	Proposed Standard	Prefix Delegation Support for Proxy Mobile IPv6
7227	BCP 187	Guidelines for Creating New DHCPv6 Options
7291	Proposed Standard	DHCP Options for the Port Control Protocol (PCP)
7341	Proposed Standard	DHCPv4-over-DHCPv6 (DHCP 4o6) Transport
7598	Proposed Standard	DHCPv6 Options for Configuration of Softwire Address and Port-Mapped Clients
7610	BCP 199	DHCPv6-Shield: Protecting against Rogue DHCPv6 Servers
7653	Proposed Standard	DHCPv6 Active Leasequery

DHCPv6 Protocol RFCs

RFC	Status	Title
7710	Proposed Standard	Captive-Portal Identification Using DHCP or Router Advertisements (RAs)
7824	Informational	Privacy Considerations for DHCPv6
8026	Proposed Standard	Unified IPv4-in-IPv6 Softwire Customer Premises Equipment (CPE): A DHCPv6-Based Prioritization Mechanism
8115	Proposed Standard	DHCPv6 Option for IPv4-Embedded Multicast and Unicast IPv6 Prefixes
8156	Proposed Standard	DHCPv6 Failover Protocol
8168	Proposed Standard	DHCPv6 Prefix-Length Hint Issues
8213	Proposed Standard	Security of Messages Exchanged between Servers and Relay Agents
8415	Proposed Standard	Dynamic Host Configuration Protocol for IPv6 (DHCPv6)
8539	Proposed Standard	Softwire Provisioning Using DHCPv4 over DHCPv6

DNS Protocol RFCs

RFC	Status	Title
1034	Standard	Domain names – concepts and facilities
1035	Standard	Domain names – implementation and specification
1101	Unknown	DNS encoding of network names and other types
1183	Experimental	New DNS RR Definitions
1464	Experimental	Using the Domain Name System to Store Arbitrary Sting Attributes
1480	Informational	The US Domain
1591	Informational	Domain Name System Structure and Delegation
1706	Informational	DNS NSAP Resource Records
1712	Informational	DNS Encoding of Geographical Location
1876	Experimental	A Means for Expressing Location Information in the Domain Name System
1982	Proposed Standard	Serial Number Arithmetic
1996	Proposed Standard	A Mechanism for Prompt Notification of Zone Changes (DNS NOTIFY)

	DNS Protocol RFCs	
RFC	**Status**	**Title**
2136	Proposed Standard	Dynamic Updates in the Domain Name System (DNS UPDATE)
2163	Proposed Standard	Using the Internet DNS to Distribute MIXER Conformant Global Address Mapping (MCGAM)
2181	Proposed Standard	Clarifications to the DNS Specification
2182	BCP 16	Selection and Operation of Secondary DNS Servers
2219	BCP 19	Use of DNS Aliases for Network Services
2308	Proposed Standard	Negative Caching of DNS Queries (DNS NCACHE)
2317	BCP 20	Classless IN-ADDR.ARPA delegation
2536	Proposed Standard	DSA KEYs and SIGs in the Domain Name System (DNS)
2539	Proposed Standard	Storage of Diffie-Hellman Keys in the Domain Name System (DNS)
2540	Experimental	Detached Domain Name System (DNS) Information
2671	Proposed Standard	Extension Mechanisms for DNS (EDNS0)
2673	Experimental	Binary Labels in the Domain Name System
2782	Proposed Standard	A DNS RR for specifying the location of services (DNS SRV)
2870	BCP 40	Root Name Server Operational Requirements
2874	Experimental	DNS Extensions to Support IPv6 Address Aggregation and Renumbering
3123	Experimental	A DNS RR Type for Lists of Address Prefixes (APL RR)
3258	Informational	Distributing Authoritative Name Servers via Shared Unicast Addresses
3363	Informational	Representing Internet Protocol version 6 (IPv6) Addresses in the Domain Name System (DNS)
3364	Informational	Trade-offs in Domain Name System (DNS) Support for Internet Protocol version 6 (IPv6)
3425	Proposed Standard	Obsoleting IQUERY
3467	Informational	Role of the Domain Name System (DNS)
3490	Proposed Standard	Internationalizing Domain Names in Applications (IDNA)
3491	Proposed Standard	Nameprep: A Stringprep Profile for Internationalized Domain Names (IDN)

DNS Protocol RFCs		
RFC	**Status**	**Title**
3492	Proposed Standard	Punycode: A Bootstring encoding of Unicode for Internationalized Domain Names in Applications (IDNA)
3596	Draft Standard	DNS Extensions to Support IP Version 6
3597	Proposed Standard	Handling of Unknown DNS Resource Record (RR) Types
3681	BCP 80	Delegation of E.F.F.3.IP6.ARPA.
3901	BCP 91	DNS IPv6 Transport Operational Guidelines
4074	Informational	Common Misbehavior Against DNS Queries for IPv6 Addresses
4159	BCP 109	Deprecation of "ip6.int"
4183	Informational	A Suggested Scheme for DNS Resolution of Networks and Gateways
4185	Informational	National and Local Characters for DNS Top Level Domain (TLD) Names
4290	Informational	Suggested Practices for Registration of Internationalized Domain Names (IDN)
4343	Proposed Standard	Domain Name System (DNS) Case Insensitivity Clarification
4367	Informational	What's in a Name: False Assumptions about DNS Names
4406	Experimental	Sender ID: Authenticating E-Mail
4407	Experimental	Purported Responsible Address in E-Mail Messages
4408	Experimental	Sender Policy Framework (SPF) for Authorizing Use of Domains in E-Mail, Version 1
4472	Informational	Operational Considerations and Issues with IPv6 DNS
4592	Proposed Standard	The Role of Wildcards in the Domain Name System
4690	Informational	Review and Recommendations for Internationalized Domain Names (IDNs)
4697	BCP 123	Observed DNS Resolution Misbehavior
4701	Proposed Standard	A DNS Resource Record (RR) for Encoding Dynamic Host Configuration Protocol (DHCP) Information (DHCID RR)
4892	Informational	Requirements for a Mechanism Identifying a Name Server Instance
5001	Proposed Standard	DNS Name Server Identifier (NSID) Option

DNS Protocol RFCs		
RFC	**Status**	**Title**
5158	Informational	6to4 Reverse DNS Delegation Specification
5205	Experimental	Host Identity Protocol (HIP) Domain Name System (DNS) Extensions [HIP RR]
5395	BCP 42	Domain Name System (DNS) IANA Considerations
5507	Informational	Design Choices When Expanding the DNS
5936	Proposed Standard	DNS Zone Transfer Protocol (AXFR)
5992	Informational	Internationalized Domain Names Registration and Administration Guidelines for European Languages Using Cyrillic
6055	Informational	IAB Thoughts on Encodings for Internationalized Domain Names
6672	Proposed Standard	DNAME Redirection in the DNS
6731	Proposed Standard	Improved Recursive DNS Server Selection for Multi-Interfaced Nodes
6742	Experimental	DNS Resource Records for the Identifier-Locator Network Protocol (ILNP)
6761	Proposed Standard	Special-Use Domain Names
6762	Proposed Standard	Multicast DNS
6763	Proposed Standard	DNS-Based Service Discovery
6804	Historic	DISCOVER: Supporting Multicast DNS Queries
6891	STD 75	Extension Mechanisms for DNS (EDNS(0))
6895	BCP 42	Domain Name System (DNS) IANA Considerations
6927	Informational	Variants in Second-Level Names Registered in Top-Level Domains
6950	Informational	Architectural Considerations on Application Features in the DNS
7043	Informational	Resource Records for EUI-48 and EUI-64 Addresses in the DNS
7050	Proposed Standard	Discovery of the IPv6 Prefix Used for IPv6 Address Synthesis
7051	Informational	Analysis of Solution Proposals for Hosts to Learn NAT64 Prefix
7085	Informational	Top-Level Domains That Are Already Dotless
7216	Proposed Standard	Location Information Server (LIS) Discovery Using IP Addresses and Reverse DNS
7304	Informational	A Method for Mitigating Namespace Collisions

DNS Protocol RFCs

RFC	Status	Title
7314	Experimental	Extension Mechanisms for DNS (EDNS) EXPIRE Option
7477	Proposed Standard	Child-to-Parent Synchronization in DNS
7534	Informational	AS112 Nameserver Operations
7535	Informational	AS112 Redirection using DNAME
7553	Informational	The Uniform Resource Identifier (URI) DNS Resource Record
7558	Informational	Requirements for Scalable DNS-Based Service Discovery (DNS-SD)/Multicast DNS (mDNS)
7686	Proposed Standard	The ".onion" Special-Use Domain Name
7720	BCP 40	DNS Root Name Service Protocol and Deployment Requirements
7745	Informational	XML Schemas for Reverse DNS Management
7766	Proposed Standard	DNS Transport over TCP – Implementation Requirements
7828	Proposed Standard	The edns-tcp-keepalive EDNS0 Option
7830	Proposed Standard	The EDNS(0) Padding Option
7871	Informational	Client Subnet in DNS Queries
8005	Proposed Standard	Host Identity Protocol (HIP) Domain Name System (DNS) Extension
8020	Proposed Standard	NXDOMAIN: There Really Is Nothing Underneath
8023	Informational	Report from the Workshop and Prize on Root Causes and Mitigation of Name Collisions
8106	Proposed Standard	IPv6 Router Advertisement Options for DNS Configuration
8109	BCP 209	Initializing a DNS Resolver with Priming Queries
8117	Informational	Current Hostname Practice Considered Harmful
8222	Informational	Selecting Labels for Use with Conventional DNS and Other Resolution Systems in DNS-Based Service Discovery
8244	Informational	Special-Use Domain Names Problem Statement
8375	Proposed Standard	Special-Use Domain "home.arpa."
8427	Informational	Representing DNS Messages in JSON
8467	Experimental	Padding Policies for Extension Mechanisms for DNS (EDNS(0))

DNS Protocol RFCs

RFC	Status	Title
8483	Informational	Yeti DNS Testbed
8490	Proposed Standard	DNS Stateful Operations
8499	BCP 219	DNS Terminology
8552	BCP 222	Scoped Interpretation of DNS Resource Records through "Underscored" Naming of Attribute Leaves
8553	BCP 222	DNS Attrleaf Changes: Fixing Specifications That Use Underscored Node Names
8305	Proposed Standard	Happy Eyeballs Version 2: Better Connectivity Using Concurrency
8501	Informational	Reverse DNS in IPv6 for Internet Service Providers

DNSSEC RFCs

RFC	Status	Title
4033	Proposed Standard	DNS Security Introduction and Requirements
4034	Proposed Standard	Resource Records for DNS Security Extensions
4035	Proposed Standard	Protocol Modifications for the DNS Security Extensions
4431	Informational	The DNSSEC Lookaside Validation (DLV) Resource Record
4470	Proposed Standard	Minimally Covering NSEC Records and DNSSEC On-line Signing
4471	Experimental	Derivation of DNS Name Predecessor and Successor
4509	Proposed Standard	Use of SHA-256 in DNSSEC Delegation Signer (DS) Resource Records (RRs)
4641	Informational	DNSSEC Operational Practices
4955	Proposed Standard	DNS Security (DNSSEC) Experiments
4956	Experimental	DNS Security (DNSSEC) Opt-In
4986	Informational	Requirements Related to DNS Security (DNSSEC) Trust Anchor Rollover
5011	Proposed Standard	Automated Updates of DNS Security (DNSSEC) Trust Anchors

DNSSEC RFCs

RFC	Status	Title
5074	Informational	DNSSEC Lookaside Validation (DLV)
5155	Proposed Standard	DNS Security (DNSSEC) Hashed Authenticated Denial of Existence [NSEC3, NSEC3PARAM]
5910	Proposed Standard	Domain Name System (DNS) Security Extensions Mapping for the Extensible Provisioning Protocol (EPP)
5933	Proposed Standard	Use of GOST Signature Algorithms in DNSKEY and RRSIG Resource Records for DNSSEC
6014	Proposed Standard	Cryptographic Algorithm Identifier Allocation for DNSSEC
6725	Proposed Standard	DNS Security (DNSSEC) DNSKEY Algorithm IANA Registry Updates
6781	Informational	DNSSEC Operational Practices, Version 2
6841	Informational	A Framework for DNSSEC Policies and DNSSEC Practice Statements
6975	Proposed Standard	Signaling Cryptographic Algorithm Understanding in DNS Security Extensions(DNSSEC)
7129	Informational	Authenticated Denial of Existence in the DNS
7344	Proposed Standard	Automating DNSSEC Delegation Trust Maintenance
7583	Informational	DNSSEC Key Rollover Timing Considerations
7646	Informational	Definition and Use of DNSSEC Negative Trust Anchors
7901	Experimental	CHAIN Query Requests in DNS
7958	Informational	DNSSEC Trust Anchor Publication for the Root Zone
8027	BCP 207	DNSSEC Roadblock Avoidance
8078	Proposed Standard	Managing DS Records from the Parent via CDS/CDNSKEY
8080	Proposed Standard	Edwards-Curve Digital Security Algorithm (EdDSA) for DNSSEC
8145	Proposed Standard	Signaling Trust Anchor Knowledge in DNS Security Extensions (DNSSEC)
8198	Proposed Standard	Aggressive Use of DNSSEC-Validated Cache
8509	Proposed Standard	A Root Key Trust Anchor Sentinel for DNSSEC
8624	Proposed Standard	Algorithm Implementation Requirements and Usage Guidance for DNSSEC

Non-DNSSEC DNS Security-related RFCs

RFC	Status	Title
2230	Informational	Key Exchange Delegation Record for the DNS
2845	Proposed Standard	Secret Key Transaction Authentication for DNS (TSIG)
2930	Proposed Standard	Secret Key Establishment for DNS (TKEY RR)
2931	Proposed Standard	DNS Request and Transactional Signatures (SIG(0)s)
3007	Proposed Standard	Secure Domain Name System (DNS) Dynamic Update
3110	Proposed Standard	RSA/SHA-1 SIGs and RSA KEYs in the Domain Name System (DNS)
3645	Proposed Standard	Generic Security Service Algorithm for Secret Key Transaction Authentication for DNS (GSS-TSIG)
3833	Informational	Threat Analysis of the Domain Name System (DNS)
4255	Proposed Standard	Using DNS to Securely Publish Secure Shell (SSH) Key Fingerprints
4398	Proposed Standard	Storing Certificates in the Domain Name System (DNS)
4686	Informational	Analysis of Threats Motivating DomainKeys Identified Mail (DKIM)
5016	Informational	Requirements for a DomainKeys Identified Mail (DKIM) Signing Practices Protocol
5358	BCP 140	Preventing Use of Recursive Nameservers in Reflector Attacks
5452	Standards Track	Measures for Making DNS More Resilient against Forged Answers
5585	Informational	DomainKeys Identified Mail (DKIM) Service Overview
5617	Standards Track	DomainKeys Identified Mail (DKIM) Author Domain Signing Practices (ADSP)
6376	Internet Standard	DomainKeys Identified Mail (DKIM) Signatures
6377	BCP 167	DomainKeys Identified Mail (DKIM) and Mailing Lists
6394	Informational	Use Cases and Requirements for DNS-Based Authentication of Named Entities (DANE)
6541	Experimental	DomainKeys Identified Mail (DKIM) Authorized Third-Party Signatures

Non-DNSSEC DNS Security-related RFCs

RFC	Status	Title
6651	Proposed Standard	Extensions to DomainKeys Identified Mail (DKIM) for Failure Reporting
6652	Proposed Standard	Sender Policy Framework (SPF) Authentication Failure Reporting Using the Abuse Reporting Format
6686	Informational	Resolution of the Sender Policy Framework (SPF) and Sender ID Experiments
6698	Proposed Standard	The DNS-Based Authentication of Named Entities (DANE) Transport Layer Security (TLS) Protocol: TLSA
6844	Proposed Standard	DNS Certification Authority Authorization (CAA) Resource Record
7208	Proposed Standard	Sender Policy Framework (SPF) for Authorizing Use of Domains in Email, Version 1
7218	Proposed Standard	Adding Acronyms to Simplify Conversations about DNS-Based Authentication of Named Entities (DANE)
7489	Informational	Domain-based Message Authentication, Reporting, and Conformance (DMARC)
7626	Informational	DNS Privacy Considerations
7671	Proposed Standard	The DNS-Based Authentication of Named Entities (DANE) Protocol: Updates and Operational Guidance
7672	Proposed Standard	SMTP Security via Opportunistic DNS-Based Authentication of Named Entities (DANE) Transport Layer Security (TLS)
7673	Proposed Standard	Using DNS-Based Authentication of Named Entities (DANE) TLSA Records with SRV Records
7816	Experimental	DNS Query Name Minimization to Improve Privacy
7858	Proposed Standard	Specification for DNS over Transport Layer Security (TLS)
7873	Proposed Standard	Domain Name System (DNS) Cookies
7929	Experimental	DNS-Based Authentication of Named Entities (DANE) Bindings for OpenPGP
7960	Informational	Interoperability Issues between Domain-based Message Authentication, Reporting, and Conformance (DMARC) and Indirect Email Flows

Non-DNSSEC DNS Security-related RFCs

RFC	Status	Title
8094	Experimental	DNS over Datagram Transport Layer Security (DTLS)
8162	Experimental	Using Secure DNS to Associate Certificates with Domain Names for S/MIME
8301	Proposed Standard	Cryptographic Algorithm and Key Usage Update to DomainKeys Identified Mail (DKIM)
8310	Proposed Standard	Usage Profiles for DNS over TLS and DNS over DTLS
8324	Informational	DNS Privacy, Authorization, Special Uses, Encoding, Characters, Matching, and Root Structure: Time for Another Look?
8463	Proposed Standard	A New Cryptographic Signature Method for DomainKeys Identified Mail (DKIM)
8482	Proposed Standard	Providing Minimal-Sized Responses to DNS Queries That Have QTYPE=ANY
8484	Proposed Standard	DNS Queries over HTTPS (DoH)

DNS ENUM-related RFCs

RFC	Status	Title
2916	Proposed Standard	E.164 number and DNS
3245	Informational	The History and Context of Telephone Number Mapping (ENUM)...
3403	Proposed Standard	Dynamic Delegation Discovery System (DDDS) Part Three: The Domain Name System (DNS) Database [NAPTR RR]
3762	Proposed Standard	Telephone Number Mapping (ENUM) Service Registration for H.323
3764	Proposed Standard	enumservice registration for Session Initiation Protocol (SIP) Addresses-of-Record
3824	Informational	Using E.164 numbers with the Session Initiation Protocol (SIP)
3953	Proposed Standard	Telephone Number Mapping (ENUM) Service Registration for Presence Services

DNS ENUM-related RFCs

RFC	Status	Title
3958	Proposed Standard	Domain-Based Application Service Location Using SRV RRs and the Dynamic Delegation Discovery System (DDDS)
4114	Proposed Standard	E.164 Number Mapping for the Extensible Provisioning Protocol (EPP)
4725	Informational	ENUM Validation Architecture
4759	Proposed Standard	The ENUM Dip Indicator Parameter for the "tel" URI
4848	Proposed Standard	Domain-Based Application Service Location Using URIs and the Dynamic Delegation Discovery System (DDDS)
5067	Informational	Infrastructure ENUM Requirements
5483	Informational	ENUM Implementation Issues and Experiences
5526	Informational	The E.164 to Uniform Resource Identifiers (URI) DDDS Application for Infrastructure ENUM
5527	Informational	Combined User and Infrastructure ENUM in the e164.arpa Tree
6116	Proposed Standard	The E.164 to Uniform Resource Identifiers (URI) Dynamic Delegation Discovery System (DDDS) Application (ENUM)

Management or Operational RFCs

RFC	Status	Title
1713	Informational	Tools for DNS debugging
1912	Informational	Common DNS Errors
2151	Informational	A Primer On Internet and TCP/IP Tools and Utilities
2606	BCP 32	Reserved Top Level DNS Names
3172	BCP 52	Management Guidelines & Operational Requirements for the Address and Routing Parameter Area Domain ("arpa")
5157	Informational	IPv6 Implications for Network Scanning
6018	Informational	IPv4 and IPv6 Greynets

Management or Operational RFCs

RFC	Status	Title
6168	Informational	Requirements for Management of Name Servers for the DNS
6303	BCP 163	Locally Served DNS Zones
6441	BCP 171	Time to Remove Filters for Previously Unallocated IPv4 /8s
6471	Informational	Overview of Best Email DNS-Based List (DNSBL) Operational Practices
6515	Proposed Standard	IPv4 and IPv6 Infrastructure Addresses in BGP Updates for Multicast VPN
6516	Proposed Standard	IPv6 Multicast VPN (MVPN) Support Using PIM Control Plane and Selective Provider Multicast Service Interface (S-OMSI) Join Messages
6586	Informational	Experiences from an IPv6-Only Network

Glossary

The key terms used throughout this book are summarized in this appendix.

- DHCP (or DHCPv4) – Dynamic host configuration protocol automates IP address assignment to network hosts or devices. DHCP technology applies to both IPv4 and IPv6 address assignment, though "DHCP" typically refers to assignment of IPv4 addresses.
    - o A-DHCP – Automatic DHCP, infinite lease
    - o D-DHCP – Dynamic DHCP
    - o M-DHCP – Manual DHCP, fixed IP address-MAC (media access control) address.
- DHCPv6 – DHCP specifically for IPv6 addresses, not version 6 of the DHCP protocol.
- DNS – Domain name system, the distributed database of Internet name, address, and other information.
- DNSSEC – DNS Security extensions provide resolution data origin authentication (the source truly published this data), data integrity verification (the data was not modified en route), and authenticated denial of existence of data (the requested data truly does not exist in this zone).
- FCAPS – An initialism of the five major functional areas of network management, namely Fault, Configuration, Accounting, Performance and Security as described in International Telecommunications Union (ITU) Telecommunications Management Network standards.
- Host – An end device which communicates on an IP network, such as a server, laptop, VoIP phone, etc. We contrast an end device with network infrastructure devices such as routers and switches.
- IP – Internet Protocol, the network layer used across the Internet and all IP networks. IP generically refers to all IP versions, while IPv4 and IPv6 denote respective IP versions.

IP Address Management, Second Edition. Michael Dooley and Timothy Rooney.
© 2021 The Institute of Electrical and Electronics Engineers, Inc.
Published 2021 by John Wiley & Sons, Inc.

- IPAM – Internet protocol address management, the disciplined approach to managing IP address space and associated DHCP and DNS services
- ITIL® – Formerly known as the Information Technology Infrastructure Library, a documented set of best practices for use by an IT organization desiring to manage, monitor, and continually improve IT services provided to the enterprise organization. ITIL was originally developed by the United Kingdom. Office of Government and Commerce, and is now managed by Axelos, a joint venture company created by the Cabinet Office of Her Majesty's Government in the United Kingdom and Capita, plc.
- KSK – Key signing key, used within DNSSEC to sign a zone signing key (ZSK), which in turn signs DNS zone data. The public KSK is published in a DNSKEY resource record within the corresponding secure zone. Resolvers or recursive servers configured to trust this zone's data must have a copy of the public KSK (or that of a parent zone's or lookaside validator's zone) configured as trust-anchors within their respective configurations.
- NAT – Network address translation – a gateway or firewall that changes (translates) an IP address within the IP packet header prior to forwarding; commonly used in enterprise networks to translate internal private IP addresses to external public IP addresses.
- TCP – Transmission control protocol, the connection-oriented transport layer protocol within the TCP/IP protocol suite. Please refer to Chapter 1 for details.
- UDP – User datagram protocol, the connectionless transport layer protocol within the TCP/IP protocol suite. Please refer to Chapter 1 for details.
- ZSK – Zone signing key, used within DNSSEC to sign zone information, meaning each of the resource record sets within the zone.

Bibliography

1. ISO/IEC (1994). *Information Technology – Open Systems Interconnection – Basic Reference Model*: The Basic Model, 2e. Geneva, Switzerland: ISO/IEC ISO/IEC 7498-1:1994(E).

2. Usage and Population Statistics (2019). *Internet World Stats*. https://www.internetworldstats.com/stats.htm (accessed 8 July 2020).

3. Postel, J. (1980). *DoD Standard Internet Protocol*. s.l.: IETF, RFC 760.

4. Postel, J. (1981). *Internet Protocol*. s.l.: IETF, RFC 791.

5. Hinden, R. (1993). *Applicability Statement for the Implementation of Classless Inter-Domain Routing (CIDR)*. s.l.: IETF, RFC 1517.

6. Rekhter, Y. and Li, T. (1993). *An Architecture for IP Address Allocation with CIDR*. s.l.: IETF, RFC 1518.

7. Fuller, V., Li, T., Yu, J., and Varadhan, K. (1993). *Classless Inter-Domain Routing (CIDR): an Address Assignment and Aggregation Strategy*. s.l.: IETF, RFC 1519.

8. Rekhter, Y., Moskowitz, B., Karrenberg, D. et al. (1996). *Address Allocation for Private Internets*. s.l.: IETF, RFC 1918.

9. Bonica, R. (ed.), Cotton, M., Vegoda, L., Haberman, B. (2013). *Special-Purpose IP Address Registries*. s.l.: IETF, RFC 6890.

10. Internet Assigned Numbers Authority (IANA) (2019). Internet Protocol Version 6 Address Space. www.iana.org. http://www.iana.org/assignments/ipv6-address-space/ipv6-address-space.xhtml (accessed 8 July 2020).

11. Hinden, R. and Deering, S. (2006). *IP Version 6 Addressing Architecture*. s.l.: IETF, RFC 4291.

12. Carpenter, B. and Jiang, S. (2014). *Significance of IPv6 Interface Identifiers*. s.l.: IETF, RFC 7136.

13. Hinden, R. Deering, S., and Nordmark, E. (2003). *IPv6 Global Unicast Address Format*. s.l.: IETF, RFC 3587.

IP Address Management, Second Edition. Michael Dooley and Timothy Rooney.
© 2021 The Institute of Electrical and Electronics Engineers, Inc.
Published 2021 by John Wiley & Sons, Inc.

14. Hinden, R. and Haberman, B. (2005). *Unique Local IPv6 Unicast Addresses*. s.l.: IETF, RFC 4193.
15. Huitema, C. (1994). *The H Ratio for Address Assignment Efficiency*. s.l.: IETF, RFC 1715.
16. Durand, A. and Huitema, C. (2001). *The Host-Density Ratio for Address Assignment Efficiency: An update on the H ratio*. s.l.: IETF, RFC 3194.
17. Ferguson, P. and Senie, D. (2000). *Network Ingress Filtering: Defeating Denial of Service Attacks which employ IP Source Address Spoofing*. s.l.: IETF, RFC 2827, BCP 38.
18. Baker, F. and Savola, P. (2004). *Ingress Filtering for Multihomed Networks*. s.l.: IETF, RFC 3704.
19. Baker, F., Bowers, C., and Linkova, J. (2019). *Enterprise Multihoming using Provider-Assigned IPv6 Addresses without Network Prefix Translation: Requirements and Solutions*. s.l.: IETF, draft-ietf-rtgwg-enterprise-pa-multihoming-12.
20. Mrugalski, T., Siodelski, M., Volz, B. et al. (2018). *Dynamic Host Configuration Protocol for IPv6 (DHCPv6)*. s.l.: IETF, RFC 8415.
21. Sun, Q., Cui, Y., Siodelski, M. et al. (2014). *DHCPv4-over-DHCPv6 (DHCP 4o6) Transport*. s.l.: IETF, RFC 7341.
22. Aura, T. (2005). *Cryptographically Generated Addresses (CGA)*. s.l.: IETF, RFC 3972.
23. Narten, T., Draves, R., and Krishnan, S. (2007). *Privacy Extensions for Stateless Address Autoconfiguration in IPv6*. s.l.: IETF, RFC 4941.
24. Gont, F. (2014). *A Method for Generating Semantically Opaque Interface Identifiers with IPv6 Stateless Address Autoconfiguration (SLAAC)*. s.l.: IETF, RFC 7217.
25. Gont, F., Cooper, A., Thaler, D., and Liu, W. (2017). *Recommendation on Stable IPv6 Interface Identifiers*. s.l.: IETF, RFC 8064.
26. Cooper, A., Gont, F., and Thaler, D. (2016). *Security and Privacy Considerations for IPv6 Address Generation Mechanisms*. s.l.: IETF, RFC 7721.
27. Krishnan, S. (2009). *Reserved IPv6 Interface Identifiers*. s.l.: IETF, RFC 5453.
28. Mockapetris, P.V. (1987). *Domain Names – Implementation and Specification*. s.l.: IETF, RFC 1035.
29. Eidnes, H., de Groot, G., and Vixie, P. (1998). *Classless IN-ADDR.ARPA Delegation*. s.l.: IETF, RFC 2317.
30. Internet Systems Consortium (2009). *dhcpd.conf man*. Redwood City, CA: Internet Systems Consortium, Inc. ("ISC").
31. Patrick, M. (2001). *DHCP Relay Agent Information Option*. s.l.: IETF, RFC 3046.
32. Volz, B. (2006). *Dynamic Host Configuration Protocol for IPv6 (DHCPv6) Relay Agent Remote-ID Option*. s.l.: IETF, RFC 4649.
33. Jones, D. and Woundy, R. (2002). *The DOCSIS (Data-Over-Cable Service Interface Specifications) Device Class DHCP (Dynamic Host Configuration Protocol) Relay Agent Information Sub-option*. s.l.: IETF, RFC 3256.

34. Kinnear, K., Stapp, M., Johnson, R., and Kumarasamy, J. (2003). *Link Selection Sub-option for the Relay Agent Information Option for DHCPv4*. s.l.: IETF, RFC 3527.

35. Volz, B. (2006). *Dynamic Host Configuration Protocol for IPv6 (DHCPv6) Relay Agent Subscriber-ID Option*. s.l.: IETF, RFC 4580.

36. Johnson, R., Palaniappan, T., and Stapp, M. (2005). *Subscriber-ID Suboption for the Dynamic Host Configuration Protocol (DHCP) Relay Agent Option*. s.l.: IETF, RFC 3993.

37. Yeh, L. and Boucadair, M. (2013). *RADIUS Option for the DHCPv6 Relay Agent*. s.l.: IETF, RFC 7037.

38. Droms, R. and Schnizlein, J. (2005). *Remote Authentication Dial-In User Service (RADIUS) Attributes Suboption for the Dynamic Host Configuration Protocol (DHCP)*. s.l.: IETF, RFC 4014.

39. Stapp, M. and Lemon, T. (2005). *The Authentication Suboption for the Dynamic Host Configuration Protocol (DHCP) Relay Agent Option*. s.l.: IETF, RFC 4030.

40. Stapp, M., Johnson, R. and Palaniappan, T. (2005). *Vendor-Specific Information Suboption for the Dynamic Host Configuration Protocol (DHCP) Relay Agent Option*. s.l.: IETF, RFC 4243.

41. Kinnear, K. Normoyle, M. and Stapp, M. (2007). *The Dynamic Host Configuration Protocol Version 4 (DHCPv4) Relay Agent Flags Suboption*. s.l.: IETF, RFC 5010.

42. Jumarasamy, J., Kinnear, K. and Stapp, M. (2008). *DHCP Server Identifier Override Suboption*. s.l.: IETF, RFC 5107.

43. Joshi, B., Desetti, R., and Stapp, M. (2013). *The DHCPv4 Relay Agent Identifier Sub-Option*. s.l.: IETF, RFC 6925.

44. Bhandari, S., Gundavelli, S., Grayson, M. et al. (2016). *Access-Network Identifier Option in DHCP*. s.l.: IETF, RFC 7839.

45. Shen, N. and Chen, E. (2018). *Generalized UDP Source Port for DHCP Relay*. s.l.: IETF, RFC 8357.

46. Kinnear, K., Johnson, R., and Stapp, M. (2012). *Virtual Subnet Selection Options for DHCPv4 and DHCPv6*. s.l.: IETF, RFC 6607.

47. Johnston, M. and Venaas, S. (eds.) (2006). *Dynamic Host Configuration Protocol (DHCP) Options for Intel Preboot eXecution Environment (PXE)*. s.l.: IETF, RFC 4578.

48. Blanchet, M. (2003). *A Flexible Method for Managing the Assignment of Bits of an IPv6 Address Block*. s.l.: IETF, RFC 3531.

49. Cherenson, A. (2010) *nslookup man page (BIND distribution)*. Redwood City, CA: Internet Systems Consortium, Inc. ("ISC").

50. Internet Systems Consortium (2010). *dig man page (with BIND distribution)*. Redwood City, CA: Internet Systems Consortium ("ISC").

51. The ITIL 4 Complete Guide (2019). *Beyond20*. https://www.beyond20.com/itil-4-complete-guide (accessed 8 July 2020).

52. Dooley, M. and Rooney, T. (2017). *DNS Security Management*. Hoboken: Wiley.

53. Huston, G. (2020). *IPv4 Address Report*. ipv4.potaroo.net (accessed 8 July 2020).

54. Statista (2020). *Global digital population as of October 2019*. Statista. https://www.statista.com/statistics/617136/digital-population-worldwide (accessed 8 July 2020).

55. Miniwatts Marketing (2020). Internet World Stats. https://www.internetworldstats.com/stats.htm (accessed 8 July 2020).

56. InternetLiveStats.com. Internet Users (2020). *Internet Live Stats*. https://www.internetlivestats.com/internet-users (accessed 8 July 2020).

57. Carpenter, B., Atkinson, R., and Flinck, H. (2010). *Renumbering Still Needs Work*. s.l.: IETF, RFC 5887.

58. Schinazi, D. and Pauly, T. (2017). *Happy Eyeballs Version 2: Better Connectivity Using Concurrency*. s.l.: IETF, RFC 8305.

59. Durand, A. and Ihren, J. (2004). *DNS IPv6 Transport Operational Guidelines*. s.l.: IETF, RFC 3901.

60. Chown, T., Venaas, S., and Strauf, C. (2006). *Dynamic Host Configuration Protocol (DHCP): IPv4 and IPv6 Dual-Stack Issues*. s.l.: IETF, RFC 4477.

61. Durand, A., Droms, R., Woodyatt, J., and Lee, Y. (2011). *Dual-Stack Lite Broadband Deployments Following IPv4 Exhaustion*. s.l.: IETF, RFC 6333.

62. Cui, Y., Sun, Q., Boucadair, M. et al. (2015). *Lightweight 4over6: An Extension to the Dual-Stack Lite Architecture*. s.l.: IETF, RFC 7596.

63. Troan, O. (ed.), Dec, W., Li, X., Bao, C. et al. (2015). *Mapping of Address and Port with Encapsulation (MAP-E)*. s.l.: IETF, RFC 7597.

64. Baker, F., Li, X., Bao, C., and Yin, K. (2011). *Framework for IPv4/IPv6 Translation*. s.l.: IETF, RFC 6144.

65. Anderson, T. and Leiva Popper, A. (2016). *Explicit Address Mappings for Stateless IP/ICMP Translation*. s.l.: IETF, RFC 7757.

66. Li, X., Bao, C., and Baker, F. (2011). *IP/ICMP Translation Algorithm*. s.l.: IETF, RFC 6145.

67. Bao, C., Huitema, C., Bagnulo, M. et al. (2010). *IPv6 Addressing of IPv4/IPv6 Translators*. s.l.: IETF, RFC 6052.

68. Huang, B., Deng, H., and Savolainen, T. (2012). *Dual-Stack Hosts Using "Bump-in-the-Host" (BIH)*. s.l.: IETF, RFC 6535.

69. Tsuchiya, K. Higuchi, H., and Atarashi, Y. (2000). *Dual Stack Hosts using the "Bump-in-the-Stack" Technique (BIS)*. s.l.: IETF, RFC 2767.

70. Lee, S., Shin, M.-K., Kim, Y.-J. et al. (2002). *Dual Stack Hosts Using "Bump-in-the-API" (BIA)*. s.l.: IETF, RFC 3338.

71. Bagnulo, M., Matthews, P. and van Beijum, I. (2011). *Stateful NAT64: Network Address and Protocol Translation from IPv6 Clients to IPv4 Servers*. s.l.: IETF, RFC 6146.

72. Leech, M., Ganis, M., Lee Y. et al. *SOCKS Protocol Version 5*. s.l.: IETF, RFC 1928.

73. Kitamura, H. (2001). *A SOCKS-Based IPv6/IPv4 Gateway Mechanism.* s.l.: IETF, RFC 3089.
74. Newton, A., Silva Berenguer, S. (2015). *Preparing Applications for IPv6.* s.l.: ARIN.
75. Dooley, M. and Rooney, T. (2013). *IPv6 Deployment and Management.* Hoboken, NJ: Wiley.
76. Montenegro, G., Kushalnagar, N., Hui, J., and Culler, D. (2007). *Transmission of IPv6 Packets over IEEE 802.15.4 Networks.* s.l.: IETF, RFC 4944.
77. Kim, E., Kaspar, D., Gomez, C., and Bormann, C. (2012). *Problem Statement and Requirements for IPv6 over Low-Power Wireless Personal Area Network (6LoWPAN) Routing.* s.l.: IETF, RFC 6606.
78. Hui, J. and Thubert, P. (2011). *Compression Format for IPv6 Datagrams over IEEE 802.15.4-Based Networks.* s.l.: IETF, RFC 6282.
79. Shelby, Z., Chakrabarti, S., Nordmark, E., and Bormann, C. (2012). *Neighbor Discovery Optimization for IPv6 over Low-Power Wireless Personal Area Networks (6LoWPANs).* s.l.: IETF, RFC 6775.
80. Volz, B. and Pal, Y. (2017). *Security of Messages Exchanged between Servers and Relay Agents.* s.l.: IETF, RFC 8213.
81. Droms, R. and Arbaugh, W. (eds.) (2001). *Authentication for DHCP Messages.* s.l.: IETF, RFC 3118.
82. York, K. (2016). Dyn Statement on 10/21/2016 DDoS Attack. Dyn. https://dyn.com/blog/dyn-statement-on-10212016-ddos-attack (accessed 8 July 2020).
83. Open Resolver Project (2016). *Open Resolver Project.* openresolverproject.org (accessed 8 July 2020).
84. United States Computer Emergency Response Team (US-CERT) (2016). DNS Amplification Attacks. US-CERT. https://www.us-cert.gov/ncas/alerts/TA13-088A (accessed 08 July 2020).
85. Drozhzhin, A. (2016). *Switcher hacks Wi-Fi routers, switches DNS.* Kaspersky Lab. https://blog.kaspersky.com/switcher-trojan-attacks-routers/13771 (accessed 08 July 2020).
86. StJohns, M. (2007). *Automated Updates of DNS Security (DNSSEC) Trust Anchors.* s.l.: IETF, RFC 5011.
87. NIST Advanced Network Technologies Division (2020). *Estimating IPv6 & DNSSEC Deployment.* NIST Advanced Network Technologies Division Information Technology Laboratory. https://usgv6-deploymon.antd.nist.gov/snap-all.html (accessed 08 July 2020).
88. APNIC Labs (2020). *Use of DNSSEC Validation for World.* APNIC Labs. http://stats.labs.apnic.net/dnssec (accessed 08 July 2020).
89. Rescorla, E. (2018). *The Transport Layer Security (TLS) Protocol Version 1.3.* s.l.: IETF, RFC 8446.
90. Hu, Z., Zhu, L., Heidemann, J. et al. (2016). *Specification for DNS over Transport Layer Security (TLS).* s.l.: IETF, RFC 7858.

91. Hoffman, P. and McManus, P. (2018). *DNS Queries over HTTPS (DoH)*. s.l.: IETF, RFC 8484.

92. Valian, P. (2010). *NetReg. sourceforge.net*. netreg.sourceforge.net (accessed 08 July 2020).

93. Ramaswamy, C. and Scott, R. (2013). Secure Domain Name System (DNS) Deployment Guide. Gaithersburg, MD: National Institute of Standards and Technology, NIST Special Publication 800-81-2.

94. Krebs, B. (2016). KrebsOnSecurity Hit With Record DDoS. Krebs on Security. https://krebsonsecurity.com/2016/09/krebsonsecurity-hit-with-record-ddos (accessed 08 July 2020).

95. United States Computer Emergency Readiness Team (2016). *Backoff Point-of-Sale Malware*. s.l.: US-CERT, July, 2014, TA14-212A.

96. United States Computer Emergency Readiness Team (2016). *Crypto Ransomware*. s.l.: US-CERT, October, 2014, TA14-295A.

97. United States Computer Emergency Readiness Team (2016). *Dridex P2P malware*. s.l.: US-CERT, October, 2015, TA15-286A.

98. United States Computer Emergency Readiness Team (2016). *Ransomware and Recent Variants*. s.l.: US-CERT, March, 2016, TA16-091A.

99. United States Computer Emergency Readiness Team (2016). *Apple iOS 'Masque Attack' Technique*. s.l.: US-CERT, November, 2014, TA14-317A.

100. United States Computer Emergency Readiness Team (2016). *Heightened DDoS Threat Posed by Mirai and Other Botnets*. s.l.: US-CERT, October, 2016, TA16-288A.

101. Microsoft Corporation (2016). TrojanSpy: Win32/Nivdort.A *Malware Protection Center*. https://www.microsoft.com/security/portal/threat/encyclopedia/entry.asp x?Name=TrojanSpy%3aWin32%2fNivdort.A (accessed 08 July 2020).

102. United States Computer Emergency Readiness Team (2016). Simda Botnet. s.l.: US-CERT, April, 2015, TA15-105A.

103. Farrell, S. and Tschofenig, H. (2014). *Pervasive Monitoring Is an Attack*. s.l.: IETF, RFC 7258.

104. Internet Assigned Numbers Authority (2016). *Root Zone Database*. Internet Assigned Numbers Authority. http://www.iana.org/domains/root/db (accessed 08 July 2020).

105. ICANN (2016). TLD DNSSEC Report. ICANN Research. http://stats.research. icann.org/dns/tld_report (accessed 08 July 2020).

106. Kolkman, O., Mekking, W., and Gieben, R. (2012). DNSSEC Operational Practices, Version 2. s.l.: IETF, RFC 6781.

107. Kumari, W., Gudmundsson, O., and Barwood, G. (2014). Automating DNSSEC Delegation Trust Maintenance. s.l.: IETF, RFC 7344.

108. Dell EMC (2016). PKCS #11: Cryptographic Token Interface Standard. RSA Laboratories. https://www.emc.com/emc-plus/rsa-labs/standards-initiatives/ pkcs-11-cryptographic-token-interface-standard.htm (accessed 08 July 2020).

109. Hoffman, P. and Schlyter, J. (2012). *The DNS-Based Authentication of Named Entities (DANE) Transport Layer Security (TLS) Protocol: TLSA.* s.l.: IETF, RFC 6698.

110. Dukhovni, V. and Hardaker, W. (2015). *The DNS-Based Authentication of Named Entities (DANE) Protocol: Updates and Operational Guidance.* s.l.: IETF, RFC 7671.

111. Bright, P. (2016). *Independent Iranian hacker claims responsibility for Comodo hack.* ARS Technica. http://arstechnica.com/security/2011/03/independent-iranian-hacker-claims-responsibility-for-comodo-hack (accessed 08 July 2020).

112. Bright, P. (2016). *Another fraudulent certificate raises the same old questions about certificate authorities.* ARS Technica. http://arstechnica.com/security/2011/08/earlier-this-year-an-iranian (accessed 08 July 2020).

113. Leydon, J. (2016). Symantec fires staff caught up in rogue Google SSL cert snafu. The Register. http://www.theregister.co.uk/2015/09/21/symantec_fires_workers_over_rogue_certs (accessed 08 July 2020).

114. Rose, S., Barker, W., Jha, S. et al. (2018). *Domain Name Systems-Based Electronic Mail security.* s.l.: NCCoE, NIST, NIST Special Publication 1800-6.

115. Hoffman, P. (2002). *SMTP Service Extension for Secure SMTP over Transport Layer Security.* s.l.: IETF, RFC 3207.

116. Melnikov, A. (2016). *Updated Transport Layer Security (TLS) Server Identity Check Procedures for Email-Related Protocols.* s.l.: IETF, RFC 7817.

117. Lewis, C. and Sergeant, M. (2012). *Overview of Best Email DNS-Based List (DNSBL) Operational Practices.* s.l.: IETF, RFC 6471.

118. Kitterman, S. (2014). *Sender Policy Framework (SPF) for Authorizing Use of Domains in Email,* Version 1, RFC 7208.

119. Kucherawy, M. and Zwicky, E. (2015). *Domain-based Message Authentication, Reporting, and Conformance (DMARC).* s.l.: IETF, RFC 7489.

120. Internet Corporation for Assigned Names and Numbers (ICANN) (2009). Factsheet – Root server attack on 6 February 2007. Internet Corporation for Assigned Names and Numbers (www.icann.org). http://www.icann.org/announcements/factsheet-dns-attack-08mar07.pdf (accessed 08 July 2020).

121. Mendel, T. (2004). *IP Address Management Market Overview.* s.l.: Forrester Research, Market Overview.

122. Morrow, S. (2019). Zero trust security: What is it? Infosec Institute. https://resources.infosecinstitute.com/zero-trust-security-what-is-it (accessed 08 July 2020).

123. AV-Test Institute (2019). *Malware. AV-Test Institute.* https://www.av-test.org/en/statistics/malware (accessed 08 July 2020).

124. Nichols, K., Blake, S., Baker, F., and Black, D. (1998). *Definition of the Differentiated Services Field (DS Field) in the IPv4 and IPv6 Headers.* s.l.: IETF, RFC 2474.

125. Boucadair, M. and Venaas, S. (2014). *Updates to the IPv6 Multicast Addressing Architecture.* s.l.: IETF, RFC 7371.

126. Park, J.-S., Shin, M.-K., Kim, H.-J. (2006). *A Method for Generating Link-Scoped IPv6 Multicast Addresses.* s.l.: IETF, RFC 4489.

127. Crawford, M. and Haberman, B. (eds.) (2006). *IPv6 Node Information Queries.* s.l.: IETF, RFC 4620.

128. Johnson, D. and Deering, S. (1999). *Reserved IPv6 Subnet Anycast Addresses.* s.l.: IETF, RFC 2526.

129. Droms, R. (ed.), Bound, J., Volz, B., Lemon, T. et al. (2003). *Dynamic Host Configuration Protocol for IPv6 (DHCPv6).* s.l.: IETF, RFC 3315.

130. Schulzrinne, H. and Volz, B. (2003). *Dynamic Host Configuration Protocol (DHCPv6) Options for Session Initiation Protocol (SIP) Servers.* s.l.: IETF, RFC 3319.

131. Droms, R. (ed.) (2003). *DNS Configuration Options for Dynamic Host Configuration Protocol for IPv6 (DHCPv6).* s.l.: IETF, RFC 3646.

132. Troan, O. and Droms, R. (2003). *IPv6 Prefix Options for Dynamic Host Configuration Protocol (DHCP) Version 6.* s.l.: IETF, RFC3633.

133. Kalusivalingam, V. (2004). *Network Information Service (NIS) Configuration Options for Dynamic Host Configuration Protocol for IPv6 (DHCPv6).* s.l.: IETF, RFC 3898.

134. Kalusivalingam, V. (2005). *Simple Network Time Protocol (SNTP) Configuration Option for DHCPv6.* s.l.: IETF, RFC 4075.

135. Venaas, S. Chown, T., and Volz, B. (2005). *Information Refresh Time Option for Dynamic Host Configuration Protocol for IPv6 (DHCPv6).* s.l.: IETF, RFC 4242.

136. Chowdhury, K., Yegani, P., and Madour, L. (2005). *Dynamic Host Configuration Protocol (DHCP) Options for Broadcast and Multicast Control Servers.* s.l.: IETF, RFC 4280.

137. Schulzrinne, H. (2006). *Dynamic Host Configuration Protocol (DHCPv4 and DHCPv6) Option for Civic Addresses Configuration Information.* s.l.: IETF, RFC 4776.

138. Volz, B. (2006). *The Dynamic Host Configuration Protocol for IPv6 (DHCPv6) Client Fully Qualified Domain Name (FQDN) Option.* s.l.: IETF, RFC 4704.

139. Morand, L., Yegin, A. Kumar, S., and Madanapalli, S. (2008). *DHCP Options for Protocol for Carrying Authentication for Network Access (PANA) Authentication Agents.* s.l.: IETF, RFC 5192.

140. Lear, E. and Eggert, P. (2007). *Timezone Options for DHCP.* s.l.: IETF, RFC 4833.

141. Zeng, S., Volz, B., Kinnear, K., and Brzozowski, J. (2007). *DHCPv6 Relay Agent Echo Request Option.* s.l.: IETF, RFC 4994.

142. Brzozowski, J., Kinnear, K., Volz, B., and Zeng, S. (2007). *DHCPv6 Leasequery.* s.l.: IETF, RFC 5007.

143. Jang, H., Yegin, A., Chowdhury, K., Choi, J., and Lemon, T. (2012). *DHCP Options for Home Information Discovery in MIPv6.* s.l.: IETF, RFC 6610.

144. Schulzrinne, H., Polk, J., and Tschofenig, H. (2008). *Discovering Location-to-Service Translation (LoST) Servers Using the Dynamic Host Configuration Protocol (DHCP)*. s.l.: IETF, RFC 5223.

145. Calhoun, P. (2009). *Control And Provisioning of Wireless Access Points (CAPWAP) Access Controller DHCP Option*. s.l.: IETF, RFC 5417.

146. Stapp, M. (2009). *DHCPv6 Bulk Leasequery*. s.l.: IETF, RFC 5460.

147. Bajko, G. and Das, S. (2009). *Dynamic Host Configuration Protocol (DHCPv4 and DHCPv6) Options for IEEE 802.21 Mobility Services (MoS) Discovery*. s.l.: IETF, RFC 5678.

148. Gayraud, R. and Lourdelet, B. (2010). *Network Time Protocol (NTP) Server Option for DHCPv6*. s.l.: IETF, RFC 5908.

149. Thomson, M. and Winterbottom, J. (2010). *Discovering the Local Location Information Server (LIS)*. s.l.: IETF, RFC 5986.

150. Lawrence, S. (ed.) and Elwell, J. (2010). *Session Initiation Protocol (SIP) User Agent Configuration*. s.l.: IETF, RFC 6011.

151. Huth, T., Freimann, J., Zimmer, V., and Thaler, D. (2010). *DHCPv6 Options for Network Boot*. s.l.: IETF, RFC 5970.

152. Polk, J., Linsner, M., Thomson, M., and Aboba, B. (eds.) (2011). *Dynamic Host Configuration Protocol Options for Coordinate-Based Location Configuration Information*. s.l.: IETF, RFC 6225.

153. Hankins, D. and Mrugalski, T. (2011). *Dynamic Host Configuration Protocol for IPv6 (DHCPv6) Option for Dual-Stack Lite*. s.l.: IETF, RFC 6334.

154. Zorn, G., Wu, Q., and Want, Y. (2011). *The EAP Re-authentication Protocol (ERP) Local Domain Name DHCPv6 Option*. s.l.: IETF, RFC 6440.

155. Lemon, T. and Wu, Q. (2011). *Relay-Supplied DHCP Options*. s.l.: IETF, RFC 6422.

156. Korhonen, J. (ed.), Savolainen, T., Krishnan, S., and Troan O. (2012). *Prefix Exclude Option for DHCPv6-based Prefix Delegation*. s.l.: IETF, RFC 6603.

157. Jang, H., Yegin, A., Chowdhury, K. et al. (2012). *DHCP Options for Home Information Discovery in Mobile IPv6 (MIPv6)*. s.l.: IETF, RFC 6610.

158. Savolainen, T., Kato, J., and Lemon, T. (2012). *Improved Recursive DNS Server Selection for Multi-Interfaced Nodes*. s.l.: IETF, RFC 6731.

159. Sakane, S. and Ishiyama, M. (2012). *Kerberos Options for DHCPv6*. s.l.: IETF, November 2012, RFC 6784.

160. Halwasia, G. and Bhandari, S. (2013). *Client Link-Layer Address Option in DHCPv6*. s.l.: IETF, RFC 6939.

161. Boucadair, M. and Pougnard, X. (2013). *Triggering DHCPv6 Reconfiguration from Relay Agents*. s.l.: IETF, RFC 6977.

162. Matsumoto, A., Fujisaki, T., and Chown, T. (2014). *Distributing Address Selection Policy Using DHCPv6*. s.l.: IETF, RFC 7078.

163. Boucadair, M., Penno, R., and Wing, D. (2014). *DHCP Options for the Port Control Protocol (PCP)*. s.l.: IETF, RFC 7291.

164. Mrugalski, T., Troan, O., Farrer, I. et al. (2015). *DHCPv6 Options for Configuration of Softwire Address and Port-Mapped Clients*. s.l.: IETF, RFC 7598.

165. Despres, R., Jiang, S., (eds.), Penno, R. et al. (2015). *IPv4 Residual Deployment via IPv6 – A Stateless Solution (4rd)*. s.l.: IETF, RFC 7600.

166. Raghuvanshi, D., Kinnear, K., and Kukrety, D. (2015). *DHCPv6 Active Leasequery*. s.l.: IETF, RFC 7653.

167. Kumari, W., Kline, E. (2020). *Captive-Portal Identification in DHCP and Router Advertisements (RAs)*. s.l.: IETF, RFC 8910.

168. Doi, Y. and Gillmore, M. (2016). *Multicast Protocol for Low-Power and Lossy Networks (MPL) Parameter Configuration Option for DHCPv6*. s.l.: IETF, RFC 7774.

169. Boucadair, M. and Farrer, I. (2016). *Unified IPv4-in-IPv6 Softwire Customer Premises Equipment (CPE): A DHCPv6-Based Prioritization Mechanism*. s.l.: IETF, RFC 8026.

170. Lear, E., Droms, R., and Romascanu, D. (2019). *Manufacturer Usage Description Specification*. s.l.: IETF, RFC 8520.

171. Boucadair, M., Qin, J., Tsou, T., and Deng, X. (2017). *DHCPv6 Option for IPv4-Embedded Multicast and Unicast IPv6 Prefixes*. s.l.: IETF, RFC 8115.

172. Mrugalski, T. and Kinnear, K. (2017). *DHCPv6 Failover Protocol*. s.l.: IETF, RFC 8156.

173. Farrer, I., Sun, Q., Cui, Y., and Sun, L. (2019). *Softwire Provisioning Using DHCPv4 over DHCPv6*. s.l.: IETF, RFC 8539.

174. Das, S. and Bajko, G. (2011). *DHCPv4 and DHCPv6 Options for Access Network Discovery and Selection Function (ANDSF) Discoveryr*. s.l.: IETF, RFC 6153.

175. Droms, R. (1997). *Dynamic Host Configuration Protocol*. s.l.: IETF, RFC 2131.

176. Alexander, S., Droms, R. (1997). *DHCP Options and BOOTP Vendor Extensions*. s.l.: IETF, RFC 2132.

177. Lemon, T., Cheshire, S., and Volz, B. (2002). *The Classless Static Route Option for Dynamic Host Configuration Protocol (DHCP) Version 4*. s.l.: IETF, RFC 3442.

178. Droms, R. and Fong, K. (1997). *NetWare/IP Domain Name and Information*. s.l.: IETF, RFC 2242.

179. Stump, G. Droms, R., Gu, Y. et al.(2000). *The User Class Option for DHCP*. s.l.: IETF, RFC 3004.

180. Perkins, C. and Guttman, E. (1999). *DHCP Options for Service Location Protocol*. s.l.: IETF, RFC 2610.

181. Park, S. Kim, P., and Volz, B. (2005). *Rapid Commit Option for the Dynamic Host Configuration Protocol version 4 (DHCPv4)*. s.l.: IETF, RFC 4039.

182. Stapp, M., Volz, B., and Rekhter, Y. (2006). *The Dynamic Host Configuration Protocol (DHCP) Client Fully Qualified Domain Name (FQDN) Option*. s.l.: IETF, RFC 4702.

183. Monia, C., Tseng, J., and Gibbons, K. (2005). *The IPv4 Dynamic Host Configuration Protocol (DHCP) Option for the Internet Storage Name Service.* s.l.: IETF, RFC 4174.

184. Droms, R. (2004). *Unused Dynamic Host Configuration Protocol (DHCP) Option Codes.* s.l.: IETF, RFC 3679.

185. Provan, D. (1997). *DHCP Options for Novell Directory Services.* s.l.: IETF, RFC 2241.

186. Woundy, R. and Kinnear, K. (2006). *Dynamic Host Configuration Protocol (DHCP) Leasequery.* s.l.: IETF, RFC 4388.

187. Drach, S. (1999). *DHCP Option for The Open Group's User Authentication Protocol.* s.l.: IETF, RFC 2485.

188. Troll, R. (1999). *DHCP Option to Disable Stateless Auto-Configuration in IPv4 Clients.* s.l.: IETF, RFC 2563.

189. Smith, C. (2000). *The Name Service Search Option for DHCP.* s.l.: IETF, RFC 2937.

190. Waters, G. (2000). *The IPv4 Subnet Selection Optoin for DHCP.* s.l.: IETF, RFC 3011.

191. Aboba, B. and Cheshire, S. (2002). *Dynamic Host Configuration Protocol (DHCP) Domain Search Option.* s.l.: IETF, RFC 3397.

192. Schulzrinne, H. (2002). *Dynamic Host Configuration Protocol (DHCP-for-IPv4) Option for Session Initiation Protocol (SIP) Servers.* s.l.: IETF, RFC 3361.

193. Agarwal, P. and Akyol, B. (2002). *The Classless Static Route Option for Dynamic Host Configuration Protocol (DHCP) Version 4.* s.l.: IETF, RFC 3442.

194. Beser, B. and Duffy, P. (eds.) (2003). *Dynamic Host Configuration Protocol (DHCP) Option for CableLabs Client Configuration.* s.l.: IETF, RFC 3495.

195. Littlefield, J. (2004). *Vendor-Identifying Vendor Options for Dynamic Host Configuration Protocol Version 4 (DHCPv4).* s.l.: IETF, RFC 3925.

196. Watsen, K., Farrer, I., and Abrahamsson, M. (2019). *Secure Zero Touch Provisioning (SZTP).* s.l.: IETF, RFC 8572.

197. Miles, D., Dec, W., Bristow, J., and Maglione, R. (2012). *Forcerenew Nonce Authentication.* s.l.: IETF, RFC 6704.

198. Volz, B. (2004). *Reclassifying Dynamic Host Configuration Protocol Version 4 (DHCPv4) Options.* s.l.: IETF, RFC 3942.

199. Kinnear, K., Stapp, M., Desetti, R. et al. (2013). *DHCPv4 Bulk Leasequery.* s.l.: IETF, RFC 6926.

200. Cui, Y., Sun, Q., Farrer, I. et al. (2015). *Dynamic Allocation of Shared IPv4 Addresses.* s.l.: IETF, RFC 7618.

201. Hankins, D. (2007). *Dynamic Host Configuration Protocol Options Used by PXELINUX.* s.l.: IETF, RFC 5071.

202. Townsley, W. and Troan, O. (2010). *IPv6 Rapid Deployment on IPv4 Infrastructures (6rd) – Protocol Specification.* s.l.: IETF, RFC 5969.

203. Klensin, J. (2010). *Internationalizing Domain Names in Applications (IDNA): Protocol.* s.l.: IETF, RFC 5891.

204. Internationalized Domain Names (IDN) (2009). International Telecommunications Union. http://www.itu.int/ITU-T/special-projects/idn/introduction.html (accessed 08 July 2020).

205. Vixie, P., (ed.), Thomson, S. Rekhter, Y., Bound, J. (1997). *Dynamic Updates in the Domain Name System (DNS UPDATE).* s.l.: IETF, RFC 2136.

206. Rose, S. and Wijngaards, W. (2012). *DNAME Redirection in the DNS.* s.l.: IETF, RFC 6672.

207. Vixie, P. Gudmundsson, O., Eastlake 3rd, D., and Wellington, B. (2000). *Secret Key Transaction Authentication for DNS (TSIG).* s.l.: IETF, RFC 2845.

208. Bellis, R., Cheshire, S., Dickinson, J. et al. (2019). *DNS Stateful Operation.* s.l.: IETF, RFC 8490.

209. Vixie, P. (1999). *Extension Mechanisms for DNS (EDNS0).* s.l.: IETF, RFC 2671.

210. Eastlake, 3rd, D. (2000). *Secret Key Establishment for DNS (TKEY RR).* s.l.: IETF, RFC 2930.

211. Eastlake, 3rd, D. (2006). *HMAC SHA TSIG Algorithm Identifiers.* s.l.: IETF, RFC 4635.

212. Eastlake 3rd, D. and Andrews, M. (2016). *Domain Name System (DNS) Cookies.* s.l.: IETF, RFC 7873.

213. Eastlake, 3rd, D. (2008). *Domain Name System (DNS) IANA Considerations.* s.l.: IETF, RFC 5395.

214. Internet Assigned Numbers Authority (IANA) (2009). *Domain Name System (DNS) Parameters.* www.iana.org http://www.iana.org/assignments/dns-parameters (accessed 08 July 2020).

215. Damas, J., Graff, M., and Vixie, P. (2013). Extension Mechanisms for DNS (EDNS(0)). s.l.: IETF, RFC 6891.

216. Austein, R. (2007). *DNS Name Server Identifier (NSID) Option.* s.l.: IETF, RFC 5001.

217. Crocker, S. and Rose, S. (2013). *Signaling Cryptographic Algorithm Understanding in DNS Security Extensions (DNSSEC).* s.l.: IETF, RFC 6975.

218. Contavalli, C., van der Gaast, W., Lawrence, D., and Kumari, W. (2016). *Client Subnet in DNS Queries.* s.l.: IETF, RFC 7871.

219. Andrews, M. (2014). *Extension Mechanisms for DNS (EDNS) EXPIRE Option.* s.l.: IETF, RFC 7314.

220. Wouters, P., Abley, J., Dickinson, S., and Bellis, R. (2016). *The edns-tcp-keepalive EDNS0 Option.* s.l.: IETF, RFC 7828.

221. Mayrhofer, A. (2016). *The EDNS(0) Padding Option.* s.l.: IETF, RFC 7830.

222. Wouters, P. (2016). CHAIN Query Requests in DNS. s.l.: IETF, RFC 7901.

223. Wessels, D., Kumari, W., and Hoffman, P. (2017). *Signaling Trust Anchor Knowlede in DNS Security Extensions (DNSSEC).* s.l.: IETF, RFC 8145.

224. Bellis, R., Clegg, A., and van Dijk, P. (2019). *DNS EDNS Tags. s.l.: IETF.*

225. Bortzmeyer, S. (2016). *DNS Query Name Minimisation to Improve Privacy.* s.l.: IETF, RFC 7816.

226. Everhart, C.F., Mamakos, L.A., Ullmann, R., and Mockapetris, P.V. (1990). *New DNS RR Definitions.* s.l.: IETF, RFC 1183.

227. Mealling, M. (2002). *Dynamic Delegation Discovery System (DDDS) Part Three: The Domain Name System (DNS) Database.* s.l.: IETF, RFC 3403.

228. Mealling, M. (2002). *Dynamic Delegation Discovery System (DDDS) Part Two: The Algorithm.* s.l.: IETF, RFC 3402.

229. Faltstrom, P. and Mealling, M. (2004). *The E.164 to Uniform Resource Identifiers (URI) Dynamic Delegation Discovery System (DDDS) Application (ENUM).* s.l.: IETF, RFC 3761.

230. Levine, J. (2010). *DNS Blacklists and Whitelists.* s.l.: IETF, RFC 5782.

231. Allman, E., Fenton, J., Delany, M., and Levine, J. (2009). *DomainKeys Identified Mail (DKIM) Author Signing Practices (ADSP).* s.l.: IETF, RFC 5617.

232. Arends, R., Austein, R., Larson, M. et al. (2005). *Resource Records for DNS Security Extensions.* s.l.: IETF, RFC 4034.

233. Josefsson, S. (2006). *Storing Certificates in the Domain Name System (DNS).* s.l.: IETF, RFC 4398.

234. Richardson, M. (2005). *A Method for Storing IPsec Keying Material in DNS.* s.l.: IETF, RFC 4025.

235. Eastlake, 3rd, D. (2000). *DNS Request and Transaction Signatures (SIG(0)s).* s.l.: IETF, RFC 2931.

236. Farrell, C. Schulze, M., Pleitner, S., and Baldoni, D. (1994). *DNS Encoding of Geographical Location.* s.l.: IETF, RFC 1712.

237. Davis, C., Vixie, P., Goodwin, T., and Dickinson, I. (1996). *A Means for Expressing Location Information in the Domain Name System.* s.l.: IETF, RFC 1876.

238. Allocchio, C. (1998). *Using the Internet DNS to Distribute MIXER Conformant Global Address Mapping (MCGAM).* s.l.: IETF, RFC 2163.

239. Crawford, M. and Huitema, C. (2000). *DNS Extensions to Support IPv6 Address Aggregation and Renumbering.* s.l.: IETF, RFC 2874.

240. Thomson, S., Huitema, C., Ksinant, V., and Souissi, M. (2003). *DNS Extensions to Support IP Version 6.* s.l.: IETF, RFC 3596.

241. Koch, P. (2001). *A DNS RR Type for Lists of Address Prefixes.* s.l.: IETF, RFC 3123.

242. ATM Forum Technical Committee (2000). ATM Name System, V2.0. s.l.: ATM Forum, AF-DANS-0152.000.

243. Hallam-Baker, P., Stradling, R., and Hoffman-Andrews, J. (2019). DNS Certification Authority Authorization (CAA) Resource Record. s.l.: IETF, RFC 8659.

244. Hardaker, W. (2015). Child-to-Parent Synchronization in DNS. s.l.: IETF, RFC 7477.

245. Stapp, M., Lemon, T., and Gustafsson, A. (2006). *A DNS Resource Record (RR) for Encoding Dynamic Host Configuration Protocol (DHCP) Information (DHCID RR)*. s.l.: IETF, RFC 4701.

246. Andrews, M. and Weiler, S. (2006). *The DNSSEC Lookaside Validation (DLV) DNS Resource Record*. s.l.: IETF, RFC 4431.

247. Abley, J. (2013). *Resource Records for EUI-48 and EUI-64 Addresses in the DNS*. s.l.: IETF, RFC 7043.

248. Nikander, P. and Laganier, J. (2008). *Host Identity Protocol (HIP) Domain Name System (DNS) Extensions*. s.l.: IETF, RFC 5205.

249. Eastlake, 3rd, D. (1999). *DSA KEYs and SIGs in the Domain Name System (DNS)*. s.l.: IETF, RFC 2536.

250. Atkinson, R. (1997). *Key Exchange Delegation Record for the DNS*. s.l.: IETF, RFC 2230.

251. Atkinson, R.J., Bhatti, S.N., and Rose, S. (2012). *DNS Resource Records for the Identifier-Locator Network Protocol (ILNP)*. s.l.: IETF, RFC 6742.

252. Manning, B. and Colella, R. (1994). *DNS NSAP Resource Records*. s.l.: IETF, RFC 1706.

253. Laurie, B., Sisson, G., Arends, R., and Blacka, D. (2008). *DNS Security (DNSSEC) Hashed Authenticated Denial of Existence*. s.l.: IETF, RFC 5155.

254. Weiler, S. (2004). *Legacy Resolver Compatibility for Delegation Signer (DS)*. s.l.: IETF, RFC 3755.

255. Wouters, P. (2016). *DNS-Based Authentication of Named Entities (DANE) Bindinigs for OpenPGP*. s.l.: IETF, RFC 7929.

256. Hoffman, P. and Schlyter, J. (2017). *Using Secure DNS to Associate Certificates with Domain Names For S/MIME*. s.l.: IETF, RFC 8162.

257. Wong, M. and Schlitt, W. (2006). *Sender Policy Framework (SPF) for Authorizing Use of Domains in E-Mail, Version 1*. s.l.: IETF, RFC 4408.

258. Gellens, R. and Klensin, J. (2006). Message Submission for Mail. s.l.: IETF, RFC 4409.

259. Gulbrandsen, A., Vixie, P., and Esibov, L. (2000). *A DNS RR for Specifying the Location of Services (DNS SRV)*. s.l.: IETF, RFC 2782.

260. Schlyter, J. and Griffin, W. (2006). *Using DNS to Securely Publish Secure Shell (SSH) Key Fingerprints*. s.l.: IETF, RFC 4255.

261. Faltstrom, P. and Kolkman, O. (2015). *The Uniform Resource Identifier (URI) DNS Resource Record*. s.l.: IETF, RFC 7553.

262. IANA (2002). *Special-Use IPv4 Addresses*. s.l.: IETF, RFC 3330.

263. Cotton, M. and Vegoda, L. (2009). *Special Use IPv4 Addresses*. s.l.: IETF, draft-iana-rfc3330bis-11.txt.

264. Deering, S. and Hinden, R. (2017). *Internet Protocol, Version 6 (IPv6) Specification*. s.l.: IETF, RFC 8200.

265. Haberman, B. and Thaler, D. (2002). *Unicast-Prefix-based IPv6 Multicast Addresses*. s.l.: IETF, RFC 3306.

266. Rooney, T. (2010). *Introduction to IP Address Management.* s.l.: IEEE Press/Wiley.

267. Microsoft (2009). *IPv6 Address Autoconfiguration.* www.microsoft.com. httpr://msdn.microsoft.com/en-us/library/aa917171.aspx (accessed 08 July 2020).

268. Loughney, J. (ed.) (2006). *IPv6 Node Requirements.* s.l.: IETF, RFC 4294.

269. Hubbard, K. Kosters, M., Conrad, D. et al. (1996). *Internet Registry IP Allocation Guidelines.* s.l.: IETF, RFC 2050.

270. Narten, T. and Draves, R. (2001). *Privacy Extensions for Stateless Address Autoconfiguration in IPv6.* s.l.: IETF, RFC 3041.

271. Polk, J., Schnizlein, J., and Linsner, M. (2004). *Dynamic Host Configuration Protocol Option for Coordinate-based Location Configuration Information.* s.l.: IETF, RFC 3825.

272. Rooney, T. (2010). *IP Address Management: Pricinciples and Practice.* s.l.: IEEE Press/Wiley.

273. Hoffman, P. and Blanchet, M. (2003). *Nameprep: A Stringprep Profile for Internationalized Domain Names (IDN).* s.l.: IETF, RFC 3491.

274. Hoffman, P. and Blanchet, M. (2002). *Preparation of Internationalized Strings ("stringprep").* s.l.: IETF, RFC 3454.

275. Costello, A. (2003). *Punycode: A Bootstring encoding of Unicode for Internationalized Domain Names in Applications (IDNA).* s.l.: IETF, RFC 3492.

276. Crawford, M. (1999). *Non-Terminal DNS Name Redirection.* s.l.: IETF, RFC 2672.

277. Cisco Systems, Inc. (2009). *Cisco Network Admission Control (NAC).* San Jose, CA: Cisco Systems, Inc.

278. Microsoft Corporation (2008). *Introduction to Nework Access Protection.* Redmond, WA: Microsoft Corporation.

279. Rooney, T. (2005). *Automating IP Address Management Workflow.* Santa Clara, CA: BT INS, Inc.

280. Tsirtsis, G. and Srisuresh, P. (2000). *Network Address Translation – Protocol Translation (NAT-PT).* s.l.: IETF, RFC 2766.

281. IETF (2016). *DNS-based Authentication of Named Entities.* IETF Datatracker. https://datatracker.ietf.org/wg/dane/documents (accessed 08 July 2020).

282. Woodcock, B. (2009). *Best Practices in IPv4 Anycast Routing.* Packet Clearing House. http://www.pch.net/resources/papers/ipv4-anycast/ipv4-anycast.pdf (accessed 08 July 2020).

283. Rooney, T. (2008). *DNS Anycast Addressing for High Availability and Performance.* Santa Clara, CA: BT INS, Inc.

284. National Institute of Standards and Technology (2013). *Digital Signature Standard (DSS).* Gaithersburg: National Institute of Standards and Technology, FIPS PUB 186-4.

285. Internet Systems Consortium (2015). *BIND DNSSEC Guide.* Redwood City: Internet Systems Consortium.

286. NLnet Labs (2016). *Unbound-anchor Man Page*. Amsterdam: NLNet Labs.

287. NLnet Labs (2016). *Unbound: How to Enable DNSSEC*. Unbound documentation. http://unbound.net/documentation/howto_anchor.html (accessed 08 July 2020).

288. Rescorla, E. and Madadugu, N. (2012). *Datagram Transport Layer Security Version 1.2*. s.l.: IETF, RFC 6347.

289. Bao, C., Li, X., Baker, F. et al. (2016). *IP/ICMP Translation Algorithm*. s.l.: IETF, RFC 7915.

290. Rooney, T. (2011). *IP Address Management Principles and Practice*. Hoboken, NJ: Wiley.

291. Klensin, J. (2008), *Simple Mail Transfer Protocol*: IETF, RFC 5321.

292. Resnick, P. (2008), Ed. *Internet Message Format*: IETF, RFC 5322.

293. Johnson, R. (2010). *TFTP Server Address Option for DHCPv4*. s.l.: IETF, RFC 5859.

294. Johnson, R., Kinnear, K., Stapp, M. (2012). *Description of Cisco Systems' Subnet Allocation Option for DHCPv4*. s.l.: IETF, RFC 6656.

295. Cheshire, S., Krochmal, M. (2020). *Apple's DNS Long-Lived Queries Protocol*. s.l.: IETF, RFC 8764.

Index

IP Address Management, Second Edition. Michael Dooley and Timothy Rooney.
© 2021 The Institute of Electrical and Electronics Engineers, Inc.
Published 2021 by John Wiley & Sons, Inc.

IEEE Press Series on
Networks and Services Management

The goal of this series is to publish high quality technical reference books and textbooks on network and services management for communications and information technology professional societies, private sector and government organizations as well as research centers and universities around the world. This Series focuses on Fault, Configuration, Accounting, Performance, and Security (FCAPS) management in areas including, but not limited to, telecommunications network and services, technologies and implementations, IP networks and services, and wireless networks and services.

Series Editors:
Dr. Veli Sahin
Dr. Mehmet Ulema

---

1. *Telecommunications Network Management into the 21st Century*
   Edited by Thomas Plevyak and Salah Aidarous

2. *Telecommunications Network Management: Technologies and Implementations: Techniques, Standards, Technologies, and Applications*
   Edited by Salah Aidarous and Thomas Plevyak

3. *Fundamentals of Telecommunications Network Management*
   Lakshmi G. Raman

4. *Security for Telecommunications Network Management*
   Moshe Rozenblit

5. *Integrated Telecommunications Management Solutions*
   Graham Chen and Qinzheng Kong

6. *Managing IP Networks: Challenges and Opportunities*
   Edited by Thomas Plevyak and Salah Aidarous

7. *Next-Generations Telecommunications Networks, Services, and Management*
   Edited by Thomas Plevyak and Veli Sahin

8. *Introduction to IP Address Management*
   Timothy Rooney

9. *IP Address Management: Principles and Practices*
   Timothy Rooney